# WINNING INSURGENT WAR

## Back to Basics

Geoff Demarest

---

The Foreign Military Studies Office
Ft. Leavenworth, Kansas

---

Published by Books Express Publishing

ISBN 978-1-780399-21-8

Books Express publications are available from all good retail and online booksellers. For publishing proposals and direct ordering please contact us at: info@books-express.com

**DEDICATION**

To Chuck's arm, which he nobly left on the other side of the world.

*About the Cover Illustration:*

All warfare is influenced by topology, but to best comprehend some conflicts, we need to look closely at the interrelationships of people with their surroundings. Insurgencies are generally determined by the same geophysical and psychological factors as maneuver wars. As stressed in this book, all conflicts have chartable and controllable profiles within the scope of long-standing principles. In that light, many constants in the dynamics of insurgency can be rendered in vivid color and detail, much like a 19th Century landscape.

In this panoramic view, Justice and Liberty are held hostage by sinister actors—control over events and power bypass questions of legitimacy (or rule of law), defaulting to whomever acts with orchestrated impunity. Consequently, the key investigative challenge in preparing for effective action and winning the peace reasonably starts with illuminating the hidden identities and interests of shadowy, but evident, perpetrators.

Accordingly, an analytic specter resembling the private eye Sherlock Holmes reflects on the literal and metaphoric guises which might be found in a conflictive landscape of this sort, or in a monograph about such a dangerous domain. The game is afoot. Ominous threats either hang dangerously like the sword of Damocles or aggressively advance—sometimes punctuating the countryside as surprising, limb-wrenching detonations. Past sins leave quiet evidence within jungle darkness, or insidiously shape essential cultural dynamics. Always aided by carelessness, human error, and illicit commerce, insurgencies more often than not endanger the innocent. Insurgency might not always be bad or endemic, but as depicted, they can be won.

Charles A. Martinson III

## QUICK START: HOW TO READ THIS BOOK

You can take a traditional approach, reading the sections in numerical sequence; or you can read the author's preface, the first seven-fifteen sections, then the last several (plus the Restatement and Synthesis), then several around the middle (say 68-76), then skip around. You could also skim the contents and go to whatever sections interest you.

Some of the sections have expansive titles like *Legitimacy* or *Human Rights*. They aren't intended to encapsulate those subjects, however, but just to tie those themes to the book's central assertions. Other titles, like *Dogs and Mules*, or *Forts and Walls*, are much less abstract, but relate to the same assertions. Those assertions, or propositions, include:

- An impunity-based definition of State success;
- Anonymity as a competitive preoccupation;
- Inventorying as an indispensible knowledge activity;
- The line of retreat as a key operational concept;
- Post-structuralism as a global ideological scoundrel;
- Geography as the academic discipline of choice;
- Property as the heart of a peaceful social contract;
- Property analysis as a way to understand power;
- Civil engineering and construction as noble activities;
- Dignity and honor as key quantities of sustainable victory;
- Adaptation of classic strategy as operational artistry; and
- Deception as an unavoidable element of strategy.

'Winning' means not just neutralizing your enemies, but doing so without creating more of them. It may also mean building places that do not create enemies.

Building such places requires that ideology, political philosophy, epistemology and engineering all get along, and so the book assumes these things cannot be distanced one from another. Below each section is a joke, quote, or piece of poetry. They are interrelated in a way similar to the text, and with the text. They are like the fins on a `59 Cadillac.

## FOREWORD

Not too long ago, our US military doctrine writers could be caught arguing about the efficacy of "design" as a thinking path to be followed prior to military planning or decision-making processes. Meanwhile, some senior military leaders began writing and speaking about an era of "persistent conflict." The *U.S. National Security Strategy* asserted a need to "pursue a strategy of national renewal and global leadership -- a strategy that rebuilds the foundation of American strength and influence." Perhaps by definition strategic pronouncements are broad and overarching, but taking stirring words and broad observations about the world's challenges and then translating them into action requires a complex pragmatism. It requires an approach to the study of war that absorbs uninspiring quantities like inconsistency, ambiguity and ambivalence without abandoning victory as a worthy and achievable goal for our Nation and our allies. "The art of war is of vital importance to the state. It is a matter of life and death, a road either to safety or ruin." If Sun-Tzu in fact said that, he would have enjoyed a book that directly ties the health and survival of states to their prospects in armed conflict.

Dr. Demarest's book gives students and practitioners a pragmatic start point rooted in the classic principles of war and simultaneously in the jurisprudential principles of impunity and culpability -- concepts that apply across the entire plane of human conflict. Demarest reminds us that success in warfare requires control of land, and so an empirical knowledge of geography, both physical and human (if the two could actually be separated) is vital.

The study of the spectrum, or firmament, of conflict -- and how principles of war apply across that firmament -- requires an unconventional approach. This is not a standard book. Student and teacher can pick up this book and start at the beginning, middle, or end. No matter the start point, the reader will find convention challenged and see that normal is no better than the cycles of a washing machine. There are no chapters in this book, and few explanatory footnotes expounding arcane academe. Demarest shakes up the growing 'laundry list' approach to war with one of his own, reaching a malleable full gross. The 144 sections of the book, short or not so, are thoughtful and thought-provoking, most spiced with humor, and some irreverent, especially as to passing and fashionable concepts. A gimmick perhaps, his frequent cinematic references together make a fabric of essential observations -- observations that can hardly be taken as superfluous in a world aching for better cultural understanding of the battlefields. The text, taken as a whole, refuses to admit distance among what otherwise seem separate compartments of thought. Political philosophy, police intelligence, military strategy, art and architecture are all presented as one ball of yarn.

Warfare in the 21st century remains an extension and means of implementing policy. We would like to think that responsible use of force as a policy tool demands some application of the intellect, however. If war cannot be well-controlled -- often assuming a momentum of its own -- at least it can be guided through thoughtful human interaction. Demarest challenges us as soldiers to think, study, and think some more so as to establish attainable goals, tied to achievable tasks and to obtainable resources. This book will make you laugh, get angry, and think -- not just idle thought, but vocational. Hopefully, the end result will be a better defense of our Republic.

Dr. Kevin Benson, Colonel, US Army (ret)

## AUTHOR'S PREFACE

Regarding the kind of conflict the book addresses, it is about a broader set of conflicts than 'insurgency.' The umbrella category *might* be 'irregular.' I defer to a section on 'Terms' in a 1960 US Army field manual titled *Operations Against Irregular Forces*. It states,

> The term irregular, used in combinations such as irregular forces, irregular activities, and counter-irregular operations, is used in the broad sense to refer to all types of nonconventional forces and operations. It includes guerrilla, partisans, insurgent, subversive, resistance, terrorist, revolutionary, and similar personnel, organizations and methods.

The word 'irregular' wasn't satisfying for use in the title, however. Too many of the draft readers thought it was dull. I throw 'organized crime' into the laundry list, and also genocide, humanitarian intervention, hybrid war, insurrection, *latrunculi*, low-intensity conflict, new war, war amongst the people, occupation, peoples' war, cocktail war, postmodern war, rebellion, anarchy, separatism, small war, manhunts, counterdrug operations, stability operations, and unrestricted warfare. You name it. I spent only a little text on the taxonomic problem, preferring instead to address what to do. The book is about almost everything other than State-on-State wars in which tank brigades maneuver against one another or countries shoot at each other with nuclear weapons. Insurgency is the center of the subject, even if it doesn't do justice to the whole range of organized violence, so please forgive occasional indiscipline regarding what may be useful distinctions of the terms.

One of my sons sent me to a website called Thesharkguys.com where they had an article offering ten pointers on how to write a pretentious book. Thank you, Shark Guys; I've tried to incorporate what I could, including use of the word *solipsistic*. This book's first pretention, however, is the first word of the title – *winning*. That word demands a definition, so I assert what contenders in an insurgent war are trying to win – what constitutes winning. Because pretending to explain how to win obliges a description of what winning might look like, the first and last sections of the book deal with *impunity*. If a society does not feature a State that holds a monopoly over the granting of impunity (that is, if an entity can grant impunity in defiance of the State), the State and the society are failing to that extent. If a government achieves a monopoly over the granting of impunity, but with that monopoly then grants impunity to a select group of people at the expense of others, the situation is likely to cause subversion.

To stop someone from being able to grant impunity, you pretty much have to find and neutralize him, and if that is what you want to do, you should concentrate your operational plans on his *line of retreat* to sanctuary. Because he keeps his whereabouts and lines of communication a secret, this book calls for deliberate attention to *anonymity.* Since, like impunity, anonymity is another word we don't see in books on military strategy, insurgency or counterinsurgency, it, too, needs some defining.

So, the book starts and ends with *impunity* (control of which the contenders are trying to achieve); the second section of the book is about *anonymity*, a practical notion tied both to impunity and to the line of retreat; and the third section is about the *line of retreat* (a geographic concept related to survival). An outlaw imperative: maintain a culture of silence to protect movement to refuge in order to keep oneself and one's comrades from being punished by the authorities.

If forced to choose from the book a single most useful theme, at least for how to win an insurgent war, it might be the control of *anonymity.* Some amount of anonymity supports freedom, but anonymity can enable impunity, and so the book highlights efforts that can appropriately sway the 'balance of anonymities.' Supporting what is outlined above, the second and related theme would be the continuing applicability of classic military operational art, especially that art's emphasis on 'lines of communication' (a concept that includes lines of retreat).

If asked to declare a third theme, it would be moving the question 'where?' toward the front of the set of questions you might use to address your war. The current tendency is to obsess over things like *why* and *how* insurgents or criminals act -- valuable questions, of course. Of greater or at least more urgent operational importance is exactly *where* the enemy is. Knowing your enemy's motives may not matter if you can't find him; he'll sneak up on you. Geography is the academic discipline that focuses on *where.* Unfortunately, Geography, like most of the social sciences, is being attacked by a politically-painted ideological fashion that tears at things like positivism, empiricism, and even optimism. Fortunately, Geography is also the home of geographic information science (GIS), which is busy restoring those things.

If imposed upon to highlight a fourth item (now risking beyond quota and patience), I would promote the general construction of a sustainable property ownership system, which we can also call the social contract. Much of the text is about closing with and destroying the enemy, but more of it is about not creating other enemies in the process. *Property* is the axial term for that endeavor.

The book is not about the US military, or about counterinsurgency (although a few sections are), but it *is* pro-American. Since the end of the Cold War, Anti-Americanism has drawn from currents that include deconstructionism, neo-Marxism, anti-colonialism, anti-capitalism, anti-globalism, anti-neoliberalism, and the reigning favorite, *post-structuralism*. These isms, and especially the latter, tend to reject maps, GIS, reason, engineering, human nature, American football and all kinds of things I like. They are annoying, especially post-structuralism, since it makes no bones about not seeking or telling an objective truth. They feed both transparent anti-Americanism, as well as a covert pseudo-epistemology that indirectly but purposefully preferences anti-Americanism -- so this book's attitude and argument oppose that conspiracy of philosophical-ideological propositions. Americans can reach into a rich inheritance of their own isms, and while this book does not delve into them at any length, some are appreciated by allusion in the selection of quotes.

Although I mentioned control of anonymity as a most useful theme, *there is no stand alone prime message in this book.* The Quick Start mentions twelve key themes, the Restatement uses seven, and I mentioned four just above in this Author's Preface. Counting is hard work; there is no utility in an integer of principles that might guide you to winning your war. The format of this book is itself intended as a reminder that words enslave and categories deceive. The ideas make a soup, not a ladder. That said, after each section, I invite you to read exactly eight other sections because I'm told 'ba' and 'fa' sound alike in Chinese -- one word meaning 'eight' and one word meaning 'luck' -- and that makes eight a lucky number.

Maybe the book's attitude will suffice as a center-pole -- that the best objective in war is to win, not 'seek a solution,' 'prepare conditions for negotiation,' or 'find a favorable outcome.' Those results might be acceptable, but this book is about how to win. Winning means defeating your enemies without creating more of them. Geometric, geologic, topologic, pragmatic, empirical, physical aspects of winning are favored in the book. Nevertheless, they cannot be honestly addressed unless they are mixed with less tangible, bigger things.

As for whom the book was written, the title seeks its audience. The text touches on a broad range of subjects. In a Memorial Day speech, Oliver Wendell Holmes, Jr., relating why his generation fought in the Civil War, suggested that we should share the passion and action of our time. Some folk may want to share that action competently. I doubt, however, I can successfully argue why anyone should read most of the material in this book. If one were to ask...

> "Why should I seek to know the secrets of philosophy? Why seek to decipher the hidden laws of creation that are graven upon the tablets of the rocks, or to unravel the history of civilization that is woven in the tissue of our jurisprudence, or to do any great work, either of speculation or of practical affairs? I cannot answer him; or at least my answer is as little worth making for any effect it will have upon his wishes if he asked why I should eat this, or drink that. You must begin by wanting to. But although desire cannot be imparted by argument, it can be by contagion."[1]

My hope, then, is that the book will find its best audience, and that some of the ideas in it will be contagious.

Geoff Demarest

**ACKNOWLEDGEMENT**

This being a disparate work, the reader will appreciate that many reviewers and counselors were abused in its making. I apologize to those who deserve personal mention here but who I forgot. Several individuals were especially generous with their time, and I in turn especially thievish with their ideas. They are, in no reasoned order: Kathleen Demarest, Kevin Benson, Scott Henderson, Tim Thomas, Ivan Welch, Jan Horvath, Les Grau, Robert Feldman, Alice Mink, Greg Fontenot, Linda Pride, Karl Prinslow, Merle Miyasato, Joel Anderson, Cindy Hurst, Brenda Fiegel, Karen Kaya, Tyson Demarest, Kayla Harford, Vince Demarest, Lauren Demarest, Chuck Bartles, Matt Stein, Patrick Reanier, Nathan Toronto, Stephany Trofino, Dennis Giangreco, Charles Martinson, Tom Wilhelm, Ralph Erwin, Randy Love, Rob Kurz, Andy Pollock, Kevin Freese, Steve Gerecke, David Spencer, James Green, James Riely, Kent Baumann, Aaron Perez, Gary Philips, Ernesto Villamizar, Anthony Scheidel, Myrna Myers, Eduardo Castillo, David Bailey, Monroe Bonfoey, Cullen Demarest, and Mark Monroe. Some of you will recognize that many of the names come from the Foreign Military Studies Office.

# CONTENTS

## *Contents*

# *Section 1,*
# *What the Pirate Said to Alexander*

St. Augustine of Hippo was a cleric and philosopher who lived centuries later than Alexander, but whose keen observations about the nature of sovereignty and power still influence us today. St. Augustine addresses moral weight in the context of State power. His assertions about the subject revolve around the word *impunity*. Impunity means exemption or protection from punishment.

Alexander the Great got great the old-fashioned way, but that's not what is important here. We turn instead to his need to deal with some less powerful contenders, a pirate in this case. St. Augustine tells us the story with the pirate as protagonist. Here is the passage:

> *In the absence of justice, what is sovereignty but organized brigandage? For, what are the bands of brigands but petty kingdoms? They also are groups of men, under the rule of a leader, bound together by a common agreement, dividing their booty according to a settled principle. If this band of criminals, by recruiting more criminals, acquires enough power to occupy regions, to capture cities, and to subdue whole populations, then it can with fuller right assume the title of kingdom, which in the public estimation is conferred upon it, not by the renunciation of greed, but by the increase of impunity. The answer which a captured pirate gave to Alexander the Great was perfectly accurate and correct. When that king asked the man what he meant by infesting the sea, he boldly replied: 'What you mean by warring on the whole world. I do my fighting on a tiny ship, and they call me a pirate; you do yours with a large fleet, and they call you a Commander.'*
>
> St. Augustine, 5th-century Cleric[2]

Man is a territorial creature who, when he gains power, doesn't like anyone else granting impunity in his space. Our captured pirate, unbowed, points out that there is little difference between him and Alexander, save that Alexander is honored for the scale of his arrogation.

This book starts with St. Augustine's pirate story because, as the title says, the book is about *winning*, and the notion of winning needs practical form. Here, that form is offered by the assertion that government wins when it is the only entity within its territory able to grant impunity. Sometimes a pirate, insurgent, separatist, warlord, or Mafioso (or even a foreign country) can successfully grant impunity in defiance of a State -- and that is the challenge addressed by this book. If an entity besides the State can grant impunity to people who defy its rules, the State fails to that extent. If no entity can defy the State's monopoly on granting impunity, the State is securely sovereign. Sometimes leaders can defy the State and grant impunity to their people because they are armed and well organized.

St. Augustine spoke through the voice of the pirate, but this book's protagonist is not the pirate, Alexander or even St. Augustine. *You* are this book's protagonist.

See Section 144, *Impunity and State Success*

---

> **Fredric**: You make it a point of never attacking a weaker party than yourselves, and when you attack a stronger one you invariably get thrashed.
>
> **Pirate King**: There's some truth in that.
>
> From the movie
> *The Pirates of Penzance* (1983)[3]

---

Anonymity is the hinge quality in irregular warfare

# *Section 2, Anonymity*

Anonymity is that obscure quality of going unnoticed or unidentified which helps an insurgent or outlaw act and move without being caught. Speed is good, too, but if there were a keyword or 'nub' to either the survival or demise of insurgency, separatist movement, rebellion, revolution, mafia and other related insults to the State, that word would be *anonymity*. With anonymity rides facility of movement, the possibility of surprise, security in escape, sanctuary, and the potential to enjoy illicit profits. Whether you are a Starship Trooper, Che Guevara, an embezzler, a whistleblower, or the Police Chief, calculated attention to the question of anonymity may be the difference between success and being shot to death in Bolivia. There are other variables, other dimensions, other preoccupations bearing on violent conflict; this book has a hundred and forty-three other sections. Failure to address anonymity, however, is a severely punished negligence.

Perhaps the single most consequential operational difference between regular (conventional, with maneuvering tank units maybe) warfare and the more common violent competitions considered by this book is anonymity, and how the contenders care for it. Your objective will probably not be to eliminate anonymity, but rather to change the balance of anonymities in your favor. For a government, this may mean the development of ways by which individual members of the public at-large can anonymously inform about illegal activities -- like an anonymous cell phone hotline. For the outlaw it can mean creating an environment of certain retribution for such 'ratting.'

For governments, public records are the traditional and proven tool for establishing a social environment in which anonymity is difficult to achieve and, consequently, anti-State behavior dangerous to attempt. Because an insurgent leader has to balance the secrecy of his whereabouts with a useful degree of public notoriety and political identity, he may be concerned more with geographic anonymity than with hiding his personal identity as an insurgent leader. Likewise, the same insurgent wants to hide the locations of his wealth while maintaining its liquidity. Hence, systems that tie specific physical locations to individual identities are especially relevant. These systems -- that tie physical geography to personal identity and wealth -- are called property systems.

Careful record keeping helps make personal anonymity hard to maintain, allowing a State to control a population with less physical coercion. Peacefully controlling Big Brother's excesses, on the other hand, can be partly accomplished by making those records publicly transparent. Transparent public records are the hallmark of a liberal State, making corruption and tyranny at least a little more difficult.

See: 41, *Whereabouts;* 73, *Property and the Social Contract*; 38, *Cultural Study for What?;* 110, *Knowledge Gaps;* 74, *Refugees and Displaced Persons;* 35, *Comuna 13*; and 16, *Keeping Secrets*.

---

"...there are advantages to being elected President. The day after I was elected, I had my high school grades classified Top Secret."

Ronald Reagan[4]

Hastings is not called the 'Domesday Battle'

# *Section 3, The Domesday Book*

Historically, few things spell Big Brother better for the English than Domesday. William the Conqueror won the battle of Hastings in 1066, but it was the census he ordered two decades later that subdued the English. That inventory, which included everything worth anything – land, cattle, everything, was put in a big registry, which became known as the Domesday Book.

If you are the counterinsurgent, you can achieve stability, governance, the rule-of-law, peace and the defeat of anti-State actors (in short, all kinds of noble goals, and many that aren't) if you do the inventory soon and well. Without these inventories, the possibilities of creating a peaceful society are dim. If you are an insurgent, you will want to confound the government's inventories, but build your own.

If you are in charge, don't let whatever crew considers itself the 'action people' wait for the 'knowledge people' to complete the inventory. Don't let any shiftlessness seep in under the guise of a debate about whether or not security comes before or after public administration, census-taking and cadastre-building. If there is to be territorial control by anyone, it will be accomplished in the long run on the basis of knowledge of exactly what and who are in a territory. If your entity (government or other) wants or occupies space, count everything in it. If you're not sure you control territory 24/7, count everything. And, of course, put it all in a georeferenced relational database because *where stuff is* is as significant as what it is. Everything belongs to someone and everyone has some kind of connection with someplace, something or someone else. Try not being anywhere! If you think a person doesn't belong in a place, you want to talk to him about it, or you might find out the wrong way. In short, any debate about whether or not intelligence runs operations or operations runs intelligence is just that and no more – a debate. If you have time to ponder whether induction comes before deduction, work on that for a while. Otherwise, proceed with the inventory with all available strength. If there is nothing else to do, take inventory.

If it is at all possible, give everybody an ID card. Biometrics can't be allowed to mean just careful physical identification of perpetrators or of someone from whom we want to deny access. Biometrics has to be applied to everyone for Big Brother to work as well as it might.

Inventories are the essential Big Brother tool, but they can be helpful for the preservation of a liberal social contract when done in the context of individual liberties and transparency. A transparent, high quality system of public records can be an aid in controlling Big Brother and for checking government corruption. This book offers few items of advice more practical to successful counterinsurgency than the creation of a complete inventory of the territories at issue. Nevertheless, it is equally true that a peaceful, liberal social contract is inextricably dependent on formalized public records of ownership. There exists, then, a singularly significant overlap of the concepts of public intelligence that underpins a peaceful society and the Big Brother intelligence that allows the State to repress resistance and opposition. The quality of the maintenance of records, and rules regarding accessibility to those records, are central factors for reaching culturally appropriate political balances. If you are not involved in this activity (determination of the types, qualities, and management of public records) or, worse, you are oblivious to it, you may have absented yourself from the main and most critical events associated with creating a sustainable environment of peace.

To be successful, 'participatory' research (in which elements of the public voluntarily join in the compilation of social data) focuses on information people will own and which empowers their control over their own wellbeing as they perceive it. When the knowledge sought is knowledge everyone needs and wants, the costs of data collection and input go down precipitously. In other words, if you design an inventory that is clearly advantageous to the flourishing of peoples' lives as they see it, the inventory will be much more realizable. Some obvious examples are inventories of water and water pollution sources, home titles and appraisals, and insect infestation or communicable disease data. Participatory research examples could also include entertainment, tourism and recreational data, or broader market information. The phone book with its 'yellow pages' is an example, likewise the social information sites on the Internet.

One of the decisions that will most bear on the acceptability of a human geographic inventory regards scale. If the people involved believe information will be public at a controllable scale, they are far more likely to participate in the inventory. The *county* (not *country*) may or may not be the right scale of formal territory, but, as a beginning assumption, the county is a better territorial scale for understanding, planning, and prosecuting military, police, or development operations than is the country.

Taking the kind of inventory suggested in this section requires technical and social training. New tools are available that can make the work faster than in 1066. Two of the best known are the GPS devices available from firms like Garmin and Trimble, or the ID-card making and biometrics suites that have come on the market only in the last decade. The taking of human geographic data, however, must be contemplated and implemented in consonance with the systems of data maintenance and retrieval. Gathering human geographic data in a piecemeal or one-off manner in order to inform a local commander or leader may be immediately, tactically useful, but it might not change the balance of anonymities for any consequential length of time. Inventorying efforts are better when tied to a relational database, a GIS, and one which will offer some immutability to the data (perhaps placed on the Internet, which can make it harder to corrupt).

The business of creating a useful inventory is an easy thing to inspect. Any leader at any level, when questioning the condition of an insurgency or its counter, for instance, will do well to ask questions about the precision, comprehensiveness, transparency, and availability of the territorial inventory. Look to see if you have a record of everyone in your territory, that any of your foot soldiers can quickly use to test the ID of anyone. If your territory has a weak record or ID-card system, that is not a good sign. Don't know where Mrs. Castro is buried? Not good. Can't quickly tell who is married to whom? Don't know the relative worth of a piece of real estate or who gets the rents from it? A cop can't quickly tell where a motorcycle was bought or where it should be parked at night? Can't say where all the licensed doctors live? These are all bad signs.

Early in 2002, the Colombian government decided to complete a titling and property formalization project for hundreds of peasant families in an area known as Puerto Leguízamo that was partly under the control of the insurgent Revolutionary Armed Forces of Colombia (FARC). To proceed, the government functionaries had to present a letter of introduction from the office of President Andrés Pastrana to the local FARC commander. The FARC commander, needless to say, knew the value of having precise public records, especially when paid for by the government.

If you are an insurgent leader or a crime boss, it is harder to protect your followers (for violent acts they perpetrate) in a land that has excellent records of who has what, and who is supposed to be where. You cannot assure the secrecy of their identities and locations. Government authorities will deny them sanctuary.

Some people will resist or demand assurances about privacy, freedoms, dignity, and the possible consolidation of an underclass (even in such places as Puerto Leguízamo). The English understood the consequences of William's inventory in the eleventh century. Should you perhaps oppose the creation of Big Brother, which this book advises as an essential undertaking for winning an internal conflict? It depends. Centralized control and manipulation of public records is dangerous to liberty. If you're an inveterate counterinsurgent, fine, GIS everybody and their dogs and their dogs' fleas. William's 11th-century book was named the Domesday Book (early English spelling) because its making was doomsday for English defiance of their Norman overlords.

For a social contract that is both sustainable and liberal, keep records local, maybe at the county-level, and do not allow public filing of much more than real estate rights, professional licenses, motor vehicles perhaps such incendiary phenomena as the location of pedophiles. This is not a counterinsurgency manual; it is about balance. The control of anonymity is necessary in order to maintain a monopoly over the granting of impunity. Human security, justice and freedom depend on and are tied to the control of impunity. If a government is allowed to monopolize access to public records, it can grant impunity to a privileged few. It becomes the brigand. It is then that you will have a reason to revolt, and you will want to grant protection to your people for defying the State.

See: 96, *Public Records*; 47, *Why The County*; 73, *Property and the Social Contract*; 51, *Underclass*; 142, *Dignity and Honor*; 66, *GIS;* 27, *Democracy*; and 49, *Territorial Scrutiny*.

---

> "This is our land. A land of peace and of plenty. A land of harmony and hope. This is our land. Oceania. These are our people. The workers, the strivers, the builders. These are our people. The builders of our world, struggling, fighting, bleeding, dying. On the streets of our cities and on the far-flung battlefields. Fighting against the mutilation of our hopes and dreams."
>
> Big Brother (voice-over) in the movie *Nineteen Eighty-Four* (1984)[5]

# *Section 4, Defining "Enemy"*

There may be nothing morally inadequate about turning the other cheek and not responding to threats with violence, even if your own demise, honor, and family are at risk. Martyring yourself peacefully is one answer to violent affront, but this book is just not about that answer. It is about winning, dominating, and it supposes winning and dominating mean violent effort at some point. The healthy path is to be careful in drafting a specific definition of enemy, and clearheaded regarding the values held at risk by the use of violence.

If you are assigned the task of stopping an enemy, have a working definition of 'enemy' on paper as well as in mind. Your definition should also be explicitly acceptable to your boss, if you have one. The Table of Organization & Equipment (TO&E) of a US tank battalion has typically started out with a mission statement something like: 'To close with and destroy the enemy by firepower, shock action and maneuver.' Such a statement could hardly be clearer, subject to agreement regarding who the enemy is. Every effort should be made to make the definition of enemy as increasingly specific as possible, in time, space and name. If 'enemy' means the seven members of the secretariat of the FARC, that may be specific enough. Maybe 'Álvaro Uribe Vélez' would be a specific enemy identity if you are a FARC leader. 'Terrorism' or 'Communism,' 'globalization,' or 'neoliberalism' might be useful shorthand for expressing solidarity, explaining positions, motivating adherents or as part of an effort to create broad alliances, but they are too abstract to solve the operational equation.

Here is a suggested intermediate definition of *enemy* for irregular conflict:

> Our enemy is a person or group the behavior of which cannot be changed by peaceful means before it does us grave harm.

This definition, rather than supposing a morally justifying context for stopping the enemy, asserts a morally compelling situation that defines an enemy. It is tied to time. It could be presented as 'What would you do if a strange man broke into your home and threatened your family? Would you shoot?' The potential tautology is obvious. We're defining enemy as someone against whom we must use force because we must. We could use the definition to justify a lot of situations. We could label as enemies a bunch of scabs who cross our picket line, given that our whole strength as a union might rest on our ability to threaten the profits of the factory owner. In other words, it is a useable, correct, but dangerous definition that is 'intermediate' because you will still prefer a by-name identity. *What is the name* of the perpetrator of the clear and present danger?

The operational equation described in Section 8 depends for its logic on the existence of enemies, supposing that if you do not have an enemy (that is, some person or group that will do you or yours grave harm before peaceful responses have time to take effect), then maybe you don't need to fight, battle is not a compelling phenomenon, you don't need to make an armed response to anything, and 'intercepting lines of communication' is an unresponsive notion. If you do not have an enemy, maybe you are not facing a conflict that you have to win by the position and movement of armed force -- unless you are happy as the aggressor, in which case you will produce enemies soon enough. There is, meanwhile, an important connection between *impunity* and *enemy*. If an organization can grant impunity in defiance of the State, it is the enemy of the State. Conversely, your enemy may be the State.

This section's definition of *enemy* suggests that, within a range of ethical considerations, we have to deem an enemy to exist before military activity makes much sense. Simplified: If he's not going to do us much harm, why shoot? The definition and its attendant logic may be too inflexible to guide your use of force in a given situation, however. You may have to apply force in order to uphold simple elements of the social contract such as the preservation of public lands, free passage on public byways, evictions of trespassers and the like. Or, you may be uninterested in supporting the legal regime, but are instead faced by opportunities for material gain and domination, or for the realization of revolutionary goals that you can achieve by the use of force. You might just want to take things, or your enemy may be an entire structure of relationships, symbols, preferences, assumptions, fashions, and teachings that keep you and yours from enjoying life as you feel you should. Armed organized violence may be the only path you have to gain what you want while you are young enough to enjoy it. As to any of these cases, you might try establishing thresholds of conflict that can be anticipated as justifying different levels of action or reaction. This section's definition can still work for you, however, in that you will define the grave harm threatened against you as the impossibility of enforcing the peace without the application of legal force, or, to the contrary, the impossibility of peacefully beating the system that denies or despises you.

See: 82, *Conflict Thresholds*; 23, *Mens Rea*; 8, *The Operational Equation*; 17, *Kidnapping*; 25, *Why Humans Don't Fight*; 138, *Roadblocks and Checkpoints*; 144, *Impunity and State Success*; and 129, *Nerd Globe.*

---

> "I believe that force, mitigated so far as it may be by good manners, is the *ultima ratio*, and between two groups of people who want to make inconsistent kinds of worlds, I see no remedy but force."
>
> Oliver Wendell Holmes, Jr.[6]

When doctrine throws out the baby

# *Section 5, Misleading COIN Articles of Faith*

Below are ten rarely questioned notions from English-language literature (including official military doctrine) on the nature of insurgency. They are not wrong, but are misleading, and most earned a separate section in this book. For the counterinsurgent, these articles of faith can do worse than misdirect -- they can disable.

**Asymmetry**
The misleading article of faith: *The unique characteristic of insurgent warfare is the great differential in resources, methods and objectives between the insurgent and counterinsurgent.*

Actually, asymmetry is the difference between winning and losing in every conflict. (See Section 120, *Turducken*).

**Classic principles of military strategy are inapplicable**
The misleading article of faith: *The vocabulary and lessons of the 19th century (and earlier) masters don't apply, are not obeyed by the insurgent, and cannot guide successful counterinsurgency efforts.*

They *do* apply; the successful insurgent obeys them diligently, and to ignore or deny them is dangerous. (See Section 6, *Classic Strategy and Irregular Warfare*).

**Decisive Battle**

The misleading article of faith: *Counterinsurgent leaders are wise not to seek decisive battle; as such an event is elusive if not an illusion.*

This is a concomitant of the broader rejection of the classic principles noted just above. When it is internalized by military leaders it can disable rational strategy. (See Section 11, *Decisive Battle*)

**Legitimacy**

The misleading article of faith: *Government legitimacy is the basis of success of counterinsurgency, and electoral democracy is the principle font of legitimacy.*

Several sections of this book are dedicated to soften this favorite. Legitimacy is as much argument as it is condition. Having even a lot of it will not assure success in irregular conflict, nor will having very little legitimacy preclude success. (See Section 14, *Legitimacy*)

**Natural Protraction**

The misleading article of faith: *An insurgent war is by its nature a protracted affair.*

It is not. Rather, the insurgent protracts it in order to survive. This misleading article of faith has been one of the most damaging to US and allied decision-making in recent years. (See Section 12, *Protraction and Diligence*)

**Nonlinearity**

The misleading article of faith: *Insurgent or irregular war tends to be nonlinear.*

This unfortunate misinterpretation of classic strategy is brother to 'asymmetry.' Irregular warfare is very linear. (See Section 7, *Nonlinear Warfare*)

**Political over Military Resolution**
The misleading article of faith: *The answer to insurgency must be more political than military.*

This assertion can be shorthand for a lot of reasonable things, but in general it is a false and disarming dichotomy. (See Section 44, *Political/Military/Administrative*)

**Popular Support**
The misleading article of faith: *The center of gravity of insurgency and counterinsurgency is the greater population.*

True and totally false. It too often begs the questions how much is enough and what to do with it once you have it. (See Section 75, *Popular Support*)

**Socioeconomic Causation**
The misleading article of faith: *The causes of or reasons for insurgency are to be found in inequitable socioeconomic conditions.*

Maybe, but it does not follow that socioeconomic improvement will help you win. (See Section 39, *Socioeconomic Causation*)

**Spontaneity**
The misleading article of faith: *Armed resistance can spring to life without hierarchical leadership or centralized design.*

Semantically it seems as though 'insurgency' necessarily contains some amount of spontaneity, but historical reflection suggests leadership is so important for the success of any organized armed enterprise that the notion of spontaneous uprising is romantic. (See Section 59, *Spontaneity*)

Maybe worse than the fact the above ideas misdirect: they displace other ideas that are more likely to accelerate effective preparation and execution of competitive strategies in armed social conflicts. (For instance, see sections 2, *Anonymity* and 3, *The Domesday Book.*)

Once again, the disclaimer: One of the favorite tricks of argumentation is to present a targeted proposition in its exaggerated form so it can be more easily attacked. The above 'articles of faith' are posed in unvarnished and vulnerable form. In fact, all of them are to be respected, but just not too much.

See: 122, *Songs of Chu*; 101, *Magical Realism*; 117, *Strategic Communication*; 141, *Seven Strategy Strains*; 83, *Conflict Geography*; 69, *Measuring Actions against Enemies*; 70, *Measuring Effects of Actions on Structure*; and 123, *Thirty-six Stratagems*.

---

"Here in America we're descended in blood and in spirit from revolutionists and rebels -- men and women who dare to dissent from accepted doctrine."

Dwight Eisenhower[7]

ઉ࿐ઉ࿐ઉ࿐ઉ࿐ઉ࿐ઉ࿐

Strategy precepts of the pre-flight era still apply

# *Section 6, Classic Strategy and Irregular Warfare*

Below is some vocabulary we associate with classic western military strategy (Jomini, Clausewitz, Rostow, Marlborough). The concepts can be applied advantageously to irregular conflict.

**Mass**

It is advantageous to marshal and concentrate force at propitious places and moments in time in order to gain at least localized and temporary superiority of force over the enemy. The notion of mass -- and that is the general's vocation to determine where and when strength will be marshaled and manifest -- is central to classic strategy, perhaps even its heart. See sections 138, *Roadblocks and Checkpoints*; and 68, *Scale*)

**Culminating Point**

The culminating point is an imaginary point in time and space beyond which the continuation of a mission (usually in the form of an offensive, attack, or a pursuit) is too risky. The culminating point is a favorite topic of discussion in military strategy and history circles. Although most counterinsurgent literature passes over this concept, it is nevertheless vital to the conduct and understanding of irregular armed conflict. (See Section 140, *Culminating Point in the Pursuit*)

**Pursuit**

After the leader of force *A* decides for whatever reason that it is time to break or avoid contact with an enemy force *B* (maybe because he thinks *A* has been or is about to be beaten by *B*), force *B* may press the confrontation in order to prevent *A*'s escape. That's when the pursuit begins. Knowing when to withdraw (and having secured a path to do so) is part of the essence of good field generalship. Knowing whether or not to pursue is also important, and the decision to pursue or not pursue is equally wrapped up in an understanding, maybe intuitive and maybe studied, of the culminating point. (See sections 140, *Culminating Point in the Pursuit*; and 2, *The Line of Retreat*)

**Envelopment**

In order to get around your enemy and to seal off his retreat, you might conduct an envelopment. If you are Field Marshal Zhukov and have 20,000 tanks at your disposal, you can envelop the German 6th Army at Stalingrad, and take 100,000 men prisoner (95% to die later in captivity). The word, according to big-maneuver people, is generally reserved for vast thrusts deep into enemy territory (ranking officers don't like to have their terms trivialized by dilettantes). A smaller-scale event might be called a 'pincer movement.' At a smaller scale still, you're a cop serving an arrest warrant on a dangerous felon, and you get a backup squad, so you send it around to the back door. All are essentially the same; you want to seal off his escape. (See Section 8, *The Operational Equation*)

**Economy of Force**

Creation of mass often necessitates economy of force. You can't be everywhere with everything, so you will decide to hold things together as best as possible with a small force in one location so you will have an advantageous correlation of force in another. (See Section 123, *Thirty-six strategies*)

**Center of Gravity**
This is possibly the most controversial of the classic strategy terms. Sometimes it refers to the place on the battlefield (or maybe a capability you or your enemy possesses) domination of which can dramatically change the probable outcome of a contest. It might be thought of as a checkmate square, or something your control of which so confounds your enemy that the result of the contest is foretold. It is a wobbly term used for all kinds of things, however. It can be confused with the 'main objective,' 'biggest advantage,' or a 'first priority.' Some strategerists enjoy arguing whether or not there can be only one or many, or if a center of gravity has to exist. (See Section 75, *Popular Support*)

**Flank (verb)**
You hit your opponent in his side, or get around his side in order to threaten his ability to safely withdraw or retreat, or because the enemy can't deliver or place as much firepower on you when you are located on his flank. It is not quite an envelopment, which you would like to effect from two or all sides, but it can be enough to win. If you're the one being flanked (or enveloped), you might have to *countermarch* (go back the way you came) in order to prevent having your supplies or your route of retreat cut off. (See Section 8, *The Operational Equation*)

**Lines of Communication**
These are the paths established and followed to send and receive supplies, orders, information; or, and this is most important -- to withdraw or retreat. If supply lines to a force are cut, that force can often obliged to surrender or retreat, hence supply and withdrawal are related. (See Section 2, *The Line of Retreat*)

**Commitment of the Reserve**
History teaches it is a good idea to hold on to some sort of mobile reserve force in case things go badly somewhere, a hole needs to be plugged, or an attack repulsed; or, in case things go well somewhere and there is an opportunity to support success and break through, pursue, or seal off your enemy's retreat. In many historical, classical battles the

contenders each had one reserve force, and there seems to have been one good time to use it. If you commit your reserve too soon, perhaps to plug a hole in the front line, and then the enemy starts to succeed in another place, and still has his reserve, you might face an unpleasantness. So knowing when to commit the reserve has been a traditional measure of good generalship. It still applies in irregular war, but the formula of types and sizes is distinct. Commitment of the reserve is associated with the notion of *mass*, either to create it or respond to the enemy's focusing of mass. 'Commitment of the reserve' also connotes a degree of timing or urgency. (See Section 121, *Commitment of the Reserve*)

**Countermarch**

This means you might just start going back the way you came. If you are taking offensive initiative and moving toward an objective (you are going to attack or take something), but your enemy threatens to (or has) crossed behind you to cut off your lines of communication, you may be forced to turn around and countermarch. When you turn around all or part of your force (because you're about to be flanked or enveloped) to confront some force threatening your lines of supply or retreat, it is usually a bad situation. (See section 2, *The Line of Retreat*)

**Correlation of Force**

This is the comparison of strength at the points of potential battle. Competent generals try to avoid battle when and where the enemy would enjoy an advantageous correlation of force. When competent generals have had to risk battle with a superior force, they manage to secure their line of withdrawal, not letting the enemy flank, envelope or force a countermarch. Whether or not the general might decide to withdraw depends in part on his estimation of the correlation of force in potential battle. The notion of mass is closely associated in that massing is an attempt to produce at least a localized and momentary advantage in the correlation of force. (See Section 8, *The Operational Equation*)

The above list gives most of the core vocabulary of classic strategy. Most of the items match or underpin 'principles,' which, like cannons or ancient wisdoms, often oppose one-another. 'Look before you leap' versus 'He who hesitates is forever lost.' In teaching these principles, or at least in the literature of classic strategy that remains, few succinct statements present the dynamics, the interrelationship, or a guiding equation using the 'principles' as variables. That interplay of principles was taught mostly through the study and comparison of many historical examples. A rare exception is a statement on a central preoccupation of generalship, which is related in Section 8, *The Operational Equation.*

Some things have changed since the Battle of Waterloo (1815), but maybe not so much. Around the turn of the 18th and 19th centuries, an army might move two hundred miles to get within that mile and a half wherein it could bring its weapons to bear. Today's weapons can be brought to bear on an enemy from almost anywhere at any distance. This is part of the reason for the rise of the idea that the old operational art of position and movement no longer matters. It is, however, exactly because weapons can be brought to bear from vast distances that people resort more to guerrilla war, care more about the balance of anonymity, dig holes, and invoke legal cover. Because of these measures, soldiers often still have to walk right up to within personal distances in order to bring their weapons to bear, which means position and movement rules still apply. By the notion of correlation of force we are reminded that the objective of classic military strategy was not to position and move in order to come into contact with the enemy, but rather to position and move in order to come into contact where and when a strength advantage could be enjoyed (at very least long enough to hit and run).

There exists a peculiar and influential protocol in today's military strategy teaching. It is a hierarchical concept about 'levels' of war generally formed of the terms 'Tactical,' 'Operational,' and 'Strategic.' Generally speaking, and with too many exceptions and arguments to bother with here, 'tactical' refers to the battle or physical engagement of enemies; 'operational' (often 'operational art') refers to movement to battle, and strategic refers to decisions about who the enemy is, how the whole force will be generated, and about the distribution of resources among elements of the force. The three terms also generally represent a scale of decision consequences. That is to say, according to convention, a solid strategy can survive an operational error, sound operational art can survive some failed tactics -- but the reverse is rarely true -- the best tactics can rarely survive poor operational decisions and the best operational plans cannot survive invalid strategy.

Although the conventional logic of hierarchical consequence can be stated in sentence form, the three supposed levels of activity and decision are actually so intimately related, the trilogy of terms can mislead. There is no magic in the terminology, and while the usual sequence of importance goes tactical-operational-strategic, even this is not always so. Some writers hold that when a general cannot succeed at tactics he is forced to resort to strategy, *strategy* meaning *stratagem* or *deception.* In short, don't worry over the word soup made by this troika; the terms gain their meaning in context. Besides, writers will at times combine or hyphenate (like 'operational strategy') or throw in adjectival wrenches like 'grand' strategy, or another level, like 'policy.' These usages don't always translate across historical periods or to other languages, and often have more to do with who is in charge of whom, and less with what to do where. Webster's 10th Collegiate does not have the same definition of *strategy* as Webster's 1st Collegiate, and yet they are both valid.

One of the most important aspects of classic strategy is not stated in the principles directly, but presumed by them. Strategy does not just happen; it is made. The creation of sufficient mass at the right time and place, for instance, is the conscious accomplishment of a leader. Without generalship there is no classic strategy. When the greats of the Napoleonic wars talked about the lessons of strategy, they associated strategic competence with some previous great such as Frederick, Marlborough, or Gustavus Adolphus. Strategy was not spontaneous. The etymology of the word strategy, at its Greek root, tells us that it means generalship.

See: 89, *The Dot Game*; 33, *Built Environment*; 109, *Hotspotting*; 63, *Cost-Distance*; 68, *Scale*; 72, *Land Strategy*; 37, *School Lunches*; and 54, *Badassoftheweek.com.*

---

"A prompt and vigorous pursuit is
the only means of ensuring complete
success."

General Phillip Sheridan[8]

Irregular warfare is highly linear

# *Section 7, Nonlinear Warfare*

Sometimes insurgencies or other forms of irregular warfare are described as nonlinear. The idea of nonlinearity is part of the misleading common wisdom about irregular war. Armed social struggles of all kinds, including insurgencies, are linear, and often extremely so. To become a believer, just accept for a moment that the important lines in classic military theory are not the lines military planners sometimes call the 'front,' 'battle line,' 'forward edge of the battle area,' or something similar to denote the face-to-face phenomena that opposing forces tend to experience in battle. The important lines are the lines of communication, especially supply lines and lines of withdrawal, and most especially the lines of withdrawal or retreat of the weaker force from places of action to sanctuaries.

If you are a single criminal suspect about to be served a warrant and apprehended in your home, the line that counts (if you intend to remain fugitive) is the line out the back door (or that secret tunnel). You intuitively understand an important part of the classic teaching about strategy -- the heart of the operational equation. For your enemy to win decisively against you, he must cut off your retreat. You figure that if he has an extra cop or two at his disposal, he's likely to send them around to the back, so you may want to get out before that happens. Or you can be like Che, who probably thought he was waging nonlinear war. The problem German General von Paulus had when facing the Russians at Stalingrad is at its root the same as that facing the single felon about to be served an arrest warrant: Once escape is no longer an option, the future can get bleak.

Just because you are having a hard time finding your enemy's lines of communication doesn't mean the lines aren't important. You better find his and secure yours.

Usually, if you hear a government briefer use the term 'nonlinear warfare,' you can confidently translate it as, 'We can't find the insurgent lines of communication.' When an insurgent uses the term, he is saying to himself 'Whew, they haven't found our lines of communication,' while to the outside audience he implies, 'Don't bother looking for our lines of communication.'

> Q. If you agree roadblocks are important phenomena in irregular war, how can you suppose irregular war to be nonlinear?

A. Exactly.

Leave 'nonlinear' out of your irregular warfare lexicon or you might leave your enemy free to use his lines of communication while he attacks yours. This does not mean you are constrained to move sequentially or make geometric moves to your points of action.

See: 19, *Extortion*; 122, *Songs of Chu*; 8, *The Operational Equation*; 2, *The Line of Retreat*; 138, *Roadblocks and Checkpoints*; 141, *Seven Strategy Strains*; 65, *Smuggling*; and 11, *Decisive Battle.*

---

> "If he were not of great ability he would have died last night. It seems to me you do not understand politics, Inglés, nor guerrilla warfare. In politics and this other the first thing is to continue to exist. Look how he continued to exist last night."
>
> Ernest Hemingway,
> *For Whom the Bell Tolls*[9]

---

The nub of classic military strategy

# *Section 8, The Operational Equation*

The practice of classic military strategy reached a zenith during the Napoleonic Wars of the late 18th and early 19th centuries. Several of the most influential writers on classic strategy, including Jomini and Clausewitz, were participants in, direct observers of, or victims of Napoleon's campaigns. This is not to say that classic strategy was invented by Napoleon, the Duke of Wellington (Napoleon's nemesis), or by any of the strategy writers. Most of the classic concepts were previously named and formally studied. Military strategy was old as an academic discipline, but it was not until arrival of the revolutionary technologies of the 20th century (aircraft and radio in particular) that the basic formulae of classic military strategy began to lose their grip. When our atmosphere became available as a plane of military action, it so changed the variables of time and distance, strategic thinking was diverted and less respect accorded to the classic principles. The older expressions were thenceforth received as archaic, and many historic battles considered obsolete in face of dramatically new technological facts and a greatly expanded battlespace.

In irregular wars, however, the use of many of the 20th century weapons is restricted either by legal and moral influences, or by even newer technologies. This section offers an explanation, written at the end of the non-flight age, of a core dynamic of the classic principles. Many of the classic principles apply (if adjusted) to all forms of warfare, and for the purpose of explaining how; this particular expression is useful and succinct.

In *Outlines of Military Geography (1899)*, T. Miller Maguire, in order to arm his students with a working concept of military strategy, stated the following:

> "Once the reader understands that soldiering and fighting are far from synonymous -- that in a campaign combats are occasional while marching is constant -- that before entering into battle a general must be most careful to secure his line or lines of retreat; he understands the leading principles of strategy, whether he can define the phrase to his satisfaction or not. He sees that a general whose road homeward or to his base is threatened or cut by a superior force must, if he loses a decisive battle, be ruined as well as defeated; while a general who has secured his line of communication will not be ruined even if defeated, but can fall back, procure recruits, replenish his waggons, and begin to fight again with a fair prospect of success."[10]

Maguire's observation remains valid today, and for every type of armed conflict. It has two parts. The first is about movement before battle. Before an action, someone is going to travel. Organized armed action means position and movement. Even the lone terrorist doesn't detonate the bomb in his own basement -- at least not intentionally. He moves it to some other place for detonation. And before that, someone united the materials for making the bomb, and motivated the bomber to act. If he is not a suicide bomber, he also faces the question of safely leaving the site of the detonation. Even threats of the use of bombs usually imply some movement before action. If terrorist organizations only threatened to blow up their own camps, they would be considerably less menacing.

The second part of Maguire's observation depends on the first, but is the more consequential point for understanding the military operational problem. The careful leader will make sure his line of withdrawal is secure in case he attacks or is met by a stronger force. Otherwise, he greatly increases the chances of his own destruction. About the only terminal mistake an insurgent leader can make is to get caught. He can recover from everything else. When the leader of the Sendero Luminoso, or the Tupamaros, or the Tamil Tigers is caught or killed, it might not take all the wind out of the revolution, but it is a severe blow. There are some organizational forms less subject to destruction by decapitation. In them, subunits act on independent initiative or the organization grooms many replacement leaders. Such independence from or depth of hierarchy doesn't change the logic or applicability of Maguire's synthesis -- it just multiplies its possible occasions. The reason armed organizations armor and vaccinate themselves against decapitation is exactly because the Maguire dilemma is ineluctable. The upshot of the equation can be ameliorated and dispersed, but essentially, ultimately, it is the basic mathematic for victory or defeat in military operations. Leadership is a precious commodity and a supremely significant element of relative power. Once that leadership is neutralized, power is neutralized.

Maguire's equation is not all about physical movement, either. It is about shaping physical reality for the purposes of acting prudently *and* to affect the perceptions and mindset of the opposing leader. Another expression from *Outlines of Military Geography*:

> "The object of the strategist in drawing up his plan is so to arrange his marches and his lines of operations that, on the one hand, if he wins the battle he will not only defeat the enemy on the field but place him in a situation of much perplexity as to his future action, his line of retreat, and his supplies; and, on the other hand, if the battle be lost, he will have secured for himself a safe line of retreat, and an opportunity of recuperating his strength."[11]

Again, there are two parts -- movement and secured options -- but this second statement weaves them together more tightly, and puts emphasis on the psychological dimension. Moving prudently means engaging a weaker enemy in order to neutralize him or fatally perplex him as to his options; or, in the event of contact with a stronger enemy force, having maintained the ability to withdraw intact. Maguire's statements remind us that contacts don't just up and happen – someone makes decisions to *be someplace.* It also reminds us that competent strategy implies the constant measurement of relative power, but with prudence to know that those measurements will often be wrong.

Maguire's statements make the line of retreat to sanctuary a central geographic concept for winning operational art. Don't think this diminishes the importance of battle, however. Maguire was emphatic in his writings about the primacy of battle. Without armed action, an insurgent is just a lawyer or a politician. Without robbery, the thief goes broke. And as far as the State goes, if it does nothing to engage the armed insurgent physically, the latter will continue to attack and grow until he *is* the State. Battle was to Maguire the ultimate military preoccupation, but he noted that it did not have to occur in order for it to be effective. The fact of potential battle, with its results and consequences as perceived in the minds of the contending leaders, could be enough.

Maguire offered his statements about movement, lines of communication, and battle hoping to illuminate the essence of strategy, although he never actually defines that essence. At that time, English-speaking military thinkers had not yet wedged much space between the terms 'strategy' and 'operations' (or had dictionary writers). Some instructors had used the idea of 'levels of war' (for instance, Jomini proposed a level called 'grand tactics'), but the idea of distinct levels was only just poking its way into doctrine when Maguire wrote. Maguire's idea of military strategy is what some military people today will insist should be called 'operational art,' thus saving the word *strategy* for bigger things. For this reason, the title of the current section changed from what it had been, 'The Essence of Strategy' to the more conforming 'The Operational Equation.' It suggests an equation because two armed contenders face the same, but opposite, formula. In irregular warfare, your strategies are more likely to succeed if your recognition of threats and opportunities, measurement of relative strengths, goal-setting, marshalling and assignment of resources, establishment of priorities and sequences, imagining and implementation of deceptions, and your positioning and movement of power are all interwoven as seamlessly as possible. This book focuses especially on the last element (the positioning and movement of lethal military power), but without discarding the others, as they are all one cloth.

The principal non-maneuver, non operational art option is a form of extortion – to cause your enemy leaders so much pain they are swayed to negotiate or surrender. The exact point of effective pain is difficult to judge, since it is dependent on factors internal to the enemy's skull, and acts that create sufficient pain may be morally untenable. Part of the eventual British strategy against the Boers was to round up Boer families and put them in horrendous concentration camps. The British had been generally unable to dominate the operational equation. They could not outmaneuver the Boers definitively. The Boers, on the other hand, could not endure their families' suffering. Causing that suffering became a column of British counter-guerrilla strategy in the face of their inability to succeed via military operational position and movement.

Of course, the two (positioning and extortion) are almost always combined. British success in using extortion against the Boers did not arrive because of total operational failure. Rather, a point came when the progress achievable by more investment in position and maneuver seemed insubstantial. The British had reached the point of diminishing marginal returns from operational art; operational art was not going to meet the British goals within conceivable time and budget. The outcome to be achieved on the basis of pure extortion was not pretty, either.

There are other counterinsurgency strategies as well, which may or may not be available. One, often suggested by the insurgent, is for the counterinsurgent government to effect those changes in society that respond to the criticism leveled against it by the insurgents. Another is to convince the population that the insurgents' argument is not valid, and so vaccinate the population against insurgent enthrallment and extortion. These two approaches work very slowly or not at all. Victory has to be secured in time, and these approaches, while they might help close down the routes of an enemy's withdrawal to sanctuary, probably will not do enough, fast enough.

Since 1990, the Colombians, for instance, have made tremendous changes in their constitution and supporting laws, greatly liberalizing the country in response to many of the criticisms long leveled against the society by the insurgent left. Those changes did little to weaken the FARC or change its azimuth toward armed takeover. Negotiating with the FARC fared no better. This is perhaps because its leaders see themselves as an ideological vanguard, a sort of secular clergy. They have explained their existence by pointing to the unjust nature of the Colombian social construct, but, regardless of any changes the society might make to address complaints about the construct, FARC chieftains intend to be in charge and untouchable. In the last decade we have also witnessed remarkable erosion in popular support for the FARC, along with a parallel increase in popular support for the government. This has indeed meant greater resources for government armed forces and greater leeway as to public acceptance of violent action on the part of the armed forces. Nevertheless, in spite of consistently high levels of popular support for the government, the FARC has not been defeated. This is because the Colombian armed forces have not been able to dominate the imperatives of military strategy as Maguire stated them. As long as the FARC maintains sanctuaries and safe routes to them, it remains a living, viable threat, even though the Colombian Army has beaten it in battle after battle, and although the FARC has almost no popular support. Colombia's inability to achieve decisive victory has little to do with socioeconomic conditions within Colombia, and a lot to do with constraints imposed by geopolitical facts on the possibilities of military position and movement. The FARC sanctuaries are too often located in neighboring countries.

At any rate, strategies based on changing the society, changing attitudes, or negotiating are, in a way, all external to our proposed definition of *enemy* asserted in Section 4 as he who will do us grave harm before peaceful measures to avert the damage of his behavior can bear fruit. If peaceful measures look like they *will* bear fruit before the violent group in question does us grave harm, then perhaps we have no enemy, just citizens with a negotiable grievance or idea. Negotiations are not necessarily bad propositions, if there is something to trade. If we are in fact dealing with an enemy, however, negotiations will be subtle, deceptive, and insincere. It can be hard to remember that when you give up something of value so that the other guy protects you from him, you are being extorted. Your enemy may be able to combine the movement and position of military power with extortion as well as you can.

Toward the end of the term of Colombian President Andrés Pastrana, he told the Colombian public it was necessary for him to accede to an ELN (National Liberation Army, a leftist guerrilla group smaller than the FARC) demand for a demilitarized zone in a strategically valuable part of the country because if he did not, the ELN could do the country a lot of harm. That was pretty much the final straw confession of presidential submissiveness. In the next election the Colombians voted in Álvaro Uribe, who campaigned on a pledge to seek peace through victory over the guerrillas, rather than appeasement.

Can two approaches -- one built upon a conviction that you must close with and destroy a foe because no timely peaceable actions will work against him, and another based on negotiations and propaganda -- exist together? Historically, it appears nearly universal and necessary. Such mixed strategies are devised around timing, separated battlefields, the need to economize force or to placate allies. The mixing of approaches is also driven by uncertainty or deception. As an insurgent, you will almost always want to mount a mixed strategy. Insurgent or counterinsurgent, and whatever the mixture of your ends, ways, and means, if your efforts do not respect the classic military operational equation, they will be far less likely to succeed. Although Maguire was emphatic about the importance of perception and the mindset of opposing leaders, he was also insistent that the best way to influence the mind in war is to create advantageous facts of power on the ground. To win decisively, there is little substitute for physically neutralizing your enemy.

See: 141, *Seven Strategy Strains*; 12, *Protraction and Diligence*; 116, *Strategy of Aggregate Tactics*; 6, *Classic Strategy and Irregular Warfare*; 59, *Spontaneity*; 11, *Decisive Battle*; 63, *Cost-Distance*; and 69, *Measuring Actions against Enemies.*

---

> "There are few generals who have run oftener, or more lustily than I have done. But I have taken care not to run too far.... "
>
> Nathaniel Greene (1781)[12]

Napoleon's masterpiece

# Section 9, Ulm and Austerlitz

Napoleon's Ulm and Austerlitz campaign of 1805 is an icon of classic military history and strategy, and the centerpiece of Napoleon's résumé -- this in spite of being Napoleon's plan B. Plan A was to invade England. In July, Napoleon was at Boulogne overseeing preparations for the invasion when information came to him that his navy would not be able to gain the necessary control of the English Channel.[13]

Napoleon soon decided to use his huge, well-drilled force by turning it westward, and in late August marching to the Rhine to meet the armies of Austria and Russia before they could join together against the French. Austrian General Karl Mack von Leiberich had prematurely begun operations, instead of waiting for the Russian army to join him from the east. The first week of October, Mack learned of the French vanguard's presence on the Danube. News of Napoleon's movements came quickly to Mack, but the reports were as much the product of Napoleon's deceptions and feints as of trustworthy observations. Mack attempted a series of maneuvers to escape from being encircled, but they were ineffective. By the $16^{th}$ of October, Napoleon had managed to encircle Ulm and most of Mack's forces. Some skirmishes occurred for a few more days as Mack sought to break out across the Rhine, but these also were too little, too late. While some parts of his force remained outside the encirclement, Mack, without a secure line of supply or retreat, surrendered an entire army, perhaps 30,000 men. Now Napoleon, with a much better prospective correlation of force, would seek battle with the oncoming Russian-led army.

The consummate battle of Austerlitz was joined December 2nd on ground west of the town in what is now the Czech Republic. French organizational excellence and logistic preparations were matched to Napoleon's tactical genius. French soldiers showed their discipline and revolutionary élan. The opposing army was soundly defeated and the alliance against Napoleon finished. At the Treaty of Pressburg, the Austrians retired from the war, and Napoleon's position on the continent became immensely more secure than it had been six months earlier.

For the Russians, the defeat at Austerlitz was grave, but it was not complete; there was a Russian retreat. Russian military leaders, including generals Mikhail Kutuzov and Pyotr Bagration, did not let the French encircle their forces as had General Mack. Positions on the ground at the time of the treaty allowed the Russian army to return home relatively intact.

The defeated Russian generals would meet Napoleon's armies several times again. Seven years after Austerlitz, the battle of Borodino in early September, 1812 (often described as indecisive) set the stage for Russian victory over the French Grande Armée. At Borodino, Napoleon atypically had failed to pursue a beaten Russian army. Bagration was mortally wounded, but Kutuzov would evacuate Moscow, retreat and refit. By late October, the Grande Armée was itself in retreat, and would be harassed to death by Kutuzov and the Russian winter. Of the half million French soldiers who marched into Russia, fewer than a hundred thousand would see France again.

**Appendix**:

The bad news that arrived in late July, 1805 at Boulogne (where Napoleon was preparing to invade England) was about the sea battle of Cape Finisterre.

The battle of Cape Finisterre is not one of military history's milestone events, but maybe it should be. Many of history's great battles were preceded by some nearly forgotten one, but which set the stage. The battle of the Corral Sea preceded the battle of Midway, Pantano de Vargas preceded Boyacá Bridge, and so on. The Battle of Trafalgar, won by Admiral Lord Nelson to establish British supremacy at sea, was preceded by the battle of Cape Finisterre.

Actually, at least two pieces of knowledge fed Napoleon's decision to abandon his plans to take England. One was the sorry performance of his landing craft, many of which floundered during an invasion rehearsal, in turn swamping some of the Emperor's confidence. More significantly, success depended on his fleet being able to control the waters of the English Channel for a period of time sufficient for the French army to cross. Napoleon's plan was daring, or tenuous -- French admiral Pierre-Charles Villeneuve was to break out of the port of Toulon (at the time being blockaded by Admiral Horatio Nelson) and sail his fleet to the West Indies where he would meet another French fleet under Admiral Honoré Ganteaume.

Ganteaume was to break out of the British blockade of Brest. By sailing to the Caribbean, ostensibly to attack British commerce, the French would pull a significant part of the British fleet in chase. Both French fleets would return quickly and overpower the remaining British ships in the English Channel, thus creating a window of time for Napoleon's army to displace before the main elements of the British fleet could get back from the Caribbean. Once Napoleon had invested Britain, he would keep the British fleet from returning to port.

Admiral Nelson did in fact chase -- that part of Napoleon's plan worked. Ganteaume, however, had not been able to break out of Brest, and so did not meet Villeneuve at Martinique as planned. Although Villeneuve got back to European waters a month ahead of Nelson, he was met off Cape Finisterre by a British fleet commanded by Admiral Robert Calder, who had been blockading the ports of Rochefort and Ferrol. The ensuing battle was indecisive, or so it seemed, and afterwards Villeneuve put into port at Ferrol. Then, although ordered by Napoleon to go north to lift the blockade at Brest and proceed on to Boulogne (the invasion plan still alive, since Nelson's fleet was still distant), Villenueve decided instead to retire to Cádiz to the south. When Napoleon heard the news of the battle of Cape Finisterre and Villeneuve's irresolute decision, the invasion plan died.

In effect, it was Calder's action that convinced Napoleon he could not carry out a cross channel invasion (rather than Nelson's victory at

Trafalgar, which did not occur until October, two days after Mack's surrender at Ulm). Neither the French nor the British commander pursued his foe after the battle, and so in that sense Cape Finisterre appeared indecisive. Each had his reasons, but each was soon condemned for failure to push to the limit of his respective culminating point. Calder was reprimanded and never commanded at sea again. Napoleon had Villenueve murdered. Calder's reasons were better than Villenueve's, and it seems from this historical distance that Admiral Lord Nelson's already immense public popularity may have been the main enemy of Calder's reputation. In retrospect, it may be that Calder's decisions saved Britain from invasion, not Lord Nelson's.

Not only do these old battles expose classic lessons, they exposed those lessons to at least one leader who would later be credited with the invention of revolutionary military strategy. Probably using these same battles as examples, the Russians taught Mao Zedong about the balance of offensive and defensive movement, lengthened and shortened supply lines, and retreat into a supportive population. They taught him the effect of distance on correlations of force, and the difference between aggressive pursuit and patient harassment. They may even have taught the wisdom of not invading an island without first securing the sea.

Irregular warfare is subject to the rules exposed by battles of the Napoleonic wars. If you can convince your enemy that he cannot withdraw to base and cannot defeat you in battle, he might surrender. If he retreats and you have the capacity to pursue but do not, he may regain strength.

See: 138, *Roadblocks and Checkpoints*; 19, *Extortion*; 88, *Sieges and Take-overs*; 8, *The Operational Equation*; 2, *The Line of Retreat*; 141, *Seven Strategy Strains*; 65, *Smuggling*; and 11, *Decisive Battle.*

---

An anarchist throws a bomb into a Paris kitchen.

Result: Linoleum blown apart.

---

The central geographic concept in armed strategy

# *Section 10, The Line of Retreat*

In order to win (decisively, definitively, conclusively, to be sovereign, to have a successful State) you want to assert a monopoly over the granting of impunity in your territory. You especially have to stop any armed competitor who figures to grant impunity in the same places as you. To discipline your impunity-granting adversary, your best bet is to go capture or kill him. To that end, the line of retreat is the central geographic concept. That does not mean retreat is the most important event in armed conflict. Battle is the most important event in armed conflict, but the line of retreat is the most important geographic concept.

Whether we are thinking of a single criminal, an insurgent column, a group of thugs, the Sixth German Army, a Costa Rican patrol boat, Darius' horde -- or you -- attention to the lines of retreat to sanctuary is a key to winning.

The line of retreat runs from a point of violent action to calm safety. If you're in opposition to government, the action may be one of your own initiative, at places you choose for a kidnapping, bank robbery, mortaring of a police station or a government convoy, making a drugs-for-money exchange, or where you plant an annoying bomb. The point of action may also be a place where a government force catches you on your way to one of your intended points of action. In either case, if you are about to engage with an enemy force of greater immediate strength than your own, you better have a secure route of escape. If you do not, you could be decisively hurt. If your force is much stronger than your enemy's, then he's the one with the retreat problem. Since it is often difficult to estimate likely comparative strengths, and the costs for guessing wrong are so steep, a prudent commander assures the security of his route of escape in all cases except those in which the superiority of his force is exceedingly obvious. Of course there are daring and brilliant commanders who sense correctly when to defy prudence.

If you think you've made it to sanctuary, but your enemy presses his pursuit and you find yourself under siege, you might not be in sanctuary, and, at best, you are still located along your route to sanctuary; and if that route remains unsecure, your participation may be about to end. So what is a sanctuary? For our purposes it is a territory in which you enjoy impunity and can plan your initiatives. The better the sanctuary, the more you enjoy.

An insurgent modus operandi or standard operating procedure may be to meld into the population in civilian clothes and disappear on the metro after an action. In such an urban setting, insurgents will fear a system that checks individual identity when persons enter the train station, or a local neighborhood full of people willing and able to report the presence of strangers. Your rebel line of retreat is made insecure to the extent you do not enjoy anonymity. Your sanctuaries may be places where anonymity is readily available, and that too could be a problem, because the government may be able to place informants there as well. Every system that makes you identify yourself (such as counterfeit-resistant ID cards, a conscription registry requirement, motorbike registration, professional licensing and so on) makes insurgent lines of retreat a little less secure. If there are several of you (and if there aren't, you haven't much of an insurgency) then the danger of exposing the whereabouts of your sanctuaries and movement to them is multiplied in relation to your number. If the government does not establish systems that endanger your anonymity as you retreat to sanctuary, you'll likely be OK. If the government has any resources at all, you will not want to be talking on the cell phone much. Don't use a credit card either, or at least use someone else's.

It is discomforting spiritually for the warrior to think of the line of retreat as the central geographic concept of operational strategy. If that's you, just try to make your lines of retreat those of orderly withdrawal and your enemies' lines of retreat those of routed panic and capture.

What is the psychology of a man on the run? Fugitives without sanctuary do not take the initiative. They concern themselves with finding sanctuary. They are on the defensive mentally as well as physically. It is tough to be both reeling and planning offensive moves. If a guerrilla cannot attack, he is stripped of identity. If your enemy is safe in sanctuary, what does he have to do with his time? Plot, of course. His mind is able to initiate; he is on the offensive. A secure line of retreat is often, for the able strategist, geography for regaining the initiative.

See: 138, *Roadblocks and Checkpoints*; 2, *Anonymity*; 16, *Keeping Secrets*; 8, *The Operational Equation*; 6, *Classic Strategy and Irregular Warfare*; 108, *Neogeography*; 140, *Culminating Point in the Pursuit*; and 121, *Commitment of the Reserves.*

---

> "Retreat is a concept which fully enters into that of the attack. I retreat over 100 to 200 kilometers so as to go over to the attack on a certain line at a certain moment decided by myself...Retreat is one of the movements in the general course of offensive operations. Retreat is not flight."
>
> Mikhail Frunze, 1922[14]

All armed struggles are decided by battle

# *Section 11, Decisive Battle*

After a decisive battle, you (if you win) can move safely to sanctuary and your enemy cannot.

Armed contests revolve around battle. Battle is as important a concept in irregular warfare as it is in classic movement and positional war, and maybe more so. Seeking decisive or definitive victory in armed engagements is a key point in the best insurgency texts. Those writings (say, for instance, Griffith's *Mao Tse-Tung On Guerrilla Warfare*) counsel insurgents to attack their State enemy without committing to a fight with a superior force unless a route of escape is secured and the State's pursuit unlikely to succeed. A battle in an irregular war is 'decisively' lost and won either when one force overwhelmingly destroys the other in the engagement *or when it leads to a failed retreat.* Either way, the winner can retire to sanctuary, and the loser cannot.

Armed groups don't arm themselves just to be armed. Folks who do that are called gun collectors. Organized criminals don't seek battle with the government most of the time, while for most insurgents, battle is imperative for existence and identity. The 'decisive battles' the insurgent wants to avoid are only the ones which are decisive in favor of the government, and in such cases 'decisive' has a crystal clear definition -- an insurgent unit's withdrawal to sanctuary (after realizing itself overmatched in contact with a government force) fails, and the insurgents are killed or captured. An insurgency without sanctuaries cannot survive long, and so the fact of decisive battle leads to the logical observation that an insurgent movement must develop reasonable sanctuaries and escape routes to them, at very least for the leadership, before it attempts battle. Of course some of the battles may be so small, or the investigative abilities of the government so insignificant, that some display of force is possible without too much care spent on sanctuary. Che never did grasp the imperatives of operational art, and thought plodding around in the Bolivian highlands would provide sanctuary enough. Nope.

For the insurgent, a damaging attack against the State that doesn't end in the destruction of the guerrilla unit may be favorably decisive. Besides, most insurgents don't plan to always be guerrillas. There exists a typical current of guerrilla thinking that looks forward ultimately to victory in more conventional battle.

For the counterinsurgent, battle should be an even more important concept. This is because, more often than not, the government units enjoy a positive correlation of force in prospective battles, which means the insurgent is the one who runs greater risk of being beaten and caught during a pursuit, cut off from sanctuary, ruined and done. The possibility of positively decisive battle is the centerpiece of the counterinsurgent's advantage. Routing the insurgent in a contact and sending him running high-tailed into the mist rarely constitutes decisive victory for the counterinsurgent, exhilarating as it may seem at the time. Such contacts may in fact be the immediate face of another decisive victory for the guerrilla. The government only succeeds decisively by way of successful pursuit. Of course counterinsurgent commanders will want to say they just won another battle, even when they did not even chance a dangerous pursuit. They may have won, but not decisively, or maybe they won decisively if the cost to the insurgent enemy during the battle was terminally high. More probably the government actually loses any time it does not win the pursuit. The cop who doesn't serve the warrant or make the arrest doesn`t go home feeling like a winner, even if he feels pretty good about still being alive.

Instead of one huge decisive battle, or five, counterinsurgent strategy may have to accept the proposition of many potentially decisive battles. In an insurgent war there may never be a Battle of Midway, but then again, there might. The Colombian Army's retaking of the remote eastern departmental capital of Mitú in early October, 1998 is shaping up historically as that kind of engagement. Before Mitú, the FARC had enjoyed a long series of successful engagements against increasingly larger army units. After Mitú, the FARC never again pretended to hold key political geography. In any case, some military historians, like Russell Wiegley, opine that few battles in any kind of war are very decisive in the long run.[15]

Battle is the quintessential military event. To the extent military events change history, they are decisive of something, but history can also ignore a lopsided military victory. That said, the counterinsurgent leader who dismisses the centrality of battle forgets his reason for being. The insurgent will always argue, 'There can be no decisive battle in this struggle, so don't look for it.' Why does he say that? He is obligated to that piece of propaganda because his whole military strategy revolves around finding opportunities for favorable little battles until he can afford to chance a big one. If he follows prudent operational art, he doesn't get stuck in contact with a superior force unless he has a secure escape route. The term 'hit and run' includes 'run.'

All the above is not to deny there may be exceptions and viable strategic options. If a guerrilla takes too many casualties during his harassments, ambushes and sabotages, he may weaken over time. It seems, however, that time is increasingly on the guerrilla's side as time goes on, and that he can paint his initiatives as victories regardless of statistics. Indeed, every little attack that is not answered with an effective pursuit by the government may be a decisive victory for a guerrilla. Even for the guerrilla, victory after decisive victory might mean nothing if no plans exist to exploit them. The potential decisiveness of a series of small successes can still be forfeited by subsequent inaction.

The term *correlation of force* comes in to play here. Seeking superior strength at the moment of battle is a no-brainer. Every commander wants to win these testing instances. In irregular warfare, the correlations of force in battle may involve very constrained tactical terrain options, small competing units and simple weaponry. They also may extend upward to thousands of men in contact, and feature highly sophisticated air power, technical communications and secret intelligence assets. Regardless of the technological scope or geographic scale of a potential battle, the counterinsurgent should not presume even a clear advantage in power sufficient *unless his concept of 'battle' includes the pursuit*. In other words, the counterinsurgent must calculate and field an advantage in correlations of force at the points of engagement such that his units can mount and succeed in the pursuit of the insurgent enemy after contacts. Then the battles may be won decisively for the counterinsurgent. Conversely, the insurgent needn't be daunted by imposing combat advantages of government forces so long as he can disengage quickly and make a safe escape.

Sometimes you may hear an expression like, 'They lost a lot of battles but won the war' or, conversely, 'They never lost a battle, but didn't win the war.' We are better off not to assert that battles are won or lost without considering whether or not the retreats were successful or unsuccessful.

Appendix: In August 1976, the Rhodesian Selous Scouts raided a large guerrilla training camp in Mozambique that belonged to the ZANLA (Zimbabwe National Liberation Army) insurgents, who were trying to replace the government of Rhodesia. The Scouts entered the ZANLA camp dressed and equipped as ZANLA fighters at a time when the garrison was celebrating and many of the ZANLA troops were in parade formation. The raiders killed more than 1000 ZANLA fighters and wounded many more. The Scouts were then able to return to their base having only suffered four wounded, making it the most successful attack of the Rhodesian insurgent war and one of the most daring and impressive raids in military history. Although the Scouts entered enemy sanctuary and greatly damaged ZANLA morale and strength, the raid was decisive of nothing. The Rhodesian government military was far too small for the territory it had to control; it had almost no operational or strategic concept; and the ultimate goal for which it fought (minority apartheid rule) was unsustainable. In 1980, Rhodesia ceased to exist. A ZANLA leader, Robert Mugabe, is today the country's dictator.

See: 119, *Huai Hai Campaign*; 2, *The Line of Retreat*; 3, *The Domesday Book*; 116, *Strategy of Aggregate Tactics*; 140, *Culminating Point in the Pursuit*; 57, *Dogs and Mules*; 138, *Roadblocks and Checkpoints*; and 69, *Measuring Actions against Enemies.*

> "The importance of the victory is chiefly determined by the vigor with which the immediate pursuit is carried out. In other words, pursuit makes up the second act of victory and in many cases is more important than the first. Strategy at this point draws near to tactics in order to receive the completed assignment from it; and its first exercise of authority is to demand that the victory should really be complete."
>
> Carl von Clausewitz, *On War*[16]

Irregular conflicts are not protracted by nature

# *Section 12, Protraction and Diligence*

Armed social struggles, including insurgencies, are not by nature protracted or prolonged. Nature has nothing to do with it. Someone protracts a conflict for a reason. A pamphlet titled *Guide to the Analysis of Insurgency* that has been kicking around the US intelligence community for decades asserts,

> "Insurgency is a protracted political-military activity directed toward completely or partially controlling the resources of a country through the use of irregular military forces and illegal political organizations. Insurgent activity...is designed to weaken government control and

> legitimacy while increasing insurgent control and legitimacy."[17]

Insurgents typically make the argument that their conflict will be prolonged indefinitely if a political solution is not found (that government concessions must be made, negotiations undertaken, amnesties granted). The counterinsurgent is often quick to repeat the assertion of conflict longevity, usually in order to explain or justify slow progress. A number of US doctrinal materials state explicitly that insurgent war is a naturally protracted affair. It is not. The Japanese were in near constant conventional campaign from September 19, 1931 until September 2, 1945, while Che Guevara was beaten rapidly and badly in the Congo and then quickly dispatched in Bolivia. This isolated and improbable comparison of the two (the warring of Imperial Japan versus Guevara's bumbling) yields a result that conventional war is some ten times more protracted than insurgent war. Such an errant statistic doesn't offer any kind of rule, but it may be closer to the general truth than what is usually asserted. If we were to include *golpes de estado* (coups) under the semantic umbrella of 'insurgencies,' then Western Hemisphere insurgencies would not average out longer than conventional wars. Some wars are short, some are long. Whether or not they are regular has little bearing on their duration compared to other factors of strength, especially how the leaders' respective strategies and resolve collide.

American observers fixate on those insurgent wars that took a long time, thereby lending tautological strength to the theory of natural protraction, but even without including *golpes de estado,* a review of insurgent efforts in Venezuela, Argentina, Uruguay, Nicaragua, Costa Rica, Bolivia, Peru, and elsewhere does not suggest insurgencies are necessarily long in duration. There are too many exceptions to the supposed rule. As to those that are long-lived, someone *protracted* them, and that someone was almost always a guerrilla leader with uncommon capability and opportunity. He was someone who understood the operational math.

Pointing out the historical occasions of abbreviated insurgencies does not erase the fact some insurgent wars of the twentieth century, including in Latin America, have been all but interminable. The case this book uses most is the struggle in Colombia, which has lasted decades. The central point here is not about average duration, however, but about the tendency to misrepresent or to lose the sense of causation by abuse of the passive voice. Statements to the effect that conflict 'is prolonged' or that guerrilla wars 'are protracted' affairs are at best lazy. Worse, they encourage a supposition that perhaps the will, attitudes and decisions of the competitors is not the source, and at different points in time during a conflict, for its pace.

Regain focus on the active voice. Insurgent, rebel, revolutionary, and criminal leaders all survive by keeping their lines of movement to refuge safe. To them, prolonging the conflict means staying alive and at large. Insurgents protract violent contests because the personal demise or incarceration of their leaders often means the end of the insurgency. Internal wars are never just protracted. Guerrilla leaders protract them as a matter of life and death – theirs.

So why isn't it practically correct, if protraction is the common result of leaders' decisions, to call protraction part of the nature of the war?

If the counterinsurgent begins his designs and plans on the assumption insurgent war is a naturally protracted affair, he is likely to suffer two negative consequences. One is a failure to recognize the precarious position of the insurgent, born of tactical and operational disadvantages as to culminating points, potential correlations of force, and anonymity, during an insurgency's early development. The guerrilla has to be wary not to attack a superior force, and when the guerrilla commander risks such an attack he has to make sure his line of retreat to sanctuary is secure. Therefore, all else being equal, the counterinsurgent should want to accelerate the war by applying as many resources as possible, especially early-on, in order to find insurgent lines of retreat and sanctuary, and to force the insurgent guerrilla into more and more encounters in which the probable correlations of force favor the government.

The second negative consequence of the natural-protraction fallacy relates to the counterinsurgent's own morale base. There are few examples of a democratic country not having their electorates grow weary of a war. This weariness is often pegged to the periodicity of elections. That is to say, the weariness can be highlighted in a political campaign at the expense of the incumbent. Weariness is often made into a political argument and asset, so any theory that assumes a conflict will necessarily last beyond the normal term of the executive is problematic. You may be setting up defeat in advance (and falling into a standard insurgent psychological strategy) by presupposing a war cannot be won during the term of a current executive. Military operational logic can in this way be forfeited to questions of strategic morale.

If, on the other hand, an insurgent leader were to assume insurgent or guerrilla war were a naturally protracted affair, he might overlook the fact that it is he who has to do the protracting.

Ongoing financial profit may also be a protracting factor. This feeds what are called the 'war economy' theories. Especially when insurgents are involved in profitable criminal activities, like the Colombian FARC, for instance, they find they can prosper without political progress, making operational strategies of prolongation more attractive to them. On the other side of the competitive ledger, some constituencies, like security guards, arms manufacturers or military sutlers, also live well on war, and thus may prefer theories that help keep a war going. These 'war economy' observations may have some weight, but they don't reverse the point. In most cases it behooves the counterinsurgent to reject insurgent argumentation that his war is a long one. A government military may sense a vested interest in persistent or prolonged conflict if it sees a link between larger budgets, organizational health, and public support. If the objective is, however, to win a war, the counterinsurgent should do everything to accelerate the insurgent's demise. It is not the reverse for the insurgent, but only the reverse until the insurgent can gain military advantage, in which case he can speed things up. It is a world of parry and thrust.

The antidote to protraction is diligence. Diligence includes the traditional military values of initiative and mass, but it also means respectful and dutiful attention to a task at hand. That means not just taking initiative, but acting in a timely way with sufficient force in the right places, and following through before the appropriate moment for action is gone.

See: *102, Negotiations*; 103, *Amnesty*; 52; *Sovereignty*; 118, *Whole of Government*; 8, *The Operational Equation*; 122, *Songs of Chu*; 68, *Scale*; and 64, *Measuring Power*.

---

> "…it is the true policy to incur even heavy loses of a few hours' fighting for an adequate object, rather than prolong a conflict for days and weeks by adopting the slower methods that in the end waste life…."
>
> A. Hilliard Atteridge[18]

No retreat, no more insurgent

# *Section 13, Puthukkudiyirippu*

The Liberation Tigers of , Eelam (LTTE) waged an on-again/off-again, but mostly on-again war against the government of Sri Lanka from 1983 until early 2009, when the Sri Lankan Army (SLA) forced the Tigers to capitulate. During the last few years of the LTTE's existence, the SLA outmaneuvered the LTTE, beat the Tigers in combat engagements, and systematically closed down its lines of supply and retreat. Finally, at a place called Puthukkudiyirippu, on the northeast coast, a little south of the Jaffna Peninsula, the Army surrounded remaining LTTE units and killed almost all of the LTTE leaders.

Sri Lanka is an ethnically diverse land, ethnicity commonly tagged as one of the ingredients that led to the Tamil Tigers' fight. According to the *CIA World Factbook*, about 74% of Sri Lankans are Sinhalese; 7% Sri Lankan Moor; 5% Indian Tamil; and 4% Sri Lankan Tamil. Religiously, according to that source, about 70% are Buddhist; 8% Muslim; 7% Hindu; and 6% Christian. The *Factbook* also indicates that 74% of Sri Lankans speak Sinhala and 18% speak Tamil. These rough ethnic statistics can only be made to overlap in a ragged fashion, so 'ethnicity' itself is a soft concept on which to hang an understanding of the Sri Lankan war.

The political conditions which many Sri Lankans found intolerable, and which to some Sri Lankans justified armed revolt, had a slow historic build. We can, however, trace the origins of the war efficiently by noting the Official Language Act of 1956. Making Sinhala the country's one official language, the Act was a statement of nationhood and a break with its British colonial past (with its English-language inheritance). The Act, democratically derived, had both a highlighting and degrading effect on the rights, honor and material well-being of the Tamil-speaking minority, and thus the Act is a milestone on the road to the Tamil insurgency. An azimuth had been struck toward the consolidation of an aggrieved yet powerful underclass identity. Sri Lankan tinkering with constitutional formulae did not derive a peaceful social contract. It led instead to a clarification of who was 'in' and who was 'out.' The basic cards given to the well-intentioned were not all good. The political history of Ceylon had rested on accreted arrogance, part of which was an advantageous relationship that an educated Tamil ethnic minority had enjoyed with the British. Then the British left.

The Cold War also provided a left-right/communist-capitalist flagging for political identity as a spur to radicalization and polarization.

The Sri Lankan mix of real and perceived advantages presented a fertile environment for leaders who could translate resentment into organized action. Velupillai Prabhakaran, charismatic, ruthless leader of the LTTE, grew to represent the Sri Lankan Tamil. He was ready to take on leftist radical signage and accept whatever foreign support came with it. Sri Lanka was to suffer its own volatile concoction of caste, communism and comeuppance.

As is typical of insurgent leaders, Prabhakaran's goal was to rule a separate Tamil country, if not become dictator of the whole island. He variously allowed speculation on the viability of federalism or partial autonomy, but, in retrospect, had always been single-minded about who was going to be in charge of any resulting polity: himself. In the course of the war, Prabhakaran eliminated competition from other erstwhile rebel pretenders. The goal of the government of Sri Lanka, meanwhile, was peace, but a peace that did not divide the island into two countries. Until 2006, the government constantly sought some sort of ceasefire or negotiated settlement, with pressure for these 'solutions' coming consistently from international forums and foreign countries.

For a while, Prabhakaran made good military decisions and, consequently, attracted foreign financial and diplomatic investment. The government of Sri Lanka took a dual path of negotiation and a slowly escalating military response that was supposed to create conditions favorable for negotiation.

Sri Lanka is one of the world's smaller countries, but it is not *that* small, with over 20 million inhabitants and an area almost the same as Ireland's. The ethnically distinct identities are not evenly dispersed on the island. The most likely supporters of the Tigers lived in the east and north. This distribution facilitated the Tigers' development of geographic sanctuaries, as well as an argument for either federalist solutions or territorially-based international recognition. Being an island, however, meant that an insurgent's lines of supply might have to pass over seawater. The most salient single piece of ground is not a salient, but a narrow neck between the main island and the Jaffna Peninsula in the north. Called Elephant Pass, it is historically the most contested piece of ground in Sri Lanka. The LTTE tried unsuccessfully to wrest Elephant Pass from the government in 1991, then did so in 2000, sweeping out a large, well-defended SLA garrison and capturing expensive pieces of military equipment in the process. The SLA did not retake Elephant Pass until January, 2009. When the government finally resolved to control the pass, its taking marked the beginning of the final chapter of the war. The LTTE won no more significant engagements afterwards.

Equality of citizen status was a perpetual issue in Sri Lanka. But for the insurgent war, Sri Lankan democracy probably would not have moved as quickly as it has to ease blatant political inequities. To Prabhakaran, inequities were to be resolved by military victory -- and his instrument was the LTTE. The government preferred the path of negotiation until the imbalance in visions about how political change was to be implemented became clearer to the Sri Lankan government and people.

After the election of President Mahinda Rajapaksa in November, 2005, he radically changed the government's military objective. Although the exact moment of epiphany is debated among Sri Lankans, the strategic objective ultimately switched from creating the conditions for a peaceful settlement to defeating the LTTE. The SLA began to win battles and gain ground, and this happened because President Rajapaska garnered substantive and extensive support from both India and China, and all but ignored the rest of the world's pleas for restraint. Rajapaksa and his military chief Sarath Fonseka resolved to eliminate the LTTE. The mechanism to resolve the conflict would be military victory, and for this the government built a more powerful military. The President and his military leaders discarded the political-versus-military dichotomy. They dumped complexity and ambiguity as guiding descriptors of the challenge. They identified Velupillai Prabhakaran as the target, and decided they would no longer let Prabhakaran grant impunity to anyone. On March 18, 2009, Prabhakaran was dead, and the war ended.

What are the lessons of the rise and demise of the LTTE?

- Evolution of a social contract that permits and ratifies the existence of a clearly identifiable underclass favors creation of an armed resistance;

- An ability to grant impunity to its followers means an insurgent group can recruit soldiers, not pay taxes, kill, kidnap, rob, trespass and nevertheless represent the aggrieved minority in foreign forums;

- Dirt and walls matter. The LTTE made extensive use of engineered earth bunds (berms and levees) in depth as fighting positions;

• The government ultimately embraced the possibilities of asymmetric weight. The big advantage available to the government of Sri Lanka was its ability to amass physical military power;

• Sea and air power proved critical for reducing LTTE lines of communication for supply and retreat;

• Insurgent leaders usually want to be the exclusive agents of the aggrieved minority, and this can become their weakness;

• International peacekeeping and monitoring missions (for instance, the Sri Lanka Monitoring Mission, SLMM) were effective only in protracting the conflict, and were not trusted by the government;

• Foreign military intervention, in this case the Indian Army (known as the Indian Peacekeeping Force, IPKF), which fought indecisively from 1987 until 1990, will do little besides prolong suffering if it is does not resolve to achieve victory. In retribution, the LTTE assassinated the Indian Prime Minister as he ran for reelection in 1991;

• Water struggles can present catalyzing events (in this case the LTTE closed the sluice gates at Mavil Oya in 2008, cutting off water to a large civilian population);

• A major natural disaster (in this case the Tsunami of late 2004) can change insurgent prospects. Because the tsunami hit the eastern part of Sri Lanka, the disaster caused havoc in rebel areas, opening the area to new observation and reporting, and perhaps shifted political attitudes in the rest of Sri Lanka ,that led to the election of President Rajapaksa;

• The question of impunity and international extradition is almost always present. The Sri Lankan government would like the United States to extradite a man they say is now the leader of the LTTE, but is in any case a United States citizen living in New York;

• Until the election of Mahinda Rajapaksa, government leaders heard 'Songs of Chu' among its people, which disarmed it and lessened its resolve (please see Section 122, *Songs of Chu*);

• The LTTE's identity, existence and survival were highly synonymous with the heartbeat of its leader, the '*mens rea'* guy (please see Section 23, *Mens Rea*);

• Territorial control became and remained a central imperative;

• Suicide bombers are weapons systems. The LTTE invented the bomb vest, and employed many women for placement and detonation, but the LTTE leaders were not suicidal. They planned to enjoy power;

• Toward the end, the insurgent leader had to resort to a strategy of hope – hope that foreigners would come to his rescue. The counterinsurgency became a siege, with the insurgents enclosed.

Sri Lanka's insurgent war has much to say, with the above list just a start. Perhaps the overriding lesson from Sri Lanka, however, is about the supposedly protracted nature of insurgent war. Sri Lanka's war was protracted only until the government resolved to win it.

See: 20, *Foreign Support*; 18, *Massacres*; 54, *Badassoftheweek.com*; 51, *Underclass*; 105, *Genocide Geography*; 27, *Democracy*; 72, *Land Strategy*; and 81, *What a Clergy Wants.*

---

"The unforgivable crime is soft hitting. Do not hit at all if it can be avoided; but never hit softly."
Theodore Roosevelt[19]

Lack of it doesn't spell defeat or a lot of it assure victory

# *Section 14, Legitimacy*

We can divide the concept of legitimacy (as in government or organizational legitimacy) into two streams. One recognizes and measures legitimacy as a degree of public opinion or support; the other recognizes and measures legitimacy according to norms of goodness and achievement. Sometimes the streams mix. If you are a contestant in an irregular armed conflict, you will want to keep an eye on the legitimacy barometers (votes, polling data, voiced opinions, investments, travel patterns), if such barometers already exist or can be devised. Be careful about defining your objectives according to legitimacy, however. Not only is use of the term *legitimacy* an invitation to debate, but all the normative legitimacy in the world won't assure your victory, or a total lack of it assure your defeat.

You can maintain a scrupulously clean behavior, but Pontius and the crowd might still turn on you (and note that normative legitimacy was not what sprung Barabbas). On the other hand, some competitors in irregular wars gain all the committed popular support they need by perpetrating the most horrendous and vicious acts imaginable. Popular legitimacy can be ephemeral, superficial, narrow, and can be based on unattractive psychological quantities such as fear, hate, humor or ignorance. Popular legitimacy can be at once democratic and foul, so a dilemma will often be created by striving for legitimacy: legitimacy-as-acceptance versus legitimacy-as-goodness.

Our hope may be that normative legitimacy will be tied to popular legitimacy, and that popular legitimacy will change conditions in the battlespace – that our increased legitimacy will tip the balance of anonymity in our favor so that so that our enemy cannot hide his whereabouts, movements and sanctuaries. We hope a high degree of legitimacy will bring more volunteers into our ranks, earn us foreign support, make it easier to finance our war plans, and even cause parts of the population to directly fight of their own accord against our mutual enemy.

According to a whole body of literature, whether you are counterinsurgent or insurgent, if you have legitimacy it means you *tax* instead of *steal*, that foreign allies rally to you, and that people voluntarily offer you information about your opponents. Legitimacy, as a north star for counterinsurgent planning, is well-argued by practitioners and theorists such as Max Manwaring and John Fishel.[20] However, striving for legitimacy begs questions. One of the most disconcerting might be what to do with legitimacy once you have it. The military challenge doesn't take care of itself just because you have earned popular support or act in a scrupulously ethical manner. You can work toward greater legitimacy for all the reasons noted above, but don't count on even perfect legitimacy to defeat your enemies.

If, as a fighter, you sense that you must use the term 'legitimacy' in the explanation of your actions, then establish an explicit set of standards of behavior and achievements that can be made publicly transparent, with a baseline, and with reasonable goals. Set your own moral compass and your own standards for success. (See Section 125, *Human Rights*)

If a criminal gang chops Stew up into manageable bits, puts his pieces in a 55 gallon plastic drum with mole, water, beer, peppers, potatoes, onions, tobacco, urine and sour cream, and leaves the drum outside Stew's mother's house over the weekend, that's not so good, either. There are, nevertheless, places not far away where groups do such things exactly, and grow in popular legitimacy on the fame of it.

Beyond the enormity of individual cases, if you believe legitimacy is better measured by ethical standards of behavior than by popular opinion, it still begs the question about what standards for legitimacy should look like. The Internet is rich with indexes of the relative performance of the countries of the world based on one or another calculation. Here is a brief sample:

> *Index of Economic Freedom*, Edwin Feulner Jr. et al., The Wall Street Journal and the Heritage Foundation, < www.heritage.org>;
>
> *Human Development Index*, United Nations Develpment Programme, <www.undp.org>;
>
> *Failed States Index*, The Fund for Peace and *Foreign Policy* magazine, <www.fundforpeace.org>;
>
> *FAST International Early Warning System*, Swiss Peace, <www.swisspeace.org> and International Crisis Group (with other relevant links), <www.crisisgroup.org> and other related data at <www.ciaonet.org>;
>
> *The Bertelsmann Transformation Index*, Olaf Hillenbrand and Peter Thiery, <www.bertelsmann-transformation-index.de/11.0.html>;
>
> *Conflict Map*, Nobel Prize Organization, <http://nobelprize.org>;
>
> *Transparency Index,* Transparency International, <www.transparency.org>;

*States at Risk and Failed States*, Marina Ottaway and Stefan Mair Carnege, Endowment for International Peace, Policy Outlook, <www.ciaonet.org>;

*All Possible Wars: Toward a Consensus View of the Future Security Environment 2001-2025*, Sam J. Tancredi, <www.ciaonet.org>;

*Happy Planet Index*, <www.happyplanetindex.org>;

*World Database of Happiness*, <www1.eur.nl/fsw/happiness/hap nat/nat fp.htm>.

Most of the indexes purport scienciness, but contain a lot of political and ideological baggage. The *Failed States* site's explanatory text carried the following lead-in: "It is an accepted axiom of the modern age that distance no longer matters." That questionable assertion will not help you win. A later sentence in the same explanation confesses something closer to the truth: "The complex phenomenon of state failure may be much discussed, but it remains little understood." All of the sites and indexes are, in some way, commentaries on legitimacy, mixing the currents of legitimacy-as-representativeness and normative behavioral standards to one degree or another.

Sometimes the indexers just can't get the numbers to come out the way they had envisioned. Investigators behind the *World Database of Happiness* had such strong negative presentiments about Colombia, which rated highly in happiness, that they astricized Colombia's rating and apologized in a footnote. Your irregular war is going to create, surface and irritate a lot of presuppositions, and will cause a lot of curious legitimacy ratings of one form or another. These may be influential legitimacy barometers. You will want to know what they are, and, although the individual sites, like the ones listed above, will come and go, the Internet is a place to start. They might help inform your strategic communications regarding current prejudices.

If you were to make a composite map of the countries that the above indexes considered to be the most failed, you would find only partial coincidence. The various indexes of state performance implicate a number of countries as likely places for internal struggle. The indexes generally agree on a few of the most obvious places, like Haiti or Zimbabwe, but we need a better method for determining what polities in the world are actually likely to fail.

The data for each country and the indexes will change, but the point remains that there exists a variety of ways to rate State success, or, as most of the listed indexes purport, legitimacy. None of the indexes is made with the definition of State success used in this book. The closest is probably the *Transparency Index* or *The Bertelsmann Transformation Index*.

If you can figure out the 'methodology' of the common indexes for legitimacy, you might be able to demonstrate progress in your programs by showing an improvement in the country's ratings (I put the word methodology between disrespectful quotation marks because some of the methodologies are un-replicable if not baffling.) Instead, set explicit standards of behavior for your force, and identify all entities able and not able to grant impunity to their people for violations of appropriate ethical standards. Doing so will build your argument for legitimacy, but it will not win your war.

See: 40, *Rule-of-Law*; 95, *Childhood*; 58, *Guerre d'Algérie*;
17, *Kidnapping*; 18, *Massacres*; 24, *Ruthlessness and Resolve*;
125, *Human Rights*; and 48, *Grading the Social Contract.*

---

**Woman**: Well, how'd you become king...?

**King Arthur**: The Lady of the Lake, her arm clad in the purest shimmering samite held aloft Excalibur from the bosom of the water, signifying by divine providence that I, Arthur, was to carry Excalibur. *That* is why I am your king.

**Dennis**: ... you can't expect to wield supreme executive power just because some watery tart threw a sword at you....if I went 'round sayin' I was Emperor just because some moistened bint lobbed a scimitar at me, they'd put me away.

From the movie
*Monty Python and the Holy Grail* (1975)[21]

State failure and the GOV-NGO tango

# *Section 15, NGOs and Unions*

Determine how you are going to deal with non-governmental organizations, international organizations, and unions.

Liberal societies honor the individual's right of association – the right to hang out with whomever we wish and to talk with them about whatever, and to obtain and spend resources together for projects ranging from dog shows to orgies. Some of the activities and organizations created in the firmament of this associational liberty tend to challenge the authority or instructions of the existing State, the government itself being but one of the organizations that the people of a liberal society form. Naturally, there is going to be some friction. In the context of a developed internal war, especially one in which foreigners take an active interest, many assemblages of people are going to try to be present to accomplish their goals, licit and illicit.

If you're willing to go just a little ways out on a philosophical limb, you could agree that all organizations that people form (if they are intended to accomplish anything as a group) are governmental. That would be to argue that 'NGO' is a misnomer and that almost all the NGOs are really non-State governmental organizations (NSGOs?). Then it's not much more of a logical leap to argue that all governments *are* the State, even if not the big formal central one, and so therefore every human organization *is* the State. You could argue that way, if you were falling in love with anarchy and wanted to confuse both yourself and others into inaction.

By 'government,' I mean the government that can impose punishment on you -- especially corporal or privative punishment -- that is, *not* grant you impunity. By NGOs, I just mean an entity (not the government) with a name, organization, plan, resolve, resources and enough presence within your conflict space that it might change the balance of prospects for or against you. It's only when one of the NGOs challenges a prerogative of the State government that a ruckus ensues. If the State wants to be into everything, obviously there is going to be more conflict or fewer NGOs, or the NGOs are going to come to some kind of compromise, settlement, agreement, relationship, etc., with the State. When an NGO is related to an insurgent or criminal entity that is also capable of punishing you or granting you impunity, things get worse.

Even when it comes to building and running highways, schools, and hospitals there are pro-State, pro-NGO, and pro-business advocates. There is plenty of logical and practical overlap between what are called 'civil society,' nonprofit NGOs and for-profit businesses. This is noteworthy because the list of activities NGOs get into does not stop short at human services, physical protection, or peaceful resolution of armed conflict. Likewise there is considerable crossover between international organizations (IOs) like the United Nations, the Organization of American States, the Pan African Union or the European Parliament.

In the coming decades, IOs especially may play increasing and increasingly independent roles as players in irregular armed conflicts. In the 1980s, a movement began in the United States to impose what some still call a 'Tobin' tax. Part of the idea, or an outgrowth of the original idea, is to automatically move small portions of international monetary transactions to a United Nations account, giving the United Nations an independent budget source based on international financial commerce. Once the United Nations is put on a more regular robust and independent financial footing, so the argument goes, it can tackle world problems like global warming, hunger, and pandemics. It perhaps could also deploy armed force with more agility in support of its resolutions regarding genocide, proliferation and the like.

Unions are a particular kind of NGO, and they are not made equally. Perhaps the archetype is a union composed of factory floor workers determined to strike and refuse both to work and to let anyone else work unless the factory owners and bosses pay a higher wage. That ideal, however, is rare today in most of the world, in part because of the distributed nature of production and the increased complexity and differentiation of people's productive contributions. So unions today are more sophisticated, interconnected and subtle in the ways they leverage what power they can attain. It is still, however, by way of geography and anonymity that the various unions can be distinguished for the purposes of your irregular war's order of battle. For instance, if a union has enough power, directly or through other agents, to demand that workers at a factory have to vote openly regarding whether or not the union will represent them, that union has greater power than if the voting among workers is done by secret ballot. A work force that does not enjoy a secret ballot as regards to unions is like a religious congregation that must go to confession. Of course, church organizations are NGOs as well. To the extent a union, church or any organization can punish people, and more so when they can provide their followers or leaders a degree of impunity from punishment, they are closer to being States themselves.

So how does all this fit together for the purpose of seeing how to win? The physical line of retreat to sanctuary (the central geographic concept in armed conflict) is often covered with people. To classify and understand the potentially most dangerous people along that line of retreat, you can start by determining what level of control of anonymity various organizations enjoy or seek. Another thing to note is the flow of rents, tithes, taxes, commissions, distributions, etc. Going beyond the formal or informal nature of the organizations' identities, if you don't know where money is coming from and where it is going, that anonymity of wealth may be dangerous to you.

The practicalities of control are not difficult math, but whether you are pro-State or rebel, you need to know both the *de jure* and *de facto* regime of rules that control various categories of NGOs, with special attention to the control of anonymity, as well as the origins and destinations of convertible wealth. Of course, as with so many things, the physical location of assets and agents is going to be critical, revealing evidence. 'GIS' everything, if you can. If you can't, keep the other guy from doing so.

See: 2, *Anonymity*; 144, *Impunity and State Success*; 20, *Foreign Support*; 40, *Rule-of-law*; 108, *Neogeography*; 56, *Militias and Gun Control*; 16, *Keeping Secrets*; and 66, *GIS*.

---

> "License to kill gophers by the government of the United Nations. Man, free to kill gophers at will. To kill, you must know your enemy, and in this case my enemy is a varmint. And a varmint will never quit - ever. They're like the Viet Cong – Varmint Cong. So you have to fall back on superior intelligence and superior firepower. And that's all she wrote."
>
> Carl Spackler in the movie
> *Caddy Shack* (1989)[22]

Don't drop the backpack

# *Section 16, Keeping Secrets*

Before declaring independence from King George, the North American revolutionaries created the Continental Army, precursor of the United States Army. They had decided that creating some ability to dominate territory and provide impunity for their followers was a good step to take before voicing their dissent. They knew that at the beginning they had to keep the fact of the army's existence a secret in order to let it gain strength. Anonymity for the army's membership was essential, but even when preserving that was no longer imperative, the ability to keep secrets remained one of the ingredients of victory.

Keeping secrets isn't easy. Rituals, rules, inspections, investigations and punishments can all help, but ultimately secrets are best-kept because of some freely-entered contract. Different ties bind differently, and among the most important are common identities based on place, common cultural experience (also tied to place), and common missions (especially if tied to place identity). There are all sorts of factors that can operate to cause people to leak information, including disaffection and dishonor. It doesn't always take big factors, either. Sex and money are often enough, or are part of the formula.

Some kinds of organizations can keep secrets better than others. Strength in keeping secrets is an attribute of winning armed organizations, whether pro-State or anti-State. International organizations, meanwhile, are unlikely to keep secrets well. They rarely have a focused and inspiring mission, exclusive membership, tight member origins, or punish disloyalty and sloppiness.

Secrets, because they are based on trust, engender mistrust. Section 18, *Massacres* mentions a case in Colombia called Tacueyó, about a FARC leader who stole a bunch of money from the FARC and created his own splinter guerrilla group. His high paranoia (fed by some very good reasons to be distrustful, such as that both the government and the FARC wanted him dead) killed almost two hundred persons, the vast majority of whom had wished him no ill. Lack of trust, in the context of an active armed competition, has separate, but equally ruinous impact inside and outside the skull.

What is the fate of spies in irregular wars, or are they even spies? Under the traditional laws of war between States in the international system of States, a spy caught by one of the parties to a declared war could be summarily executed, or at least executed after the briefest of military tribunals. If, however, that spy were to avoid capture or escape, and make it back to his own side's lines, he was no longer to be considered a spy and could not be punished, even if he returned to the area of his enemy (that is, if he were no longer spying, of course). In other words, the traditional statute of limitations on punishment for spying was the spy's success at evasion. In these irregular wars there is no rule like that. What do you do when you find spies (maybe better to just call them infiltrators or moles) in your organization? Summarily dispatching them may be seen by the public as unpleasant. Most insurgent groups and most criminal gangs, however, don't just kill moles – they torture them to death. About the only category of human out for which worse punishment is meted is the traitor/deserter. If you are a traitor-deserter-spy, good luck with that. Ethel Rosenberg was executed for spying. The first electrocutions didn't work, so she was strapped back in and electrocuted some more.

A government law enforcement unit finding moles from a criminal gang (and who are citizens of the same country as that government) will arrest them and charge them under a number of available statutes. A government counterinsurgency force finding moles from an insurgent organization (also their citizens) will probably arrest them and charge them under a variety of statutes, perhaps including an espionage or treason statute. If they are from another country, but there is no war extant between the countries, the statutes will be a little harsher, the punishments probably a little more severe and the protections fewer. In addition, there may be some diplomatic interchange as the government of the foreign country in question may wish to protect its citizens.

But what if a foreign force is helping an allied government with counterinsurgency and has its own troops in the territory of the foreign ally? The problem gets stickier. The government being defended is supposed to be the only one exercising a monopoly on the granting of impunity inside its territory, or at least that often seems to be the goal. All else working well, the visiting troops, if they were to find a mole in their midst, could turn the perpetrator over to the host government and the appropriate prosecution would proceed. If the host country is not in condition to successfully prosecute, however, the mole might be released. That would be tantamount to allowing the mole's parent organization to grant the mole impunity. In such a condition, the visiting government is not keeping secrets well, and not doing the basic job of providing protection for its own soldiers.

One way of sorting things out is by defining sub-territories. The foreign force can set out a zone or zones of occupation. Inside those zones, the questions of justice, prosecution and impunity would be retained by the visiting government for the purposes of this one kind of offense. It is a partial or sliced sharing, or a loan of sovereignty. Another way is for the visiting force to participate in the processing of the captured moles. That could present some difficult language problems and surface some cultural divisions.

The question of what to do with moles is further complicated by differences between forensic evidence and military secrets. Most of these kinds of problems can be reconciled by thoughtful status of forces agreements, but the basic rules for winning armed conflict and the basic responsibilities of a government are clear. A military command that cannot maintain its secrets (perhaps by allowing infiltrators in its midst to go unpunished) is not responsibly protecting its soldiers.

In 1973, Fabio Vásquez, a leader of the ELN (now a waning guerrilla group) dropped his backpack during a skirmish with the Colombian Army. The backpack had in it a notebook with a long list of names of members and collaborators. The loss of the notebook all but doomed the ELN, which only survived on a thread for years. Similarly, when the Colombian government killed FARC leader Raul Reyes in a 2008 raid across the Ecuadoran border, it found computers with similar, much longer lists. The loss was to that point the FARC's biggest single setback of the long war, and may have constituted the decisive turning point in the fortunes of the FARC (rather than the Battle of Mitú, mentioned in Section 11). The next big blow to the FARC came in 2010 when another major FARC leader, Jorge Briceño, was killed -- and even more digital files taken. Gangsters and insurgents need to keep records, and the loss of those records is costly in the extreme. The business of keeping secrets goes both ways. Not only do insurgent leaders have to enforce secrecy among their followers, they have to keep secrets. There is no way to just remember every person, place and thing. There has to be someplace to keep the records, and while the flash drive seems like a good idea, it is as dangerous as it is practical. Losing secrets means you are not controlling the balance of anonymity.

The right to speak is often not as significant as the right not to speak. Some labor union organizers, for instance, thrive best where ballots are not secret. They prefer to disallow anonymity to workers for fear that the workers will not choose the union as their exclusive agent. One of the less-debated freedoms of functioning democracies is the freedom not to speak, and the freedom not only of association but of discreet association, and the right to reject association. Some feel that democracy is only valid when each vote is transparent, and each individual accountable to the whole group for his or her vote. This view of democracy, while sometimes attractive and just, is one that invites not only group pressure, but extortion and bullying as well. Anonymity is a primary theme of this book exactly because control of anonymity lies at the center not only of what it takes to win an organized struggle, but of the central values of the social contract.

Anonymity and secrecy are tightly related, with the word secrecy connoting a contract and intimacy, while anonymity connotes something impersonal. Rooting out traitors is a search for those who you feel have broken a trust, an intimacy -- but a law that limits expression can actually lend anonymity to your opponents by suppressing their revelation of disaffection. The Constitution of the United States makes a big deal about labeling people traitors, and this is understandable considering who penned the document and when. Americans don't like to have the term traitor thrown around too lightly, given the American fondness for insurgency. Laws that limit free expression deter people from exposing themselves. Making it illegal to burn a certain flag, in other words, means suppressing the most obvious evidence of who would burn that flag.

You can lose secrets because of spying, treason, and your own sloppiness. All three can unbalance anonymity in your disfavor. In the process of fighting these things, however, you might create conditions that make your opponent's secrecy problem easier.

See: 3, *The Domesday Book*; 2, *Anonymity*; 134, *Luigi Galleani*; 108, *Neogeography*; 78, *Personal Identity*; 15, *NGOs and Unions*; 124, *America's Insurgent Stamp*; and 2, *The Line of Retreat*.

---

"The first rule of fight club is don't talk about fight club."

Tyler Durden in movie
*Fight Club* (1999)[23]

---

The basic extortion

# *Section 17, Kidnapping*

Kidnapping is extortion, but it is a version so mean that it deserves its own policy prescriptions, and its own counter-strategy planning and resourcing.

Kidnapping is the ultimate protection racket. If you are the kidnapper, you promise to protect the hostage from harm if the hostage's family (or company, government) pays up. Interestingly, although kidnapping is on
e ruthless option to military operational math, the industrial version appears to be dependent on mastery of similar map algebra. The kidnapping mastermind establishes a formula to communicate terms, setting up contacts and exchanging goods in such a way as to minimize the risk of having the victims pursue his people with any success. He attacks in such a way that he can withdraw to sanctuary, and then negotiates in such a way that the mechanisms of negotiation do not give away the geography of his lines of communication.

High kidnapping rates spread wildly from Colombia to Argentina, then to Mexico and other places after the FARC learned to industrialize it, formalize it, and give business clinics on how to make a safe and profitable go of it. Part of the genius of the industrial kidnapping business plan is a total consciousness of geography. Time, distance, and location are key factors in successful industrial-scale kidnapping.

Of course, control of anonymity and secrecy are central to success as well, making a secure means of communicating with the mark critical. Therein also lays a major weakness for kidnapping as a criminal enterprise. Security of communications is always dependent on codes, technology and tradecraft, and those are always subject to compromise.

Given the nature of this particular criminal enterprise, tied as is so closely to anonymity, a trend of increasing kidnapping can be seen as a measure of State failure. If you are the counterinsurgent and you cannot stop kidnapping, you are doing poorly. If you are the insurgent and you can kidnap with impunity, you are doing well.

See: 95, *Childhood*; 14, *Legitimacy*; 24, *Ruthlessness and Resolve*; 2, *The Line of Retreat*; 138, *Roadblocks and Checkpoints*; 143, *Is It an Insurgency?*; 25, *Why Humans Don't Fight*; and 90, *Prisons*.

> "Kidnapping, extortion, bank robbery, and drug trafficking -- four favorite insurgent activities -- are very lucrative."
>
> US Army Field Manual 3-24,
> *Counterinsurgency*[24]

Mile markers of armed conflict, their details surprise

# *Section 18, Massacres*

Internal conflicts are often chaptered by massacres. A massacre can change the direction of public psychology, mark changes in the fortunes of contending groups, and expose severe internal divisions or loss of leadership in a government army or inside a violent nongovernmental armed group. Sometimes massacres are just horrible mistakes or the work of the criminally insane.

Be aware that there are various working definitions, and that the definitions have an effect on statistics and stories. One recognized measure of a massacre is four persons killed in a single incident. I was told by a Colombian official a number of years ago that if fewer than ten persons – soldiers, policemen, civilians – were killed in a single incident, the Colombian public wouldn't take notice, inured as it was to news of homicide. He felt that to earn the term 'massacre' an event had to reach some appreciable level of public recognition and impact, which meant at least ten dead victims. Another word, *atrocity*, is commonly used in propaganda pieces. Atrocity spans both massacres and genocides, but the word seems to have gained no legal or mathematical definition as have the other two.

The counterinsurgent especially should be prepared in advance for the certain occurrence of massacres. Below are four notorious Colombian cases, out of many dozens, highlighting divergence in the nature of massacres. They are all named after the place in which they occurred.

> **Tacueyó** – A man named José Fedor, who had been a trusted member of the Colombian communist insurgent group, the *Fuerzas Armadas Revolucionarias de Colombia* (Revolutionary Armed Forces of Colombia, FARC), fell into disfavor with the FARC senior leadership sometime late in 1981, stole a lot of money from the organization and with it founded an even more radical splinter group called the Ricardo Franco Front (after a former guerrilla leader). Many of the foot soldiers of Fedor's dissident group came over from the FARC, and he recruited others. Paranoia got the best of him and in late 1985 he perpetrated an especially vicious torture/execution of between 160 and 180 of his own men, a very few of whom might have been infiltrators and all of whom he suspected of being infiltrators. The massacre came shortly after an unrelated guerrilla takeover of the Colombian Supreme Court Building, a coincidence that would amplify the public impact of the massacre. Although it was mostly FARC renegades killing themselves, Tacueyó not only left an impression on the Colombian public, it is generally marked as the event that took away much of the opinion (held perhaps by a majority of Colombians) that the FARC was a guerrilla with noble goals.

> **Bojayá** – In 2002, the FARC launched gas cylinders at a church in which maybe five hundred civilians were taking refuge from an ensuing battle between units of the FARC and units of the *Autodefensas Unidas de Colombia* (AUC), an anti-Communist

guerrilla group (generally categorized as a 'paramilitary'). The gas cylinders are a primitive style of artillery, but effective. One of them went through the roof and exploded on the altar, killing around 120 civilians, many of whom were children. Although the AUC was cited by the United Nations for violating human rights (using the villagers as a shield and pillaging), there was no way for the FARC to avoid international condemnation. The government, meanwhile, was also found culpable of not doing enough to have stopped the event, having been warned that the two warring parties were in the area.

The Bojayá massacre occurred in the context of a battle between two contending guerrilla groups (there were instances in which the government and the AUC colluded, but this was not one of them). However, the incident cemented an idea that the government could be condemned and sued for a failure to protect its citizens, even if the government was not itself a participant or perpetrator. This result suggested a bit of a military operational problem, implying that the government was obliged to assign forces to protect civilian populations on the basis of information about pending clashes between other armed groups. Needless to say, a lot of initiative could be stripped away from government military leaders. Under such rules of legal obligation, anti-government forces could disperse or deceive the government into reactive defense.

**Trujillo** – Trujillo is a county north of Cali, Colombia. Trujillo is actually the name given to a series of massacres in about the same place. Well over three hundred persons were killed by members of the AUC and the Cali drug cartel, who dumped most of the body parts into the Cauca River. Almost all of the victims were union activists or others accused by the perpetrators of supporting the leftist guerrillas. Some collusion occurred, at least early on, by officials of the government armed forces. The details form a complex drama that is still being investigated by a truth commission.

**Jamundí** – In 2006, an army unit, on orders from a drug lord, ambushed and killed all the members of an elite counternarcotics police unit that had been trained in good part by the United States. In Colombia, both the national police and the army belong to the Ministry of Defense. The shock wave of questions, investigations, inter-institutional accusations, self-doubt and slumped morale was palpable, even while the action was only tangentially related to the insurgent war.

The above massacres weren't perpetrated using planted explosive devices, although there have been many deaths from explosive artifacts, including some notable urban bombing attacks on civilian targets. None of the above-listed massacres involved contact between an anti-government armed group and a unit of the government armed forces, either. Plenty of those occurred, too, but these highlight the environment of violent habit and impunity that allows an odd array of excesses, each with its own character. The reasons for massacres are usually control of territory, paranoia, or revenge. They are very often tied to the preservation of anonymity and silence regarding illegal and materially profitable activity.

Many of the massacres in Colombia have been followed by forensic efforts, some better than others, but getting better over time. That has meant a growing body of evidence that can be made available not only for criminal prosecutions, but for civil litigation. Briefly, the difference between the two (criminal prosecution and civil litigation) revolves around burden of proof. Although the particulars of this concept are not universal, they are becoming continuously more so. That is to say, we are experiencing a globalization of legal processes. In civil litigation, the presumption of innocence can be shifted. For instance, instead of having to prove guilt beyond a reasonable doubt, it might only be necessary to show that a conclusion of culpability would be reasonable. Instead of having to get a unanimous decision out of a jury, maybe only a majority is necessary, etc. Why does this note move from the poignancy of horrendous murders to dry instruction about civil procedure? It is in order to illuminate a special challenge of today's armed conflicts. If a guerrilla or criminal force (or for that matter, a government unit) commits a massacre, how is a government going to be able to offer amnesty to the perpetrators? Impunity and amnesty are related terms.

Massacres, a category or scale of unethical killing that falls in our understanding somewhere between simple murder and genocide, will probably mark and possibly define your irregular war. Their occurrence will be used propagandistically by you or by your opponents. You will do better to have stated, then inspected and enforced your intentions to discipline all who you call your people against massacres, and to investigate and illuminate massacres as quickly and completely as is practicable and beneficial.

See: 104, *Extraterritorial Jurisdiction*; 49, *Territorial Scrutiny*; 105, *Genocide Geography*; 86, *Shifting Covet-Geography*; 136, *Weapons*; 28, *Oviedo*; 103, *Amnesty*; and 40, *Rule-of-law*.

---

> "Yesterday, about 1 P.M., Brydon, an Assistant Surgeon, of the Shah's Service, reached this place, (on a horse scarcely able to move another yard) wounded and bruised from head to foot with stones, and he, alone, has arrived to tell the fearful tale."
>
> Account of Dr. William Brydon's report of the massacre of a British army in Afghanistan in 1842[25]

I'll protect you from me

# *Section 19, Extortion*

Extortion is one of the crimes, like smuggling, that all but defines organized crime. It is also one of the main strategy alternatives applied by both regular and irregular armies everywhere.

Every extortion is a protection racket. Extortion means you create a threat to your target and allow him to buy his or her way out of the threat. You offer to protect your target from you. Sometimes you have to communicate the threat discreetly, because a sense of dishonor can increase the stakes. Sometimes you have to communicate the threat more openly, but in every case you have to make the threat credible. If your target does not believe that you will carry out your threat, your extortion won't work. You may want to make a threat especially indiscreet, so that others can be extorted more easily. Mexicans, for instance, are hard to impress, so if you are a Mexican gangster, you may have to roll a half dozen or so heads (formerly attached to the bodies of some of your enemy's employees) onto a nightclub dance floor. Extortion knows no scale limits. You can make money by protecting a parked car from having its paint scratched (by you), or assure an emperor that you won't destroy any more of his cities.

Kidnapping is the queen of extortions. You take something of the highest value, a daughter maybe, and ransom her back to her distraught father. If you do this well, you can make it seem as though you're the good guy for sparing her delicate life.

Extortion's little cousin, bribery, requires less technical expertise and physical risk than kidnapping or outright theft, and requires less post-act logistical preparation for product movement, storage and fencing. You might be able to bribe a government official with some money to allow you a particular privilege, speed a bureaucratic process or overlook an infraction, and maybe this can proceed with no threat of violence. For this reason, bribery is often considered less of a crime than extortion. Bribery leads quickly to extortion, however, when the government official starts getting uppity and asks for too much, or doesn't respond to your needs diligently, in which case you may have to threaten to expose his corruption, along with the photos you took of him with that one prostitute. Be careful with police officials, however. You need to know how far their corruption has reached. The police department has guns, too, and you could start a fight you cannot afford. Your extortions have to be in proportion to your ability to fulfill your threat and to withstand any incidental retaliations or mistakes.

Extortion warfare might be a suitable term for the course of action most favored by gangsters, insurgents, or terrorists. Extortion may be collective or very individual, and is often both. The particular tactic of communicating a threat might be a letter to a local government, a kidnapping or bombing, or just a kiss on the right cheek, but kidnapping defines a recourse to violence that can be applied in the absence of revolutionary strategy, with or without a political goal, and *almost* regardless of advantageous correlation of forces save that advantage gained by amorality. Extortion is an available option for a whole array of identities, and is aided by every advance in communications and information technology. It is supremely flexible in that some form of violence can be leveraged against almost any vulnerability.

Successful extortion, as well as resistance to extortion, requires detailed knowledge of the wealth to be extorted and where the extortionists can most efficiently and safely endanger that wealth. The extortionist must nevertheless have a sanctuary and be able to move to it safely in case the target resists. So, while the use of extortion can sometimes free a leader from having to find his enemy's line of retreat and maneuver accordingly, it does not mean he can then ignore operational equation of classic strategy. If you resort to extortion, you not only have to be sure you can make good on the threat (actually you might be able to deceive that part), you will probably run some risk of exposing your own route to sanctuary.

Extortion is the principle alternative way to defeat a foe besides confounding his route of retreat to sanctuary. The key is to threaten something of such essential value to him that he is compelled to surrender to you in exchange for its salvation. For instance, if NATO begins to destroy all of Belgrade, the Serb Army, otherwise neither perturbed nor dislodged, gives up. Or, in the face of spectacular and disheartening loss, the Japanese Emperor spares the Americans a counter guerrilla campaign on the main islands of Japan. The strategy of holding at risk things of value requires a certain flexibility of moral boundaries, a requisite level of ruthlessness. In a sense, extortion is an attack on the sanctuary of the spirit from which there is no physical retreat.

Another strategic approach, gentler, and one to which we might aspire under the moniker of legitimacy, is to create a social contract within which (A) a great majority of citizens enjoys a sense of belonging, and (B) anonymity for reporting illegal behavior to the State is assured. Under such conditions, resistance forces cannot plan secure routes of escape to sanctuary; and their management of risk for an anti-State movement is problematic at best. It is then hard for a rebel organization to enjoy the secrecy and impunity needed to grow, or when beaten, to return. Unfortunately, while positive changes in society can rarely be made to outpace changing grievances, there is always time for extortion.

See: 95, *Childhood*; 17, *Kidnapping*; 135, *Bank Robbery*; 2, *The Line of Retreat*; 141, *Seven Strategy Strains*; 81, *What a Clergy Wants*; 74, *Refugees and Displaced Persons*; and102, *Negotiations*.

---

"Catapultam habeo. Nisi pecuniam omnem mihi dabis, ad caput tuum saxum immane mittam."[26]

Insurgencies are international conflicts

# *Section 20, Foreign Support and Foreign Perspective*

**Foreign Support:**

An insurgent or separatist is more likely to win with foreign support than without it, or at least that's the rule. We can go a step farther, however and say that there are no wholly internal conflicts. Ok, there are probably a few, but the proposition is strong enough to switch the burden of proof onto those who would argue that anti-State armed groups (or at least those that last any appreciable amount of time) ever succeed without foreign support. So are these, then, not international wars? The answer is yes; almost all internal wars are international wars.

Even if a foreign government does not support an insurgency directly or openly, it can lend a blind eye to movement into and through its territory, allow the issuance of false passports, vote in favor of international recognition, block international police investigations, etc. This accessorial behavior is probably the most common form of effective support, and it relates directly to one of the principle themes of this book – the central importance of lines of communication, especially the line of insurgent escape to sanctuary. Because the line of retreat to sanctuary is the central geographic feature of military strategy, any time those lines pass into or through a foreign country, and that country abets or remains indifferent, it is effectively an accessory and participant in the war. It behooves the insurgent in such cases, which is most cases, to cultivate those public arguments about the nature of his war that diminish the importance of lines of communication. Instead, he will highlight the importance of psychological, political and socioeconomic factors. The insurgent rarely wants to have a bright light shined on the classic military dimension of the war: his lines of communication.

Foreign countries also often facilitate insurgent finances and fiscal anonymity. Moving, storing and converting money is essential to the longevity and success of insurgent and criminal leaders. In the case of the FARC, some countries have found it in their best interests to appreciate the FARC as a legitimate social movement in order to perpetuate a lucrative banking service, giving the FARC asset liquidity and forensic security for many years. European protection of FARC wealth makes the aerial spraying of coca leaf (which was supposed to reduce FARC financial strength) seem ineffectual. If foreign banks had revealed FARC finances years ago, the damage such transparency would have done to FARC logistical strength might have been far greater than the damage done by killing coca plants.

In May 2008, the government of Colombia attacked a FARC camp across the Colombian border a couple of miles into Ecuadoran territory. Aerial bombs not only killed Raul Reyes, a principal leader of the FARC, they also opened a can of geopolitical worms. It appeared convenient to the government of Ecuador, spurred on by Hugo Chavez, dictator of Venezuela, to call the incident an international invasion of Ecuador by Colombia. Ecuador had either been allowing or hosting the presence of FARC camps on its territory for some time. Maybe an aggressive diplomatic offensive seemed to the Ecuadoran government the best defense against accusation of being a surreptitious ally of the FARC, and therefore complicit in illicit drug trade and terrorism. The relationship of the Ecuadoran government, and even more so that of the Venezuela regime, to the internal armed struggle in Colombia is historically typical of internal wars.

Foreign support in internal or irregular conflicts can have more facets than just surreptitious support to an insurgency by an outside government. A short list might look something like this:

1. Support from a foreign government to a government or to an insurgent, separatist etc., movement;

2. Support by international organizations to a government or to an insurgent or separatist movement;

3. Support from international non-governmental organization to a government to counter an insurgent, separatist etc., movement;

4. Support to a government or to an insurgent or separatist movement by foreign volunteers and facilitated by a foreign government;

5. Voluntary participation by foreign individuals to a government or to an insurgent or separatist movement;

6. Support to foreign non-governmental or proto-national entity resisting a foreign occupation.

7. Protection by a foreign government, international organization, international NGO, or foreign private firm of criminal activities by an anti-government armed group.

Because the consequences of exposing and declaring an international conflict seem both unpredictable and vast, governments prefer to maintain diplomatic fictions regarding the international character of armed conflicts that are supposed to be 'not of an international character.' What you don't want to do is fool yourself regarding the geographies of the lines of retreat, supply, finance, recruiting and diplomacy. This book is especially about operational art, and as such it focuses on the geography of the lines of communication, and especially lines of retreat to sanctuary. If the Mexican government gives refuge to Guatemalan insurgents, it is very unlikely that the Guatemalan government can muster enough power to conclude the war entirely on its terms. If the Indian government denies sanctuary to the Tamil Tigers, but instead helps the Sri Lankan government prevent their escape, then the Sri Lankan government has a chance to win big militarily.

**Foreign Perspectives:**

Most relevant foreign perspectives are manifested in foreign languages. An irregular armed conflict will not only have an international component, that component may be its driving or sustaining force. Is it unreasonable, then, to suggest that foreign viewpoints, analyses, perspectives, and decision paths be discovered and considered in one's own planning and decision-making? Americans especially are notorious for incapacity in foreign languages, and a weak base in foreign languages makes gathering and absorbing foreign perspectives difficult. Mastering an irregular armed conflict inside a foreign land is even more unlikely.

It can be an indicator of a knowledge weakness if formal country-to-country diplomatic channels are your default source for gaining knowledge of foreign perspectives. The formal diplomatic channels, in a world of varied, massive and open information flows, can, especially in the context of an irregular armed struggle, be easily manipulated, and as noted above, diplomats are in charge of diplomatic fiction. Many strategists believe strategy and deception are synonymous, and that strategy and stratagem cannot be far apart. As a starting rubric, it is best to consider all irregular wars international, and that diplomats will believe they have something to hide and something to gain by lying. In addition, if you are limited to the use of local interpreters, you will face the problem of the interpreters' tendency to filter and adjust communications in accordance with their own perspectives, goals, fears, and foibles.

Among the economic investments any government or anti-government force can take in advance of anticipated irregular armed challenges is to increase capacity in relevant foreign languages. There are few irrelevant foreign languages. The anthropologists' attitude is valuable in this. They tend to think small. It isn't enough for them to know that in Guatemala they speak Spanish. They recognize that in Purulhá, Guatemala, Spanish may be the second language. If you are planning to meddle in the problems of a foreign place, and you aren't sure you even know the locale's principal language, you're traipsing close to the edge of cross-cultural disaster. Start out a campaign profoundly ignorant of cultural basics and you will concede the weight of those key factors to your enemy. Foreign support is always at risk of foreign misunderstanding.

See: 13, *Puthukkudiyirippu*; 122, *Songs of Chu*; 2, *The Line of Retreat*; 136, *Weapons*; 68, *Scale*; 52, *Sovereignty*; 53, *Hohfeldian Grievance Analysis*; and 117 *Strategic Communications*.

---

> "I learned that Japan was a weird foreign country that was for some reason under almost constant attack by giant mutated creatures. Godzilla was the most famous one, of course, but there were also hyperthyroid pterodactyls, spiders, etc., all of which regularly barged into Tokyo and committed acts of mass destruction."
>
> Dave Barry[27]

A hidden conventional story

# Section 21, Iximché

A lot was going on in Guatemala in the early 1980s. This rendition of the conflict highlights a relationship between small battles in Guatemala City and guerrilla warfare ranging the mountains west of the capital. The underlying war of position and movement, obedient to the principles of classic military theory, was more consequential than most histories remember. A major operation and turning point was named after an ancient Mayan ruin and piece of key terrain called Iximché. Of the personalities involved, Colonel Manuel Antonio Callejas y Callejas, who at the time directed the Guatemalan intelligence service (D-2), had the greatest individual impact on outcomes.

Sometime early in 1981, a member of the ORPA (Revolutionary Organization of the People in Arms) rented a big house from a dentist in the upper middleclass neighborhood of Vista Hermosa along the highway heading east out of Guatemala City toward El Salvador. The new tenant was a foreigner, apparently a Salvadoran who used falsified documents. His house guests, ORPA guerrillas, converted the home into a revolutionary headquarters, explosives and propaganda factory, and materiel transfer point. From there they supported guerrilla units marshalling in the highlands about fifty miles west of the city. Careful at first, they grew lax in their security under the growing weight of preparations for what was intended as a huge 'final assault' on the city sometime around Christmas that year.

At 9:45 AM on July 9th, the house was surrounded by upwards of 200 policemen and another 200 soldiers. The army sealed off the neighborhood with armored cars and troops from the Honor Guard Brigade. Kids at the nearby American School, attended by many children of embassy personnel, were kept at the school until 4:30 PM, well past their normal dismissal. Schools in the area were closed on the following day as well. Efforts were made to secure the surrender of the besieged guerrillas using loudspeakers, but the guerrillas disdained the ultimatums, choosing instead to fight it out. Around noon, one of the army's M-8 armored cars opened fire with its 37mm cannon. The explosion did more damage than expected, setting off a huge secondary explosion inside the house (no wonder, since the occupants were busy making landmines). The entire roof nearly collapsed. Fourteen guerrillas were taken out that day and another three bodies were taken out on the 10th. Four of the dead guerrillas were women. One soldier from the D-2 fell through the roof and died. There are conflicting reports as to whether any of the guerrillas were taken alive. Perhaps the army was able to conduct a few rudimentary interrogations. Regardless, the tenacity of the guerrillas in defending the safe house can be explained by the value of the house's contents. Not only did the army find an impressive stash of weapons and explosives, it also claimed discovery of guerrilla plans and valuable lists of other guerrillas.

The D-2 may have been tipped off by an insider. Two ORPA guerrillas had been taken captive and shown off in public two weeks earlier, on June 26. Both were young *campesinos* who had been taken prisoner in a rural area. In their public admissions, they spoke of their recruitment and international training, and they probably gave far more information to their interrogators. Mario Payeras, leader of another leftist insurgent group, the EGP (Guerrilla Army of the Poor) later suggested that the captives might have described the interior of the house, and with that information the D-2 could deduce its type and neighborhood and then slowly check lists of rentals. In the search of those records, they would have been attracted by the suspect documents of this particular renter. Apparently, earlier in July, the D-2 had received a call from a neighbor's domestic servant reporting odd goings-on next door -- too many lights on too late at night, too many adults and not enough children. The G-2 confirmed the neighbor's suspicions and mounted the assault.

Mario Payeras wrote in *Trueno en la Ciudad* (*Thunder in the City*):

> "According to the classic principles of war, any army, knowing that the fundamental factors on which it has based its strategy are threatened, had better change that strategy. To the extent that a severance of support between rearguard services and the frontlines occurs closer to the front lines, the effect is more immediate. The closer the severance is to the rearguard, the more global the effect. Inside the urban Front a similar military doctrine applies: to put the enemy commander in a dilemma. Either leave the city or risk having your forces destroyed in position.... In synthesis, that is what occurred. In the following weeks, having destroyed the rearguard, the anti-guerrilla offensive would have to proceed in phases in the countryside, exploiting the initial success and maintaining the initiative. It was the difficult logic of the laws of war that we were learning then. We paid for the lesson in blood."[28]

In the weeks that followed the July 9th assault in Vista Hermosa, the army was able to mount a series of attacks on insurgent safe houses that devastated the guerrillas' presence in Guatemala City. Army morale skyrocketed. Cracking the Vista Hermosa safe house was the good news the army had long needed, and as it would turn out, the officers correctly sensed that the 9 July attack was a major turning point in the war, perhaps *the* turning point.

The previous week, on July 4, the EGP held a dedication ceremony for two squads belonging to their urban military unit. On that day, the guerrillas noted an eerie calm in the city that they thought might presage bad news -- perhaps the government was planning a house-by-house sweep (*cateo*) of the city -- but the guerrillas discarded that possibility because of the huge number of soldiers it would take. The army couldn't afford to dedicate the men needed to make such an operation worthwhile. Nevertheless, in the first week of July, normal vehicle checkpoints in the city had all but disappeared. This might have put the guerrilla more on alert, but they attributed the situation to impotence on the part of the government. The Guatemalan president, General Fernando Romeo Lucas García, reconfirmed the insurgents' predisposition with a public speech wherein he admitted how strong the guerrillas were.

After the events of July 9, it might have seemed more obvious to the insurgents that indeed they had observed the calm before the storm, but instead they attributed the attack on the ORPA's Vista Hermosa safe house to errors made by that cell. The EGP did not yet sense an immediate danger to its own urban operations. The next day this hopeful perspective was demolished. On July 10th, a second redoubt was taken, this time EGP. Twelve more guerrillas were killed. Although the guerrilla counted on informants inside the government, the speed of D-2 operations outpaced the speed at which the insurgent moles could inform. Within one month, dozens of safe houses had fallen, and although the D-2 continued to clear some safe houses well into 1982, the ORPA and then the EGP was forced to abandon almost its entire urban presence.

Each week, Colonel Callejas would brief Minister of Defense Aníbal Guevara in increasing detail on two phenomena (coup plotting and climactic events in the guerrilla war), but the arrogance of the minister and his boss, Romeo Lucas, was by then strong enough that neither could process the information. The defense minister was devoting his attention to his personal destiny – which he thought meant becoming President, and his busy preparations for that end made him oblivious to both the political and military upheavals that were taking place around him.

The public psychology in Guatemala in July 1981 is both difficult to capture and significant for understanding the shift in momentum that was about to disfavor insurgent plans. For some time the revolutionaries had succeeded in creating that magic mixture of revolutionary messaging -- that insurgent strength was growing; that the government military was impotent to fix and destroy them; and that insurgent success was inevitable. Guerrilla strategic communication, if formulaic, had the desired effect of garnering supporters from throughout the economic spectrum and internationally. It has to be said as well that the insurgents broadly transmitted the message of their inevitable rise to power while at the same time never ringing the alarm bell of the Guatemalan Army's hierarchy.

Both guerrilla military powers, the EGP and ORPA, hid the size of their military preparations by disciplined avoidance of head to head contests with any sizeable Guatemalan Army units. Now, however, after the first of the safe houses had fallen, the G-2 was gaining convincing evidence about the magnitude of the guerrilla challenge. More importantly, the public as much as the army noticed the vincibility of guerrilla units. The raids also alerted the entire urban population to be curious about what was going on over at their neighbors.' Finally there was a palpable demonstration of public support; the D-2 began to receive hundreds of phone calls.

The anniversary of the Sandinista Revolution in Nicaragua was also in mid July. Nicaraguan President Daniel Ortega gave a long, Fidelesque speech to commemorate the occasion, and it fell hard on attentive ears in

Guatemala. In his speech, *Comandante* Daniel laid out emphatically and with little ornamentation the radical course that had been mapped for the Nicaraguan revolution. Property confiscations were the order of the day.[29] The *Comandante* also outlined and justified control of the press, including the highly regarded newspaper *La Prensa*. Guatemalans of any material means were offered a stiffening reminder of the consequences of socialist revolution.

The number of guerrillas or guerrilla leaders captured or killed in the raids was by no means crippling, or was the loss of materiel. The D-2's urban success had, however, four overarching consequences, as follows:

> 1. The raids greatly changed the distances of logistical supply to the guerrillas' rural units. The insurgents had to switch (quickly) what had been a main line of communication running thirty to sixty miles from Guatemala City into the mountains to the west. Now they had to run their support activities from Mexico -- nearly a 180 degree reverse. In their urban raids, the D-2 had found hospitals, landmine factories, propaganda centers, and weapons smuggling devices. The bulk of these activities would now have to be conducted at five times the distance. The D-2 also uncovered things like papier-mâché facemasks, uniforms, national police car license plates, and so on. These anonymity and infiltration activities would have to be re-constructed to be suitable in their Mexico context. At least, as the new intelligence also made clear, the insurgents could count on collaboration from within the Mexican government. They could obtain, for instance, official PEMEX (Petróleos Mexicanos, the national petroleum company) pick-up trucks to haul explosives.
>
> 2. They shifted the psychological momentum, giving the Guatemalan Army a vital morale boost at a critical point in the war, and making key sectors of the public reassess the possibilities. The D-2 had muffled the 'Songs of Chu.'
>
> 3. The raids unlocked a door to intelligence information that would help make the next chapter in the war unfold in the Army's favor. Between mid-July and mid-October, the D-2 obtained sufficient hard information not only to see the marshaling of guerrilla forces for a major offensive against the capital city, but to convince the Chief of Staff, General Benedicto Lucas Garcia (the President's younger brother) to

act diligently. This was no small task considering the environment of cocksure oblivion into which the regime's leaders had fallen. Colonel Callejas arranged a helicopter tour of key points in the highlands for the new Chief (who had been transferred from command of the distant Poptún Brigade in mid-August). They flew to the nearby mountain village of Chupol where the General saw a network of Viet Cong-style defense trenches, tunnels and booby traps installed by the guerrillas. Finally, the senior military leader was a believer that Guatemala had a war on its hands, and not just a few annoying rebels. The resolve of the Army's leadership changed tenor, and planning for a rural counteroffensive began immediately.

4. They eliminated part of the guerrillas' operational formula, which was to distract a major part of the Guatemalan Army's overall combat power in reaction to guerrilla urban actions and provocations.

The D-2 followed up on leads, uncovering a series of older rural insurgent materiel depots, as well as rural logistical improvisations that were occasioned by the collapse of the urban safe houses. Soon, Colonel Callejas could outline the shape of the planned insurgent offensive, measure its strength and point to its geographic heart.

**From urban to rural**. Although it is hard to recognize on a tourist map, or during a quick drive along the Inter-American Highway, the ground around the Indian villages of Chupol and Xepol in Chimaltenango Department has always been a military geographic prize. The space that runs roughly from Chupol and Xepol, to Tecpán Guatemala and the ancient ruins of Iximché, and through Patzún dominates both east-west and north-south passage through the mountains. These towns sit near the continental divide – waters to the north flowing to the Motagua River and the Atlantic, and streams to the south flowing to the Coyolate River and the Pacific, or into Lake Atitlán. The departmental boundaries of Chimaltenango, Quiche and Sololá meet in the area, as do the *de facto* boundaries of three major (and historically contentious) ethnic groups, the Quiché to the north, Cakchiquel to the southeast and the Tzutujil to the southwest. These indigenous boundaries are not contiguous with the modern departmental limits.

The territorial organization of the army (into *zonas*) had been based on the assumption of external invasion rather than an internal challenge, so the Xepol-Patzún axis was not a focal point for the design of the major military commands. A boundary between two military zones ran across the area, their headquarters located in distant Huehuetenango and Guatemala City, respectively. Insurgent choice of the environs as a focal point of extraordinary revolutionary effort was no accident, and was not predicated on proletariat ripeness or ideological romanticism. The insurgents selected what history, movement, and enemy order of battle all indicated was key terrain, if not the geographical center of gravity. Both the ORPA and the EGP, whose territorial boundaries also met there, recognized the same military criticality as had the pre-Colombian Mayas, and conquistador Pedro de Alvarado.

The Army kicked off Operation Iximché at one o`clock on the morning of November 15, 1981 with about 1,900 soldiers. The terrain objective was that key crescent of land in northwestern Chimaltenango Department, but the underlying goal was to break up guerrilla preparations for their anticipated Christmas offensive, and to wrest control of the rural highland approaches to Guatemala City. The guerrillas, overextended, overconfident, and not alert, were badly routed. The guerrillas had not anticipated the weight of the attack or the ferocity with which the army dealt with some of their most supportive villages. A clear message raced through the highlands: The revolutionary left, with its selective terror and Marxist bravado, was no match for its better-armed opponent. Insurgent marshalling for a Christmas offensive was dead. The army gained strategic initiative. The long-term implications could not be immediately seen by either side, and Operation Iximché, which was supposed to last 10 days, essentially went on for two years. The guerrillas would try to adjust, but they had no adequate 'Plan B.' They reeled, and in 1982 the army made surprising adaptations to exploit gains and frustrate any effective guerrilla return.

Beyond a final assault on the Capital City, what was the insurgent plan? It is not clear the major groups within the insurgent political umbrella organization, the URNG (Guatemalan National Revolutionary Unity) ever shared the same vision, but militarily there was some concurrence. They would isolate the northwestern areas of Huehuetenango and Quiché from Guatemala City and the eastern provinces, proclaim a liberated territory backed by broad international support (especially Mexican), then leverage this nascent autonomy for concessions from a besieged central government. For this plan to work, the Xepol-Patzún axis had to be effectively controlled both day and night. The territory would be defended by a deep battle zone that extended east to Guatemala City, to be supplied from out of the northwest (especially after the Guatemala City guerrilla infrastructure was decimated). Guerrilla positioning and attacks would dissipate Guatemalan army strength by coaxing the army into static defenses and reactions against urban guerrilla initiatives. The 'final assault' might or might not take the capital, but the army's strategic reserve (comprised mainly of units in the urban area) would be so stretched to protect the city and its suburbs that it could not effectively answer the insurgents in the highlands.

If the urban guerrilla infrastructure was back in place in three months (as EGP leader Ricardo Asturias later claimed), it was back in place on a much smaller, more timid scale, like a re-grown salamander tail. The urban rearguard was no longer able to fill the same role. Three months, moreover, (in fact, it was more like six) meant that the urban front could neither distract army forces away from Chupol when the army launched its rural counterattack in November, nor disrupt the general elections the following March. Whatever lessons the urban front might have learned, and however well organized it might later become, its moment had gone. It had three main missions: supply the rural units, misdirect Army resources, and confound the elections. It could do none of these. Now it just served to prove the guerrilla still had a pulse.

Destruction of the guerrillas' Guatemala City network of safe houses was the first clear strategic defeat suffered by the guerrillas. Alone it would not have been sufficient to unsaddle revolutionary plans, but the urban campaign led almost immediately to the army's rural counterpunch. That punch caught the revolutionaries overextended and in the midst of marshalling for their attack on the city, and not preparing for the army's move. The balloon of guerrilla geographic presence quickly deflated, sending insurgent cadre streaming back into Mexico.

The Guatemalan Army could not definitively beat the URNG because insurgent sanctuaries lay inside Mexican territory. Eventually, the contenders would come to a negotiated agreement; the army had to accept a bitter half loaf. The Guatemalan government just didn't have the power to beat an insurgent foe that had Mexico as an ally. But inside Guatemala, in 1981, the Guatemalan Army, guided by Callejas y Callejas – a student of geography, history, and strategy – beat a huge insurgent force militarily.

Colonel Callejas later became Army Chief of Staff, retired, and is aging gracefully. He is one of the graduates of the School of the Americas about whom the radical left is most resentful and vituperative. Mario Payeras lived anonymously in Mexico City and died young in

1995. His remains were exhumed by thieves, and scattered. He left behind an appreciable body of literature, however, and he has become a minor martyr in the leftist revolutionary firmament.

In review, then, what are some of the relevant lessons from this obscure history?

* Smart guerrillas think about the classic principles of military strategy;

* Police forensics can have military operational impact;

* Public records are powerful resources;

* A guerrilla sanctuary in a foreign country presents a difficult operational and geostrategic challenge;

* Internal wars are international wars;

* Leadership is critical;

* Timing matters;

* Rural and urban are connected operationally;

* Cottage industry explosives had become an insurgent staple;

* Kidnapping had become an insurgent staple.

See: 34, *Urban or Rural*; 16, *Keeping Secrets*; 140, *Culminating Point in the Pursuit*; 64, *Measuring Power*; 53, *Hohfeldian Grievance Analysis*; 117, *Strategic Communication*; 36, *Foreign Support*; and 96, *Public Records*.

---

"Crowded the nations there were (Tzatz ri amaq' chu k'oje'ik).
Not counted people (Mawi ajilan chi winaq).
Warriors (E aj lab'al),
Also killers (E pu kamisanel),
Murderers (E kamisay),...
Not only two eight thousands (Mawi xa ka chuy),
Three eight thousands of nations (Ox chuy chi amaq')
They encircled (Xkotkomij)
Around citadel (Chirij tinamit)."

Allen J. Christenson
*Popol Vuh: Literal Translation*[30]

මහින්ද රාජපක්ෂ

# *Section 22, Badassoftheweek.com*

Who leads insurgencies, drug mafias, separatist movements and the like? So many great examples are noted on the website *Badassoftheweek.com* it just seemed fair to name this section after the website, presented by Ben 'Amazing' Thompson. A lot of Thompson's heroes are fictional, some aren't even human or even vertebrate, but that doesn't matter. There are still plenty of historic examples to profile the kind of person who becomes a successful anti-State leader. There is no single profile of attributes, but most of the successful leaders are most of the following:

> Aggrieved; Athletic; Brave; Charismatic; Creative; Egoistic; Horney; Male; Perseverant; Rich; Risk-taking; Ruthless; Smart; Student of military art and history.

There are plenty of examples of great insurgent leaders. I already mentioned George Washington. Spartacus is a standout. Pick your own; they all understood and respected the operational equation inherent in classic military strategy. Washington was especially careful to secure his lines of retreat. He didn't enjoy too many straight up victories in battle against the British, but he never got caught. Spartacus, in a funk, finally defied one time too many not just his Roman masters, but the timeless principles of war.

Note that 'male' is not on the list of successful insurgents' basic characteristics. Few women rise to lead major criminal or rebellious armed organizations, although it happens, and Badassoftheweek.com honors a few. The vast majority are male, gender holding true more than the other characteristics. Guerrilla war leadership is an alpha boy's club.

As for counterinsurgent heroes, it's harder to find historic cases. Abe Lincoln might be up there, depending on how you define things, and no, it is not simple jingoism that I pick Americans, and it's no coincidence either. Lincoln might actually fall into both categories, insurgent and counterinsurgent. Colombia's president, Álvaro Uribe, might be in the making as one of history's most successful counterinsurgents, but we'll have to wait a little longer to see. Sri Lanka's President Mahendra Rajapaksa or even his former Army Commander, General Sarath Fonseka have solid resumes, and some would include Francisco Franco on the short list. Whether or not the successful counterinsurgent personality is the same as that of the insurgent is a question beyond the reach of this book, but it might be so.

Mao was not the prettiest man, but he beat the Kwomintang using strategies that have become clichés of irregular warfare. Che was hunted down and killed by a Cuban-American who is still alive forty years later drinking rum and coke and telling the story. While Che wasn't smart enough to hide his campfires, Mao mastered military strategy. According to some, Mao's last words were 'There is a serious tendency toward capitalism among the peasants.' Che's last words are debated, but were probably not as his iconographers relate. I suspect he said, 'Gee, I wish I had secured my line of retreat.'

The competent insurgent or gang leader can grant impunity to his underlings in defiance of the State. If an insurgent leader is dead, however, he is not going to grant impunity to anyone, so one conclusive measure of success, say, against a given insurgency group, is the destruction of its leadership. This destruction may not have to mean killing; it could mean disrupting the means of communication between insurgent leadership and subordinates, or the suppression of receptiveness to the insurgent leaders' message within a relevant population. I believe, however, that the physical bodies of the leaders are the preferable target. Some will argue that some insurgent movements are spontaneous, or that 'networking' or other phenomena of the age make the replacement of insurgent leaders all but endless. I reject such a notion. We just don't know of any insurgency that succeeded without effective, named, flesh-and-blood leaders anymore than we know of effective governments without human heads. Effective leadership is a rare commodity, and in the majority of successful insurgencies the leadership appears both stable and jealous. Besides, spontaneity grants very temporary impunity, if any at all. Somewhere someone is granting impunity in defiance of your assertions of territorial sovereignty. That's got to stop. If you gain physical domination over the granter of impunity, he isn't going to be a granter of impunity any longer.

The above observation does not imply that a counter-leader strategy is the only useful approach; either in counterinsurgency or insurgency. It does not dismiss other parallel, complementary efforts. It only insists that, ultimately, the engine of an insurgent movement is its leaders. Everything else about the insurgency -- its financial strength, its public support, its international support -- are important to the insurgency's maintenance, and so are worthy of targeting in an overall counterinsurgent plan. It may be a similarly useful part of an insurgent's plan to attack public and international support for a government, or to attack the economy. Nevertheless, all organizations are forfeit to a lack of leadership. The heart of an insurgency is the insurgent leader; of the revolution the vanguard; of the mafia the mafia don; of the dictatorship the dictator; and as long as leadership remains at large, it can prolong or revive the insurgency (or revolution, rebellion, or criminal gang). The fact that many counterinsurgents can't find and fix their insurgent enemy's leaders does not make the point any less valid. It only means the counterinsurgency has not succeeded, usually due to an inadequate intelligence function or simple lack of will to act.

Chairman Mao and George Washington deserve their own sections as revolutionary military leaders, but only Washington as planter of revolutionary change. The example and direction the latter set, and the propositions for which he led, survived his death by centuries.

See: 12, *Protraction and Diligence*; 8, *The Operational Equation*; 109, *Hotspotting*; 18, *Massacres*; 23, *Mens Rea*; 1, *What the Pirate Said to Alexander*; 143, *Is It an Insurgency?*; and 81, *What a Clergy Wants*.

---

Before the boogeyman goes to sleep at night,
he checks under the bed for Chuck Norris.

Scientific fact

Who is the culpable author of the crime?

# *Section 23, Mens Rea*

*Mens rea* means criminal intent. Someone can be held responsible, accountable or culpable for criminal and insurgent activity. That someone is the intellectual author of violence. This book is about winning organized armed violence, and so, tautologically-speaking, if it is 'organized' violence, someone organized it. The system or the structure of society might indeed be unworthy, and its own quiet organizer of violence. Maybe that unworthiness is a motivating factor for the intellectual authors of resistance or insurgency, but insurgencies don't just up and happen as a result of injustices.

Some academics disdain the notion of human nature, and diminish concepts like guilt or shame as products of social constructs, the legitimacy of the latter being subject to constant reevaluation. Some of that may be true, but it is a tough wave for the jurisprudentially-inclined to ride. We are asked to take a difficult leap of logic to accept the argument that human nature is 'merely a human construct,' together with the consequence that by so saying, human nature is invalidated as a reference for determining how to deal with our miserable species. In other words, since guilt is a social construct and not really real, *mens rea* is also a social construct, so we shouldn't be focused on capturing and punishing the intellectual leaders of insurgencies or crimes, but rather on fixing the things in society that create the resistance or survival desires and behaviors. If you are inclined to resistance against the establishment, if you find wisdom in the post-structural arguments, you will want to press the argument that your criminal behavior is not your fault, but the fault of the system. The argument does not fall on deaf ears only; it might get you out on parole earlier, or give you a few more minutes to escape capture, or formulate a plea bargain, but don't convince yourself.

The above, post-structural viewpoint notwithstanding, *Mens rea* remains a basic element of criminal jurisprudence in our and in most societies. Fault, culpability, criminal intent, authorship of crime, badness – *mens rea* is Latin for an important part of why someone deserves to be punished. It is also an important concept for winning armed conflict. It is connected with the definition of enemy. 'Public enemy number one' is a phrase the substance of which depends not just on the behavior of an individual, but on the intent of that individual, as interpreted by the rest of us, to lead himself or others to future unpleasant behavior with which we cannot abide.

We might agree that: Public Enemy Number One's mother didn't love him; he was poor and just learned to survive; his Dad was an abusive alcoholic; and even that all these things might have been the result of a poorly formed society which spawned an underclass in which such conditions are woefully normal. Agreeing to all that, we might still disagree as to whether or not such observations should force us to transpose anger from the individual to the society, and so justify chancing his raping and stealing on a continuing basis. Maybe some Public Enemy Number One crowns himself agent and vanguard of proletariat retribution, even though he is not poor, but rather a scion of an upper middleclass champion of selfishness. Either way, if his is the skull within which plans are made for doing harm to others, and especially if he is intelligent, guileful, ruthless and charismatic, he will guide others into violent action.

*Mens rea*, the guilty cogitation causing violent actions, can be located and followed. Bad things sometimes just happen, but usually they are the product of nasty thinking. If you have no sub-plan to hide your nasty thinking, or to locate the physical geographic locus of your foe's nasty thinking, you are making a competitive mistake. Killing Adolf Hitler might have worked. Capturing *Presidente* Gonzalo (*nom de guerre* of insurgent leader Abimael Guzmán) stopped the Peruvian Sendero Luminoso insurgency in its tracks. As time passes for an insurgency (or even for an unjust social structure) the *mens rea* can be spread out a little bit (more leaders, more places), making it a little harder to corner. The *mens rea* of insurgency or crime has precise geography, while the guilt of a faulty social construct has a nebulous geography. Insurgents would of course prefer to blame the construct; they do not want to be located.

See: 54, *Badassoftheweek.com*; 2, *Anonymity*; 42, *White Bird*; 51, *Underclass*; 79, *Suicide*; 41, *Whereabouts*; 25, *Why Humans Don't Fight*; and 2, *The Line of Retreat.*

---

> "You can't hold a whole fraternity responsible for the behavior of a few, sick twisted individuals. For if you do, … isn't this an indictment of our educational institutions in general? I put it to you…isn't this an indictment of our entire American society? Well, you can do whatever you want to us, but we're not going to sit here and listen to you badmouth the United States of America."
>
> Otter in the movie
> *Animal House*[31]

Some believe that people respond best to threats

# *Section 24, Ruthlessness and Resolve*

If you are not willing to kill someone, you won't win your armed conflict. You might get lucky, of course, and not have to, so if hanging on to that hope is helpful to you, OK. But I assume somebody has the willpower to kill you, otherwise we'd just be talking politics or global warming.

Roger Trinquier wrote a book titled *Modern Warfare*. He is one of a pair of deceased French Army officers often referenced in US military writing about counterinsurgency. The other is David Galula. Section 58, *Guerre d'Algérie* talks a little about that war, so suffice it here to say it was probably the worst counterinsurgent effort in history, or at least since the French Revolution. Trinquier, however, thought he was doing pretty well as a counterinsurgent, for a short while at least. (Some characters in Jean Larteguy's novels, *The Centurions, The Praetorians,* and *The Hounds of Hell,* may have been inspired by or based on the life of Trinquier.) Trinquier attributed his success to attitude, as much as to specific tactics or strategies. The marrow of that attitude was a conviction that the populace had to be put in mortal fear -- scared to death or put to death.

I was told in Guatemala that the Communist guerrillas and the Guatemalan Army each had to prove to villagers of the mountain tribes that their opponents could not protect them. In other words, the guerrillas argued that the army could not protect a tribe from the guerrillas and the army would argue to the same tribe that the guerrillas could not protect it from the army. Each side would present their version of the argument by graphic example.

A culture of violence can become draconian inside guerrilla bands. Leaders of the Colombian *Ejército de Liberación Nacional* (National Liberation Army, ELN), for instance, thought it necessary to require from its recruits a proof of willingness to kill, a proof that could only be met by killing. They also required acceptance of death as a penalty for even relatively minor infractions, and certain death for betrayals, with betrayal sometimes defined broadly to include even minor infractions. In other words, to be part of the unit, you had to be willing to kill and die cheaply. Anonymity was especially important, and death was therefore the penalty for breaching anonymity. From *Lapham's Raiders*, about American and Philippine guerrillas fighting against the Japanese in World War II, we read,

> "First off, to be successful a guerrilla leader must become, in one way or another, the de facto ruler of the territory in which he operates. Failure to achieve authority will defeat all his plans and hopes. From this it follows that he must maintain the loyalty of local officials and local people, making it safer for them to give him such loyalty than to pursue any other course. That, in turn, requires that spies, collaborators with enemies, and anyone else who breaks down the trust between himself and the local population must be eliminated or neutralized without pity. Nothing less will suffice."[32]

The two centrally significant violent events in mafia or gangster culture are retributions for bearing witness or informing against the organization (death to traitors) and proof of loyalty by way of the commission of murder and torture (can get the job done). For efficiency's sake, the victims of the proof-by-murder will be persons who resist the payment of ransoms or for whom ransoms are not paid. These deaths are not part of the culture *per se*, but rather part of the business. The similarity to guerrilla violent culture, however, is evident.

Spanish Professor Jorge Verstrynge (See Section 98, *Jorge Verstrynge and Pio Moa*) praised the resolve shown by Islamic fundamentalists. His admiration was not so much for those who commit suicide-murder, but for the engine that ties existential ruthlessness to a project of resistance -- that the radical Islamicists can convince and send people to commit suicide-murder on behalf of a grand concept which they framed. Therein lays one cutline between resolve and ruthlessness. The Islamicists as Verstrynge admires them are both ruthless in their willingness to expend human life, and they are resolute in their defiance of the great Satan, America.

A British officer once explained the Irish problem to me succinctly: that the Irish were stubborn and the British resolute. Resolve is neither the opposite of ruthlessness, or always to be combined with it. Resolve is obviously a significant quality, both for resistance to the Man, and for resistance to the kinds of cultures of violence that sometimes grow in guerrillas and mafias. Willingness to suffer and regain defiance in the face of extortion and proofs of ruthlessness, or to resist enslavement, is not the human norm. Most communities fold.

See: 132, *Brigands*; 16, *Keeping Secrets*; 4, *Defining Enemy*;
140, *Culminating Point in the Pursuit*; 56, *Militias and Gun Control*;
58, *Guerre d'Algérie*; 18, *Massacres*; and 23, *Mens Rea.*

---

"Okay. You wanna play rough?
Okay. Say hello to my little friend."

Tony Montana in the movie
*Scarface* (1983)[33]

It's cheaper not to

# *Section 25, Why Humans Don't Fight*

It might help you to know why you want to fight and why your opponent wants to fight. It might be more helpful to know why people don't fight.

**Why humans fight:**

A. 'That's my stuff.'
B. 'That's my girl.' (Or 'You hurt my feelings,' 'You dishonored me.')
C. 'I'm nuts.'

The three mix. 'That's my stuff' is easiest to understand, the most important and the most common. Some people are purists on the matter: 'What's mine is mine and what's yours is mine.' Or, as Ben Franklin advised, "Mine is better than ours."[34] A tendency toward arrogation is one of those things some folk call human nature while others, who do not believe so much in the concept of human nature, will say it is the product of a flawed social construct. Either way, we try to tax other people's wealth so that we don't have to work so hard at just stealing it. If we can be the government, we can be legitimate thieves, or, instead of self-righteous philanthropists, we can redistribute un-earned wealth to the downtrodden. Meanwhile, a standard act of insurgency is to not pay the king's tax. We might even rob from the government tax collector. Ours is better than his.

'That's my girl' alludes to emotive reasons generally. Violence may be response to dishonor, revenge, or it could even be an arrogation of spirituality. Someone may hold an object of veneration, but have sufficient ego that he wants the rest of us to venerate it along with him, led in worship by him. Naturally, he will tax us for the education. The object of veneration may be God or a theory, but, since the effort to impose communion requires so much ego, the personality of the priest himself becomes the object of veneration. Lots of people are enthralled by and apologize for what today is called a 'populist.' Others prefer mullahs.

'I'm nuts' might be less common, but people do fight because they are not healthy psychologically. Many successful violent populists have seemed to be partially nuts, bi-polar nuts, or drug-induced nuts. We always ask if a leader who seems a bit eccentric or radical isn't actually a little insane. We often enter into debate about whether the leader of some foreign government whose behavior offends us is or isn't a little off his rocker. Are Ahmadinejad or Chávez messianic, crazy like foxes, or do we just not understand? The right answer is...they're probably a little insane. But we all are to some degree, and we often admire and follow those who are just a little nuttier than ourselves, perhaps confusing irrationality with commitment or resolve. We often look to our radicals, to the activists, to the obsessively invested, for leadership. Resolve is necessary for action, and extreme resolve is sometimes necessary for mortal action. We admire single-mindedness and perseverance against adversity. It just happens that these qualities aren't as sane a set characteristics as those that guide us to staying comfortable and taking the easy pathways.

There is a longer list of possible reasons why people fight. Domination and violence seem pleasurable to some people. There is also the notion of war economies, meaning that some people simply benefit economically from selling this and that to violent competitors, so it behooves them to warmong; and there are Hegelian-type notions that war is a crucible of history and nationhood, meaning that leaders feel and encourage the unifying emotions of mortal challenge.

Use of the concept of *mens rea* builds on these possible reasons for organizing to violence. Knowing the motivation of the authors of mortal action helps measure the possibilities for prosecution, compromise and restitution, or to temper vindictiveness. Organizationally speaking, it also helps us consider the likely effect of a change of leadership. If we capture Gonzalo, will his revolutionary organization keep the same unity, purpose and determination, or will it fold? If the country's president loses the next election will there be a change of strategy toward us?

As noted in Section 23, some scholars reject the overall parameters of thought within which the concept of guilt or criminal intent (*mens rea*) is a feature. These folk are more likely to express causation as a product of social forces, like the slow violence economic privilege perpetrates against an underclass. They are more likely to excuse the violence of an individual as being the product of an unjust social contract the construction of which the individual had little input. This 'resistance' perspective, with many sincere adherents, is perfectly subject to the three general categories of why people fight. Although the resistance perspective justifies violent actions of the underdog, the justification still accuses some elite or oligarch of a culpable *mens rea*, and still prescribes justice in the form of punishment. It is still a 'you've got my stuff' or a 'you've got my girl' proposition.

**Why humans don't fight:**

A. Peaceful conflict resolution is cheaper
B. They don't think they can win
C. They are convinced fighting is wrong

To ask why humans fight presupposes that peace is the normal human condition and war or violent conflict the exception. If, however, the base condition of man is violent and territorial, and peace a recent improvement, then the efficient question is why peace occurs. Sir Michael Howard (*The Invention of Peace: Reflections on War and International Order*) would probably agree.[35] A point made by John Powelson in *The Story of Land: A World History of Land Tenure and Agrarian Reform* becomes all the more intriguing. He noted that no country without a formal system of land ownership and written contracts has ever enjoyed long periods of internal peace.[36] In everyday legal parlance, land outside the lines of formal property is subject to 'possession by force.' Without the unique controlling institution of formalized property, violent conflict is inevitable.

Looking at thresholds of peace instead of violence, we also see an inverse of the transaction cost approach taken by Douglass North and Robert Thomas (Please see Section 82, *Conflict Thresholds*). People are more likely to turn to peace when the cost of peaceful transactions is perceived to be less than the cost of violence. Peaceful transaction costs became less than the cost of violence when systems that encouraged fulfillment of contractual obligations were emplaced. These include things like statutes of fraud and land surveys. If you are the counterinsurgent trying to win an internal armed conflict of some kind, it means that you will not achieve a condition of generalized human security and social peace without the tedious forms, papers, signatures, photocopies, files and maps of obsessive public administration. And...although indispensable, that will still not be enough. You will still need property courts, markets and elections. If you are an insurgent, the fluid functioning of these things could do you in. You might want to put a wrench into them.

Humans fight because our neighbor has stuff we want, or for pleasure, dominance, revenge, or because we're insane, or some combination or inverse of these. The idea of a peace threshold is more concerned with the when, where, who and how people come to live within a peaceful social contract. It doesn't delve so much into the basic question of *why* we fight as it does how we might create an environment where it is easier not to fight.

Jealousy, greed, revenge, and fear are common departure points for explanations of why people fight. All knowledge is grist to the mill, and it would be nice to know why you and your enemy are fighting. However, for winning you want to know your enemy's whereabouts. You want to attack his geographic anonymity. If you know where but not why, your chances of winning are greater than if you know why but not where. Moreover, to sustain peace and not create enemies, you want to know why people do *not* fight. You will want to encourage the historically-proven institutions that help people reach and maintain the threshold of peace. Chief among these is administration of the social contract based on transparent distribution of property.

See: 86, *Shifting Covet-Geography*; 82, *Conflict Thresholds*; 73, *Property and the Social Contract*; 51, *Underclass*; 142, *Dignity and Honor*; 103, *Amnesty*; 2, *Anonymity*; and 3, *The Domesday Book*.

---

> "Peace is not absence of conflict; it is the ability to handle conflict by peaceful means."
>
> Ronald Reagan[37]

Start small, think mean

# *Section 26, How Violent Groups Form*

Some conditions favor and some disfavor the germination and coalescence of violent groups, and we can predict which places are most likely to harbor or grow them, even if the exact mechanisms and processes of group formation are not well known.

**General Conditions Likely to Stimulate Germination**:

A. Availability of a franchise package for violent resistance behavior.

There may be an attractive strategy-set available (objective, method, resources, ethic), which we can call a franchise package, that provides a ready-made theology/ideology;

justification (of violence); pride identity/symbols; methodology; resources; objectives; and maybe active guidance. Detailed expression of a felt grievance may be significant in some contexts. Most people can't invent these things on their own. Examples include Marxism, Maoism, fascism, and various forms of religious fundamentalism. These do not just arrive as lone ideas; they often come in packages that include the elements just noted above. As with a typical peaceful business franchise, there is often a buy-in fee, a corporate headquarters, standards, inspections, rents, and even uniforms.

Not all of the above-listed franchise features are necessarily provided by each package, or are needed, and, unlike hamburger restaurants, they can overlap. One currently recognized and seemingly ascendant package is radical Islam (especially radical Wahabi Islam). A form of Marxism-Leninism (revamped postmodern or post-structural socialism/communism) has cachet; and the Soprano (gangster, FARC, etc) package is also popular and seems to require a lower start-up investment. Bolivarian-Liberation is brisk right now in Latin America. Not all packages or features are available worldwide, and there are many variations.

B. Inadequacy of establishment inspiration. The 'establishment' may fail to garner respect or to motivate. The government may be a violent criminal actor itself, an authoritarian regime or it may be a gentle, liberal, but existentially uninspiring democracy. The important condition for germination of violent groups is that the establishment or reigning structure fails to inspire or channel the energies of those otherwise disposed to opposition violence.

C. Existence of attractive franchise motivational propaganda. If the possibilities of adopting a resistance franchise is made known to those disposed to participate in resistance activity, a resistance organization is more likely to germinate (it pays to advertise).

D. Existence of successful franchise examples. A person or entity that has taken up the franchise, been honored as a result, and (perhaps) not effectively repressed by the establishment, is a positive stimulant.

E. Elements in the cultural environment (legal, political, social) that make repression of resistance conduct more difficult.

**Local Conditions Likely to Stimulate Germination**:

A. Absence of resolute establishment authority. If the local institutions supposed by the population to wield physical force are reluctant to do so (or simply are not present) then a vacuum of resolve exists that can be filled by another, ruthless group. Impunity is quickly sensed, so any reluctance on the part of the establishment to apply force in uncommon circumstances (to stop looting after a natural disaster, for example) can quickly lead to group creation around ruthless actors.

B. Inadequacy of establishment inspiration. At the local level there may be a variety of competing legal and illegal visions for channeling energies (especially of young males). If they do not inspire, persons seeking inspiration will find it in an alternative franchise package.

C. Absence of outlets for sexual expression, especially male.

D. Presence of pro-franchise charismatic leadership. An opinion leader seems to be an important stimulus. Leadership counts.

E. Availability of enabling resources. Vision without resources is fantasy. The abject poor, left alone, have rarely posed a violent threat to the State.

F. Effective presence of an agent of the franchise package. An expert is someone from out of town, especially if the agent offers money and adventure. An agent in command of an armed team of insurgents may be still more convincing.

G. Contested wealth, especially real estate, without a functioning conflict resolution mechanism.

H. Unaddressed grievances with a definable defendant(s).

I. Successful violent actions (success = accomplished with impunity).

**Strategic Conditions Likely to Counter Germination**:

A. Existence of a favorable option or leader opposed to violent behavior. -- Gandhi, MLK Jr., The Peace Corps.

B. Detailed expression of plans to address and redress grievances. -- affirmative action, apologies, monuments, employment opportunities, upgraded services.

C. Adequate establishment inspiration: Focusing on a common, out-group enemy, or on a unifying mission. This includes potential within the system for aspiring leaders to ascend via peaceful mechanisms (elections, education, military rank).

D. Attractive non-violent motivational propaganda and counter-propaganda and education.

E. Presence of successful non-violent examples.

F. Elements in the cultural environment that make repression of deviant conduct easier. Cadastres, stable addresses, ID cards, complete census data, licensing, registries.

**Local Conditions Likely to Counter Germination**:

A. Resolute local establishment authority. Criminals are captured and punished. Impunity is denied. Orderly responses are made to environmental crises.

B. Adequate establishment inspiration. Local government, schools, civil society, churches exist to channel aspirations.

C. Existence of outlets for sexual expression, especially male.

D. Presence of charismatic leadership that is not pro-resistance.

E. Absence of contested wealth.

F. Existence of a functioning conflict resolution mechanism for contested wealth.

G. Availability of establishment enabling resources, and capacity to repress violent franchise-enabling resources.

H. Capacity to deny the presence of agents of a resistance franchise package. Elements exist in the cultural environment that make repression of resistance easier. Cadastres, addresses, ID cards, complete census data, registries.

**What to do:**

1. Establish a priority of localities requiring more study. Promote outside multidiscipline research of select localities.

2. Identify the worst places. Locate the congruence of conditions that favor the germination of violent resistance groups as described in the above paragraphs, highlighting

the qualitative as well as quantitative characteristics of those places.

3. Shape conditions so that information on local conditions is freely available and willingly provided. Promote comprehensive, accurate census, personal ID, cadastral, mobile property and other property registry records, as well as inventory systems for dangerous instrumentalities.

4. Apply control technologies where your resources allow, and establish a continuous reliable information flow. Apply secret resources only where necessary.

5. Study the propaganda environment. Identify ways to diminish elements of the opposition message.

6. Neutralize opposition agents in locales and reduce the delivery of resources to them. Identify their lines of retreat and their sanctuaries. This requires comprehensive cultural knowledge.

7. Violent actions, especially those accomplished with impunity, are important indicators of favorable conditions for the germination or expansion of violent actors. Whether you are a pro-government person or an insurgent, you probably want to make details of violent events available to outside researchers in order to establish a favorable public record for later use.

8. Gather knowledge about all groups and institutions, not only of resistance franchise packages and agents, but of the groups and institutions they oppose.

9. Identify grievances and contested wealth. Comprehensive conflict analysis identifies grievances and contested wealth, party (claimant) identities associated with these grievances or wealth; determines the locations of members of the claimant groups (cognizant that claimant group memberships will overlap, and that an individual can belong to numerous claimant identities and even belong to competing sides of the same issue); learns what will satisfy grievances or wealth claims; and measures the capabilities and capacities of the claimant identities. This knowledge is necessary for resolution of conditions likely to stimulate the germination of new violent opposition groups. (See Section 53, *Hohfeldian Grievance Analysis*)

10. Build actor-origin databases. In order to help test hypotheses regarding the details of local conditions conducive and not conducive to the germination of violent actors, the database of origins and motivating factors of known violent actors should be expanded, unified, and perfected. Compare the coincidence of that data to physical geography (origins of perpetrators against localities identified as having favorable conditions) to improve understanding of the conditions and where they exist.

This section makes 'how groups form' seem a lot like 'where groups form.' As such, the listed implications (What to do) may seem to be entirely about gathering knowledge and not about doing something more active. No. At some point, you might have to go kill someone, and the idea is to be especially careful about that.

See: 143, *Is It an Insurgency?*; 54, *Badassoftheweek.com*; 34, *Urban or Rural*; 25, *Why Humans Don't Fight*; 53, *Hohfeldian Grievance Analysis*; 4, *Domesday Book*; 23, *Mens Rea*; and 99, *Postmodern and Post-structural.*

---

Three German soldiers are sitting around drinking beer in a Bavarian pub after WWI:

**Eric**: So, Hans, what are you going to do now that the war is over?

**Hans**: I'm going back to Hamburg; my father has a sausage works there. Where are you going?

**Eric**: My dad has a watch shop here close-by. I'll apprentice with him. How about you, Adolf?

**Adolf**: Oh, I'll think of something.

Free and fair elections are the small part of peace

# Section 27, Democracy

The word democracy is not mentioned in the Constitution of the United States. Democracy was not its purpose. People like electoral democracy, however, especially if they haven't had any, and many of its proponents use the word democracy to mean 'good.' Elections are better than no elections, but beyond that they are no guarantee of good governance or a peaceful social contract, and holding them will not necessarily help you win a war. Elections, even if open, egalitarian and fairly administered, can be counterproductive. The same characters who were the owners of everything before there were elections can hijack the new gift, or if popular legitimacy is awarded solely on the basis of an initial electoral victory, it might be the last election.

There is a big difference between a cult of the elected and regular elections. The ultimate purpose of electoral democracy should not be peaceful selection of leaders, but the peaceful change of leaders. Few historians will make the claim that the founding fathers of the United States thought democracy was a great deal. In fact, several of the founding fathers saw in democracy another form of tyranny that needed to be constrained. Electoral democracy encourages those elected to believe they have earned a right to rule, instead of having been lent a privilege of service. The elected like to believe that a popular preference, measured at an instant in time, transfers to them a mandate that lasts forever. That partly is why the framers of the US Constitution sought a formula that could keep the ballot box from creating more problems than it solved.

Democracy is an overused term in discussions about successful counterinsurgency. Plenty of governments that use the term cynically (and allow little of it) are nevertheless good at counterinsurgency. Insurgent organizations that use democracy to pick their leaders are rare. The list of adjectives that describe the *typical* insurgent leader does not include modest, restrained, or democratic.

The United States pushes democracy in places where it can, but that is because Americans haven't maintained cultural memory of the less-positive aspects of democracy about which the founders of the United States warned. Likewise, Americans don't sufficiently value their political inheritance of formal property, and how a just property regime, as much as elections, underpins peaceful social relations.

If you are in charge of planning or leading counterinsurgency, and cannot escape the word democracy, at least define democracy to mean the whole basket of institutional contraptions that limit the concentration of power and that allow for the peaceful replacement of leaders. Selection of the right leaders might have a lot to do with winning the struggle. Admirers of democratically elected Colombian President Álvaro Uribe Vélez think so. However, putting the process of selecting civilian political leaders at the center of counterinsurgent planning could be a distracting and disappointing mistake. Creating an insurgent-resistant society requires an acceptable social contract. As much as vibrant electoral politics, it takes efficient, transparent administration. Elections are interesting. A formal property system is not, but it is a more substantial achievement.

At the time this section was being written, a couple of world events occurred to put extra spin on this theme. The President of Honduras, Manuel Zelaya, was visited at home by members of the Honduran military who brusquely escorted him to an airplane and then dropped him off on the tarmac in neighboring Costa Rica. The immediate widespread reaction, including from the US government, was to condemn the actions in Honduras as dangerously reminiscent of an earlier time in Latin American history that had supposedly passed. Some first impressions are hard to reverse, but in this case it shortly became apparent that all the other civilian institutions of the Honduran government were in favor of the ouster. The military, sworn to obey civilian leadership and law, had found itself between two legitimacies: their President, and the rest of the government that wanted him arrested for unlawful acts. Although a dilemma, the arrest orders from the Honduran Supreme Court were from a unanimous decision, and the whole panoply of government institutions were in agreement, to include almost all the congressional members of President Zelaya's own political party. The Honduran military command agreed afterwards that although the arrest was a legal, constitutionally supportable exercise, it had not been legal for them to take President Zelaya out of the country.

Some say that whatever the ouster's constitutionality, it only highlighted the underlying undemocratic nature of the constitutional order. Such viewpoints tend to coincide with a broader 'post-structural' attitude which observes that institutional scaffolding of legislatures, courts, statutes, and other social accoutrements merely serve an entrenched and oppressing hierarchy of power. Their argument uses logic unlike what most of us have come to understand as the math of electoral democracy. They argue that numerical majorities from an oligarchic legislature or court are inherently insubstantial. According to their new math, President Zelaya genuinely represented the downtrodden; his original election was therefore an 'ontologically' democratic moment that should not be overturned by any subsequent majorities that are the product of an elaborate, structural neoliberal trick.

At any rate, the Honduran elections, which had been previously scheduled and with candidates already chosen, went off without a hitch.

A relatively liberal new president, Porfirio Lobo, took possession in late January of 2010.

One of the interesting details of the Honduras saga was part of an effort that got President Zelaya arrested to begin with. It had been a design of Zelaya's to hold a public opinion poll using ballots and counting mechanisms imported from Venezuela and apparently paid for by a non-Honduran fund. The radical international left employed numerous means to support Zelaya's bid to return to power, and thereby maintain the Honduran State within their Latin American alliance. Fomenting and paying for controlled electoral formalisms while simultaneously creating an image of popular spontaneity and mass support had become a standard element of the international leftist energies.

The latest presidential elections in Honduras may be an apogee in the swing of an ideological pendulum in Latin America, which is possibly now moving back toward political liberalism and away from populism. More significant for the purposes of this book, however, is noting the power of a vision of electoral democracy that doesn't just question details of representation, but simply rejects the entire envelope of mathematical concepts on which most understandings of democracy are built. Democracy's meaning is gutted by this 'post-structural' understanding. In the case of Honduras, it appeared that many governments and international organizations sided with the new understanding, rather than the old.

See: 129, *Nerd Globe*; 14, *Legitimacy*; 52, *Sovereignty*; 98, *Jorge Verstrynge and Pio Moa*; 96, *Public Records*; 125, *Human Rights;* 55, *Staute of Frauds*; and 137, *Declaration of Counterinsurgency.*

---

> ""Democracy" is often used as shorthand for the Western form of government. But the framers of the U.S. Constitution knew that voting is far from a sufficient guarantor of good government. Nor does it forestall dictatorship. From Azerbaijan to Benin, from Serbia to Sudan, tyrants have learned how to get themselves elected. ... In favor of democracy, it is true that power is best divided and checked by a popular chamber. But democracy should be viewed as a means, not as an end, and voting as an official act, not as a universal right.'
>
> Tom Bethel
> *The Noblest Triumph*[38]

When does revolution begin?

# *Section 28, Oviedo*

In early October, 1934, the city of Oviedo, (in the Principality of Asturias, Spain) suffered a violent leftist revolutionary attack. Military and police garrisons loyal to the Spanish republic resisted the uprising, other government troops were sent to relieve the besieged, and in two weeks order was restored. More than seven hundred buildings in a city of about 100,000 inhabitants had been gutted or leveled, almost entirely by the insurgents. The revolutionaries willfully killed a number of unarmed civilians, including clerics, some of whom became the first Roman Catholic martyrs of the 20$^{th}$ century as recognized by the Vatican. Government forces also committed un-justifiable killings. Both sides, however, acted with more discipline and charity than was painted by the propaganda that followed. The Republican government threw almost 30,000 rebel leaders and followers in jail. Oddly, because many remained in jail so long without disposition of their cases, their plight became a highly influential issue in the elections that were called for 1936. Section 98, *Jorge Verstrynge and Pio Moa*, mentions a debate about the start-date of the Spanish Civil War. This section adopts the view that it started that first week of October, 1934 with the armed uprising in Asturias and complementary events in the rest of Spain.

Remembrance of the Spanish Civil War is a matter of academic faith that continues to fuel emotional and political contentiousness. In many Spanish hearts the war did not end; its causes and debts have never been reconciled. Some Spaniards will say that today's youngest generation of voters is no longer knowledgeable or cares about the events of the 1930s, but the shadow of those events is a long one, and it is impossible to escape the war's influence on political philosophy and political organization. The flags of political parties in Spain are designed, in one way or another, in relation to the civil war. Both leftists and rightists tend to record, if not remember, Spain of the 1930s in romanticized, vituperative, and moralizing political tones. In the English-speaking countries, meanwhile, that war is all but unknown and of no emotional stature, except among a few Europe-historians and the ideologically-inclined far left, for whom it remains an icon. The ideological left (Marxists, post-structuralists, some socialists) prefers a selection of facts about the events of the 1930s that forms a sort of liturgy and leftist imaginary. That liturgy, chanted not just by the Spanish left, but worldwide, intones the Spanish Civil War as a robbery of democracy by fascists.

The principle sources for this section were, in Spanish: Juan Carlos Laviana's *La Guerra Civil Española Mes a Mes (The Civil War Month-to-Month)*; Ricardo Cierva's *Historia de España Para Niños* (History of Spain for Children); and Pio Moa's *1934: Comienza la Guerra Civil Española* (1934: The Spanish Civil War Begins). The principle English-language sources were: Stanley Payne's *The Spanish Revolution*; Paul Preston's *Revolution and War in Spain 1931-1939*; and Gabriel Jackson's *The Spanish Republic and the Civil War, 1931-1939*; The Spanish authors listed above are not supportive of the leftist view, and no pro-leftist Spanish-language titles are in the bibliography, although there exist hundreds of them. That said, this section is no apology for any of the Spanish contenders in the war, or of political views that any of them might have held or hold.

Some basic facts: Nobody knows exactly how many Spaniards died in the war, but estimates start in the hundreds of thousands; the contending armies reached perhaps a million armed participants each; Francisco Franco came out the leader of the winning side in 1939 and stayed in power in Spain until his death in 1975.

Why had the Spanish left decided to take violent revolutionary action in October, 1934? The timing related back to a victory by rightist and center-right parties in the general elections held in November of 1933. Further back still, in June, 1931, Spain had held its first constitutional elections. In those first elections, Largo Caballero's PSOE, *Partido Socialista Obrero Español* (Spanish Workers Socialist Party), won the largest number of parliamentary seats (115 of 272). There were over thirty political parties at the time, but while it was necessary to make alliances in order to form a government, the numbers greatly favored a leftist direction away from the monarchy and dictatorship of the past. The Spanish Second Republic was under weigh (the first experiment in republican democracy was a disastrous mess in 1873-1874). The 1931 elections were a huge victory for republicans and socialists, and a defeat for monarchists and religious conservatives. In that environment, Caballero was offered a cabinet post as Minister of Labor and Social Services, an offer he accepted. During the ensuing two years, the Republican government implemented a number of policies that promised to change Spanish life greatly. One aspect unpopular with many Spaniards (perhaps more than half and including the sitting President) was that of turning a blind eye to physical attacks against the Roman Catholic Church. These were perpetrated by leftist radicals and anarchists. No doubt the Church was a bastion of the old system and a direct participant in traditional governance, but the burning of churches, basilicas, and Catholic icons did not set well in a still deeply religious land.

In anticipation of the elections in November of 1933, and in light of considerable social unrest, Caballero resigned his ministerial post. He had probably been an active fomenter of the growing social unrest. During most of 1933, and although he was a cabinet member, Caballero's PSOE organized a series of strikes, including a general strike in Zaragoza that lasted over a month, as well as a widespread agricultural strike. Then, in the November elections of that year, the PSOE only won 58 seats. This time parties tending toward the ideological right achieved a sweeping victory. The political map had completely changed colors. Now, instead of left and center-left, the parliament was right and center-right. Ironically, one of the major democratic reforms of the new republic had been women's suffrage. The numbers suggest they voted heavily for social peace and for the church.

In the formation of governments, it was generally expected that the parties would be represented in accordance with the number of parliamentary seats they had won in the most recent election. In other words, the president would choose cabinet members from the various parties in some ratio appropriate to the level of representation that the parties had demonstrated in the elections. The number of cabinet members (ministerial posts) that a party might fill was a rough measure of the practical political power gained, given that the ministers had broad authority to act within their portfolios. The PRR, *Partido Republicano Radical* (Radical Republican Party), had been the winner of the second greatest number of seats in both the 1931 and 1933 elections. In a sense, the PRR was a more centrist party, although definitely republican and generally anti-clerical. To form the first three governments following the 1933 election, the PRR was offered the greatest number of cabinet seats. The right-leaning CEDA, *Confederación de Derechas Autonomas* (Confederation of the Autonomous Right) was offered no ministerial portfolios in the first two governments formed, even though it had won the highest number of seats (115) in the elections. Later in the year, however, on 4 October, the president formed a government that included three CEDA ministers, in Labor and Social Services, Justice and Agriculture. It looked to the PSOE that what it considered social progress was about to be undone, and therefore the continued utility of the electoral process was questionable. Caballeros and other leftist leaders apparently felt that the value of the electoral process had run its course and that the left would not again be able, or perhaps allowed, to re-take the reins of government. To the PSOE and other parties of the

Spanish left, the historical moment for implementing violent revolution was at hand.

The revolutionary planning, however, was incomplete at best. The Socialists' estimates of relative physical power at any place and time were overly optimistic, their alliances shaky and resources inadequate. Caballero was not a consolidating charismatic figure -- no Hitler or Mussolini -- and had to share power and influence across a range of personalities. Spain had little experience with parliamentary democracy or socialist revolutions; the many political parties were bound to the foibles of their leaders, and to tenuous sources of financial support. Opinions on all sides indicate Caballero was a scrupulously incorruptible, personally disciplined, and nationalistic man. His fortune at the time was the failure of his opponents to wholly understand that his was the *mens rea* behind a lot of violent subversive activity. His misfortune was being a poor military strategist. By mid November, he found himself in jail for treason.

There cannot be any real-world histories more convoluted and multi-faceted than the Spanish Civil War. No single book could possibly do the drama justice. Militarily, however, the actions in Asturias in 1934 are relatively simple to understand. Asturias presented a most favorable human and physical geography for a leftist armed revolution. On Spain's northern coast, its millennial ports of Avilés and Gijón connect the Iberian Peninsula to the ports of northern Europe. Inland, the Cantabrian mountains are home to coal mines and coal miners. For years, communists, socialists and anarchists had organized coal miners, stevedores and factory workers. Oviedo, in the center, is the principality's capital. By 1934 it and the surrounding area were also home to several weapons and munitions factories, and to a few major banks. Had the armed uprising enjoyed better cooperation among the leftist parties, been led by more militarily capable leaders, or witnessed any appreciable success elsewhere in Spain, Asturias might have proven a formidable refuge and springboard for further revolutionary action.

From Madrid, the Socialist leaders sent orders via Oviedo to start the uprising in Asturias. They also sent the basic military plan, which was for the local committees, using the union locals, to take over several key towns in the mining areas, and then march on Oviedo. The thought was to secure the center of political and economic power. Radical leaders initiated military actions in mining areas of the high grounds south of Oviedo. Mieres was the first significant town controlled by the revolutionaries, and from there, as well as from near Trubia to the southwest (where there was a munitions factory) and La Felguera to the southeast, revolutionary columns marched successfully to Oviedo against some government resistance. The Minister of Defense in Madrid, counseled in part by General Francisco Franco, sent a column of regular troops commanded by General Bosch-Balmes north from Leon toward Oviedo, but this approach was ably blocked by revolutionary militias. The main government column, led by General López de Ochoa, approached from Galicia in the west, moving north to Avilés and then south toward Oviedo. Another column was sent from the east, passing the port of Gijón and then moving south to the La Felguera region east of Oviedo. Finally, a column that included a contingent of legionnaires from was sent by sea from African posts, disembarking at El Musel just west of Gijón and then marched south to Oviedo.

Anarcho-syndicalists who controlled much of Asturian port and coastal factory labor were slow to contribute to the uprising and proved irresolute. Had they planned and resisted the movement of government troops into and through the northern ports, the outcome might have been significantly different. For their part, the communists and socialists were slow to provision the anarchist elements with weaponry and munitions. Bitter dissention among these revolutionary groups had been bandaged over by agreements together called the Worker's Alliance, but remaining distrust contributed to failure in Asturias. In total, revolutionary leaders probably motivated around fifty thousand people to participate directly in the uprising. The government suppressed the rebellion with a total of about eighteen thousand soldiers and constabulary. The government troops had to travel far greater distances than the revolutionaries to arrive at the points of contact, but the insurgents were only able to stop one of the government columns, in the mountainous terrain with which the miner militias were most familiar.

The leftist leaders did not respect the northern approaches to Oviedo, did not close the backdoor. In retrospect, they did not think in terms of operational art or classic military strategy. They did not plan in accordance with the central significance of lines of communication. They were in effect hoping to control an area that could resist long enough that larger political truths might allow local gains to stabilize; but hope is not strategy. What they had done was take a centrally-located city, becoming themselves surrounded, and this only after ruining the electrical power and fresh water supply. By the short time it had taken to dominate most of Oviedo, the uprisings in the rest of Spain were already cold dead. There could be no effective international support in such a situation as the Asturian Worker's Alliance had created, and the possible routes of escape for its leadership closed fast. The revolutionaries had quickly captured enough weapons with which they might have armed all of their supporters, but the military moved immediately. The most effective aspect of the government response to the revolution was its diligence.

General López, in charge of the overall operation to repress the uprising, was a decided republican, an atheist, and not a rightist. There is no evidence that he acted other than honorably in his treatment of the defenseless, yet, in an injustice normal to the civil war, he was assassinated in 1936, having gained a reputation as the 'Executioner of Asturias.' Francisco Franco, who later led the rightist Nationalists in the later phase of the Civil War, did not arrive in Oviedo until after the uprising had been suppressed. Almost no *falangists* (far right or fascistic elements) participated in the repression of the uprising.

Simultaneous events in Barcelona were curious in that Barcelona separatists attempted to exploit the rest of the uprising for purposes of independence, and inside that movement rightist nationalists took the lead. In other words, Barcelona experienced a brief alliance of purposes between the far right and left. Josep Dencas, a murky Catalonian radical separatist, tried to foment a national socialist rebellion in the midst of a socialist-communist one, but ended up having to escape through the sewer system, which he apparently knew well, to Mussolini's Italy. One of the few charismatic leaders in the drama was leftist Lluís Companys, head of the Catalan government and leader of the insurrection. He was arrested by a pro-left General who was loyal to the Spanish Republic. The uprising in Barcelona, which easily could have been as violent as that in Asturias, lasted for a day. In Madrid, the violence was widespread, but not intense. The left apparently counted on a spontaneous uprising, but while there were some enthusiastic participants, they were all to be disillusioned by the lack of a plan and by the quickly faltering resolve of the leaders.

Several individuals were executed for treason following the October events, but hardly any of the leaders. In fact, many of the leaders were then able to commune in jail. In a sense, they had made it to the sanctuary they needed -- fed, housed and clothed by the government where they could review failure and better plan the next attempt. Largo Caballeros was let go after a few months. The left propagandized widely on the issue of releasing the rebel prisoners, and successfully accused the government of heavy handedness and cruelty during the suppression of the Asturias revolt. As the February, 1936 elections approached, the right and center right form a loose political alliance, and the PSOE and parties furthest to the left formed the more successful Popular Front. Although the division of votes was close, the newly formed government greatly disfavored the right. The new president, Manuel Azaña, put only leftists in the government. He quickly released all the 30,000 leftist prisoners and restored the positions of those who had led the uprising of 1934. (Although he opposed union cooperation with the republican government, Largo Caballero would become Prime Minister and Minister of Defense in September, 1936.) The PSOE instigated 'victory parades' that often turned into provocative street demonstrations. President Azaña reposted General Franco to virtual exile in Tenerife, a move that would turn out to be one of Azaña's gravest mistakes. Church properties were newly under attack, and the Spanish right, scared and now seeing no possibility of another electoral opportunity, would implement the next armed uprising in July. It would be against the Republic incidentally, while decidedly against the Socialist, Communist and Anarchist left. It would be much better led militarily than the revolutionary attempt of 1934.

The themes illuminated by just the 1934 beginning phase of the Spanish Civil War are countless. They include as a minimum the relationship between urban and rural, the timeless importance of leadership and lines of retreat, money, foreign support, massacres, elections, religion and the prerogatives of clergy, prisons, amnesty, strategic deception, the artificial creation of history, vanguards as clergy, weapons, and the value of sea power. The Spanish Civil War is often seen as a precursor of WWII, rather than as an independent, but related phenomenon. It is more valuable as a font of lessons about insurgent war. The 1934 Asturias Revolution was the beginning of the Spanish Civil War. Although it involved some foreign ideological presence, especially from the Soviet Union, it was relatively free of foreign meddling. Still, Europe was lurching toward Armageddon. Spain's internal struggle was greatly influenced by the ideological battle between fascism and communism.

But why all the fuss about exactly when the war began? It is important because of the assignment of blame, and more importantly today because of competing claims over the word 'democratic.' The ideological left maintains the argument that the Republic was forced to resort to violence only after the repeated violent provocations of the right -- that the fascists tried to rob the people of their democracy -- and then did so. According to the facts, that is, to the places and timing of acts of violence and the names of the perpetrators, the left's assertion of innocence and self-defense is unsupportable. Without siding ideologically with the Spanish monarchy or the power of the Roman

Catholic Church, we can say with little doubt that the *mens rea* causing the Spanish Civil War resided first and most in the minds of socialists, communists and anarchists. They believed power grew out the barrel of guns and that revolution had to be won by force. Their use of republican, parliamentary electoral processes was convenient and insincere. Republic became just another word for Revolution. Spanish leftists use those two words interchangeably, and then assign along with them a kind of divine bolshevist right to rule, a right they call democratic. Thus, writers with a leftist sympathy today will see a Honduran like Mel Zelaya as a minor Largo Caballero who they claim would only use violence in self defense of democracy. The most radical will see a fascist tyranny like that in Syria or Iran, however, and give it an ideological pass. This is because what matters is not about left versus right, or about religion, but about the divine right of vanguards; about upholding a value system of power forged in the crucible of violent struggle and concentrated in the most ruthlessly resolute individuals.

Again, the above comment is not a support of an ideological position, but is offered to strongly suggest that you cannot separate ideology from its influence on the outcome of your insurgent war, and, whatever propagandistic tact you allow yourself, you will do better not to be fooled, including by yourself, by the magical realism. When you decide to apply organized physical force, remember the basic principles of position, movement and strength.

See: 16, *Keeping Secrets*; 144, *Impunity and State Success*; 14, *Legitimacy*; 27, *Democracy*; 118, *Whole of Government*, 52, *Sovereignty*; 19, *NGOs and Unions*; and 132, *Brigands*.

---

"Concentrated power
has always been
the enemy of liberty."

Ronald Reagan[39]

Caterpillars are bugs, too

# *Section 29, Heavy Machines*

Section 139, *UAAV*, is about a transformational new machine. The cell phone is an influential technology; DNA research has changed forensics and the concept of personal identity; and of course there is the suite of machines that make up GIS technologies and the Internet. The landmine was the most important insurgent weapon of the late 20th century, and the radio-detonated explosive device the most troubling so far in the 21st. This section underscores something old-school – not electronics or high-tech items, or even weapons, but big wheels, levers, drills, etc. – heavy machines. We have not neared the limits of creativity in the use of heavy machines in irregular wars, especially in support of the counterinsurgent. Some off-the-shelf machines are already available. It may be due to conservativism or to failed experiments, or to the competing fascination with electronics and miniatures, but here are some machines we may yet see take on more of a role in irregular armed conflicts:

> – 800-ton bulldozers. (The biggest commercial bulldozer is the Komatsu D575 at about 150 tons) There are a lot of huge dump trucks and cranes. Eight hundred tons is not a fanciful size for a machine. Such a bulldozer just wouldn't be designed for crossing European bridges. It would have to be moved modularly and its purpose would be to flatten urban terrain and reform it with favorable observation, fields of fire and control.
>
> – Boom guns. Putting remotely fired machine guns or sniper rifles on 100-foot cherry-picker boom-extension trucks is a natural. New tactics have to be devised to best exploit the advantages.
>
> – Trenching Machines. These are for starting tunnels and digging across them.
>
> – Tunnel Boring Machines. These are also for tunneling and tunnel discovery. Hezbollah has employed these to great effect.
>
> – Barrier Transfer Machines or Zipper Machines. These allow for high speed barrier emplacement in urban environments.
>
> – Scissor-lift trucks. (like those that lift the food and water onto commercial airplanes) These are a throw-

back to medieval siege engines, allowing protected access to upper stories in an urban area.

Cities are man-made geographies, and heavy machines allow the side that has them to more rapidly change physical geography to its advantage. Big machines can give prohibitive advantage in *The Dot Game* (see Section 89, *The Dot Game*). Today most machines can be operated remotely, without a human occupant, like the new aerial vehicles.

Some people think the tank has run its historical course as a weapon system, but don't count on it. Infantrymen are vulnerable and therefore admire and respect things that are faster, better protected or carry bigger guns. Something like the US Stryker may prove itself soon enough, although that vehicle is getting mixed reviews out of Afghanistan. Technical trucks (a Toyota Hilux with a machinegun in the bed) still provide mobility and firepower, and heavy robot tanks are definitely coming soon. Not having tanks and being an insurgent is a coincidence of poverty, but cost-points change. The boom machine suggested in the list above is, in a way, a form of tank, if a tank is a vehicle that combines mobility, firepower and protection. The protection comes from not having to be on the vehicle itself and the firepower from the increased urban visibility that a huge articulated boom affords the gun position.

Because of the resources required to develop and deploy them, we can suppose that the potential advantage of huge machines would go to governments, as opposed to the enemies of government. It may be that fashion and fascination with electronics, miniaturization and flight has caused a major area of potential advantage to be overlooked. Asymmetry does not spell disadvantage to the side with more weight.

The other side of the coin comes from intemperate application of heavy machines. Scenes like a large armored vehicle crashing into the Branch Dividian compound in Waco Texas, or of Israeli armored bulldozers flattening parts of Jenin may cause a reaction that makes their immediate effectiveness counterproductive. In any case, when and where to use a bulldozer, or any heavy machine, is a significant question for urban conflict. A potential advantage held by most counterinsurgents is the ability to design, acquire and employ heavy technologies.

See: 34, *Urban or Rural*; 31, *Holes in the Ground*; 89, *The Dot Game*; 88, *Sieges and Takeovers*; 138, *Roadblocks and Checkpoints*; 91, *Forts and Walls*; 33, *Built Environment*; and 36, *Engineers*.

**Mr. Prosser**: Do you know how much damage this bulldozer would sustain if I just let it roll over you?

**Arthur**: How much?

**Mr. Prosser**: None at all.

From the 2005 movie
*The Hitchhiker's Guide to the Galaxy*[40]

Big Brother likes cameras

# *Section 30, Control Technology*

There are always new technologies available for invading people's privacy, and most of them have other, positive uses, so these things will become cheaper and won't go away. Control technologies, however, are found along a wider gamut than just electronic devices. Walls, overhead walkways, even gondolas can be part of a control design. Electronics and architecture do not exist in different worlds. As expressed in Section 64, *The Statute of Frauds*, legal and organizational innovations combine with new uses of physical technologies to form part of the suite of available control technology.

Personal identification cards (IDs) are not very good unless they can be made much more cheaply than it is to counterfeit them. 'Good' for an ID card means accurate, inexpensive and hard to fake, unless you're the one trying to remain un-identified, then what you want is a bad ID card system.

Accurate, durable, easy-to-read, hard-to-fake cards can now hold or cue up more and more personal information. For the controller, an important upshot of comprehensive ID-carding is not determining who someone is, but rather who is a stranger -- someone who is out of place. 'What are you doing here?' is an easier-made and stronger question if everyone has to carry an ID card and every ID card tells a story. Apparently, unique systems are under development that don't require 'carding,' but instead can make near-perfect identifications on the basis of facial recognition technologies. Wearing masks is likely to become more popular.

If you are planning a revolution or an insurgency, start propagandizing against government individual identification systems (sometimes referred to as *biometrics*), and, when the time comes, try to sabotage the digital archives.

Mass, remote photography can help detect anomalies in human activity, especially when the collected images are combined with automated change detection technology. One of the latest related technological curiosities is GigaPan® and its similars. Used during the Obama presidential inauguration, it makes taking comprehensive photography of big areas inexpensive and easy.

Vehicle GIS registries are another thing. To help control truck traffic and truck-born contraband, you could require that all the trucks carry GPS tracking devices. Tagging select purchase items can also be a powerful aid, especially when combined with camera monitors.

Another interesting technological development is shipping containers with GPS activated locks that only open at pre-set destinations, thus helping to control shipment pilfering.

City governments have historically controlled their populations through bureaucracy, statute, religion, education and by:

- Controlling commodity access;
- Segregating castes, races, classes, and trouble-prone businesses into designated neighborhoods;
- Controlling movement to and through key neighborhoods and centers;
- Controlling services, especially waste removal;
- Maintaining a system of rewards and punishments for public behaviors;
- Establishing a routine of entertainment and socializing times and spaces, such as stadiums;
- Controlling demonstrations, marches and parades via licenses and fixed routes.

These aspects of urban control can help further military and police objectives. Some cities have rebuilt key centers to incorporate control architecture. While perhaps appearing to improve access to an area, this new architecture actually allows a small security element to control or deny access. Many of these city centers are self-contained, with their own water, food, and electrical supplies. All of the control measures can be augmented with electronic monitoring technologies.

Some technologies especially contribute to the efficiency and impact of urban forts. Extensive, closed-circuit television (CCTV) monitoring is a fact of life in most European, Japanese, Canadian, and US cities. CCTV watches high-traffic areas, high-crime areas, isolated loading docks, passenger terminals, store displays, parking lots, and the like. The average urban US citizen might appear on a CCTV screen many times in the course of a normal day of city living. Traffic light and speed zone automatic cameras increase this coverage.

The counterinsurgent will want to install CCTV throughout as much of the urban area as possible, starting with high-incident areas and key facilities, but then surreptitiously along theoretical routes of insurgent escape to sanctuary. CCTV and other sensors, mounted on buildings, vehicles, robots, aerial vehicles, fencing or even tethered blimps provide semi-permanent urban and even outlying rural coverage. The urban fortress provides a safe place to house or monitor the various electronic sensors.

Land-use planning can incorporate sustainable security (meaning that it can be maintained indefinitely because it is acceptably unobtrusive, doesn't eat up too much of the personnel budget, and works) into spatial planning, and control technologies can be a cost-effective part of the design.

Control technologies make it harder and harder for a dumb insurgent to succeed in urban areas. Strangely, although the global population is on the rise and we are finally admitting the imperative to address security challenges of the urban environment, there seems to be more and more accessible and relatively unpopulated rural space, and increasing reason for insurgents to design their survival as a rural formula. Maybe the world is not shrinking and the conflicts not necessarily going urban. There are few histories of purely urban or rural insurgencies. They are more likely both.

See: 92, *Land-use Planning*; 34, *Urban or Rural*; 40, *Rule-of-Law*; 72, *Land Strategy*; 83, *Conflict Geography*; 36, *Engineers*; 91, *Forts and Walls*; and 106, *Tourism.*

---

> "It seems that you've been living two lives. One life, you're Thomas A. Anderson, program writer for a respectable software company. You have a social security number, pay your taxes, and you... help your landlady carry out her garbage. The other life is lived in computers, where you go by the hacker alias "Neo" and are guilty of virtually every computer crime we have a law for. One of these lives has a future, and one of them does not."
>
> Agent Smith in the movie
> *The Matrix* (1999)[41]

One technological answer to the Man is to dig

# *Section 31, Holes in the Ground*

By holes in the ground I mean holes in the ground. Digging, making bunkers and tunnels and improving caves was a feature of State military expenditures long before the appearance of the airplane, but has become more so since. The same activities have also been life-savers for insurgent organizations and anyone without enough money to gain air superiority. The tendency increased with WWI and has been so strong since World War II that any consideration of the military operational environment that does not address the unseen underground geography is incomplete. The under-dirt-and-rock realm is the fourth plane of today's military operations.

Many strategies, such as 'peoples' war' strategies, depend greatly on underground facilities for headquarters, communications, population protection, materiel storage and so on. Underground facilities analysis for irregular conflict, or about places most likely to suffer unconventional armed conflicts, is rare. Nevertheless, history tells us that the subservice world is extremely important in irregular war. In Colombia, the government only recently uncovered 'Mono Jojoy's Caves,' where the FARC maintained a headquarters for years in spite of dogged efforts by the Colombian government to find it. Vietnam was a tunneled war. Much of the arms trafficking into Gaza is through tunnels. The Hezbollah dug tirelessly in southern Lebanon – far more than the Israelis estimated. Add to this the vast below-ground built environment of almost every modern city.

Underground battlespace doesn't just demand special tactics, techniques and procedures. It calls for explicit strategies, intelligence efforts, and equipment acquisition. Today, the price of machinery for digging, hardening and preparing underground facilities for occupation are high enough to give an advantage to governments, but as the sophistication of Mexican drug trafficking tunnels attests, advanced underground works are within the reach of many organizations. The tunnel is a technology of secrecy and anonymity.

It would be a good idea to address the underground explicitly in your strategies, training and equipment. Classic strategy demands attention to the security of your and your enemy's lines of communication to sanctuary. In the century of the UAAV (see Section 132), many of these lines will run under the surface of the earth.

See: 2, *The Line of Retreat*; 29, *Heavy Machines*; 34, *Urban or Rural*; 33, *Built Environment*; 16, *Keeping Secrets;* 67, *Points, Lines, Spaces*; 65, *Smuggling*; and 57, *Dogs and Mules.*

---

"Food for five years, a thousand gallons of gas, air filtration, water filtration, Geiger counter. Bomb shelter…. Underground... goddamn monsters."

Burt Gummer in the movie
*Tremors* (1990)[42]

ઊઊઊ

RIP

# Section 32, Graves Registration

You will want to know all the laws, customs, expectations and sensitivities related to the care and disposition of human remains. Be scrupulous, disciplined and respectful in preparing and registering all human deaths. Caring for only the mortal remains of your own people can become an offense of its own. The first and most important step is to precisely identify cadavers and to safely record that information. Today, there are no unknown dead, only remains that might be temporarily difficult to match to their correct name; every human corpse has a unique genetic identity. With some ugly exceptions, there is normally little reason to be anything but exact as to the identity and burial or storage of remains.

Informal burial has been a constant, poignant and politically abused issue in Colombia. Recently, as the country overcomes organized violence and increases the rule-of-law, it faces the question of thousands of nameless remains buried in hundreds of counties. Eventual identification of these remains is expected to clarify the fate of tens of thousands of individuals who have been reported missing over the past few decades. One locale becoming an emblem of that challenge is in a remote area southeast of Bogotá known as the Macarena. A few NGOs (all with a leftist ideological lean) announced the existence of an unmarked site with almost 2,000 corpses – what would have been the most horrendous mass grave since the war in the Balkans. The attending accusation was that Colombia's national army had negligently or criminally disposed of the bodies in order to hide extrajudicial killings of one sort or another. The Macarena area is all the more significant because it had for years been a stronghold of the FARC until after 2002 when the government began to reoccupy the region. Extensive multi-agency investigations, however, have turned up no such common gravesite, and none of the accusers provided evidence of a specific place, leading to counter-accusations about the propagandistic nature of the accusation.

A large gravesite does exist in Macarena, however. It is a formal cemetery next to a military camp. Some four to six hundred persons were buried there in recent years, but individually and on many separate occasions. According to the government, the cemetery is open to the public and has kept careful records of each interment. Nevertheless, the government also says that the vast majority of those buried were members of the FARC, or other illegal armed groups, killed by the army in combat actions. Exhumations and autopsies may have revealed that a handful of the corpses correlate to what are called 'false positives' in Colombia. That medical reference is to a scandal in which at least one military unit murdered innocent young men in order to claim higher numbers of killed enemy guerrillas. That accusation is also subject to a judicial process still under way when this was written.

A mix of statutes and administrative processes causes the government of Colombia to pay indemnities for murders or wrongful deaths for which it is responsible. This legal responsibility may, depending on the circumstances, even include deaths directly caused by armed enemies of the State -- or at least that is an active legal theory. This potential for financial restitution has spurred the government to greater care in protecting basic rights, but also acts as an incentive to accuse the State and generate evidence against it for the independent purpose of profitable litigation. In the case of the Macarena gravesite, the curator claims to have been offered bribes to say that unregistered burials had occurred. The curator also asserts that his family received death threats for refusing the bribes.

All in all, the human remains of the armed conflict are a persistent evidentiary, jurisprudential, emotional, and therefore political lesion. One of the wisest things that Colombian senior military leaders did in the last few years was to order scrupulous record-keeping of interments of all corpses. Not to say that the orders were everywhere followed, but they at least generated a record of accountability and due diligence regarding dignity in death, rule-of-law as to the location of a person's mortal remains, respect to surviving family and estates, and the preservation of forensic evidence. The Macarena case, instead of becoming the emblem of government human rights abuse, was reduced to its still formidable role as emblem of a complex national challenge to correctly honor the deceased, heal anguish, and strengthen the rule-of-law.

Also related to the Macarena accusations, the government counterattacked, in a sense, releasing news of a whole series of informal grave sites encountered and recorded over the past several years in territory previously dominated by the FARC or one of the other illegal armed groups. Rather than a single huge common grave, some 400 bodies were distributed into about forty grave sites, mostly unmarked. The remains are thought to be of guerrillas who were executed for having committed disciplinary infractions. The disposition of these former guerrillas may take some time, but as that time passes, more and more friends and relatives of deceased guerrillas will be willing to come forward and express their concern or curiosity. Because the government captured FARC computers with files containing the names of thousands of guerrilla foot soldiers, it is at least possible that many of their fates eventually will be revealed. It is doubtful, had the FARC gained political power or even been able to remain sovereign in the Macarena, that it would have done anything to reveal the whereabouts of the remains of these departed.

The process of resolving missing person cases, especially of rural teenagers in the most conflictive counties, is a morbid prologue of the conflict. The war in Colombia is hopefully winding down now, and as it does more and more disappearance and missing person cases will be closed. Since there is no statute of limitations on murder, the process could conceivably generate a continuing flow of homicide cases as well, although not only is the evidence deteriorating; many of the responsible leaders are themselves dead. Plus, extracting a financial recovery from the defendants is much more likely if the defendant is the government and not, say, the FARC.

Prerogative writs. Prerogative writs are orders from superior courts to other courts or government organizations that they do or stop doing something -- and that the burden of proof for showing that a writ is unreasonable belongs with the government, not with the citizen petitioner. The historical appearance of prerogative writs was a significant step in Western liberal governance, although most of the writs have counterparts in other jurisprudential cultures. The writ of *habeas corpus*, which means 'produce the body' or 'show the body' is probably the most commonly known. The idea is now related to imprisonment -- that a custodian of a captive person must show he has detained someone, why and usually where. This is connected to the theory that a person cannot be held '*incommunicado*,' that whatever offense or crime he might have committed, a person has a right to communicate his or her existence to the outside world. The idea of clandestine imprisonment is in turn connected to that of clandestine disappearance, kidnapping, murder and obstruction of justice. According to many thinkers, clandestine confinement is almost the same as burial. Secret confinement is often done as part of some anticipated extortion -- e.g., kidnapping. Clandestine imprisonment, informal burial, and kidnapping draw very close to one another. The prerogative writs are an historical expression of preoccupation about the right to personal identity, to proof of life, and to proof of death. The writs have been advanced in the past forty years by technologies named GIS and DNA.

Today it is harder to escape the forensic unraveling of a crime if bodies are buried or discarded. Not only is it harder to get away with murder in a world of genetic mapping, it is harder to get away with false accusations of human rights abuses, this not only because of new technologies, but because researchers, journalists and even common citizens are equipped and increasingly expected to give plausibly accurate location data with their denunciations. Rule-of-law is about people knowing and believing in certain rights. It is also about things written down -- like the prerogative writs, and maps. Human identity carries into death.

Because human identity, dignity, place, and liberty so overlap, it behooves you, if you are involved in an organized violent contest, to be respectfully scrupulous regarding human identity, even after death. The writ of *habeas corpus* is one of our great jurisprudential inheritances. It was invented with the understanding that human rights have a geographical reference. Where people are is part of *that* they are.

See: 18, *Massacres*; 38, *Cultural Study for What*; 49, *Territorial Scrutiny*; 69, *Measuring Actions against Enemies*; 16, *Keeping Secrets;* 90, *Prisons*; 78, *Personal Identity*; and 142, *Dignity and Honor*.

---

Here Rests in
Honored Glory
An American Soldier
Known But to God

The Tomb of the Unknown Soldier

It can be rebuilt to suit

# *Section 33, Built Environment*

'Built environment' is a term for all the man-made physical terrain we associate mostly with cities, but also other man-made elements outside the cities -- buildings, roads, dams, cell-phone towers, etc. It includes things built with stone, sand, mud, wood, glass or steel. It connotes a broader range of geography than the word infrastructure, in that burned-out factories, abandoned quarries, filled graveyards, or even agricultural terracing are all part of the 'built environment,' but rarely considered 'infrastructure.' The shape of the built environment can advance or impede the competitive aims of parties to almost any conflict, and so competitors with the capacity to change the built environment to their advantage should probably do so. Oddly, beyond the scale of single buildings and some business parks or downtown areas, few counterinsurgency or irregular warfare planners seem to have latched onto the advantages available through the calculated re-design of the built environment.

Urban land-use planning theory in the United States seems preoccupied with aesthetic arguments, like density versus sprawl, and not so much with the challenge of organized violence. Not all foreign cities have been able to afford that indifference. Medellín, Colombia is an example of a city where planners have had to build ease of policing into their concept of land-use sustainability.

Space is a key concept in Geography, and for our purposes we'll focus on spaces of association and communications. A lot is said of the revolution in electronic communication that defies both space and distance. A chat room doesn't need a room and the geographic distances between individuals in the virtual room don't matter. Nevertheless, when armed conflict comes into play, the weapons weigh something, and people have to get together. Bigger spaces are needed as organizations grow, and to remain geographically anonymous, the spaces are either going to be hidden in difficult terrain, like caves and jungles, or hidden in plain view, like hotels and churches.

The synagogue, in fact, may be one of the most important architectural precursors in modern times. Synagogues may have inspired the most important association and communication spaces in more than half the world. It isn't just that the church building is used for something spiritual or religious, but that for centuries it was often the only space available for indoor meetings. For clergy, the church building represents a way to get people together for the purposes of guidance, comfort, harangue, organizing for action, and financing.

Architecture (design at the scale of single buildings or complexes), while important, is dependent on urban land-use planning, which is more concerned than architecture with the relative location of urban elements – with distances.

Distance is a geographer's obsession, and it is with distance that engineering of the built environment can have the greatest impact. In cities, the calculus of distances in time between your or your enemies' likely sanctuaries and likely targets is based on the structure of the built environment. You can rearrange that structure to your advantage. If you have no plan for doing so, you are leaving that initiative to your enemy by default.

See: 92, *Land-use Planning*; 91, *Forts and Walls*; 29, *Heavy Machines*; 36, *Engineers*; 2, *The Line of Retreat*; 34, *Urban or Rural*; 106, *Tourism*; and 135, *Bank Robbery*.

---

"If it ain`t baroque, don't fix it."

Les Grau, attributed

City is where insurgency goes to die

# *Section 34, Urban or Rural*

We all know what a city is, but what does the difference between city and country mean for winning and losing an armed conflict? Many writers will refer to an armed group, like the Colombian FARC, as a *rural* insurgent group, but what does that observation mean and what we do with it?

Urban means a lot of buildings and people. Exactly where rural ends and urban begins geographically and historically is a question we will skip for the most part. Some of the answer is statistical protocol. The United States government, for example, uses several categories for a variety of purposes, including a thing called the Standard Metropolitan Statistical Area (SMSA) which is somewhat arbitrary, but more or less means a place with a core of more than 50,000 persons and a surrounding population of more than 100,000. Definitions also often include a legal concept such as incorporation of some kind. Urbanites generally share services such as a power source, entertainment, potable water, and a sewer. Some would say that a restaurant is the beginning of urban.

In rural environments people supply their own basic services. The more rural, the fewer shared services, until there are so few shared services, an area is no longer considered even rural, but primitive or wild, so maybe 'rural' correlates to independence. Bottled propane is a sign of ruralness in some countries. Propane can be sent through a pipe network or delivered in a truck. If your place is so rural you have no delivery system but have to get it yourself, then you might be rural. If you are using wood and coal you mined yourself, you're really rural, although you just might be so urbanite you can play at being rural. At any rate, more rural means less dependence and fewer networks. It does not necessarily mean less wealth. There are many areas in rural America where farmers own half million dollar tractors they use only for pulling against other tractors. It is rural to dedicate expensive machines to pulling against each other in pulling contests, so economic measures may not be the best distinguisher of rural versus urban.

Maybe eighty-five percent of Colombians live in cities of over fifty thousand people, most of which have centralized sewer systems. Debates about rural versus urban are often won with behavioral and linguistic arguments rather than according to infrastructure statistics, however. Where rural and urban begin and end in Colombia are academic curiosities and matters of self-identity. If a person rides a *chiva* (a colorful bus-like truck conversion with a wooden cabin, no doors and a pithy saying on the bumpers) as an economic necessity, he or she probably calls the *chiva* a *misto* and is almost certainly a rural Colombian, scientifically speaking. The geographic extents within which *chivas* roll as *mistos* has shrunken a lot because suburban areas have reached out, roads have improved (allowing lighter-framed buses), and fewer people live in some of the more remote areas. If you live in Colombia and regularly ride what the city folk call a *chiva*, but which you call a *misto*, you have also ridden a lot of mule, and you are a rural person, a *campesino*.

A map of Colombian National parks gives a 75% solution to the location of guerrilla sanctuaries inside Colombia. The parks are remote. If we were to identify those points in Colombia farthest from the cities and from the main roads in terms of cost-distances, those points would mostly fall within areas Colombians considered suitable for designation as national parks, and that is where the FARC established its refuges. The FARC is or was a rural movement, which makes sense because its early leaders were born in rural areas, but also because it has had to depend on lines of communication that lead out of the country. Remote locations are also distant from the controls that government can efficiently put on anonymity. Together, staying rural and remote meant learning how to walk (a lot). Rural people can walk. Because of the need to maintain long lines of communication in rural areas, FARC leaders had to depend on rural people, and consequently assumed many of the perspectives, knowledge, habits, and values of rural life. The FARC has had urban cells and urbanite leaders to be sure, but general description of the FARC as a rural insurgency is apt. For many years, the overall strategy of the insurgency was to surround and then take the cities. In the forty plus years since the beginnings of the FARC, however, Colombia has seen a huge increase in urban life while the percentage of the population that can still be called rural has greatly shrunken. The cities to be surrounded grew larger and larger while the rural population on which the insurgency depended grew smaller and smaller. The FARC did not implement or change its strategy fast enough to keep up with the pace of Colombian demographic change. Paradoxically, much of the impetus for urbanization in Colombia came from the violence that the FARC embraced in rural areas.

Cities seem to be where insurgencies go to die. This is probably because the insurgent organization cannot control anonymity there. There is so much anonymity available as a consequence of urban life that too many people can safely inform on the outlaw. This depends, however, on how the insurgent uses city terrain, and on timing. On moving into the city, the insurgent may encounter criminal organizations already in control of key neighborhoods and key smuggling routes. The criminals are urban, with urban skills at controlling anonymity, keeping secrets, and imposing violent will. The rural insurgent is used to walking, while the criminal gangsters roll. They are more used to the speeds, technologies, timing and pitfalls of urban life. This presents a challenge for the rural guerrilla wanting to 'take' a city. He confronts a paradox of city life: the city offers the possibility of great anonymity, but simultaneously presents an organization with greater difficulty in controlling that anonymity. Gangsters and guerrillas alike depend on codes of silence, but enforcing that code in a city with which you are not familiar is a trick.

Some urban geographies are more amenable than others to the insurgent. One is the university campus, especially in Latin America, where a great deal of tolerance and amnesty is available for youthful and scholarly reflection and expression. On the campus, a radical can get away with having some public personality profile and remain at large. The poor, mostly peripheral, and densely crowded neighborhoods are also more likely to host insurgents and crime bosses. People refer to relatively poor urban wards in US cities as slums, which suffer some unique challenges associated with phenomena like high crime rates and illicit drug use. The mix of social characteristics that cause people to refer to neighborhoods as slums in the United States, however, is not quite the same as in the marginal, informal sprawls in the developing world. The zones that we might casually refer to as slums in Latin America (known variously as *favelas*, *turgurios*, *barrios populares*) are heavily populated, covered with ramshackle housing, and perhaps suffer a lack or shortage of waste removal systems, potable water or electric power. They are often exposed to costly environmental events like mudslides or flooding. They may be home to populations with nowhere better to go. Although these areas are almost always worse off in terms of basic services and conveniences than the slums of the more developed cities in the United States, that disadvantage does not equate to a community of incapacitated people, broken families, criminal culture, academic underachievement or even lack of hope (although some of these ailments are patently present). The human capital in the slums of many cities is often capable, mobile and successfully aspiring.

The most obvious distinguishing characteristics of a Latin American underprivileged urban area may indeed be the most easily changed. The civil engineering, or physical arrangement, architecture, street pattern and urban plan can greatly assist government or anti-government elements. It behooves the side with the capacity to reform the built environment to do so in its favor.

The kinds of things that can be done to gain advantage from the physical environment include the creation of controlled passage-ways and elevated bridges, and construction and relocation of walls. These things are sometimes called control architecture. The advantage normally pertaining to the government stems from greater capacity to change the physical structure. Administrative devices, such as the imposition of street naming conventions and the formalization of addresses, also break down anonymity. Re-organizing streets and traffic to speed the safe flow of persons, especially children and home makers to and from schools, as well as unimpeded, un-extorted access to basic services also seem to give government an advantage over insurgents and criminals.

For understanding geographic advantages and disadvantages in irregular war, it appears there really is an important difference between rural and urban. Rural ethics, habits and necessities don't always mix well with their urban counterparts. However, concentrating too much on the distinction between rural and urban might itself throw us off. The in-between, suburban or transitional areas may be the hardest to understand and the greatest challenge. It is too easy to speak of urban conflict as distinct from warfare 'in the field.' The most difficult and important areas are the transition zones around cities.

See: 49, *Territorial Scrutiny*; 33, *Built Environment*; 37, *School Lunches*; 91, *Forts and Walls*; *89, The Dot Game*; 107, *Price of Real Estate*; 92, *Land-use Planning*; and 72, *Land Strategy*.

---

"The lowest and vilest alleys in London
do not present a more dreadful record of sin
than does the smiling and beautiful countryside."

Sherlock Holmes in
*The Adventure of the Copper Beaches*[43]

---

The Hunter's redemption

# *Section 35, Comuna 13*

On the 30th of May, 2002, Medellín's mayor, Luis Pérez Gutiérrez, assembled his municipal cabinet and a group of newspersons, mounted a tour bus and headed over to the western hillside borough known as *Comuna 13*, or San Javier. People of the borough had been complaining. A major police sweep into the borough a week earlier had left bitterness and bad publicity. Public order was flagging, and so the mayor decided to visit the borough, take a sounding, and show his interest. As they arrived, a lead car was shot up and immobilized by gunfire, blocking the way. The adrenalined bus driver managed to back up to safety from the bullet storm. The residents' complaints had been understated. For the mayor it was a frightening experience, but it was also degrading and embarrassing to realize, finally, that an entire sector of his city was completely outside the constituted government's civil authority. *Comuna 13*, an area of over seven square kilometers and a hundred thirty thousand people, had fallen outside the *de facto* territorial limits of government control. Outlaws, rebels and gangsters had gained a zone of complete impunity from government authority. For several years they had been fighting mostly among themselves for dominance. The population of the zone, many with few economic options, had become terrorized by that fight, and were all but enslaved by the various violent groups.

The month before the mayor's bus ride, the country's president, Andrés Pastrana, ordered the Colombian Army to retake what was known as the *Despeje*, a demilitarized zone in south-central Colombia that Pastrana had conceded to the FARC for the purpose of conducting a national peace process. Pastrana had been elected on a campaign of seeking a negotiated settlement with the insurgents, and he had fulfilled his promise through a series of demarches and concessions. After what seemed to the public and government to be a long, violent series of insincerities on the part of the FARC, President Pastrana reversed course, and ordered the *Despeje* to be retaken by the Colombian State.

The end of the peace process led to a changed security dynamic in Medellín. During the years of efforts to maintain cease fires with the rebel groups, the Pastrana administration had been loath to authorize substantial offensive operations. During the peace process period, the FARC planted units outside Medellín and attempted to create a presence within the city, or at least within a few of its peripheral zones, *Comuna 13* in particular. The FARC took active measures during the peace process to improve its geographic positioning. It exploited the depressed pace of government military initiative. Now the peace process had collapsed, and to a degree the green light went on for more aggressive counterinsurgent operations within Medellín. Attention and resources from Bogotá, however, were to be aimed at retaking the *Despeje*, to addressing the presence of FARC units nearer to the capital, and toward the upcoming presidential elections. Also, the scale of urban insurgency in Medellín may not have been correctly measured in Bogotá, or even seen as an integral part of larger insurgent strategies. At any rate, Mayor Pérez would not find a responsive ear in Bogotá until after the inauguration of a new president.

On May 21st, that is, a week before Mayor Pérez' rejected visit, about seven hundred police officers and soldiers implemented Operation Mariscal, descending more or less simultaneously (in this case more like *ascending* since the borough is almost all hillside) mostly on residential addresses in the borough. The objective was to issue outstanding warrants to members of the various armed groups and to interdict what government intelligence warned might be an organized attempt to disrupt the presidential elections that were scheduled for May 26th. Mariscal, which met with organized resistance, indicated to the public forces how thoroughly infested the borough had become. It also exposed some weakness in government operational practices. Three children had been killed and 31 other civilians wounded.

Liberal party presidential candidate Álvaro Uribe Vélez won the May 26 elections by a large margin. He had campaigned on a platform of toughness against the various insurgent enemies of the State, especially the FARC. Colombian voters not only rejected the failed Pastrana 'peace process,' they were attracted to the idea of beating the FARC definitively. Uribe's inauguration in early August marked not only a sharp turn in national military strategy, but a change of fortunes for *Comuna 13*.

Medellín was returning to hyper-violence. During some days as many as twenty five murders occurred. The city suffered over two thousand murders in the first half of 2002. The violence actually never deteriorated to the levels suffered during the early 1990s before Pablo Escobar was taken out, but the people of Medellin had every reason to fear it might.

On October 14, during a spike in inter-gang violence in *Comuna 13*, a stray bullet entered an apartment in an adjacent sector of city, killing the beautiful only daughter of one of the mayor's friends, a prominent doctor. At the wake, the mayor was not only moved by the total deflation of his friend, but by the parallel depression of another man whose college-age son had suffered the same fate. The war had reached the heart of an otherwise oblivious elite. Calculating that the city itself did not have the resources to deal with the problem at the appropriate scale, Mayor Pérez called the new president on the phone, asking for help with *Comuna 13*. President Uribe picked up the phone and ordered the head of the chief of the armed forces to take back the borough.

On October 16, 2002, a joint force of Colombian army, national police, municipal police and other government agencies, a force more than twice as large as in Mariscal, surrounded and entered the borough to serve arrest warrants. This 'Operation Orion,' the shooting part of which lasted only twenty-four hours, resulted in about four hundred detentions. Not all the warrants were served, the government forces suffered several casualties, and more civilians were killed. It was the single biggest urban operation ever attempted in the country, however. It did not bring economic equality to the borough or eliminate desperation in the lives of many of its residents. It was a successful counterinsurgent event nonetheless.

On Tuesday, October 21, Mayor Pérez again loaded up his cabinet and a bunch of media people and headed for *Comuna 13*. This time he went to the middle of the borough, led a public prayer, raised the national flag, and took a long march up and down the borough's labyrinth of stairway streets. Colombian flags had been distributed generally and were flying and hanging everywhere. There was cheering, no shooting, and no mistaking that a change had occurred.

Orion was the last of a series of operations, but it was different than its predecessors. Previous operations had failed to create a permanent government presence. Government units had gone in, often with uncertain destinations, to serve warrants on the basis of fairly good information about suspects, but not about the overall operational options of the enemies they faced. They had approached the problem as police, without visualizing the flow of movement in and out of the borough, nor had they planned any assault on the relationship between the enemy and the population. They had not assembled sufficient resources to remain with sufficient power to address that relationship -- especially to change the nature of the competition for information. Although the authorities had always hoped to enter and stay, they had never assigned enough personnel even to protect the policemen themselves.

Finally, after Operation Mariscal revealed itself as another wrung on a ladder leading nowhere, an army intelligence sergeant with an integral view of the problem (perhaps from the experiences of a humble background) spoke up at a brainstorming meeting and laid out all that had to be accomplished. The authorities had to seal off the zone, go in big, clear the entire area, stay there, and then create conditions in which the residents were confident that they could talk to the police so that it would be easy to sort out the criminals. That meant involving everyone in and with the government, including engineers, social workers, teachers, local NGOs -- everyone -- and that meant not offending the population with high-handedness or mistakes. The military and police commanders, and the city's civilian leadership listened.

Lessons from *Comuna 13* include, in no particular order, the following:

**Achieve resolve at the top**. If the bosses aren't on board, failure is likely. In the *Comuna 13* case, the president and the mayor were resolute and committed. Sadly, the resolve came only after a long period of obliviousness, wishful thinking and half measures.

**Effect military-police coordination**. Operation Orion was unusually favored in this regard. The senior police officer was General José

Leonardo Gallego, and the senior army commander was General Mario Montoya Uribe, commander of the army's 4th Brigade, headquartered in the city. The two were friends, familiar with each other and the area since boyhood. This relationship did not hurt. The two knew the practical capabilities and cultural expectations of their forces as well as the personality of their partner, so appropriately dividing up roles and missions was not a difficult challenge.

**Surround the area**. The terrain in and around *Comuna 13* is steep and broken, with a mixture of built environment (much of it of precarious) and undeveloped rural terrain. Surrounding the neighborhood could not be done with police assets alone, and, in fact, was never completely accomplished by the army. Sealing off the borough had several positive effects. One was to keep out reinforcements from nearby rural-based insurgent units. Another was to frighten insurgent leaders within the borough to try to escape. (perhaps the fact that holes remained in the cordon actually lessened the violence) Another was to secure dominant terrain so that the outlaw groups would not take the best firing and observation positions. Finally, the cordon also helped prevent innocent civilians from accidently straying into harm's way.

**Take dominant terrain and own it**. The mayor had given an order well before Operation Orion for the police to buy key properties on which to build new local police stations. Getting hold of those properties took a little more legal and financial effort than originally anticipated, but the decision to dominate key ground permanently proved smart in the long run. Covering militarily significant terrain with a police fort makes future control of the area by an insurgent force much more difficult.

**Start building**. The city determined that staying in the borough meant making a constant effort to improve everything to the extent resources allowed. A huge highway tunnel project, a gondola extension off the city metro line, and a major urban housing project all evidenced government presence and commitment.

**Control anonymity**. One of the most important controls on anonymity was the simple presence of more policemen. Less visible, but effective to the mid-term success of the operation, was a local one-stop center where residents conducted mundane business with the city (connection of services, payment of fees and bills, enrollment of children in school).

The building was organized in such a way that residents felt confident of their anonymity should they choose to denounce criminals in the neighborhood. A small architectural and administrative innovation helped the city attack the 'law of silence,' or 'mafia rule.' Such rules of silence are built partly on a foundation of loyalty and mostly on one of fear -- but such fear does not constitute an intractable cultural human condition. A simple opportunity for discreet conversation can defeat it.

Control of the balance of anonymities became a focus of the government's operational design, ideas to address anonymity then came easily, and the whole outlaw 'culture of silence' was put at risk as the flow of information from the public to the government authorities increased. Because the carrying of cell phones had become common in Medellín, an anonymous call-in number to the police was maintained. Vehicle registries were also groomed as anonymity-control measures. Anonymity became an increasingly more difficult necessity for a stranger to gain or maintain inside *Comuna 13*, and easier for peaceful citizens to exercise.

**Control the location and movement of children**. As noted in Section 37, *School Lunches*, a number of programs were developed to address the quality of life for children in the borough. Schools were the natural geographic focus of these efforts. Since 2002, horror stories about accidental shootings, drug-related kidnappings, and other tragedies in *Comuna 13* have occasionally been published, but most stories coming out of the borough are hopeful.

**Encourage community**. Medellín's public administrators built a modern library and funded parades, art programs, and other events to garner participation, encourage joint effort, and engender community pride. These things were not relegated to the status of details. The government, in conjunction with local and international NGOs strived to increase the provision of basic services to the area. City administrative leaders saw equitable, orderly distribution of services (as opposed to violent pirating) as intimately connected with civic culture and education.

**Address cost-distances**. City planners poured over maps to determine service access, school locations, military outpost locations, transportation locations, and adjusted these to the extent possible. Medellín's municipal management corporation, *Empresas Públicas de Medellín*, is highly GIS competent.

**Support rule-of-law systems.** The city's security office coordinated with other city managers to perfect street names and the formal addressing of residences and businesses. This facilitated the formal service of criminal process by prosecutors. Before the streets and addresses were formalized, it had been difficult to serve warrants and to follow other rule-of-law practices.

**Add local support to demobilization, disarmament and re-insertion/reintegration.** The city government also collaborated with national and international organizations to conduct DDR programs of ex-guerrillas and paramilitaries. While these have had mixed results, most observers praise them over the alternatives. (See Section 103, *Amnesty*)

**Be careful making alliances.** An accusation exists that the precipitous drop in crime after 2002 was not due to the government's new presence, but because the government aided select outlaw groups. The history of collaboration between the government and illegal rightist armed groups in Medellín is yet to be fully exposed or understood. Some coordination and alliance occurred in Antioquia as elsewhere in Colombia, especially between the government and elements of the United Colombian Self Defense Forces, AUC. As the AUC evolved into an uglier and uglier component of the country's outlaw violence, however, those associations became an embarrassment and a political yolk. Some of the calm reigning in *Comuna 13* since 2002 may owe to the dominance of a single surviving criminal gang. The larger truth, supported by a great deal of evidence, is that the borough returned to the fold of municipal, civil governance. It is no longer being organized politically or militarily by insurgents.

**Don't take victory for granted**. As great as the Operation Orion victory was, underlying weaknesses in the social contract, especially in the control of corruption and the power of illicit drug organizations keep *Comuna 13* vulnerable to social deterioration. In late 2009 and 2010 Medellin and *Comuna 13* experienced a renewal of high violence levels, even if not compared to earlier periods. This violence was apparently the result of turf battles between small, ascendant new criminal gangs battling over the same drug trade corridors.

**Go in big and stay**. 'Take, hold, build' has no better example than Operation Orion. After all, operational art in irregular warfare isn't just about the lines of communication and not getting caught during a retreat; it is also about not retreating. Start with unified, resolute leadership. It took a couple of epiphany moments for Medellín's mayor to commit, but when he did, he not only went to his president to assure support, he listened to a sergeant explain what governance meant.

**Understand the connection of rural and urban**. *Comuna 13* lies along the main east-west route in and out of the city, and not going through the borough entails a costly detour for people, materiel, and merchandise moving between the Panamanian isthmus region and the middle of Colombia. Outside *Comuna 13*, a number of insurgent and criminal groups maintained rural connections for supply and escape.

**Buy informants**. The city created a hefty fund to pay for informants inside the borough. This direct assault on anonymity paid dividends quickly.

**Expect legal attack**. First General Gallego and later General Montoya would suffer legal demands and accusations stemming from their conduct of operations in Medellín. A cursory check of Internet sites reveals a cyber realm populated mostly by left-apologetic criticism of these officers, their institutions, and the results of their efforts, especially Orion. The Colombian government branches are differentiated and independent enough that accusations of government abuse can be effectively forwarded regardless of the political or ideological stripe of the chief executive. That's the good news. The bad news is the degree to which radical anti-State individuals gained positions within the government, the low prices at which some government personnel were purchased, and the ease with which outside perceptions were manipulated. Had these two officers acted during the regime of a different president, they might have been far more vulnerable to legal attack, independent of the nature, ethic or effectiveness of their decisions. Paradoxically, an important factor in making these two leaders vulnerable was the spectacular degree of their counterinsurgent success, especially in Medellín.

**Remember terrain**. Although *Comuna 13* is an urban area, it is very vertical. High ground in and around the borough is key terrain. This matters in even the lowest-intensity of armed encounters, especially due to the new prominence of snipers.

**Train for explosive booby traps.** One of the first serious government casualties in the borough was produced by a cadaver-bomb.

**Find money.** The actions, activities, and programs required money. Medellín was lucky enough to have had some. Peace requires a social investment. Medellín has been trying to make that investment, and, sincere arguments to the contrary notwithstanding, recent history tells that in the midst of a larger, complicated national armed struggle, Medellín tackled what seemed to be an intractable problem and succeeded. The self-concept of the people of Antioquia, *Paisas* as they are known, is one of can-do problem solving, and in that spirit, the *Paisas* opened their checkbook. They are not much for existential angst. Post-structuralism is not catching-on in Medellín.

The physical and human geography of *Comuna 13* is unique, and the lessons are not all easy to generalize. This recounting of a successful counterinsurgent vignette doesn't delve into the identities of the anti-State actors or the causes of the conflict. For that background and additional sources there are three books of note, all in Spanish. They are: Ricardo Aricapa's *Comuna 13*; Yoni Rendon's *Comuna 13 de Medellín*; and Pablo Angarita's *Dinámicas de guerra y construcción de paz*. Of particular interest in the history of the conflict is an episode of organized land squatting.

See: 78, *Personal Identity*; 49, *Territorial Scrutiny*; 74, *Refugees and Displaced Persons*; 51, *Underclass*; 109, *Hotspotting*; 58, *Guerre d'Algérie*; 106, *Tourism*; and 95, *Childhood.*

---

**Riff**: We gotta stand up to them Doc; it's important.

**Doc**: Fighting over a little piece of street is so important?

**Gang**: To us it is!

**Doc**: To hoodlums it is.

**Gang**: Who're you callin' a hoodlum?

From the movie
*West Side Story* (1961)[44]

Building things trumps blowing things up

# *Section 36, Engineers*

Today's would-be or self-styled counterinsurgents haven't seized the initiative in civil engineering. To gain counterinsurgent initiative would mean identifying what the engineer should be asked to build that would make the insurgent have to react. These things include walls and forts, bridges of course, and also urban plans that shape the built environment to create advantage in anonymity, and make the *Dot Game* easier for a government to win.

If you ask Engineers to build something, like a bridge, they will, regardless of how wide the gap or difficult the terrain. They will, in fact, design and build anything, but they are generally not so good at deciding why. We also know that if engineers are not given something to design or build they can still figure out how to blow stuff up -- which goes to a significant mistake in counterinsurgency thinking and preparation over the last half century. The most creative and influential participation of engineers in irregular warfare has been the 'blow stuff up' part.

Insurgencies, or at least the leftist revolutionary insurgencies of the recent past, are about tearing at the fabric of the establishment or of the system. Even insurgent philosophers use terms like 'deconstruction,' hence a convenient marriage between the violent political activist and the indolent engineer. The counterinsurgent, meanwhile, has not found enough ways and occasions to tell engineers what to build where. Civil engineering's contribution to recent counterinsurgency has been late in coming and reactive. It has been how to make a vehicle that is harder to blow up, or how to make a device that will make it more difficult for an insurgent to detonate his bomb.

In 1994 author Mike Davis wrote *Urban Control: The Ecology of Fear* on the control architecture of Los Angeles (really how engineers were being put to the service of the establishment to make protest and resistance difficult). What Professor Davis saw was actually the rarest of exceptions. Davis' fears were drawn from the modest assumption that more than a handful of persons were as astute as he, and had figured out the urban Dot Game. In fact, few government planners have taken full advantage of civil engineering as a means to control civil resistance, with the Israeli government being a possible exception.

So much of the world is urban now, you almost have to build or rebuild something if you are going to contribute to the structure of life. The question should almost never be whether to build, just what to build with the money and expertise available, and where. Bridges are usually a great choice. Sports complexes seem to be what the Chinese like to build, maybe partly because schools and hospitals, though they sound good, are like churches in that they are not just structures, but include the people and institutions in them. They require educated professionals and professional materiel. It's easy to build a school building, but if the educational effort is not sustainable, the psychological effect of an empty school building can be a worse than no school at all. Pure water systems are a contribution in most places, but they always seem more expensive than expected because of environmental impact and competition for source waters. Sewers are good, especially when the engineers find an adequate place for the waste material to go.

Roads are also good, but not necessarily so much as people will claim. Every road benefits someone more than someone else. The road-building constituency rarely talks about the differentials. Road building can be a great idea, but it is not a great idea *ipso facto*. As some folk say, 'The insurgency begins where the road ends.' Most roads have two ends, and if you don't have a good idea in advance about whom specifically a road will favor and who it will disfavor, you might want to re-think. Not every road improves your strategic map algebra.

If one party to your conflict keeps building things that are useful and help people live better, and the other side keeps blowing things up, eventually people are going to interpret that formula to the benefit of the builders. 'Engineering' means building thoughtfully. The counterinsurgent can win by way of engineering, but not if the constructive advantage in civil engineers is not engaged, or is only reacting to engineers who are blowing things up. An assertion here is that an engineer's mind works a bit differently than, say, a poet's or a lawyer's. Engineers live near breweries. This is a scientific fact – which can be proven (or perhaps disproven) using the precise, amassed temporal and spatial correlation data available using GIS. Engineers like GIS almost as much as they like beer, at least if GIS can get them closer to the brewery.

See: 89, *The Dot Game*; 94, *Poop*; 138, *Roadblocks and Checkpoints*; 92, *Land-use Planning*; 111, *Knowledge Cultures*; 91, *Forts and Walls*; 29, *Heavy Machines*; and 33, *Built Environment.*

---

> A doctor, a priest, a lawyer and an engineer are waiting to tee up, but they have to wait an inordinate amount of time. The club pro explains that the foursome ahead of them are firefighters who lost their sight saving children

in a local school fire, and that the club lets then play any day they want. The golfers answer the pro:

**Pastor**: Forgive my impatience, I'll pray for them.

**Lawyer**: Well, the club should give us a discount.

**Doctor**: Maybe they can be cured; I'll talk to my ophthalmologist friend.

**Engineer**: Why can't these guys play at night?

Not all social programs are bad

# *Section 37, School Lunches*

Several sections of this book are dedicated to the simple idea of cutting the enemy off at the pass, that to win armed struggles you better pay close attention to physical routes of escape to sanctuary, yours and his. It is about the bottom line of biological survival, about beating your enemy in physical time and space. That is indeed the book's attitude, so admiring mention of a social program like government provision of school lunches might seem out of character. Not at all. Routes are composed of people, not just space and distance. The time scale of strategy includes time to recruit, to convince, to be the legitimate font of power and governance, or not. This book does not suggest that the essence of strategy is all geometric, all physical or all anything. It doesn't even define the essence, except to tie it to an equation about the timing and placement of power by strategizing enemies. To win at irregular war requires having a grasp of victory in time. Is victory or defeat to be determined after a week, a decade, a century? Winning at irregular war can mean just eliminating the enemy, or it can mean that plus achieving a social condition less likely to spawn new enemies. Besides, a meal can keep a child in a building, and off the street, during that one critical hour.

A school lunch is probably a good thing in its own right. A hungry student is not a good listener, and is a poor learner. Beyond compassion and beyond the logic that human brains are society's most important natural resource, and that the bodies housing and fueling those brains need to be nourished, there is the goal of this book – to win. If a child is inside a school building to get fed, he or she is not being a messenger or a look-out or a carrier of contraband, or a thirteen-year-old assassin. The child is not participating to change the weight of a factor in the operational equation.

The geography of armed conflict does not get much simpler than this. Programs are good that keep children in safe places where it is difficult for some gangster to recruit them. If children are progressing in peaceful pastimes, that's good. The ancillary benefits for the responsible insurgent or counterinsurgent leader, or for law enforcement, is the better development of human resources coming out of childhood.

This book chooses school lunches because government programs to provide meals have been shown, in places like Medellín, Colombia, to be effective in drawing underage participation away from armed conflict. There are probably other useful programs as well. Western militaries are fond of completing certain kinds of projects in foreign countries that take advantage of what seems to be excess engineering capacity. They like to build schools and medical clinics. The 'build something' notion promises an amorphous if ephemeral change likely to benefit the builder. The basic idea is that doing something useful will be appreciated. It probably will, but a school is not just a building, and a *good* school is much more than a place of learning. It is a place where kids are taught by competent teachers who are not teaching hate. The building, faculty, administration and families all factor in to what defines a good school, and how the educational environment will resist the recruitment of underage children into armed conflict.

Seek programs that keep children in safe places advantageous to them and to you. A building alone is never a school. Create places that protect, inspire, equip and enlighten. Keep track of the enemy's side of the school question. Plenty of places dishearten, instill hatred, teach methods of destruction, and preach slavery. Those places are schools, too, and may even have school lunch programs. It would be a shame if you were helping to pay for such a negative education.

See: 33, *Built Environment*; 95, *Childhood*; 77, *Sex*; 14, *Legitimacy*; 90, *Prisons*; 17, *Kidnapping*; 16, *Keeping Secrets*; and 30, *Control Technology*.

---

> "The miser, starving his brother's body, starves also his own soul, and at death shall creep out of his great estate of injustice, poor and naked and miserable."
>
> Theodore Parker[45]

# *Section 38, Cultural Study for What?*

Interest in foreign cultures is now fashionable in military educational circles. The new interest, however, begs a question: What is the purpose, from a military, competitive point of view, of understanding foreign cultures? The answer can be divided into five parts as follows:

1. To find people and things. Cultural knowledge helps locate individuals, their wealth, and their supporters. ('Locate' means establish their precise whereabouts -- where they will sleep tonight, where their mother is buried, the number of their bank account, where their motorcycle is sitting, their email address, where and when they play golf... and where they feel safe.). For the competitor in a violent struggle, this is the first and most important reason for cultural knowledge. It is what Sam Spade, the private investigator, knows. The rest is important too, but if he knows where you are, but you don't know where he is, you are prey.

2. To communicate good. Cultural knowledge can improve communications with others so as to endear and not offend, to facilitate collaboration and compromise, and to settle disputes peacefully when preferable. This involves language beyond the verbal, and into customs, prejudices, habits, mores, expectations, fears, historical grievances, community pride and the like. All knowledge is grist to the mill. Especially important is to identify any aspects of the culture related to honor and dishonor.

3. To identify objects of desire, sources and holders of power, grievances, agents, resolution mechanisms, debts, tax relationships, jurisdictions and expectations. In short, to comprehend the territorial geography of conflict and conflict resolution -- the ingredients of *Hohfeldian Grievance Analysis* (see section 53).

4. To set reasonable objectives. Knowing how or if to change the social contract, how long such change might reasonably take to implement, and how long they might last.

This may include determining the interrelationship between peoples' behaviors and their surrounding environment in order to derive sustainable improvements in human flourishing and harmony. When good intentions are not built on sufficient knowledge, the reward may be a set of nasty unintended consequences. In a domestic legal setting we demand due diligence of doctors and lawyers -- that they avoid negligent practice. Strategic due diligence presupposes the applied, programmed and resourced study of foreign culture in order to avoid strategic negligence.

5. To get the joke. Jokes work the same mental pathways as military deceptions. For practical purposes. military deceptions *are* jokes. Irregular armed conflicts are generally clothed in law, economics, propaganda and other aspects of quotidian, civilian life. Not being able to get civilian jokes means being vulnerable to the dangerous, military or criminal ones. Just as the insurgent can move from military uniform to civilian attire, so can military thought hide in civilian guise.

It is hard to know what relevant cultural knowledge looks like or how to get it. In any case, the best time to gather and produce relevant cultural knowledge of a place is well before participating in organized armed violence there. It is never too late.

See: 49, *Territorial Scrutiny*; 53, *Hohfeldian Grievance Analysis*; 73, *Property and the Social Contract*; 120, *Turducken*; 43, *Sam Spade*; 80, *Why You Should Like Geography*; 78, *Personal Identity*; and 54, *Mercatus*.

---

A Moscow radio host puts out a question on his call-in show:
"Какая часть речи диван?"
(What part of speech is 'couch'?)

After receiving various incorrect answers, e.g., "A noun?", "A verb?", the show host gives the correct answer:
"Это местоимение."
(It's a pronoun.)

Of course, so what?

# *Section 39, Socioeconomic Causation*

Improving overall socioeconomic conditions in a country suffering some kind of organized armed internal strife probably won't help the counterinsurgent win, and might just as likely do the opposite. Economic development measures often aren't targeted so as to influence the specific sets of individuals positioned to help the government in counterinsurgency. Furthermore, there are examples of violent inconformity, such as Spain's ETA, about which the economic causation model seems wholly irrelevant.

The idea that insurgency can be traced to human suffering has been lavishly serviced by studies sponsored by the US government and others. For example, the 1966 *Human Factors Considerations of Undergrounds in Insurgencies*, one of a series of works from the Special Operations Office at American University that, during the Vietnam War, held considerable sway on US government counterinsurgency thinking. In 1966, word was that "There are few comprehensive studies on the relationship between economic factors and insurgencies."[46] The work mentions that one contemporary comparison of Gross National Product (GNP) and domestic political violence showed low levels of violence in countries with very high levels of GNP and with a very low level of GNP. The middle range countries seemed most susceptible. In Latin America, the work noted, some of the highest economic achievers relative to the region – Colombia, Venezuela, and Cuba – had suffered insurgencies while others had not. (Since 1966, Argentina, Colombia, Uruguay, Chile, Nicaragua, El Salvador, Peru, and Guatemala have all been stricken with insurgencies, as well as other countries to a lesser extent.)

A more recent and influential example of the kind of effort sought by the 1966 study is a sequence of three reports on "state failure" by the State Failure Political Instability Task Force (PITF), the latest of which is titled *Internal Wars and Failures of Governance, 1955-Most Recent Year*.[47] The PITF authors define "state failure" as revolutionary wars, ethnic wars, adverse regime changes, and genocides or 'politicides.'[48] A 1995 version of the report found that three factors predicted seventy percent of all insurgency problems: failure of international trade, high infant mortality and undemocratic elections.[49] Near the center of their analyses lay the same unshakeable assumptions regarding the significance of underlying socioeconomic conditions as a cause of state failure and insurgency.

The big danger of the assumption of socioeconomic causation to your winning is this: constant mention of socioeconomic performance leads inexorably, even if unintentionally (but it is probably intentional), to prescriptions aimed at improving general socioeconomic conditions. Unfortunately, *nobody* has a clue about *how much* overall economic performance improvement might move a given society away from spawning, harboring or empowering insurgents or terrorists. Worse, little has been done to trace the effects of an economic assistance program on insurgent or criminal finances. Likewise, a little improvement in, say, electoral democracy might not be a stabilizing move, all else remaining equal. According to one of the later PITF reports, the "odds of state failure was seven times as high for partial democracies as for full democracies and autocracies."[50] Sidestepping the issue of the validity or usefulness of the reports or the definitions on which they were based, it seems on the surface that moving a place from really poor to poor (or from poor to a little less poor and from undemocratic to somewhat more democratic) might increase instability.

Colombia is a mixed or middle-performing country economically. Things inside Colombia aren't the same everywhere. There are 1,100 counties for which there is pretty good socioeconomic data and pretty good violence data. Some of the 1,100 counties are poor, some rich, some violent and some not. The country isn`t geographically homogenous as to violence or economic prosperity. According to a 2002 study by Mauricio Archila, et al titled *25 años de luchas sociales en Colombia 1975-2000* (25 years of social struggles in Colombia 1975-2000), there was little correlation between poor counties and violence in those counties, but there was some correlation between violence and counties that were doing better economically.[51] Counties with the most protests and the most violence didn't coincide with where there was the most poverty. According to the authors, Colombians didn't exactly appear to fight because they were poor. They fought because they perceived that they were *comparatively* poor; or, more probably, because they were led to perceive their comparative poverty and then organized to fight.

Some years ago I was shown a georeferenced map of Colombian counties where the government had mounted economic assistance programs, and other georeferenced maps where the worst armed violence had occurred. Nothing jumped out of the maps regarding a possible correlation between the programs and the violence, and the briefer claimed that none existed. Enough longitudinal (over time) data was available that such a correlation analysis could be made. It is often against bureaucratic interest to make any such careful analyses because what is suspected might be proven true -- that there is little correlation geographically between changes in violence and the economic assistance programs. More troublesome is that it is probably now possible to overlay maps of the timing and location of assistance programs to parasitic and extortion efforts of insurgents. There may have been a correlation between economic assistance programs and successful efforts by the Colombian insurgents to siphon off much of the wealth distributed or created by those programs.

We can assert there might have been little spatial correlation between economic assistance programs and amelioration of violence because so little effort was put into auditing the effects of the assistance programs. (Apparently, by the way, things have improved in recent years.) Having accused those aid programs of little correlation with achievement of counterinsurgent goals (and this is only correlation, not causation), however, there surely have been some significant exceptions, with the best of these exceptions situated geographically along insurgent lines of communication.

If you are able to provide economic aid, be careful to analyze the effects by starting with a geographic detailing of where comparative wealth will be generated and what the psychological effects of changed wealth comparisons is going to be. Oftentimes, roads don't make people richer; they make *some* people richer. More important is to have some way of measuring if the wealth your programs create ends up in the hands of your enemies, keeping in mind that the amount of financial wherewithal a typical insurgent needs to create an explosive device may be one tenth what the government will need in order to deal with it.

A poor insurgent might wish to find ways to quietly encourage all kinds of foreign economic assistance programs, especially going to locales where you enjoy impunity. Those programs will rarely be formulated so as to reduce your impunity, and you will be able to find easy ways to take much, if not most, of the money generated by the programs. Protect the program administrators and implementers from harm (unless they start talking against you).

Geographic specificity of economic programs is extremely important because dominance of the operational equation demands relevant placement and timing. Every attempt should be made to anticipate the likely effect of an economic program on insurgent sanctuaries and routes to and from those sanctuaries -- and this holds true if you are the insurgent or the counterinsurgent. If program proponents cannot address this relationship, a program may be counterproductive in the extreme.

Insurgents justify violence by pointing out economic suffering. Governments, however, are usually only able to make slow changes in economic performance. Because of this slow pace, the socioeconomic argument is never taken away from the agile insurgent. Socioeconomic improvements may be good ideas in their own right, but an observation regarding socioeconomic injustice should not be misinterpreted as the first part of a logical syllogism that offers socioeconomic improvements as a strategy for winning. In the long run, they might be. In the short term, they are probably not.

Miserable economic conditions are a motivating factor for foot soldier recruitment, especially among young males, but this is as true for a government army as it is for an insurgency. Economic assistance can also motivate individuals to inform, but the most effective of such programs pay informants directly -- perhaps not something you would want an organization like the United States Agency for International Development to be doing.

If you are the counterinsurgent, you will prefer that government economic programs not fund your armed enemy. You want to have a way to measure the extent to which money spent ends up going to your enemy. Even if you do have such measures, you will want to know not just how much socio-economic progress has been achieved, or even how much this may have bought you in terms of the public attitude. You need a measure of the change in the balance of overall advantages between you and your foe within the relevant frame of time. That is a tall order.

See: 71 *Measuring Effects of Actions on Structure*; 66, *GIS;* 54, *Mercatus*; 80, *Why You Should Like Geography*; 144, *Impunity and State Success*; 74, *Refugees and Displaced Persons*; 122, *Songs of Chu*; and 86, *Shifting Covet-Geography*.

---

> "We must reject the idea that every time a law is broken, society is guilty rather than the lawbreaker. It is time to restore the American precept that each individual is accountable for his actions."
>
> Ronald Reagan[52]

The rule-of-law is written

# *Section 40, Rule-of-Law*

We hear a lot about the rule-of-law these days, and a lot of programs are sold as providing or supporting it. I can suggest no single title to read, but advise you start with Wikipedia and go from there. On the other hand, *property* (ownership systems; how a society divides, distributes, and recognizes rights and duties; how these rights and duties are recorded and observed; and how conflicts over important disagreements are resolved)) is, as a practical concept, inseparably tied to the rule-of-law. There are a number of good property titles, some noted in section 73, *Property and the Social Contract*. In the end, for winning, the key to grading a rule-of-law program will be whether or not it helps you gain advantage in anonymity and a monopoly over the granting of impunity.

There are two principal currents of thinking about the rule-of-law. One current argues that rule-of-law is about the process and coverage of law, but doesn't speak to the normative goodness of the laws themselves. In other words, we would credit a place as following the rule-of-law if the people had stable expectations about the consequence of behavior, and if everyone were treated even-Steven, regardless of whether or not the laws were harsh and stupid. According to this current, a tyrant could run a rule-of-law country wherein no other entity besides his State could grant impunity, even if the tyrant were consistently cruel. The other branch of opinion sees rule-of-law as a normative condition of justice. By this way of thinking we would praise a society as upholding the rule-of-law only if the laws and their application are reasonable, equitable and meet some minimum standards of gentleness. The two currents are similar to those attending *legitimacy*. One approach to legitimacy depends on acceptance and stability, but not a normative standard of behavior, while the other current asserts minimum behavioral standards. As with legitimacy, the currents that define rule-of-law are almost always mixed.

A notion commonly associated with rule-of-law is that nobody be above the law. You have to ask, however, *whose* law is it above which nobody can be. The relationship between corruption, rule-of-law, and impunity – one of sordid intimacy – comes into play here. When government officials sell impunity, it is corruption. If a government then grants its own members impunity, we can say not only that the government is above the law, but that it has dragged others above the law with it. The geography of sanctuary for such corruptionists is the geography of the government itself.

Many of us would prefer to believe that real rule-of-law cannot exist under a tyrant or a corruptionist, no matter how accepting, obedient and pacific a people becomes. We would prefer to reserve the term *rule-of-law* for something better. In the cruel world, governance is easy without the rule-of-law; you can win at irregular war by assuring that only *your* State, good or bad, can grant impunity. If in your State the Man happens to be one man, then it is his law, his property, and he is the lord and ruler. A dictator can win an armed social struggle, an internal war, and an insurgency. It happens all the time, and some would say that dictators often implement the rule-of-law. There are proponents of strong-arm caudillos in Latin America who will support a government that, while itself 'above the law,' rules in such a way that other entities can't grant impunity to their own underlings for crimes against the public. Many Latin Americans are so starved of a peaceful social contract that stable expectations, procedures and institutions for quotidian conflict resolution are worth the price of losing the power to change away from the tyrant. They become willing to democratically vote themselves into slavery. That is the price of a flaccid standard for the rule-of-law.

Creating the rule-of-law entails two challenges. One is building stable expectations, procedures and contraptions for conflict resolution -- all of which can slow government down. For instance, under the best rule-of-law, civil courts expect to see contract documents, and police officers have to go get warrants before they make arrests. The other challenge is cultural education and acceptance. Rule-of-law is elusive where people are ignorant of their rights according to the written law, or if they have so little faith in the execution and defense of the written law that the writings are empty and merely hypothetical. Some countries are chock full of legalities and statutes that purportedly protect everyone and everything, but the level of impunity is such that most of the paper is meaningless. So there are two important parts to creating the rule-of-law: paper and education, but they are both forfeit to impunity.

It is not uncommon in embattled areas to find individuals who are motivated only by the threat of violence or by money. They readily believe threats of force made against them because they are aware that the perpetrators are ruthless, practiced, and likely to go unpunished for the violence they commit. A victim population won't help the gentler opponents of the perpetrators, whatever the attraction of their gentleness, because victims fear the immediate cost of violating the rules of silence imposed by the ruthless. Rules of silence substitute the rule-of-law. Money, meanwhile, often represents the value of a victim's risk, a value measured by how much it will cost to escape the ruthless tormentors. Violence is relatively cheap conduct, as is accessorial behavior that fears defying the perpetrators of violence. In such a situation, many people find the immediate cost of siding with a gentle opponent (who would establish a system of formalized justice) too high.

The rule-of-law will not exist if the side determined to impose a gentle peace does not control the balance of anonymity and close down the routes of the ruthless to their sanctuaries. Little progress can be made against a ruthless, organized enemy who can hide, or can hide corruption. Fortunately, many of the same processes that break down anonymity also serve as a foundation toward sustainable peace in which the cost of peaceful conflict resolution is less than that of violence. The rule-of-law is a combination of written evidence, institutions, and expectations regarding how evidence will be used by those institutions. To win peace and sustain it -- to create the rule-of-law -- means *written* inventories, statutes and procedures. There is no rule-of-law without all the penmanship.

Rule-of-law does not mean more policemen. The two main parts of rule-of-law are documents and public attitude about the documents. If those two parts aren't constructed, it doesn't matter how many more policemen you put on the street, unless you are satisfied with a tyrannical rule-of-law, and individual liberties are of little importance. In this latter case more policemen might be a good idea as long as they don't form a union or identify a leader prettier than you or your tyrant (which tends to happen).

If you are going to win an internal armed struggle, your side has to dominate the granting of impunity. That is not the same as saying that people can't get away with crimes. Your side, your government, can grant impunity, but it has to be the only organization in the territory that can do so, otherwise violent conflict is still likely. If you want to keep organizations that challenge your monopoly (on the granting of impunity) from forming, then you are going to have to spend resources on the design of the society. A very repressive society can succeed at eliminating competition in the granting of impunity. Liberal societies find it harder for the obvious reasons that people exercise rights of association, privacy, and owning weapons. If you want to design a liberal society that also can dominate the granting of impunity, then you have to work harder. You have to create a lot of documents, and a lot of people that read them and believe in them. It takes readers, and that takes education, and that takes time. You need transparent markets, too, especially for the most important stuff, like land.

If someone is trying to sell you a program purporting to advance the rule-of-law in some territory, think through what the program does to the granting of impunity within the territory. One possible indicator toward that end is the relationship of the program to the balance of anonymities. If you cannot predict the effect of the program on anonymity or impunity, maybe the program is a misnomer and you can seek clarification. If you are trying to shut down an enemy armed organization, you don't want a rule-of-law program that does no more than provide your enemies a new avenue of legal escape. If, on the other hand, a program seems reasonably designed to create stable records and conflict resolution institutions, and to educate people as to the economic and moral value of peaceful conflict resolution, it might very well be a good program.

See: 48, *Grading the Social Contract*; *73, Property and the Social Contract*; 128, *Global Insurgency and Global Trespass*; 143, *Is It an Insurgency?*; 1, *What the Pirate Said to Alexander*; 14, *Legitimacy*; 81, *What a Clergy Wants*; and 106, *Tourism*.

---

> "There is no person in this room whose basic rights are not involved in any successful defiance to the carrying out of court orders."
>
> Dwight D. Eisenhower[53]

---

If you can't find your enemy, he is sneaking up on you

# *Section 41, Whereabouts*

'Place' is a central theme of this book. The idea includes 'sense of place,' and distance, especially as understood by costs in time, money and cultural affinity. Putting 'where' back into the 'who, what, when, where, why, and how' question set is an important contribution of Geography. To do so (to put the *where* back), helps resist concentrating too much on why governments fail or why there are insurgents, or why there is crime. Not that these aren't good questions, but being an insurgent or a criminal is about keeping your whereabouts and the whereabouts of your sources of power hidden from your enemies. It is especially about protecting the routes of escape that you and your people may have to take between the places of their offensive actions and their sanctuaries. For the counterinsurgent, if you know exactly where your insurgent enemy is, but can do nothing about it, that's called a political problem. If you can't locate your enemy or the sources of his wealth, that's called an intelligence failure. If you know where he is exactly and can confound his retreat to sanctuary, that's called the cusp of victory.

It is hard to hide in a land where there are excellent public records, people are clearly identified and it is difficult to move without having to prove one's identity and purpose. It is hard to maintain wealth in a land where wealth is tied by files to individuals, families, businesses, and specific places.

Most people, bad people included, have a mother or a mother-figure they favor. The relationship they have or had with their mother is an important factor in their makeup (or so Sigmund tells us). Finding where a person's mother is or is buried can be a significant start to fixing the whereabouts of a person in time, and for better understanding that person, if that's worth something. If you're serious about finding a hard-to-find enemy, go find his mother, and if you are really serious about finding enemies plural, establish systems that make finding everyone's mothers easy. Fowling this up is also a good way to create all the enemies you'll ever need. Don't disrespect peoples' moms in the process of figuring out where they are. There aren't that many cross-cultural constants on which we can depend, but this is one of them. Most mom's love their babies. Maybe there is some culture that doesn't love its mothers. I am not aware of any.

See if your system of knowledge regarding your enemy or potential enemy, or his supporters or yours, includes knowledge about where everyone's mothers are, and especially when and where mothers are likely to get a visit or a message from an adult son. Don't forget your own mothers; protect and love your mommas.

Big Brother is not built on weaponry; it is built on scrupulous civil administration and cultural knowledge. To the extent whereabouts cannot be hidden, insurgency is difficult. The prospective insurgent must learn to live 'off grid,' but, if he were to stay entirely off-grid and completely anonymous, how would he accrete and maintain fungible wealth sufficient to present a threat? How would he gain broad popularity? It is tough to be public and private at the same time, to move from a latent stage of insurgency to a mobile stage without exposure. For many, it is tough just to keep from communicating with their mothers.

See: 66, *GIS;* 2, *The Line of Retreat*; 67, *Points, Lines, Spaces*; 3, *The Domesday Book*; 96, *Public Records*; 2, *Anonymity*; 1, *What the Pirate Said to Alexander*; and 110, *Knowledge Gaps*.

---

"It's not fer me, it's fer me ma."

Mickey from the movie
*Snatch* (2000)[54]

---

Retreat without strategy

# *Section 42, White Bird*

I distilled this section from four sources: Jerome Greene's *Nez Perce Summer 1877*, Elliot West's *The Last Indian War*, Helen Addison Howard's *Saga of Chief Joseph*, and Bruce Hampton's *Children of Grace*. Although an American vignette and long ago, it is illustrative.

Near Slate Creek, on the Salmon River in Idaho Territory, on 14 June, 1877, three young Nez Percé warriors went on a killing spree in revenge for unpunished crimes, including murder and rape, by white settlers against Nez Percé families and the tribe. Chief Joseph had recently decided to capitulate to the federal government's demand that his band of the Nez Percé move to the Nez Percé reservation where the bulk of the tribe had already resettled. Joseph had his people busy marshalling at Tolo Lake for the trek to the reservation. In line with the Nez Percés' form of shared governance, Chief Joseph did not enjoy unchallenged authority. Other, more militant and recalcitrant chiefs spurred the three warriors to change facts on the ground. Chief Joseph's efforts to keep his band out of an unwinnable war were now futile, and Joseph was obliged to lead about 100 warriors and 500 women, children and elderly toward sanctuary across the Canadian border. On October 5, after an 1,100 mile retreat and more than a dozen battles, Chief Joseph surrendered at Bear's Paw, Montana Territory, about forty miles from the Canadian border.

Joseph incorrectly measured the strength of a treaty agreement he thought he had with the Crow, who ultimately sided with the US Army. He also did not gauge the resolve of Brigadier General Oliver Howard, Commander of the Military Department of the Columbia, to pursue him; and he did not correctly measure the impact of modern communications, which enabled the US Army to timely deploy columns to intercept his route from distant garrisons. Joseph hoped, in vain, that the Lakota Sioux would come to his aid, but they would not endanger themselves for the sake of the Nez Percés. During the long retreat, combat decisions of the Nez Percé warrior chiefs were brilliant, and the actions of the warriors exemplary in competence, valor and discipline. Chief Joseph's operational and international strategies, however, were based almost entirely on hope. He was moving away from the sanctuary of the greater tribe, not toward it. He was moving instead toward a sanctuary that did not exist.

Responding as best he could to what many regard today (as then) as a righteous indignation of his people, Chief Joseph acted on the presiding emotion and not the imposing geography. This is not to say Chief Joseph was foolish. He figured, probably correctly, that the invisible line between the United States and Canada would protect his people as it did the Lakota Sioux. Given Joseph's acceptance of federal demands (before the June killings) that he remove his people to the reservation, he apparently understood how poor the band's chances of escape were. Still, Joseph did what was expected of him to uphold the three avengers and their warlike Chief, White Bird. Under the justice of the United States, they surely would be found guilty of murder. Joseph had to know that the coming retreat and the battles which now underwrite his military renown were, if not hopeless, more likely to be paid in honorable memory than in land.

Of perhaps 800 of the non-treaty Nez Percés (some had joined the march after the events along the Salmon River), probably 350 died. Almost all of the warriors and their chiefs had committed themselves to what they determined to be an honorable fate in the service of those they were stewarding. By the time they arrived at Bear's Paw there was less need to protect the young hotheads who precipitated the war. Two had died fighting. Their fate, at least, would not be as convicts, but as warriors. A third escaped to refuge in Canada, and later returned to the Nez Percé reservation where he lived in anonymity in order to avoid prosecution.

It seems no amount of valor could survive this ill conceived retreat, but that's not entirely true. Chief White Bird was one of the war chiefs. He had been one of the older men who roused the younger warriors to fatal action back at the Salmon by challenging their manhood and courage. Unlike Chief Joseph, White Bird intended to fight from the outset; his was the *mens rea* mind. He is also probably due more credit than Joseph (along with other war chiefs including Joseph's younger brother Ollokot) for the band's military successes during the retreat.

White Bird and more than two hundred others, a quarter of the band, escaped during the battle at Bear's Paw or shortly after the surrender. Most of those made it to sanctuary in Canada among the Sioux, and some, including Ollokot, eventually returned to the treaty reservation in Idaho. White Bird didn't like the Sioux all that much, but was murdered in 1882 by a Nez Percé tribesman. White Bird had counseled honor killings and was a victim of one. He was never prosecuted or captured. He is not remembered or revered as is Chief Joseph.

The band led by Chief Joseph Hin-mut-too-yah-lat-kekht (Thunder-rolling-in-the-mountains) played a poor hand expertly, but it was not enough. Chief Joseph had reluctantly gone to war, and lost. Masterful tactics could not redeem a forfeit strategy. Most of his band was captured and made to live in the Oklahoma Indian Territory. Chief Joseph was never allowed to return to the Nez Percé homeland to live, and was not buried near his father.

What can we learn from the Nez Percé war?

*The Nez Percé did not have foreign support

*Joseph did not measure his enemy's strength well

*Young men sparked the violence

*Most of the war was movement

*Tactical supremacy could not overcome operational error

*Scale counts. Eight hundred was not a big number

*Being trapped en route to sanctuary means decisive defeat

*You cannot retreat to a sanctuary that does not exist

Other relevant lessons are available from a more thorough read of the history. For instance, all the four sources note that agents of the United States told the Nez Percés a series of lies, as was almost habitual in dealing with Indian nations. They were treated as foreign nations; strategy and stratagem were considered intimately related. The Indian nations were not quickly or fully welcomed into the social contract. A land privatization program was part of the approach to dealing with the majority of the Nez Percés who accepted the treaties. The events were broadly publicized; commanders acted in the light of nation- and worldwide journalistic attention. The treatment of the non-treaty Nez Percés after Bear's Paw was almost as controversial a history as events of the retreat itself. Military decision-making was influenced by the dramatic loss to the Lakota Sioux at the Little Big Horn only one year earlier. Surprisingly, it is difficult to argue that there was a lack of cross cultural knowledge or understanding. The two sides seemed to understand each other extremely well. The Nez Percés were expert militarily before the famous retreat, and enjoyed a reputation as dominantly competent warriors; but they did not get that way fighting against the United States government.

See: 41, *Whereabouts*; 79, *Suicide*, 78, *Personal Identity*; 38, *Cultural Study for What?*; 142, *Dignity and Honor*; 96, *Public Records*; 73, *Property and the Social Contract*; and 2, *Anonymity*.

---

> "The Battle of Adowa, fought on March 1, 1896, between Menelek's huge army of semi-barbarian warriors and Baratieri's Italian regulars and native levies under European officers, was an epoch-making event. It was the first great victory won by a non-European race over the white man which had lasting and decisive results."
>
> A. Hiliard Atteridge,
> *Famous Modern Battles* (1913)[55]

Why private detectives find their mark

# *Section 43, Sam Spade*

Probably every plaintiff's law firm in the United States has on staff or contracts a private investigator, a PI, a Sam Spade. That's because in America, if you want to stick it to someone else using the legal system, you or your lawyer have to find your target and give him or her a piece of paper. That is what Sam Spade is paid to do: find your opponent and give him an unfriendly piece of paper that puts him on notice or calls him to court. 'You've been served.' It is called *service of process*, fair processes being considered an indispensable element of justice. Your lawyer also wants the PI to find your nemesis' things – a car, boat, house, bank account – because lawyers want to be paid. Sam Spade does too, and to keep putting food on the plate he has to find his mark, and he almost always succeeds in spite of not having satellites or phone taps, and maybe not even a very good camera. There are two main reasons why Sam Spade succeeds. The first is because he knows local culture. He knows what's going on in his town or county. He has few local knowledge gaps, and he doesn't have to ask 'cultural study for what?' For him, every bit of knowledge about the local culture helps him with the whereabouts. He knows which bumper sticker goes with what congregation, what kinds of vehicles will show up in the parade, who organizes the service club charities, etc. He follows all the sports teams and every public event. He knows the favorite cigarette brands. He understands sex and sexuality.

The other big reason Sam always finds his prey is that he is familiar and competent with public records. He can get hold of school registration lists, team rosters, cadastral records, and can decode the license plates. He can read a map. Sam might not contemplate the role of public records as evidence of the social contract, or worry that for a liberal society to thrive, the public records must be transparent and stable. For him, public records are simply part of what makes it possible to find people and their property so that he can successfully serve process. If the public records are shoddy and inaccurate, if they are hidden from inspection, are not comprehensive or are subject to manipulation and fraud, it is harder for Sam to succeed – and the social contract is at risk.

If you want to measure the progress of an ongoing counterinsurgency campaign, and you are apprised of the fact that the public records remain in poor condition as to their accuracy, completeness, or transparency, you can be sure that the counterinsurgency program is not sustainable and not really going that well. No social contract will be sustainable without solid evidence. It is like a contract with no writing. Would you buy a house or a car and not get a written document of the transaction? A society without solid, accurate, comprehensive public records is a society that will be in conflict. Sam Spade will fail, and with him the likelihood of peaceful conflict resolution. As a counterinsurgent, you might not be able to teach the would-be sleuths enough culture, or give them tracker's instincts, but you can work to improve and perfect the system of public records. Big Brother keeps book.

There are Sam Spades around the world, and there are other categories of people, like real estate agents, prostitutes, bar tenders, truck drivers and taxi drivers, who have inside knowledge of local culture, and know where people are likely to be when. They are the best computers for finding people, and they are most effective when transparent, comprehensive and accurate public records are available to them.

See: 107, *Price of Real Estate*; 49, *Territorial Scrutiny*; 78, *Personal Identity*; 3, *The Domesday Book*; 110, *Knowledge Gaps*; 90, *Prisons*; 2, *Anonymity*; and 41, *Whereabouts*.

---

> **Kasper Gutman**: You're a close-mouthed man?
>
> **Sam Spade**: Nah, I like to talk.
> **Kasper Gutman**: Better and better. I distrust a close-mouthed man. He generally picks the wrong time to talk and says the wrong things. Talking's something you can't do judiciously, unless you keep in practice.
>
> From the movie
> *The Maltese Falcon* (1941)[56]

Can you find those files or not?

# *Section 44, Political / Military / Administrative*

It takes administrative effort and excellence to create a peaceful, liberal society. Aside from that, it takes administrative effort and excellence to win militarily, at least in some armed struggles.

Too often, conversations about how much military effort is appropriate begin with 'military' somehow counterpoised against 'political.' This is especially curious coming from the pens of Clausewitzophiles, one of whose mantras is that 'war is politics by other means.' Most of the time we have a pretty good idea how to translate the terms, though: shooting people is an activity thrown into the 'military' column and building a society in which people are not disaffected or indifferent is thrown into the 'political' column. The distinction makes some sense, and echoes the two goals of neutralizing the enemy and not making more of them. A website called *The Mudville Gazette* has a little piece called '20%military80%political' that outlines arguments attending the war in Iraq. The question really being asked, however, is whether military organizations should do all the things that are not archetypically military.

If a military goes someplace and destroys or clears away enemies, that military will still have to remain in place facing the question of what to do so that it can leave and not have its efforts wasted. Large spaces have to be occupied, even if the enemy is only located in a few small places. As a result, militaries are forever confronted with challenges that they may not deem spiritually martial.

A lot of the sections of this book are about the traditional martial vocation -- how to close with and destroy the enemy -- which is a notion dependent on the definition of enemy. A soldier might like to say that either there are battles, or potential battles, or, if not, then let's go home. Experience tells us, however, that there is a lot else that the soldier (or the insurgent) can or has to do besides combat. The situation boils down to this: You are there, someplace, and you can't just stand around whittling, not able to get that decisive battle to occur. What do you do?

The answer about what to do is spread throughout a number of the sections of this book. Mostly they are engineering, knowledge creating, or administrative. The proven innovations in long-term conflict resolution aren't headline-worthy, like combat or elections. They are folded into the boring details of civil administration. The long-term stability of a society seems to require many different pieces, but a lot of those pieces depend on things like statutes of fraud. The statutes of fraud require written evidence of duties and rights in order to ease administration of justice and services. Uninspiring, perhaps, but therein lies another question....Can peace be solidified administratively? The answer is: Apart from whether peace can be solidified, it cannot be solidified *without* administrative excellence. It might not be enough, but it is essential.

The good news is that not only can conflict resolution mechanisms be designed and implemented, but the exact same civil systems that operate to release people from the perceived advantages of everyday violence can also provide a system of intelligence that helps expose the lines of communication and retreat of intelligent enemies.

Don't hesitate in creating the inventory, your *Domesday Book*, on which administration excellence depends. Build what almost every sheriff uses to find a perpetrator, fugitive, or witness. The human environment can be shaped administratively to cough up detailed information about the connections between individual habits and precise locations. This means that the military may have to attempt what would ideally fall to civilians – to create a comprehensive, precise and transparent census, impose a system of individual identification cards for everyone, and map exactly who owns what and with whom, who is resident where, what the tenancy and debt relations are, the marriages and business associations, tax duties and destinations, the descriptions of cars, bicycles or mules, who has licenses to practice medicine and law and to sell real estate, cut hair, ordain, or circumcise. It means street signs, phonebooks, and license plates. With the availability of GIS technologies, the locations and linkages can be exposed almost instantaneously, once the data is input. Will there be gaps in the data; will people try to hide their assets and identities? Of course, but so what? That's all detective fodder. When soldiers start talking "take, hold, build," they're right, but probably the first thing to build is the inventory.

If this smacks of Big Brother, it should. Both the rule-of-law and population control are created on the basis of records, not batons. If a person wants to create impunity for his actions, he is generally obliged to maintain anonymity for himself and his wealth. Once the authorities know the particulars of his motorcycle, phone, or apartment, it is harder to act outside the law without consequence. It is difficult even to stand distant from home without that fact being apparent.

As long as no system of institutional knowledge regarding individual identity and wealth is created, other cultural and physical geographic knowledge is rendered less valuable for the capture of enemy leaders. If the lines of communication, especially the lines of retreat and sanctuary of enemy leadership, are not identified, military success against that enemy is not likely. In order to see the finely-scaled placement geographies of insurgents, as opposed to the LOC of an army tank corps, maps must be drawn on the basis of individual identities linked to wealth. That wealth exists everywhere in the form of preferential rights to the use of places and things. Such recognized preferential rights are what we have come to call property, and records of such rights either exist or can be created. Once a system of laws and administrative and technical capacity are married in such a way as to enable the mapping of property rights, then control of a population is, if not easy, practicable. So maybe Hans Morgenthau was right about power, that it is simply influence over behavior. Influence over the behavior of a population lies in the condition and use of mundane administrative records.

See: 45, *Police or Military*; 3, *The Domesday Book*; 66, GIS; 72, *Land Strategy*; 4, *Defining Enemy;* 73, *Property and the Social Contract*; 40, *Rule-of-law*; and 144, *Impunity and State Success.*

---

"Throughout past history liberty has always walked between the twin terrors of tyranny and anarchy."
Theodore Roosevelt[57]

ଓଃଓଃଓଃଓଃଓଃଓଃ

Real distinctions beneficially observed

# *Section 45, Police or Military?*

Americans distinguish between what is police and what is military. They know that, at least archetypically, one wears blue and the other green; one makes arrests and the other goes overseas. Further articulating the differences gets a little harder, but one of North America's criticisms of Latin America in the second half of the 20th century centered on militarism -- that Latin America had too many military governments or too many military men in power. In most cases, military governance tended toward a rightist and 'anticommunist' flavor of oppression. As such, this military governance was often excused and sometimes coaxed by the United States government during the height of the Cold War against the Soviet Union. As the Cold War played out, the US expected rightist regimes to democratize and armed forces to go back to the barracks and away from political life. To a considerable degree this did indeed happen, such that by the mid-1990s almost all the countries of Latin American were experiencing democratic electoral practices and were putting civilian institutions in charge, even if the armed forces in many States continued to wield political influence.

Although the negative term 'police state' might have been used here and there to describe dictatorial regimes, the core offense was called 'militarism,' even while, in the firmament of disabling *isms*, fatalism, medieval Catholicism, sexism, and cronyism probably played greater roles in maintaining what for many seemed a stagnated and unjust status quo. Militarism was targeted, especially by academe, as the most offending *ism* because it was rightist and because it was conveniently wearing a uniform (often designed after a US or German uniform). With this as the inferential parameter, aid from the US to Latin American countries after the Cold War took a shift toward police organizations and away from the military, even while an analysis of the effective differential in repressive capacities of the two types of organization was hardly attempted. The differences between what is police and what is military, under-studied, is nevertheless central to understanding of the rule-of-law, limitations on political power and the control of government excess. Furthermore, few conversations can go to the marrow of irregular warfare more quickly than those about the proper separation of things police and things military.

Legal distinctions between what is police and what is military vary from country to country, and many countries have organizations that seem to confound distinction. The linguistic cognates are treacherous in translation. The variation should interest us because the nature of public forces influences counterinsurgency efforts, the rule-of-law, and even reflects traditions about the definition of tyranny versus good governance. Americans may take the concept of police for granted. For instance, the word 'police' is used at least 183 times in the US military manual *Counterinsurgency*, but the definition of that word has to be inferred. Also, the question 'What is the difference between a police officer and a soldier?' is a little different than the question 'What is a police situation and what is a military one?' We'll go over both. Below is a list of hints from a North American cultural and institutional perspective.

A. *In flagrante delictu.* Obligations are as defining a set of distinctions as authorities. Obligations are intimately tied to public expectations and police ethic. Police officers have an obligation to pursue persons in the act of committing a crime. Military personnel normally do not. If a crime is not in progress, but the police know, or are pretty sure they know, who did it they have to go get a warrant to that effect from a judge, or assure that an arrest warrant is extant. In many jurisdictions, if the police have time, they are required to present it to the suspect at the time of arrest. In normal military circumstances, even if the military know who they are going to go 'arrest,' they don't need a warrant.

B. *Dead or alive.* Police are granted leeway in applying deadly force in their self defense or the immediate defense of others. The 'dead or alive' announcement, however, is one in which prosecution and sentencing have been achieved before capture, this because someone is considered so dangerous that nonlethal action is deemed ineffective in stopping grave harm (See Section 4, *Defining Enemy*). The use of snipers is an interesting area of overlap and of definition between police and military. Police snipers are ready to kill someone who poses an immediate threat because they are armed and dangerous, are holding hostages at gunpoint, or are threatening a vulnerable public personality. Military snipers are often able to take targets of opportunity, kill enemy leaders, take out vehicle drivers, and so on. Police and military snipers are distant relatives in terms of their respective authorities. Military personnel are granted advance immunity from prosecution for premeditated killing. The police sniper's State-granted immunity will be more limited than that of the military sniper. Theoretically, the police officer will not enjoy impunity. He is not going to rest beyond the reach of indictment and judgment if his target's status and behavior did not rise to the thresholds that permit the sniper to kill. The military sniper, on the other hand, might be granted impunity by his State in defiance of any moral or legal characterization that another State or entity might make of the sniper's action. Killing by the military sniper is a creature of state sovereignty. His State might discipline his excesses or misjudgments, but, theoretically, will not allow any other entity to do so.

C. *Incoming.* Military people are authorized to use indirect fire weapons and area weapons in certain contexts. This again is tied to what I call the premeditated immunity of the State as it applies to weapons that are generally useless for making an arrest. (if a war were deemed unjust, the immunity might be considered impunity) We should hope it would be an extreme situation wherein the police would use an unoccupied armed aerial vehicle, for instance.

D. *Not on my beat.* Police are commonly used as a deterrent presence. That is to say, the police chase and capture perpetrators and serve warrants, but they also just cruise for the purpose of dissuading criminal acts. Criminals are the police's counterpart and are often distinguishable from insurgents because criminals usually do not attack government forces, while insurgents make it their business to do so. You can hardly be an insurgent if you don't attack your enemy. You're a dumb (or a tad crazy, and that's not so uncommon) criminal if you make it your business to attack the police. Hence, it is reasonable for a police officer to be on patrol deterring criminals from acting, whether or not that officer is looking for any particular criminal or intent on serving some warrant.

The soldier can be put at risk patrolling if the patrol is simply mounted to deter insurgent action, and not for the purpose of closing with the insurgent at a known location. A core objective of insurgent initiative being to attack government forces, the soldier might be no better than bait that causes insurgent action, rather than a deterrent to insurgent action. When soldiers are sent on deterrence patrols, it is often said that they are on police missions. Nevertheless, in a broader plan of patrols designed to perplex insurgents as to their lines of communication, what seems like a deterrence patrol becomes a key activity in offensive operational art.

The above delineations expose what in some situations can be a principal conceptual error in counterinsurgency. We may like to say that the police are the backbone, or should be the backbone counterinsurgent force. In a way this is certainly true, since good governance, application of the rule-of-law and so forth will provide the best long-term counterinsurgent condition. Nevertheless, if a violent armed insurgent force exists, it may, as is generally the case, conduct premeditated attacks against police. In such conditions, a counterinsurgent force often cannot safely conduct itself under a police ethic of criminal deterrence. When the public force is the natural target of a politically motivated armed enemy, to send elements of the force out without a fixed notion regarding when and how to enter into battle is to leave that force at a disadvantage in terms of initiative and strategic planning. Not only is it not the predator, nor even prey, but simply bait.
Here are some other relevant tendencies:

E. *Plea bargains*. The military might turn a prisoner over to the police, but when would a police unit turn a prisoner over to the military? (This may have been the case, briefly, with Abdulmutallab, the Nigerian bomb terrorist in late 2009.)

F. *Evidence versus intelligence*. Eventually the police (in situations we would honor as within the rule-of-law) must expose the source of their evidence in order to succeed in bringing a suspect to conviction. The military is not expected to reveal its sources. Police intelligence is constrained by prospective use in a court as evidence, while military intelligence is constrained from using information as evidence in order to protect sources and methods. This is not simply a matter of habit. It is also one of the reasons that the wistful goal of world government will not be realized in our lifetimes or those of our children.

G. *Longevity of personal relationships*. Police officers are usually permanent members of communities, married-in. Soldiers are more often from somewhere else. The soldier is naturally a traveler and a visitor. Local cultural knowledge, including of public records and community ethics, takes a longer time for the soldier to grasp. The soldier is someplace foreign exactly because something *there* has offended something *elsewhere*, whereas the policeman is from there, and is the more appropriate repressor when the problem is from within.

There are also some distinctions especially important in the United States domestic context:

H. *Territorial scale.* Police ranges are often delimited by the legal relationships that a police department or office has with the judicial institutions that empower it with warrants, prosecutions, etc.

I. *Chains of command.* Military personnel often report up through a chain of command that is within or leads into the federal government, while most police chains of command do not. Many military combat units suppose the maneuver of at least dozens of elements, while only the largest and most complex police operations suppose the coordinated physical movement of more than a few elements.

J. *Crew served and fully automatic weapons.* When would an American police organization appropriately use a machine gun?

K. *Knowledge cultures.* Police investigators tend to form investigations around clues and focus their theories on suspects. Military intelligence officers tend to form collection around requirements and concentrate analyses on enemy units. The difference draws the importance of personal identity. These days, criminal gang membership has created an overlap in this tendency.

These secondary differences between *police* and *military* can be significant in the aggregate.

Within the United States, when a situation occurs in which internal organized violence poses a threat to the viability of the State, the economy of part of the country, or to some basic value of our national exceptionalism, the difference between police and military moves to the top of national political debate. Use of the military along the Mexican border is a recurring issue, some politicians and pundits calling for more military and others calling for less. I personally prefer the no-military option. I think the US Border Patrol is the correct force for that job. I also think that the events in Waco, Texas in 1993, during which federal police tried to serve an arrest warrant on David Koresh at a compound of the religious sect called the Branch Dividians, and the events at Ruby

Ridge, Idaho in 1992, should be required curriculum material for both federal police agents and US military officers. The Wikipedia site for Ruby Ridge includes the following sentence: "FBI HRT sniper Lon Horiuchi was indicted for manslaughter in 1997 by the Boundary Court, Idaho prosecutor just prior to expiration of the statute of limitations for the crime of manslaughter, but the trial was removed to federal court and was quickly dismissed on grounds of sovereign immunity."

Sometimes key violent events can supply aspiring insurgents with what they perceive to be legitimate purpose, argument, rallying cry, and targets. Timothy McVeigh cited the events at Ruby Ridge and Waco as motivations for his bombing the Alfred P. Murrah Federal Building on April 19, 1995, the second anniversary of the Waco siege.

If police can adequately suppress crimes (including such crimes as sedition, insurrection or subversion) within the confines of police attributes and the rule-of-law, then counterinsurgency is perhaps *ipso facto* successful. If the capacity of the police is exceeded and the State finds itself obliged to employ military units to suppress crimes, such a condition may be evidence of an organized, armed challenge to the State, and at least of inadequate police capacity. If a State must employ military force to stop some organization from granting impunity, the condition begins to define State failure, at least in those areas where the State's monopoly on granting impunity is defied. Employing military force, meanwhile, can exacerbate lawlessness, making it harder to regain a police ethic and the rule-of-law. A State may, instead of employing military units, change the attributes of the police toward those of a military organization. That too may be evidence of a failing rule-of-law or of failing counterinsurgency.

See: 52, *Sovereignty*; 8, *The Operational Equation*; 82, *Conflict Thresholds*; 37, *School Lunches*; 13, *Puthukkudiyirippu*; 51, *Underclass*; 144, *Impunity and State Success*; and 139, *UAAV*.

---

**Ludwig**: Tell me, Mr. Papshmir, in all the world, who is the most effective assassin?
**Papshmir**: Well, I would think anyone who manages to conceal his identity as an assassin.
**Ludwig**: Yes, but there is even a more ideal assassin - one who doesn't *know* he's an assassin.

From the movie
*The Naked Gun: From the Files of Police Squad!* (1988)[58]

# *Section 46, Taxation and Debt*

Taxes are one of the two certainties. If you are in charge of some sort of effort involving organized armed human conflict, violent competition, or internal war, and you don't know who is able to tax whom and how, you need to eliminate that ignorance.

The power to tax is the power to destroy, and taxes aren't necessarily called taxes. If an entity is redistributing wealth it did not earn, it's probably a theft or a tax. In *The Geography of War and Peace: From Death Camps to Diplomats*, one of the authors, David Newman, looks at tax boundaries, tax-taking records and evidence, because tax so often appears as a theme in genocide research.

Debt and taxes are closely related. When someone is owed money they usually want to collect it. Of the various lines of investigation that this book advocates for unraveling and dominating armed conflict, knowledge about debt is one of the least practicable to obtain, but most likely to prove useful if obtained. Who owes what to whom is a significant index of power hierarchy. Part of that relation can be painted by understanding taxation. Debt can itself be treated as property in that it can be bought, sold, given, or inherited.

Debt systems can exist at many scales. A tribute system is a kind of debt arrangement that is almost purely extortion-based. The Ottoman *vilayets* and *sanjaks* are sometimes cited as examples. Very little administration or governance service was provided by the greater Ottoman State in many of these territories. Internal matters were left to local custom and structure, but an imperial tax was nevertheless collected.

Purgatory is a virtual geographic space invented by religious clergy. It is not a nice place, either. It is worse than the mortal vale -- it is a place where the soul suffers. The amount of time one spends in purgatory is correlated roughly to the quantity of un-absolved sins one commits here on earth, but even in a 'state of grace' some believe that additional purification is needed to assure speedy entrance into heaven. There is little about purgatory in the Bible, so why the invention? Because as clergy you can collect an *indulgence* from your parishioners that they, through your intervention with the Almighty, might reduce time spent there. Since being rich is almost synonymous with needing more purification, the Roman Catholic clergy managed a progressive tax scheme (or reverse toll) that extracted more indulgence money in accordance with your wealth. Improvements to the innovation came soon enough -- parishioners could pay to shorten the suffering in purgatory of relatives already deceased. In the face of such an option, clergy could profitably encourage a sense of guilt on the part of family members for allowing their stinginess to let their deceased relative suffer. The collecting of indulgences continued for centuries even past Martin Luther's protest against the extortion. It funded the construction of magnificent cathedrals in many parts of the world, especially Latin America. The cathedrals became toll booths to heaven.

Purgatory is an invented geography over which the church had sovereign tax authority. For efficient collection of that tax it was necessary for the clergy to develop and cultivate a belief among the congregants that such a place existed, that the congregants had a debt to pay, and that the clergy were exclusive agents of intervention. Many debts and many taxes, although not be as obviously fanciful as indulgences, depend at least in part on the establishment and maintenance of a belief that the taxes are necessary, or a debt owed, and that the tax collectors are the rightfully exclusive recipients of the money.

The issue of taxation and debt are woven into your war. They are a likely cause, shape the locations of your war's costs, guide the struggle over anonymity, and determine power to make war. The most consequential objects of debt and taxation are highly physical, like land, but can also be entirely fabricated. Find them.

See: 73, *Property and the Social Contract*, 65, *Smuggling*; 81, *What a Clergy Wants*; 48, *Grading the Social Contract*; 96, *Public Records*; 105, *Genocide Geography*; 135, *Bank Robbery*; and 19, *Extortion*.

---

"Someday, and that day may never come,
I will call upon you to do a service for me."

don Vito Corleone in the movie
*The Godfather* (1972)[59]

ଔଷ ଔଷ ଔଷ

A more useful scale than country

# *Section 47, Why the County*

Almost every country in the world has an administrative or formal territorial unit approximately equivalent to what in the United States is known as a county. In Iran they are called *rayons* and in Colombia *municipios*, etc., and they generally have a great deal in common as a geographic unit. They are often the object of considerable local geographic data-collection. Most Mexican counties (also called *municipios*), for instance, have their own website, which is usually very informative. In Colombia, every *municipio* government is required by national law to prepare a land-use plan (*Plan de Ordenamiento Territorial* or POT). Even rural, under-populated and poor *municipios* often produce sophisticated POT. For instance, Toribío (a conflictive *municipio* in southern Colombia through which FARC smuggling routes pass) received an international grant and the help of foreign specialists to prepare its plan. It is exquisitely detailed, and includes numerous GIS-based maps that represent physical and cultural phenomena. Included are the lines of privately owned plats, along with tribal boundary lines, township lines, and environmental risk areas.

The Canadians have managed to confuse the county level of governance, but within most of their Provinces they have something akin to the county. A few of the smaller US States have eliminated the county. Counties today are one of the greatest employers of practical geographers, who earn their livelihoods on the basis of expertise in geographic representation and analysis. For them, GIS has almost become the universal epistemology for land-use planning, and precise geographic predictions regarding traffic, floodplains, or development costs have become an administrative expectation at the county level. County governments do almost nothing in the absence of knowledge about land ownership.

Not only does most knowledge about real property ownership reside at the county level, the size and shape of the county is often intimately associated with familial histories and shared ownerships, physical compartmentalization of terrain, peculiar economic phenomena such as a mine or a popular beach, and other fairly obvious factors that guide decisions, affiliations and identities. For internal or irregular armed conflicts, the county is probably a good choice of scale for analysis and operational design -- or at least a good place to begin. The county is usually a good place for which to build an understanding of the relationship of residents with their surrounding environment, and of the local fit in the greater world. In many countries, including most in the Western Hemisphere, the county is a focus for tax distribution, developmental programs, land-use planning and reform programs, quality of life statistics, distribution of government services, voting representation, marriages, notaries, cadastres, school planning, etc.

To not have a collection of county-level data and a grasp of problems at the county scale might equate to being out of touch with the most revealing administrative events and social performance facts. Rural insurgents especially know counties; understand differences among counties; and deal with county governments. Innumerable popular seasonal events ranging from religious celebrations to concerts, fairs and contests are planned and organized at the county level. Many profitable extortions occur at the county level as well. In Colombia, for instance, the central government redistributes a percentage of the national oil, gas and coal production profits to county governments, with counties that produce hydrocarbons receiving a larger percentage. From some rural counties the FARC would threaten away large portions of those hydrocarbon royalties.

Mexico has about 1,500 counties and Colombia about 1,100. China has about 2,000. Iran has over 300 and Liberia about 15 (which have Senators). The point is that while the country, national or federal level is impressive, the right knowledge or operational starting scale for your approach to an internal war might be the next level down (state, province, department), and probably the next one down from that. If there is a rule regarding scale, it is probably that we should not bite off more geography than our resources can chew. Also, it is good to dominate land and property knowledge, details of which are often only available at the county scale.

This book stresses the importance of lines of communication, and the lines of communication of almost any armed group will lead in and out of a county, which means that the county level will almost never be the right scale for the whole geography of winning. Nevertheless, it is probably a good idea to orient your search for relevant geographic knowledge at the county level. You can adjust.

See: 49, *Territorial Scrutiny*; 80, *Why You Should Like Geography*; 38, *Cultural Study for What?*; 110, *Knowledge Gaps*; 26, *How Violent Groups Form*; 48, *Grading the Social Contract*; 86, *Shifting Covet-Geography*; and 78, *Personal Identity*.

---

> "My first book on Faulkner bears the title Yoknapatawpha: Faulkner's Little Postage Stamp of Native Soil." The title of this volume was chosen to signify that I am following Faulkner's progress from the provincial to the universal...."
>
> Elizabeth Margaret Kerr,
> *William Faulkner's Yoknapatawpha: A Kind of Keystone in the Universe*[60]

# Section 48, Grading the Social Contract

The first and last sections of this book (and several places in-between) assert a definition for the success or failure of a State. That definition concentrates on *impunity*, holding that competitors who can grant impunity are enemies of the State. Normative qualities of State behavior are also touched-on throughout the book. They have similar relation to impunity that 'neutralizing the enemy' has to 'not creating more of them.' This section deals with the normative condition of a society's social contract, especially the extent to which, as a system, it is likely to create enemies. 'State' is not equivalent to 'society.' The book presumes that government could be minimal, but also that a healthy social contract nevertheless requires a healthy government.

Many thoughtful scholars believe, kindly and with reason, that not only is it a dubious exercise to make normative judgments about the quality of a foreign society, it is the kind of presumption to which US Americans are especially prone. Let's do it anyway. Some cultures or polities are more likely than others to promote human flourishing and to exist in a sustainable relationship with the surrounding natural environment. Some social contracts are more sustainable environmentally, more peaceful, more successful materially, and happier than others. Some are just plain offensive. In the long run, any claim we might make to victory in an irregular conflict will be vulnerable if we can't accept the notion that it is acceptable to judge societies. After all, revolutionaries have all judged their society -- have critically measured society and are motivated to 'improve' it. Only the inveterate counterinsurgent would rest assured that all societies are equally valid. What follows is a way to measure better and worse:

Describe in as much detail as possible the following three aspects of the real property ownership system:

1. Quality of the evidence that delineates rights, duties, and the identity of owners of valuable things (this is sometimes referred to as *clarity of allocation*);

2. Capacity of owners (or claimants) to act on conclusions logically drawn from the evidence (this is in some contexts

referred to as *ease of alienability* or as *security from trespass* depending on the mix of owner rights and government duties involved); and

3. Basic rules delimiting contract participation (this we at times refer to as *liberality*).

'Valuable things,' by the way, means land, water, transportation means, taxation and creation and control of negotiable instruments, but especially real property. What we are measuring is the quality of the social contract using one of the closest proxies, the real property regime. We can break the three streams of inquiry down further, as follows:

1. Quality of the evidence delineating rights, duties and owner identities is determined by three characteristics:

A. Accuracy (or precision. How accurate technically are the geographic or physical descriptions, and how accurate legally are they in terms of owners and rights, and perhaps how accurate in terms of market value);

B. Comprehensiveness (what is the coverage of the system both geographically and in terms of the percentage of owners and the possible rights involved);

C. Transparency (the visibility and availability of the data and its resistance to corruption and fraud).

A. Accuracy

1. Extent to which ownership registry and cadastral descriptions are unified;
2. Existence of a statute of frauds and related statutory requirements;
3. Availability and use of title insurance;
4. Accuracy of surveying technologies;
5. Monument quality and density;
6. Age of records;
7. Capacity of cadastral and registry bureaucracy;
8. Appraisal cost and availability;
9. Relationship of tax assessments to market value appraisals if applicable.

B. Comprehensiveness
   1. Percentage of the geographic surface represented in cadastral maps;
   2. Percentage of owners whose properties are represented in cadastral maps;
   3. Difficulty of registration;
   4. Percentage of properties with tax appraisals;
   5. Percentage of properties with market appraisals.

C. Transparency
   1. Access to cadastral information;
   2. Access to land-use data online;
   3. If paper records available for public inspection;
   4. Where records are kept;
   5. Are registries and cadastral records digitized;
   6. Are cadastral maps digitized and vectorized;
   7. If government development projects are advertised online and GISed;
   8. What records cost.

2. Capacity of owners (or claimants) and the government to act on conclusions logically drawn from the evidence (sometimes *ease of alienability* or *security from trespass* depending on the mix of owner rights and government duties involved). It also can be reduced to three parts:

A. Marketability;
B. Protection from invasion, and;
C. Protection of the social contract generally.

A. Marketability
   1. Ratio of properties bought and sold to total properties in a given time;
   2. Existence of a professional real estate industry and its measures of professionalism;
   3. Regulatory limitations on sale commissions, and their effect;
   4. Real estate price controls and what is the effect;
   5. Where zoning laws exist;

6. If deed restrictions and other controls on alienation are used, where and for what;

7. Existence of an electronic market property listing service;

8. What collateral is accepted for loans and what are standard rates across types of real estate.

B. Protection from invasion

1. How long it takes to file a quiet-title claim;

2. If there is a grievance mechanism against real estate professionals;

3. How much it costs to conduct a quiet-title action;

4. If there are established rules for ownership through adverse possession.

C. Protection of the social contract

1. How often the statue of frauds is applied;

2. If agency contracts are used;

3. If sales contracts are used;

4. Whether or not the police use formal records to resolve property disputes;

5. Professional standards of real property sales or appraisal force;

6. Professional standards for appraisals;

7. Prenuptial requirements (is there a statutory requirement, what are the choices, what is the intention, how do they limit alienability).

3. Basic rules delimiting the contract participation (at times called *liberality*). The three general determinants of liberality are:

A. Inclusiveness (who can effectively be owners);
B. Divisibility (how thoroughly the various rights associated with things can be divided);
C. Alienation -- what rights supposed owners have as to the disposal of real property.

A. Inclusiveness

1. If women can own property;

2. If foreigners can own property and to what extent, where, etc.;
3. If religious or ethnic identities are excluded.

B. Divisibility
1. If subsurface rights can be bought and sold;
2. If innovations such as time shares, condominiums, joint, common, partnership, incorporation, etc. are used and is there data on geographic distribution and percentage of types;
3. If any studies relate ownership and tenancy forms to violence, migration or illicit narcotics production or trafficking.

C. Alienation
1. If real property can be freely bequeathed by testators;
2. Who can give away real property and to whom;
3. How intestate estate property is disposed by statute or custom;
4. If life estates are used;
5. Standard tenancy patterns (leases, sharecrop arrangements, *ejidos*, communes, family corporations);
6. If land is otherwise fully alienatable (mortgaged, sold, rented, lent).

Of all the above items, transparency or its absence may be the first clue to the overall condition of the social contract. One of the three qualities of evidence in a functioning liberal social contract, transparency is the principal antidote to government corruption. It is a natural tendency of government to want to keep some information close-hold, and there are many seemingly valid justifications for doing so. The same is often true regarding the most significant public records, such as family census and cadastral records. Nevertheless, no amount of technical precision or completeness of coverage will cause a system of public records to serve the purposes of human flourishing if those records are kept for the exclusive consideration of a few. Sometimes lack of transparency may seem to be due not so much to some attempt to hide data as it is to the simple lack of record systems. This may be true, but if a leadership group exists, and that leadership is able to aggregate wealth, then there are probably records someplace and that leadership group controls them.

See: 73, *Property and the Social Contract*; 72, *Land Strategy*; 95, *Childhood*; 109, *Hotspotting*; 27, *Democracy*; 110, *Knowledge Gaps*; 70, *Measuring effects of Actions on Structure*; and 96, *Public Records*.

---

"There's only two things I hate in this world:
people who are intolerant of other cultures,
... and the Dutch."

Nigel Powers in the movie
*Austin Powers in Goldmember* (2002)[61]

---

Overlapping territories exposed

# *Section 49, Territorial Scrutiny*

Territorial scrutiny is a map-based investigation and analysis method that is built upon human territorial nature. The idea is to expose, understand and relate the nature of conflicts through territorial mapping. It happens that over time and because of new technologies, human territoriality has become increasingly mappable. The issue of what actions to take on the basis of detailed territorial knowledge is considered elsewhere throughout the book. A few suggestions about how to organize human territories, based in part on the theories used in this section, can be found in Section 92, *Land-use Planning*.

If, by the way, you insist on starting from a philosophical position holding that the idea of human nature is an invalid construct, a fallacy or superstition; and that humans are not instinctively territorial, then this territorial scrutiny stuff won't make sense to you. That is exactly where the post-structuralists would like to have you.

Below are several initial points about territorial scrutiny that can help you collect and organize knowledge useful for winning, and maybe for shaping the social contract to reduce the likelihood of future armed violence.

People's rights, duties, privileges, delimitations, obligations, powers, capacities, and trespasses are almost all associated with territories. It might be a shoe salesman's territory, a telephone billing exchange, a sports league school set, a catchment area for insurance patients, fire vulnerability zones, a language-group density gradient, a

Kiwanis club membership spread, and on and on. It might also be something more legally formal and consequential, such as a gas or water line easement, a building setback line, or a noise abatement zone. There could be a theoretical area where people might be at risk of mud slides, or where they might be fearful of UFOs. It could be a territory where people pronounce a word in a curious and distinguishing way. It might be the estimated borders between the zones of action of two gangs or guerrilla groups, or it might be the series of way-stations used to move stolen emeralds. It might be the boundary of duties or privileges to organize a public event (such as a religious celebration or parade) in one locale as opposed to another.

With some exceptions, there exists a potential conflict whenever territories overlap. This is true almost irrespective of the type of territories involved. If you overlay the map of a ditch easement with the map that shows where monarch butterflies light and then overlay those two with a map showing the boundaries of the various Boy Scout troops, you might discover a conflict. If a gas line easement crosses a water line easement, there is a potential problem. So one step in territorial scrutiny is naming and mapping all the relevant territories you can think of and seeing which ones overlap. As a general proposition, the more geographic knowledge you have, the better your decisions as to what territories you select as most consequential. Some categories are suggested in Section 53, *Hohfeldian Grievance Analysis,* as a way to begin.

*Nested Identities* is the title of an interesting and useful anthology edited by Herb Guntram and David Kaplan.[62] Some human collective identities coincide with administrative or formalized territories, and people often have a hierarchically/geographically-based set of identities typically growing from the self to the family to the school to the town and so forth to the nation-state. As such, you will want to name, to your own satisfaction, the competing identities related to the place you are scrutinizing. This is not to suggest that individuals who are members of a given competing identity will necessarily be located in the place you are studying, just that they have some influence on the rights, duties, conditions and events in the place. Try to map the whereabouts of the identities' members, what the members of each identity consider to be 'theirs,' where the agents or representatives of the identity are located. Map all the significant administrative territories. See which administrative concepts and identities are cozily nested and contiguous, that is, if the power identities and administrative boundaries are copacetic.

The likelihood that a territorial overlap exposes a conflict increases as the distance between the proponents of each of the territories increases. In other words, if the engineer who is in charge of servicing the water line is the same individual who services the gas line, then the distance between the proponents is nothing. The guy might have a conflict in his own head about whether the gas line goes over the water line or vice-versa, but that hardly presents much fuel for armed social conflict. Maybe he just says to himself something like, 'I'll run the gas line over the top of the water line since it is smaller and it is more urgent that I get to it quickly if there is a problem.' Not much of a conflict, and conflict resolution is easy. If, on the other hand, the water pipeline engineer sits in Omaha in a large company with a number of subordinate engineers, and the gas line company headquarters is in Wichita, then there could be some digging arguments, and they will be harder to resolve. If instead of talking about a couple of simple utility easements, we are talking about a couple of lucrative drug smuggling routes, overlapping turf boundaries of two violent cartels, a fiber optic cable line, and the edges of two soccer team fan-bases, the conflict is going to be rougher.

In the context of armed conflict, especially if it has been ongoing, the organization with the headquarters that is further away from an area in question is probably the more powerful organization overall. This may seem counterintuitive since one of the basic theories of geography is that everything influences everything else, and that closer things influence more than distant things. It takes strength to maintain armed force at a distance, so, therefore, if an organization can maintain defiant armed force a long way from its base, it is probably powerful in accordance. (More on the relationship of distance and power is considered in Section 64, *Measuring Power*.) This does not mean that the identity with the more distant HQ is the more powerful organization in that one little place at a given moment in time, however. Also, again, distances should be measured as cost-distances, not just Euclidean distances.

Let's say that a local family gang has a little pickpocketing territory in town, but a group shows up called the Tri-State Crypts, who don't want attention from the cops in the new drug distribution territory they are trying to establish, so the Crypts courteously invite the local pick-pocketing gang to stop work. The Tri State Crypts have more members and money than do the local pickpockets, and the Crypts sport a well-advertised degree of existential resolve. Still, although the identity whose headquarters is the farthest away is generally the more powerful, it is not always more powerful at the local point at a moment in time. It has to want to focus its power locally. If the pickpockets are clever enough, they can distress or unhinge the Crypts' business in 'their' town. At any rate, it is useful to know the relative distances to all the decision-making loci of competing identities. Distance should be measured as *cost-distance*. What if the headquarters of two competing groups is in the same place? Such a condition won't last long. The point of the rule is not that there aren't constant exceptions, but that the trend, due to territorial behavior, will quickly move toward the condition if any shooting starts. Can treaties be reached? Of course. In such a way a distant power can create a system of tribute. A foreign power only has to convince the locals that, however distant and foreign, it is willing to focus on and transport its power to the locale. Sometimes another, closer power won't go along, and will sink your fleet off Tsushima or someplace.

The scale of map images matters. A current fashion holds some phenomena to be 'flows' as opposed to 'spaces.' That's fine, especially since in the context of visual analysis some territories are more easily depicted as lines such as airline routes, or retail distribution networks. They are territories nevertheless, and so exposure of the legalistic and strategic-competitive importance of relationships (such territorial jealousies) has to be guarded from semantic distraction. Don't let words like 'flow,' 'network,' or 'assemblage' distract you from exposing territorial overlaps. You are seeking to unravel organized human conflict and that means analyzing places and privileges (territories) that are coveted enough for humans to fight over. Those things are going to have a spatial manifestation or reference. Scale mistakes are easy to make. Pick the right scales for the interpretation of territorial conflict, but think beyond scale. Do not let your thinking become frozen at one scale of space or time. An image of a network of airline routes can give the impression of 'flows' in and out of territories. When the pilots land, however, they will do so under some territorial agreement allowing them to fill a passenger gate or refuel. All routes are territory.

There exists an interesting literature on frontiers and border cultures that, to a useful degree, opposes and belies the idea that lines drawn as territorial boundaries necessarily make sense. In fact, there are plenty of occasions when a line would be less visually meaningful than a fade from one shade density or color to another. That, however, is because of an overlap of some concept, perhaps an unresolved dispute about tax territories, ethnic affinities, or maybe just some territorial indifference because nobody lives in an area between two more formalized ones. Many such places exist, and other lines that were drawn as theoretical propositions and no more, are later taken to represent something grounded. There are lots of misleading and stupid things that can be done with mapping or in the name of territorial scrutiny. One of the current conversations in international matters revolves around the present meaning of some national borderlines drawn long ago by the cartographers of colonial powers. Sometimes observers accuse the lines as being artificial, arbitrary and damaging because they were originally drawn indifferent to or disdainful of local territorial matters such as tribal or economic relationships. Commenting on the British challenge in the northwest of India in 1893,

> "Sir George Robertson, an expert in frontier politics, puts the matter so clearly that his words on the subject may be quoted at length: – 'To the superficial observer,' he says, 'nothing could seem more statesmanlike that to lay down distinct boundaries demarcating respectively the spheres of influence of the Amir of Afghanistan and the Government of India, and so to prevent all fear of collision of those two powers. A weal point, however, in the plan, was the practical ignoring of all the intervening tribes, who, as they owed allegiance neither to the Afghan chief nor to the Government of India, not unnaturally objected to what they imagined was the parceling out of their country without their consent."[63]

The lines, however, were in very few cases arbitrary as to the relationships between the colonial powers. Today, although they may be locally dysfunctional, present-day national governments are generally loath to change the colonial lines.

It is important to map identities of persons and collectives who consider themselves to be in the legitimate current exercise of significant rights ('owners') as well as groups and individuals who are not in exercise of those rights, but claim they should be ('claimants'). When nominating owner and claimant identities it is important to keep in mind that any given individual can belong to multiple, competing identities; can be ambivalent, capricious and indecisive over time; and that some identities can be as fleeting as they are powerful. As I expressed in *Geoproperty: Foreign Affairs, National Security and Property Rights,*

> The ownership status of individuals can be credited to multiple owner identities. One... might fit all of the following groups: mother of children who cross that piece of land on their way to school, citizen of Overland Park, Kansan, Black, Dominican, owner of ten shares of Texaco, property tax payer, Republican, speedboater, female, Baptist, wife, Irish, short person, twin, lefty, kids hockey team representative, mother against drunk drivers, and alcoholic. Each descriptor can be

> matched to a right related to land that the mother is variably willing to defend or attempt to obtain. As a Black person, she may be fiercely opposed to badges of racism. As a mother of school children and payer of property taxes, she may be just as opposed to allowing undocumented immigrant Mexicans from attending school in the district. Other identities may be at odds with one another as far as property rights are concerned. For instance, she may find it difficult to vote for a proposed ordinance against serving alcohol. She is both an alcoholic and a member of Mothers Against Drunk Driving."[64]

The fact that owner identities (which for a lawyer might become classes of plaintiffs or defendants) can overlap even while the territories in question don't appear to overlap, is what makes territorial scrutiny a 'postmodern' concept. A collective identity has members, but is not necessarily an organization, and it is not the same as the sum of its membership. Collective identities are key to your conflict analysis to the extent they influence the conflict at particular moments in time and in places important to you.

Territorial scrutiny is suitable for use in forensics, but also in support of a property-based approach to understanding and improving a social contract. By specifying the spatial and temporal condition of territoriality, the manifestations of abstractions like sovereignty, human rights, civil rights, property rights, power and wealth can be visualized and analyzed on the same plane. Territorial scrutiny can reveal the practical overlap of those concepts. The object of conflicts is often reflected in tax plats, resource concessions, easements, building codes, land-use plans, development and aid schemes, service boundaries and schedules, school districts, and sports events schedules. The movement of objects of desire (opium, emeralds, water, prostitutes, bananas…) is also consequential. These details of property (or power relationships) can be visualized, compared, correlated, even modeled because of the GIS revolution. Ultimately, all territorial lines represent power relationships. Every formal territorial construction reflects preferential rights and duties that together reflect at least part of a social contract. These reflections of related power can be collated and correlated, and in so doing many dangerous imbalances can be recognized. This potential to read power from the aggregate minutia of overlapping territorial spaces forms part of the logic of territorial scrutiny. Given enough data, a GIS can be used to produce territorial trends and display theories or predictions about territorial change over time.

It has to be taken for granted that the universe of overlapping lines cannot be seen, much less comprehended on one visualizable map or screen image. The complexity of created, shared, traded, excluded and denied rights pertaining to a locale is something that a GIS can allow people to play with and to test, the various layers and scales of territorial information resting in unseen relational databases. The images and maps that a GIS produces cannot safely be considered the final 'products' of the GIS. The maps and images are better taken just as partial products and windows into the dataset, with the ultimate product being the understanding that the person playing with the data can achieve. This means that the person doing the playing has then to find a way to explain the understanding to which she or he has arrived. This can only partly be achieved by construction of derivative images.

Doing careful territorial scrutiny can be time-consuming and expensive. Maybe prioritize the most coveted geography, and concentrate along the most likely or favorable lines of communication to sanctuaries. Also, territorial scrutiny can itself cause harmful conflict. Many people do not want to have the boundaries of their territories exposed, especially when the exposed territorial boundaries are of private property and wealth.

Lines on a map can show the physical boundaries of preferential and shared rights and duties, that is, they can express human power relationships, as well as relationships with the natural environment. In those places where the details of competitive territoriality have not been recorded in maps, revealing lines and spaces can be created. Territorial scrutiny can even provide some visual insight into factors such as indifference, ambivalence, distraction, confusion, whim, anger, forgetfulness, etc., when these are discovered by suitable methods. It can, in other words, allow for rational input of the seemingly irrational.

See: 53, *Hohfeldian Grievance Analysis*; 66, *GIS*; 38, *Cultural Study for What?*; 3, *The Domesday Book*; 80, *Why You Should Like Geography*; 25, *Why Humans Don't Fight*; 73, *Property and the Social Contract*; and 107, *Price of Real Estate.*

---

> "Why should we think upon things that are lovely? Because thinking determines life. It is a common habit to blame life upon the environment. Environment modifies life but does not govern life. The soul is stronger than its surroundings."
>
> William James[65]

# *Section 50, U.S. Persons*

The saying, 'Countries don't have friends, they have interests,' is a realpolitik staple ascribed to de Gaulle, Kissinger, Bismarck, and numerous other geopolitical alpha males of lore. We want to be careful with its use these days, even if it still serves to explain some government decisions and behaviors. The United States is home to so many families with international membership that in the case of some countries, US bilateral relations are not just a matter of friendships, they are a matter of families. To suppose that a democratic government could rise above those familial relationships to assert an ostensibly greater national interest is the more naive view. It isn't just the United States and its 'US Person,' either. Irregular conflicts will involve many countries with shared families, companies and migrants. Millions of Colombians live in Venezuela and vice versa, for instance. For the United States, the obvious examples are Cuba, Colombia, the Dominican Republic, Israel and Mexico. The existence of family ties is a complicating factor that itself should invite careful examination, not just at the philosophical level, but at the operational one.

There now are several overlapping definitions of 'US Person' that can be easily Googled, but, more or less, a US Person is a United States citizen, a permanent resident alien, an unincorporated association substantially composed of United States citizens or permanent resident aliens, or a US corporation unless directed and controlled by a foreign government or governments. You may see the inclusivity expanded or contracted a bit depending on the agency and context, but in any case, US Person status engages a range of constitutional protections including those relating to illegal government searches, invasion of privacy, and warrantless arrests. It is an example of a self-imposed dilution of State power. For many law enforcement purposes, the rights accruing to United States citizens have been extended beyond US borders. Along the US-Mexico border, US federal officers apply a broad interpretation of US Person. Guided also by the intent of another requirement, the Posse Comitatus Act limiting military authority in domestic territory, US federal officers are normally cautious, presuming almost anyone within the United States to be a US Person. They may presume, for instance, that anyone heading toward Mexico from the interior of the United States to be a US Person.

The 'US Person' is a human identity category that can be traced at least back to a Ronald Reagan executive order (No. 12333), and it was a substantial invention. To a degree it mooted many arguments about whether or not the US Constitution applied to noncitizens. The rights of Americans are not granted by the US Constitution; rather the Constitution asserts protections of human rights from infringements by the US Government. It is perhaps an interesting historical note that the US government would constrain itself as to infringements on the rights of persons who are not citizens of the United States, but creation of the 'US Person' was born of the same spirit that motivated the founding fathers to keep the government at a distance from tyrannical practices. Creation of the US Person was recognition that to lord it over the relatives or foreign interests of US citizens was too close to infringing on the rights of the US citizens themselves. Does it make law enforcement harder? Yes. Does it lessen the rule-of-law? Perhaps not.

Every day the number of persons who fall into the US Person category increases, especially in the United States' near-abroad. Any irregular conflict in which forces of the United States government might find themselves engaged in the Western Hemisphere will encounter an ever-increasing proportion of US Persons. If we were to add to the definition, as is likely, close family member of a US citizen, it would be exceptional in a country like the Dominican Republic to find a non-US Person. Today, for the United States, in the context of some potential irregular wars, the idea that countries have interests and not friendships becomes a dangerous intellectual anchor. Beyond friendships there are families by the hundreds of thousands. The implications of operational law in such situations, tied as families are to democratic politics and to tort law if nothing else, should sober all commanders to think about the golden rule. It would be the exception for the United States military to find itself in a place in the Americas where they would not be at once in a foreign land -- and not so much. Many Americans outside the US know this better than do Americans inside the US. An operations plan for a United States government unit that does not explicitly address the phenomenon of the US Person might be a dangerously incomplete plan. The depiction of an operational environment that does not attempt to define the social and legal geography of the US Person might be a dangerously incomplete depiction.

Anonymity is a central theme of this book. The fact of the US Person cuts in both directions as far as the creation and control of anonymity is concerned. On one hand, the individual rights of US Persons, backed by their access to grievance mechanisms, can hamper investigation and surveillance. On the other hand, the condition of 'US Personship' can make the establishment of comprehensive biometrics, perfection of public records, or the creation of Big Brother easier. In any case, and for all parties, the extent and implication of US Personship should be a matter of attention, as should analogous conditions elsewhere.

In the 1970s, a dominant current of American opinion and emotion, soured from the Vietnam War, turned against what was perceived to be overreaching by the federal government in the name of national security. The Church Committee, among other things, investigated a project carried out by the US Army called COINTELPRO, under which military intelligence personnel secretly collected and filed private information about US citizens, especially on college campuses within the United States.

In the spirit of discipline imposed by public reaction to the perceived violation of civil liberties, the Federal Bureau of Investigation and the Central Intelligence Agency were led to maintain separated geographies of responsibility. The FBI worked inside the country and the CIA worked outside the country. They rarely traded files, and when the 2001 World Trade Center attack came, this failure to share information was perceived as a weakness. New laws, The Patriot Act among them, increased cooperation between the two agencies (broke down the geographic boundaries), as well as among other principle components of the US intelligence and law enforcement communities.

In 1983, Executive Order 12425 gave the International Criminal Police Organization (INTERPOL) status as a public international organization entitled to enjoy the immunities accorded under the International Organizations Immunities Act of 1945. The 1983 order expressly excluded some immunities regarding search and seizure, as well as regarding taxation. Some tax exclusions were dropped in 1995 (Executive Order 12971). In 2009, Executive Order 13524 further amended EO 12425, exempting Interpol from search of all INTERPOL properties and files. In other words, the 2009 amendment released INTERPOL from oversight by the United States. It is too early to say if the 2009 order means that INTERPOL is beyond the reach of civil actions for abuse of process, or if it is relieved from Freedom of Information Act requests. However, it seems that, whereas the US Person executive order was designed to limit infringements by the US government on the rights of individual humans, even if not fully US Citizens, Executive Order 12425 goes in the other direction, releasing a foreign police organization from accountability regarding the rights of US citizens within the United States.

The US Person is an invention in law; the measurement of your performance in irregular war is subject to such legal inventions; and therefore your winning could depend on how well you understand concepts of identity such as the US Person.

See: 2, *Anonymity*; 51, *Underclass*; 49, *Territorial Scrutiny*; 104, *Extraterritorial Jurisdiction*; 45, *Police or Military*; 52, *Sovereignty*; 128, *Global Insurgency and Global Trespass*; and 90, *Prisons*.

---

"If I were to live my life over again,
I would be an American.
I would steep myself in America,
I would know no other land."

Henry James[66]

Trouble when dishonor shares identity

# *Section 51, Underclass*

Underclass is not used here in the way Karl Marx used *lumpenproletariat* -- a refuse class, but rather as a term for any collective identity that suffers an inferior social status compared to the societal norm, or even compared to some other minority collective identity. It is a dangerous condition, and while its mere existence might not cause an irregular armed conflict, it is safe to assert that it can contribute.

Perceived relative deprivation has for some time been observed as a causal condition for criminal behavior and posited as a motivator of rebellion. Professor Ted Gurr (*Why Men Rebel*) can be credited with the observation, but so can Karl Marx and maybe some long-dead Greeks. (The observation can be inferentially tied to egalitarianism, e.g., if everyone is in about the same material condition there will be less discontent and less conflict.) The opposite view is that plenty of us are actually not content unless we have more than others.

A category of people sharing some cohesive identity and perceiving a shared grievance can be a recruiting, financial or leadership source-bed for insurgency. It can facilitate the identification or creation of routes and places of anonymity and refuge. If there is an underclass, a perception of grievance can be created even if it does not already exist.

Careful analysis and self inspection of a territory for the existence of an underclass can advance understanding of the potential for internal conflict or its amelioration. The perception of membership in an underclass can itself be constructed. Construction of the perception of the existence of an aggrieved proletariat, for the purposes of furthering class conflict, is perhaps the classic example of the 19th and 20th centuries. Today, aggrieved identities are sometimes defined as ethnicities or religious affiliations, but some astute leaders learn to aggregate the action of much smaller groups of the disaffected. Álvaro Garcia provided a chapter titled 'The Multitude' to Oscar Olivera and Tom Lewis' *Cochabamba!: Water War in Bolivia*, wherein he examines the trend away from organizing plant or factory labor and toward the necessarily more nimble engagement of disparate social groups that have a variety of demands and grievances.[67]

The national identity of Americans includes a current flowing historically from the pre-constitutional existence of a Black underclass. The evolutionary erasure of that status continues to encourage and dismay, but is nevertheless part of what paints collective attitudes about the fairness and stability of a social contract. Meanwhile, however, the United States has allowed the growth of a new underclass of foreign nationals, mostly of Mexican origin, who are illegally present in US territory. This condition has not been adequately addressed in terms of its potential as a cause, kindling, or enabler of irregular conflict in North America.

Whatever the scale of the territory, it is a good idea to check for the existence of an underclass. Do not start with the assumption that there is none. The underclass can be an amalgam of disaffected identities. This said, you will do better to steer clear of 'class warfare' or 'class struggle' as an approach to conflict analysis, except maybe for propaganda purposes if you are so inclined ideologically. Lots of plaintiff's lawyers would like to come up with a good class, the word just a synonym for a human collective or category that can be reasonably said to share an actionable grievance. So in a way, all of your analyses will be class analyses if they have anything to do with conflict and competition. One of the weaknesses of Marxist class analyses, however, has always been the contrived and amorphous nature of the classes chosen. If enough people are convinced they're in the 'proletariat' or that they're 'workers' or something, and that some other people are in an abusive 'bourgeoisie' or 'elite,' then maybe some of the vocabulary from that construct can still have some meaning.

See: 53, *Hohfeldian Grievance Analysis*; 26, *How Violent Groups Form*; 79, *Suicide*; 1, *What the Pirate Said to Alexander*; 72, *Land Strategy*; 73, *Property and the Social Contract*; 134, *Luigi Galleani*; and 27, *Democracy*.

---

"Most people don't know that appending the name 'gypsy' to my people is both wrong and pejorative…"

Ian Hancock (Romani: Yanko le Redžosko)[68]

I own this place, not you

# Section 52, Sovereignty

Some political scientists like to define sovereignty as a *summa potestas*, a unified authority supreme in internal affairs and independent with respect to external affairs. Anytime anyone invokes sovereignty, however, they are almost sure to be saying something pretty close to 'I'm the owner of this place and you're not.'

There are some particular ownership rights and duties that we can usefully tie to the word sovereignty or to territoriality at the level of States in the international state system. The trick is to determine what individuals control these rights, where those people sit, how much power they have to exercise their claimed rights, and how much we can expect them to meet any duties we suppose them to have. How do we know if a State is a sovereign owner of land?

1. It alone can conscript soldiers from the population in its territory;
2. It can impose exclusive tax authority within the territory;
3. It can deny entrance to the territory;
4. It sends delegates, who uniquely represent the territory, to international organizations;
5. It has a monopoly on granting impunity for acts committed within the territory.

When the State in question is not the only entity to effectively grant impunity, adherents of some other entity will not only enjoy impunity for acts of violence, they probably choose not to pay the State's taxes, won't serve in its army, and can come and go as they please. Things break down. Impunity and sovereignty are linked. Sovereignty, in a sense, is the geography of impunity. Everything else is details. Salient among those details, however, is international recognition that allows the State to send representatives to international forums and to mutually respect the above list of five items. Things like extradition and rendition are tied to this sovereignty-by-recognition, so this aspect of the concept is also tied to impunity.

As with property regimes at every scale, there is an international membership society that recognizes boundaries for the purpose of conflict avoidance and resolution. Land outside the formal lines of property ownership is possessed by force. It has been a long time since the world had much territory outside formal international boundaries. Almost all the land on earth now falls within the lines of some recognized country, although there is still some irredentism. This isn't the same as saying that the boundaries and borders all work, just that somebody thought they were divvying up rights and duties and made some commitment, idle or otherwise, to help enforce the club's regime of rights and duties. Almost all borders and boundaries are related to a commitment to effect eviction (to deny entrance or use by someone who has no right according to the agreement of the social contract).

The idea of international recognition seems to throw people off. It shouldn't. If the United Nations uses the argument that it is protecting the principle of sovereignty when it goes in to kick the Iraqis out of Kuwait, it is saying that the club leaders made agreements about the lines, and that they aren't going to accept a violation of those lines.

The rules of the club come from multilateral agreements like the UN Charter, from customary international law, from bilateral treaties and from business contracts, but the point is always the same. There are some agreed-upon rights associating States with specific land and water. The agreements are in place to avoid constant fighting. Some people suggest that there is no international law or that international law doesn't work, but this is simply not true. Most leaders of States want to have recognized property rather than constantly have to possess by force. Otherwise, there would be a lot more international fights than there are. A leader wanting to gain more rights on the other side of some internationally recognized line may have to trick or defy the rules.

The club of countries in the international property system grants representational recognition. One of the big benefits of membership in the club of countries is that (for the most part) club members agree to do business only with one recognized representative entity. The United

States has one government that gets to send a representative to the United Nations, not fifty. Someone gets to go to the club meetings. There are exceptions and odd cases. For instance, Puerto Rico sends its own representatives to some international bodies.

If a State can't maintain a monopoly over the granting of impunity within its borders, it probably can't maintain other characteristics of sovereignty. A State member might not even be the only entity allowed to send a representative to the meetings of an international club. Recognition in international forums of an entity such as the Palestinian Liberation Organization is an example. We might argue that a 'non-State' entity does not deserve recognition (in the normative sense of ethical of standards) that should allow it to send its representatives to international forums, or to send ambassadors to other sovereign States. Conversely, we may determine that a State needs the assistance of the other members of the club to help it regain rights lost to unworthy trespassers, claimants, and usurpers.

These questions come up all the time. Sometimes the cases are clear-cut. In South America, the Venezuelan Dictator Hugo Chávez proposed that the international clubs recognize the FARC as a legitimate international representative of Colombians. His idea was a direct insult to the Colombian government's claim of unique sovereign representation in the international system. In a way, Chavez' assertion made sense. The FARC was able to grant impunity to its members in much of Colombia, FARC members could come and go against the wishes of the formal State, didn't pay government taxes, assessed their own taxes, and conscripted soldiers. Chávez' proposal came at a time when the fortunes of the FARC were waning precipitously, however, and when the hyper-violent modus operandi of the FARC had become more evident to the world. If Chávez had been acting as a good member of the international clubs, he would have supported the rules of those clubs recognizing and guarding Colombia's sovereignty -- which includes Colombia's right to a monopoly over the granting of impunity within Colombia, and the right to send unique representatives to international forums. He would have helped seal off the FARC routes to sanctuary in Venezuela, and helped eliminate the FARC's granting of impunity. Chávez did not want to be a good club member -- and Venezuela had enough power that he didn't have to be.

A more recent and confusing political drama in Honduras raised questions about the nature of the international property regime. Various components of the Honduran State decided that their president was breaking the law. He was arrested and spirited out of the country. There was no internal armed conflict going on in Honduras and hopefully one was not planted by the history surrounding the removal of their president and the attendant foreign involvement. If there is an armed conflict, it will be hard to establish an international consensus regarding the rights to Honduran sovereignty.

There is a house in Boiling Springs, Pennsylvania that was owned by abolitionist Daniel Kaufman, who provided a way station on the 'underground railroad' established to secret slaves out of the antebellum South and to freedom in Canada. Maryland slave owner Mary Oliver sued Kaufman in property court and won, costing the Northerner about $4,000.00. Although the North had abolished slavery, and many of the North's citizens were morally offended by the institution, Southern property laws were respected among all the states under the principle of comity (by which courts of one jurisdiction give effect to the laws of another). Citizens of the North had admitted the owner status (human status) of Blacks, but the State of Pennsylvania, under the club rules of the United States, felt obliged to respect the ownership laws of another state where Blacks were not considered owners, but rather part of what could be owned. The legalistic result was not only that a citizen of the North did not have the right to defy a law of the South, but violation of a Southern property law drew a sanction. The example illuminates a central fight-causing problem of sovereignty in international relations today. Nice people advocate cross-cultural understanding and tolerance, but the most conflictive aspects of culture involve property. It may seem that varying systems of property can live together in a globalized world, but there really is no way to respect sovereignty while simultaneously defying property laws. Sovereignty and property are the same quantity. When the ownership regimes of two States differ radically in terms of the basic rules regarding who can own what, the potential for a fight exists.

At the beginning of this section is a list of five ownership rights that most typically compose national sovereignty. Transnational gangsters often recruit foot soldiers within a particular ethnicity or linguistic group, tax a select set of products, smuggle across international boundaries, and protect their members from State prosecution. They mock the territorial map (and therefore the whole scheme of rules) of the countries in the international club. That's why pirates and terrorists are explicitly considered enemies of the State system. It boils down, again, to the words territory and impunity. Anonymity remains the sibling of impunity at the international scale. If a State, supposedly a member in the club of sovereigns, provides anonymity for the identity and wealth of a transnational gangster, that State is really violating the terms of the club agreement and undermining someone's national sovereignty. Some bankers have been so good at maintaining fiduciary discretion (euphemism for secret bank accounts), and so many people appreciate the anonymity that they have provided for individual wealth, that they have been given a pass on what most analysts understand as willful, continuous accessorial behavior to massive international crime with purposeful disrespect for international sovereignty. Secret international bank accounts constitute major sanctuaries in the firmament of irregular wars. Of course, if your cause is legitimate or your government a tyrant, you will not consider your secret banking accessorial behavior; but rather a noble risk.

If you are a married male, go around your house thumping your chest and saying '*Summa Potestas, Summa Potestas.*' It'll help, try it.

See: 144, *Impunity and State Success*; 40, *Rule-of-law*; 24, *Ruthlessness and Resolve*; 105, *Genocide Geography*; 73, *Property and the Social Contract*; 48, *Grading the Social Contract*; 20, *Foreign Support*; and 31, *Holes in the Ground.*

---

> "The fundamental difficulty of subjecting states to the rule of law is the fact that states possess power. The legal control of power is always difficult, and it is not only for international law that it constitutes a problem."
>
> J.L. Brierly in *The Law of Nations*[69]

---

Lawyers are lazy

# *Section 53, Hohfeldian Grievance Analysis*

The name of this section is both an admiration of and theft from Wesley Newcomb Hohfeld's ideas about how to analyze complex cases (especially property cases) in civil legal practice. He's been dead for many decades, so he won't mind; apologies to his great-great grandchildren.

Hohfeldian Analysis is adapted here as a practical way to dissect existing or nascent violent organized struggles for the purpose of determining the likelihood that one party or another will prevail, how much effort that might take, and the best way to win. It could be applied to forecasting future conflict, but for explaining if or why a given society is likely to experience continuous or repeated conflict, I recommend something more like what is offered in Section 48, *Grading the Social Contract.* For identifying which of the many locales in the world might demand the attention of their neighbors because of such problematic conditions, I suggest something like what is in Section 109, *Hotspotting.*

Every day, some process akin to Hohfeldian Analysis is applied by practicing civil lawyers for quickly analyzing the situation of a prospective client during initial consultation. Let's say the lawyer is competent, honorable and wants to give the prospective client an honest estimate regarding his chances for a positive outcome. This actually happens, really. The lawyer will try to accurately identify:

1. The object(s) of the conflict;
2. All rights and duties potentially at issue;
3. All interested identities of potential parties to the issue as they relate to each right and each duty (and the identities' agents and overlaps in identity membership and affinity);
4. Preferred and acceptable goals of each interested identity (and of the leadership agents of each identity);
5. Resources and capabilities that each of the identities can bring to bear on the issue (especially of the prospective client: Get the money up front!);
6. Jurisdictions (derived from the location of the objects, rights, parties, and courts);
7. Mechanisms of resolution (court, settlement, police, prayer) and rules;
8. Likely outcomes under a variety of circumstances; and
9. The likely costs and risks of distinct courses of action.

There aren't many 'simple' civil cases, and so this process goes on in one form or another, at varying levels of efficiency, thousands of times every day, and it generally leads to favorable results for someone, even if only for the lawyers.

The identities of the parties may be precise, like 'Cullen Barclay Demarest,' or they may be amorphous, such as 'theatergoers,' 'the environmentally responsible,' or 'patriots.' The membership of the identities can overlap, and members can enter and drop out of an identity at will, even whimsically. The significant identities exhibit some level of intent and resolve, however (this often depending on the quality of their leadership or agents), and one key to a useful analysis is to correctly match the objects at issue with the right identities, and the identities to their resolve, resources and objectives. If this is done well and quickly, it is then not so hard to determine jurisdiction, resolution mechanisms, chances for success either in settlement or trial, risks, costs and potential rewards. It is also easier to game the inevitable counterclaims and cross claims.

To best analyze property disputes, Hohfeld pointed out the relevant rights and duties were not derived from relationships between persons and things (like land or personal possessions) but between and among persons. Rights, according to Hohfeld, are formed by the nature of multiple interrelated relations among people. In this light it makes some sense that 'social contract' be understood as almost synonymous with 'property regime.' Terms like 'rule-of-law,' 'justice,' 'sustainability,' or 'peace,' fit comfortably within the meaning of the social contract and within Hohfeldian analysis. When contemplating and listing the 'objects' of a civil conflict, it is an easy shorthand to say, for instance, 'the lot at the northwest corner of 121st and Washington streets,' but the object is really a less tangible set of rights and duties, such as the right to exclusive use of that lot along with duties to pay taxes and keep it safe. We say that the thing is the object, but we are really talking about a concert of rights and duties that will be recognized by the rest of the community. That is what transforms the lot from being a mere thing into being property.

A similar process, with some adjustments, can be helpful for the analysis of armed conflicts of the type contemplated by this book. As to armed conflict, however, we'll add some elements to the question list.

> To number 5, resources and capabilities of the parties, for instance, we'll highlight the capability to maintain or dominate anonymity.
>
> To number 7, the mechanisms of resolution, we can add 'physical elimination of the enemy.'

> We could add a specific 10th question directed directly at sanctuaries and routes to and from sanctuaries, or we could consider physical sanctuaries as part of the jurisdictional problem contemplated by number 6.

Please note that this is a heuristic device. That means it is built for speed. It is supposed to assist your common sense in getting to some practical answer to a problem. It does not matter which of the categories of analysis you land on first -- the identities, the objects, the agents, etc. It also does not matter if they overlap a little. Keeping the identities consistent with their agents and understanding the real power of those agents *is* important. Section 64, *Measuring Power*, looks closer at the question of measuring power. After all, part of classic strategy is not engaging a stronger foe unless you have a secure route of escape. You don't want your measurements of strength to be faulty.

A country like Bolivia, with a constant, complicated internal struggle that includes competitive, overlapping identities, organized criminal activity, strong political parties, high regional income differentials, regionally specific international economic dependency, a politically astute population, and so on, is a laboratory of social conflict. We can usefully dissect that conflict by applying the Hohfeldian lawyer's laundry list suggested earlier. Part of it might look like the chart on the next page. A caution, however: Some institutions are infatuated with matrices -- so be careful it doesn't turn into a check sheet. The matrix below is a way of explaining the method, and if it helps you remember key questions to ask, that's good. It might even serve for the paragraphing of some sort of report or article. Checking boxes, however, can threaten thought.

| The Object of Conflict | Rights & Duties Disputed | Claimant Identities (Parties to Conflict) |
|---|---|---|
| hydrocarbons | Concession fees and royalty destinations (here will be a consideration of the pairings) | Central government party in power; Bolivian hydrocarbon companies in Santa Cruz; Petrobras from Brazil. |
| lithium | concessions, licenses | Local land owners in |
| path to the Pacific | Sovereign taxing rights, flagging | Bolivians generally, |
| tax authority | Central government | Political party |

| | authority to appraise and tax land | agency |
|---|---|---|
| Reparations | Peaceful enjoyment | Displaced Persons |
| Goals of the Contenders | Contender Capabilities | Where |
| Control reception and records of income from companies | Can overcome source locations with national army | Specific locations in Santa Cruz Department |
| ? | Controls anonymity using biometric census | ? |
| Resolution Mechanisms | Likely Outcomes | Costs and Risks |
| ? | ? | ? |

Depending on who 'we' are, however, the scale of our contemplation might be outsized in relation to our interests and power, or at least it might be too large a scale for efficiently dissecting the relevant interests and identities at play. The Department of Santa Cruz, Bolivia, for instance, might be an appropriate scale of analysis. Time is the other inescapable scale-setter. If we were to need final resolution of some issue within the period of a president's remaining term in office, the relevant objects, identities and goals would take a different form than if we were serenely planning the inheritance of our great grandchildren. In this regard, the fashionable term 'sustainability' seems to argue a lengthening of the time period for valid objectives. One of the common sources of self-delusion or confusion, and a technique for deceiving others, is the mismatch of practicable scales of time and space with proposed goals and rationales. You can always stump your opponent or yourself by lowering or rising to different scales in time, geography or concept.

A weakness inherent in many approaches to the analysis of human competition is insufficiency in identifying and locating the agents or brokers representing an identity to the conflict, or their sources of power, their ability to maintain anonymity, and the locations of their sanctuaries and routes thereto. Hohfeldian Analysis is vulnerable to criticism as a technique for irregular armed conflict because of the anonymity typically at play in armed struggle. The dispute environment in which Wesley Hohfeld proposed his formula was, and remains, one in which 'discovery' is enforced by the regime of laws, and in which public records can be made transparent if they are not already. The lawyers' environment is one in which all parties are forced to submit to a common information rule, and where unnamed entities rarely exist or where at least their agents are made known. Not being able to establish the identities, home ground and wealth of the competition identities and their agents precisely can make Hohfeldian Analysis hard to employ. This fact serves to highlight again the importance of *anonymity* as a central issue of irregular conflict. It also suggests another way to determine how well things are going in an insurgency or counterinsurgency. That is to say, if Hohfeldian Analysis cannot be effectively practiced, it is probably because anonymity reigns, in which case we can be sure that measures of qualities like the 'rule-of-law' or 'monopoly on the granting of impunity' are not going to look good for the government. In any case, consideration of an armed conflict using something like Hohfeldian Grievance Analysis will speed planners and leaders to reasonable appreciations more quickly than the application of PMESII (see Section 112, *DIME & PMESII*).

Hohfeld asserted that relationships among people regarding valuable things (land especially) could be paired as correlatives or as opposites. Hohfeld also insisted on the need for clarity and precision in the use of the language. Let's just say, however, that his pairings were not patently clear, and so we'll take the liberty to change those pairings a little in order to further our aims as to the analysis of armed conflict, as follows:

> **Correlatives:** Right/Duty; Privilege/Restriction; Power/Duty; Immunity/Liability

The pairings can be useful for testing the relationships associated with objects of contention. If you gain a right related to a piece of land, what are the duties and to whom do they belong? If you gain some power, such as to control who gets to take the SAT exam, what duties of fairness do you incur? If you win the privilege of serving as mayor, what restrictions does that place on the other aspirants? The same kinds of questions can be asked in relation to events in complex internal armed conflicts.

Adding one more twist to the process, we can apply a jurisprudential contribution of one of Hohfeld's contemporaries, Oliver Wendell Holmes, Jr. Holmes is credited with what is called 'legal pragmatism.' The gist of legal pragmatism is the idea that the duty owed as a result of making a contract is not to fulfill the contract, but rather to fulfill the contract *or* to pay the monetary consequences of not fulfilling it (often called damages). This was a big deal, a significant innovation, because it took away some of the sense of revenge and punishment in civil law, thus ameliorating the judgmental logic of morality, and replacing it with a practical, or pragmatic, sense of restitution or fairness. This is valuable to your analysis of grievances because it can offer an easier path to conflict resolution. It is not a universally understood or necessarily cross-cultural concept. In other words, the philosophy of justice with which you begin your analysis of a fight will also impose itself on the options you have for conflict resolution. You might have to teach legal philosophy.

See: 48, *Grading the Social Contract*; 109, *Hotspotting*; 68, *Scale*; 49, *Territorial Scrutiny*; 70, *Measuring Effects of Actions on Structure;* 112, *DIME & PMESII*; 40, *Rule-of-law*; and 13, *Puthukkudiyirippu.*

> "Common sense and a sense of humor are the same thing, moving at different speeds. A sense of humor is just common sense, dancing."
>
> William James[70]

Suffering is a price and a product offered

# *Section 54, Mercatus*

Economics is decidedly relevant to the cause and resolution of your war, but economic concerns are difficult to isolate from everything else. That said, there are four theoretical points that might be especially useful and are favored in this book, all related to markets. They are: 1. Transaction theory and peaceful conflict resolution; 2. Borrowing and speculation as causes of organized violence; 3. The certain existence of markets in things tangible and intangible (especially land), and; 4.The unlikelihood of beating the market through central planning. These four are themselves all intermixed, so the following text is not perfectly divided accordingly.

You cannot: separate the market from the world; separate the market from money; or separate armed conflict from the future value of money. Money is both a measurement and a promise. Stable, agreed-upon measurement is one of the original human inventions for conflict resolution, an accelerator of trade, and a creator of trust. When we talk of the future value of money, we are talking about gambling and speculation, or about investment. Some friend of yours may disdain commoditization, mercantilism, commercialism, and Bill Gates' cats.

That attitude will not succeed to separate markets from the environment of your irregular war; don't let it disjoin your study of markets from your understanding of that environment.

Financial debts created under duress might be called an extortion market or time-fused extortion. The fact that people take advantage of others' needs by creating untenable debts or charging usurious interest rates is the fuel for entire political philosophies, religious edicts, works of art, and revolutionary thinking. What is an ethical price for the current use of future value? What is one's ethical obligation to give of one's surplus, and what right should individuals have to decide where their surplus should go? Can central planners decide the best use of private surplus better than a free market? What right should an individual or group have to decide on the divestment of someone else's surplus?

If you are in charge of a military occupation, however (and 'occupier' might also be appropriate if you are an insurgent guerrilla leader) then the first question is whether or not you know who owes what to whom. If you pretend that there is no market for the current value of future wealth, you're lost. If you pretend that the lending of wealth for the purpose of investment is not happening or that it does not create resentments as well as appreciations and loyalties, you are likely mistaken. If you do not know if there is a collective identity of debtors and another of creditors, you may be missing an underlying factor of organized violence. If you do not know who has debts, who pays them and who collects them, you cannot be fully aware of the dynamics of violence.

It is not uncommon for some organizations to actively, purposefully create or promote a violent environment favorable for their investment. Shakespeare's Falstaff (*Henry IV, Part I*) says "you may buy land now as cheap as stinking mackerel." Falstaff, a swollen bag of dropsies, was looking forward to the bargains (not just in land, but in young maidens) that would present themselves due to the civil war passing through. The FARC, and its opposite, the AUC, would create geographies of fear and violence in order to suppress the market value of land, and then extort its sale.

Speculation about the future value of things, including money, is a frequent cause or catalyst of armed social conflict. A debt is often the product of a loan, interest accruing. People don't always want to pay up. Debts can take on sophisticated forms, too, like 'national' debts, worker pension plans or sub-prime mortgages, and it is common to create secondary markets for debts owed, and to provide secondary insurance for that debt, thus creating a speculative market regarding the payment.

This latter form of market is essentially a betting pool on whether or not the debt will be paid, and on whether or not the insurance will be paid if the original debtor doesn't pay. Other lenders will pay off (assume) debts now in return for a higher probability of payment, perhaps over a longer period. All this 'securitization' can be confusing, but essentially it is all about the future value of money now. Knowing all this, and that it is really not complicated, can be a great advantage to you in armed social conflict, but you have to start by understanding there is a market for important things, and that the first important thing is land. There is also sex, retribution, absolution, etc., but start with land. It tends to stay put.

There is always a market in land. You may want to suppose not, because the form of ownership and the nature of records may be unusual to you. A right to charge rents may be ecclesiastical or clan-based, or the rents paid in kind, labor or military service. If someone has the authority to determine a land-use, occupancy, or to exclude the presence of certain people on any areas of land -- those authorities and powers are rights in land. The rights and their exercise can be traded and almost always *are* traded. Any trading in the privileges associated with determining rights to passage, occupancy, free use and enjoyment, rents or the distribution or alienation of such rights and duties constitutes the market.

Find out all about the market in land. You can intervene in this market, changing debt relationships, thus changing the cost of future value now. In fact, if you are involved in an armed conflict in some way, you probably are changing the market in land whether you know it or not, so it behooves you to know how, and to at least have some control or initiative over it. It is an easy condition to test. If you do not know who controls or exercises basic rights and obligations regarding occupancy, rents, access, divestment, etc., of key pieces of terrain -- of any terrain -- then you are probably not aware of the conflict-consequences of your actions or those of anyone else. The inevitable result is your not being situated to take efficient measures, or anticipate unintended consequences of your work and presence.

Banking is a realm into which few soldiers enter, but where sophisticated forms of parasitism have long been known occur. Sometimes they cause a war. In the late 19th century, the government of Colombia began to use a combination of tax and monetary policies to divert an increasing share of the country's convertible wealth into the incumbent political party's coffers. Coffee growers, at least those of the opposing political party, were acutely aware of the profit their lands might earn in international markets, and how much they were losing to inflation and to taxes. They resented the forced cheapening of the local currency, matched by having to pay export taxes in stable dollars. The government's attempt to redirect the rents of private land, via banking, and without returning value through public works, was one of the underlying causes of a costly civil war.

'More absolution, less tithing' is not a slogan likely to gain converts to a new religion, at least according to one observant economist, Larry Iannaccone. The Marine Corps recruiter who tells high-schoolers that being a Marine is easy won't meet quota nearly as fast as the one who tells the kids "You're not good enough, go home, you're a weenie; if you don't want to get yelled at, humiliated, exhausted, ridiculed and abused, don't waste my time." The market for some things seems to go against logic, but it doesn't really. As Iannaccone observes, you just have to know what's being sold and bought. The Marine recruiter is gleaning for the candidate looking for challenge, camaraderie and honor. The Marines figure those prime recruits are especially not looking for comfort or efficiency. Honor is also in the mix for the Islamic radical. For the recruiter of the suicide bomber, the pitch includes existential meaning -- an answer to desperation and despair.

Few Colombian Catholics are going to commit suicide for a religious or political purpose, and especially not for seventy-two virgins. Aside from suicide being one of the mortal sins, sex between men and women is apparently a less guarded event in Medellín as compared to, say, Fallujah. Nevertheless, Pablo Escobar knew what the local cultural equivalent to Jihadist suicide looked like. He knew he could recruit a young man to go assassinate someone, even though to do so meant swift and certain (or rather, near certain death) for the assassin himself. The offer was to buy the young man's poverty-stricken mother a house, and to throw the boy a celebratory party. No shortage of takers. The parallels are easy to identify. They have to do with dignity, honor, hopelessness, disillusion, and are tied to territorial identity, local culture, and the future material value of current action. It seems that many Muslim fighters who volunteer for suicide missions are also aware of the material support likely to be bestowed on their families as a result of their sacrifice. Honorable death often leaves a residual of material benefit. It can create a form of debt.

At some point or other, you have been abused by thinkers who don't like market forces and consider them an over billed, false God of neoliberal capitalism, and a cynical justification of ethically undesirable outcomes. Some of that may be true, but if you so despise Adam Smith's invisible hand that you deny its presence and power in your thinking and plans, you will probably lose your war. Marxist revolutionaries, for instance, have often turned into some of the best, if most vicious capitalists. They want you to think the market is not happening, and that price is a fiction, while they work the market hard to their business advantage. Post-structuralism (the Zombie of Marxism-Leninism) argues that power flows throughout the social discourse, that all actors, to include perhaps even things, have immanent power that emerges in the context of specific events and struggles. Ethereal sounding, the economist might just call that same dynamic interplay of desires and influences the *market*; and might call *price* the market's way of measuring manifest power at a moment in time and place. For the purpose of winning your war, don't fall in love or hate with any academic discipline's way of explaining things, but definitely do not talk yourself out of the existence of markets and market mechanisms just because you like philosophers more than economists.

The great names in economics were, at any rate, almost all social philosophers. "...[T]hough the sole end which they propose from the labours of all the thousands whom they employ be the gratification of their own vain and insatiable desires, they divide with the poor the produce of all their improvements."[71] The quote is from Adam Smith, who was talking about unintended but beneficial consequences of a free market, and about the role of morality in all social dealings, including those most closely associated with money and trade. He was of course talking about the 'invisible hand' of the market, but the quotation is not from *An Inquiry into the Nature and Causes of the Wealth of Nations* but rather from *The Theory of Moral Sentiments*, which was published some two decades earlier, in 1759.

Unintended consequences always seem to tide in when a government bureaucrat or politician supplants the priest or hacienda owner as philanthropist or patron. Among the unintended consequences are those related to the generalized payment of what some people call the 'social debt' -- a debt supposedly owed by the more powerful to the less powerful. People don't always recognize a debt, or want to pay the debts they do recognize, and creditors naturally get anxious when they feel some debt is due. The radical activist advises the downtrodden not to ask for what is rightfully due, but to demand it. Some government ratifies such social debts, reinforcing the idea that payment is due, will be taken from the rich debtors, and paid to the poor. In the process, the government often collects from the supposed social debtors, pockets a handsome commission for the service, and makes the population of supposed creditors wait patiently in line for the rest of their lives.

How you define this basic question of credit and charity (spiritual, social, and personal debt) may come to backstop the approach you take to your irregular war responsibilities. You might dutifully repeat the notion that the government (a government that you might *be*) is justly measured in accordance with the services it provides. Good luck with that; the list of services demanded can expand fast, and a population that is given much might produce little.

Speculation and debt are under-considered causes of organized violent conflict. They are all traded in markets, and there is also always a market for land, the most important object of desire. Know the markets -- for souls, money and especially land.

See: 61, *Who Sins More?*; 65, *Smuggling*; 46, *Taxation and Debt*; 74, *Refugees and Displaced Persons*; 19, *Extortion*; 83, *Conflict Geography*; 3, *The Domesday Book*; and 72, *Land Strategy*.

> "The King of England brought seven dollars, and his prime minister nine; whereas the king was easily worth twelve dollars and I easily worth fifteen. But that is the way things always go; if you force a sale on a dull market, I don't care what the property is, you are going to make a poor business of it...."
>
> Hank in Mark Twain's,
> *Connecticut Yankee in King Arthur's Court*[72]

Giving memory a boost

# *Section 55, The Statute of Frauds*

(Adapted from *Property & Peace*)

In 1677, the English Parliament passed the Statute of Frauds, which would survive to become one of the most durable instruments in English-speaking law. More than just a convenience for the court, it was a moment of recognition that physical technologies, and persons who could put them to use, were available in sufficient quantity that they could be applied to thwart human dishonesty. From that point on, any important agreement in the realm (anything dealing with land was considered important) would have to be in writing if it were to be recognized and enforced by the State. Later, agreements would have to be signed, then witnessed, then notarized, then copied, photocopied, distributed and even put on the Internet. All of the requirements go to the same end -- to make evidence more reliable and court decisions more effective. Subornation, perjury, contempt, and vigilantism are more likely contained, and systems of commitments can span beyond human memory and familial control. The jurisprudential event of 1677 was a milestone in the evolution of an innovative discipline that had not been so formally appreciated since the time of the Romans. The simple rejection of oral evidence became a competitive advantage of Western civilization. The West systematically prepared the legal environment for peaceful conflict resolution. That the pen is mightier than the sword is more than shibboleth. The importance of this cultural inheritance may have been overlooked, forgotten or taken for granted, but it is a key to peace. The requirement that the evidence of human agreements be precise, comprehensive and transparent is much of what makes life in your county peaceable. It is what keeps so many of today's practical geographers to work at the county courthouse or office of the city manager. There they maintain ownership maps, land-use plans and the like. If not for such records, their maintenance and the courts and markets that apply them, we would live in a world of possession by force -- a continual physical struggle.

Useful public records are created through innovative mixes of law and physical technology, like the statutes of fraud. Those innovations respond to an observation about human nature -- that humans tend naturally toward territoriality, lying, and violence. Some political philosophies (which I lump together as post-structuralism) argue that the whole idea of human nature is itself a human invention; that there is no basic human nature of territoriality, lying and violence; and that the innovations of the White, European, Christian, male-dominated structure (maps, property, statutes, guns) are contemptible tools that service and motivate neocolonialism, imperialism, neoliberalism, and racism. Wars, according to this view, are not caused by human nature, but rather by the social construct that all these other things built and protect. It is a philosophy that counsels against your application of the central, proven innovations for building peace. The single greatest innovation for conflict resolution -- property -- is despised by post-structuralism because it works.

See: 72, *Land Strategy*; 25, *Why Humans Don't Fight*; 100, *What the Foucault*; 40, *Rule-of-law*; 54, *Mercatus*; 108, *Neogeography*; 64, *Measuring Power*; and 48, *Grading the Social Contract*.

---

**Lt. DeBuin**: How many are watching?
**Ke-Ni-Tay**: One man see as many as ten.
**Lt. DeBuin**: Can we find him and kill him?
**Ke-Ni-Tay**: You cannot.
**Lt. DeBuin**: But Ke-Ni-Tay can?
**Ke-Ni-Tay**: nods yes.
**Lt. DeBuin**: But will he?
**Ke-Ni-Tay**: Ke-Ni-Tay sign paper. Ke-Ni-Tay soldier.
**Lt. DeBuin**: All right. Find him and kill him.

From the movie
*Ulzana's Raid* (1972)[73]

Self-defense units, paramilitaries, vigilantes…

# *Section 56, Militias and Gun Control*

Here *militias* represents an entire set of armed groups that aren't national armies, gendarmeries, police or national guards, and aren't necessarily anti-government insurgent armed forces or criminal gangs, either. That may seem a long list of what militias might not be, but the naming conventions can include paramilitaries, community self-defense forces, private armies, private guard forces, tribal militias, political party armed wings, vigilantes, and posses. All the names and definitions are contextual, overlap, and are subject to imperfect translations. Whatever these less formal armed forces are called, they can change the face of an irregular war and change prospects for the success of any of the players. Notably, the framers of the Constitution of the United States used the word *militia*, and used it in the same paragraph as *arms* (firearms), closely associating the two with an essential political right.

Don't be diverted by debate about whether or not militias can be effective against insurgents or criminal bands. They can be. They might also *become* the insurgent or criminal bands. Any debate will depend for its logic on local situational variables, but the bottom line is that when it comes to the question of whether to design, create and employ irregular forces, all sides of an irregular war *will* consider it.

The fact that there are so many names and organizational formulae for militia is hint enough toward a method for categorizing, evaluating and treating these organizations. Don't do so according to their name. You don't have to call anything a militia, but there are a number of characteristics that demarcate the interest you will take in militia-like organizations. A number of other notes in this book cover the pertinent characteristics of armed forces and the milestones of armed conflict. You will recognize some of them in the discussion below.

Foremost is the question of impunity. Let's say for the sake of fluidity that you represent a national State. You want to know if some militia under consideration is able to grant impunity to members of its force. If the militia can grant impunity independent of your grant, then you have a problem. If, on the other hand, you can arrest and punish members of the militia, including its commander, then that militia is part of your armed forces, and you might be responsible for its actions. How you delimit its missions, territories, obligations, armament, and recruiting is of interest, of course, and is in no way a mystery. If, on the other hand, the militia can grant protection to its members from punishment by your government, you might want to ask the following four questions:

1. Is the militia leadership able to convey some sort of immunity to its people for violent acts in accordance with some form of written social contract such as articles of confederation or a hierarchical system of sovereignty that limits the types of actions for which immunity can be granted? In other words, maybe the members of the militia enjoy some sort of immunity apart from what would be granted by the central government, but it is limited within a known geographic space, or only applies to certain kinds of acts or categories of person. Instead, the militia might enjoy impunity because of some written or unwritten negotiation or treaty-like agreement that your State acceded to because the militia in question was strong enough to force it, or because you wanted that militia's help to defeat some other armed force. It happens all the time, even in the context of major wars, e.g. the Sicilian mafia and its dealings with the United States government during World War II.

2. What are the militia's obligations and authorities? Is it required to muster and deploy if there is a natural disaster? Are its members obliged to serve warrants, or chase a criminal *in flagrante delicto*? Can they implement dead-or-alive orders such that they do not have to attempt capture and arrest? Do they have formal geographic limitations or otherwise observe jurisdictional or territorial boundaries outside of which they do not go? If so, you will want to know exactly why, because the answer might form the basis of a method for your re-asserting control over it later.

3. How hard is this bunch? Levels of ruthlessness and resolve often come into play when dealing with a militia. What is it, by the nature of its membership, willing to do? The platoon chasing Rambo in the movie *First Blood* might be about average for a militia. That comedic militia was willing to shoot at Rambo, but not if doing so entailed any danger.

4. Finally, there is the mundane and sordid question of how rich the militia is. Does it have its own trucks? Transportation forms half of Maguire's operational synthesis, and if the members all have to walk, it is not the same kind of militia as the volunteer force of private pilots and plane owners that helped the Guatemalan Army during the 1980s. The other half of Maguire's formula is about battle strength. How much machinegun ammunition can the militia get or carry?

These are the four big questions (impunity/authorities and obligations/resolve/wealth), but the militias theme is better divided into two parts. One is legalistic and turns almost completely on the question of who can grant impunity, and for what acts. That part relates directly to State success. The observation about impunity implies that you seek a complete understanding of the legal framework within which a militia exists, to include what flexibility you have to influence the laws or other rules that limit the militia in terms of leadership, territorial powers and obligations. If what you confer is the only immunity or impunity the commander and personnel of a militia are likely to enjoy, then it is your militia and its actions are probably your responsibility. The other part is the practical one revolving around what the militia can do for you, independent of the impunity question. That part can be tallied according to the last three questions about the militia's obligations and authorities, its psychological hardness, and its material capacity.

OK, the question was just divided into four parts, then put back into two parts and now we will try three parts: A local militia might be an autochthonous organization (locally birthed and not created by the central state as an extension of its power), or it might have been created by an outside entity, but the challenge for the State regarding a militia can almost always be divided as follows: (1) how to maintain its discipline and loyalty, (2) what to specify as its missions and mission parameters, and (3) how to get rid of it when it is no longer needed or goes bad.

To maintain discipline there are some tried and true aids. One is recordkeeping. Another is control of material sustenance. Another is co-opting or extorting its leaders. Training and indoctrination can also help a little. Section 49, *Territorial Scrutiny*, mentions imbrication and tessellation. Correct tessellating (assuring clear, non-overlapping administrative boundaries) and imbricating (assuring an overlap of identity) can be useful. If you do not maintain discipline of a militia, it will obtain its own power to grant impunity and it will become part of your State's failure. Even in a condition of pure challenge to the State, however, a militia can be of assistance in defeating another State enemy. There is little doubt that the United Self-Defense Forces of Colombia (AUC), for instance, became a tremendous problem for the National Liberation Army (ELN) guerrilla in some locales. Meanwhile, as the AUC grew in power, it also grew in its capacity to defy the Colombian government. Eventually the Colombian government had to defeat and dismantle the AUC.

The missions and parameters you give to a militia should be limited geographically if at all possible, and specific rules of engagement delivered and explained. Militias can be immensely useful in a conflict that features many roadblocks and checkpoints. Your government's (or maybe your insurgent movement's, if you are the insurgent) monopoly over the granting of impunity should be made explicit and proven at early opportunities. The militia's mission types and territorial limits should be clearly expressed in terms of the impunity. In other words, if one of your militias has a member operating outside its designated territorial space, you want to have the militia itself punish the infraction, and if it does not, you will probably want to punish the commander of the militia. Such a move can entail a price in loyalty and effectiveness, however, so you will have some weighing to do in relation to every militia.

Technically-identified militias, such as civil air patrols, can be very useful and easy to control because they depend for their existence on outside deliverables such as fuel, and their activities are easy to monitor. One of the tricks to creating effective militias is control of their initial identity and role. Weapon types are consequential. You cannot make an arrest with a mortar, nor can an armed unit that does not have indirect fires compete against an enemy unit that does. If you are going to deny indirect weapons (or other crew-served weapons) to a militia as a control measure, for instance, you might want to assure that, if necessary, you can provide timely artillery cover. If not, you are setting up for some kind of failure. The introduction of un-occupied armed aerial vehicles (UAAV) complicates the matter.

If a militia defies the central State's asserted monopoly on the granting of impunity, the State might have to fight militia as it would any other insurgent organization. Autochthonous militias more likely to form where the State (via either the central government or some subordinate or affinity government) is not providing the service of conflict resolution and justice, especially as those terms apply to questions of land and trespass on land. If the State is not present in the land/trespass equation (if the government cannot effect legal eviction), the result historically and universally is violent self-help. When no effective property regime defends the lines of land ownership, the almost certain result is devolution to a condition of possession by force. Unless your government or the society through some working division of obligations and authorities provides a service of eviction of trespassers, you will more than waste your time with a decree that there be no militias. Such a decree will be worse than idle. Not only will militias form, they will do so out of resignation to the fact that your government is not adequate. The militia will form in a context of disrespect to your State. It will be born with a need to grant impunity to its members and with a need to organize surreptitiously for the use of armed force.

Once a militia begins to use force, it will harden. So, although a decision to form militias must be tempered by the fact that disciplining militias entails high risk, keep in mind that militias will form where the State does not provide property conflict resolution. If militias do not form even though a *de jure* government is not providing property services, it is probably because those services are being provided by an insurgent or organized criminal. Some anti-State group is probably now sovereign over that land. That is State failure.

Debate about militias is tied to debate over gun control, and to the issue of autochthony. Gun control is a visceral issue for many Americans. The founding fathers of the American republic decided on language in the US Constitution that tied citizens' right to bear arms to a co-relationship between a free State and a 'regulated militia.' Nobody at the time supposed that the militia they had in mind would be regulated by the central government, however. The militia was conceived as all able-bodied males and the regulation they had in mind was locally autochthonous. Many of the American revolutionaries felt that political power grew out the barrel of a gun, and that the technology of firearms was singularly significant to the experiment in liberty.

Rounding up all the weapons seems to be an historically popular measure for governments and occupation forces to take when they set out to pacify or bring stability to an area. It is what the Romans did in Britannia. However, a generalized condition of gunlessness can make extortion of a local population by insurgents or organized criminals easier. Numerous indigenous villages in Colombia have found that out. Militias that are truly autochthonous, meanwhile, are likely to seek independent sources of weaponry.

More weapons in private hands can also challenge a government that improperly grants impunity to itself. If a government, especially a local government, does not have a monopoly on the use of force, but grants its own agents improper levels of impunity, that government faces a formula for effective insurgency, or for suffering discipline from some outside entity.

If you do a good job of organizing local militia, the militia may end up being called the police. If you do a really good job organizing local militia, they not only end up policing, they will not grant themselves impunity for violent acts. If you are insurgent or counterinsurgent, your success may well be tied to the formation of militias, whether they are formed by a central government or autochthonous -- and tied to that formation is the question of who gets guns and where they come from.

A State's monopoly on the use of coercive force is not as great an element in State failure as the monopoly on granting impunity. Either wider or more restricted dispersion of lethal tools might help a State maintain unity and control over the granting of impunity, depending on other factors.

See: 45, *Police or Military*; 82, *Conflict Thresholds*; 44, *Political/Military/Administrative*; 19, *NGOs and Unions*; 138, *Roadblocks and Checkpoints*; 49, *Territorial Scrutiny*; 2, *Anonymity*; and 85, *Gun Control.*

---

"Who has seen a militia without weapons?"

Hugo Chávez[74]

Dogs are heroes; mules are mules

# *Section 57, Dogs and Mules*

Dogs are good people. There are bad dogs, and for those of you who don't believe in the concept of human nature or dog nature, consider at least if it is possible to build a social construct for bad dogs. In the sixteenth century the Spanish created the Canary Island Hound, a vicious canine used to threaten, scatter and tear apart indigenous villages and villagers in the Americas. But those aren't our dogs. Our dogs find people buried in the rubble, check luggage for drug shipments, find landmines even if there is no metal in them, and protect our bunker from rats. In the context of irregular war, dogs are generally counterinsurgent, but with the right indoctrination and some rib roast, they could be insurgent.

It is good to have a plan for the treatment and employment of canines, and, depending on the human cultures involved, to make evident their alliance and care. No insurgency or counterinsurgency was ever won or lost on the basis of canines; canines are no 'center of gravity,' but, again, they are good people. In Colombia, the government army and police have used dogs extensively for mine clearing, drug sniffing and victim recovery.

Mules and other beasts of burden (mules get to represent the set) may or may not be endearing, but their care and application lie closer to the nub of winning and losing, at least in the context of active insurgency. A 'demobilized' FARC guerrilla leader related to the author that mules were an integral part of FARC logistics and operational movement. For years it was puzzling and reassuring to the guerrillas that the Colombian army disdained the use of *bestias*. The guerrillas, meanwhile, maintained sizeable units dedicated to animal husbandry and pack-loading. The mule provided a means to transport mortar components too heavy for the individual guerrilla fighters. They also changed the formula of speed and distance when the government units were pursuing them in rough terrain, which Colombia has. The mule was a significant element in the strategic math of creating advantage in aggregate culminating points. The landmine was an extremely influential to this same end, but mule-handling was also a technology that gave the guerrilla an ability to gain separation from pursuing army units. The culminating points of army units in contact were shortened by landmines and those of the guerrillas lengthened by mules. While a simplification to be sure, in general this is a formula that worked hundreds of times over.

Search for applicable technologies that change weights of the variables in the operational equation, most of which has something to do with movement, time, distance and weight. The Colombian State sought the help of dogs, who have given their lives in combat and have been honored for their service. FARC snipers have shot many dogs trying to sniff out landmines. The government, however, had until recently been less astute than the FARC in the use of animals that could change advantage in operational art, this in spite of Juan's *bestia* Conchita radiant on the national coffee symbol. By the way, dogs often make heroic sacrifices, but never commit suicide. Mules, on the other hand, have been known to shoot themselves in the head.

See: 116, *Strategy of Aggregate Tactics*; 140, *Culminating Point in the Pursuit*; 8, *The Operational Equation*; 95, *Childhood*; 63, *Cost-Distance*; 84, *Cultures of Violence*; 31, *Holes in the Ground*; and 41, *Whereabouts*.

---

"Well! The last to go will see the first three go before her.
And her little dog, too."

Wicked Witch of the West in the movie
*The Wizard of Oz* (1939)[75]

ثورة جزائرية: Worst counterinsurgency ever?

# *Section 58, Guerre d'Algérie*

On November 1, 1954, the Front du Liberation Nationale (National Liberation Front, FLN), launched the 'day of insurrection' against France's sovereignty in Algeria. That day become a fabled milestone in, if not the start of the Algerian resistance and independence movement. Charles de Gaulle pronounced Algeria an independent country on July 3, 1962. France lost over half of its territory, and the lowest estimated death tolls from the war claim around 350,000 dead. Otherwise, it was a disaster. The constitution of France was replaced, military mutinies mounted, and millions of persons displaced. The history of French Algeria is one of insurgent victory and near total counterinsurgent failure. Dedicated insurgents and counterinsurgents do well to study French experience in Algeria. Here is a very brief English-language bibliography on a subject worthy of its own course:

•Alexander and Keiger, *France and the Algerian War 1954-1962: Strategy, Operations and Diplomacy*;

•Aussaresses, *The Battle of the Casbah: Counter-Terrorism and Torture*;

•Chaliand, *Guerrilla Strategies: An Historical Anthology from the Long March to Afghanistan*;

•Galula, *Pacification in Algeria, 1956-1958*;

•Horne, *A Savage War of Peace*;

•Johnson, "Algeria: Some Problems of Modern History" (*Journal of African History, v, 2, (1964), pp. 221-242*);

•O`Balance, *The Algerian Insurrection 1954-1962*;

•Shrader, *The First Helicopter War: Logistics and Mobility in Algeria, 1954-1962*;

•Stora, *Algeria 1830-2000*;

•Talbott, *The War Without a Name: France in Algiers, 1954-1962*;

•Trinquier, *Modern Warfare*;

•Wall, *France, The United States and the Algerian War.*

Maybe we can derive some military operational lessons from the civil-political or socio-psychological ones. As for the latter (given French objectives, the moral balance, and the abysmal results) the case of French Algeria seems to present all bad examples, and only a few related to operational military matters are especially positive. Among successful French counterinsurgent operational innovations, however, are their use of the helicopter, territorial barriers, detailed census records, and the creation of anonymous reporting systems. The use of militias and of propaganda seem to have had mixed results.

The French also recognized how central to the conflict questions of land-use and ownership equities were, including inequitable relationships between ownership rights and tax burdens. Recognizing is not the same as doing something, however. The French did not do enough to change the basic unfairness of the Algerian social contract, or at least failed to change perceptions of inequality. Even though it recognized severe inequities, the French government did not make decisions or implement enough changes to quell insurgent energy. This central feature of the Algerian case -- that real estate ownership and taxation matters were basic issues to be resolved -- might serve as a guiding lesson for almost every internal conflict.

The French military had earlier absorbed a defeat in Indochina. Their recent failure had been built on disrespect for their North Vietnamese enemy, and on disregard for the basic lesson of classic military strategy. Dien Bien Phu became a place from which there was no route of withdrawal in the face of an enemy who grew to have a four-to-one firepower advantage.[76] Dien Bien Phu was indeed an historically decisive battle, booting French colonial power out of Indochina. The Algeria challenge, however, was closer, much more important to Paris, and the results far worse.

The Algerian War naturally draws attention today, given that the principal insurgent identity was Islamic, and the counterinsurgent a western power with an apparent technological, logistical and financial advantage. Algerian physical geography also seems similar to Iraq's in that it features a dominant urban area surrounded by a harsh hinterland. Passing these similarities, the differences are considerable. Physically, the aggregate logistical distances challenging France in Algeria were one-tenth what the United States faces in the Middle East or Southwest Asia. Moreover, the cultural barriers to effective French counter-insurgency (especially the language barrier) were not nearly as severe for the French in Algeria.

French objectives were also inherently different than anything the United States has or is likely to have anywhere. The French government and people, and most of the people of northern Africa and the world, believed Algeria to be part of France proper. The French government's aim, at least at the outset, was to maintain its sovereign territorial status. Today, American goals in whatever theater are unlikely to include the protection of long-established settlements of Americans inside US borders. The American Southwest might someday make for an interesting exception.

Because counterinsurgent operational plans should be linked to strategic objectives, some significance attaches to differences or commonalities of purpose in overall national strategies. That is to say, because the geographic relationships and national strategic objectives were so radically different for the French in the 1950s as compared to the Americans in the 21st century, it would require quite a logic stretch to apply the Algeria experiences to United States overseas operations. Algeria is frequently mentioned in US military curricular materials, however, prompting the following observations:

**Torture**. The French used systematic torture, which some, like Paul Aussaresses, have since justified. The United States manual *Counterinsurgency* is explicit, repetitive, emphatic and unequivocal about the illegality and immorality of using torture. A typical sentence on the subject in that manual states, "Torture and cruel, inhuman, and degrading treatment is never a morally permissible option, even if lives depend on gaining information. No exceptional circumstances permit the use of torture and other cruel, inhuman, or degrading treatment." The fact that US manuals seem to dote on French operational experiences in Algeria should not be taken as a ratification of the French officers' attitudes toward interrogations and interrogation techniques.

The application of torture and terror is presented by French military writers as a factor in whatever success they think they achieved. Another simple fact is that just a few years after the French military withdrew, it was clear that they had achieved nothing positive. The link between the two (French ruthlessness and their strategic failure) is not necessarily causal. Several other factors are implicated in the French defeat. Nevertheless, in a final section of *Pacification in Algeria*, David Galula lists what he considers the three principal causes of failure in the execution of counterinsurgent strategy in Algeria. One of these three he says was "lack of firmness toward the population."[77] In this regard, Galula apparently advises that…"it is necessary to punish in exemplary fashion the rebel criminals we have caught…The Rebels' flagrant crimes must be punished immediately, mercilessly, and on the very spot where they took place."[78] I seriously doubt that the spectacular French loss was due to their coddling of the rebels or the population, and I believe this remarkable assertion by Galula indicts his mindset. This kind of language, by the way, does not appear in his derivative *Counterinsurgency Warfare*.

**Psychological warfare**. Some French planning officers stressed psychological operations designed to wrest control of the civilian population from the enemy (meaning generally the FLN). According to Jorge Verstrynge (see Section 98, *Jorge Verstrynge and Pio Moa*) many of the French officers favoring psychological operations were influenced both by Goebbels and by Soviet doctrine, or by Marx himself. Verstrynge mentions the 1938 work *Viol des foules par la propagande politique*, (Rape of the Masses through Propaganda) by Serge Tchakhotine. Apparently that book appeared in a new French edition in 1952. Roger Trinquier (*Modern Warfare*) participated in a counterpoint or complementary current to the French enthusiasm for psychological operations. Trinquier defined the Algerian war as a clash of systems -- political, economic, psychological, and military. Trinquier, like most of the pro-psychological operations thinkers, instructed that the support of the civilian population was the *sine qua non* of victory; that, taking from Mao, it was as important to the combatant as water to fish. For Trinquier, popular support had to be spontaneous, and terrorism an effective technique for inspiring spontaneous support.

**Population control**. The importance placed on organizing the civilian population led Trinquier to criticize exclusively psychological methods. He saw it necessary to dismantle the political-administrative structures of the enemy, and then to build similar, affinity organizations. Such work could take place concurrently with psychological activities, but the goal was to control movement and infiltration. In ratification of his thinking, the French high command authorized Trinquier to deploy the Dispositive du Protection Urbaine (DPU, Urban Protection Detail) in the Algerian capital. Jorge Verstrynge writes in his book *La Guerra Periférica y el Islam Revolucionario*,

> "DPU operations were based on a tactic of population classification, using coordinated neighborhood volunteers who contributed information about the goings-on of these areas. Within this system, each house was given a number, which was the equivalent of a record containing the number of inhabitants, profession, etc., by which it was possible to control any kind of change. To a certain extent, the DPU became the French equivalent of the Organisation Politique-Administrative (OPA, Political Administrative Organization) of the FLN, although this organization invented by Trinquier -- which was commonly referred to as *the GPU* in reference to the Soviet political police -- did not generate any kind of economic funding. Proof of the system's effectiveness came after information provided by DPU members led to the arrest of Ben M'hidi, one of the FLN's leaders in the battle of Algiers."[79]

It seems that operational theories adopted by the French officers, in conjunction with disillusionment with Paris politics, emboldened them to consider themselves legitimate fonts and representatives of political power. Perhaps because things political and ideological were woven into the new counterinsurgency theory as part-and-parcel of the war effort, it was natural that the officers would begin to assign themselves political and ideological roles and responsibilities. It seems these new 'military' responsibilities had spread from the informational and administrative requirements of occupation. Some officers considered expropriating large colonists' agricultural properties to redistribute them as part of a kind of national communism. Many officers ended up participating in mutinies against the government of France.

**Galula or Trinquier?** (Some of this material was repeated in the **July-August,** 2010 *Military Review* article 'Let's Take the French Algeria Experience Out of US Army Doctrine.') A brief 1965 book review in *International Affairs* of both Trinquier's *Modern Warfare* and Galula's *Counterinsurgency Warfare* (both were first published in English in 1964) favors Galula's work, asserting that "Mr. Galula has a much wider view of the problem, partly no doubt because his professional experience is wider."[80] The reviewer also supposes for his readers that Trinquier, having first published his book in French in 1961, may have at that time still held false hope that the war offered a positive conclusion for the French. Available biographic information about Trinquier and Galula, however, indicates that Trinquier was older, more experienced, a more prolific writer and much more widely known than Galula. Alistair Horne, in his 1977 *A Savage War of Peace* (widely considered a seminal English-language work on the subject) indexes Trinquier heavily, but Galula not at all. Jean Lartéguy apparently modeled characters in his novels after Trinquier, but it is unknown if the life or experiences of Galula impressed that author at all. It is hard to believe that Trinquier and Galula were not familiar with each other, and especially that Lieutenant Colonel Galula was not perfectly aware of Colonel Trinquier, at the time a chief of intelligence in Algeria. Still, Galula, although he almost undoubtedly read Trinquier's *Modern Warfare* before working on his own 1963 *Pacification in Algeria* (from which his less-revealing *Counterinsurgency Warfare* was then derived), does not cite Trinquier in either of his own works. The curious absence of citation by Galula to Roger Trinquier invites us to consider professional jealousy, personal differences, or a rule of silence (in view of possibly feared prosecution) as reasons.

Regardless of the interpersonal or professional relationship of the two Frenchmen, it is not reasonable to assert that Galula's writing is more reflective of French military thinking about Algeria than Trinquier's. Galula seems to take a less brazen stance in favor of the use of torture and terror for breaking into the cellular organization of the Algerian insurgency, but maybe Galula was just coyer. Note for instance, his comment, "Under the pressure of a press campaign against "tortures" (in my [Galula's] view 90 percent nonsense and 10 percent truth), a special unit was created in the fall of 1957 under the name of D.O.P."[81]

In *Pacification*, Galula offers some basic laws, or principles, of counterinsurgency, to replace the classic ones, as follows:

> 1) The objective is the population
>
> 2) The support of the population is not spontaneous. It can be obtained only by a minority among the population that supports the counterinsurgent
>
> 3) A pro-counterinsurgent minority among the population will emerge, but only if the counterinsurgent is seen as the ultimate victor. An early success is necessary
>
> 4) Effort must be concentrated area-by-area. "Which side threatens the most, and which offers the most protection?"[82]

Like Trinquier, Galula intones that the counterinsurgent should dominate the psychology of fear, so even his easy advice about the importance of psychological operations is overshadowed by uncertainty regarding exactly what messages he felt should be sent by those operations. It is not clear from the English literature what is meant by his principle number 4 in the above list. Did Galula imply, as Trinquier made explicit, that the counterinsurgent must present himself to the population as a more palpable and certain physical menace than the insurgent?

The Algerian armed struggle is a nutritious episode for any student of insurgency and counterinsurgency. It should be approached cautiously and from several angles. The French did not do well. Either the French lost because of something they did, or in spite of what they did. Only a few activities fall clearly into the latter category. These include the use of the helicopter, careful inventorying of the population and geography, the construction of border barriers, and the organization of neighborhood watch organizations. In the not good category we can put systematic torture, terrorizing of the public, and failure to make property ownership equitable.

This book bangs into the word *strategy* from a number of different angles. On the one hand, it insists that classic principles of military strategy (operational art) apply mightily in irregular war. In this regard the French military commanders did what they could to lengthen the distances to friendly units' culminating points, confound enemy lines of communication, and contain the enemy's movement options. The lesson of Dien Bien Phu had been learned. The significance of *anonymity* is a related highlight. The French were attentive and industrious to reduce insurgent anonymity.

The following, insightful text comes from Edgar O'Ballance's *The Algerian Insurrection*:

> The barriers on the Algerian frontiers were a far greater success than has been realized. Publicity was usually given to the few insurgents and small quantities of arms that got through, but less was said about the thousands of armed and trained ALN soldiers who were forced to remain in helpless idleness because they were physically unable to enter Algeria.
>
> Although claiming, and at times practicing, a right of pursuit over the frontiers, the French stuck to the rules -- ...Not enough is made of French restraint in this matter. Such an action (pursuit of the ALN across the national borders) might have caused international repercussions, but it would probably also have destroyed the conventional part of the ALN....[83]

O'Ballance and others also point to Charles de Gaulle's resolve to let Algeria go as an ultimately decisive ingredient in the French loss. Therefore, in light of four huge things: the immense operational impact of a simple physical innovation like the border barrier; failure to attack the enemy army concentrated in its nearby sanctuaries; inattention to land and tax inequity; and (perhaps the trump) that the senior political leader resolved to not win the war -- in light of these huge things, what relative weight should we assign to arguments about the efficacy of psychological operations aimed at parts of the population?

Another issue might be the overall strength of French counterinsurgency forces in-theater. French counterinsurgent troop numbers (It is not clear who-all to count, but probably European-France-originated troops, French Foreign Legionnaires, Francophone Algerian police, etc.) seem to have been at least several hundred thousand.

The *Guerre d'Algérie* didn't only leave us positive lessons in military operational art along with negative lessons in overall counterinsurgency; it fueled left-leaning resistance philosophies, centered in France, that all but formalized anti-Americanism.

Please see sections: 73, *Property and the Social Contract*; 125, *Human Rights*; 3, *The Domesday Book*; 91, *Forts and Walls*; 48, *Grading the*

*Social Contract*, 105, *Genocide Geography*; 2, *The Line of Retreat*; and 100, *What the Foucault?*

---

> "You don't understand our mentality -- the French officer mentality. At first, we lose in Second World War. I don't say that you Americans win, but we lose. In Dien Bien Phu, we lose. In Algeria, we lose. In Indochina, we lose. But here, we don't lose. This piece of earth, we keep it. We will never lose it, never!"
>
> Hubert in the movie
> *Apocalypse Now* (1979)[84]

Rare, but technology helps

# *Section 59, Spontaneity*

Spontaneous public action, in favor of one side or another in an armed contest, is an ideal, more urban legend than historical phenomenon. Maybe it happens, but it is rare. Most of the time in most places, peoples' actions are organized, fomented and directed by nameable leaders. Here is a famous episode in Mark Twain's *The Adventures of Huckleberry Finn* in which Colonel Sherburn faces down a mob that has come to his home, ostensibly to lynch him.

> "'Why don't your juries hang murderers? Because they're afraid the man's friends will shoot them in the back, in the dark -- and it's just what they WOULD do. So they always acquit; and then a MAN goes in the night, with a hundred masked cowards at his back and lynches the rascal....You didn't want to come. The average man don't like trouble and danger. YOU don't like trouble and danger. ...But a mob without any MAN at the head of it is BENEATH pitifulness. Now the thing for YOU to do is to droop your tails and go home and crawl in a hole. If any real lynching's going to be done it will be done in the dark, Southern fashion; and when they come they'll bring their masks, and fetch a MAN along. Now LEAVE -- and take your half-a-man with you' -- tossing his gun up across his left arm and cocking it when he says this."[85]

Mark Twain tells us that the courage of a crowd and most of the individuals in it is derived from its leaders. Lenin criticized what he called the cult of spontaneity. He believed the great problems of history had to be resolved by force, and that meant a militant organization, and that meant leaders. Today, myriad post-structural activists may halfheartedly distance their philosophizing from Lenin's, but regarding this insistence on the necessity of a vanguard they remain constant. The proletariat might sometimes just up and do something, but for that something to induce class struggle, it must be directed. Much of leadership in armed conflict is 'encouragement' and the amelioration or control of fear. This aspect of human nature can be adjusted in the short term by alcohol, drugs or enthrallment. In the longer term anonymity helps, as does superior firepower. Training and indoctrination is a proven tool, and engagement with the courage of a leader is heralded in literature and art. Not all groups have a 'fearless leader,' even while leaders invariable are so-called. There are few psychological operations more effective than convincing a mass following that their fearless leader is actually a coward. Although spontaneity of action is rare, spontaneous dissipation of mass action is common. After a crowd is panicked or disheartened, whether by gas canisters in a plaza or by exposure on an Internet chat forum, followship is hard to regenerate.

In January 2008, Carlos Andrés Santiago, a 22-year old pharmacy student, initiated a march against kidnapping and against the FARC guerrillas. The result was a protest march of more than four million persons against the leftist revolutionaries, an odd event given that mass action was supposed to be the domain and purview of popular leftist movements. It must have been disconcerting for leaders of the FARC to witness the new technologies of globalization being used to turn the vehicles of concientization and public mobilization against them.

There exists what might be called a Hobsbawmean effect, in which the power of the mob or potential power of the mob is harnessed and leveraged by leaders adept enough to attach themselves to certain identities and grievances. The grievances do not have to be against the establishment, as proven by Mr. Santiago.

Many palpable, shared grievances need little organized leadership for translation into action. One of the legendarily effective propaganda messages of World War II was a simple poster of how to prepare a Molotov cocktail (wine bottle half filled with gasoline and a kerosene rag). The resistance did not need much by way of orders or messages. Those inclined got the message.

The leader who successfully represents the potential mob can transmute mere potential into leverage against almost whatever group might be harmed by mass action. The leader who learns to influence a small group of psychologically tenuous individuals has a related and potentially more fearful power. If the leader can convoke a crowd to listen to her sing, she's an entertainer. If she can convince a lot of people to go vote for her, maybe she's a democrat. The point being that motivational ability is not what separates those who would form an anarchic mob from those who would motivate us to go to a concert or vote. The difference is in the match-up of a propensity in the audience to do something violent and individual *mens rea.* When an audience is motivated to take mortal action, there is almost always a pre-existing propensity combined with leadership, and the leadership will include an element of ill will. If we are talking about 'organized' violence, someone provides the organization.

In 2009, Ms. Susan Boyle sang in a television competition called *Britain Has Talent.* She was an unlikely competitor. Few occasions are filmed in which a crowd is caught being so genuinely, universally and spontaneously surprised and delighted. Well, they weren't asked to go kill anyone. More importantly, the promoters who had encouraged Ms. Boyle to sing were backstage, and they were absolutely certain about what the crowd reaction was going to be. So it was not spontaneous reaction. The crowd had been targeted.

Because of the new huge anonymous communications, a lot of people can be motivated very briefly to do little things, bad and good, like send a few bucks to save a kitten from microwave doom. For the audience there is no fear, no mortal risk, no accountability, no Colonel Sherburn to face -- just the amassed gratification from a million poignant instances of no moral dilemma at all. The generated poignancy is then fungible. That is, the organization dedicated to saving kittens can also be putting up roadblocks. Although Lenin was correct that there is little spontaneity, we have to add that now there is a huge Internet-resident crowd that has within it every human propensity and impulsivity.

There are no spontaneous armed uprisings, no rhizoidal insurgencies, no headless, starfish armies. There might be some interesting and annoying phenomena, like flash riots, that you will want to keep your eye on that don't entail much central or hierarchical direction. Not all armed organizations are built like a German battalion, either. If, however, you are in an armed competition, it's being organized and led by somebody. Someone has the *mens rea*, or is the intellectual author, the distributor of funds, the cheerleader or ideologue, or plans to be the vanguard or the clergy. If there were an insurgency and no one in it intended to take over, what would that leave, exactly? For some inexplicable reason, it seems to be those most taken to cults of leadership who most talk up the idea of chaos and spontaneous movements. If there is one thing we have learned from twentieth century revolutionary movements, it is that the anarchists get killed by the organizers.

See: 51, *Underclass*; 54, *Badassoftheweek.com*; 2, *Anonymity*; 56, *Militias and Gun Control*; 76, *NGOS and Unions*; 16, *Keeping Secrets*; 23, *Mens Rea*; and 142, *Dignity and Honor*.

---

> "A human group transforms itself into a crowd when it suddenly responds to a suggestion rather than to reasoning, to an image rather than to an idea, to an affirmation rather than to proof, to the repetition of a phrase rather than to arguments, to prestige rather than to competence."
>
> Jean François Revel, attributed[86]

May I vote myself into slavery?

# *Section 60, Slavery*

Slavery is the opposite of liberty, but it is difficult to make a useful statement as to where either condition begins or ends. Because this book is about winning irregular conflict, it must be admitted up-front that holding slaves can help you win. Many humans will accept being your slaves if you feed, clothe, entertain and keep them more or less healthy and safe physically. They may even give you their loyalty and fight for you.

On the other end of the spectrum, however, lives a stubborn minority for whom no amount of care is sufficient to compensate enslavement. They would rather be sick, poor, and ignorant than dominated by you. They can be problematic, too, especially if they can find a leader. For them, a central question arises over the need to recruit, organize and proselytize: Does a people have a right to choose slavery for itself or not? It is the one question that forces the theme of slavery to be included as a section in this book. Can a people freely and willingly vote itself into a condition of slavery, or must that particular free act be opposed? It is one of the main questions of the age. Unfortunately for practical opposition, the choice toward slavery is rarely made in one big leap, but rather in a series of comfortable increments. This leads to a closely related question: Can a majority in a democratic polity vote away the rights of a minority, slice by slice? Does the fact that such slicing is the result of peaceful, predictable, open, mathematically democratic elections make the slicing toward slavery and away from liberty legitimate?

It is bad press for you to be in favor of slavery, to allow slavery, or get anywhere close to slavery. Americans especially are touchy about the subject. If you fancy yourself anti-American, and especially if your organization runs a risk of inviting the Americans to come visit you, armed, don't expose yourself as slaveholder, slave trader, slaver, or even as a slave.

Like *legitimacy*, *democracy*, *rule-of-law*, and *sovereignty*, the term *slavery* does not have an official, commanding definition, nor is there a clear boundary between when it exists and when it does not. There are, nevertheless, some conditions about which there is little argument. If you have enough money, but cannot leave a place, then you are probably a slave or a prisoner. You might be a debtor. Debt servitude gets pretty close to slavery. If you can be corporally punished for not paying a debt, or for something you say, then you might be a slave. If you are good to your children, but they can be taken from you anyway, you're probably slave. If you do not have the right to *not* speak, you're probably a slave. Study your social contract. If you are more part of what can be owned than part of who can do the owning, you might be a slave. If you can decide at whim the important outlines of other persons' personal identity, you are tending toward being those persons' owner, or at least toward being perceived as such.

In the past, *Webster's* defined *enthrall* as "1. To make a slave of; enslave; hence, 2. To put or hold under strong influence; captivate; enchant; fascinate. The words "Now rare" appear before the first meaning in more recent *Webster's*, and most new American English language dictionaries start with the second denotation – that of enchantment. I don't often cite dictionary definitions, but I couldn't escape the term's grasp. To me, more of the first meaning should be returned to the word. Enthrall is what charismatic political leaders do; enthrallment is what charisma allows. Attractive in small doses, its excess is a near constant in today's conflicts. To enthrall rather than to convince distinguishes the intentions of fascists, Bolsheviks, Rasputins, or populists in general. Post-structuralists are captivated by populists. Theirs is a voluntary slavery, which they often commend to, or even prescribe for others. The question of slavery, and whether or not a people can choose slavery, may be at the heart of your insurgent war.

See: 125, *Human Rights*; 77, *Sex*; 124, *America's Insurgent Stamp*; 62, *Illicit Commerce*; 95, *Childhood*; 105, *Genocide Geography*; 17, *Kidnapping*; and 46, *Taxation and Debt*.

> "Perhaps the fact that we have seen millions voting themselves into complete dependence on a tyrant has made our generation understand that to choose one's government is not necessarily to secure freedom."
>
> Friedrich Hayek[87]

Where best do we spend our money?

# *Section 61, Who Sins More?*

'¿Quién peca más, la que peca por la paga, o el que paga para pecar?' ('Who sins more, she who sins for pay or he who pays to sin?') Sexist saying? Maybe. As for an answer to the question: Who cares? That's not the point. This Spanish saying is often used to introduce an important, heartfelt argument from Latin Americans about the drug trade and drug war. The allusion is to prostitution, but is extended to the relationship of men and women generally in machismo society. The strategic application of the reference is obvious enough (at least as extended to the illicit drug trade) -- that buyers of illicit drugs are as bad as sellers. The idea of she and he is then combined with a personalization of countries, as in 'The United States buys the drugs, so why is Mexico any more of a sinner for selling them?' The practical application of the saying is connected to arguments about whether to attack illicit drugs at their source or instead to invest in demand reduction -- source versus destination/supply versus demand. The argument is not weightless, and when made by the agile lawyer always seems to resonate, especially inside the stereotyped 'Protestant mind' wherein a little sense of guilt can go a long way to unhinging logic. Here are three defenses to keep in your mind, whether you are on the defense or not:

1. The great majority of persons in both seller and buyer countries don't participate in either sale or purchase of illicit drugs. The dichotomy, if not entirely false, is one of displacement and projection of identity. The battle is between, on the one hand, those majorities in all countries who neither

sell nor buy, and, on the other hand, those individuals involved in illicit trade, whether producing, processing, moving, wholesaling, retailing or consuming.

2. Regardless of any moral equivalence between seller and buyer, the suppression of illegal drug use at the demand or user end invariably means invasion of private space. In the process of empowering police to inspect and repress the use of drugs, there will be a costly consequence in terms of civil rights. One might say, 'Well, that is what you get for bogarting that joint, Buddy,' but law enforcement often entails an invasion of the spaces and rights of third parties, and a destruction of privacies and associations that touch accidentally beyond the use of illicit drugs only because of physical geographic proximity. In the process of empowering police to repress drug use, it is impossible not to both empower but also embolden police to peek at other behaviors and effect other intrusions into private lives on the wings of expanding and maybe enjoyed suspicions. Drug use suppression at some point has the side effect of violating citizens' rights. Suppression of the seller, on the other hand, has a distinctly different geographic signature. Sellers must build contraband routes, supply chains, production facilities and source contracts. Clearing *marijuaneros* out of a national park is not the same as searching an apartment.

3. Illicit drug production and sale enterprises cause more governmental corruption than do drug use activities. The money at the profit end, and the structures needed for the industry, are far more toxic to the functioning of government than the post-distribution use of illicit drugs. Use-suppression does little to relieve the extortive pressure put on governments in illicit drug producing lands.

Offering the above arguments is not to say that demand reduction is not worth doing, and the ever-present if wistful 'third way' is legalization. Legalization is a chimera, however. In a world of tort law wherein cigarette manufacturers are sued for producing something patently poisonous, and secondhand smoke is so intolerable there are few public places left for it, it is hard to see how a more dangerous poison could be made legal and also lawful. Unless lawful, a black market will still reign, and along with the black market all the other unpleasantness follows. Anyway, we tend to forget *mens rea* in our economic analyses. What kind of person knowingly sells dangerous drugs to children?

Not all drugs are equal. A weakness in commentaries about the drug trade (including the one above) comes from throwing all illicit substances in the same bag. Marijuana is not the same as heroin. Growing habits and habitats, processing needs, transport challenges, effects on the human body -- all are distinct one from the other, and suppression of their markets are likewise dissimilar, except for the fact that the same criminals often are involved with trade in various drugs. Suppressing the dealers usually means suppressing someone who is responsible for a variety of nefarious behaviors. Suppressing drug use of one kind or another does not offer the same, multiplied benefit.

Illicit drugs are a feature of many irregular wars, and probably a feature in yours. It may even be the central feature, motivating its own outlaw, national, and international armed strategies; there exist large, resolute, well-organized and well-equipped criminal drug-armies that rudely defy the State by granting impunity to their members. The drug trade may also be an important logistic element to an insurgent's, or even to a government's ability to sustain their war efforts. In any case, there exists a constant debate about whether resources, perhaps resources that would flow toward you, should be used to suppress illicit drug use or drug supply. You will want to have an opinion on the matter.

See: 65, *Smuggling*; 54, *Mercatus*; 62, *Illicit Commerce*; 95, *Childhood*; 23, *Mens Rea*; 77, *Sex*; 2, *The Line of Retreat*; and 34, *Urban or Rural*.

---

> "And now, my pretties, something with poison in it,...but attractive to the eye, and soothing to the smell... poppies, ...poppies,...poppies will put them to sleep."
>
> Wicked Witch of the West in the movie *The Wizard of Oz* (1939)[88]

ଔଓଔଓଔଓଔଓଔଓଔଓ

Who will pardon what?

# *Section 62, Illicit Commerce*

Successful illegal business requires organization and secrecy. Organized armed groups already have some organization and enforce what secrecy they can. They also are always in need of funds, so they get mixed up in capitalist enterprise. Meanwhile, even criminal gangs dedicated to direct robbery (rather than to the sale of some desired commodity) find themselves in business because they have to launder stolen money, fence stolen goods, or negotiate ransoms. There seems no way for the outlaw to avoid stretching out to Adam Smith's invisible loving hand. It's out there, even where the long arm of the law can't reach.

Among commodities traded illicitly, cocaine and heroin seem to have the greatest impact on armed conflicts today. Colombia and Afghanistan, respectively, are the obvious focus countries. Marijuana and methamphetamines also weigh in as kindling for organized internal and international armed conflict. Illicit agriculture, or agro-industry, is distinct in its physical geographical footprint. Crops take up rural space, which changes the dynamic of communications routes, who is likely to control access or to tax, and where labor will come from. When smuggling is tied to rural lands, the geographic distribution of money is also distinct. Someone has to pay someone else for labor and inputs, as well as for raw harvest and production.

A prevailing theory in the early years of Colombia's struggle with the coca leaf was simple: Money from coca was the lifeblood of the FARC and other major criminal organizations plaguing Colombian society and challenging the Colombian government; reducing illicit income from the coca agro-industry would reduce the power of these antigovernment armed groups; and as a result, the government would be able to gain the upper hand.

President William Clinton's Presidential Decision Directive/NSC 73, August 3 (PDD/NSC 73), published while US support to the Colombian government was picking up momentum. The decision explicitly distanced counternarcotics from counterinsurgency, allowing the former but not the latter. Here is the text again:

> *As a matter of Administration policy, we will not support Colombian counterinsurgency efforts....This Administration remains convinced that the ultimate solution to Colombia's longstanding civil conflict is through a successful peace process, not a decisive military victory, and believes that counterdrug progress will contribute to progress towards peace.*

The directive made spending money in favor of the Colombia's fight against its armed opponents confusing if not more difficult, since the insurgent FARC was already up to its bandoliers in the cocaine trade.

Organized armed groups have to feed and pay their soldiers, so they get money from someplace. It could be a foreign State, legal enterprises, direct predation, or it could be from illicit commerce. If it is illicit commerce, the organization's lines of withdrawal to sanctuary are likely contiguous with the lines of commerce (product-to-market; inputs-to factory) because of the need for secrecy.

Money laundering and fencing are downstream crimes or after-the-fact crimes. They can be a weakness of almost any criminal enterprise. After something is taken illegally, it has to be bartered or converted into a liquid asset. Cash, although liquid, has both physical form and unique identification. In most organizations the handling of money is delegated to persons whom the top leaders trust, or it is not delegated at all. For this reason, the geographies of illicit money transactions are often the geographies (sanctuaries and lines of escape to them) of the leaders.

The world of irregular conflict is linear, and the important lines are often those along which illicit product, inputs, and financial instruments flow. The physical and human geographies of lawbreaking, whether simply criminal or politically insurgent, overlap so much that policies which artificially distinguish them can be counterproductive.

See: 138, *Roadblocks and Checkpoints*; 61, *Who Sins More?*; 135, *Bank Robbery*; 46, *Taxation and Debt*; 132, *Brigands*; 54, *Mercatus*; 7, *Nonlinear Warfare*; and 65, *Smuggling.*

---

**Peter**: (about a conspiracy to embezzle) Before we go any further, all right, we have to swear to God, Allah, that nobody knows about this but us, all right? No family members, no girlfriends, nobody.

**Samir**: Of course.

**Michael**: Agreed,

**Lawrence**: (through a wall from the apartment next door) Don't worry, man. I won't tell anyone either.

**Michael**: Who the **** is that?

**Peter**: Uh, don't worry about him. He's cool.

From the movie
*Office Space* (1999)[89]

How far away is it really?

# *Section 63, Cost-Distance*

The whole discipline of Geography obsesses over distance, and it should be a key obsession for any military planner involved in irregular armed conflict. An accurate sensing of relevant distances is indispensible, especially when a leader dares to defy the classic principles of war. Additionally, distance in organized armed conflicts cannot be separated from factors of time and weight.

Distance has an inverse effect on power. Power diminishes as distance increases. As we travel farther away, our choices about what we can do at the end of the trail diminish. When you calculate relevant distances to likely confrontations in an armed struggle, the distances will have an intimate relationship to correlations of force at the points of probable contact. If the point of contact with your enemy is so distant that you will have inferior relative strength at the points of contact, you are overreaching. The Dutch have a museum at Arnhem where they go to discuss this very topic.[90]

Distances in irregular warfare are best measured as cost-distances and relative cost-distances. Cost-distance is such a common concept we forget about it. How far it is from Colorado Springs to Denver in terms of the cost of gas, or time, or some other factor is cost-distance. The distance between Colorado Springs and Denver is longer or shorter depending on the vehicle, the price of gas, the weather, the traffic, and so on. In urban areas, cost-distances can be especially complex, even involving such quantities as the emotional cost of fear due to criminal risk, or the opportunity cost of aesthetic preference (as in: you would have preferred to walk through the park).

Multiplicity of route options complicates comparison of the relative cost-distances, that is, your cost-distances relative to those of your enemy, or, say, of a riot population relative to riot control personnel. Construction of a public mass transportation line can drastically change relative cost-distances, as can the interruption of bus service, or the location of public transportation stops and stations. What slows you down may or may not slow down your enemy *as much*. Manipulations of the built environment, especially the calculated use of walls and bridges, can change the aggregate cost-distance advantages as to specific human collectives. Student protestors, for instance, tend to move via public conveyance from a university; farm protesters tend to drive tractors in from farms; and so on. An armored vehicle might shorten a cost-distance by reducing a risk factor, but simultaneously lengthen a cost-distance by increasing the factors of time and fuel -- and exposure. Many military people are familiar with a form of cost-distance known as the 'culminating point.' The culminating point sets at a theoretical distance in time and space beyond which your risks of continuing are too great. The culminating point for an infantry patrol in combat might be highly affected by how much water the soldiers can carry. In a city, meanwhile, one step into a gang's territory might be a 'bridge too far' for a couple of beat cops.

A lot is made of how modern information technologies shrink distances. Compared to just a couple of decades ago, it takes a lot less time to spread an idea to millions of people on the other side of the globe, but the amount of time it takes to send a rifle bullet or a grand piano has not changed much. Ideas are powerful, to be sure, but when you determine to apply physical force, the mass inherent to the exercise slows things back down, lengthens the cost-distances. In most irregular wars, the world is not so much smaller than it was when T. Miller Maguire made his observations about globalization. (See Section 130, *Globalization*)

Because they seem to live in a realm of pure math and electrons, computer trespassers give the impression they act beyond the parameters of the military operational equation. Nerds seem to escape the concept of those distances which impel classic military strategy. They seem to escape the bounds of mortal earth on gossamer boogers. False. Think in terms of cost-distances: In the case of a computer criminal, the distance from his keyboard to the desk of some FBI agent correlates with the protection the criminal is afforded by the legal and political regime of the place where the criminal sits at his keyboard. For the FBI agent, the distance in flight hours might be longer from the agent's desk in Miami to Memphis than it is from his desk to the criminal's keyboard on some island in the Caribbean. The real distance between the FBI agent and the perpetrator may nevertheless be far greater than the distance to Graceland because the government of the country where the criminal sits has created a condition of anonymity and impunity that immensely changes the relative cost-distances for the FBI agent. Practicably, it is a much longer trip from the agent's desk to the criminal's keyboard. Measured as Euclidean problems, distances are reduced to getting airline tickets and taxis. Measured in terms of impunity, however, the comparison of distances involves visas, extradition orders, local police cooperation, or maybe the costs of a military operation in defiance of sovereignty. Such impunity cost-distances can nevertheless be mapped and measured. Sometimes, just the cost of an airline ticket creates enough distance to abet impunity. On the *Michelle Malkin* blog, 'Hangfire' stated,

> "Bad guys here (and the cops) count on visitors not being able to come back to Hawaii to testify against the perps. If you have to save money for years to spend five days here, you really can't afford to come back and spend weeks in a hotel waiting for the defense to stop all delaying tactics. All the defense attorneys here demand that their client face their accuser in person, as is their right. Written affidavits just don't cut it."[91]

Historical affinities can also change the map of psychological cost-distances. Perceptions make some places closer in terms of political action, and these, in turn, can bear on the factors noted above. Many Americans perceive the Philippines to be closer to the United States than Nigeria, even though the air distance from Los Angeles to Manila is about 7,300 miles and from Miami to Lagos only about 5,600 miles. Influence of one group of humans on another is usually greater as distances are closer, and again, influence-distance (or culture-distance or affinity-distance) is a cost-distance.

The maps that are appropriate for the accurate use of artillery fire, with their scale representations of almost frictionless distance and their gridded division of two dimensional space may be perfectly inappropriate for expressing distance in the usual conflicts where artillery rarely is used.

This is not a call to take charts away from artillerymen or pilots, but it is a suggestion that in your irregular war you might do better to configure some maps in terms of relevant cost-distances, which are likely to include factors as seemingly abstract and unrelated to distance as fear, law or aesthetics.

See: 89, *The Dot Game*; 68, *Scale*; 138, *Roadblocks and Checkpoints*; 80, *Why You Should Like Geography*; 65, *Smuggling*; 140, *Culminating Point in the Pursuit*; 66, GIS*;* and 129, *Nerd Globe*.

---

> A psychologist experiments with a mathematician and an engineer. He puts a slice of a mouthwatering chocolate cake in one corner of the room and the mathematician on a chair in another corner, and tells him: 'I'll halve the distance between you and the cake every five minutes, and you're not allowed to stand up.' the mathematician leaves, yelling: 'In that case, I'll never get to the cake!' Then the psychologist takes the engineer and tells him the same plan. The engineer starts grinning. The psychologist asks him: 'but you'll never reach the cake!?' The engineer tells him: 'Yeah, but for all practical purposes it'll be good enough.'[92]

Distance, size and resolve

# *Section 64, Measuring Power*

Since one of the keys to winning armed conflicts is to pick fights with weaker opponents (or at least a place and moment in time when an opponent is most likely to be weaker), it is good to practice measuring relative strength. A lot of measuring the strength of armed groups has to be done the old-fashioned way, with spies and photos and bean-counters. Below are a few tips relevant to some of the new kinds of armed groups. One is based on distance and how distance and power correlate. Another has to do with what is called a 'power-law,' and the third is more *stochastic*, which may mean it's just wild guesswork, but it still works.

1. **Distance**. The scale of a group's territory or the distance from its boss to his foot soldiers is one way to measure the group's power relative to other groups. Distance diminishes power, so any sustained presence of an organization's people at a distance from its headquarters can be correlated to its relative overall power. For instance, in Medellín, Colombia, during the height of the violence in the mid 1990s, a neighborhood might suffer the presence of any of more than a half-dozen illegal armed groups. The least powerful groups would be the ones with little territorial scope, and whose boss was close-by. These would include small neighborhood groups of locally-spawned bullies organized around control of pirated and makeshift services such as water hoses, power lines, or TV cable lines. Other small groups organized in response to dishonors associated with the lack of sewage and refuse removal.

The Medellín Cartel was a little less local and a lot more powerful. Its boss lived on the other side of the city, and his organization controlled high-profit crime in most of the city. Cali is another Colombian city about 200 miles away. If the Cali Cartel could maintain personnel with impunity in Medellín, it was either because it could defy the Medellín Cartel or because the two had come to some kind of an agreement. Meanwhile, the national-scale revolutionary movements, like the FARC and the ELN, wanted to establish their own territorial advantages inside a few of the boroughs of Medellín. Their headquarters were in distant parts of Colombia. They were more powerful organizations than the cartels.

Being a more powerful organization overall does not mean it has more power *in the neighborhood at a given time* than one of the more local groups. The FARC might have enough power, and reputation of power, to keep someone on the block for a while, but even the most local thugs get good information on the outsider's location and habits, and maybe don't like the way he looks at their girlfriends. The FARC guy may be a tough from the country's most powerful illegal armed group, but he is at the edge of that power and may have to negotiate, bluff, or die.

This understanding of power according to distance does not give absolute power. It is just a quick observation that an armed group that can maintain presence at a distance from its boss is usually more dangerous than one that cannot, but not necessarily the more dangerous at a very specific place or given moment.

2. **The power law**. It proves something with math and economics that soldiers have known for a long time.[93] You don't want to attack an opponent unless you can marshal enough force to get the job done safely. It is the operational equation again. What the power law predicts is that, given a rational guerrilla force, the guerrillas are going to make smaller attacks and kill fewer people per attack if they can't marshal enough force at a given place and time to do something bigger, safely. Over time and in the context of a lot of space, it is logical that if the guerrillas' attacks begin to cause larger numbers of casualties, and they attack larger size government units or other targets, that they are getting better at marshalling forces, which means they are getting stronger. Changes in weaponry can make a difference, as can improved transport, information, etc. This is where the ideas of correlation of force and creation of mass apply to irregular war. However, while it may seem that the economic 'power law' only proves the obvious, it at least provides a way to extract from many disparate events (which individually may not say much) some indicator about the course of the combative capacity of a guerilla force. It also suggests a way to classify individual events as being unique or not.

With the above in mind, one of the most useful indices of power you can note in irregular armed conflict is of a group's ability to block a road. A landmine can certainly block a road for a while, but the convocational ability of a group may be more important. As Section 138, *Roadblocks and Checkpoints* notes, the ability to create a crowd for a roadblock can be extremely important in the operational math of irregular war. Notice that like the business of marshalling for an attack, this is also a power law-type of ability. It is the power to achieve what the classic military strategists call mass, and even though the manifestation is just a road blockage, when road blockages are timed and placed in obedience to the rules of classic strategy (to the operational equation), they become, in the aggregate, a powerful phenomenon in armed competition.

3. **Improving your guess with categories**. The following components are proposed for improving you calculation of the relative power of competing illegal armed groups: *cohesiveness of identity, leadership, wealth, and technological capacity.*

a. Cohesiveness of identity is a good starting point for calculating power. Cohesiveness is the source of shared resolve. Communal resolve connotes perseverance and willingness to sacrifice to achieve an end. One might say that the group's leader must translate cohesiveness into resolve in relation to a given project. Measuring the level of resolve, however, is sometimes only possible by way of observing a group's commitment to a particular goal, and so the measurement only reveals the quantity in the course of its own consequence.

b. Whatever the cohesiveness of a group's identity, leadership initiative must be present in order for power to have any active meaning. Effective leaders build cohesiveness, translate cohesiveness into resolve, and preserve resolve. Measuring effectiveness of leadership is a lot harder than determining who the leader is. Leadership effectiveness, like cohesiveness, is easily measured only after displays of success or failure.

c. Wealth is an obvious component of power.
Wealth is determined to an extent by physical geography, which is to say basic factors such as location, space, access to water or population, weapons and fungible assets like cash. With great wealth, average leaders can successfully undertake projects that do not enjoy a high degree of resolve. Wealth is both means and end. It is also an important clue regarding who holds power because wealth (more than cohesiveness, resolve, or leadership skill) can be pinpointed, traced, counted, followed, ruined or confiscated.

d. The right technologies can help coerce, capture or kill people, and can help gain and protect property. Technologies are as often organizational as physical, and are often

> second-hand. Al Qaeda's innovative use of airliners as bombs, of individual suicide bombers or improvisation of remotely detonated bombs has been a hallmark of that organization's enterprise. Without strategic use of the landmine the FARC would never have succeeded, but it also invented industrial kidnapping and other predatory schemes.

Measuring power in irregular warfare cannot be done in the same way as it is done to compare nation-states in contemplation of some international inter-State war. It has to be done at the appropriate geographic scale and more carefully address the effects of power on the ability of the State to maintain or gain a monopoly on the granting of impunity.

See: 53, *Hohfeldian Grievance Analysis*; 69, *Measuring Actions against Enemies*; 89, *The Dot Game*; 68, *Scale*; and 143, *Is It an Insurgency?*; 2, *Anonymity*; 56, *Militias and Gun Control*; and 63, *Cost-Distance.*

---

> "**Zander**: My God. How could this happen?
> **Carmen**: We thought we were smarter than the Bugs."
>
> From the movie
> *Starship Troopers* (1997)[94]

Action is movement, and most secret action is smuggling

# *Section 65, Smuggling*

Smuggling means moving valuable things secretly and contrary to the law. Pretty much all criminal organizations have to smuggle, and smuggling almost defines the difference (as well as the overlap) between an archetypal mafia and an archetypal insurgent organization.

We know that the prudent leader does not risk getting into a shoot-up with a stronger force unless he has secured a route of withdrawal to sanctuary. The insurgent, however, wants to maintain the initiative, looking to effect battle against government forces whenever the conditions are favorable. The criminal leader, on the other hand, is not looking for that battle, but almost always to avoid it. There are in-between cases, but by-and-large, that's the operational difference – the insurgent is looking to take shots against the army or the police, while the criminal is not. Still, in both cases, the successful leaders will have secured their routes to sanctuary just in case they suffer a run-in with a stronger force.

An insurgent's routes of supply are a significant determinant (as they are for every army) of his units' culminating points (how far they can go in time and space before they assume too much risk). The quality of his units' supply routes (and these may be highly dispersed) delimit the strength that the insurgent's units will enjoy at chosen points of attack and during his units' escapes to sanctuary. The routes are an integral ingredient in the insurgent's ability to battle the government forces successfully. We know that the routes of insurgent supply are often the same as the routes of withdrawal. For the smuggler, the routes of supply are obviously indispensable and integral to his enterprise, but they are not established or maintained in order to enable expenditure in battle against the government. For the smuggler, any battles against the government constitute overhead that should be reduced as much as possible. The smuggling routes are for moving merchandise from source to buyer without being taxed (and that's if the goods are otherwise legal). Secure routes for the smuggler are part and parcel of the main event, and their quality determines the margin of profitability. The supply route is what the smuggler does and who he is, while the insurgent is defined by battle, with continuous success in battle dependent on the routes.

If advanced in his art, the head smuggler will only sometimes be found along the smuggling route. He will rarely be involved directly with the activity. The operational equation, however, tells us that he will almost always stay on what amounts to his route of escape to sanctuary (or in it). The accomplished insurgent leader often has a different leadership problem, and may have to place himself where battle might occur, or along supply routes. If he is a survivor, however, he will rarely move without confidence in a secure escape route to sanctuary.

Smugglers and insurgents, often the same entity, make every effort to establish relationships with people at important way points and constrictions along smuggling routes and along safety valve escape routes to sanctuary. These relationships may be coerced, but they are often romanced and voluntary.

When smugglers and insurgents share or intend to share the same geographic space, a common problem imposed by physical geography is likely to occur. The smuggler is probably going to know the best routes, have the informants and have imposed the necessary silence. As a result, the insurgent is likely, unless he is one-in-the-same with the smuggler, to be the newcomer. While the insurgent might get lucky and be able to bring coercive, extortive force to bear against the smuggler and his family, it is also highly possible that the smuggler will hold an advantage of knowledge. The insurgent will likely have to negotiate and use the same routes for supply and escape. The latter is especially significant, because unless the insurgent has achieved some semblance of peaceful coexistence with the smuggling organizations, the insurgents' movements to sanctuary from points of contact against government targets could be compromised by the smugglers. Failing to pay old smugglers their due can be counterproductive.

Smuggling is done by amateurs, individual professionals, and by experienced organizations. Basic smuggling for individual consumption or sport-risk differs in a number of ways from the smuggling conducted by organized criminal organizations, but the most important difference for our purposes is the development of established routes. Routes can be graded as good or not so good in accordance with their security, throughput, and speed. There is no single business model for establishing and protecting a viable smuggling route, but achieving and maintaining the silence of persons along the route or who participate in storage along the route is always a central feature.

A criminal smuggling organization will often use newbies or 'virgins' as a method for testing security systems and other observation. This is akin to flying over radar stations so that they will turn on and identify their frequencies and fans. The more mature smuggling organizations will also preplan cooperation with official agencies of governments by giving up hapless or rival smugglers to the authorities. This tendency to compromise, as well as what appear to be natural phases or stages in the life of smuggling organizations, suggests opportunities for cooptation by insurgent or counterinsurgent organizations.[95]

Not all smuggling is going to be seen as a bad thing, even by the most respected governments. Rare earth elements are critical to Japanese manufacturing, Japan getting most of its rare earth from China. Maybe 20% of that arrives via the black market, so maybe the Japanese government isn't going to mount an aggressive campaign against that particular smuggling phenomenon. Meanwhile, some governments, like North Korea, have been accused of being outright sponsors of smuggling, including of outlawed commodities.

People smuggle things with very little weight, like personal identification cards, to heavy things like people and weapons. Smuggling is an indispensable action in armed social conflicts. It is very linear (there are no nonlinear armed social conflicts or irregular wars). Where there is organized smuggling, you might have an apparent rule-of-law, but not an applied rule-of-law. Usably, criminal smugglers tend toward political compromise.

See: 140, *Culminating Point in the Pursuit*; 25, *Why Humans Don't Fight*; 138, *Roadblocks and Checkpoints*; 2, *The Line of Retreat*; 139, *UAAV*; 3, *The Domesday Book*; 80, *Why You Should Like Geography*; and 67, *Points, Lines, Spaces*.

---

> "... I admire all nations and hate all governments, and nowhere is my natural anarchism more aroused than at national borders.... I have never smuggled anything in my life. Why, then, do I feel an uneasy sense of guilt on approaching a customs barrier?"
>
> John Steinbeck,
> *Travels with Charley: in Search of America*[96]

---

The new empirical

# *Section 66, GIS*

GIS stands for Geographic Information Systems or Geographic Information Science. Sometimes the 'G' turns up as *georeferenced* or *geospatial* and the 'I' as *intelligence*. The term is thrown around freely to encompass the physical and organizational technologies that together allow data on every kind of phenomenon to be organized in database form – perhaps to be visualized on a computer screen and made subject to calculations and analyses otherwise difficult for the human mind.

As a knowledge revolution, GIS is almost as important as the Internet. Tens of thousands of licenses for commercial GIS software are sold all around the world to academic, governmental and nongovernmental organizations, which are using the software suites in combination with GPS-derived data to create massive files on everything from endangered species to real property ownership to the wiring of buildings. GIS is not new epistemology, but it might be thought of as empirical epistemology revisited and restated to engage the new technology. Because the technology is so powerful, and investments in it so great, it is hard to see a reasonable way around it short of something like deep ecological rejection of and abstention from history. That might be a good idea; let's not reject the option out-of-hand. Nevertheless, for those of us at least temporarily committed to vacuous and futile human competitions, GIS is big.

For decades, the US military has taught as doctrine a process of information management, visualization and analysis known as Intelligence Preparation of the Battlefield (IPB). IPB goes in and out of popularity, probably depending on how welcome or unwelcome the word *intelligence* is at any given moment. At any rate, the purpose of IPB is to define the battle environment, describe the likely effects of that environment, describe human threats within it, predict the likely actions of those threats and identify propitious times and places for action. GIS is applied to a much greater and more complex set of variables and endeavors, many not associated with a threat, but, practically speaking, GIS is how civilians spell IPB.

A consolidating set of analytical and presentation protocols also emerged in the wake of recognition of the suite of technologies associated with the term GIS. Consensus as to what constitutes a best-practice in GIS methodological science to some degree depends on the specific practical application or on theoretical preferences and traditions within a given academic discipline. Perhaps because the explosion of GIS is occurring within and as part of the accelerating pace of globalization, the currents of GIS knowledge and method are highly internationalized.

GIS is the certain future of both intelligence organizations and public administration, too, and therefore the technological/ methodological key to a universe of knowledge in the files of government agencies, public administrative units, non-governmental organizations, business enterprises, and in the best-practice research efforts of university scholars. GIS is raising quality standards in social science research, making the research of disparate disciplines compatible for comparison and enrichment, and allowing research to be more easily tested for veracity and scholarly diligence. The same tools, the same processes and almost the exact same body of knowledge that allows citizens to check tax equity, the effects of and responsibility for environmental harm, or optimal traffic design, are those that can help you find your enemy before he finds you. The universe of GIS-based knowledge, almost wholly unclassified and outside formal government intelligence, has within it the material needed to name your enemies and to trace their wealth.

The US federal government has barely applied GIS to questions of national security. As yet, almost all of the extensive investment in GIS by the various US government agencies still revolves around the precise location and representation of physical phenomena. Government interest in GIS is tied to remote sensing, targeting and precise movement of friendly units. While this is all useful, the US government has only very recently picked up on the importance of GIS for building knowledge about human geography -- about culture, cost-distances, whereabouts, ownership, land value, and the integration of these with the many other themes scattered throughout the sections of this book. Although some might fear so, the US military has not yet figured out Big Brother.

We might already be going into a post-GIS era in which the so-called *neogeography* is the more powerful, if dependent phenomenon. Not really as new a term as it seems, *neogeography* refers to disperse, nearly spontaneous and generally voluntary public participation in creating GIS data files about all kinds of interesting phenomena. An age of nearly spontaneous map creation by millions of personal GPS recorders is beginning. How to influence this phenomenon of casual geographers could become an important advantage in human competition.

The way knowledge is organized and presented is important to the success of any endeavor. The way words and terms are related and distributed in the columns and lines of a GIS makes a difference in the way priorities will be determined. The human mind, however, does not seem to work like the GIS we've created with computers. The human mind is still better at the most complicated things, and the most important things. So the interface between GIS and humans will remain an uncomfortable one. There are some people, 'deconstructionists' perhaps, who see GIS more negatively still. They see GIS as some ultimate perfection of a Western, positivist, realist, rationalist, and imposed reality that is, for them, not the best way to go. They might be right.

As far as armed competitions go, however, if you build a good GIS and your anti-GIS enemy doesn't, he'll be explaining it to you from prison.

Military planners are forever being asked to think critically, meaning be aware of logical fallacies and impoverished assumptions. One of the logical fallacies of which we are constantly being warned is called *post hoc ergo propter hoc*, or the rooster fallacy, or 'after this therefore on account of this.' It is risky illogic because events are not necessarily caused by preceding events, however proximate they are in time and however often the correlation occurs. The rooster crows, then the sun comes up, but it is illogic to assert that roosters cause the sun to rise. *Post hoc ergo propter hoc* fuels jokes and deceptions, but this fallacy is not the rooster booster of evil logic. In social science it is more probably the inverse. Although a correct sequence of events does not necessarily evidence causation, it is a rare phenomenon indeed that does not obey logical sequence of causation. This is where the disciplining value of GIS comes in. A common laziness (or perfidy) allows excessive abstraction in place or time. The assertion, 'The very year the new national government was elected there were seventeen murders of union leaders,' is not the same as saying 'Seventeen union leaders were murdered in Gong Province in June of 2007, and national elections occurred in September of that year.' The first sentence is a typical dissemblance, implying that the government was connected with the murders. The second tends, by the logic of sequence, to argue the opposite. Lies often appear on thematic maps that aggregate statistics in time and space.

Responsible GIS uses a scale and resolution of data that is as consistent geographically and as sequential in time as the data will allow, or at least that confesses whatever geographic or temporal illogic might hide in the representations. GIS will not establish many theories of causation with certainty, but it will demolish many theories of causation. We can suppose that some social scientists do not care for the challenges of GIS-based research because the demand for precision is made greater and because the logic of temporal sequencing and physical proximity is likely to ruin pet theories of causation. For this reason and others, the measurements and observations of a place experiencing organized armed conflict should be mounted in a geo-referenced relational database if at all possible within the technical and financial means available. GIS is no secret to success, but it is the best methodological lie detector of the age.

GIS is not really a category of research. The term is better used just to represent the tool and technique. 'A' GIS might be no more than a spreadsheet of no greater value than the data that goes in to it. On the other hand, it can allow transparency of knowledge and replicability of method. In studying places, it can make for better science.

See: 112, *DIME and PEMISII*; 108, *Neogeography*; 47, *Why the County*; 67, *Points, Lines, Spaces*; 111, *Knowledge Cultures*; 2, *The Line of Retreat*; 85, *Gun Control*; and 144, *Impunity and State Success*.

---

Q. What do you call a map of outhouses in the woods?
A. A shaded relief map.

Gishumor.com

If you like pencils, this can be useful

# *Section 67, Points, Lines, Spaces*

When faced with the need to manage violence over a large area, thinking in terms of points, lines, and spaces can be a valuable exercise. A lot of this book is about returning the strategist's mind to the importance of 'where.' 'Where' has a shape, and that shape determines a lot about how to find the *right* where and what to do with it after it's found. At different scales the *wheres* change shape. On a 1:100,000 scale map, a family residence, if it can be fairly depicted at all, is but a point. To the owner of that lot, meanwhile, a problem with the neighbor over the common fence line is a big deal. One man's point problem is another man's line problem.

If a proposal arises to disassemble a crew of malevolent computer geeks, the appropriate force selection might be a special operations or SWAT team; if closing off an enemy tank army were a valuable strategic option, some powerful set of fast, armored maneuver units would be the better fit; or if the general's problem were returning a whole province from internal violence to a peaceful social contract, then a larger force composed of police, medical, engineering, intelligence, and social service personnel might be the right prescription. Depending on the scale of map, these three challenges might be fairly characterized and depicted as point, line, and space, respectively.

Geographic Information Science (GIS) is heavily invested in the trigon of visual power just described. But the point is not that because programs like ArcGIS® are glued to a line-point-polygon mental skeleton, the strategist should follow suit. Rather, when the designers of ArcGIS® attacked the problem of organizing knowledge for ease of analysis and depiction, they responded to the common conditions of life and language as we see and hear them. Things happen at a point on the ground, or a 'point in time'; or they happen along that river or ridge, or 'over time'; or they happen in that county, along that road, or during that period. That's the way things are as we generally conceive of them -- as points, lines and spaces. The GISers, figuring within the confines (or liberty) of 0s and 1s, saw that lines could be formed of points and polygons of lines -- albeit when we get right down to pixelating things it's hard to say if the pixels are points or little boxes. No need worry about that. It's not about following the GISers, it's about following what they followed.

Part of what is successful in 'Western' culture revolves around the innovations that moved talking to publishing -- ink, paper, Gutenberg, and all that. Mapping is part of it. Having the right maps at the right scales depicting the right points, lines and spaces will help you win. Without them, the mind has to work harder to reach useful interpretations of physical and cultural phenomena.

See: 8, *The Operational Equation;* 68, *Scale*; 66, *GIS;* 73, *Property and the Social Contract*; 129, *Nerd Globe*; 47, *Why the County*; 80, *Why You Should Like Geography*; and 111, *Knowledge Cultures.*

---

**Rat**: How many languages do you speak?
**Dr. Zimsky**: Five, actually.
**Rat**: I speak one: One, zero, one, zero, zero. With that I could steal your money, your secrets, your sexual fantasies, your whole life; in any country, any time, any place I want. We multitask like you breathe. I couldn't think as slow as you if I tried.

From the movie
*The Core* (2003)[97]

Size matters in things, time, and ideas

# *Section 68, Scale*

You will want to create hierarchical systems (of administration, control, law, representation) of the appropriate size, with the right intermediate levels, and covering the right amount of space. Creating organizations or territories, or conducting analyses at inappropriate levels, or thinking in inappropriate amounts of time (using inappropriate scales) will hurt you.

Cartographic scale, sometimes called representational fraction, is a neat invention that gives map readers a useful idea of the relationship of distances on a map to distances on the ground or sea. Map people also use the word *scale* as a synonym for extent (usually the extent of earth represented by an image on paper or a computer screen), or they will use it in the sense of granularity, resolution or detail, that is, the amount of information on a map. All these definitions of scale are interrelated, and around them swirls a lively intellectual debate. But that debate is not what this section is about.

Scale is also used by geographers and others to classify levels of phenomena. This meaning of the word *scale* can be related to its meanings noted above, but it is more of a homonym. It sounds and looks the same, and in a given case may even share some meaning, but it is a different concept. The fact that the concepts sometimes appear in the same paragraph or sentence is confusing. Geographic scale, for the purposes of this section, is not about how big you make the squares on your map -- it is about your selection and ordering of categories of human activity, their relationship, how much territory they cover on the ground, and how much time they consume. You can make the map later. Having said that, you will probably have to use a map to establish your scales.

The phenomena you categorize will have some human ingredients and some non-human ingredients. Water catchment areas are a good example. Part of what defines a water basin, and therefore part of what would define the categories or levels (scales) of water catchment areas, will include ancient geological formations, the fact that water flows downhill, and rainfall. Another part of what defines the categories will be dams, pumps, aqueducts and water laws. Your scaling, in other words, will be informed by a combination of manmade contraptions along with factors that are not manmade.

You will probably find many scaled territorial units already established in the geography of your armed conflict, and others you can find and map if you look. The scales you find are not magic. If they don't work for you, if they do not distribute power, provide justice or services or security in a way that you think is optimal, you can change them. People get used to the inefficiencies and injustices they have, however, so do not trifle with administrative territories. Still, if you don't like the voting districts, or the school tax districts, consider changing them.

Imagine if you came into a large area where there was some kind of water management problem, but you knew neither the administrative history of water districts, where to find the records, nor the people in charge. Nevertheless, you want to study the stewardship and application of the water resources. You would want to select some scales at which to study the phenomenon of water management. In other words, you need to be able to say this much water comes from this watercourse, goes to this use, and is taxed this much within such and such a sub-territory. You might invent a set of categories that exactly matched the categories as were invented by the people who set up the system that is already in place, or your research scales might be different. If different, it will be hard to use older data. If it is overly focused on the non manmade aspects of the resource (like how much water is in the various watersheds and sub-sheds) then you might find that your categories don't match the political boundaries where water decisions are made, or at which money is accumulated for a project. This is no small problem since the scale at which decisions are made to fund and build dams might not have much of a relation to where the water naturally flows.

Water is valuable, but the section is not about water. It is about proper scaling as it applies to water, militias, taxation, church dioceses, school boards, electric power, cell phone use, county commissions, zoning ordinances, sports leagues, and on and on. All these things will impinge upon the lines of communication and existence of sanctuaries. If you have the power to impose a hierarchy of territories, it is one way you can structure the social contract to concentrate or distribute political influence, to create or dissipate grievances, and to reveal relationships. In your study of administrative scales, explicitly address the scalar distribution of political power relevant to the particular issue at hand.

Some phenomena are only revealed at certain scales. For instance, if high school textbook content decisions are made by a federal-level board whose members are elected to life tenures by representatives of an international association, then studying the preferences of schoolbooks among students, teachers, schools or even school districts might be a waste of time. They maybe aren't the right scale. You might do better to go directly to the level of the international association, unless perhaps you wish to show that the textbook choices do not reflect the needs or desires generated at lower scales.

False study categories will throw off your understanding, and clumsy administrative categories could cause you to lose your war. Strategies for social development, security, knowledge generation, or whatever can be greatly enhanced by the explicit discovery and recognition of scales (particularly administrative power scales), and especially of hierarchical and nested scales.

Scales are cultural, and often natural. The term 'natural' is derided by some social scientists as a semantic contraption, but consider the difference between woodworking and house-framing, that is, between furniture or cabinet-making and home construction. These are two closely related but distinctly different scales. At the furniture scale, the direction and appearance of wood grains is a significant matter, the aesthetics of visible joints a concern. Distances are related to things like the height of human knees when sitting at table, or the width of an average human derriere. The house builder is not as often worried about wood grains, but is worried about insulation and roofline. Furniture fits inside the house, not vice-versa. The scales are distinct, if they overlap a bit, and are commonly related to the normal size of the human body. They, like most scales in human geography, are in this sense natural.

The measurement of distance and location are intimately tied to the passing of time, so to ignore or mistake the scale and form of places or spaces is a formula for mistaking the relevant quantities of time. Carpenters like to say 'Measure nine times, cut once.' Many philosophers like to throw space and time together, which usually means they like to see geography and history thrown together as well.

Add weight to the mix of scale problems. Distances seem to be shortened by speed. Karl Marx, commenting on the role of capital on globalization back in his day said space was being annihilated by time.[98] He was saying that capital was shortening distances to markets by technological advancements in the speed of product movement. In the 19th century, however, Karl could not send a grand piano over the telegraph lines. If something is heavy, it can un-annihilate space. Appropriateness of scale applies to space, time, weight, and, if you want to get fancy, resolve.

In an armed conflict, the scales of knowledge and the scales of organization and operations have to be in sync. Learning that most of the people in Mexico speak Spanish doesn't help as much as knowing that in that one county where the dental unit is going to work most people speak Tenik, a rare indigenous language. To say that there are only 8,000 FARC guerrillas left in Colombia might be good, but if you are going to a *municipio* where 2,000 of them are running around, your concern should mount. *Scale* and the classic military concept of *mass* are closely related, as are scale and the relative measurement of power. Your care in determining scale will weigh heavily on the time it takes you to win.

Seeing things as scale problems can help you measure those things in better geographic detail. Not seeking the geographic footprints of problems (in other words, calculating the balance of resources, objectives and methods in the abstract and apart from geography) is a formula for failure. To a lesser degree, so is indifference to administrative power scales. Time is the same way. All things are possible in time, they say, but they don't say how much.

See: 63, *Cost-Distance*; 67, *Points, Lines, Spaces*; 49, *Territorial Scrutiny*; 66, *GIS*; 2, *The Line of Retreat*; and 116, *Strategy of Aggregate Tactics*; 12, *Protraction* and *Diligence*; and 47, *Why the County*.

---

> "What is this? A center for ants? How can we be expected to teach children to learn how to read... if they can't even fit inside the building?… I don't wanna hear your excuses! The building has to be at least... three times bigger than this!"
>
> Derek in the movie
> *Zoolander* (2001)[99]
>
> (on being shown a mock-up of the proposed 'Center For Kids Who Can't Read Good And Wanna Learn To Do Other Stuff Good Too')

ꕥꕥꕥ

It's not that hard

# *Section 69, Measuring Actions against Enemies*

People find, given war-making and other cultural habits, that efforts to stop an existing enemy are not always entirely consistent with the job of bettering the physical and psychological conditions that help create more of them. This section and the next deal with the problem of how to measure the effect of action in terms of a reasonably expressed goal -- a problem in this case complicated by the confounding relationship just noted. How do we measure progress in neutralizing enemies and simultaneously determine if we aren't creating more of them?

The first and last sections of this book define State success in terms of impunity. State failure by this definition can be measured, and ideas for that measurement are offered later in this section. The immediate subject is how to measure progress against an organized armed enemy -- how well you are doing to close with and neutralize him. In international warfare, surrender of the enemy's generals, demobilization of his soldiers, and confiscation of his weapons are good signs of military victory, and these things occur in irregular wars as well.

Usually, however, when an armed conflict doesn't rise to the level of international war in which a country's government might be able to surrender, evacuate territory and pay reparations, the word victory can be more argument than substance. Citizens, soldiers and comrades demand and deserve to know how things are going -- what their blood and treasure are paying for, and if their aspirations are being fulfilled. Leaders often don't want them to know, afraid that the resolve of their followers may not be equal to their own; or they want to hide failures; or maybe it doesn't matter to them how the enterprise is going as long as they are doing well personally. Leaders tend to want to keep their jobs. There also exist good, honest, competitive reasons for not letting your enemy know how well you think you are doing.

Measuring success in armed conflicts shouldn't be difficult unless the goals are wobbly. Criticism to the contrary notwithstanding, the United States national security goal for places like Iraq, Afghanistan, the Philippines, or Colombia is obvious enough: that those places not be cradles, harbors and exporters of contraband and murder. Whether the specific object of smuggling is drugs, people or plutonium; or if murder is perpetrated by way of suicide, landmine or a weapon of mass destruction, America's best understanding holds some places more likely than others to be enablers or source-grounds of internationally dangerous behavior. When you cannot timely deter smugglers and murders from doing you grave harm, you might label them enemies and try to visit violence on them. The lead documents of US national security strategy name a few such enemies as the US sees it, and also express the observation that negative underlying social, economic and cultural conditions help a place to become one of those wherein enemies of the US are formed or aided. The United States expressed a reasonable challenge: to protect itself; and has asserted a reasonable hypothesis: that to do so it must destroy an intractable enemy, but must also ameliorate the conditions that create enemies. Side with the United States or not, but the logic is straight forward.

Relevant public and individual psychological attitudes are not constrained such that we can easily label them enemy or friendly attitudes. Apathy, fear, ignorance, indifference, capriciousness, curiosity, fecklessness, and passive resistance all weigh on levels and types of participation in activities we either promote or feel we cannot abide. We can measure some of these mental quantities, but not all of them, and rarely well. For this reason, psychological measurement, while not wholly rejected here, is not central to this conception of measurement.

Finally, distinctions between criminally and politically motivated action (distinctions often confounded and belied by the nature of many of today's armed organizations) are still useful. For efficiency, however, most of the following presentation refers to the various forms of enemies of the State as insurgents.

We can divide our measurement instrument into three levels as follows:

> CONCLUSIVE: Measurement of the extent to which a government action or program has ended an opponent's power to grant impunity. Tied closely to this is whether or not the government has captured or killed the insurgent, and tied closely to this is whether or not the government has blocked the insurgent enemy leaders' routes of escape, denying their sanctuaries. The insurgent commanders' strategies for survival are almost opposite: To maintain routes of withdrawal and lines of communication; maintain sanctuaries so as to retain the ability to recruit, train and supply, and, foremost, to grant impunity.
>
> CONDITIONING: Measurement of decisions and actions taken by senior leaders over time to improve the probabilities that subordinate leaders will encounter the enemy, and that in any given encounter subordinate leaders will enjoy an advantage in correlations of force and culminating points.
>
> ENCOUNTER: Measurement of decisions and actions taken immediately before and during encounters with enemy elements that result in local victory or defeat.

Of these three, it must be noted that only the first category, CONCLUSIVE measures, are measures of results, while the other two are measures of inputs.

**(1) Indices of conclusive success**: If you are the counterinsurgent, your ultimate grade depends on whether or not you have stopped a challenger of the State from successfully granting impunity in defiance of your State. If your enemy has a name and you kill him, that person, at least, is not going to protect anyone from your laws and punishments. If you do not identify your enemy correctly, however, your real enemy will continue to protect his followers from your ability to punish them for wrongdoing. Honest measurement is tied to correctly and precisely defining your enemy. Of the indices of conclusive success, however, first and foremost is the measure of impunity being granted by an identity other than your State. (Let's be nice for a moment: You *might* not have to kill the guy. You might be OK just capturing him, or 'psyoping' his people against him, or taking away all his financial strength.) Regardless of how you achieve it, if you have not stopped the unauthorized granting of impunity by your enemy, you have not beaten him.

> 1. Are elements of the enemy organization able to commit crimes and not get caught; get caught, but not be prosecuted; or be prosecuted, but escape from jail? *If insurgent leaders are effectively protecting their agents from punishment by the State, the State and probably the society are failing, and if you are the purported* counterinsurgent *military leader, so are you.*

Everything below this first measure is a secondary measure. They are still *conclusive* under the assumption that you can correctly identify your enemy. If so, your goal is easier, because you do not have to measure success on the basis of whether or not impunity is being granted in defiance of the State generally, but only if your *named enemy* is granting impunity in defiance of the State.

> 2. How many of the enemy insurgent leaders have been eliminated by surrender, capture, death, coercion, buy-out or deception? *Either they have been neutralized or they have not. If, by the way, an insurgent leader can be timely turned or purchased, and he ceases to provide impunity to his followers, then the logic here is that he or she is thus neutralized.*
>
> 3. How many of the identified enemy insurgent leaders have been located? *Of course, how many is not as good as how many out of the total and how important is each.*
>
> 4. How many enemy insurgent leaders have been identified? *If they have been identified, then some insurgent security is breached. If the leaders have not been identified, locating them is all the more difficult, as is counting them.*

If you are going to kill or capture your insurgent enemy, you will have to block his route to sanctuary. (Remember, if you catch him in his sanctuary or close his sanctuary, it is not his sanctuary.) In order to establish indices to measure success in blocking your enemy leaders' lines of retreat to sanctuary, you first have to find the enemy lines of communication (LOC). If enemy LOC haven't been found, some measurement of their being blocked may nevertheless be possible, but it is then logically a more difficult task. The most senior insurgent leaders sometimes reside outside the territory at issue. If a FARC Commander, for instance, is sleeping someplace in Venezuela, he at least keeps some subordinate level of command inside Colombia. To close with and destroy second-tier leadership, the same truth reigns, however: counterinsurgent military success revolves around closing the routes of escape of the insurgent leaders. (Although 'closing' need not necessarily be conceived in a physical sense. That is, if the enemy leader cannot move along his chosen route of escape fast enough to prevent effective pursuit, the route is effectively closed. It does not have to be crossed in a purely geometric, two-dimensional or Napoleonic sense.) So, how do we know if lines of communication have been effectively blocked behind an insurgent leader? We identify him, fix him in space or time, and capture or kill him. For some this may be a daunting metric to impose because it is so obvious and so difficult. Regardless, it is a conclusive measurement for defeating an enemy. Please don't take this assertion as a defense of the counting of dead insurgent soldiers; the count of neutralized insurgent leaders is far more indicative, the higher a leader the better. Sometimes they surrender. If it has become impossible for your enemy to grant impunity for actions his people take in your territory, that is a conclusive sign of success, and if the condition can be indefinitely maintained, victory.

5. How many wounded insurgents are returned to action by the insurgency? *If captured guerrillas have been previously wounded and successfully returned to combat functions, it is a clear sign that the insurgent LOC-to-sanctuary was viable. We can suppose that it remains equally viable for an insurgent leader.*

6. How far from combat actions are insurgent hospitals? *Distance from the point of injury to medical care is a clear indicator of ability to maintain the LOC-to-sanctuary.*

7. Do insurgents receive training outside their areas of operation? *Similarly, the more it appears that training is conducted remotely, the more evident a healthy LOC-to-sanctuary.*

8. Is there evidence of general support maintenance of enemy equipment? *Some maintenance activities are unlikely to be conducted close to the point of operations. Evidence that such maintenance is occurring is again evidence of a healthy LOC-to-sanctuary.*

9. Are insurgents recruited from areas distant from their areas of operation? *This may not be a strong indicator of LOC-to-sanctuary health, but sufficiently varied data can indicate recruit source preferences and changes in likely sanctuaries over time.*

10. Can insurgent leadership travel abroad legally? *If insurgent leaders are showing up in foreign capitals, it is clearly a sign of LOC-to-sanctuary health.*

11. How well are the insurgent junior leaders and foot-soldiers trained? *This may or may not be a sign that the leaders' LOC-to-sanctuary is healthy or their ability to muster resources intact. The insurgent leaders may be choosing not to expend or risk resources.*

12. How new are insurgent weaponry and other equipment? *This may or may not be a sign that the leaders' LOC-to-sanctuary is healthy or the ability to muster resources intact. The insurgent leaders may be choosing not to expend or risk resources.*

13. What is the pattern and pace of visits by leaders to subordinate leaders? *This may or may not be a sign that the leaders' LOC-to-sanctuary is healthy or the ability to muster resources intact. The insurgent leaders may be choosing not to expend or risk resources.*

14. What is the number and rate of valid, un-coerced informant reports? *This may be one of the most revealing indicators of LOC-to-sanctuary health because it implies a breakdown of security for the LOC. This, however, is one of the types of indicators that must be closely held.*

As a parallel we can consider what the insurgent leader's measures of conclusive military success are. If the insurgent kills or captures all counterinsurgent leadership, he wins conclusively, but that is an unnecessarily radical requirement for conclusive evidence of success. A national leader might negotiate terms (which for the insurgent is equivalent to partial victory), may be booted out by his own people, or even abandon the country. It may be that staying in the business of insurgency is a sufficient level of success for the insurgent, and so the measures become almost synonymous with measures that prove the avoidance of failure. The insurgent leader might measure the safety of his enterprise as follows:

1. Is my bank account increasing or decreasing? *If it's beating inflation, I'm OK.*

2. Has the government identified any of my lines of communication? *(Has it found a bank account, broken one of my codes, stopped a shipment of weapons, intercepted the visit of a subordinate commander, or prevented out-of area training?) If it has, it may find more, my sanctuary is tenuous, and I might have to run.*

3. Is my family safe? *If not, and I care, I'm in trouble.*

4. Can I travel to country X? *If not, my sanctuary options decrease, and my safe lines of retreat are fewer.*

5. Can I meet with subordinates easily? *If not, my power to effect things on the ground is limited.*

6. Are my people being killed or captured? If they are captured, can I get them back? If I can fulfill my grant of impunity to my people, I'm doing well. *If the State can enforce its monopoly on granting impunity, my end is nearing.*

7. After contact with government forces, are my subordinate units successful in escaping?

This is what the insurgent leader needs to know, depending on his patience and goals. His ultimate questions are 'Am I still able to garner resources without being trapped by my counterinsurgent foe?,' and 'Can I still protect my followers from punishment by the government?' If the answers are yes, the insurgency conclusively is in good shape. We might ask if the government's ability to recruit soldiers wouldn't be a significant metric by which the insurgent could measure the progress of the insurgency. Ease of government recruitment could not be taken as a good sign for the insurgent, but it would hardly be conclusive of anything.

In a liberal democracy, counterinsurgent leadership is on loan. The ultimate decider of the professional fate of counterinsurgent leadership may be a voting public. That public may be wise, valiant, knowledgeable and persevering, and guided by selfless volunteers. It may also be flighty, uninformed, fearful and misled. Measures of personal success of an insurgent do not generally apply to the liberal politician or his generals.

**(2) Indices of conditioning success:** These items help measure the extent to which the counterinsurgent military leadership has improved the probabilities that in any given combat action their subordinate commanders will enjoy advantages in correlation of force. It also includes measures taken to assure anonymity for counterinsurgent information providers and take away anonymity from the insurgent enemy (improve the balance of anonymities). Metrics of conditioning success might include the following:

1. How many insurgent supply caches have been found? How large are they?
2. How many persons are killed in individual insurgent attacks?
3. What are the locations and numbers of insurgent landmines and other explosives?
4. What category of targets is being chosen by the insurgent?
5. What is the location of the targets chosen by the insurgent?
6. What are the relative sizes of forces engaged in combat actions?
7. What is the condition of captured insurgent weapons, rations?
8. What are the ages of captured enemy soldiers?
9. What is the ability of the insurgent enemy to recover wounded?
10. What is the relation of friendly casualties to insurgent casualties in firefights?
11. What is the extension of illicit crops?
12. What do extortion and other crime statistics indicate?
13. What is happening to the number of un-coerced informant reports?

To these indices might be added, not as conclusive measures, some advantages that may be given to the counterinsurgent force or taken away from the insurgent force. For instance, if the counterinsurgent force has been given better rifles, more training, or more mobility, these things might be assumed to give a relative counterinsurgent advantage, all else remaining the same. They should not be given too much weight, since they are all means toward the goal, not the goal itself. Supposed, or potential advantages for creating superiority in culminating points and correlations of force might not be applied; or they might be countered by other loses, or overmatched by enemy adjustments. A counterinsurgent force might obtain more helicopters, for instance, but that change is not a good measure of greater counterinsurgent success.

The insurgent leader's measure of his conditioning success will be very similar. Since he may be in the business of simple survival as an entity, or, like the Colombian FARC, simply in business, measures might also include such things as the number of subordinate elements meeting or exceeding previous financial contribution quotas, the territorial area under control according to tax revenues, customer complaints, etc.

**(3) Indices of encounter success:** The indices in this sub-section help measure the success of decisions and actions that directly cause victory or failure during an encounter with the enemy (battle). The encounter might be police in scale or considerably larger, or might entail the destruction of materiel, capital assets or inventory. They might be simple terror attacks. The indices should not be used to measure success in the overall insurgency or counterinsurgency, but rather to validate the selection of techniques, tactics, procedures, combat leaders, equipment and intelligence categories. Record of these indicators might be kept on a national scale for a variety of reasons. (See, however, sections 11, *Decisive Battle* and 116, *Strategy of Aggregate Tactics.*) They are highly situation-dependent and in the aggregate can mislead. Nevertheless, over time a change in the averages may indicate some change in the overall relative strength.

1. How many enemy soldiers were captured alive or surrendered in an action?

2. How many enemy soldiers were killed in an action?

3. How much materiel was decommissioned in an action?

4. How much insurgent capital inventory was destroyed or taken in an action?

5. Did the local, national and international media pick up the story of an action?

6. How do the above compare with friendly losses and capital expenditure in comparison with other encounters?

7. Was contact with the enemy followed with a pursuit of the inferior force by the superior force?

8. If pursuit followed a contact, was the inferior force overtaken?

The last two questions, about pursuit, are especially significant in the aggregate. If pursuits are never successful, it almost becomes a conclusive measure of insurgent success and counterinsurgent failure.

The three categories, Conclusive, Conditioning and Encounter, are important in that order, and whatever success story the conditioning and encounter numbers might purport, it can be cogently argued that a counterinsurgency is not progressing well if the conclusive numbers are not improving. However, if the enemies who we have identified as having wielded the power to grant impunity are dead or in our controlling custody, *and* our measures of unauthorized impunity show that our State has regained a monopoly on granting impunity, we've won, at least for now.

Unfortunately, if in the society you are trying to defend, impunity is the norm for criminal behavior – because of the lack of law enforcement, generalized corruption, prosecutorial ineptitude, lack of judiciary resources or institutional infrastructure, overcrowded prisons…whatever – it will be pretty hard to tell if the insurgent you've named as your enemy is protecting his followers from government punishment or not, since the system isn't punishing *anyone* on an equitable basis. Since this is often the case, you may have to settle for a count of dead or captured insurgent leaders as the conclusive measurement, rather than of the monopoly of State impunity. At least the entity you named as your enemy will no longer be protecting their members from government punishment for having illegally taxed, blown things up or otherwise offended your sovereignty.

A lesser counting problem for conclusive success is evident when the number of insurgent leaders you've caught, or at least identified, cannot be represented as to its portion of the total in existence. It may be hard to know how much of the insurgent leadership must be neutralized before you have doused the *mens rea.* Much of this ability depends on the capacity of the insurgency to replace its leadership. For this reason, 'conclusive' progress counts are best when accompanied by measurements in the conditioning and encounter categories.

At some point we can assume that an insurgency has been effectively reduced if no more insurgent leaders can be identified, no insurgent actions are undertaken and no insurgent leaders can protect their followers from government punishment. If there are no remaining insurgent leaders at-large, and there is no insurgent activity, then there is probably no insurgency, at least for a while.

Some intelligence, insurgent or counterinsurgent, cannot be made available to the public, but battles and other actions are hard to hide, and should be carefully recorded as to time, place, participants and results. Governments, at least, are wise to make data about actions public as soon as possible so that a public ground truth stabilizes. This can go a long way to avoiding false accusations and claims, but obviously, if the government has done something wrong, such as a clear human rights violation, it may find itself on the wrong side of life's ledger. Individual government and insurgent leaders may calculate that covering things up is to their personal advantage. These days, 'truth commissions' or 'truth, reconciliation and restitution commissions' are common features of the political landscape. The data on which these commissions rest their findings is often opaque, but does not have to be.

Reasonably, some data cannot be released to public scrutiny until after an appropriate time lapse. This is because the public includes violent partisan members, and some information has a time value that directly influences military or forensic operations in progress. Some information is kept confidential because public exposure is too likely to adversely affect the acquisition of more information or hurt an informer. In some individual cases, child or other victim protection is involved. For instance, the results of prisoner interrogations, if made public, could discourage cooperation from prisoners, endanger their lives or change the quality of information. Nevertheless, ultimately public opinion matters, and there probably exists a publicly presentable truth about every event that is precise enough for public decision-making, not detrimental to current operations and not likely to endanger anyone.

Depending on the situation, it may be useful psychologically and practically to identify publicly some or all of your targets in advance, and then to announce their demise. The deck of cards of most wanted Saddam Hussein regime leaders worked well for the Americans in Iraq, and the rapid crossing-out of the top fifty of the ousted regime clearly showed progress against the former regime. That set of leaders is not coming back. In Colombia, a similar set of cards was proposed and prepared, but Colombian leaders made a determination that its use there was inappropriate. The insurgent can make similar public announcements and tallies to considerable psychological effect.

Some information can be more powerful if made public, the location of landmines being the obvious example. Not only does public knowledge of the presence of landmines in an area directly increase safe practices, it encourages submission of information on landmines that only the public might possess.

The ultimate standard of measurement of counterinsurgent success cannot be predicated on a hope that the enemy insurgent leaders will give up without being forced to do so, that their ability to recruit will be rendered ineffective, or that their means of communicating with followers impeded. These later concepts are useful, but they are *ipso facto* secondary. The most conclusive measure of victory over your enemy is his death. As often underlined, however -- if you isolate on this measure alone, over-emphasize it, or over-rely on it and the operational methods leading to it, then you are likely to suffer the unintended consequence of creating more enemies.

See: 4, *Defining Enemy*; 66, *GIS;* 106, *Tourism*; 49, *Territorial Scrutiny*; 107, *Price of Real Estate*; 144, *Impunity and State Success*; 2, *The Line of Retreat*; and 48, *Grading the Social Contract.*

---

> Strategy is for winning. The best strategies reconcile goals, resources, courses of action and ethics. Good strategies economize the expenditure of power; they gain, create and defend property. Great military strategies perplex the enemy -- conditioning, channeling and frustrating the enemy's perceptions of power and options. The best leaders strategize not only when a disadvantage dictates, but at all times, especially in comparative strength, in order to preserve the most precious resources. Strategy is the identity, mantra and beloved of all war colleges. It is also their mother and their father. Strategy covers all things, it has faith in all things, it hopes in all things, it endures in all things.
>
> Anonymous

Will the place you create spawn enemies?

# *Section 70, Measuring Effects of Actions on Structure*

The last section suggested ways to measure the impact of actions taken to close with and neutralize an armed enemy. Those actions can affect both the enemy and conditions in the society, conditions which in aggregate we can call the structure. Your actions might further the creation of more enemies, or not even address whatever conditions helped spawn, motivate or empower your enemies. So you might try to measure what effect your actions against the enemy have on the structure of life, in addition to measuring those actions you take to change the structure directly, if you are taking any at all. As with section 69, this section is not so much about what to do; but rather how to measure the effects of what you do.

Besides closing with and neutralizing an enemy, success in armed social conflicts may mean establishing conditions from which new enemies do not spring. Maybe if liberty and property are protected, and material progress is a reasonable expectation for everyone, such conditions are met. We see that even in places where all parts of the trinity of human flourishing -- freedom, security and material prosperity -- are abundant, disaffected elements exist, armed and angry. Misery does not equal insurgency, either. In many of the poorest, disease-ridden, illiterate areas of the world, where the populace is barely eking out an existence, the people do not rise against the government. Conversely, there are insurgencies or violent opposition groups in economically developed, healthy, literate countries, and leaders of the discontented often emerge from the educated, upper-middleclass children of privilege. It seems that the measure of successful action against an insurgency cannot validly base itself on an assumed correlation to material improvements.

Whether or not the poorer strata of a population are provided with government services may be crucial or of little importance. A population may tolerate government corruption or fight it. Good governance to some societies may mean an all-encompassing social welfare system, whereas other societies may view good governance as non-interference in the lives of the populace. Measuring the success of governance, therefore, may require some measurement of popular perceptions and expectations. New schools, roads and inoculation programs are often popular, visible signs of government interest, but are they measurements of counterinsurgent success, the basis of better propaganda, or nothing at all?

Violent insurgent ideologies today are described as religious, nationalist, ethnic or regional, or still of a Marxist tint, or ambiguous in their intellectual determinants, and they often involve competing armed groups vying for supremacy over control of the movement in question. Regardless, economic and political power will remain ultimate insurgent goals, and financial profitability and renown are available in sufficient measure by merely surviving. Therefore, the success or failure of an insurgency should not be measured by its having attained or having failed to attain some stated political goal, or even by having such goals.

Measurement of overall violence would seem to contribute, but if violence spikes, does that mean that the government is losing ground? Or if violence slowly diminishes, does that mean the government is doing something right? The 'right' answers may depend on numbers of incidents of violence, or on intensity, identity of the victims, number of victims per event, identities of the perpetrators, or the purposes of the violence, etc. Whether the violence occurs in primarily one-sided attacks or in clashes between armed groups is also significant. One-sided attacks indicate initiative or maybe the capacity and resolve to bully and extort. An increase in attacks or clashes initiated by government forces against an outlaw armed force may mean that the government is gaining ground. Even this may be a false reading, however, as the initiative of government forces may be due to an increase in resources or of aggressive and effective leadership. Evidence that government forces are taking the fight to outlaws (and perhaps thereby protecting the civilian population) may be a positive sign of effort, but the same evidence may tell us nothing about the overall condition of the society as to its likelihood of producing more outlaws.

Offered below is a laundry list of indices that might serve to measure progress of a counterinsurgency to establish conditions of human security, along with an improved likelihood that more insurgent enemies are not being created.

Measuring human security:

1. Real estate prices
2. Migration rates
3. Vehicle-miles traveled on selected roads without incident (incidents per vehicle mile)
4. Tourist destination bookings and visits
5. Civilian landmine injuries and locations

6. Tip-offs to government regarding criminality
7. Kidnappings reported
8. Number of resolved real property civil court case
9. Transparency of public records
10. Levels of smuggling activity
11. Number of peacefully achieved arrests by warrant for felonies
12. Bond rates

Measuring prosperity:

1. Real estate prices
2. Tax collections to tax rates
3. Percent of formally owned land
4. Bond and insurance rates
5. Vacation patterns

Measuring freedom:

1. Real estate prices
2. Ballot access
3. National tourist origin-destination
4. Immigration rates
5. Registered NGOs
6. Cell phone dispersion and use rates
7. Internet logon rates

Measuring public will to support the social contract and defeat insurgents:

1. Informant tip-offs
2. Voter turn-outs and votes
3. Emigration and immigration
4. Volunteer participation in public forces by youth members of the elite

You, being cynical, will say that many of the above indices are inappropriate to the level of education and economic development in some societies. True, but some are highly universal. One is tourism, and so tourism is addressed in a separate section, although there are few societies where tourism will not provide a useful measure for changes in human security. Another is the price of real estate, and so that has a separate section as well.

**Regarding baselines, stability and testability:** Whatever the indices used, you may want to fix a baseline for measurement, as well as durable increments of measurement. Our ruler should be armored against manipulation, or it cannot give an honest measure over time. It should resist change. To aid in credibility, the instrument must be subject to repetition and testing by those disinterested in the upshot of the measurement, as well as by those who are stridently invested in the arguments that the data might support or undermine. Be careful with definitions used in statistical presentation. For instance, in regard to landmines, 'Known Landmine Locations as of 01/11/2008' is a more durable map title than 'Landmine Locations,' given the typically incomplete nature of these datasets, not to mention the danger and liability caused by a map negligently claiming to display all current locations.

**Regarding the availability of data**: It would be a formula for frustration, misdirection and loss of credibility to establish a system of measurement based on indices that are practicably unavailable or that could become so. The best data is data that is least subject to purposeful influence either by an enemy or by opponents and proponents of the policies under scrutiny. It is also data the collection of which does not depend on an unsustainable infrastructure of collection assets.

**Regarding causality**: Can you ever be sure of causation? Even if available data clearly show the insurgent force to be weakening and the conditions of society improving, it may be difficult to claim that the government's policies caused these trends. What is to say that other policies might not have worked better? There will always be room for logical (never mind merely argumentative) attack. However, faith in data can be built on the basic logic of proximity in time and space. As mentioned in Section 66, GIS events can strongly suggest causation when there is a continuing pattern of correct temporal sequence and spatial proximity. Although anecdotal evidence might suggest that the implementation of a particular government tactic was followed by a reduction in political violence, a much stronger argument for causation is available if that same tactic, implemented in town after town, were followed by a similar decline in violence in each place. In such a scenario, the burden of proof regarding causality reverses, and those who would deny causality are invited to prove their contention with better data. Because of the logical power of physical proximity and temporal sequence, the most convincing indices of causality (convincing because of their durability under honest examination) are those that can be presented geographically over time. Although causation is hard to prove, factual misalignments in time and space can easily disprove many theories of causation. For this reason, relational GIS databases are a salient technology for useful measurement.

**Regarding State failure**: A map can be made of the sub-territories within a State where some entity other than the State can successfully grant impunity. The map will show where the State is failing. If it shows few places where impunity can be granted by any entity other than the State, the State is not failing. Conversely, if the map shows that in the greater portion of space and population the State does not have a monopoly on the granting of impunity, how can the territory function as a democracy, and why should that State be considered a legitimate representative of the people? The answer is by no means automatic. It may be that the State has an attractive philosophy, sincere leaders and many loyalists, but is simply under successful attack. The measure of State success proposed herein does not say that the successful State is necessarily a good one, but it also does not say that the failing State is necessarily a bad one.

It may be possible to form a baseline of data regarding how many felonies are committed in relation to cultural norms. A map can be created based on the number of felonies that the State fails to investigate, lead to arrests, successfully prosecute or punish. Such data gives an idea of overall impunity for the commission of crimes, but the impunity may be caused by simple State inefficiency or prosecutorial weakness. If the impunity is particular to a specific entity (say, to members of a specific mafia or guerrilla) then it becomes apparent that the State does not have a monopoly on the granting of impunity.

In some places, data on felonies is so hard to build and the prosecution of felonies so unlikely that the above measures are impossible to create or are meaningless. Still, if such is the case, what level of respect is the State then due as a representative of the territory or the people in it? Perhaps some States should have their legitimacy as representative bodies qualified to no area greater than the sub-territories in which they maintain control over the granting of impunity. This is exactly the argument that some insurgent groups will make, given that they, through ruthless efficiency, strictly prosecute crimes, and simultaneously do not let the formal government do so. In many cases these may produce an unsustainable result. Just because a State is successful, doesn't make it ethical, and just because it is not completely successful, doesn't mean it is unethical.

Human security is a complicated concept, but that also can be measured, as Section 75 on tourism and Section 44 on the price of real estate both suggest. The problem of fair measurement is itself a matter to be considered in any formulation of a peaceful society. Andro Linklater's *Measuring America* is one of the least heralded, but most remarkably well-argued books on this point. It is about the forming of the United States, but it frames that story within an observation about stable measurements and measuring devices as central innovations in human conflict resolution and in the creation of human wealth.

The 'gram' or the 'yard' reveal themselves as so obviously valuable that we are impressed to return to our plans to see if we have overlooked fairness and stability of basic measures as a concern in our plans for peaceful territories. That is a theme of *Property & Peace*, and of the sections in this book that deal with the formalization of property ownership. The regulation of measurement goes beyond that, however, to the expectations of monetary stability, time periods for governance, the value of a single vote, number of public school days, etc. The question of stable measurement as a column of conflict resolution reminds the most libertarian among us of the role that government might have to play in conflict resolution, a role that depends on something we so easily overlook -- that an ounce needs to be exactly an ounce every time if we are to avoid fights.

See: 66, *GIS;* 106, *Tourism*; 49, *Territorial Scrutiny*; 107, *Price of Real Estate*; 144, *Impunity and State Success*; and 48, *Grading the Social Contract*; 53, *Hohfeldian Grievance Analysis*; and 90, *Prisons*.

---

> "Some people wonder all their lives if they've made a difference. The Marines don't have that problem."
>
> Ronald Reagan[100]

Land promise

# *Section 71, Jerusalem*

The Hymn *Jerusalem* (built on William Blake's poetry from the early 19th century) as well as the histories of the song, the poem and the artists fit several themes of this book. Here are the lyrics:

And did those feet in ancient time
Walk upon England's mountains green?

And was the Holy Lamb of God
On England's pleasant pastures seen?

And did the Countenance Divine
Shine forth upon our clouded hills?
And was Jerusalem builded here
Among those dark Satanic Mills?

Bring me my Bow of burning gold:
Bring me my Arrows of desire:
Bring me my Spear: O clouds, unfold!
Bring me my Chariot of fire!

I will not cease from Mental Fight,
Nor shall my Sword sleep in my hand
Till we have built Jerusalem
In England's green and pleasant land.[101]

'Dark Satanic mills' became Brit-speak for poor human stewardship of the natural and human environment. It has been interpreted in other ways, all subversive, and it could have become a catch phrase for the global insurgency, or at least parts of it. Maybe it is paradoxical that the music now mated to the poetry was written during World War I in an effort to brace British resolve. In one way or another, the poetry is seditious, protesting as it did the failed observance of labor rights and women's rights, and the rights of British subjects generally. It speaks of the desire to create the idyllic Jerusalem, the just City of God, in England, and became a beloved national song representing the best that the British would believe about and aspire for themselves. Its singing in the 1981 movie *Chariots of Fire* brought the hymn to the American ear in a particularly apt way.[102]

At the beginning of the movie, a young Jewish sprinter is singing the hymn along with the rest of the Cambridge choir. He is both a great sprinter and self-consciously Jewish, and not far removed is the allusion to a contemporary Zionist movement that would like to see Jerusalem created on earth. The Zionists don't see Jerusalem being built in England any time soon; the Jerusalem they have in mind is *the* Jerusalem.

This brings us to the central issue confronting Zionist strategists between about 1897 and 1949, which was the mortal vulnerability of the European Jewish population in its dispersed condition. The Zionists reasonably feared massacre. In response, they resolved to create an independent Jewish state in Palestine, but the Nazis (rather than the Russians as earlier Zionists had predicted) engaged in murder at a pace and scale that overcame the capacity of the Zionist enterprise. Before the appearance of the Nazis, however, and before Arabs in Palestine could consolidate a common identity with leadership able to oppose them, the Zionists had already formulated and launched their unique land strategy.

As it formed in the 19th century, the national purpose of the Jewish collective contained within it three parts. One was fulfillment of the scriptures as interpreted by Jewish religious leadership; a second was simple survival in the midst of variously hostile polities; and a third was prosperity. Establishment of a Jewish presence in Palestine concerted with the first of these purposes. Redemption was to come through human effort to gather the scattered of Israel into the Holy Land. By the end of the 19th century the still small but growing set of Zionist leaders interpreted the messianic significance of redemption in and from Palestine as necessary for the second purpose, survival. Regarding the third purpose, prosperity, those same Zionist leaders had to create arguments and conditions to overcome inertia of complacency, logical doubt, intra-ethnic distrust, and divided national loyalties among elements of the geographically disperse European Jewish population.

Jewish grand strategy, or strategic vision, would be provided by Zionist leaders. If we begin in the late 19th century with Theodor Herzl and Chaim Weizmann, we can say that Zionist leaders faced not only the task of translating national purpose into a practicable vision, but also the task of consolidating Jewish cultural and religious identity into a national secular one accessible to Zionist strategic leadership. In this respect, these late 19th century Zionists already enjoyed a strategic legacy of sorts. One of the innovations necessary for a project of national geographic consolidation was the secularization and broadening of the study of Hebrew as a language. Earlier leaders, beginning perhaps with Yehuda hai Alkalai, willed Hebrew to become not only suitable for religious purposes, but for secular communication among Jews for the explicit purpose of enabling a common Jewish political life in Palestine. To this we can add strategic recognition by the Zionists of a relevant global trend: accelerating globalization.

Globalization was more than a phenomenon at which to marvel; it meant opportunity to communicate and implement an un-Diaspora that had not previously been practicable. It allowed Zionists to apply tithes and other donations from areas where economic conditions or moral empathy provided surpluses to fund migrant families from other areas where the domestic environment and social conditions created pressures for migration. Like today, globalization meant more than advances in financial communication and transportation technologies. The expansion of free market principles also eroded feudal land ownership patterns within the Ottoman Empire, opening a door for Zionist strategic thought. For the Zionists, useful globalization occurred incrementally. The occasions during which liquid financial means, effective diplomacy and travel potential coincided with localized Jewish demands for an escape increased throughout the period.

Growing nationalism, especially in Eastern Europe, was another relevant international trend that Zionists recognized as both a force for Jewish unification and a factor increasing discrimination and ethnic resentment. Warfare in the Balkans before World War I spurred a varying mix of local alliances and coalitions that in every case seemed to prejudice Jewish populations. They not only produced waves of migration, but specific national and international policies based on ethnic movement and redistribution. In every case, the central issue was land ownership.

In order to implement Zionist national policy, the construction of a strategy formulation process was also necessary. On October 29, 1897, Herzl and other continental Zionist leaders convened the First Zionist Congress in Basel, Switzerland. This was the beginning of a process of process-formation that resulted in increased capacity to excite solidarity, marshal resources and induce action from a dispersed and disparate collective identity. By 1903 and the Sixth Zionist Congress, Herzl was trying steer the concept of a Jewish homeland toward a site in eastern Africa -- not a concept appealing to other Zionists, including Weizmann, who considered the notion a betrayal of the national purpose. When Herzl died in 1904, Zionist leaders, led especially by Weizmann, who became president of the World Zionist Organization (WRO), permanently returned the decision azimuth toward Palestine.

Herzl's assessment of the risks of a Palestine strategy appears to have been correct. We might say that according to Herzl's analysis, the Palestine goal would achieve the desired ends, the Jewish population would support it and consider it entirely ethical, but it was not feasible in that the means did not appear to exist. The rest of the Zionist leadership, which would prevail, made a different assessment, believing that an Africa strategy was not suitable because presence in Palestine was an element of the basic national identity that gave the strategy meaning.

Whether in Palestine or eastern Africa, the national objective of the Zionists from the outset was the construction of an independent Jewish homeland. Although Herzl ultimately despaired of its being established in Palestine, there was little divergence among Zionist leaders that an independent state was the goal. The Jews needed a place where the granting of impunity did not belong to their enemies.

The operational strategy to support that goal centered on incremental migration and real estate purchase and development. It was not a land strategy in the abstract. It was a buy land and live on it strategy. This reconciled well with available Jewish national power in the form of intermittent flows of migrants, a growing amount of financial capital, but very limited physical force. It could be tailored to disparate and incremental migrations at the family and community level. It also presented a legal approach that did not challenge ethics shared by Jews with non-Jews. Furthermore, it entailed less risk of sparking Judaeophobic reaction, and it was subject to support by quiet diplomatic efforts tailored to whichever geographic, judicial and bureaucratic paths presented themselves.

This real property strategy had to be supported by the creation of specialized organizations and processes, key examples among these being the Palestine Land Development Corporation and the Committee for Population Transfer of the Jewish Agency, which were ultimately comprised of specialists in the areas of land purchases, settlement, economics, law, and local Arab culture. Also indispensible was the development, beginning in 1921, of a loyal, organized armed force. This became increasingly important as strategic competitors analyzed Jewish intentions and began to take and execute decisions against the Zionist strategy.

The Zionists recognized they could begin the process of land acquisition with a company chartered from the Turkish government, this in spite of protestation from some anti-Jewish Ottoman diplomats to whom the strategy was transparent. Up until World War I, official Turkish resistance was also subject to amelioration indirectly through intervention by the British government. After the war, the Ottoman strategic actor disappeared, but the fact of Ottoman governance had postponed consolidation of other Arab Palestinian leadership entities.

The League of Nations Mandate to the British ratified and legitimatized British pretensions of rule in Palestine, making the Zionists one of the first non-state actors to be a significant party to a decision of a 20th century international organization. The Zionists with whom British functionaries dealt were often patently British (Chaim Weizmann's youngest son died serving as a Royal Air Force pilot in World War II) and some of the functionaries were themselves Jewish. As 20th century time passed, the British Imperial Self surrendered to the fact of diminished British power. Meanwhile, the claim of a Jewish right to a homeland grew morally attractive in the Anglophone popular imagination. The British government also did not understand their own constant contribution to the foundation of Zionist operational power inside Palestine. British institutions and economic assumptions furthered the secularization, bureaucratization and marketing of real property, thus facilitating an 'asymmetrical' strategy that British military experts would not grasp.

The Zionists, meanwhile, recognized the long-term weakening of the British imperial proposition. They also recognized that moral support against that proposition could be translated into operational power as financial contributions allowed land acquisition through purchase, especially growing contributions from the United States. Finally, the Zionists understood that the land acquisition strategy was difficult for the British to see, and therefore difficult to oppose by force. Significantly, Zionist strategy was not dependent on British goodwill or reactive to British imperialism. It attempted instead to maintain initiative through broad diplomatic maneuvering and resource positioning that would produce the greatest amount of migration to and land acquisition in Palestine. Key events such as the Balfour Declaration are milestones in the relationship between the British Government and the Zionist project, but the overall Zionist strategy was to constantly change the facts on the ground, plat-by-plat. The idea was not to seek grand strategic acts, but to constantly act with strategic intent.

Raphael Lemkin, one of the 20th century's most famous activists, conducted a parallel media and diplomatic effort. Lemkin, inventor of the term *genocide*, dedicated his life to the idea that 'sovereignty' should not lend impunity to a government for collective murder. (Lempkin's efforts are put into context by Samantha Power in *A Problem from Hell.*) Lemkin immersed himself in the history of the massacre of the Armenians. Although his celebrated campaign was not about Zion or the Jews, the underlying connection with Jewish history was easily inferred, especially in North America. Lemkin's personal strategy was to build the structures of international law that might help protect peoples from their own governments. The Zionists felt a less idealistic approach was necessary. Neither strategy, as it turned out, was fast enough.

So did implementation of a patently land-based strategy itself delay fulfillment of the objectives? If Uganda or perhaps Arizona had been acceptable as a substitute for the literal Palestine, or if Jerusalem could have been built in England's green and pleasant land, would the strategy have had a better chance to succeed on time? Sunk costs were of a spiritual and millennial nature. Another refuge might only have been temporary, a return to Holy Lands remaining the mythical redemptive prize.

The Zionist effort was briefly supported by the Nazi's themselves. It was also underpinned by the British, but was simultaneously resistant to British military response. It matched details of facts on the ground to national purpose, national interests and operational objectives. So powerful was the Israel land strategy, it is now being imitated by Hezbollah.

See: 66, *GIS;* 106, *Tourism*; 49, *Territorial Scrutiny*; 107, *Price of Real Estate*; 144, *Impunity and State Success*; and 48, *Grading the Social Contract*; 53, *Hohfeldian Grievance Analysis*; and 90, *Prisons*.

---

> "Our forces saved the remnants of the Jewish people of Europe for a new life and a new hope in the reborn land of Israel. Along with all men of goodwill, I salute the young state and wish it well."
>
> Dwight D. Eisenhower[103]

From agrarian reform to ethnic cleansing

# *Section 72, Land Strategy*

Unless the duration of your role in your conflict is going to be breathtakingly brief, and regardless of what side you're on, you need a land strategy. If you ask your people 'Who owns the land here?' and they can't say, then the chances are you don't have a land strategy, and you need one even more. If you do not have a grasp of how the land is owned, you cannot really win one of these conflicts. The best you might be able to do is get things calmed down a bit so you can yell 'victory' and get out. The winners will outlast or trick you, but they won't listen to you, because you don't know enough about them.

Land is very important. To win, know what the relationships are among your people and among others regarding land so that you can change what is possible in favor of your goals, not unwittingly let someone change something that you don't see, and not try to change what is impossible to change. Tenancy is complex. These days, people don't just own land in fee simple (meaning the entire basket of possible rights). They hold life-estates or occupancy certificates, or they sharecrop, suffer debt servitude, and on and on. Land reform is not a detail to be left to any anthropologist. It has to be at the heart of *your* understanding of the society and the possibilities for change. You especially want to know exactly who will gain and who will suffer from transference of rights related to the most important pieces of land. Some of the most important pieces of land are sitting along your enemy's lines of retreat to sanctuary, or yours, or may be the source ground of his wealth and power to fight you. Some of the most useful cultural questions are about land and how it is owned. If you have a bunch of cultural experts running around and they do not know all about land ownership, well, they perhaps are not the cultural experts you need.

It may be that all the dimensions of land ownership are so ingrained and cemented in existing cultural, administrative, legal and customary practices that your leeway for change isn't great. You will nevertheless want to know this. More than likely, if there is an internal armed competition, it is exactly because something is wrong with the property regime.

Your entrance onto a piece of land might be denied by barriers and destructive fires (as in artillery fires, landmines, bombs). If you have enough gas for your tanks and they don't have enough barriers and destructive fires to stop your tanks, then you can enter. That's in big maneuver wars. In these other types of war you're already on that land and probably so is your enemy. If you haven't located your enemies' lines of communication or their sanctuaries, some of the public is helping your enemy, or, covering their bets, helping both sides. And there might be more than two sides. And people might change their minds three times a day. Unfortunately, because of all this, you might want to think that the conflict is not about taking land. It is. It always is. It is just that owning land is a beautiful thing, not a perfect thing. Maybe you only have the right to be inside that restaurant while you eat and buy drinks, then you're expected to leave. Maybe you have the right to be there, but not to smoke. Maybe you have the right to be there, but not go upstairs. It will be a matter of law and culture. Nevertheless, all the rights to every square inch are divvied-up somehow. If nobody has the right to exclude anybody else or keep them from doing anything, it is called no-man's land and it is either worthless or people will fight over it.

If you are a United States American, your entire political heritage is wrapped up in land strategy and property. In 1785, the Congress of the Confederation (which had been the Continental Congress and would become the United States Congress) owed debts to officers and men of the Continental Army. The Congress worried about the land west of the

Appalachian continental divide, and wanted to seal the principles of the revolution. So, in fulfillment of the Northwest Ordinance, it sent surveyors out west to measure the land with chains. The survey started at what the surveyors called The Point of Beginning along the Ohio River where East Liverpool, Ohio is today. The parcels were sold at auction in New York City in fee simple absolute. That means you bought the whole thing, all the rights from the heavens to the core of the earth. You could do what you wanted with it and all the government kept was the duty to make sure that what was yours was yours.

That was a land strategy. It manifested a revolutionary change in the relationship of the individual to the government; it placed an affinity population in an area that might have otherwise been populated by opposition identities; it paid down a national debt; and it ignited an era of exploration and productivity. It framed the relationship that Americans were developing among themselves. Those relationships were about the land, but among people. Most of the founding fathers knew well that the ugly exception, slavery, was an error that would exact its payment. Slavery was made unlawful in the Northwest Territory even before it had been banned in some of the northern states. Writs of *habeas corpus* would be respected. Proof of one's whereabouts was to be part of an individual's right to live. Government was not to 'disappear' people.

America's revolutionaries understood that land rights, civil rights and human rights overlapped almost completely. Rights enjoyed are enjoyed in places, and they will be enjoyed in those places only in the context of a social contract that is the result of an actual strategy. Sometimes part of the strategy has to include force and weapons.

The American revolutionaries had a lot of land, no money and a revolution to manifest. They sold land. The Zionists had no land, some money, and a people to save. They bought land. These are two huge examples of land-centered strategies. Each of the land strategies is wrapped up in questions of property and property regimes.

Land reform is a broad-brush label given to a wide array of land-focused strategies for resolution of political struggles. Many land reform schemes were promoted by the ideological left during a twentieth-century in which geopolitical advantage was often tied to polarized ideologies. Results have been mixed and depend ultimately on subjective measures. Too many land reform notions, however, have been bad ideas.

Any strategy aimed at attaining objectives beyond the immediate physical possession of terrain, and maybe even those, are land reforms. Their flaw has usually been a presumption that the land itself is the dominant source of wealth, and therefore political power. Lost has been a full understanding of the nature of property. Property, even real property, is not the thing, but rather the concert of rights associated with the thing. Strategies that begin with a complete understanding of the preferential rights and duties of all owner interests are more likely to succeed than any strategy that only envisages preferential occupancy of a delimited space. It is hard to find a land reform project that hasn't suffered unexpected and unintended effects of tinkering with forces and relationships that were incompletely understood. For those interested in securing and centralizing government power, however, land reform has had a long record of successes. Economic progress, individual liberty and upward mobility have not fared as well. As Professor John Powelson expressed in *The History of Land*, "The most disheartening conclusion...may be that whenever a reformer (such as a king, a government, or a revolutionary junta) has changed the land tenure system by fiat, he, she, or it has retained a substantial portion of the rights instead of yielding them to the peasant."[104]

The concert of rights that constitutes land ownership includes the right to divest, sometimes called the right of *alienation*. This single characteristic of ownership can probably be blamed for half of the whole failure of land reforms. If a peasant is given redistributed land, he will sell it unless he can afford to be the owner and wants to be. If a plan includes incentives for the peasant to stay on rural land – seed credits, extension service advice, and technical capitalization – the government is in effect entering the agricultural industry in a pervasive and very expensive way. Even with all necessary aid having been provided to the small farmer, there is little a government can do to assure the market value of food staples.

The next logical step is price support buying by the government, or other interventions into the market mechanism. Pressures build toward re-redistribution of ownership portions, either in new mortgages, resale to original owners, or uneven taxing schemes. In order to avoid the immediate frustration of land redistribution programs (caused by individual decisions to sell and go elsewhere), reform regulations tend to include tenure requirements such as residence during a fixed minimum number of harvests before the occupant receives title. In these cases, not only is part of the ownership retained by the government, the government has created a new form of serfdom. As with most government intrusions, the process is subject to corruption and to loopholes that allow the black market sale of quit claims, false appraisals, and so on. What the head of land reform programs always seems to understand best is how to sell the program, and almost never understands the nature of property. Property is a relationship among people. Land is a most important object of the social contract, but it is not the substance of the contract.

In order to influence the lives of a large number of persons, land or 'agrarian' reforms too often involve overarching central government control of prices and movement of labor. If successful on a large scale, agrarian reforms can slow a process of urbanization that, however painful, may be necessary to shift an economy away from subsistence farming. Having said this, there have been occasions in which the forced reapportionment of rural terrain may be said to have positively supported strategic interests because of the changed property relationships. Accordingly, land reforms sometimes appear at the outset to be good ideas even to the anti-statist. A quotation from the United States military governor of Korea in 1945 says everything:

> The program of Military Government included taking over all Japanese properties as rapidly as possible for the benefit of the Korean people, relieving labor from the conditions of absolute servitude under which it has existed for the last forty years, returning to the farmers the land which had been wrested from them by Japanese guile and treachery, and giving to the farmer a fair and just proportion of the fruit of his sweat and labor, restoring the principles of a free market, giving to every man, woman and child within the country equal opportunity to enjoy his fair and just share of the great wealth with which this beautiful nation has been endowed. (Gary L. Olson, *US Foreign Policy and the Third World Peasant: Land Reform in Asia and Latin America*)[105]

In post-World War II Korea, land reform measures were taken by a military occupation force that followed another foreign occupier. Probably the most determinant policy impetus was a desire to undermine the appeal of socialist and communist arguments within a large rural population. In that case, large tracts of virtually ownerless properties were available for redistribution.

We also learn from Olson that in the case of the American occupation of Japan, the number of pure owner-cultivators was increased from 52.8 percent of the total farming households in 1946 to 61.8 percent of the total in 1950. Pure tenant households dropped from 28.7 percent to 5 percent. In the process, one million former landlords were dispossessed. Rights in land had been purchased by the central government by instruction of the Supreme Command Allied Powers. The plan had its roots partly in pre-war academic appreciations of a relationship between feudal tenure systems in Japan and the power of militarist elites. General MacArthur's directive to the Japanese government stated in part:

> In order that the Imperial Japanese Government shall remove economic obstacles to the revival and strengthening of democratic tendencies, establish respect for the dignity of man, and destroy the economic bondage which has enslaved the Japanese farmer for centuries of feudal oppression, the Japanese Imperial Government is directed to take measures to insure that those who till the soil shall have a more equal opportunity to enjoy the fruits of their labor. (Also from Olson, *US Foreign Policy and the Third World Peasant: Land Reform in Asia and Latin America*)[106]

It is speculative to claim that these land reform efforts led to the economic successes of Korea or Japan; too many other factors weigh in. At least they did not prevent economic development, and perhaps the redistribution of wealth broadened the base of material expectations. The land programs in both countries seem to have had a direct effect on elections that favored pro-United States elements. One observation is essential: These reforms were imposed. In one case they were imposed on a defeated enemy. In the other they were imposed on a country that had been previously occupied by a foreign army. The observation does not lead to a conclusion that such changes must be imposed, but it does discredit off-hand pandering that changes must be indigenous or locally motivated, even while that might be preferable.

In summary, if what you are doing is to be of any sustainable consequence, you need a land strategy. If what you want to achieve has any chance of longevity, you need a land strategy. The American Revolutionaries had one, the Zionists had one, the occupiers of Korea had one. It can't be a complementary notion, a detail or add-on to your overall design. It has to be the main thing. Someone may try to sell you on the idea that the centerpiece of your effort should be the 'rule-of-law.' That's OK. Rule-of-law for a Kansan means that if she is in her home, and the police want to come in to arrest her, they need to have a piece of paper with her name and address on it signed by a judge. Part of the Kansan land strategy says there are some private spaces where strangers need special permission to enter, including -- and especially -- agents of the government. She also has rights on the street in front of her home, including a right to be safe and not harassed. You might be thinking I'm stretching the meanings of strategy, land and property, so that they are forced to overlap. No, they just do overlap. By the way, closing off your enemy's route of retreat to sanctuary is a land strategy.

See: 73, *Property and the Social Contract*; 40, *Rule-of-law*; 2, *The Line of Retreat*; 48, *Grading the Social Contract*; 105, *Genocide Geography*; and 39, *Socioeconomic Causation*; 86, *Shifting Covet-Geography*; and 91, *Forts and Walls*.

---

> "When the Argives were disputing land boundaries with the Spartans and were maintaining that theirs was the fairer claim, he (Lysander) drew his sword and said: "The man who has this within his grasp argues best about land boundaries."
>
> Plutarch, quoting Lysander (circa 395 BC)[107]

---

There is no private property

# *Section 73, Property and the Social Contract*

(Much of this section is adapted from *Property & Peace*)

Property is not a tangible object, but a set of recognized rights and duties associating a tangible item (perhaps a place) with an owner-identity. Those rights and obligations constitute the details of a contract among a society's members. The social contract is an agreement to enforce lesser agreements (and to resolve disagreements) regarding advantages and disadvantages. So the property is not the place, but the mix of recognized rights and obligations that some group of persons has sorted out among each other about the place and things in it. 'Creating property' means the entire process of establishing and solidifying an *agreement about agreements* regarding rights and duties associated with places and objects. The creation of property is a process of institution building.

If a place does not have a formalized property ownership system, it will not be peaceful or materially successful.

If the property system of a country or a county or anyplace is not formalized – that is to say, the evidence of who owns what is not precise, comprehensive and transparent, that place is not going to enjoy peace for long, or at least it won't live in peace and also enjoy liberty. For humans to flourish in today's world (for them to enjoy material success, establish human and spiritual relationships as they see fit, and to treat their surroundings with respect), the social arrangement has got to include a formalized system of property ownership.

You are probably wasting your time engaged in a project, program, strategy or movement aimed at improving the material performance of an economy if that effort is not built around, cognizant of and informed by the construction of a formal property regime. Property is man's most successful conflict resolution invention, and I know of no examples, save isolated and very small communities, where peoples have long survived in peace, or even enjoyed long periods in the absence of violence, where the property regime was not formalized.

Saying that a place will not enjoy peace unless there is formal property is not the same as saying it will have peace if there *is* formal property. The assertion is unfortunately negative. Formal property is a necessary but not necessarily sufficient condition for social peace. The formalization of property is mostly to be associated with the evidence of ownership. There still needs to be ways to do something with the evidence. That is to say, there must be property courts, markets and democratic processes. Then, even if the evidence of ownership is excellent and there exist vibrant courts and markets, there is still likely to be trouble if the basic rules of ownership are illiberal or out of balance with the basic expectations of the culture.

If you are a natural rebel, taken to the language of resistance, you would be wise not to reject out-of-hand this assertion about the importance of formalized property. The question does not revolve around the epochal and fantastic battle of private versus public property. There is no private property. When things are 'owned' outside the bounds of community formalities, they are merely the objects of possession by force. They are only 'property' as the result of a community's agreement. If you're an up-and-coming gangster, then you want to have records of who lives where and who owes you money (unless you're content to be a very small-time gangster and can remember all that in your head). If you fancy yourself the vanguard of the proletariat, you will eventually need records of who is supposed to be where, and what they and the bourgeoisie and elite have (unless you are content to represent and redistribute to a very small proletariat). If you fancy yourself as intermediary between a flock of souls and a spiritual master, you will need records of who the sheep in that flock are and what is ten percent of theirs (unless you are content to be a very poor pastor of a very small flock).

Still, the upshot of the assertion about formal property is that you, on whatever side of social conflict and irregular war you find yourself, will want to have some plan, program, intention -- something -- that directly addresses the administration of evidence of ownership. This ought to start with real property -- with land and the things attached to it, but it should reach into all significant forms of wealth, from motorcycles to bandwidth, attorney's licenses, savings accounts, phone numbers, voter registration, even names. If you have no good plan to win administratively, you do not have a winning plan.

*Property & Peace* is pretty good, containing some of the points made elsewhere in this book, plus a few others. You can download it free in pdf form from the Internet. It is not the best book on property. Several that are better include Tom Bethel's *The Noblest Triumph*; Andro Linklater's *Measuring America*; Richard Pipe's *Property and Freedom*; John Powelson's *The Story of Land*; Hernando De Soto's *The Mystery of Capital*; and Douglass North & Robert Thomas' *The Rise of the Western World.*

A property regime is *formal* to the degree that documentation regarding ownership and tenancy is accurate, comprehensive and transparent. The regime is effective to the extent people observe the agreements and can do something with the evidence. It is liberal to the extent that many individuals can participate in the distribution of the rights and duties. The property system probably cannot be effective or definitely won't be liberal unless it is also formal.

A column of Western cultural progress is the use of technology to improve the faithfulness of evidence regarding everyday rights and duties, including the duties of government. Formalizing real estate records can involve considerable technical effort -- interviewing, surveying, monumenting, mapping, registering, filing, digitizing, web-mounting and so-on.

Much of the success of Western societies, and much of what is often alluded to as the American Way, is bound to the systemic creation of irrefutable evidence regarding rights and duties related to things, and particularly to real estate. However good the evidence, rights remain inchoate unless they can be exercised. This exercise of rights requires that an authoritative body (a court) can consider and act upon the evidence if the rights are disputed, or that a functioning market exists within which rights and duties can be traded. That is why we judge the strength of the social contract according to its *observance*, by which we mean to tie the evidence together with its practicable consequence. Observance of the social contract: the combination of solid evidence and the realistic possibility of doing something with that evidence, gives the contract strength within its basic rules. These basic rules, however, may still be unjust according to one perspective or another. For instance, if we can determine easily to whom rights and duties pertain within the system, and all of the designated owners have access to efficient enforcement mechanisms; but there nevertheless exists a category of people that is excluded from owning; then there still exists great potential for conflict. Such a system, well-named 'apartheid,' can be quite formal.

Some people are stressed by the very word *property*. They become preoccupied with the idea that it is synonymous with 'private property' and a tattoo of capitalism and Western cultural arrogance. Indeed, formalized property is a hallmark of Western culture and a basic institution in most materially successful economies, if not all. The most defensible goals of human development: freedom of expression, association, movement, worship, physical health, and non-violent resolution of conflict, are more likely achieved where rights and duties associated with land are formalized -- regardless of the name given to the overall political system. Private property and semi-private property exist everywhere, whatever the nature of a property regime's broad outlines. These property advantages can be made explicit and protected wherever the social contract agrees to their existence.

Property systems are *agreements about agreements* or *contracts regarding contracts*. Contracts are best made freely among parties somehow capable of negotiating terms, albeit at times indirectly. To the extent fewer-and-fewer individuals exercise more-and-more of the rights we associate with real estate (access and exclusion, profit, safe enjoyment, alienation, preservation, collection of rents, distribution of occupancy) a property system tends toward tyranny. Tyrannies in a property regime may grow from the cultural fabric as much as from political formulae. One way of slowly reducing the number of persons who actually exercise rights, and who determine the distribution of rights and duties related to land and other material wealth, is through taxation.

*Liberal* and *formal* are not the same qualities. Formal property ownership entails comprehensive, precise and transparent evidence of ownership, the logic of which can then be duly enforced. *Liberal*, meanwhile, refers to the most basic rules delimiting the distribution of rights, however evidenced. A property regime is more or less liberal to the extent different categories of persons are admitted as owners and a broader array of rights are obtainable. The ultimate expression of private ownership -- total, independent, unencumbered and uncompromised individual exercise of rights in land -- may not constitute property ownership at all. Such a condition is sovereign lordship (meaning that an owner enjoys complete impunity for whatever he does on his land), which must be defended by unyielding force. It is only when lords reach agreement with their neighbors that property is created. That is to say, in order to speak of property at all, an agreement must exist regarding conflict resolution -- which leads inexorably to the recognition of a role for government. Mundane facts of ownership show how complex and subtle the lines between private and common ownership rights actually are. So, rather than focusing solely on owner rights, we want also to underline duties, and especially those of government in the social contract. We see that where the State fails to shoulder its immediate duties (conflict resolution and prevention or amelioration of trespass) the property regime is less likely to promote human flourishing, and that the reverse is true also: to the extent governments *do* shoulder duties; the balance in the social contract favors the prospects of peace, prosperity and freedom. Rather than claim that this or that balance between individual and communal ownership is best, the argument here favors liberal property regimes featuring fluidity, divisibility, precision and transparency in determining the balance.

There are, then, two broad points about property: The first is about formality because without precise, clear, stable evidence regarding who claims what, any question of how to divide the pie is subject to corruption, deceit and extortion. Clear evidence makes the observance of contracts far more likely and peaceable. There is almost no practical amount of additional formality in a property system that would be detrimental to the cause of peace, and without formality, no long-term peace is likely. The second point is about liberality. A liberal property regime maintains a broad range of potential owner-identities and allows those identities to exercise and protect the fullest range of rights by way of efficient courts, free markets and a participatory democracy. If a property regime encourages flexible, rapid and precise markets for rights in real estate, it may be more conducive to peace than one in which decisions are made more centrally or by political processes. In this, however, there reside questions of balance and timing, the optimal measure of liberalness being susceptible to specific cultural and political details. As we tinker with who is allowed to own what in a society foreign to our own, we can directly threaten cultural basics. The property rules related to gender that the West confronts in Islamic lands present an interesting example. As a property regime becomes more liberal it may become more conducive to social peace, but disclaimers and exceptions are obviously required. To the extent a system of ownership is informal, however, liberality is an empty notion and the prospects of peace dim.

Property is relatively new as a theme in Political Science, development and conflict studies. Most of the books noted earlier were written as the Soviet Union died or shortly afterwards, with the exception of *The Rise of the Western World.* Back in the nineteenth century the topic had been shuffled off to law schools as of only local vocational interest. The Communists painted the whole notion of property as theft and a trick of the capitalist system. One of the benefits of victory over the Soviet Union is the re-positioning of property as a topic of political discussion.

How does this assertion about property relate to winning your war? Why is creating a property system indispensable? Classic military strategy is about possession by force. When an army takes land, it tries to become, in the pure sense, the owner of the 'fee simple absolute,' the owner of all the rights, protected by force as the sovereign lord, exempt from the law of the previous owner, and able to maintain a total monopoly over the granting of impunity within its conquest -- at least for a while. However, everything that is not quite classic international warfare is subject to some kind of property rules. In other words, if some other law is still extant, if some sense of the previous social contract remains, or if one is immediately being implemented somehow, then the military commander is obliged to know the property regime or build one.

Section 72 warns that a land strategy has to be a property strategy if it is going to have any longevity or effectiveness. That and other sections of this book divide the irregular war challenge into two parts: One is how to get rid of enemies and the other how to not make more of them. The creation of a formalized property regime can help you succeed at both the military challenge of closing with and destroying your enemy and with the additional chore of creating a society that does not spawn and abet your enemies. Some of the classic principles of military strategy apply, but their application does not imply the renunciation of civil law.

Property is much of what distinguishes classic war between States from the irregular wars that are the subject of this book, and which puzzle so many leaders today. In classic (declared, international) war, the relevant property regime is a very thin set of agreements among the States of the international community. In irregular wars, the relevant property systems are rich, detailed, culturally specific, and often broken or inadequate.

Do not separate the idea of property rights from human or civil rights. They are quickly recognizable as the same quantity. A property approach, however, puts a lot of emphasis on 'where,' and 'who.' It allows the application of our best innovations, like maps, cadastres and quiet title courts. It helps redirect thinking toward the lines of communication and the question of anonymity.

The question may arise whether or not to adjust an existing social contract, leave it to its own evolution, or scrap it and start over. While there is no rule for that question, it is a cinch that your answer will be very risky if it is not built on thorough knowledge of the existing contract and on an informed feel for the potential of cultural change. If you are not familiar with the concept of property and property systems, and with the specifics of the property ownership systems pertinent to your war, you can improve your chances of winning by gaining that knowledge.

See: 72, *Land Strategy*; 92, *Land-use Planning*; 3, *The Domesday Book*; 48, *Grading the Social Contract*; 46, *Taxation and Debt*; 60, *Slavery*; 105, *Genocide Geography*; and 2, *The Line of Retreat.*

---

> "Logic…has never played more than a small part in the history of weights and measures. The rest has been about the distribution of power. In its rawest guise, greater accuracy has given empires the power to explore new areas and to exploit them at the expense of the less accurate. But measurement is also about the power of society to allow a just exchange of goods and cash, and at its most fundamental level it has, like language, the power to express a personal value between the individual and the material world."
>
> Andro Linklatter *Measuring America*[108]

---

Confounding place, identity, and impunity

# *Section 74, Refugees and Displaced Persons*

Out-of-place people are a regular feature of organized armed conflict. Generally, the connotation of refugees is of people away from their country homeland, perhaps exiled. 'Displaced persons' usually connotes displacement within a country, the currently fashionable term in international organizations being Internally Displaced People (IDP), of which there are tens of millions in the world. For our purposes, all persons who are forced away from their homes are dis-placed, or out-of-place, the significant aspect being separation of the human body from its owner's preferred place of identity and geographic connection to livelihood.

Internal armed struggles invariably displace persons, families, communities, or even whole populations. At one end of the gamut are peoples removed by force, the option being death, while at the other end an insecure environ contributes to voluntary decisions to uproot. The displacement may be an emigration from the country and continent, or it may be a house change from an outlying area to a nearby city. Every point on the plane of displacement types and motivations has some effect on your prospects for winning. In one way or another, the demographics of where people go to live affect your chances of success.

Displaced persons are a challenge and an opportunity. They are displaced for a reason and sometimes there is someone to blame. Many persons are displaced by disasters of one kind or another. It should be obvious how useful it can be to gain an understanding of where displaced persons have come from, where they wish to go, the impediments they face, what their survival needs are, and why they are displaced. Certain population cohorts can show distinct behaviors during forced relocations. Young men especially tend to leave refugee flows in order to forage or find some answer to their displacement, and sometimes to seek revenge.

Nomads can be refugees. Nomads have a special sense of place that connects to seasonal activities and special events. Their place identity is tied to a set of rights and duties they claim or expect in various places. The lives of nomads are less revealed by such contraptions as cadastral maps, but the rights and duties pertaining to, presumed or demanded by nomads can still be mapped.

Some displaced populations, or parts thereof, may be participants or pieces in a concerted strategy that uses migration to change demographic facts, and thereby gain political leverage. The speed of such migratory strategies or policies can vary, which will in turn influence what possible responses a destination polity might make. Whether to welcome, resist, or take indirect measures is dependent on so many factors, it is futile to make any non-contextual suggestions. Still, it behooves you, if population displacement is a factor in the midst of your insurgent war, to consider if any part of it is the product of a competitive strategic design.

Displaced persons can be offered new identities, but usually only if that identity is accompanied by acceptable new places. In some situations, the longing for original lands is inconsolable and cannot be assuaged except by commitment to help return people to their former places. It can be difficult to fulfill a promise to make full restitution to a displaced population, but the effort can be a powerful motivator. Meanwhile, forcing displaced persons into camps, although it can ease logistical burdens related to the immediate needs of a displaced population (and concerns in hosting locales), can quickly sour any advantageous human potential that a displaced population might have presented. Displaced persons had rights in land somewhere beforehand, a right to *be* somewhere. What were those rights and what happened to them? You can probably best express solidarity with groups of displaced persons by actively addressing questions about rights and duties that previously existed.

See: 72, *Land Strategy*; 78, *Personal Identity*; 109, *Hotspotting*; 105, *Genocide Geography*; 90, *Prisons*; 96, *Public Records*; 95, *Childhood*; and 51, *Underclass*.

---

> "I prayed for twenty years but received no answer until I prayed with my legs."
>
> Frederick Douglass[109]

---

You may have to do something with it

# Section 75, Popular Support

The importance of 'popular support' as a theme in American counterinsurgency literature can be summed up by the clichéd admonition, 'The civilian population is the center of gravity.' After all, if we are not servants to the betterment of the condition of our people, what are we? A problem quickly arises, however. Once we have asked the big softball question, 'Are the people most important?' and answered purely, 'Yes, of course!' the challenge of the enemy still remains. Depending on how one measures it, there is little to suggest that broad popular support is necessary for the success of an insurgency, even though logic insists that such support would be helpful. Any cursory review of insurgencies in Latin America reveals that some of the longest running 'revolutionary movements' have continued to profit, protect and encourage their insurgent leaders for decades on the back of marginal public support. The numbers in Colombia speak clearly. President Álvaro Uribe was elected with over 62% of the popular vote during a first round election that was essentially a referendum on his hard line against the country's illegal armed groups. He was then reelected with undiminished support for having progressed militarily in the war. Active supporters of the leftist insurgent guerrillas probably do not exceed 2% of the population, and some indications hold it as low as 0.2%. It appears that only the amount necessary to secure routes of escape, places of refuge, and a surviving black market is actually necessary for FARC survival. With sufficient financial and international support, the FARC barely needs any Colombians at all.

The mixture of relevant public psychological quantities includes ambivalence, apathy, fear, confusion, etc. These vicissitudes all bear on the resources and options available to the contenders in an internal conflict. It would be foolish to suggest that public psychology does not matter. It does, and so contenders in internal wars attend vigorously to the various components and dimensions of public attitude. That said, the optimal public attitude for successful insurgency or counterinsurgency is situation-specific, and valid knowledge about that attitude is usually sparse. Ignorance on the part of the majority population may alone suffice for the outlaw, and a little fear among the right sectors seems to go a long way. Yes, the government could usefully expend resources on the general morale and behavioral propensities of the population, and more particularly on those elements of the population that can immediately assist in defeating the insurgent. Obviously, depending on its type and level of command, a given military unit might be wholly dedicated to the material wellbeing of a civilian population. A construction battalion working on a hospital can easily assert that the civilian population is its 'center of gravity.'

The counterinsurgent operational planner might do better, however, to not swallow whole insurgent arguments that the conflict is principally a psychological question, an ideological fight, a political contest or a fight for justice. It will be all those things, but insurgents' arguments that fix on public attitude are almost always obedient to the knowledge that danger lies in being captured, not in being out-debated. They know the names and addresses of the few members of the civilian population to whom they need to apply the effective dose of persuasion. A government usually does not know the names and addresses of these persons, and so the government usually administers its psychological medicine *en masse*. The wholesale dose rarely has the intended effect on the specific individuals needed by the insurgent, and the government effort often suffers the side effect of enlarging the profile of the insurgent. As long as an insurgent leader enjoys the minimum overall mix of public attitude and consciousness that allows his secure movement from points of action to sanctuary, he will be able to prolong his insurgency. With rare exception, an insurgent leader must be physically defeated or be made to conclude that his physical defeat is unavoidable. The same holds true for the warlord, mafia don, etc.

The above argument downplays popular support and emphasis on the civilian population in operational planning in favor of physically intercepting insurgent leadership. Don't fall in love with the argument. Successful interception of insurgent leadership can depend on active support of the population at large, and there may be a direct relationship at the national level between popular support and a counterinsurgency budget, or between popular support and a preferred counterinsurgent strategy, or between popular support and international support to the government or to the insurgent. Still, watch out with the 'center of gravity' stuff. If you're the counterinsurgent, the indices of support for you, your efforts, and the government can skyrocket -- and you could nevertheless have an enemy as strong as or stronger than ever. The argument warns -- especially if you are planning or leading something in the military dimension of counterinsurgency -- that your job focus is the enemy, and that public support needs to be sought, aimed or translated in such a way that you can better adjust the variables of the operational equation to your advantage. If you are the insurgent and find that you enjoy a lot of public support, hey, run a candidate. It worked for the Spanish Communists in 1936.

Information from members of a motivated public often exposes insurgent leader *whereabouts.* However, the counterinsurgent leader can take a lesson from the Colombian electorate. President Andrés Pastrana was elected in 1998 on the promise to engage the FARC guerrillas in negotiations to seek a peaceful settlement of the war. By 2002, the electorate came to perceive that the FARC had not negotiated in good faith and the public persona of their president had been reduced to one of submissiveness. Their reaction was to elect Álvaro Uribe, whose stated intention was to defeat the FARC militarily. Since Uribe's election, the Colombian government and military have enjoyed high levels of public support, but the chore of defeating the FARC remains. The challenge of popular support for the Colombian military is clear: you might gain and enjoy high levels of public support, but the public will expect you to do something with it. Without public support, counterinsurgent success is unlikely, but support of the people is a tool and an advantage, not the goal. It might be appropriate as an intermediate goal, but it is not the goal. The Colombian military still has to close FARC lines to sanctuary.

Mao Tse-tung said, "Propaganda materials are very important. Every large guerrilla unit should have a printing press and a mimeograph stone."[110] Also, "There are some militarists who say: 'We are not interested in politics but only in the profession of arms.' It is vital that these simpleminded militarists be made to realize the relation that exists between politics and military affairs. Military action is a method to gain a political goal. While military affairs and political action are not identical, it is impossible to isolate one from the other." Mao also said, on the question of the relationship between the people and the troops, "The former may be likened to the water and the latter to the fish who inhabit it. How may it be said that these two cannot exist together? It is only undisciplined troops who make the people their enemies and who, like the fish out of its native element, cannot live." This last statement may be the most often cited, especially in support of the idea that the people are the center of gravity for counterinsurgency. Mao's comment was made in the context of the war against a foreign occupier, the Japanese. It follows a list of rules for the troops, guiding them to not steal, to replace what they borrow, be honest in their transactions, etc. Much of the rest of Samuel Griffith's *Mao Tse-Tung On Guerrilla Wafarer*, the text from which most of these ideas entered American strategy literature, is about movement, speed, position, mass, correlation of force, the goal of constructing regular units, etc. The rest of the book, in other words, is about the operational equation.

See: 8, *The Operational Equation;* 41, *Whereabouts* ; 98, *Jorge Verstrynge and Pio Moa*; 6, *Classic Strategy and Irregular Warfare*; 38, *Cultural Study for What?*; 54, *Badassoftheweek.com*; 39, *Socioeconomic Causation*; and 60, *Slavery*.

---

"It is anchor 'man,' not anchor 'lady.'
And that is a scientific fact."

Champ, in the movie
*Anchorman:*
*The Legend of Ron Burgundy* (2004)[111]

Half the world, a twentieth of the violence

# *Section 76, Gendering*

Killing and dying in irregular wars is done or suffered at a rate of about twenty young males or more to each female.[112] Twenty times as many males as females are mortal victims in most armed conflicts, and the ratio of male killers to female killers far higher still. In some other difficult cost categories, like limbs lost to explosives, the ratio of males to females is also much higher.

Very few females become leaders of armed guerrilla or criminal organizations, and even in the most female-welcoming guerrilla armies, the female roles tend strongly away from combat action and toward service, supply and information. Irregular warfare is a young man's game, the few exceptions proving the rule.

Having asserted the above about the male character of armed conflict, most governments, and maybe most insurgent groups would be better situated to succeed in irregular conflicts if they counted on ground forces with much closer to a fifty-fifty gender mix. For readers who take that assertion as disqualifyingly un-macho, here is the disclaimer: combat actions, whatever their level of conventionality or regularity, will continue to be athletic events that generally favor the male. That is to say, there is a significant dimension of strength, physical exertion, and prowess on which success in irregular warfare depends, and in which males will best, in the aggregate, females. At least this will be true for ground combat, especially combats in 'low intensity' contests. The National Hockey League hardly fears that crazed gendermongers will prevail upon its teams to put two or three women on the ice every shift.

If there is anything that can change the above assertion, it is the Unoccupied Armed Aerial Vehicle, UAAV, which markedly decreases the physical strength needed to bring death at a distance, and simultaneously lowers the level of ruthlessness and spirit of physical domination that seems necessary in order to kill.

In the government armies of Latin America, young women appear to have contributed to counterinsurgent success beyond the weight of their relative numbers. Guatemala's special operating forces (including the renown *Kaibiles*) began assigning women in the 1980s to civil affairs and psychological operations duties. Women in many of Guatemala's highland tribal groups would only talk with other women. To open communication with what amounted to an unheard half of the population, the army applied the parsimonious solution of adding women to their force structure. The result was a flood of useful information about guerrilla infiltrations and whereabouts.

Women influence formal armies more than people realize. In Guatemala, a senior retired army officer told me about the matriarchy. Whenever a coup threatened (often), the intelligence unit in charge of suppressing such things fanned out to spy on some women's coffee clutches. As it turned out, several generals didn't wear the pants in their families, and officer assignments were made by the older wives. The assignments were indeed a feminist conspiracy.

In cities suffering extreme violence, like Medellín, Colombia, the vast bulk of all violence is done by males. In contrast, the bulk of actions like lobbying for community services and infrastructure improvement, self-help education programs, food distribution and child care are conducted and led by women.

Colombia's FARC has had a relatively high percentage of women, at times as high as 30% according to some sources, even in some combat units. Colombian army observers say that the female guerrillas are often competent, durable and committed fighters, but that during ground pursuits they are often caught first because they are slower runners. Most women who have reported their experiences in FARC and other guerrilla ranks claim having been subjected to demeaning and sexually abusive treatment. They also become pregnant, which, if not forced to abort, further slows their track times and often inspires them toward nurturing and protecting their young, away from killing and dying. Go figure.

Having asserted that combat will continue to be an athletic event, one of the most often fronted arguments in favor of equal gendering in armies touches on the fact that so many women in military service have to endure equal endangerment -- that is, the positions in which women find themselves are equally dangerous when compared to those in which the men find themselves. This equality of danger is, in an appreciable portion of cases, the truth of the matter. Less debated (often ineffable), but more poignant, is the duty to kill. The positions of most maleness in the US military are those in which the soldiers anticipate and are expected to kill, and to do so at a close enough range to lend a personal aspect to the act. Whether or not a society would or should place female youth in that drama is a central question.

Back to the assertion about 50/50 gendering in government armed forces: To improve the overall capability of a force to win in irregular war, a military should aim toward a 50/50 balance of men and women, both in leadership and in the ranks. Most military tasks do not directly involve killing. Instead, they are jobs like psychological operations, police investigation, civil affairs, medical attention, and road building. Failure to include sufficient women in the forces is a failure to recognize that the populations with which militaries will deal are 50/50, and that gender-match matters.

See: 115, *Transformation of Armed Forces*; 77, *Sex*; 95, *Childhood*; 96, *Combatant Status*; 92, *Land-use Planning*; 28, *Oviedo*; 94, *Poop*; and 24, *Ruthlessness and Resolve.*

---

"Women hold up half the sky." (Mao, attributed)

"Does not Wisdom call, and does not
Understanding raise her voice?" (Solomon, attributed)

"Women fill all the best bleachers." (Yogi, attributed)

Motivating environmental changes

# *Section 77, Sex*

Sex is attractive, powerful, dangerous stuff. It is more of an element in armed conflicts than people want to admit. For many people, it is a more delicate subject to address, ethically and emotionally, than even the most extreme violence. Sex, or human sexuality, is a driving factor behind or within many conflicts.

> Sex influences physical and social differentials in the built environment of cities.
>
> Sex provides a basic way to make money, which encourages agency (pimping).
>
> Sex increases affective values that can make extortion and kidnapping more lucrative. It is difficult to distance kidnapping, illicit trade and slavery from the subject of sex.
>
> Sexual taboos and constraints related to ethnic, religious or other collective identities can be indicators

of the existence of an underclass or of a group potentially the victim of massacres or genocide.

Sex affects soldier and unit performance.

Sex drives power relationships that cause some groups to dominate sexual opportunities or to carefully control sexual property (as in the maintenance of sexual roles, privileges, and constraints).

To a degree, cities organize around sex. This is due to the nature of markets, moralizing tendencies, and sometimes fear, especially of sexually transmitted diseases. City leaders often try to concentrate prostitution, or at least low-price prostitution, into 'red light' districts where bordellos, strip clubs and streetwalkers are more densely situated. It isn't just that cities have pay-for-sex areas. Young single people also seek healthier sex, and this hunt manifests itself architecturally in bars, nightclubs, singles gymnasiums, restaurants, etc. Married couples often seek to gain some separation from the hunt, and look for places to live and work that are specifically not close to the places of sexual fervor. Tourist hotels begin to distinguish themselves according to family atmospheres or hunting atmospheres. Accordingly, some locales will have architectures favoring safety, parental control and movement limitations, while other architectures are designed to provide intimacy, anonymity and suggestiveness, along with the opportunity for contact and negotiation (not to mention the coincidence and varying permissions of alcohol). Hence, there occurs within most cities a sexual geography, a geography with which police detectives are familiar.

A similar sexually-induced or influenced geography can be seen at the scale of the single home or at the global level. Some places become known for particular practices, sexual license or taboos. Because of the taboos and the social and physical dangers attendant to sex, discretion (anonymity) is often sought as a complement in sexual endeavors. As a result, those geographies that provide anonymity are often used not only by those with rarified sexual hunting practices, but by those with anti-State anonymity requirements. In other words, the whereabouts of non-standard sexual practices and insurgency or organized crime can coincide because of the care taken to provide secrecy.

Criminality is integral to most irregular armed conflict, and as a rule one thing leads to another. There are all kinds of illicit trade, and once criminals get the hang of keeping secrets, making bribes and smuggling, they tend to diversify and rarely specialize in a single sin. The sex trade probably got started fairly early in human history. Maybe the trade is one of the negative phenomena of globalization, or perhaps its exposure an achievement of globalizing information. Some places are more notorious than others for some kinds of sex trade, but there is little to indicate that the industry is weakening. Greater awareness of the international sex trade, including human slavery and even including child sex slavery, has sparked some increase in direct international law enforcement cooperation.

Prostitutes learn a lot and, apparently, don't always keep the knowledge secret. Madams and pimps, if they are going to do well in the business, need to keep records, and these records, which tend to get subpoenaed, often become trading chips for other information.

The lines of withdrawal to sanctuary for many leaders in irregular conflicts take detours through sexual geographies. To be more specific, insurgent leaders are especially likely to visit their wives, lovers or favorite prostitutes, or have boys, girls, or women shipped to them. This is a traditional security weakness.

Venereal diseases can have a destructive effect on small unit efficiency. Guerrilla units often detour from preferred mission routes or risk exposure in order to seek medical attention for all kinds of diseases, but sexually transmitted diseases are high on the list.

Proscriptions against sexual contact between members of separate races or religions are common worldwide, and where those proscriptions are formalized they may be a very good indicator of the existence of an underclass, and of a potential victim identity. Interracial, interethnic or intercommunion sexual liaisons and marriages, on the other hand, may be indicators of group adhesion, or they may be a warning of social stress if the sexual intermixing causes determined reaction against it.

Cross-cultural sex shock can cause barriers to communication, disagreement and distrust between allies. Typically, the US Americans are subject to sex culture shock, especially when confronted by some of the practices of soldier-aged young men on other continents. By and large, they seem to do all right with the women.

Religions, castes, and classes can diverge as to sexual privileges. A clergy or a dominant caste may create and maintain special sexual privileges for themselves, as well as permit or foster a market for the satisfaction of sexual desires. These systems of preferential property rights in sex rarely favor control by females. Females in most societies have less negotiating strength regarding the value of sexual acts and opportunities. Among males, small minorities often control the market for the highest-value sexual prizes. Because of systemically weaker power positions, most females face highly circumscribed sets of sexual choices, while some women are reduced to outright sexual slavery. Many children, sharing a similar relative weakness, are also reduced to being sexual commodities. These relationships, in which women and children have little negotiating power regarding themselves as objects of sexual desire and performance, are often perceived as being integral to a culture. However, what members of one society might paint as a cultural norm, members of another may see as violation of physical integrity, or as an illegitimate discrimination against a category of humans.

When a power relationship considered normal within one social contract is perceived from the context of another social contract as the perpetration of a crime, the question of impunity can become a cause for inter-cultural conflict, even among allies. What if nobody in a neighboring county investigates or prosecutes what in your country is considered sexual abuse? Legalistic contraptions intended to respect the neighboring State's monopoly on the granting of impunity, like extradition, cease to work. It becomes harder for one society to respect the prosecutorial culture of another. Lines of retreat to places of impunity begin to follow cultural differentiation. Sexuality is not the least of factors that drive such differences.

Open discussion of sexual topics can exact responses of embarrassment, revulsion, titillation, or fear. It is nevertheless advantageous to surface those sexual issues that will affect your likelihood of having to fight, where to fight, and winning. Your military efficiency especially can be negatively affected by ignorance regarding sexual practices. In addition, sexual practices and geographies present an exploitable link to information about the whereabouts of your enemy, or even regarding impending violent events.

See: 76, *Gendering*; 81, *What a Clergy Wants*; 62, *Illicit Commerce*; 65, *Smuggling*; 17, *Kidnapping*; 105, *Genocide Geography*; 49, *Territorial Scrutiny*; and 142, *Dignity and Honor*.

---

> "I am a very good shot. I have hunted for every kind of animal. But I would never kill an animal during mating season."
>
> Hedy Lamarr[113]

How many names can a person have?

# *Section 78, Personal Identity*

Anonymity and personal identity are inseparable. Anonymity means you cannot be identified as you, nor your things and relationships as yours. Personal identity, beyond simply being the most particular of ownerships, often rests on our relationships, possessions, memories and aspirations -- these things and our personal identity might be considered co-constitutive. If you gain perfect anonymity, you run the risk of losing personal identity, or maybe the ability to express that identity. You might suffer…an identity crisis. Spies sometimes suffer these, insurgents not so much perhaps -- maybe since at some point they have to express their identity if they are going to translate it into power. Anyhow, anonymity is a dilemma for the insurgent. Criminals, meanwhile, want to enjoy their ill-gotten lucre, and so they're often in the same boat as the insurgent, needing to keep their anonymity, but finding that conspicuousness was one of the goals of their behavior. Finding the right balance of anonymity and profile is of central importance in every thoughtful, organized challenge to the structure of things, and so the destruction or preservation of personal identity is concomitantly important.

Careful ID carding of populations, and centralized ID inventories, can serve either to protect or to endanger personal identity. Creating firm evidence of identity is a practical step against theft or fraudulent use of personal identity. On the other hand, identity and marking systems have been implicated in assisting the perpetration of genocides, so ID cards are not necessarily or always a positive tool of peace or moral behavior. Nevertheless, no property system that orders rights and duties related to land, professional licenses, bandwidth, etc., can be fully functional as a tool of a peaceful social contract unless there is a parallel, transparent method of ensuring correct personal identification. Owner and owned are absolutely co-constitutive. Accuracy and transparency of the things owned is almost meaningless without accuracy and transparency of the identity of owners. This might seem to create a practical and philosophical dilemma with privacy values, but not really.

Moderation and reasonableness in transparency as to types of wealth, location, timing, etc. are built into the best identification systems. For instance, while real property might be subject to the transparency of public knowledge, purchases of personal items should not be. Although records pertaining to real property might be available for public inspection, the property itself (at least from the ground) should not be.

While there might be a requirement to carry an ID card, a requirement or the right of the government to inspect the cards can be limited to specific places and times. In this regard there are common and varying practices in jurisdictions around the world – which should suggest considerable room for creativity in balancing the needs of anonymity and privacy against the needs for transparency and forensic power.

Recent discoveries about DNA coding have so changed television crime stories it is a wonder anyone watched them before. We also have to wonder, however, if DNA falsification and planting (instead of dropping a weapon at the scene of a crime, a lot of faked DNA gets spilt around) isn't coming soon. In the meantime, all personal identity systems are two-edged swords that can favor good governance and bad.

**Sense of Place**. 'Where you from, Son?' must be the number one cliché question that the General asks the Private. Trite, expected and unimaginative, everyone likes it and is almost always happy to answer. The General can't go wrong because it is an essential question for most people. It is almost like asking 'Who are you, really?' Personal identity, who we are, is often tied to physical geography, and even to some imagined and remembered physical geographies. We might be Southerners, Yankees, Paisas, Texans or whatever, and we can be more than one thing at a time and feel ourselves more from one place than another depending on a whole rafter of other situational factors, including not only where those making up the rest of the 'we' are from, but where 'they' are from. Some say it is harder to get people to fight for the revolution than it is for them to fight for Mother Russia. Strangely, we can be *we* and keep them *they* for only the duration of a basketball game, or for generations. Section 92, *Land-use Planning*, notes how place identities can be nested just like the territories themselves. When nested identities become un-nested, internal conflicts of identity can grow, as well as conflicts of loyalty.

Creating and tapping into sense of place are staples of effective leadership. A country with powerful national symbols can motivate citizens more easily toward national missions. The United States, held together with frail ideas, nevertheless counts on many symbols of the whole – The Stars & Stripes, Statue of Liberty, Rock and Roll, the Golden Gate, hamburgers, Coke, Mt. Rushmore, Muhammad Ali, the ice cream cone,.... The master of irregular conflict will know place-identity language, what symbols say what to whom, and will try to manage them accordingly. It is not just about psychological operations or diplomacy either. Knowing where people are from helps identify where they are.

'Everywhere we go-oh, people wanna know-oh, Who we ah-are, where we come from.' Pride of action is pride in place. The city where you find yourself might be pleased at having a sister city wherever you came from. If both those cities are proud of what you're doing, that's good. If not, it behooves you to know why. When Americans are abroad, they should never be just from America. America is all the places from which its citizens hail. There are some persons for whom this rule (that identity is tied to locale) does not apply, and some persons who have become so traveled and sophisticated they take pride in everyplace and no place. Most of us aren't like that.

See: 105, *Genocide Geography*; 49, *Territorial Scrutiny*; 93, *Diseases and Disasters*; 74, *Refugees and Displaced Persons*; 96, *Public Records*; 3, *The Domesday Book*; 95, *Childhood*; and 2, *Anonymity*.

---

"To kill a human being is, after all,
the least injury you can do him."

Henry James[114]

Is what's worth dying for worth living for?

# *Section 79, Suicide*

Eschatologists generally agree that King Solomon wrote the Book of Ecclesiastes, a middle portion of the Christian Bible. It is an existential essay by a man who has everything and is yet tortured by a sense of meaninglessness and hopelessness. Solomon believes, however, that something exists greater than his self, and that a savior is to come. Solomon banks his hope in that salvation. It's a sizeable chunk of the Christian message, even though at first glance the book seems so out of place that some think it is a wonder it was included in the Bible at all. It doesn't say much about the history of the Jewish nation or the old covenant, or anything about the life of Jesus and the new covenant. It is, however, about hopelessness, meaninglessness, and that these afflictions are not limited to the poor. Christ's mission, apparently, was about this health and sickness of the soul, rather than about material well-being. Nevertheless, although hopelessness may be dispensed irrespective of worldly fortune, worldly misfortune can create and conjoin with hopelessness. Furthermore, luck often has nothing to do with it. Other men are sometimes to blame straight up for creating or allowing conditions that engender and fuel existential crises. These conditions are well known to us -- poverty, degradation and physical illness can weaken the spirit. Sometimes suicide is late evidence of something or somebody in the human experience that needed fixing. Who should have fixed it is a question we often find at the heart of armed struggle.

Some of us, not as astute as the leaders just mentioned above, notice that some of the other kids in high school are into a bunch of seemingly unhealthy, counterculture, gothic, *emo* psycho-babble. We do not grasp why they don't stop all the whining and go out for wrestling or cheerleading or something. Not afflicted, we have a tough time sensing the urgency of the search for the meaning of life, or why 'existentialism' should be counted as a movement of literature and art (often foisted on us) instead of being roundly dismissed. Most American art tends to be pretty sweet. Beer commercials, mostly; good stuff. There is another vein of art however, including American, that taps into, exposes and expresses Solomon's suffering. It is so much present in the art world, and so many souls drawn to that art, that many critics don't admit art as being art unless it suffers. Authenticity becomes a reflection of some sort of pain. Everything else is mere illustration or commercial schlock.

How does existentialism, depression and pained-art lead back to winning insurgent war? It is because of their connection to the perception of *them* versus *us*, insiders and outsiders, the resistance and the system. It is also about the strong connection between failed or missing dignity and honor. Dignity and honor bear especially on the mindsets of young men, many of whom are attracted to violence. Desperation, existential dilemma, unhappy sexual outlet, the search for honor, testosterone and guns make for a common and volatile soup. The mix doesn't necessarily lead to suicide of course -- homicide is often sufficient. It only needs an organizer for it to become organized homicide.

Once in a while, an individual gifted with the requisite combination of charisma, intelligence and wealth recognizes existential stress in others (perhaps, but not always wrestling with it themselves) and can translate that stress into action. Sometimes this same leader is ruthless, selfish, creative and energetic. That's when things get interesting.

The person resolved or coerced to commit suicide-homicide is someone's enemy, but the intellectual author of the suicide-homicide usually survives. The intellectual author usually just commits homicide, or perhaps just an efficient act of war. Most suicides are committed by heroes or chumps. The worse enemy is the leader who spots, vets, develops and convinces chumps and heroes to become suicide-homicide weapon systems. The leader (agent, intellectual author, or *mens rea* guy) is the more difficult operational challenge for his enemies. An act of suicide-homicide appears to present no route of withdrawal to sanctuary, but that only seems true because focus is drawn to the weapons system and not to the *mens rea* author. The latter scrupulously observes the operational equation by launching a weapon that affords himself, the intellectual author, a short distance to sanctuary. If he is really good, he can establish not only the appearance that there is no line of retreat, but can motivate heroes and chumps in such a way as to create the public notion of spontaneity and broad moral acceptance, whereas in fact, he is a much more unique and vulnerable leader.

The attentive criminal, insurgent or counterinsurgent leader will seek to dominate the explosive mix of existential stress, the search for honor, and violent propensities. However, local cultural knowledge is more useful than vague acceptance of the existence of existential plight. While a good deal is made today of the willingness of some radicalized Islamicists to commit homicide-suicide, the phenomenon is cross-cultural. Only the details differ. As Section 54, *Mercatus* noted, recruiting assassins requires an understanding of the local interpretation of the dilemmas presented by poverty, honor, faith and suicide. Drug lord Pablo Escobar contracted young Medellín men who knew they would be killed after they made a hit. But the deal included a guarantee that the hit man's mother would have a house provided for her to live in for the rest of her life. The local envelopment of happiness, home, motherhood, and honor with the meaning of life were served in the sacrifice. Of course, the police were *Paisa*, too, so eventually the tracing of moms with new houses, dead sons and going-away parties started leading back to the *mens rea.*

Please read 142, *Dignity and Honor*; 59, *Spontaneity*; 81, *What a Clergy Wants*; 94, *Poop*; 13, *Puthukkudiyirippu*; 23, *Mens Rea*; 98, *Jorge Verstrynge and Pio Moa*; and 51, *Underclass.*

---

> "There is as much courage in supporting with firmness the afflictions of the soul as there is in standing steady under the grape of a battery of guns. To give one's self up to grief without resistance, to kill one's self to escape it, is to abandon the battlefield defeated."
>
> Napoleon Bonaparte (1802)[115]

"When the nerves break down, there is nothing left but to admit that one can't handle the situation and to shoot oneself."

Adolf Hitler (1943)[116]

ଔଓଔଓଔଓଔଓଔଓଔଓ

The propaedeutic of winning

# Section 80, Why You Should Like Geography

All kinds and categories of knowledge, all disciplines and all approaches can help the astute competitor win an armed conflict. Among the modern academic disciplines, however, Geography is probably the one that gets to the most relevant knowledge fastest. It obsesses about distances, fascinates about the interrelationship between human activity and the natural environment; and revels in travel and exploration. Vocationally, geographers solve transportation puzzles, order ownership records and land-use plans, and calculate the environmental costs of human activities.

Property is where Geography, Law and Economics cross. It is difficult to understand property regimes, urban planning, or agrarian reform on any significant scale without a grasp of geographic theory. Peaceful design depends on geographic knowledge. So does not-so-peaceful design.

Geography is probably the most hyphenatable discipline. Most geographers in the major geographical societies of the United States consider themselves to be human geographers of one stripe or another. They are economic geographers, cultural geographers, and so on. The common denominator of Geography, however, is recognition of the importance not only of place and distance, but of differentials in environmental conditions, human approaches to that environment and the potential for peaceful, or conflictive interaction.

Again, all knowledge is grist to the mill, but Geography should be the discipline of choice for those who want to win violent struggles. It teaches the measurement of distances, inventorying everything, cultural exploration, precision mapping in time and space. It accepts a broad range of the meaning of truth, without abandoning latitudes, longitudes, wind directions and soil samples. Below are ten reasons to favor Geography and geographers:

**Distance** --- perhaps the most profiting theoretical concepts special to Geography revolve around distance. The dissipation of power as distance increases, or the increase of influence and identity as distance decreases; the idea of cost-distance and its various measurements by time, money, fear, fuel, risk, etc.; and distance as a question of cultural affinity or perception -- these are easy to Geography. Distance is passed over by other disciplines even while it is so central to the study of armed conflict.

**Place** --- Place is also prominent in other disciplines like Anthropology and Sociology, but concepts of place-identity and the relationship of these to nested and un-nested, formal and informal territoriality is more richly considered by Geography.

**Maps** --- Attacks on mapmaking by 'critical geographers' may be all the evidence the discipline needs of its theoretical uniqueness. Even English Literature cannot claim language or writing as a special purview, while maps and mapmaking are stuck to Geography. As one of the first and still spectacularly effective methods to communicate ideas, maps belong to the discipline.

**Inventories** --- While the tendency to catalog and count is derided by some, it is a theoretical as well as a habitual strength of Geography in that it bespeaks a basic empirical intention. Truth, for most geographers, is not a floating matter of pure perception and human invention (although these matter), but is still an objective quantity that, more than likely, has a latitude and longitude, a moment and second.

**Exploration** --- Other disciplines explore, but geographers will explore anyplace. Going out and reporting back is more than research, it is search and research.

**Hyphenation** -- Geography is always a willing partner to other disciplines. Geography is often the ecumenical keystone of many multidiscipline research efforts.

**Embrace of Technology** --- It isn't just that Geography dominates GIS, but that as a thought culture, Geography embraces new ways to make its maps, descriptions and discoveries. GIS allows us to better match the right temporal and spatial scales to our objectives, projects, and analyses.

**Environment and Human** --- The interrelationship of humans and the environment has always been one of Geography's central themes. Man's domination of that environment (and of other men and women) has been more prominent in, and more favored by Geography than by other disciplines, but this fact does not diminish the strength of its methods and habits in service to other passions.

**Conflict** --- Geography is criticized as a discipline of empires, but what is lost in such criticism is that Geography has been the one discipline to take head-on the question of power and human competition in ecological space. Nothing in the discipline today insists on taking one side or another in human competition, only that the natural environment, distance, weight, time and space are central considerations. Terrain and weather do not favor one side or another in warfare, but only the side that understands and engages them best; likewise, the discipline of Geography.

**Fun** --- Some of the criticism brought against Geography is subliminal, and is about geographers as much as it is about Geography. It is by and large a happy discipline, optimistic -- a celebration of humanity and nature. It is a problem-solving discipline. Other disciplines offer more psychological space for accusing and lamenting. The admiration of cynical perspective and of suffering-as-authenticity is notably less present in Geography than in other social sciences. Geography's tone of discovery is buoyant. Such optimism and egoism can engender resentment and fear. Well… be afraid, non-geographers, be afraid.

See: 41, *Whereabouts* ; 73, *Property and the Social Contract*; 63, *Cost-Distance*; 49, *Territorial Scrutiny*; 66, *GIS;* 8, *The Operational Equation*; 108, *Neogeography*; and 38, *Cultural Study for What?*

---

"War is God's way of teaching Geography."

Attributed to everyone from Alexander von Humboldt to Winston Churchill to George Carlin

# Section 81, What a Clergy Wants

Clergies want to provide a service, which can be valuable. They want to be paid for that service as well. Clergymen would like to be your agents, middlemen, go-betweens, representatives, spokespersons, lawyers. When life is good for the clergy, the clergy invents its own vocabulary or speaks its own language, has its own licenses and schools. When things really get good for a clergy, it no longer has to expend energy selling the idea of their agency to the clients. They just presume clergy is a natural and necessary part of life. Tithes, indulgences, pledges and donations are too often the equivalents of commissions, retainers and fees. Offensive as it may sound to put lawyers and sports agents in the same bucket with religious clergy, the point here is not about charlatanism or even about religion, but to remind that religious spirituality is often a question apart from religion's leadership, just as ideological sense is a question apart from the quality of the vanguard, or the justness of the law distinct from the caliber of the bar and the judiciary.

The concept of clergy and exclusive agency are almost the same; only the linguistic protocols for their use vary. A vanguard of the proletariat seeks almost the same kind of exclusive agency as some religious leaders do, so when I use the word clergy, I don't mean to disparage religion, but only warn that clergies bear watching because of their tendency to seek exclusive agency.

You will be helped in your armed conflict if you understand the rents of agency, especially exclusive agency. Where rents of agency are collected, who exactly pays them, to whom they go and what they pay for is key. It is a property issue. The places and methods of delivery of tithes and indulgences, the catchment areas and variety of paid services all have a geographic mark, and as the clergy system becomes more complex, it begins to consecrate seminaries, require examinations and ordinations. There arises a concomitant sense of jealousy and fierce protectiveness regarding the 'right' to exclusive agency. If there are too many lawyers, it will cheapen the bar. Bolsheviks don't abide by other Communists wanting to be the vanguard. Remember, by clergy I don't just mean religious clergy; I mean a collaborative institution of exclusive agency.

The insurgent and the counterinsurgent need to take inventory of agents and agency of all kinds, because through clergies flow matters of morale, followership, enthusiasms, and enthrallments.

Freedoms of and opportunities for speech and of assembly are closely tied to some powers and opportunities for representative agency, and it can be hard to remember that the profitable feature of exclusive agency is not freedom of action and expression, and not fiduciary responsibility, but *exclusivity*. Separating the two for analysis can be difficult and has been a thorny question for Americans since the founding of the Republic. It appears in the form of a debate about whether or not churches, for instance, should be taxed or whether a given organization even is a church such that it should not be taxed.

Where is all this going? The last section of the book is about a successful State versus a failed State, and that a successful State has an exclusive power to grant impunity. Religious clergymen (at least your ambitious types) aspire to be the exclusive granters of absolution. If they get enough power they will protect that exclusive agency (that they will call a right) with apparatuses like inquisitions, and with the simple control of private spaces. Impunity and absolution are not so far apart that if you can combine the Church and the State, there is hardly any difference at all. You can ease the defense of your right to exclusive clerical agency by building a theology and creating a religious belief among followers -- your clients -- for whom you intend to be the exclusive agent. Please keep in mind that defining the success of the State in accordance with its ability to maintain exclusive agency in the granting of absolution (impunity), is not to say that such success makes the State good -- just successful at being a State.

When a State asserts that to be successful, a State has to provide this and that material benefit, it might be a subterfuge for claiming a right to exclusive agency. Once people are convinced that their care is properly in the hands of a good State, then it is a lot easier for those lucky and wily enough to put themselves in charge of the State to establish the same sense of exclusive agency that clergy wants. They will claim that *only* the State can rightly provide this and that.

Hopefully the concept of exclusive agency makes it easier to see why some religions want to make sure they control the State and why some States want so badly to either *be* the religion or kill off religions, or at least organized clergy. Whenever you see a group bent on maintaining any kind of exclusive agency, and especially when they try to get others to believe they have some spiritual right to exclusive agency, you have also found a font of grievance and resistance.

Exclusive agents, by the way, tend to create specific geographic spaces for the exercise of their advantage. It is easier for a rabbi to create and maintain influence if he has a synagogue. If you want exclusive agency for bringing big league football to the American fans, you need stadiums. If you are going to maintain exclusive agency for the provision of civil justice, you want court buildings. These spaces are not hard to find, and they lead back to the operatives and owners. As is highlighted in other parts of this book, it is often easy to find geographies of power, and if you have the capacity to change the built environment; you have the capacity to greatly adjust the shape and possibilities of exclusive agency.

It can be dangerous to posit one religion as better than another, either for the good of the universe, or for winning your war. Consider, nevertheless, a handful of desert prophets -- which of them did not kill and which did; and consider, from among the beliefs and religions they inspired, which are oriented toward sparing souls from desperation and hopelessness, which are based on free will, which demand taxes, which invite or exclude, and which are jealous.

See: 144, *Impunity and State Success*; 124, *America's Insurgent Stamp*; 128, *Global Insurgency and Global Trespass*; *143, Is It an Insurgency?*; 19, *NGOS and Unions*; 122, *Songs of Chu*; 53, *Hohfeldian Grievance Analysis*; and 46, *Taxation and Debt.*

---

> "The real religion of the world comes from women much more than from men - from mothers most of all, who carry the key of our souls in their bosoms."
>
> Oliver Wendell Holmes, Sr.[117]

---

You cannot make an arrest with a fighter jet

# *Section 82, Conflict Thresholds*

Sometimes we claim armed struggles fall along a 'spectrum' of violence (less to more), a convention that may or may not reflect the relationship of one conflict to another, or be helpful for determining which struggles are more urgent than others, or when to change our strategies for dealing with them. There are some thresholds, however -- ethical, technological, economic, legal, territorial and emotive -- that are distinct enough to help guide our strategies. None of them exists independently. They don't act sequentially to announce the status of a conflict, nor do they, singularly or in the aggregate, describe war.

Thresholds nevertheless illuminate a field of organized human conflict that includes thermonuclear war and peasant roadblocks. A few of the thresholds inspire other sections of this book, like *UAAV*, *Mercatus*, *Kidnapping*, and the last section, *Impunity and State Success*. Conflict-as-thresholds is a device, not a philosophy. Some of the thresholds might be milestones in a struggle with which you're dealing. If you establish a shared understanding of the thresholds relevant to your struggle, you might be able to anticipate arguments and decision-points, and maybe even push the thresholds backward or forward in time a little.

**Ethical Thresholds** -- In the ethical category, the premeditation of impunity is a gateway to explaining other thresholds. An example of its practical manifestation can be taken from another threshold category, technological. It is difficult to make an arrest with a 203mm howitzer. A potential act of killing has been anticipated before its use. The cannoneer who pulls the lanyard, and all ranks above him to include those who ordered the forging of the tube, presuppose their impunity from prosecution for the potential future, willful act of killing. A distinct, ethical threshold is passed when the cannon fires, but even before the tube had been forged and the artilleryman trained, impunity had already been bestowed and the possibility of an act of war foreseen.

Another ethical threshold is that which justifies the killing of persons who are clearly not resolved participants, such as children.

**Technological Thresholds** -- Use of a cannon heralds and emblemizes war beyond the expectations of trial justice, to say the least, so obviously the categories of threshold overlap. Other technological thresholds include manufacture and use of the unmarked landmine, instruments which are also extremely difficult to employ within contemplation of a law enforcement process. They come into play beyond the normal rule-of-law. The employment of an unoccupied armed aerial vehicle would be a clear technological threshold. Use of this technology is too new historically to allow us to analyze its full impact on armed struggles, but it is clearly new grist for impassioned debate, especially as the low per-unit cost of the machinery spreads the technology to more and more potential contenders.

**Economic Thresholds** --- In *The Rise of the Western World, a New Economic History*, Nobel laureates Douglass North and Robert Paul Thomas outlined the idea of transaction cost as that concept related to conflict.[118] They asserted that people resort to violence when the cost of violence is perceived to be less than the cost of nonviolent transaction.

The nation-state, they argued could afford high end means of applying organized force, and so could make the costs of violence seem very high to a would-be challenger to the nation-state's authority. (Here we would say that impunity is the absence of such a cost for violence.) Peaceful transaction costs would generally be higher than the costs of violence if it were not for the invention of systems that encourage fulfillment of contractual obligations. Focusing on offenses or trespasses, if the costs of transacting a peaceful resolution to a conflict in land, for instance, are calculated as uneconomically high within the sense of time available, parties to the conflict are likely to resort to violence. Depending on whether or not you are the insurgent, you may or may not want to see an administrative and judicial environment in which land disputes can be resolved economically.

**Territorial Thresholds** --- The economic thresholds strongly influence another category -- territorial. These are perhaps the most naturally understood thresholds in that they relate closely to what many think is a natural element of human character. The title to Robert Ardrey's popular work, *Territorial Imperative*, is succinct. The territorial thresholds are reached by the physical act of crossing a demarcated boundary in a way not authorized by the occupiers (perhaps sovereigns). The invasion of Kuwait by Iraq or the taking of the Falkland Islands by the Argentineans are easy examples, but so are property trespasses by squatters, or tossing a bag of excrement onto the roof of a downhill shack. In the broader range of human conflict, almost every territorial trespass is subject to spatial mapping, and those territorial violations that imply war are often the most ardently mapped. Spaces outside the lines of formalized mapping are known as no-man's land and are usually subject to possession by force.

**Legal Thresholds** --- Legal thresholds overlap the territorial thresholds, and tend to delimit the geography of military action, rather than the geographic object of the conflict. For instance United States domestic law places clear boundaries on the physical space of action of the United States military. The Posse Comitatus Act exists because of concerns that the whole panoply of American civil rights and duties might be overmatched by an organized armed force, however noble its leaders, whose members might enjoy immunity from civil prosecution and, as the reasoning goes, impunity for socially dangerous behaviors. Thus, with exceptions, the US Army does not operate within the geographic boundaries of United States territory.

The Colombian government has had to face many of these questions in recent years. For instance, in 2008, the Colombian armed forces raided just across the Ecuadoran border to take out a major FARC headquarters. The Ecuadoran government claimed the attack was a violation of Ecuador's sovereignty, while the Colombians saw it as more of a hot pursuit of a terrorist organization and an action within the common defense agreements of the two neighbors. Some Ecuadorans have moved to prosecute the Colombian Minister of Defense in their or international court. Our first reaction to that notion might be 'Fat Chance.' Nevertheless, the Ecuadoran stance does encumber the Colombian State, not to mention the defense minister. In this kind of context, the denial or rejection of extraterritorial jurisdiction can be considered a threshold marker.

**Emotive Thresholds** --- Any dehumanization or demotion from privilege can become or lead to a conflict threshold. We are talking here about the formalized establishment by fear and hate of vulnerable and resentful collective human identities. Persons committing trespasses or violence against such a collective are sometimes led to expect impunity for those acts. In other words, a nation, premeditating impunity, could designate a category of humans as a target, abuses against which impunity would be granted. The Nazis, for instance, not only crossed the threshold of publicly identifying Jews, they premeditatedly established a public understanding of impunity for violence against them. This is an historically extreme example, but by no means the only. A sense for those locales around the world where human disqualifications occur would be a good start to predicting organized violence that could escalate toward war, or toward genocide. As with the disqualification of the European Jews, disqualifications often start in the realm of property rights, reaching the thresholds of war only in late stages. The emotive threshold can become wrapped tightly to other thresholds, such as the territorial. For instance, Bolivians have indoctrinated themselves to hold the loss of Pacific coastal territory as a shared emotional void, the recovery of which is now an article of patriotic faith.

We might hope that our domination of the technological thresholds of war will appropriately match our understanding of the other thresholds, but we probably always perceive an imbalance. Israeli angst in their decisions to use a 500-, 1,000-, or 2,000-pound bomb is exemplary. Might we conduct war with nonlethal weapons that stun and disable without permanent harm? Using nonlethal force where possible (in order to meet standards of proportionality and discriminate use) may be a good thing in its own right, and might secure the blessing of Sun Tzu's ghost. The overmatching advantages that perplex and confound an enemy can sometimes be found beyond lethal weaponry.

In *Makers of Modern Strategy from Machiavelli to the Nuclear Age*, contributor John Shy quotes of Jomini, "strategy, like politics, must find some '*juste milieu*' between wars of the past fought by professional armies and the new yet old barbaric warfare unleashed by the Revolution."[119] Jomini was talking about the French Revolution. The 'Revolution' is a little different these days. The thresholds may arrive as dissonance or cacophony. In the analysis of irregular wars globally, however, a solid sense of the thresholds can be useful. The passing of various thresholds fuels premonitions that the time is coming when established governments will launch militarily against enclaves that harbor, train, promote or aim powerful math minds against digital systems. Meanwhile, more athletically-oriented organizers of violence will continue to manage the more traditional kinds of violence.

See: 144, *Impunity and State Success*; 104, *Extraterritorial Jurisdiction*; 39, *Socioeconomic Causation;* 129, *Nerd Globe*; 4, *Defining Enemy*; 109, *Hotspotting*; 24, *Ruthlessness and Resolve*; and 25, *Why Humans Don't Fight.*

---

Watch out for canoneers. Often hooded,
they fire ethical and legal principles at you.

---

Amplius prodest locus saepe quam virtus

# *Section 83, Conflict Geography*

Military geographers have their own specialty group in the Association of American Geographers. Conflict Geography this book foresees for irregular armed conflict would emphasize *where* and *when* without overlooking who, what, where, why, and how. While Conflict Geography might presume to help avoid or resolve conflict, it would be as ethically comfortable seeking victory and dominion. Here are some proposed methods and principles of Conflict Geography, in no particular order:

Selection of appropriate scales for time, space, and weight is a useful exercise, especially for expressing ideas about distance and location across academic and professional disciplines and across other means of communication than the map. Scale helps conform thought, but it can restrict creativity as well, so remain flexible to the constant dynamics of scale and to the possibilities of limitless or not-scaled concepts.

Maps, photography, models, verbal and written description, poetry, plastic art, and performances are all useful for describing the nature and importance of places. Today, GIS provides the most significant and useful inventorying and epistemological framework to combine subjective descriptions with technical specificity as to absolute and relative location, time and weight.

Territorial boundaries (as drawn on maps and sometimes on the ground) represent agreements, desires, impositions, natural phenomena, theoretical phenomena, descriptive categories or perhaps technical limits. They come in all sizes shapes and scales, representing things like cell phone tower ranges, school catchment areas, sales territories, water easements and historical trends. When these territorial lines overlap, however, the overlap almost always betrays a conflict or a potential conflict.

While most territories can be visualized as areas, most networks are easier to draw with connected lines, but they, too, have a geographical reference or limit. Usually they can be drawn in conjunction with the territories. Sometimes the networks can also be called flows, and sometimes the flows or networks create their own territories (like bandwidth or a gas line easement).

Many human identities can be depicted in two dimensions as well. Sometimes territorial ranges and identities match, and sometimes they don't. A mismatch indicates a potential conflict. For instance, you could probably make a two-dimensional boundary around where inhabitants who identify themselves as Kurds predominate, but where the tax and other boundaries suggested in Section 52, *Sovereignty*, will not match your 'Most of us call ourselves Kurds' boundary.

Some kinds of data can only be drawn appropriately in point form, depending on the scale. Many geographically relevant concepts, including cultural affinities, fears, aspirations, economic trends and the like may be better expressed in ways other than the map, and in conjunction with maps.

Power diminishes with distance, like the light from a light bulb. The geography of competing powers and influences in a given locale is rarely so complex that the major elements cannot be both identified and their relative power understood.

Euclidean distance is the standard baseline, but the determining distances in Conflict Geography are friction or cost-distances. More than time, fuel or money, the measurement and analysis of distances should include factors such as fear and extortion, legal constraint, anonymity, public will, and especially impunity.

Conflict Geography must more fully incorporate the underground plane of physical conflict. Underground is added to sea, aerospace and land.

Irregular warfare unfolds in the context of dynamic legal and economic relationships. Armed competitors are nevertheless still subject to the classic principles of warfare, albeit with adjustments due to a wider gamut of scales as to numbers, weight, time, and space. The operational math is always subject to the kinds of friction distance mentioned above.

The propensity of a place to be the venue of irregular armed conflict can be estimated by careful consideration of the social contract, and the social contract can be best understood in terms of property relationships, especially as regards land and the system of land ownership.

Successful strategies in active armed competition will obey classic rules of movement and position, and within these rules the central geographic feature is the line of retreat. Lines of retreat lead from some sort of target or contact to a sanctuary.

Successful strategies for long-term peace will be land-based strategies that are built on an understanding of the relative worth of real estate and the relation of places and their worth to human identity.

Technological and other innovations constantly change the variables of friction distances, and therefore the power that can be exerted in a given place.

Earthquakes, volcanoes, epidemics, hurricanes and similar phenomena can have major predictable and unpredictable influence on the environments in which irregular wars unfold, and are therefore a staple consideration.

Among those preoccupations from broader human geography, conditions providing anonymity (of person, wealth and relationships) are paramount. For long longer-term strategies, the system of land ownership is the preoccupation.

Conflict Geography, like the discipline generally, has to remain hyphenatable. It can't be just geography, but has to be medical-geography, historical-geography, business-geography, etc. It has to strive (against the disdain of post-structuralists) to be as objective as possible in its measurement of the world and the battlespace. This is not to say it cannot or should not takes sides in a fight.

See: 14, *Legitimacy*; 141, *Seven Strategy Strains*; 140, *Culminating Point in the Pursuit*; 144, *Impunity and State Success*; 125, *Human Rights*; 66, *GIS*; 2, *Anonymity*; and 8, *The Operational Equation.*

---

> "Territory is not the cause of war. It is the cause of war only in the sense that it takes two to make an argument. What territory promises is the high probability that if intrusion takes place, war will follow."
>
> Robert Ardrey,
>
> *Territorial Imperative*[120]

---

Silence and bloody proof

# *Section 84, Cultures of Violence*

Culture is a broad, amorphous term. For the purposes of winning, it is useful to talk of 'Mafia culture,' 'gang culture,' 'guerrilla culture,' and to avoid painting a whole people as having a violent culture. There are two principal characteristics of violent organizational behavior that focus the attention in this regard. One is the rule or ethic of silence (or a culture of anonymity), the other is proof of resolve to kill (or a culture of ruthlessness).

Colombia is a violent place, but a look through the ample Colombian literature on violence reveals that some physical object of contention is always present in the formula (some piece of *Covet-geography*), not just human foible. Violent behavioral habits exist, but they matter in the presence or absence of certain characteristics of the political, administrative and economic surroundings, many of which can be changed rapidly. Peace might be achieved more surely by changing administrative conditions than by trying to change human behavioral dispositions. Colombia is a violent place, but Colombians aren't innately more violent than anyone else.

According to economists like John Umbeck, people resort to violence when the cost of so doing is perceived to be less than the cost of nonviolent transaction.[121] In practical terms, governments create a chance for peaceful coexistence when they put in place rules and mechanisms for peaceful conflict resolution. Establishing institutions to resolve conflicts about the use and occupation of land is positively consequential. Large polities have done this successfully only with the use of written records and some kind of property court. The likelihood of social peace increases as more agreements are openly published, land ownership mapped, titles granted, and courts made available for eviction of trespassers.

Does all this disciplining of contractual obligations constitute culture? Arguably, yes, but the suite of innovations that make a social contract stronger does so in great measure because of the simple destruction it causes to anonymity. That is to say, in peaceful societies, the right to privacy has some very specific exceptions. The identity of wealth, especially the nexus between individuals and valuable property (real estate, vehicles, significant chattel) can be made precise, comprehensive and transparent. Doing so leads to accountability, tax equity, environmental responsibility, etc. In an administratively open society it is hard for individuals to hide their personal identity in relation to quarrels about land.

Cultural understanding – knowledge of pertinent elements of human psychology, sociology and geography can further success in internal conflict. That said, practical, mechanical, organizational innovations are readily available that trump and obviate many human phenomena that we might too respectfully honor with the term *culture*. Colombia is violent, but it is becoming more peaceful as its leaders finish putting in place those innovations proven to strengthen the social contract and alleviate simple human urgencies that can be exploited by amoral entrepreneurs and charlatans. That optimism stated, Colombia may never be able to build a peaceful society if powerful armed groups, bent on defying the Colombian government's monopoly on granting impunity, enjoy sanctuaries in countries neighboring on Colombia.

Systems that limit one competitor's anonymity, and provide anonymity to the informants of another provide a competitive edge in irregular war. Property maps tied to transparent ownership records, along with courts to give them meaning, are a related proposition for the longer-term. Infrastructure investments that alleviate dispiriting conditions and invite human aspiration are also powerful in the long term. To the extent these kinds of things (transportation systems, toilets, property registries, school lunches) are cultural, so be it. They can beat the cultures of violence.

See: 38, *Cultural Study for What?*; 2, *The Line of Retreat*; 126, *Particularization of Power*; 108, *Neogeography*; 37, *School Lunches*; 96, *Public Records*; 43, *Sam Spade*; and 36, *Engineers*.

---

"Where's my money, man."

Stewie on the television show
*The Family Guy*[122]

Bombing oil and leaves

# *Section 85, Ploesti & Putumayo*

(adapted from *Property & Peace*)

In 1943, allied war planners suggested that a bombing raid on the Romanian oil fields around Ploesti could be a knockout blow to German war-making capacity and thereby shorten the course of World War II in Europe. Churchill called the Ploesti fields the taproot of the Nazi war machine, so a huge air raid was mounted against the fields. The Ploesti raid was no knockout blow; the immediate results were insubstantial. Fifty-four of the 177 B-24 Liberators sent on August 1, 1943 did not return. A resilient, determined enemy took countermeasures and found alternatives. Eventually, Nazi use of Romanian oil was reduced by as much as 85%, at least by the time the Russians occupied the fields in 1945. Hurting the Nazi oil resource base was a good idea, and later bombing campaigns against Nazi fuel infrastructure did speed the end of the war. The Battle of the Ardennes in late 1944, in which the final German offensive stalled for lack of fuel, is often cited as evidence.

Starving the Nazi war machine of Romanian oil was accomplished far more by railhead interdiction and destruction of rolling stock and production facilities within Germany than by bombing facilities in the production fields. Not only that: airpower may have been most effective in Europe when, during major allied ground operations after D-Day, it weakened Wehrmacht operational reserves. The strategic air campaigns attempted to hit as many critical industries as possible, but ultimately, for Nazi Germany to be defeated, the Allies had to close with and destroy the Wehrmacht on the ground.

How does the history of Ploesti apply to irregular conflicts? The aerial glyphosphating of plants in the coca fields of Putumayo, Colombia, for instance, proved inefficient in hurting FARC guerrilla finances (never mind stopping the market flow of cocaine). Massive aerial attack against the dense Putumayo coca crops was supposed to cause grave harm to the FARC's cocaine-based financial health -- just as the raid on Ploesti was to deprive the Nazi war machine of its supposed lifeblood. (Colombia, by the way, is five times the size of Romania.) The coca fields were seen by some planners as the taproot of the FARC war machine. Perhaps if aerial spraying could have been done simultaneously throughout the entire coca cultivation area, it might have had the intended effect, but that was never physically possible. Putumayo was densely cultivated in coca, and therefore the locus of a significant amount of the FARC's overall war-making strength. The long-term value of eradication spraying has turned out to be, as many of us anticipated, underwhelming. Spraying achieved the immediately visible result of knocking out a lot of commercially valuable vegetation, but the guerrillas shifted to other income sources, protected other crop areas, dispersed cultivation, replanted, improved the species genetically, shipped from storage, increased kidnapping and other extortions, exerted political pressure to end the spraying, and took other countermeasures. Aerial eradication made it a little more difficult for the guerrilla groups to fund their respective wars, but they did.

Neither the raid on Ploesti nor the Putumayo coca eradication was an abject failure, even if neither were decisive blows. The costly experience at Ploesti led to better planned and executed follow-on operations that evolved with the broader counter-oil strategy. Like Ploesti, the coca field targeting may have been the result of the obvious. That is to say, oil field infrastructure in the World War II case, and coca plants in the Colombia case, stuck out in aerial photos, prompting a planning momentum that left little room for the painstaking identification of less dramatic and more disperse transportation nodes and infrastructure. Had there been a methodology in place that could precisely scale the relative economic-military value of European transportation terrain, then perhaps the Ploesti fields themselves might never have been rated as an optimal target as compared, say, to railheads. In Colombia, while drug traffickers use all means at their disposal for product shipment, cost constraints have them employ roads and rivers, probably in a measure consistent with the routes' carrying capacities.

The Putumayo aerial eradication strategy recognized a place in Colombia as particularly valuable economically to the outlaw enemy, and therefore, a valuable military target. Unfortunately, the Putumayo spray plan, like the Ploesti bombing raid, was not based on a sufficient understanding of the relative economic value of terrain as a targeting guide. The Putumayo plan didn't do enough to identify terrain that might have influenced the overall value of the final product, cocaine, more than the coca fields. It was not based on a geographic concept of inputs that included transportation routes as being of equal or greater importance than raw material source locations.

The importance of the coca plant itself was perhaps over-rated as a factor in the commercial value of cocaine. Consider another widely available product on which there can be some physical dependency -- water. Bottled water is an extremely lucrative offering in the United States, and bottled water can sell for more money than the soft drink on the shelf next to it, even if the water was drawn untreated right from a municipal water service. This might make you question the value of sugar, but don't be fooled into thinking the price of bottled water is closely associated with the quality of the $H_2O$. The plastic in the bottle is not worth much either. To choke off water-profits from some ill-doing water-trafficker, we might try drying up the sources of water, maybe because it is easy to see an offending lake on an aerial photo, or find a water main. That strategy seems unlikely to succeed. It would be more efficient to knock off the truck on the way to the store. Where is the most valuable geography in the bottled-water industry? It is not the lake, but the bottling plant or some point on the road to the convenience store, or maybe the shelf in that store. The value of bottled water is the fact that it is found in a portable form *in the convenience store*, not that it is water.

While this analogy of water to oil or coca is soon overdrawn, the question it highlights regarding relative geographic value -- ingredient source vs. factory vs. route to market -- is valid. The coca fields are not as important as they appear in an aerial photo. They are more replaceable than other parts of the product-to-market geography. This question of relative geographic value is much more easily understood when land is considered as property, and that lines of communication are more important than destinations. Maybe in all cases the most critical geography is that which sets between the ears of the *mens rea* mind.

See: 61, *Who Sins More?*; 65, *Smuggling*; 131, *Sea and Aerospace Power*; 62, *Illicit Commerce*; 57, *Dogs and Mules*; 139, *UAAV*; *86, Shifting Covet Geography*; and 19, *Extortion.*

---

**Joe Dirt**: You're gonna stand there, owning a fireworks stand, and tell me you don't have no...spleen spliters, whisker biscuits, honkey lighters, hoosker doos, hoosker don'ts, cherry bombs, nipsy daisers, with or without the scooter stick, or one single whistling kitty chaser?

**Kicking Wing**: No... because snakes and sparklers are the only ones I like.

**Joe Dirt**: Well that might be your problem, it's not what you like, it's the *consumer*.

From the movie,
*Joe Dirt*[123]

The cause of the where of violence

# *Section 86, Shifting Covet-Geography*

Some places are more desirable than others. Organized armed violence happens where the relative value of real estate changes and there are no systems in place to handle the change peacefully. Simple. A physical geographic index of market value can be highly revealing, if not the easiest thing to make, if you want to anticipate the changing places of armed conflict in the world. When something new, like oil or another saleable commodity is discovered, people fight over the source locations, transport nodes, labor, tax revenues, insurance coverage, proximate business locations, and even related trademarks. Everything that can be sold, traded, or held at risk for the purposes of extortion: water, coal, bananas, guano, cardamom, feathers, emeralds, coca, heroin, ink, cattle, gold, silver, salt, bandwidth, goldfish, babies, hardwood, medical cadavers, rare earth, and on and on, will be violently fought over in the absence of alternative means of coming to agreement about ownership.

The cost of violence takes its own geographic shape (where the natural environment is damaged, landmines are placed, people thrown in unmarked graves, innocents hit by stray bullets). The phenomenon is true at every scale. The 'where' of the cost of violence can be mapped. The reasons *why* the costs of an armed struggle are located *where* they are located can be explained by changes in the geographic locations and values of saleable material.

The above assertion about *where* is not the same as stating why people resort to violence, just why the costs of violence fall where they fall. The logical leap from *why-the-where* to just *why* isn't that far, however, except that for the latter we would have to rest on some philosophical assumptions about the nature of man, the nature of social constructs and all that falderal. The question of *why-the-where* speeds us to doing something about the situation, however, whatever the shape, purity or complexity of our competitive goals.

There is a major exception to the above observation that armed conflict and the costs of armed conflict correlate to changes in the commercial value of places. The exception is battle plans. When groups travel to attack each other in obedience to their understanding of the military strategy, the places where battles occur are generally not related to changing differentials in real estate values, but to the possibilities of attacking a foe and either being able to withdraw safely or pursue successfully. The terrain of operational art and the terrain of real estate values coincide in some way. Perhaps it is exactly when the terrain of organized violence is not related to commercial value that it must be related to military strategies.

See: 25, *Why Humans Don't Fight*; 80, *Why You Should Like Geography*; 53, *Hohfeldian Grievance Analysis*; 47, *Why the County*; 2, *The Line of Retreat*; 72, *Land Strategy*; 49, *Territorial Scrutiny*; and 83, *Conflict Geography*.

---

> "Unfortunately there is one thing standing between me and that property: the rightful owners. …Wait a minute... there might be legal precedent. Of course….Land-snatching. (He thumbs through a legal casebook index.) Land, land...(He finds the entry he is looking for): 'Land: see Snatch.' Ah, Haley vs. United States. Haley: seven; United States: nothing. You see, it can be done."
>
> Hedley Lamarr in the movie
> *Blazing Saddles* (1974)[124]

Denying water, destroying water, and not having enough

# *Section 87, Water Wars*

It wouldn't seem that water would be much different than any other commodity, or that it is so scarce it would merit constant mention. However, the human body is 95% water, and can't go without replenishment for very long. We can divide water conflicts into three categories: Water we need for combat; water we possess or can control in order to make money; and water we figure to deny others because we just hate them and want them dried-out dead.

1. Water for fighting. Soldiers in the United States military are logistically well-supported, but still sometimes run out of water at the front, which endangers them and impairs their fighting effectiveness. At the fighting end of logistical distances, which might just as likely be measured in yards as miles, the weight of water is increasingly felt. Water doesn't move over the Internet. A soldier has to carry it, and he

consumes it more rapidly as he does more work, so getting an ocean tanker full of fresh water to the closest port may not be enough, close enough. Big-war water moves in huge ships, cisterns and pipes, but in the more usual conflicts it is a canteen problem. From Colombia, which is one of the four or five freshwater-richest lands in the world, come many anecdotes of soldiers and guerrillas fighting fiercely over some damp streambed during the dry season, or at altitude during a dry spell. When soldiers find themselves too many hours away from water resupply, other determinants of strength begin to fade toward insignificance. In the aggregate, small unit water problems can spell a significant strategic advantage for the side better able to assure that its fighters have water. More water is one of the classic ingredients of superior culminating points and correlations of force. It might even constitute a fair distinction between police work and a military operation, because military operations so often require consideration of water's urgency.

2. We want a better deal. Contests over the price of water are ubiquitous and happen at many scales, from small urban residential areas to bordering nations. Sometimes you or the neighbor, the municipality, the evil corporation or the uphill country wants a better price, or maybe even needs it to keep providing the water. Water sources, courses and distribution systems that serve multiple ownership identities are always a potential object of conflict. That is why water courts of all kinds exist, and why there is a whole regime of international water law. One of the best-used arguments is that water is so elemental to human life it should be free and not subject to commercialization. This is a great emotional argument that works all the time, but it is also highly problematic. If water is worth something, then waterworks, water delivery systems and water storage facilities are worth financial investment, and that means dealing with the market for money, which means borrowing, which means we get to the question of interest rates and how much is a usurious rate and how much isn't. This generally gets us to a question of who gets to commit extortion, the guy with the water, the guy with the money, or the guy that organizes a bunch of people who demand water, but don't want to pay its worth. Sometimes the water is tied indirectly to a parallel problem of money and future value, such as when the water is contained in order to produce electricity.

3. Thirsty? Restricting water as a toll of extortion is common in irregular war. FARC units have on many occasions isolated and shut off intake pumps or interrupted municipal aqueducts in order to announce

their presence and power, and therewith to extort concessions from towns in Colombia. If the international conventions held sway, which they don't, such actions would be in violation of the rules of war as postulated. I mention those wistful rules only to point out that some deliberative bodies, interested in the normative course of civilization, have at times concluded that leveraging the scarcity of water to extract concessions is illegitimate behavior. It seems, however, to be effective.

If there is a fourth category it is the unintended effect of changing or damming a watercourse -- ruining its drinkability with toxic waste; overtaxing it; or changing its course and destroying habitats in the process. This kind of water negligence or crime can cause human population displacements and armed conflict. They are not exactly about water, but a result of poor resource management or stewardship.

The rise of Evo Morales to power in Bolivia is tied in recent urban lore to his participation as a leader of the aggrieved underdog in a 'water war' in the medium-sized city of Cochabamba. The facts revolve around a municipal potable water distribution system the management of which had been privatized. The company may or may not have overreached on prices, but in any case made a few boneheaded and culturally unacceptable revenue strategies. Evo Morales' personal participation or effectiveness in the actual events is debatable, and the whole history is a lot less engaging than the term 'war' merits, but in the end, water, its distribution and appraisal, was a catalyst for political competition, some of it violent. Meanwhile, the Bolivian government, backed by everyone along the Bolivian political and ideological spectrum, was claiming from Chile a higher price for water that flows from Bolivia into Chile and which is used there by a combination of residential areas and mining concerns.

Water is one of many natural resources over which people fight. It has some special characteristics, not the least of which is the fact that it flows downhill. Watersheds and streams often mark human territories. Availability of water often determines the relative value of real estate. Entire court systems are built around the need to resolve conflicts over water. Today, there may be a few places in the world where water could spark an international incident or even start a larger war. Those rarities aside, it is highly likely that the irregular war in which you find yourself will feature within it one or more of the types of water fight listed in this section. Don't lose the water fights.

See: *25, Why Humans Don't Fight*; *54, Mercatus*; *142, Dignity and Honor*; 26, *How Violent Groups Form*; 53, *Hohfeldian Grievance Analysis*; 86, *Shifting Covet-Geographies*; 85, *Gun Control*; and 107, *Price of Real Estate.*

---

"Moisture is the essence of wetness, and
wetness is the essence of beauty."

Derek in the movie
*Zoolander* (2001)[125]

ƇƎƆƇƎƆƇƎƆƇƎƆƇƎƆ

Negotiate or die

# *Section 88, Sieges and Takeovers*

Sieges attempt to turn sanctuaries into the last stop on someone's line of retreat. Let's say the Grand Vizier surrounds your town and bombards it with dead horses and rutabaga. If the Vizier can breach the walls, enter, and start slaughtering everyone, and you have no escape, you better have some sweet negotiating skills or you are about done. However, it is often just as hard to keep a siege army fed and watered as it is to keep the people inside a castle fed and watered. In order to beat the siege, you want to stay alive and resisting, your walls more or less intact, until his provisions run out and it is too risky for him to continue. The Grand Vizier will have to lift his siege if some Polish field army threatens his Janissaries and his line of withdrawal. On this matter, Machiavelli had counseled,

> "I judge those (princes) to be in constant need of help who cannot take the field against their enemies, but are obliged to retire behind their walls, and to defend themselves there."[126]

Maybe you're just in a small castle and don't have Polish king friends. You do your calculations and decide it best to negotiate, so you offer to give back your besieger's daughters and to offer him a higher percentage of the water that runs through your little realm, or maybe just to pay him the tribute he asked for to begin with.

Things haven't changed. The castle might only be a remote police station or a forward operating base, but the math is the same. How good are the walls and roofs; how much food, water and ammunition have you stored up, and how resolute are you? Do you have a field force, or allies that can interrupt the siege? Do you have an escape route? Sieges are a permanent feature of armed conflict. They are communal tests of will, and resolute resistance to sieges provides the material of military legend and national heritage. Texans have the Alamo, the Spanish Numancia; the French Camerone, the British Khartoum, and so on. Sometimes it is the siege that provides national pride, like the Vietnamese victory at Dien Bien Phu. Sometimes these battles are merely heroic footnotes and sometimes they are milestones of change in political history. If you build a fort or fortify a town, provision it well. If you conduct a siege, bring extra lunch and be sure to keep your route of withdrawal secure.

Takeovers (say, of a governor's office, or a foreign embassy, or a court building) are a common feature in many of today's armed conflicts. The takeover is usually done by an insurgent or resistance group, followed by a siege of sorts from the authorities. In a typical takeover, the insurgents intend from the outset to negotiate. When you conduct a building takeover, you turn your nose up at the operational equation. You don't expect to escape, but rather you have such confidence in the negotiating position that you have or will gain that you figure you'll walk out with a net win. Your withdraw plan leads out the front door after having gained the respect of your opponent.

Building takeovers are spectacular and daring. Like roadblocks they combine classic strategy (operational art) with extortion. There are some rules, however. You need to assure you have the necessary provisions, and you need to measure the psychology of your opponent correctly. If at all possible, you want to have help on the outside.

One of the most famous takeovers in history occurred in Bogotá in 1985. The M-19 guerrilla group invaded the Colombian Supreme Court Building and took all of the judges and a bunch of other people hostage. The takeover had been carefully planned, even to making sure weeks' worth of extra food was on-hand in the cafeteria. The M-19's idea was to put the president of the country, Belisario Betancur, on trial. While they prepared the show trial, they were also going to destroy some prosecutorial files pertaining to some drug lords, including Pablo Escobar, who had funded the operation.

It might have gone well, but these things are subject to chance and confusion. Supporters of the M-19 were supposed to produce a huge student & worker demonstration in the great plaza outside the court building, which would have made military and police siege operations difficult. Unfortunately for the insurgents, some local army units reacted immediately, beating any large crowd to the scene. Then government leaders made an early decision that there was going to be no negotiating with the guerrillas. The M-19 had expected that President Betancur would capitulate, but communication with the president was all but shut off. The building caught fire, and while the details of who and when are still being debated to this day, the result was that the building burned. The invaders executed most of the judges, but could not themselves escape the conflagration. Most of the assailants and many of the hapless bystanders died. The event invited a national soul-search, and to major political changes, including a new and more liberal constitution. Within five or six years, however, the M-19 was almost completely disappeared.

That the M-19 risked such a violation of the principles of operational art might seem curious, except that they had successfully taken over the embassy of the Dominican Republic in Bogotá in 1980, a hundred diplomat hostages being ransomed for a lot of money and a flight to Cuba. They had also stolen Simon Bolivar's sword (still missing) and in a separate coup robbed thousands of weapons right out from under the Colombian Army's nose. The M-19ers were takeover champions. They calculated well and were immensely daring, but the operational equation always includes chance, and some days the bear just gets you. By the way, the M-19's legendary co-founder, Jaime Bateman, had died in an airplane crash in 1983. That'll happen, too. The other co-founder, Alvaro Fayad, died holed-up in an apartment in Bogotá in 1986.

Takeovers don't need to be strategy-defying all-or-nothing rolls of the extortion dice, either. They can be planned so that escape routes and outside help are in place, and they can be combined with other strategies, perhaps to lure your enemy into a trap from which *he* has no viable escape. Takeovers of the right places can yield useful things like money, information, hostages, and munitions. In an urban world, if you are a rebel and you never takeover anything, you're not much.

On the other side of the ledger, you want to pay attention to control architecture so that takeovers of your most valuable places are more difficult and containing a takeover is easier. Inspect your reaction plans building-by-building, site-by-site, and make sure that the reaction plans are not one-size-fits-all. Every takeover force will have different capabilities and different leadership. In a given case it might be best to do very little. Just waiting may be enough to disarm an opponent who is inside a building. There have been some terrible siege force failures. One occurred in Waco, Texas in 1993.

See: 91, *Forts and Walls*; 2, *The Line of Retreat;* 8, *The Operational Equation*; 140, *Culminating Point in the Pursuit*; 34, *Urban or Rural*;

33, *Built Environment*; 144, *Impunity and State Success*; and 123, *Thirty-six Stratagems.*

---

"It is sometimes wise, Gordon Pasha, to provide the man with a few sunny hours of fraudulent hope so that when night comes he will have a more perfect inward vision of the truth of his hopelessness."

The Mahdi in the movie
*Khartoum* (1966)[127]

Take, hold, sign

# *Section 89, The Dot Game and Go*

**The Dot Game** is a fine and dangerous pastime if you're the parent of a small child -- fine because little kids love it and can play it for hours on a long road trip; and dangerous because you, the parent, are delighted in it for about two minutes. Beyond that, it is instructive as the essential 'Take, Hold, Build' game. Try it out. Make a bunch of dots at the interstices on a page of graph paper. As a first move, you draw a line between any two points on the board, then let your doobie-picking opponent take a turn. When you can make an enclosed square, you can mark that square with your initials -- it's yours. Also, whenever you fill in a square, you get another turn. The winning objective is to end the game (when all the dots are connected and squares signed) with more squares than your opponent. It might be the most basic territorial board game possible.

But what if you could take three turns to every one of your progeny's? You could destroy the child's fun and self-confidence, and save some time in the process. In armed struggle, while the dots have to be adjusted to the nature and value of the landscape, you will do pretty much the same thing, especially in an urban setting -- gain moves to possess more squares. Just as in the dot game with your kid, the lines don't always have to be drawn contiguously. Unlike the kid's game, you can create urban lines with physical barriers, and control technologies that especially favor your side. And you can apply various methods in various parts of a city simultaneously. Your priorities regarding which squares to possess will usually be based first on control of movement and then on control of market value, the latter related to the former. The right choices will maximize placement of your signature on the most valuable pieces of terrain and deny use of those pieces to your enemy. It apparently took a while for US forces to figure out the imperatives of the dot game in Iraq.

Think about what it means to put your signature on an urban square. Hopefully it means your enemy cannot move into it, and at least not through it. Scale is important. Scale is important; don't make the squares so big that you might not be telling yourself the truth about being in control before initialing.

Unlike the dot game you play with your kids, you won't concede any territory in armed conflict that you don't have to, so if your enemy puts his initials on a block, you'll want to go after it and get it back -- but maybe not right away.

**'Go'** is an old Chinese board game played on a 19x19 line grid. While the Dot Game becomes predictable almost immediately, Go is unrelentingly complex. Played by two, the object is to control more of the board than your opponent by denying him options for movement while maintaining your own. Players have to find a balance in the use of their resources (the playing stones) between close in and more distant positioning. An earlier name for the game was *weiqi* (pronounced wei ch' i) meaning 'encircling territory.'

See: 49, *Territorial Scrutiny*; 47, *Why the County*; 92, *Land-use Planning*; 33, *Built Environment*; 67, *Points, Lines, Spaces*; 66, *GIS;* 30, *Control Technology*; and 2, *The Line of Retreat.*

---

"But Big Jule cannot win if he plays with honest dice."

Harry the Horse in the movie
*Guys and Dolls* (1955)[128]

School of resistance, extortion inventory, place of shame

# *Section 90, Prisons*

Prisons can be places where human rights are violated, or where gangs form or insurgents communicate, recruit and train. People organize amnesties and prisoner exchanges around prison populations. Prisons always seem to be too small for the number of prisoners, and when the prison capacity grows, that growth just seems to invite judges to send more prisoners. There never seems to be much racial or social equity in prisoner mixes, either. Some scholars will argue that prisons are the architectural manifestation of a system that punishes behavior that is itself the result of the way the system is organized. The difference between some prisoners and some prison guards is just a matter of conviction. Prisons can become high value targets for armed groups wanting to spring their comrades. Wardens and staff become targets for kidnappings and vengeance attacks.

Given the above litany of prison problems, it should be clear that where you put them, how you build them, who you put in them and for how long, and who guards the prisoners are all substantial issues. If you are not going to kill all of your opponents, you need a system of incarceration. Having to maintain a growing prisoner population is one of the accelerating costs of allowing a war to drag on. This problem alone is a big reason why you ought not to accept the notion that insurgencies are by their nature prolonged.

Courts are intimately tied to prisons. While the functioning of a court is not as dependent on the architectural design of its walls as is the prison, the courts' functioning and rules are closely tied to the functioning of the prison walls. If legal requirements are such that prisoners are too easily released, the historical result in insurgent-type warfare can be a tendency on the part of those doing the capturing to choose a more severe and immediate justice, i.e., killing instead of capturing.

What to do with abandoned children is a related and potentially sensitive question. Institutions like orphanages and reform schools quickly approach the status of prisons. Actually, a lot of schools do, too. The inconsistent functioning of other architectural manifestations of the social contract, like old folk homes and insane asylums, influences internal armed conflict to a lesser degree.

Invest in an optimal built environment for detainees, prisoners, captives, the incapacitated, and highly dependent populations. Design policies that do not confound their use. Get your conflict over with as quickly as possible. It does not have to be protracted. If you let it be, you will have a prison problem and a prisoner problem. That said, all of these comments about government prisons pertain to an insurgent force as well. Even maintaining a population of kidnap victims in miserable conditions became a major operating cost for the FARC.

See: 37, *School Lunches*; 142, *Dignity and Honor*; 96, *Combatant Status*; 95, *Childhood*; 110, *Knowledge Gaps*; 12, *Protraction and Diligence*; 8, *The Operational Equation*; and 69, *Measuring Actions against Enemies.*

---

"Me they can kill... You they own!"

Papillon to Dega in the movie *Papillon* (1973)[129]

Someone there is who doesn't love them

# *Section 91, Forts and Walls*

T. Miller Maguire, whose words are used in Section 8 to help introduce the operational equation, believed that nobody could build an impregnable fort. He said, "A fortress once invested is certain to fall, unless a relieving field-army can beat the besiegers away."[130] He also claimed forts were almost indispensable in both the defense and offense. While chiming in with the maneuver generals' contempt for fortifications, Maguire included a clear exception when it came to the "works devised by ourselves to meet the exigencies of irregular warfare." One read on the subject of forts in irregular war is a *Military Review* article by me and Les Grau titled 'Maginot Line or Fort Apache.' Military architects are rare today, but in a world ever more dominated by urban terrain, built environment, building takeovers and sieges, disdain for forts and walls just can't be right.

As for walls, the Chinese didn't keep building their Great Wall because it didn't work. Forts and walls, like locks, are best rated according to the cost, time, or effort it takes to breach them or go around. Forts and walls work best when part of a greater system of defense or offense that is planned around cost-distance.

The venerable 1940 US Marine Corps *Small Wars Manual* recommends establishing fortified advance bases for logistics support to units moving inland from the coast. What does that say? It reflects the fact that for the American Marines, their line of supply or withdrawal ultimately led to the US Navy. It also says that to be effective inland, the Marines had to lengthen their culminating points. They had to change the geographic facts of cost-distance. Forts have always been part of the military answer to geographic reality, even when not recognized as such.

Almost every port becomes a fort. The Marine manual said their little forts would:

> 1. cover productive areas and their lines of communication with their markets;
> 2. afford protection to the local population in that area;
> 3. form a base of supply, rest, replacement, and information.

Forts can be an effective part of an offensive campaign when placed across enemy LOCs, placed to endanger enemy lines of retreat, shorten the distance in time and space to enemy culminating points, and lengthen the time and distance to friendly culminating points. The Marine manual put less emphasis on using forts to interdict enemy LOCs because identifying the enemy line of retreat or lines of resupply had been so difficult. If you cannot find your enemy's lines of communication, it is harder to place your forts correctly.

In the 16th and 17th centuries, the forts of continental Europe were deployed in such a way as to promise an invader that, if he did not take them, the forts' garrisons would play havoc on his line of communication and retreat. The forts were located not so much for protection of the area where they were built but as part of a greater strategy of defense in depth. They also served expansionist aims by extending and protecting friendly lines during strategic advances. In 21st century Colombia, many new, fortified police stations have been placed along known guerrilla LOCs. The police presence serves to counter the isolation and marginalization of rural communities affected by the internal conflict as well as to increase the operational range of friendly military forces by maintaining supplies. The driving idea behind the location of the new stations is to change the shape of the Colombian battlefield by confounding guerrilla resupply and making guerrilla escape routes less tenable in the face of Colombian military pursuit. In other words, while police stations will help protect and service remote communities, the strategic logic for geographic placement is part of a military offensive plan, not simple defense of towns or infrastructure.

The offense-minded Colombian military logic followed an appreciation of Colombia's compartmentalized geography and a mutually supportive relationship between police and military. The police, anticipating being magnets of attack by the FARC, fortified their stations. The military high command knew that almost any station was subject to siege and to being overrun if a relief force could not be dispatched on time. 'On time' is a math that correlates the speed and weight of the relief column with the amount of time the fort design affords its defenders. In other words, the architecture of a building can have the same kind of influence on the military operational math as the speed of the maneuvering force. A fort and a helicopter have something in common.

Fortifications can be permanent or temporary. They can be large, super-modern government or commercial buildings or a knocked-together site consisting of barbed wire, an observation post, and a communications center. They can also be used in urban networks to disrupt enemy movement, fragment enemy neighborhoods and safe havens, and force the enemy to abandon key corners. The key is location, location, location.

A one-story police station in a high-rise neighborhood located at the end of a dead-end street might not be well-placed. Fortifications are best situated to dominate their surroundings and allow rapid deployments in multiple directions. Obviously, it is not the building itself, but the forces it protects that must be enabled by location to disrupt enemy ability to move, marshal, and transport. The best fortifications are located and constructed for ease of defense, ease of relief, and ease of launching raids, sweeps, and counterattacks. Fortifications are often necessary to support a system of roadblocks or checkpoints, the positioning of which should also support offensive operations. Like the forts, checkpoints work best as a network designed to shape the battlefield.

Forts can help you...

- Seal off distinct, reasonably sized sectors;
- Back up patrols with a reserve force;
- Provide or withhold from the residents access to electricity, fuel, water, and food, as well as services such as medical care, sewage processing, garbage collection, and firefighting;
- Segregate or isolate suspect individuals from the general population;
- Protect shipments and convoys;
- Remind the population of your presence and strength;
- Support networks of roadblocks or checkpoints.

Well-placed fortifications (combined with normal city infrastructure such as freeways, tunnels, railroad yards, rivers, factory blocks and walls) can seal off areas to create funneling and filtration points. Forts should provide control, information and ease of action, and deny these to your enemy. Forts can also provide a useful show of force. Also, fixed fortifications can allow foreign contingents to participate in a coalition strategy without the political exposure of direct offensive action. If your forts do none of these things, you might want to close them down or move them.

Insurgent forces must maintain access to their supplies, redoubts, arms caches, hospitals, and sanctuary areas, both internally and in neighboring countries. When government fort placements disrupt insurgent LOCs, constraints on the insurgents mount, and the probability of insurgent tactical advantage in any given encounter diminishes. A government fort system that focuses exclusively on friendly force protection or the protection of economic targets is not as dangerous to the insurgent as one designed to create operational advantages, to disrupt guerrilla operational and logistics movements, to shape the battlefield, to be part of the offense, and to wrong-foot the insurgent. The insurgent line of withdrawal to sanctuary is the most significant geography.

Forts have been shortchanged in recent military technological innovation efforts. Insurgencies end in various ways, often including political and economic agreements, sometimes on the basis of military actions, and not on the application of any single technology. Forts, however, can be an effective part of either counterinsurgent or insurgent effort.

Walls, like forts, are supposed to slow people down. The wall systems you devise will be tested in the context of a movement and space-control game with your enemies. Can he out-race your reactions to his attacks or he to yours? You want to anticipate pursuits after contacts to see how a wall affects or might affect the relative culminating points and probable next-contact moments. Walls are for keeping people out or in, and for separating groups one from another. Wall placement can make a checkpoint plan more effective, can separate licit from illicit commerce or help protect valuable infrastructure. Walls aren't high tech, but you need a wall plan, especially in an urban environment, even if you are the insurgent. In San Salvador in the 1980s the Communist guerrillas created some almost invisible routes and walls by opening a series of holes through the adjoining walls of adjacent urban homes. The routes were protected from visibility by the street-facing walls, allowing the movement of combatants parallel to streets without being on the street. Walls change the advantages in the *Dot Game* that is urban warfare. Forts and walls begin to be the same thing at certain scales. A gated community, for instance, starts to look like a fortress.

Gain confidence in rebuilding the urban 'built environment' to your competitive advantage. The walls you build can be above or below ground, just as are the routes of approach and escape. Heavy machines can help you control the pace of change in the built environment to your advantage. You want to build your walls and tear down his at the speed that best suits your analysis of the moves. Deciding to design forts and walls into a strategy is also a decision to revisit the design of heavy machines.

While placement is the first, most critical question for putting forts and walls into a security strategy, fort and wall locations in large urban areas can incorporate other design elements. The war will eventually be over, and the structures will either be used for something else or destroyed. They can be constructed for multiple uses so that the eventual success of a military strategy does not have to lead to scrapping the structures.

Because forts and walls can contribute to offensive or defensive strategies, your engineers might revisit control architecture, doctrine writers look to where forts and walls are missing in their literature, planners practice geographic analysis for the proper placement of forts and walls, and police organizations consider the manning and provisioning requirements implied by a fortification strategy.

You can put debates about the primacy of defense versus offense behind you. Insurgency is a world of block and tackle, parry and thrust, tae kwon do. You sometimes have to rest and refit in order to not pass your culminating point. In irregular war, if you are the government, you want to be on the offensive as much as possible because if you are not on the offensive, you are either being beaten or you are just allowing your enemy to gain strength. Forts and walls are not inherently defensive. They are terrain that you can build to suit your rhythm of defense and offense at the scale of time and space that you can best handle. They can be placed to help you to gain or regain the balance of advantages in culminating points and the probable correlations of force in battle. Proper urban forts can help you gain advantage in the balance of anonymities. Ultimately, if your enemy is alive and well, you have to close with and neutralize him.

See: 63, *Cost-Distance*; 2, *The Line of Retreat*; 140, *Culminating Point in the Pursuit*; 33, *Built Environment*; 8, *The Operational Equation*; 31, *Holes in the Ground*; 88, *Sieges and Takeovers*; and 29, *Heavy Machines*.

---

> "And he...showed me the holy city Jerusalem...having a wall great and high; having twelve gates...on the east were three gates; and on the north three gates; and on the south three

> gates; and on the west three gates. And the wall of the city had twelve foundations...and he that spoke with me had for a measure a golden reed to measure the city, and the gates thereof, and the wall thereof....and he measured the wall thereof, a hundred and forty and four cubits, according to the measure of a man, that is, of an angel."
>
> from the *Book of Revelations*[131]

The bookend to Madisonian property

# *Section 92, Land-use Planning*

**Centralized value decisions.** Land-use planning is a counterweight to Madisonian property systems (those based on a market for highly divisible real estate rights), or a complement to them, depending on your ideological preferences. Land-use planning has become a universal language among city government managers. The term ties itself to central planning and government-oriented and directed solutions, so for some it carries a degree of anti-private property bias. Zoning is an early and still popular form of urban land-use planning, but the theories have evolved to tackle issues like density versus sprawl, or saving cultural patrimony. The 'built environment' is land-use planning's result, but preservation of the non-built environment is typically part of the concern. One of the bywords of land-use planning is 'sustainability,' which supposes a balance or reconciliation of environmental stewardship, social equity, and economic maximization over the long term.

Municipal and regional land-use planners in Medellín, Colombia internalized the design values supposed by 'sustainability,' but the city had to wrest land-use dominance from violent illegal armed groups. To provide the urban population with both immediate security and longer-term conflict resolution services, the *Medellinenses* have had to innovate beyond the confines of mainstream urban planning theory. 'Sustainability,' in a violent urban geography, has to comprehend security goals. In the long run, attainment of basic sustainability goals should facilitate a peaceful social contract and vice versa. Urban designs that consider ease of policing, and in the near-term even military success against an intractable enemy, are likely to be more successful.

Sustainable land use plans for cities suffering organized violence have to assess control architecture and technology, address disputed territories, measure citizen cost-distances in terms of fear and extortion, and measure the relative power of numerous armed groups.

If your war is going to unfold in an urban environment, it behooves you to be familiar with the vocabulary, theories, methods, and fashions of land-use planning.

**Nesting, Tessellating, and Imbricating.** When an administrative territory or jurisdiction fits neatly within a single level of a hierarchy, we say it is nested (townships 'belong' to one county, counties to a state, the states to the federal union). By and large, nested territories are less conflictive than un-nested territories. (As noted in Section 49, *Territorial Scrutiny*, overlaps in territories mean conflict) If you are looking to stabilize things, pacify and the like, then by and large you want to nest territories, at least administrative territories. If you don't know what territories to look for or how to determine if they are appropriately nested or not within a geography that interests you, then you need to fix that knowledge deficit in advance of being asked to do something else.

If you are trying to build a more peaceful society, you won't want to tolerate geographically overlapping tax, service, and representation territories if you can help it. Administrative territories, say, an Afghan *alaqadari*, have boundaries that were established by someone for a reason. That reason had some administrative logic associated with something such as water conflict resolution or taxation, or the edge of an ethnic group, watershed or village clustering. You want to know the original logic of the boundary to see if the logic is still valid and still has meaning. The lines, in other words, represent something or represented something. You want to know the history of the reasoning and of the parties to the reasoning. You may, on the basis of that knowledge, decide to adjust the boundaries or attempt to give them a new meaning. Lines (or fades or measles, whatever) may not have much meaning at all to some local societies, but that does not mean they can't have a lot of explanatory meaning for you, and a lot of value at different levels of conflict. If you are in a military, you are comfortable with the idea of a battalion sketch delineating the areas of responsibility between two subordinate companies. Your enemy might like to know where that delineation is as well. As for other people's maps, including those showing some national borders, the people who made the lines originally might not have been any smarter than you. (*Might* not have been.)

As far as achieving a peaceful social contract is concerned, while administrative units are best nested, it is sometimes good to have human identities overlap. Such an overlap can mean that the human tendency toward 'we versus they' is softened. This is in line with the frontiers theories mentioned earlier.

'Imbricated' means overlapping in a pattern, like roof tiles or fish scales. 'Tessellated' means a butt-up against each other pattern, like the squares of a checkerboard. You'll want to imbricate your roof and tessellate your floor so you won't trip up on the tile edges of the floor or on water leaks from the roof. As mentioned above in terms of nesting, you'll generally want to assure that public administration is tessellated. Mostly you'll want the identities (like Nijmegenites and Arnhemites) to match the nesting of the administrative units, that is to say, be likewise tessellated. That way you won't have administrators tripping over each other or playing we-and-they with physically proximate communities. But some of the identities you'll want imbricated. (There is a city-region called Arnhem-Nijmegen ) Court jurisdictions, for instance, especially for real property matters, need to be tessellated according to the location of the land in question. At the same time, jury catchment areas can be imbricated, depending on the nature of the case, because their function is one of cultural leavening and disinterest. When people have tried to tessellate transportation districts, they have sometimes ended-up with one width of railroad track meeting another width at the territorial border. This can perhaps promote the cohesion of a national identity, but doesn't keep the train on the rails. What you tessellate and what you imbricate is a choice you will make, consciously or unwittingly, when trying to implement a social contract. Cultural affinity and sensitivity is hard to tessellate. So in the process of territorial scrutiny it is not only important to notice the nesting and overlapping of territories, but patterns of tessellation and imbrication as well.

Land-use planning, as a modern professional and academic endeavor, depends heavily on GIS technologies. It daily concerns itself with the interface between the logic of sustainability and the logic of optimal positioning for collective land uses, especially public enterprises such as airports, parks, water systems and other infrastructure. However, although land-use planning usually connotes this technical approach to the spatial distribution of human activities, it is also inextricable from political philosophy about the social contract -- the relationship among members of the polity within geographic space.

This book was written in Kansas. Ft. Leavenworth is located near the geographic center of the United States, and was seen from its founding as an appropriately central launching place for military operations intended to dominate and pacify much of a continent. When historians return, as they regularly do, to the entertaining debate about where the Old West began, Ft. Leavenworth has a good argument, as do Abilene and Dodge City. Although Kansas is a sparsely populated state that derives much of its identity from a 1930's movie, it is also nicknamed *The Free State*, after a role it played at its birth -- a spark in the timing of the American Civil War. Liberty, as an American proposition, has been a land-use plan, an idea about human nature tied to land, boundaries, and the administration of the social contract. Kansas is one of those imagined and then executed plans for a better world, and to a degree it is because of Kansas that American exceptionalism is more than a notion, but a provable fact on the ground. The idea of Kansas was not just a territory, it was a land-use plan.

See: 49, *Territorial Scrutiny*; 94, *Poop*; 91, *Forts and Walls*; 47, *Why the County*; 106, *Tourism*; 118, *Whole of Government*; 77, *Sex*, and 54, *Mercatus*.

---

> The construction of Popular Power is based on the territorial-organizational emphasis that the New Geometry of Popular Power gives us. With this emphasis, the strengthening of the base social movements is promoted.
>
> United Socialist Party of Venezuela in the *Red Book*[132]

Predictable unpredictables

# *Section 93, Diseases and Disasters*

This section was written in the wake of the 2010 earthquake in Haiti, mooting any intended assertion that disasters are practicably predictable. Every once in a while a disaster will be of such a magnitude that 'no one could have predicted it.' Not only was there no way to anticipate the level of need that the Haitians would face, there is no rationale and logic that can be emotionally adequate in the face such enormity. More people died in Port au Prince than in Hiroshima. Nevertheless, so many earthquakes, hurricanes, and volcanic eruptions occur in Central America and the Caribbean Basin it seems irresponsible to call them unpredictable. We might not know exactly the where and when of an earthquake epicenter, but our response preparations can cover quite a range of effects. The effects of floods are more predictable still, and we at least know from where most of the volcanoes will spew.

Attacks from weapons of mass destruction are more frightening because other humans are working the surprise issue, and diseases seem so egalitarian and cruel that, regardless of our knowledge of their method of reproduction, we are afraid. Still, locations of populations at risk, and the calculation of probable material and environmental costs in the event of a given occurrence, is the work of an increasingly competent community of scientists and humanitarian workers.

Predictable or not, big events can change the direction and character of irregular war. A big earthquake in 1976 in Guatemala was followed by a long civil war. That may have been mostly coincidence; the timing of the internal conflict may have had more to do with the lives of the revolutionary leaders and the development of external support in relation to the Cold War in the late 1970's. That said, a lot of political history is blamed on the earthquake and on the nature of aid programs and the intentions of foreigners during the response and reconstruction stages. New money, coming in on top of a people whose normal leadership hierarchies and expectations had been disrupted, gave space to new organizational forms, new ideologies, and new debt relationships. How such things might play out in Haiti or elsewhere is to be seen, but there is no doubt that big events can be game changers providing competitive advantage and opportunity.

In Guatemala, the activist left not only did a good job inserting itself in an organized way within communities affected by the earthquake, it also did a good job propagandistically, painting the government and allied aid as self-interested and as privileging the already-rich. Regarding reconstruction after the earthquake, one anthropologist who had long worked in Guatemala, Robert M. Carmack, asserted in *Development and Social Effects of the Guatemalan Earthquake*: "The wealthy, who owned the materials, vehicles to transport them, and companies of construction greatly profited from the earthquake. Engineers, lawyers, architects, and other 'professionals' similarly benefitted from the increased need for their services. Many of them raised their prices, an added burden partly shouldered by the already broken poor."[133]

Devastation from the tsunami of 26 December, 2004 drove both the government of Indonesia and the Islamic separatists on the island of Aceh to resume peace talks. The same tsunami had a dissimilar effect in Sri Lanka, where the eastern coast was hard hit, weakening the position of the Tamil insurgents, who controlled that part of the island.

Depending on the physical geography, it will behoove you to create a plan for the next natural disaster and the situation of populations it puts at risk. Plan accordingly to quickly and effectively ameliorate suffering, set a sustainable course for recovery, and take political and military advantage of changed conditions as appropriate. Address within the plan how to keep your enemy from being advantaged by disaster conditions. Apply to disasters the adage that luck is where preparation and opportunity meet. Check to see if the balance of anonymity is radically changed for or against you because records have been destroyed, control of human movement made impossible, etc. Act quickly if key walls and bridges are compromised, which might give your side a distinct physical advantage. Determine if there will be a displacement of communities.

Dealing with diseases is its own reward. A competitive advantage lies in the legitimacy of doing the best work that resources allow on behalf of those afflicted, and in appropriately condemning practices of your enemy that reduce chances for medical progress. Governments are usually far more capable than antigovernment challengers to work on disease prevention and control.

One of the entertaining characteristics of the old 90-millimeter recoilless rifle was the speed and volume of the ignition of the rocket when the shooter would depress the trigger mechanism. Its firing was a surprise to the person shooting it, even thought he was entirely in charge of the timing. Some things will be surprising if they are big enough or happen fast enough, even if they are perfectly predictable. Don't be surprised by something you set off.

Eyjafjallajokull... (See Section 13, *Puthukkudiyirippu*).

See: 121, *Commitment of the Reserve*; 74, *Refugees and Displaced Persons*; 90, *Prisons*; 114, *R.V. Jones*; 91, *Forts and Walls*; 2, *Anonymity*; 122, *Songs of Chu*; and 50, *US Persons*.

---

**Markoff**: How do you feel tonight, Lieutenant?

**Lt. Martin**: I'm dying.

**Markoff**: I hope not, sir.

> **Lt. Martin**: I'm going to die. I'll be buried under the sand and forgotten. When I was a little boy, I thought soldiers always died in battles. I didn't know there were so many soldiers...and so few battles...
> and so many fevers.
>
> From the movie
> *Beau Geste* (1939)[134]

Excrement meets dignity

# *Section 94, Poop*

A poignant, irritating and significant section in Mike Davis' *Planet of Slums* is titled "Living in Shit."[135] Unvarnished is hardly a sufficient descriptor. The paragraphs examine a pitiable human urgency and failure of decency on a massive scale due to the lack of basic facilities. Davis describes, for instance, how whole populations of Moslem urban women cannot evacuate during the daylight hours. This tactical, personal matter presents both strategic necessity and opportunity, but not if it goes unmentioned. Excrement, with its frustrating disposal and dishonoring presence, has been shown repeatedly to be a factor in generating the kind of existential despair that can inspire violent behavior. The geography of fecal matter matters.

This subject of excrement is so disagreeable it is usually ineffable, but it can't remain so for the person asked to win a war or enable social peace. It is in some places tied too closely to the problem of human honor and dignity; to the practicalities of security architecture; and to securing the support of the population.

From the history of Medellín, Colombia we learn that during the worst of the uncontrolled 'squatting,' in which marginal neighborhoods rapidly overpopulated, some shanty dwellers couldn't or wouldn't take the time to act civilly. Ricardo Aricapa writes,

> The problems arose as the squatting [no pun intended] increased, the distances to the ravine grew; and people forgot their decency. They then preferred to do their business inside their shacks and later put their bodily waste in black plastic bags – there was always someone who used transparent bags – which they would throw wherever, as slyly as possible, like someone pretending not to have thrown the rock by hiding the hand. These flying leftovers almost always landed

> on the roofs of other homes.[136] [my translation from the Spanish]

To this unpleasantness is reasonably ascribed a portion of the city's gang formation and no small number of machete events.

In the Johnson County, Kansas *Rural Comprehensive Plan*, considerable attention is paid to issues such as density versus sprawl, aesthetic and lifestyle preservation, environmental stewardship and so forth. Chapter Eight, however, wherein the hydrological engineers opine, reveals something at the heart of what is urban -- what to do with wastewater. The problem of city annexation, questions of density, economic development, environmental carrying capacity and ecological protection depend in many places on the flow of water and the flow of human waste. This is true in Johnson County, one of the very richest, flattest American counties. It is more so in most of the rest of the world. The processes of city annexation, at times contentious and at other times collaborative, are built around a well-established mix of rights and duties -- the city's right to plan and tax matched against a duty to provide services. Among the most coveted and valuable services is sewage removal and processing. As it turns out, the stuff indeed flows downhill, and so it is that the sewage engineers have more to say about the efficient shape and growth of the city than other planners who might prefer to concentrate on higher-order, more genteel challenges such as cultural heritage. The poop has to be made to make its way to places where it can be processed or dispatched. That problem resolved, engineers can tackle roadbed suitability, provision of potable water or electrical lines -- but the real challenge is sewage. To be urban is easy; to be a functioning city takes a sewer.

Poop is nasty. Doctors associate it with diseases that can have an unpredictable and never pleasant impact on the course of any kind of warfare. Waterborne illnesses, such as cholera, are spread through sick people's poop that contaminates the water supply. You might want to have a plan for poop. Find someone who can explain to you in detail the cultural and engineering condition of human waste in the battlespace of concern to you. You might have a clean, clear opportunity to take positive action. This argument about the management of excrement applies also, with different variables as to cultural sensibilities and physical mass, for other forms of human waste -- trash, garbage, grey water -- these are all consequential substances.

See: 142, *Dignity and Honor*; 79, *Suicide*; 33, *Built environment*; 89, *The Dot Game*; 36, *Engineers*, 138, *Roadblocks and Checkpoints*; 26, *How Violent Groups Form* and 80, *Why You Should Like Geography*.

---

> "Our errors are surely not such awfully solemn things. In a world where we are so certain to incur them in spite of all our caution, a certain lightness of heart seems healthier than this excessive nervousness on their behalf."
>
> William James[137]

孟母三迁

# *Section 95, Childhood*

We like to think all peoples prize their young and place them in a special, separate category of protection. Legal concepts like statutory rape, custody, guardianship, or juvenile prosecution all draw off social norms that set the developing human-being apart from the fully-formed adult. Most societies recognize that the child is not yet sufficiently developed emotionally, physically or mentally to make valid independent decisions. We want the human child to have the opportunity to grow up -- *then* do stupid things. This separation of status -- child or adult -- is significant to the shape and conduct of armed conflict.

Childhood becomes an issue in irregular war in a variety of ways. The most obvious is in the recruitment of the under-aged for soldiering. While there is a general international standard of eighteen years for military service in more formalized armies, many national militaries allow for voluntary service by seventeen-year-olds, and there are many stories of successful military service of younger soldiers who lied about their ages. In guerrilla armies, the foot soldiers are often younger. Use of preteen children as lookouts, couriers and servants is common, as is sexual enslavement of teenage girls. International slave trading is becoming ubiquitous or at least has become more visible. In other theaters, children are paid to deliver or even plant explosive devices or pieces of them. Simple abandonment of children is also normal in the context of hostilities and forced displacements.

Theories asserting a causal relationship between distressed childhoods and internal armed conflict can be tenuous or confused, however. After all, it seems the leaders of insurgencies, criminal empires and revolutions are as often the scions of the rich as they are the sons of poverty.

Sometimes the criminal gang or rebel army improves the condition of an abandoned child, giving identity, respect and material opportunity. It is hard to say with any exactitude what physical or psychological malnourishment is produced by a sociopathic parent as opposed to a noble rebel. Regardless, it takes no leap of faith to believe that the neglect of children leads to bad results for any society. Societies suffering internal conflict always seem to experience the exacerbating participation, at one level or another, of abused or neglected children, and of adults whose childhoods were less than ideal.

Children can in fact make good soldiers. A fourteen-year-old can be a ruthless, obedient, enthusiastic, courageous fighter. Kids are easier targets for recruitment arguments and lies. In sum, it makes sense for an armed group to recruit children when older youths are resistant.

Programs, laws, and campaigns that address the fate of marginalized children are more than a good idea. They might not only shrink the universe of potential recruits for your enemy, they increase human capital capable of finding peaceful pursuits and solutions.

Organized crime often leads to the organization of youth groups and the outsourcing to such groups of specific criminal activities. The go-betweens or intermediaries between children's gangs and adult organizations should be an early target of investigation. Separation of the two entities is a step toward possible recovery of the younger participants.

International sex tourism is often linked to child abandonment, abuse and use in other organized criminal behavior. Governments can profile and monitor sex tourism as a method for identifying child abuse and tracing that abuse to other criminal organizations.

An appendix to the US Army's field manual *Counterinsurgency* has a warning to "keep the children at arm's length."[138] It may be necessary to teach rules of engagement for how soldiers are to interact with the children they meet, and care must be taken that those interactions don't individually or in the aggregate endanger either the soldiers or the children. This section, however, is about the larger question of where children should be, who should be taking care of them, what they are being taught, what their aspirations become, etc. It is about the structure of life that can lead to a need for a specific set of rules of engagement with them. If the instruction that must be given is to harden one's heart, then there should be another set of instructions that deal with the reasons for why that first, unfortunate, instruction is necessary – so as to make it not the case. It takes five years for a twelve-year-old to become a seventeen-year-old. If you are going to let a war go on for six years, then how you treat a twelve-year old may be how you are treating a future combatant.

Childhood deserves direct, formal consideration by any who presume to make plans and decisions in the context of an armed struggle. Assertions abound as to the legitimacy of governments, insurgents and social movements. In this one area, however, we have a sort of litmus test. If an organization willfully abuses children, that organization should not be considered legitimate. If you are not explicitly, actively considering children who are vulnerable to conditions imposed by armed struggle, you have an opportunity. The actions you take to address the fate of children can change the nature of your physical lines of communication and those of your enemy. They can also build substantive legitimacy.

See: 14, *Legitimacy*; 51, *Underclass*; 74, *Refugees and Displaced Persons*; 78, *Personal Identity*; 115, *Transforming Armed Force*; 90, *Prisons*; 19, *NGOs and Unions*; and 48, *Grading the Social Contract.*

---

"Which brings me to my second point, kids: Don't do crack."

Lawrence Taylor in the movie
*The Waterboy* (1998)[139]

---

Legitimacy meets impunity meets amnesty

# *Section 96, Combatant Status*

We can address some of the more consequential characterizations of anti-State actors by using the lens of impunity. Who can confer impunity, and where might that person go to enjoy it? Let's say a guy who is not a US citizen sets off a bomb in the United States, but gets caught. If he then were to escape, where would he go? Or rather, will authorities where he goes extradite him back to the United States, or will they absolve and maybe protect or even honor him? If the person were designated a combatant, he might enjoy some exception from an extradition treaty, and maybe therefore impunity for his actions. A foreign country might protect him from the processes of justice in the

United States, and do so while remaining within the rules of the club of countries. Like other things, the concept of impunity has a relationship to geography. Generally, distance and time from the place of the action lessen the power of the State and increase the possibility of impunity.

Gaining 'belligerent status' could be a useful achievement for an insurgent force on its way to becoming more than an insurgent force. As influential as words like *belligerent* and *combatant* can be, they beg a warning about cognates in foreign languages: These terms and others that surround them are translated with fair consistency within the formal regime of international law pertaining to armed conflict. There is less consistency among interpretations inside various countries' legal systems and still less consistency among arguments, commentaries, and their translations.

What it means that an individual prisoner be classified as a *combatant* or as an *unlawful combatant*; or that an armed political movement gain *belligerent* status, are not questions to address haphazardly. Planners and their leaders should build an early, shared understanding of the pros and cons of attaching these legalistically-charged terms to specific sets of individuals, and should not allow such understanding only to stay within legal staffs. Try to establish theoretic coordination and agreement among those in charge of your operations, legal analysis, and propaganda (among lawyers, press secretaries, ambassadors, and commanders). The bottom line has to be tied to the State's monopoly on the conference of impunity.

The documents and concepts of international humanitarian law generally express aspirations for humane behavior and treatment, especially as to defenseless humans, the natural environment and cultural patrimony. At its best, humanitarian law can be used to protect people by overcoming or sidestepping arguments about the categorization of individual participants or entities. In practice, however, international law can be as much political argument as it is juridical statute and process. It is itself subject to use as leverage in irregular conflicts.

An approach that neither dismisses the importance of legalisms nor relegates the discussion to lawyers is to frame the semantics according to their effect on your gaining or losing the monopoly your organization seeks on the granting of impunity. Especially to be considered in this regard is the effect on likely lines of retreat to sanctuary. If, for instance, a majority of members within the international club of countries were to accede to Hugo Chávez' argument that the FARC be considered a belligerent, the lines of escape for FARC members to sanctuaries within Venezuela would be strengthened.

See: 90, *Prisons*; 144, *Impunity and State Success*; 44, *Political/Military/Administrative*; 104, *Extraterritorial Jurisdiction*; 103, *Amnesty*; 40, *Rule-of-law*; 133, *Snipers and Assassins*; and 28, *Oviedo*.

---

> "...the generation that carried on the war has been set apart by its experience. Through our great good fortune, in our youth our hearts were touched with fire. It was given to us to learn at the outset that life is a profound and passionate thing. While we are permitted to scorn nothing but indifference, and do not pretend to undervalue the worldly rewards of ambition, we have seen with our own eyes, beyond and above the gold fields, the snowy heights of honor, and it is for us to bear the report to those who come after us. But, above all, we have learned that whether a man accepts from Fortune her spade, and will look downward and dig, or from Aspiration her axe and cord, and will scale the ice, the one and only success which it is his to command is to bring to his work a mighty heart."
>
> Oliver Wendell Holmes, Jr.[140]

Culture, land, measurement, whereabouts

# *Section 97, The Denver Broncos*

Entertainments, including sports and games, tell a lot about a culture -- about society, including how people from or within that culture are likely to fight. Knowing thoroughly about entertainments also helps in the control of anonymity, because entertainment locations and activities are valuable property.

**The fall football schedule:** In Oklahoma, on a Friday evening in October, a small town high school will host a football game. That game was scheduled in advance and the schedule published on the Internet, carried home as flyers by members of the student body, put up on posters in local businesses and printed in the local newspaper. All of the town's high school players are listed by name and position. It will also typically include their year, weight, height, and jersey number. The high school football schedule is a formal property record. In fact, it is one of the most formal and most effective property records in the society. It states exactly where a very specific group of humans has a right to do a very specific thing at a very specific place and time. The individuals who have a right to play almost always show up to do so. The record is accurate, rarely in error, and transparent. The system of such records is comprehensive in that all the high schools in the league also have schedules. Rarely do more than two teams show up for a ballgame. The document is the most disseminated of a larger weave of other documents that the schedule reflects. In that weave is a league charter, an agreement regarding gate receipts, about contracting referees, about the location of the playoff and championship games, and so on. The football schedule is what we see of an entire rule-of-law apparatus of written documents.

The schedule also reflects a central aspect of community identity. The football game is a moment of collective expression. The players represent not just a town, but a dimension of life. Meanwhile, and while participating in that moment of hotdogs and energy, Spencer, a private investigator, sees the football game and the football schedule from a vocational angle. He knows that the coach will put Grayson, a fast, fearless kid, in for the kickoff as the 'gunner,' whose job it is to fire himself down the field at 'breakneck' speed to tackle the also-fast kid who will catch the kickoff. Spencer knows Grayson will be standing on one of the forty yard hash marks at seven o`clock on the evening on 8 August wearing the number 3 on the back of his jersey. He also knows that Grayson's mom and dad will be in the north stands wearing the school colors, one or both of them even wearing a matching number 3 jersey. That's when Spencer will politely (since Spencer's daughter is one of the cheerleaders) serve Grayson's dad a summons to appear in court.

**The game itself.** American football explains a lot about America, and a description of that sport can illuminate many of the themes in this book. A football field is divided by many lines, with the opposing teams fighting not only for every yard, but for every inch. A pair of officials on the sideline measures progress with a chain, not coincidentally evocative of the survey chains used to square up the new territories of the early republic. Other officials keep time, because the game requires constant decision-making regarding what is time-in or time-out. Different amounts of time are accorded to different activities, and these are measured to the second. Lack of promptness is invariably punished. While the number of players on the field is unremarkable, each has a specialty. Many of these specialties match patterns of natural gifts -- a 230-pound athlete will more likely be a linebacker, whereas a fleet 160-

pounder more likely a wide receiver and a 300-pound youth an offensive lineman. The coaching staffs and batteries of officials are organized by specialty as well. The game requires a lot of gear. Players are variously armored, electronic communication is ubiquitous, and practice fields are replete with blocking sleds, targets, and obstacles. Football is an athletic contest, but games are considered incomplete if not surrounded by collateral activities. There are bands, cheerleaders, food, coronations, awards, recognitions, lotteries, food, parachutists and even jet planes if you've got `em.

The rule book for American football is about eight-feet thick. Few living humans know all the rules, such that games require a committee of five people to regularly confer. The players' jerseys are all numbered and most leagues require players' surnames be put on the jerseys. This helps the officials control anonymity and assign accountability for infractions. Once every few years, the sports journalists report a football game in which no infractions occurred, but most games don't go five minutes without some rule being broken. Many of the coaches' playbooks are immensely complex, the combinations and permutations of their strategies being marvelously varied. This leads to a whole industry of scouting and spying, since a marked advantage goes to the defensive coordinator who anticipates his opponents' plays. Not only are the players specialized as to their skills and attributes, they each have a particular task to complete during a given play -- a specific block, running pattern or throw to make in order for the team to effect any of the myriad plays the coaches devise. Any failure of individual responsibility can cause failure of a play, meaning that teamwork is built on responsibility for completing individual assignments.

Finally, and essentially, American football is violent. People regularly promote efforts to tame the game, or at least make it safer and less likely to injure the players. Violence, however, is part of what makes the game not only enjoyable and exiting, but probably why so many young males are attracted to it, and so many young females attracted to them. Accordingly, with this atavism undaunted, each new generation of linebacker defines the game and the linebackers' personal mission in it as one of separating quarterbacks and running backs from a few moments of light.

American football is territorial, flamboyant, sexual, and (perhaps being repetitive here) violent. It is also complicated, technology-heavy, legalistic in the extreme, and incrementally and minutely measured both as to time and space. It is tied inextricably to money, contracts and place identity. It is about individual prowess and responsibility in a group context. It is serious business and fun at the same time. Especially...it is violent, but the violence is poured on and poured over by a thousand rules and banks of judges. It is a legitimated violence. Rarely do young men fight in the stands at American football games. Most of those young men are on the field getting their faces smashed.

There are two major points that this section tries to make, and they are not about American football or the Denver Broncos (paragon of the activity). The two points are: First, many cultural activities, especially entertainments, are inseparable from place identity. Entertainment activities imply sets of rights and duties that people are highly likely to exercise – because they want to. Knowing about these activities is to know, with actionable accuracy, where groups and individuals will be, what they will be doing, and who they will be supporting. Property systems are social contracts among people, but associated with specific places and rights. Property analysis means knowing what, why, how...and especially *where* and *when.* The second point, related to the first, is that enjoyable voluntary activities describe manners of thinking and organizing. They will even reveal hierarchies and interpersonal relationships that will carry over into what might seem to be more serious enterprises. If you disdain learning about fun and pastime, you will fail to learn who people admire, to whom they sense a debt, who they voluntarily follow, and most of all, when people are likely to be where.

See: 47, *Why the County*; 3, *The Domesday Book*; 27, *Democracy; Unions*; 48, *Grading the Social Contract*; 73, *Property and the Social Contract*; 78, *Personal Identity*; 16, *Keeping Secrets*; and 55, *The Statute of Frauds*.

---

> "Football is an honest game. It's true to life. It's a game about sharing. Football is a team game. So is life."
>
> Player Joe Namath (quarterback)[141]

> "Football linemen are motivated by a more complicated, self-determining series of factors than the simple fear of humiliation in the public gaze, which is the emotion that galvanizes the backs and receivers."
>
> Player Merlin Olsen (lineman)[142]

"When I played pro football, I never set out to hurt anyone deliberately – unless it was, you know, important, like a league game or something."

Player Dick Butkus (linebacker)[143]

Is authenticity at odds with honesty?

# Section 98, Jorge Verstrynge and Pio Moa

**Jorge Verstrynge**. For about a decade until the late 1980s, Jorge Verstrynge was an active member of the conservative *Alianza Popular* political party of Spain, but after leaving the party, his writing veered almost 180 degrees. He is now an anti-globalist Marxist professor at the Compultense University in Madrid. He is author, among other works, of the 2005 book *La Guerra Periférica y el Islam Revolucionario: Orígenes, reglas y ética de la guerra asimétrica.* (I clumsily translate this to 'War in the Periphery and Revolutionary Islam: origins, rules, and ethics of asymmetric warfare.').

In *La Guerra Periférica*, Professor Verstrynge weaves together total war, unrestricted war, insurgent war, every kind of war (or perhaps warfare). His definition of asymmetric warfare was for the most part not new, touching on the now common or passé terms 'fourth generation,' 'network,' 'irregular' and so on. There is something significant about the book, however, that arises partially from its admiration of Islamist radicalism.

Asymmetry is a word some Americans hoist to lament the fact that weaker countries sometimes win, because the United States is easy to surprise, or because nobody will stand up straight and fight Midway rules (aircraft carrier-a-aircraft carrier). Professor Verstrynge effectively co-opted the term and nudged 'asymmetric warfare' toward meaning 'The Asymmetric War.' Professor Verstrynge's explanation is fluid and measured. He treats Mao well, Che roughly, and discusses the Algerian War with care.

In the course of Professor Verstrynge's presentation in *La Guerra Periférica*, asymmetric warfare ceases to be merely a taxonomic category of warfare in which ostensibly weaker forces fight against ostensibly stronger ones. Instead, while maintaining a format of academic indifference, Professor Verstrynge's definition of asymmetric warfare becomes fighting against the United States, its interests and its allies. *Resistance* would at times be a more appropriate term than fighting, however, and broader concepts such as globalization, the North, the West, neoliberalism, capitalism, etc., could be substituted for United States in a given instance. Hence, what might have been a workmanlike explanation of 'postmodern' warfare escapes revolutionary disdain for being naïve or edgeless. It escapes being a book for the mere trade unionist. Instead of leaving 'asymmetric' as only a category of conflict to be compared with other types, or filled-out by other terms, Professor Verstrynge clothes it as a stage in the evolution of conflict, mimicking the idea of capitalism being an evolutionary step toward communism. For him, the asymmetric war is not just total or unrestricted war, it is tantamount to the 'totalitarianization' of war. Asymmetric becomes the same as the Chinese 'unrestricted' war.

Professor Verstrynge's work hit a perfect note for someone in Venezuelan President Hugo Chávez' position. Hugo Chávez set his chips down as being anti-American, and he seems to need anti-Americanism as part of the signage on his jacket, although he may not actually be much good at military art. He was, after all, the militarily least effective leader among the plotters in their failed 1998 coup attempt. Chávez, like Verstrynge, admires the existential willingness of radical Islamicists to take mortal risk and to kill for a great project. Chávez made *La Guerra Periférica* required reading for his military officers. Fighting The Asymmetric War seemed to justify much, and to attract appropriate company.

Aside from philosophically framing opposition to the United States for the likes of Chávez, Professor Verstrynge's book offers another little problem for global security. It advises countries 'in resistance' to obtain nuclear weapons. It is pro-proliferation, and in no uncertain terms. 'Asymmetric' includes nuclear deterrence in this formulation.

> "Let us be clear: true sovereignty now means possessing 'the bomb.' Furthermore, today, those who can, will, in search of maximum efficiency, combine nuclear, conventional, and asymmetric warfare to achieve maximum effectiveness. No potentiality is ruled out, in the manner that today the fighters are volunteers and conscripts, professionals and mobilized forces, unpaid soldiers and condottieri, reluctant heroes and kamikazes, old men of the Volkssturm or members of passive defense, and child soldiers, i.e., everyone and everybody... Nothing is disdained in the war..."[144]

Nevertheless, and following Chairman Mao on this point, Professor Verstrynge opines that the war will ultimately be won by regular forces.

**Pio Moa**. Pio Moa is another Spaniard, maybe the un-Verstrynge; or conversely, Verstrynge is the un-Moa. During his youth, Moa was active as a militant for GRAPO, a Maoist armed wing of the Spanish Communist Party. (Moa the Maoist) President Franco, good at counterinsurgency, caught young Pio and threw him in jail. Not idle in captivity, he used the quiet time to educate himself and study history. His learning journey steered him away from the radical left, and to a transformation diametrically opposite that of Professor Verstrynge. Moa published several works around the time that Verstrynge's *La Guerra Periférica* was published, including *1934: Comienza La Guerra Civil Española* (1934; The Spanish Civil War Begins). It is really a popularization and summary of several more involved investigations Moa did of the Spanish Civil War. The title itself was an instant provocation because establishment academia in Spain, Europe and beyond holds the Spanish Civil War to have begun in 1936. The difference in starting dates reflects uncomfortable historic facts.

As Moa points out, the men and women who became the leaders of the Spanish Republicans (the 'left' during the war) were the same violent subversives, armed radicals, and Communists who had tried to take power by violence in 1934. Mr. Moa's statement is clear and his factual assertions well documented. The radical armed leftists who failed in 1934 to take power by way of arms subsequently succeeded through organization, luck, and the democratic electoral process, but they never had any intention of preserving a system that might put their party out of power again, peacefully or otherwise. Just as Moa doesn't see anything unusual about communists calling themselves republicans, he also doesn't equivocate in pointing out that *how* the Communists took power in Spain is relatively insignificant in the face of the fact that they planned to quickly dismantle the system that elected them.

It can be said that the Spanish Civil War is still played out daily in Latin America. Manuel Zelaya, for instance, after almost a full term as President of Honduras, was booted out of office by nearly the entire political elite in Honduras. He started to smell to them like the Spanish Republicans of 1936 -- elected, but planning to dismember the democratic framework in order to stay in power.

In his youth, Pio Moa was a genuine violent revolutionary. His insurgent activity and the consequent jail time lend Mr. Moa's perspective a street credibility and authenticity that Professor Verstrynge lacks, thus fixing for us a neat question. Is Verstrynge's work edged and authentic because it admires the un-tethered ethic of political resistance, and Moa's work the dull servitude of a man beaten down? – Or, is Vertrynge's the work of second-hand experience and jilted ego, while Moa's a reflection of earned experience and unpressured scholarship? Asking the question from a distance, it appears Mr. Moa tends toward confident, informed argument, and Professor Verstrynge toward romanticized argumentation.

In any case, this pair of personalities and experiences frames for us a major portion of today's ideological struggle, as well as the relationship of that struggle to the prosecution of irregular conflicts influenced by it.

See: 23, *Mens Rea*, 90, *Prisons*; 128, *Global Insurgency and Global Trespass*; 99, *Postmodern and Post-structural*; 124, *America's Insurgent Stamp*; 100, *What the Foucault?*; 81, *What a Clergy Wants*; and 122, *Songs of Chu.*

---

> "Perchance he for whom this bell tolls may be so ill, as that he knows not it tolls for him; and perchance I may think myself so much better than I am, as that they who are about me, and see my state, may have caused it to toll for me, and I know not that."
>
> John Donne,
> *Devotions upon Emergent Occasions* (1623)[145]

Feeding the zombie of Marxism-Leninism

# *Section 99, Postmodern and Post-structural*

For our purposes, 'postmodern' is best used as an adjective for the style of warfare that a sophisticated insurgent, or maybe counterinsurgent, might wage these days. 'Post-structural' is more appropriate for labeling the kind of attitude and political philosophy held by many current activists and apologists for armed violence, especially if it has an anti-American scent. The two terms are related, but not the same.

**Postmodern**

The etymological roots of 'postmodern' lead back through, among other things, the study of architecture. The Sony Building in New York City, built in 1984, is a normal-enough, boxy-looking building -- except that it has a Chippendale top: a skyscraper with a sense of humor. It is often cited as an example of the postmodern style in architecture. In general, architectural postmodernism is (or was) characterized by at least partial rejection of the starkness and pure functionality of modernism. Modern meant carrying building design to the limits of technological possibilities (Sears Tower in Chicago), while postmodern teaching encouraged incorporation of evocative symbolism touching on group identity, and even ornamental inefficiencies related to human characteristics such as whimsicality. It also rejected purity in design styles, allowing combinations of formality and informality, traditional and 'pop,' federal and baroque, etc. The term postmodernism was then applied to all kinds of creative efforts from literature to factory assembly lines, and with a variety of intentions all the way from making material things more ergonomic (or less boring to assemble) to the rejection of imperialism. For a lot of people postmodern pretty much came to mean 'better considered than just modern.'

Postmodernism can be tied to a sequence of design time-periods, but, in the true spirit of the idea, that's not necessary. The 1959 Cadillac had huge fins, a design element common to numerous makes and models around that time. By 1964, no more finned models were offered, and American cars were squared-off, modern. The 'fifties' cars were postmodern and the 'sixties' cars modern. Detroit made the fifties cars look like aircraft dream machines, flamboyant, sexy and confident, and today the fifties cars are preserved and cherished more than the sober, boxier cars of the sixties. And just to bring the idea back to buildings, the Chrysler Building in Manhattan, with its hubcap and hood-ornament gewgaws, remains one of the most beloved and valuable icons in the world. (In a standard art history book, the Chrysler building would be more likely found under *Art Nouveau* or *Art Deco*, and not *Postmodern*, but so what?) For the purposes of understanding irregular warfare, we can get a lot of mileage out of the term postmodern, as follows:

> ***Beyond hybrid***. Postmodern architecture is associated with a pastiche, mixture, or cocktail of styles and themes. Today's irregular wars may be hybrid, or as the *Turducken* section quips, one thing inside another. A more encompassing description, postmodern, would have them as an uncertain mixture of components and conflict types in varying measure.

***More than technical.*** Postmodern architectural design often made a direct appeal to human emotion, or at least obeyed a logic informed by human vicissitudes. In irregular conflict, related, partly-related or unrelated human identities can seize on emotional quantities as weighty as liberty or as flighty as sport. Motivations can include long-term financial gain or a moment of schadenfreude. Decisions may seem premeditated in agile yet patient calculation, or they may look like dumb mistakes that appeal to people anyway. Leaders, especially insurgent leaders, will put together coalitions of groups for very temporary purposes using what seem to be highly inconsistent and unrelated motivations. What holds them together logically is something like a roadblock strategy, as described in section 138. The only thing that the various groups have to do in consonance is stop traffic at the same time.

***Spatially aware.*** Architectural postmodernism recognized sense of place. Community styles, like Spanish Colonial style in Albuquerque, relate architecture to peoples' sense of pride, heritage and recognition of home. Successful leaders of contending identities in postmodern warfare are cognizant of the same sense of place and identity. They almost invariably try to connect the legitimacy of their leadership and the cohesion of the identity they are purporting to lead with place-association, even if it means creating identity out of whole cloth.

***Technologically advanced.*** Postmodern buildings still incorporate modern technological advantage. Although postmodernism was a rejection of the tendency to build to the limits of technological possibilities at the cost of other values, it was not a rejection of technology. The idea of combining successful styles allows acceptance of high technology as long as that does not inhibit affective expression. Today's irregular conflict winners are ready to combine obscure mysticism with cell phones, Twitter, or whatever gizmo and organizational innovation seems to further the cause. Postmodernism admits human complexity, and remains pragmatic.

A couple of Chileans wrote well about postmodernity and armed conflicts. One is Arturo Contreras and the other Cristián Garay.[146] Neither of their books is in English, however. The term postmodern fell on hard times since the heyday of its use in English academe in the late

1980s and 1990s. Apparently, it is now academically behind the times to be *postmodern*, or even to talk about postmodernism without a disclaimer. Rejection of postmodernism in liberal arts perhaps rested on the observation of overuse. Not only was every un-rebellious Tom, Dick and Harry calling himself a postmodernist, he was using the term to justify old modern, structural stuff, too. Postmodernist posing made it harder to authentically represent the suffering human condition as a rebel and still call oneself postmodern. You could hardly take it to the Man and call it postmodern while some petite bourgeois just opens a Starbucks® in a hotel lobby and calls *that* postmodern.

**Post-structural**

When applied to political ideology, political philosophy, or geopolitics, postmodernism was supposed to be a resistance movement, that is, an expression of rejection of modern structures, the United States or neo-liberalism being prominent among those structures. Discerning intellectual anti-ists (maybe that global subversive who rejects colonialism, imperialism, capitalism, commercialism, commodity-ism) started using *postmodern* before the end of the Cold War, before the failures of the two Communist giants. Many of these resistance postmodernists might also have identified themselves as Marxists or Marxist-Leninists. At some point, say, in the late 1960s, the philosophical left began to see the Soviet Union as overbearing, overly 'modern' and too 'structural.' Slowly, some erstwhile Marxist-Leninists would become just Marxists, and/or something else.

For them, however, deflation of the term *postmodern* led not so much to *post-postmodernism*, but to *post-structuralism*. Some of the latter term's heritage can be traced to *deconstructionism*, which was connected to literary criticism. In other words, part of what today is called *post-structuralism* has some parental lineage in architecture (postmodernism) and some in literary criticism (deconstructionism). From the latter parentage especially comes the idea of tearing something down – to tear at its basic vocabulary, assumptions, institutions, mores, codes, and so on. Tearing at the structure or at structuralism, which is like tearing at modernism, allowed you (as a Marxist) to go after errors of the Stalinists and Maoists, and remain a Marxist. This is significant when we consider the timing of the appearance of the terminology, given that many political/philosophical unhappy types struggled with a conscious or subconscious need to recalculate, re-justify and reinvigorate Marxism in the face of the geopolitical mega-failure of the Soviet Union and the capitalistic treason of Red China. By the time the Parisian philosophical left officially snubbed postmodernism as passé, some momentarily would-be 'post-postmodernists,' looking to put radical edge back into whatever postmodern no longer was (and to raise and include all kinds suppressed grievances), began denying they were post-structuralists. And thus post-structuralism was born. Whenever it was exactly, it was not on a 4th of July.

If you are anti-globalist, against neo-liberalism and opposed to US hegemonic power, you could call yourself a post-structuralist (but probably won't since that would seem conformant). The bulk of post-structuralism-speak seems to originate from within a European and particularly a small French philosophical community that has a number of its own codes and characters. That community is born and embedded in the strain of French thinking that is viscerally anti-American.

There are several reasons why the terms postmodern and post-structural should interest you. For one thing, you may notice them in what you read; you may notice someone calling themselves, or an analysis or perspective, *post-structuralist*. They might just be pandering, mimicking or posing, but if you're anti-American he is probably your ideological fellow traveler. Another reason has to do with the shape of your arguments and the flexibility of your own designs for winning. Note that postmodern architectural or engineering style was a near universal success. It really was better than modern for all the reasons noted. You probably want to be postmodern in your design philosophy. Curiously, the post-postmodernist, or post-structuralist (that person who thinks postmodernism went sour, wants to remain a Marxist, but has to get over the sweeping failures of Marxism), can't do better than postmodernism for designing armed conflict. Still, the post-structuralist's critique of 'postmodern' includes its supposed moral devolution into compromise with the old modern structures. That means he thinks postmodernism sold out to the establishment.

Here is a convoluted example of what may be happening in the world: Hugo Chávez is trying to mount a postmodern war. He is flexible and creative in combining old styles and new, in accordance with whatever seems to work at the moment (warfare that some people might want to call 'hybrid,' or other people want to call 'unrestricted'). He weaves together appeals to peoples' sense of place, historic inheritance and current ethnic identity, age-relevance, and once in a while even an accountant's logic. He would be undeterred by any suggestion that baseball, Bolivar, Marxism, pre-Colombian ethnicity, beauty contests, hip-hop and Persia might not be happy companions. He buys tanks, digs holes, nationalizes factories, hosts a TV show, and meddles in foreign electoral politics.

Chávez also likes the FARC. Pensive post-structuralists may see the FARC as a successful postmodern guerrilla movement that devolved morally, and so might reject as merely 'postmodern' much of what the FARC has become. Chávez, by association, may be seen by them as a post-structuralist poser, that is, a self-interested charlatan postmodernist – a user of rebellious style without revolutionary moral substance. Meanwhile, the hard-core anti-American post-structuralists reject such moralizing tones, and embrace Chávez' Realpolitic.

Fortunately for the enemies Hugo Chávez has chosen for himself, he doesn't seem to be too good at classic military strategy. Bolivian President Evo Morales and his Vice-President Álvaro García Linera, on the other hand, not only have figured out strategic postmodernism, they have intellectual post-Soviet post-structuralism figured out as well. Fortunately for *their* enemies, they're stuck in Bolivia.

*Postmodern* relates to a design freedom and creativity that at its best doesn't throw out proven practices, technological advances or working structures. *Post-structural* is globally recognized code for a stance against what is perceived to be the whole symbolic, semantic, jurisprudential, moral, institutional and geopolitical structure of the overdog (the US, the West, neo-liberalism, globalization, capitalism, rapacious environmental irresponsibility, anthropogenic global warming denial, etc.) *Postmodern* is more design style; and *post-structural* more political flag. The first has little to do with existentialism; the latter tends to seek and apologize for an existentialism centered on the will to kill.

See: 98, *Jorge Verstrynge and Pio Moa*; 120, *Turducken*; 26, *How Violent Groups Form*; 13, *Puthukkudiyirippu*; 128, *Global Insurgency and Global Trespass*; 100, *What the Foucault?*; 66, *GIS*; and 54, *Mercatus.*

---

> "And new philosophy calls all in doubt,
> The element of fire is quite put out;
> The sun is lost, and the earth, and no man's wit,
> Can well direct him where to look for it."
>
> John Donne,
> *Devotions upon Emergent Occasions* (1623)[147]

The intellectual détritus of French Man's defeat

# *Section 100, What the Foucault?*

Section 99 mentions post-structuralism. If you are involved in an organized armed conflict these days it is advantageous for you to know a little about the idea and where it comes from. In sum, it is the zombie of Marxism-Leninism. It lurches around, soulless, on the same campuses and in the same agencies and headspaces trying to eat the flesh of the surviving 'structure', which it still calls capitalism, neo-liberalism, or something related. Post-structuralism is also the name of an ideological franchise package that can be adopted and adapted very broadly -- more broadly than Marxism-Leninism could be. It appeals to many identities who feel they are on the outside of power or consider themselves the despised 'other' or underdog. It exists as a movement that a left-leaning intellectual can join if he or she has a need to belong. In this respect it is both a presentation to and a request for participation in a population of persons who want to follow something that they can believe is ethical, intelligent, has a political effect or purpose, and is not a lackey of or apology for the Man.

About the time of the American military involvement in Vietnam, a small group of French ideologues nearly cornered the trademark of Philosophy. This didn't happen all at once and was never complete, but under the auspices of the authority gained, post-structuralism was slowly spawned. Some of the French person's names, in no particular order, are Jacque Derrida, Jean-François Lyotard, Jean Baudrillard, Luce Irigaray, and Gilles Deleuze, but chief among them was Michel Foucault. He died, apparently of AIDS, in 1984 at the age of 57. A little bit of his intellectual popularity is as a sort of martyr. At any rate, below is my take on the history of why Marxism didn't just stay buried, and why post-structuralism prospers either to give an intellectual backstop to your war aims, or to cause you a headache as it makes it harder and harder to tell the truth.

The pertinent history doesn't begin or end at any special moment, but to lighten the load I'm going to start with Blackjack Pershing and the American Expeditionary Force, the AEF, in World War I. Blackjack was an American alpha male. He refused (more or less) to have American soldiers fight except as an army unit, instead of becoming a troop replacement pool (thus telling the French that the American wasn't just there to help, but to *be*), and ultimately the AEF tipped the balance in the war in favor of the Allies. Even though the Allies won the war, the French alpha males did not fare especially well. This failure of France's

Man opened a little space in the French discourse (about strategy, politics, power, philosophy and, well, everything) to other voices besides that of the French Man. Notably, Marxism-Leninism was taking off in a big way just at that time, with the Russian Revolution in full swing when World War I ended.

Paris became the kitchen for ideas that would take on monikers like existentialism, nihilism, structuralism, etc. Long a philosopher's destination, it becomes even more so, especially for Marxist philosophers, as Germany is then tending toward fascism. When World War II arrives in France, France's Man does far worse than in World War I. In fact, he is an abject failure. Unable to protect France, in comes German Fascist Man in his place. This opens up more room in the discourse. American Man looks potent by comparison, and, again, saves France. After the war, France's Man takes a beating in Southeast Asia from Vietnamese Man. Then, in almost the instant that French manhood is embarrassed in Vietnam, he decides that he will regain dominance or at least face by winning at all costs in Algeria, but that turns out to be the cost France pays. France loses terribly, and French Man with it. This opens up a tremendous amount of room in the French discourse for 'other' voices, and what those voices are saying especially includes an abiding anti-Americanism. This anti-Americanism is conveniently agreeable to the Marxist-Leninist currents for the obvious reasons of the competition between the Soviet Union and the United States.

As the Cold War progresses and many in Europe begin to sense the stale quality of Soviet governance and promise, some of the French philosophers, who by this time have constructed the parameters of fashionable European academe, begin to think in terms akin to the postmodernism described in Section 99. The year 1968 looms large in all this since it was a good year for dissidence in the United States and a very active year of rebelliousness in Europe. Distaste for the high handedness of the Soviet Union sent some erstwhile Marxists looking for something to spruce up their resistance thinking.

Sooner than they might have predicted, however, the Soviet Union was in full collapse. In the face of political reality, their philosophy had to evolve quickly. The result was a contraption that took big chunks from Marxism (criticizing the self-perpetuating structure and voracity of capitalism), still garnering for itself the look of moral preference for the downtrodden, but escaping the need to consolidate any specific outcome or vision. There was no longer a new communist man, or a communist condition, or some substitute utopia to which aspirations had to be aimed. It became a sort of anarchism with social empathy that could take or leave bombs as suited. It is sort of a virtual, linguistic framework for radical goodness in which almost any grievance can be made to fit, although there have always been some conditions. It claims, falsely, to have invented critical thinking, and it eases its own burden of illogic by disdaining things like objectivism and realism. It tells scholars that they should include emotive, affective, and politically responsible content to their analyses, and that *responsible* means *progressive.*

There are gatekeepers to post-structural approval. To be gonged post-structural, and therefore enjoy some of the other benefits of membership such as being called progressive, one must pay homage to that group of French founding fathers and preferably to a coterie of other popular Marxist or 'new' Marxist thinkers. Also, there are a number of issues the wrong side of which you must not fall. For instance, it appears difficult to gain post-structural approval if you are pro-Israel, do not agree that carbon emissions from North America are the main cause of global warming (and that therefore the United States should pay a monetary debt); or express faith in Christ (you may, however, worship Allah).

Less and more than a philosophy, post-structuralism is a political platform the planks of which are provided by leftist-radical *du jour.* Older leadership is peopled by radicals from or supporting organizational remnants of Cold War communist or socialist political parties. The Forum of Sao Paulo is a good example of a consortium of these parties. Although the followship may not be as responsive as what we might have sensed in the relationship of Marxist-Leninist thinkers to the geopolitical agendas of the Cold War communist parties, there is nevertheless a strong connection. It is, as the systems theorists like to say, a complex system, but there is a clear, namable community of leadership and guidance (the descendant and inheritor of what used to depend on auspices of the Soviet Union or Communist China) to which many self-described post-structuralists attune. The activist post-structuralists rail about the false dichotomies of conservative thinking, but they are themselves often guilty of a Manichaen (old religion from Persia that stressed a lot of Light versus Darkness) tendency to line up everything as either good or neoliberal.

It is not a black and white world, but take note of all who claim they're post-structural. Of course, sneaking, some of the ideologically contentious may call themselves postmodern, while admiring others as post-structural. If they also admire that French crew, they are quite possibly post-structural ant-Americans, and you'll want to know why.

See: 124, *America's Insurgent Stamp*; 101, *Magical Realism*; 99, *Postmodern and Post-structural*; 128, *Global Insurgency and Global Trespass*; 79, *Suicide;* 58, *Guerre d'Algérie*; 5, *Misleading Counterinsurgency Articles of Faith*; and 83, *Conflict Geography.*

---

> "It's a complex fate, being an American, and one of the responsibilities it entails is fighting against a superstitious valuation of Europe."
>
> Henry James[148]

ঔ ঔ ঔ

The WWF and the NCAA Both Wrestle

# *Section 101, Magical Realism*

Sometimes the search for truth is hard to satisfy with scrupulous science and measurement. In your war, truth will also be a product of propaganda and its delivery. The construction and reconstruction of reality itself, activities off-putting to some of us, will be a feature of your war. The 'post-structuralist' especially seeks to own the construction of truth, so the observer of and competitor in today's irregular wars need to be keen to the making of truth beyond the arguments and beyond the numbers.

'Magical Realism' is a genre of fictional literature, born in, associated with, and even emblematic of Latin America, that intermixes attention to worldly detail (respect for 'objectively' factual conditions, events, locations and time of occurrence) with fantastical interludes, incorporeal characters, and intangible dimensions of human experience. Genius writers bring us the interplay between greater truths of the spirit and the mundane or technically necessary. More than requiring a suspension of disbelief, magical realism requires an intention to understand larger truths about life, love, and justice: truths that perhaps cannot be explained without the intervention of the supernatural or whimsical. Gifted novelists tease out of magical realism the most difficult to explain quantities – like dignity, honor, fate, or even environmental determinism. When in the hands of a less gifted writer, magical realism becomes a cheesy trick to get the plot out of some corner.

When some story tellers attempt to explain the meaning of life they create an existentialist marvel. Gabriel Garcia Marquez is an often-cited master of magical realism, but hardly inventor of the style. Argentinean Jorge Luis Borges might be closer to the creative beginnings, while another Colombian writer, Jose Rivera, can be credited with innovating a precursor or perhaps parallel style known as the jungle novel. These writers and their emulators also owe a great deal to their Spanish inheritance, but that's not the point -- the point is that there exists a named style of literature in which the supernatural is accepted not as science fiction or horror or fantasy, but as a dimension of reality that exceeds the boundaries and importance of the thought processes or social expectations we build around the idea of 'objective' truth. Magical realism proffers a truth of equal or greater importance than the truth of our five senses. It is the literary rejection of corporeal realism, positivism, empiricism, etc. Just because things happen, or just because you can prove they happen in logical space and correctly sequenced time, doesn't make them the truth that we should care about.

So why talk about magical realism? Because of its evil political twin. Magical realism serves an entire universe of ethical justifications in politics and ideology. It not only encourages 'ends justify means,' but glorifies use of what used to be called the 'big lie' as more than an admirable propagandistic achievement. Beyond propaganda tactics, it forms up an alternative beauty and an alternative honesty. It encourages and praises the creation of identities, histories, grievances, hate memories, and absolutely anything that furthers political goals. After all, it can be cogently argued that truth does not exist outside the mind, that it is all perception. This understanding of truth is called solipsism. Magical realism in fiction, which draws in some way on solipsism, can be a powerful aid to understanding. In politics and war, it can destroy the ethic of replicability in science, of trust in fiduciary relationships, and of pride-worthy historical inheritance. The political version of magical realism is not a calm romanticism; it is a license for strident partisanship. It is not an egalitarian proposition available to all contenders, either, but rather a purely competitive reality trick that feeds cults of personality and vanguardism.

**Argumentation and argument.** There are two principal categories of wrestling in the United States. One is called amateur or folk style, and in that category we can include intercollegiate rules and the Olympic styles called freestyle and Greco-Roman. The other category can be subsumed under professional wrestling, featuring organizations such as the

Worldwide Wrestling Federation, WWF. My favorite US professional wrestler was 'The Rock' (Dwayne Johnson), with his 'People's Elbow,' 'People's Eyebrow' and other gimmicks the infringement of which could cause one to find out "what the Rock was cookin'" and be slammed by the bad end of the 'Rock Bottom.' It is wrong to say that professional wrestlers like Mr. Johnson are not great athletes or that the winners of a professional wrestling match are not winners. It is a different victory, and it is a different set of attributes that takes a professional wrestler to the top of his profession than the set of attributes that takes an amateur wrestler to the state finals or the NCAA Championships.

We can liken folk style or intercollegiate wrestling to argument and professional wrestling to argumentation. When we see a hand raised in amateur wrestling, we are confident that the athlete won on the basis of a superior set of athletic attributes -- quickness, strength, durability, resolve. The athlete paid in advance in hours of physical sacrifice, discomfort, disappointment, and foregone social opportunity. It is unlikely that his hand was raised because of the votes of the fans, because the referee was bribed, or the rules unevenly applied. Neither poverty nor wealth, while they might have helped, was the reason for his victory. His opponent probably won't claim to have failed because of other people, either; he will blame himself.

In the other world of wrestling there are other qualities, qualities of showmanship that reward and understand the aspirations and self concept of followers, of the balance between dangerous physical maneuvers and the way they appear to the audience, of the close connection between skill during interviews and skill in the ring, and of money and social timing. These professional skills are just as, if not more, precious than the difficult moves learned by the intercollegiate wrestler, but the skill sets are not the same.

In the world of legal argument and argumentation, a good lawyer cannot scoff at one or the other. He has to master both. Johnny Cochran was known as a master of argumentation, just as Dwayne Johnson was a master of professional wrestling. Mr. Cochrane knew how to apply 'tricks' like juxtaposition, change of subject, or other techniques that can lead a jury to nullify legal and factual argument, but Mr. Cochrane was hardly helpless in the realm of argument. He knew the law, what motions had to be made to the court and when, why one logical argument was more dangerous for his client than another. He made sure his team dominated both worlds. He knew when argument might not be enough to win; when it was time to resort to argumentation.

Magical realism as it is expressed in politics and ideology is like one side of that Johnson/Cochranesque professional wrestling/trial lawyering dimension of today's political truth-making. Somewhere else in the book I might refer to it as an element of postmodernism. The postmodern designs are strongest when they don't reject the old reality, new technology or the physical realm of time and space, but still pay particular attention to personal and place identity, imaginaries, self-concepts, grievances and all the vicissitudes, curiosities and ailments of the human mind that allow a competitor to build an alternative reality if the 'objective' one does not suit competitive purposes.

What do you do about this political magical realism? Use it, or, to confront it competitively, you may want to go back to sections 54, *Badassoftheweek.com*, and 2, *The Line of Retreat*, remembering that ultimately we are not talking about some reality floating around inside a propagandist's or intellectual's head, or about the reality he is trying to create inside the heads of the people, but about the bone skull housing and gooey brain of the *mens rea* guy itself. Don't get thrown off. If you have an enemy, he sleeps and defecates. He has or had a Mom. If he is armed and intends to do you harm before you can bring arguments to bear, you want to close off his line of retreat to sanctuary, put that brain in a cell and *then* talk to him about all kinds of fun philosophical stuff.

Magical Realism can be easily dismissed by the technical mind, or compartmentalized as a frivolous enjoyment. That would be a competitive mistake.

See: 114, *R.V. Jones*; 129, *Nerd Globe*; 23, *Mens Rea*; 142, *Dignity and Honor*; 77, *Sex*; 122, *Songs of Chu*; 117, *Strategic Communication*; and 123, *Thirty-six Stratagems*.

---

"Who ya gonna believe, me or your lyin` eyes?"
Marx[149]

"You cannot know yet whether what you see
is what you are looking at
or what you are believing."
William Faulkner,
*Absalom, Absalom!*[150]

A move, they are not the goal

# *Section 102, Negotiations*

This is a recurrent topic in insurgent wars, and there seems to be a school solution for both the insurgent and counterinsurgent. For the insurgent, it is always a good idea to appear willing to negotiate, and to do so if the government is willing to give ground on something valuable, perhaps a demilitarized zone, some sort of international recognition for the movement, or the exchange of prisoners. A moderately successful insurgent (one who has mastered the operational equation of classic military strategy) holds the advantage of being able to offer a non-thing and make it seem as though it is a something. That is to say, the insurgent can offer to explode, rob, and kidnap less in exchange for some kind of actual advantage such as the trappings of international recognition, which could quickly lead to a belief on the part of members of the international State community that the insurgent organization has the *right* to grant impunity to its soldiers for acts of armed violence against government targets. There is never a right to grant impunity.

Since almost all insurgents hold a relatively weaker position geographically and militarily, if not financially, the insurgent is generally more careful about the security of routes to sanctuary. The result is that the insurgent usually needs to play it safe and prolong his life, and that in turn means prolonging the conflict. Negotiating can help do just that, so one of the first negotiating goals for many insurgents will revolve around the negotiation process. The process itself may offer much of what the insurgent needs, if that happens to be time, and it often is, so delaying is good, for as long as possible, if it can be done, until it is annoying. Requiring a specific geographic area for negotiations is a ploy that can provide useful temporary sanctuary. Extending the timeline of the negotiations by seeking 'honest brokers,' working around executive schedules, getting sick and the like can provide the insurgent with months of government latency and lack of substantive diligence.

The government should always appear willing to negotiate, provided that the government actually means it will offer the insurgent leniency or amnesty upon surrender. If the insurgent makes reasonable demands, such as a change in patently unfair labor practices or the failure to prosecute known criminals, the government might do well to just resolve those issues without attributing its decisions to the insurgent demands. On the other hand, it might behoove the government, if it intends to take certain actions anyway, to appear to concede the points in return for surrender. The government should waste no time in the planning processes of the negotiations, for the reasons expressed above. The government should not in most cases unilaterally establish a cease-fire or lift military pressure due to the negotiations. The principal negotiating chip possessed by the government is the offer to lift the military pressure, and thereby lessen the possibility of the death or capture of the insurgent leaders. The exchange should be their surrender. Some will argue that this is a best-case answer, or that this attitude toward negotiating strategy is logical or available to the government only if it is clearly superior militarily and is in a position where such arrogance might bear fruit. Perhaps, but if this were not the government position, it is because the government is willing to give up something that does not belong to it, or it is being forced to surrender something of great value, like land. Sometimes a government must give up space for time.

The release of kidnap victims in exchange for the release of imprisoned insurgents is a touchy dilemma, so to announce a fixed or school solution would presume too much, and it would be gratuitous given that the relevant executive decisions are always from a subjective and pain-ridden point of departure. The notion of cold objectivity is too cheap. Here's a school solution anyway: Offer leniency for the release of hostages; do not allow family members, even and especially those powerful families with political influence, to direct and pressure the government position. The necessary separation can be created by isolating the chief executive by way of a series of lesser negotiators. The insurgent will, of course, demand that the chief executive be directly involved in negotiations. A chief executive should avoid being an active negotiating element.

The principle strategy against kidnapping should never be to negotiate, even if an occasional negotiation is done covertly because of some especially valuable hostage. The smart insurgent will try to gain politically influential hostages. If the play works even once to secure a valuable negotiation, the insurgent is well paid for the behavior.

See: 120, *Turducken*; 24, *Ruthlessness and Resolve*; 103, *Amnesty*; 8, *The Operational Equation*; 12, *Protraction and Diligence*; 17, *Kidnapping*; 90, *Prisons*; and 104, *Extraterritorial Jurisdiction.*

---

"Diplomacy is the art of saying 'Nice doggie'
...until you can find a rock."

Will Rogers[151]

# Section 103, Amnesty

Amnesties are like a mix of plea-bargaining, granting of executive pardons and conditional surrender. Their significant political and ideological content raises the stakes for all sides to a conflict, and the hinge issue is usually how an amnesty candidate is likely to fare after he is given amnesty.

Considering the first assertion of this book -- that a State fails to the extent some other entity can grant impunity, the negotiation of amnesty can be seen as an admission of State failure. Once again we are back to the word impunity, but in this context it is impunity that the State would grant in the context of a process of reconciliation. The State's options are influenced by the bargaining power of the perpetrators, but also by how the balance of justice is perceived by victims and their agents.

As with so many things, an amnesty plan has to be culturally appropriate. Considerable cultural space exists in Latin American culture for the design of amnesties. In Colombia they have been a recurrent strategy, if with mixed results.

A Google search for discussion of amnesty will hit on Amnesty International, but that organization is as interested in the justice of punishment as it is in amnesty, a phenomenon that marks the theme generally. Amnesty sounds nice, but it has become complicated by the global spread of 'Western' law. It is one of the ironies of ideological history since World War II that justice activists have achieved not only the spread of public criminal law in order to confront what they see as State impunity for the violation of human rights, but also the spread of civil tort law, including internationalized mechanisms not only of institutionalized forensics but of civil discovery. International (or extraterritorial) jurisdiction has spread civil actions such as wrongful death. As a result, it is now difficult for a government to grant amnesty to an insurgent leader if that leader has been the intellectual author of, or accessory to, kidnapping and murder. To provide effective amnesty, the government would not only have to forego its criminal prosecution, it would have to extend special legal and physical protection for perpetrators against the motions of civil claimants or foreign prosecutors.

An essential function and economic contribution of formal penal processes is the dampening of the human tendency (or perhaps satisfaction of a perceived human necessity) for revenge. In other words, good governance includes keeping people from taking violent revenge on their own initiative – no vigilantism. The world of extraterritorial civil law can undermine this State function, punishment sometimes being driven more by third party observers than it is by the victims. International activists begin to define justice on a global scale, rather than on a local one, and provide otherwise unavailable resources to fuel the pressing of grievances. For better or worse, your enemy may be able to find international support for the idea that he should be granted amnesty for his felonies, while the people on your side of the ledger should be subject to the justice of punishment. This is the stressful formula that many Colombians have had to face.

The book, *Walking Ghosts*, by journalist Steven Dudley, is a riveting and enlightening account of an 80s-90s peace process in Colombia that included the creation of a political party, the Patriotic Union, from amnestied ex-guerrillas. It didn't go well. Many of the open members of the Patriotic Union were murdered, and the party eventually withered away. Many ex-guerrillas, officially amnestied by the government, were forgiven neither by some of their former enemies nor by some of their former comrades. Regardless of what a legal process is called, or what it pronounces, perpetrators and participants may go un-forgiven, and the goal of the system, to control revenge, unmet.

Don't throw the idea of amnesty around as though it is an automatically good idea. The potential to offer an amnesty should be thoroughly reviewed in terms of victim acceptance, participant survival, international jurisdiction, and the effect of precedent setting.

Dilemmas are created by the spread of the rule-of-law. As courts, legal theories and investigations become more available to victims, amnesties can become more difficult to devise. How would Pablo Escobar have ever atoned had he been captured and not shot down? His history alone is a roadmap of the difficulties presented. Earlier he had surrendered to the law to wait comfortably in a luxury non-prison until he decided he had had enough of that gambit. Finally, the only logical end for Pablo Escobar was to be killed like a rabid dog. In 2009, Pablo Escobar's son, emotionally burdened, reached out to the families of some of his father's victims, asking for their forgiveness. At least by some, it was granted without reservation.

In the last decade, the Colombian government has gained the surrender of tens of thousands of guerrillas, mostly former members of the *Autodefensas Unidas de Colombia* (United Self-Defense Forces of Colombia, AUC). The process has included a variety of programs for their reinsertion and reintegration into the fabric of peaceful society.

Generally these are referred to as Demobilization, Disarmament and Reintegration (DDR) programs. The Colombian effort attracted some international funding, but was not one of the seven or so ongoing UN-mandate DDRs. There have been successes and failures, the latter caused by lack of resources, bungling, resentments and unmet expectations. Beyond the fact of forgiven crimes, the programs had at least the appearance of giving ex-outlaw fighters more economic and educational assistance than what the government gave to ex-soldiers who served in the army. In addition, jobs are often not available, appropriate or appealing enough. As a result, crime bosses can still bid successfully for the combat experienced manpower.

Smaller, functional amnesties and rewards programs such as drug material amnesties and gun amnesties can give some individuals a second chance, take dangerous instrumentalities out of circulation, and are relatively painless. Having a set of amnesties of this nature can be a good idea. On the other hand, they can also confound some evidentiary efforts and give the wrong kind of second chance. That is to say, criminals can game such programs to ditch evidence.

Some amnesties have taken the form of buy-in programs. In El Salvador in the 1980s, for instance, the government initiated a program that not only gave amnesty to individual guerrillas who surrendered; it gave them an amount of money if they turned in a rifle. The purchase was of a weapon, but really the government was buying a cooperative interrogation in order to find caches of other weapons. The program met with some success, although a lot of worthless weapons were purchased and there is a distinct possibility that some of the money was funneled to the guerrilla command. Adam Smith's invisible hand can slap you.

Note the relationship of amnesty to our definition of State success. A State with a monopoly over the granting of impunity never has to grant amnesty. Nevertheless, by so doing, a challenged State can return rule-of-law initiative to itself. Amnesties are culturally sensitive and their success may be inseparable from questions of honor and dignity. If you don't know much about the culture, maybe don't take it upon yourself to design an amnesty.

See: 84, *Cultures of Violence*; 95, *Childhood*; 38, *Cultural Study for What?*; 104, *Extraterritorial Jurisdiction*; 90, *Prisons*; 20, *Foreign Support*; 110, *Knowledge Gaps*; and 88, *Sieges and Takeovers*.

"May you grow to be proud, dignified and true
And do unto others as you'd have done to you"

Rod Stewart (and Bob Dylan?) from the song
*Forever Young*[152]

Modern paradox of hypocrisy?

# *Section 104, Extraterritorial Jurisdiction*

In the next several years, extraterritorial jurisdiction, as a feature of the global legal environment, is most likely to increase. It can have a dissimilar effect on insurgent and counterinsurgent. Under a theory of extraterritorial or 'international' jurisdiction, a foreign court might successfully order your arrest, prosecution and incarceration, or that of one of your people. A foreign court might even have ability to self-initiate criminal or civil process. Such events can be highly politicized and the prosecutions finely targeted. There are a lot of problems with extraterritorial jurisdiction, some of them mentioned below, but the consequences could be game changers.

As this section is being written, one of the twists of the conflict in northern South America is that of a judge in Sucumbios Province, Ecuador, summoning the former Colombian Minister of Defense (and now President) Juan Manuel Santos to answer charges in connection with a raid into Ecuadoran territory that killed a number of Colombian FARC guerrillas plus some nationals of other countries, including Ecuador.

The territory presumed by the word extraterritorial is the national State (member of the world's international club of countries), and a counterpart term would be 'extradition.' The various countries of the world keep treaties between and among other States within the system, and under the terms of the treaties one State will deliver up a fugitive to the authorities of another.

An extradition treaty is a recognition of State sovereignty and particularly a State's right to disallow other entities from granting impunity. Extraterritoriality is a denial of national sovereignty, and an assertion that the State in question should not have a monopoly on granting impunity. The concept of extraterritoriality can be a bit softer on the civil side than on the criminal side, if the courts in question obey some distinction between civil and criminal law. That distinction has been closing over the decades, even while civil process has been globalizing. No one statement can be made about the effect of international jurisdiction on the war you are in, except to say that the legal environment as regards extradition treaties and extraterritoriality are worthy of your concern. They relate to the physical and temporal geography of your potential sanctuaries and the impunity you can practicably grant to your people, and for how long.

A favorite current of jurisprudential thought holds that no entity should be 'above the law.' For this reason, American courts tend to stress protection of the rights of individual defendants. Say a suspect in a criminal case has been arrested and charged with a crime. The government tends to protect its investigatory and prosecutorial agents, even when they overreach. If they follow the wrong suspect, interrogate him brutally, don't chase other reasonable leads, or drop an extra weapon at the scene of a crime, the tendency of the State agencies is to protect their own and to believe their own. Thus, in the process of providing the service of justice, the State tends toward providing impunity for a whole slew of process-induced crimes of its own. Since Americans don't like the granting of impunity, they have laid on a lot of rules that protect individuals against abuses of the State and allow accused citizens to take legal actions against the government on the grounds of unjust processes.

The tendency of government entities to provide impunity for their own abuses, and the cultural response that favors the individual underdog against the State overdog, is significant for understanding irregular wars. If a foreigner, that is, someone who is neither a US citizen nor a US Person, commits a crime inside the United States, Americans usually confer on him the protections against the government that are afforded to citizens. Again, Americans don't like the State to grant its own agents impunity for their abuses. However, what about a case, such as the 2009 Detroit underpants bomber, who appeared to represent a foreign organization dedicated to waging war against the United States?[153] In that case, a question arose as to whether or not the bomber should have been tried in an American civilian court, where all the protections against the abuse of process would apply, or be tried in a military court where the protections *might* be fewer.

In the underpants bomber case, some protections against abuse of process would have existed in either the civilian or military routes. In fact, a nearly simultaneous case involved a US Army major at Ft. Hood, Texas who was being tried in military court for killing fourteen people.[154] The major, a US citizen, was being tried in military court, while the foreigner was being processed in civilian court. In this we witnessed the tension between competing values of sovereignty and civil liberties. How much protection should be offered to defendants from abuse of governmental process as compared to the protection lost by victims to some foreign entity (to which both those defendants seem linked)? How much defense of American sovereignty is lost as a result of the formalities of domestic criminal law? This is an American example, but it is broadly generalizable.

Let's say that a US military court were to convict and condemn a defendant (such as those noted above) and the defendant were executed without his having been given the full panoply of protections from abuse of process normally enjoyed by US citizens. In such a case, would and could the United States Government protect the members of the military court from prosecution by some foreign court?

Status of forces agreements (SOFA) cover some of the legal relationships, rights, duties, privileges, etc., pertaining to the military personnel of one country when they are invited to stay in another. Sometimes these agreements can require that the visiting soldiers relinquish the protection of their State from foreign prosecution. If soldiers of one country are operating in an allied country, they might or might not be subject to prosecution by the courts of that ally, or in turn by an international court. Such situations are problematic, given that the protections against abuse of process may not be the same in the various courts. This problem of abuse of criminal process, however, is usually generated in the context of some crime committed outside the soldier's official activities. In other words, if a soldier is downtown shoplifting, or date-rapes someone, the sending country is likely to accede to the local jurisdiction.

The problem is much different when a killing is done during activities related to the sending government's reason for their soldier's presence in a foreign land. In those cases, the sending State is greatly responsible for the situation in which its soldiers (or some other category of agents) find themselves. In those cases, it may be deemed irresponsible on the part of the sending government to relegate its agents to a lesser level of protections than what would be afforded in their native land. Moreover, the sending State may wish to assert not just its sovereign immunity, but its monopoly over the granting of impunity. This is logical because, in situations that are politically, geopolitically and ideologically charged, some other entity (another government or a non-state actor) can use the jurisprudential system as an attack mechanism. Thus, a foreign entity is able, premeditatedly, to grant impunity to its own agents for the purpose of attacking the agents of a foreign government, and thereby attack that country. It is indeed an attack on sovereignty.

The above may seem merely an opinion regarding the legalistic parameters of extraterritorial jurisdiction potentially affecting your irregular war. You are forewarned that any applicability of extraterritorial jurisdiction to your war will be determined by some set of 'opinions,' and you will want to know exactly what those opinions are, whose they are, and where they sit. Depending on your status and the policies of your government, you could win your war, and then go to jail for it in some foreign land.

See: 144, *Impunity and State Success*; 20, *Foreign Support*; 96, *Public Records*; 96, *Combatant Status*; 28, *Oviedo*; 40, *Rule-of-law*; 130, *Globalization*; and 129, *Nerd Globe.*

---

> "Behind every scheme to make the world over, lies the question: What kind of world do you want? The ideals of the past for men have been drawn from war, as those for women have been drawn from motherhood."
>
> Oliver Wendell Holmes, Jr.[155]

Slicing away at a people's property

# *Section 105, Genocide Geography*

*Genocide* is a 20th century word with a legendary etymology. Invocation of the word is used to overcome the barrier of sovereignty, that is, to justify physical intervention into the internationally demarcated territory of a foreign State. Genocides are bigger than massacres. For one thing, genocide has legalistic import as an accusation of the breach of international humanitarian law, and it carries greater emotive power related to the targeting and destruction of whole human collective identities. The topic is included in this book because: when a State kills its own people, it is intending to grant impunity to itself for clearly immoral acts; mass killing is a reasonable motivator for those being killed to start an insurgency; and almost all insurgencies are also international conflicts. If your definition of the rule-of-law is overly tied to the stability of laws (or to popular legitimacy or democracy), at least note that the actions the Nazis took against the Jews were legal. It may be hard for you to justify intervention into a foreign land absent some other quantity of national interest, but you may not have a choice. Places that suffer genocide will face internal violence afterwards. Survivors or perpetrators will fight over whatever the dead leave behind. Genocides cause flows of refugees, and it is unlikely that post-genocide violence will obey the proscriptions of international borders. This section is about where genocide occurs and where it is likely to occur. Public knowledge about genocides can be readily improved, the signs are fairly obvious; and, better armed with knowledge of the reality, you can better decide the morality.

Public knowledge about genocides can be placed into seven categories, each connected to the global attention paid to the phenomenon, as follows:

1. Long-term (years) warnings regarding the likelihood of or heightened vulnerability of a people to genocide.
2. Creation of human inventories (which might themselves deter mass killings).
3. Forensic geography conducted before events that can support prosecutions after the fact. This category serves both as a deterrent and as a support to justice.
4. Midterm (weeks and months) warnings that can mobilize attention and pressure against potential perpetrators and in favor of potential victims.
5. Occurrence reporting and recording to inform the world community of ongoing genocidal events.
6. Prosecutorial discovery and post-crime forensic mapping.
7. Recovery mapping.

Below is the start of a little taxonomy of indices of vulnerability, danger or murderous intent that we can place under the seven categories suggested above:

1. Longer-term warnings:
   a.) clearly identifiable collective identities, especially linguistic, national, ethnic, religious, and racial;
   b.) high contrast and proximity of collective identities;
   c.) inability of a collective identity or members of a collective identity to defend itself/themselves.
      1.) Improbability of physical escape from the actions of a likely perpetrating entity due to:

A. physical isolation,
B. lack of material wherewithal,
C. existence of legal prohibitions on personal movement,
D. lack of welcoming destinations;

2.) Lack of representation in executive, administra tive, legislative and judicial forums;

3.) Lack of reporting and warning capacity due to:
A. lack of journalist presence,
B. lack of academic presence,
C. lack of technical communications means,
D. existence of legal restrictions imposed on A-C,
E. existence of legal restrictions imposed on communications;

4.) Existence of collective cultural disrespect evi denced as follows:
A. explicit insult in educational materials,
B. explicit insult in governmental documents other than above;

5.) Lack of effective weaponry due to the following:
A. Laws monopolizing or restricting the ownership of weapons,
B. Lack of sufficient wealth for armament,
C. Existence of cultural norms deterring the ownership and use of suitable weaponry;
D. High differentials in tax burdens;
E. General inability to migrate due to the fol lowing [see also 1. c.) 1.), above]:
1.) enforced legal restrictions on migration,
2.) physical barriers to migration,
3.) enforced legal restrictions on immigration to best destinations;
F. Proximity of high value physical geography, including the following
1.) source locations of commercial exportable things,
2.) best routes of movement of commercial exportable things including contraband routes,
3.) chokepoints and nodes in above routes,

4.) properties or terrain with high market value for any other reason;

2. Inventories of potential victim populations (deterrence mapping). Geographers can inventory the following:
   a.) representative (tracking) individuals in victim-likely populations;
   b.) property rights pertaining to victim-likely collective identities and/or pertaining to tracking individuals in those collective identities;
   c.) property rights pertaining to perpetrator-possible identities, both individual and collective;
   d.) cultural signatures of victim-likely collectives;
3. Pre-forensic preparatory mapping in support of prosecutorial discovery after the fact (deterrence mapping and justice support):
   a.) geographic forensics baseline preparations;
   b.) human-caused physical destruction and obstruction;
   c.) mapping of wealth of hate-agents and leaders of perpetrator identities;
4. Mid-term (weeks and months) warning in order to mobilize attention and pressure against potential perpetrators and in favor of potential victims:
   a.) presence of effective hate agents;
   b.) permissive rules of hate speech;
   c.) collective sense of loss, especially national, in a potential perpetrator identity;
   d.) collective sense of impending or threatened loss, especially national, in a potential perpetrator identity;
5. Occurrence reporting and recording:
   a.) mapping communications potential from within a risk geography;
   b.) inventory and mapping of reporting networks;
   c.) fear mapping;
6. Prosecutorial discovery and post-crime forensic mapping:
   a.) geographic forensics;
   b.) mapping areas of evidence destruction and obstruction;
   c.) mapping of wealth of hate-agents and other leaders of potential perpetrator collective identities;
7. Recovery mapping:
   a.) damage mapping of dwelling places;
   b.) defensible terrain mapping;
   c.) logistics mapping for temporary sustainment;
   d.) line of communications damage mapping;
   e.) NGO or government support systems mapping;
   f.) remnant victim-group mapping;
   g.) donor and potential donor inventory and mapping;

h.) cultural symbols damage assessment and mapping;

Occurrence reporting (#5) is often the purview and expertise of journalists, or of government personnel dealing with classified means, so it is only touched on here. As for recovery mapping (#7), that is a question of logistics, humanitarian aid and reconstruction, a function for which there already exist massive datasets, preparations, bureaucracies and even industries. That said, changes in aspects discussed in the other categories may well shape and add to the effectiveness of these functions.

Although there are a number of obvious warning signs that remote technical sensors can provide (villages burning, for instance), cultural geographic knowledge reveals more about potential mass murder. Multidisciplinary geography expeditions could be used to create a fairly continuous presence of outside observers in locales with susceptible populations. Such an enterprise would depend, however, on some system of hotspotting in order to reduce the number of places to be scrutinized. There are maybe 75,000 county-level territorial units in the world, and if only a tenth of one percent of them are potential scenes of mass killings, it means people live at risk of mass murder in 75 counties. If this is indeed a reasonable guess regarding the scale of genocidal danger in the world, it nevertheless implies a need to expose which 75 counties, which implies the building of an organizational engine that can maintain the fielding of considerably more than 75 academic research efforts at a time.

Research on genocide points to authoritarian, radical or dictatorial regimes as a common characteristic correlated to mass killings. A number of national-level regimes exist in which power is highly concentrated in a single ruler or clique, and where peaceful change away from that leadership is unexpected. Liberal regimes that undergo regular peaceful selection and de-selection are relatively unlikely to perpetrate mass killings.

An ongoing armed conflict is logically to be associated with the potential for mass killings. This is evident from killings in Rwanda, Bosnia, Cambodia, the Ottoman Empire, and many others. The logic is self-evident. The potential for a mass killing increases rapidly when undisciplined young men are armed, gain a habit for killing, need to secure a line of communication, do not have ready means to care for prisoners or refugees, feel that a population poses a risk or believe a population gives aid to their enemy, or that a population is guilty of past offense against them. If a logical line of march for an armed contingent passes through a locale, that locale should be a prime candidate for monitoring. Depending on the circumstances, what might have been a massacre can expand into genocide.

Another characteristic worth monitoring is the inability of a potential victim population to escape due to terrain, lack of mass transport, etc. Lack of ready means of communication and expression with the outside world is a logically dangerous condition, especially if combined with others. This is also a phenomenon that is readily detectable and mappable. Those counties in the world that are without Internet service, cellular or older telephone systems may be more vulnerable due to the perception of anonymity that such incommunicado conditions logically create. A world map of counties with the poorest communication to the outside world could be created.

Collective legal impairments can exist for years without there being a mass killing or genocide, but changes in the impairments can be a valuable clues. Changes in legal systems that clearly weaken the power or ability of a potential victim group to protect itself should be considered endangering. If a clearly contrasted collective identity exists within a polity (especially if led by a dictatorial regime) and government leadership does not belong to the potential victim identity, then the occurrence of *newly* prejudicial legal and administrative impositions can mean impending trouble. The following list of impairments is adapted from Raul Hilberg's *The Destruction of the European Jews*.

•Restrictions on professions

•Restrictions on divestment and purchase of real estate

•Special physical or clothing markings

•Special naming conventions

•Marriage and intercourse restrictions

•Off-limits locations or concentrations

•Any form of mandatory migration

•Marking of transactions

•Special taxes

Restrictions on intermarriage and sexual relations are especially significant as in-group/out-group separators. Such restrictions are easily detectable as either a social norm or formal restriction, and may be a condition imposed from within the potential victim identity or by the potential perpetrator. This classic phenomenon is an inspiration for literature, art, and feud, and is also one of the clearest markers of group cohesion and inter-group friction.

Taxation is another item worthy of special note. Few other subjects mark and measure the physical territorial limits and spaces of human conflict, or are able to measure conflict as precisely in time or material as is taxation. Tax differentials, tax anomalies, tax evasions and tax inequities can be detected, described, measured, and mapped. It can be fairly stated that wherever a severe tax inequity is matched to a vulnerable collective human identity, that tax announces potential violence.

Another indicator of potential mass killing is hate language, and especially official hate literature. For instance, in Rwanda *Radio Television Libre des Milles Collines* helped fuel Hutu anger at the Tutsis before the genocide there. Hate literature that appears in schools should be of special concern. If the hate literature appears in texts that are centrally published or are the product of educational literature review boards (as is often the case) the phenomenon can be documented and mapped. At least the addresses of publishers, review boards, or schools have specific physical geographic signatures, and mapping such signatures can have a pronounced effect on one's ability to influence the hate.

Another possible predictor is high contrast in ethnic, racial or linguistic identities. A good deal of ethnographic mapping has already been done in the world, and along with updates to local census data, a worldwide by-county inventory of highly contrasted populations can be made. There have been genocides and other mass killings not associated with highly contrasted linguistic, ethnic or racial identity (Cambodia comes to mind, but even in that event anecdotes suggest that 'educated' speech was a sufficiently contrasting determinant for selection for elimination).

Impunity is a key feature in genocide history. As noted by Benjamin Leiberman (*Terrible Fate: Ethnic Cleansing in the Making of Modern Europe.*), when Nazi Germany expanded into neighboring lands, the newly arrived German overlords did not have to force foreign populations into violent action against Jews. The Germans had only to establish the enabling environment of impunity and its psychological complement of release from ethical dishonor. With those conditions emplaced, many populations willingly and perhaps eagerly set about to destroy their Jewish neighbors. Pre-existing anti-Semitism was a factor. Hitlerian plans called for much more than just the displacement of the Jews, however, although the value of the Jew as a scapegoat was never underappreciated. Hitler's plan for the Reich was such an immense ego-national project that mass murder could be reduced to a mere technical and administrative challenge.

Some of the activities proffered above to predict genocide could actually facilitate genocide. For instance, ID-carding and human inventorying might be used to monitor the protection of a human identity, but it might also be used by a genocidal government to more carefully and completely single-out members of the identity for destruction. In some cases, the very effort to discover, monitor and report could increase danger to an at-risk group.

A debate exists among those peoples with the capacity to stop genocides. One side of the debate (the side less inclined to act) often summarizes its argument as an absence of 'national interests' at stake. The other side of the debate invokes a higher, moral responsibility to act. In this I am going to take sides, but without detouring into much argument. If a nation has the wherewithal *competently* to prevent genocide, it should do so. Genocides, however, are rarely just based on hate. They are never just disasters or spontaneous combustions, either. They are politically motivated, and so any response designed only to stop immediate killing is probably only going to be temporarily effective. The political structure that emboldens and empowers groups to commit murder with impunity has to be changed. The *mens rea* of genocide has to be located and nullified.

The *Convention on the Prevention and Punishment of the Crime of Genocide*, adopted by the United Nations General Assembly in 1948 (combined with the Security Council Resolution of 1674 of 2006) offers an international legal path to override formal State sovereignty and legitimize foreign intervention into lands whose States appear guilty. The existence of this line of formal international law presupposes its eventual use.

*See: 109, Hotspotting; 48, Grading the Social Contract; 78, Personal Identity; 66, GIS; 108, Neogeography*; 49, *Territorial Scrutiny*; 40, *Rule-of-law*; and 52, *Sovereignty*.

---

> "The territorial imperative is as blind as a cave fish, as consuming as a furnace, and it commands beyond logic, opposes all reason, suborns all moralities, strives for no goal more sublime than survival."
>
> Robert Ardrey,
> *Territorial Imperative*[156]

The true measure of security?

# *Section 106, Tourism*

Tourism locations, patterns and rates provide one of the most significant measures of human security, especially if we expand the idea of tourism to include recreation and entertainment. If people are willing to vote with their feet and wallets to be someplace other than their home because to do so is pleasurable, it says a lot about a place. In addition, data for tourism and recreation is relatively easy to find, establish and maintain.

Recreation and tourist sites can include anything from religious pilgrimage destinations to neighborhood swimming pools. The point is that people make voluntary decisions to be someplace, and people don't keep going to places that are too unsafe, expensive or not pleasurable in some way.

Tourism and recreation geographies include the destinations and the routes to and from them. The geography of tourism can be organized along common scales according to tourist origins and administrative peculiarities. For instance, international tourists need to obtain passports and visas, exchange money and make travel and destination bookings through travel agents. Local recreational sites have other fiscal and territorial features. In every case it is possible to create a baseline of destinations, origins, and visits, and maybe amounts of money spent.

Tourism and recreation measurements (such as the number of miles traveled, by how many people, and down what roads or to what ports) can provide a publicly accessible and geographically clear appreciation of the progress of an internal armed conflict.

As a measure of progress in providing human security, there are few things that a government can do that are more innocuous (even helpful) than the careful calculation and transparent presentation of tourism and recreation data. Tourism industries, their expansion and success, are heavily dependent on the built environment. Tourism is cosmopolitan and urban, even when it is nature or eco-touring. As such, there are few things more subject to planning, or more subject to the market. A tourism plan has to be a business plan.

An insurgent group may wish to create a psychology of insecurity, or follow a counter-economy strategy in which tourism and recreation are targets. Measuring tourism is then all the more instructive, and its presentation may have the added benefit of exposing destructive extortion strategies.

See: 70, *Measuring Effect of Actions on Structure*; 68, *Scale*; 107, *Price of Real Estate*; 53, *Hohfeldian Grievance Analysis*; 47, *Why the County*; 80, *Why You Should Like Geography*; 2, *Anonymity*; and 107, *Price of Real Estate.*

---

**Guard at Walleyworld:** That's not a real gun, is it Clark?

**Clark Griswald**: Are you kidding? This is a Magnum P.I.

**Guard**: It's a BB gun.

**Clark**: Don't tempt me. I could put an eye out with this thing.

**Guard**: You couldn't even break the skin with that thing.

From the movie
*Vacation* (1983)[157]

The price of real estate traces key terrain

# *Section 107, Price of Real Estate*

There are several connections that tie the price of real estate to winning an insurgent war, especially if the conflict is widespread.

**Key terrain is key terrain.** Military people are used to the idea of key terrain and what makes the terrain so key, or at least so they think. What terrain is most important in an irregular conflict may have little to do with cover from weapons fire, and everything to do with the marketplace. People tend to fight over the places of greatest value in relation to material wellbeing, and while some places may have great emotional value, and others may have purely military value, a good way to detail variation in value over a broad area is to encourage and allow a market in real estate to operate, and to create mechanisms that reflect the price decisions of that market.

**Measuring Success**. Regardless of what else might be used to measure operational success in an insurgency or counterinsurgency, some success over time will manifest itself in an improved overall value of the real estate. For an organized crime boss, the overall value of *his* real estate is a pretty good measure of *his* success.

**Find extortions, corruptions and money laundering.** Abrupt changes in market prices bespeak all these things, but if the market is invisible, so too are these activities. Make the market for real estate both vibrant and transparent, and by so doing, many activities and places will be vaccinated against violent illegalities.

**Pay for the conflict.** There is often a spatial logic between where the costs of conflict fall and who owns land and other valuable things. Find out what the spatial logic is and propose that the persons causing or benefiting from the placement of the costs of the conflict are those burdened.

**Real estate people know everything.** If there is a real estate market, there is someone who will set himself up as an agent for sale and purchase. To be an effective agent for the exchange of something valuable, the agent needs to know about the thing being sold and about both buyer and seller and about the environment. Few people know more about the details of value in a community than do real estate brokers and appraisers.

**Property is the foundation of conflict resolution.** Property statutes, courts and processes lie at the heart of day-to-day conflict resolution, but much of the content of arguments over real estate have to do with the real estate's value. Where there is no market to establish value, there is only the argument.

**Help those who help you.** Land strategies can work, but they should not be attempted in the absence of knowledge about what places are really valuable and which places aren't.

If you fancy yourself as a planner or leader in irregular war and you have little clue about the market value of land in the operational area, you'll want to change that. If other people are around who are acutely aware of the market value of real estate, they almost certainly know more than you do about what's going on in that place.

Look for cadastral records. Cadastral records are usually tied to a land taxation system that is based on value appraisals done by a government or by certified professionals, and the appraisal values are generally tied by formula to an anticipated market value or to a theory of tax equity. If the cadastral system is broken, fix it. If there is no cadastral system, maybe create one. Societies do exist where literacy is the exception; resolution of land conflicts follows patterns of familial seniority or ancient feudalism-like inheritance; evidence is oral; debts are paid entirely in kind; and there are few public records. Such places are rare. They are themselves not likely to be the source grounds of much danger to the world. To the extent they become so, due perhaps to foreign presence, the creation of formal records can still proceed if it can be shown, especially to those who make decisions regarding occupancy of land, that a material and social benefit will accrue from the records.

See: 73, *Property and the Social Contract*; 64, *Measuring Power*; 81, *What a Clergy Wants*; 72, *Land Strategy*; 69, *Measuring Actions against Enemies*; 40, *Water Wars*; 85, *Ploesti & Putumayo*; and 92, *Land-use Planning.*

---

"Out of the land we came and into it we must go
- if you will hold your land you can live - no one can rob you of land –
if you sell the land, it is the end."

Wang Lung in Pearl S. Buck,
*The Good Earth*[158]

Tai Shan is a great mountain

# *Section 108, Neogeography*

The word *neogeography* is not as new as it sounds, but for the past few years, the cell-phone-with-embedded-camera-and-GPS has spurred mass collaboration of non-expert participants in knowledge collection and transmission. The life and impact of this collaboration and its impact on public knowledge depend on a mix of personal liberties, continued distribution of the devices, creation of forums (like Google Earth®, Twitter® and YouTube®) and a vast array of GIS machines and wiring. It also depends on the absence of high-end investment (notably by governments) to suppress it.

A couple of decades ago, law enforcement agencies in the United States experienced an abrupt increase in accident and crime reporting from the general public that coincided with the explosion in cell phone ownership. The cell phone phenomenon is highlighted here not because they can be converted into deadly bombs or into listening devices, but because they are a base technology that allows broad public participatory exposure of movements, ideas and networks. They also leave a trace. The fellow who allegedly tried to blow up Times Square in 2010 left a cell phone trail from the family that sold him the vehicle he used. Notably, cell phones have empowered publics to hold police more accountable for their behavior as well.

A technology is not just the gizmo itself, but also includes the relationship of the gizmo to people and how the gizmo changes relationships among people. I like to think Stephen Wozniak and Steve Jobs took down the Soviet Union. The Soviets could steal their design of the Apple II® computer, copy it, make some poor quality production runs, and even decide to distribute thousands of them, but they could never have the technology, because it just couldn't be had by Soviet Russia. The personal computer is a piece of property. That is, the box of wiring is tied to a liberal social contract, a basket of recognized rights and duties, which allows ideas to be exchanged from one possibly anonymous inventive head to another. Without the social contract, the personal computer 'technology' doesn't exist. In a society with a social contract that is untrusting, things like desktop publishing cannot really flourish -- the personal computer cannot actually exist. The Soviets got a taste of it, though, knew it was out there and knew their social contract spoiled it. So, at the dawn of the Internet, the Soviet dialectic locomotive went off history's tracks. There is admittedly a bit more to the story of the Soviet collapse. Ronald Reagan, for instance, told them they were the empire of the *mens rea*, and that helped, but give Wozniak and Jobs their due.

The same observation about technology applies to less electronically advanced places and less exotic things. Even a simple water well can disrupt existing social relationships in a remote village. It can create new patterns of movement and distribution of wealth. Here, however, the observation about technology-beyond-the-thing concerns a trend toward mass participation in providing public knowledge, including about violent conflict. The 'technology' might be mistaken as a small electronic gizmo.

Whether or not this movement of electronically-armed crowds constitutes an insurgent or counterinsurgent advantage depends on far more than the gizmos. Like physical terrain, the leader who understands and exploits the potential will gain the advantage. *Crowdsourcing* is another current term for the phenomenon, and especially for efforts to encourage, orient or corral public participation in creating geographic knowledge.

There is a lot in this book that might seem old-school troglodytic. Praise for a Victorian strategist's military geography, for instance, or assertions about the continuing power of mule handlers and bulldozers. Still, the quip that 'nothing is new under the sun' is not welcome here. No one claiming leadership in the conflicts of this century will succeed on a sincere claim of being Luddite. Innovation helps win wars, and even simply noting and applying old innovations can help win.

In the context of recent conflicts comes the story of the avocational descendants of British bird watchers/train watchers began recording aircraft tail numbers. The tail watchers were able to trace aircraft they suspected were being used for rendition flights carrying captured terrorism suspects. That was a few years ago. Now huge followings of participating tourists upload tens of thousands of images to the Internet and map whole cities in ill-matched and patchy detail. The fearful will highlight crowdsourcing's lack of discipline, consistency and quality control -- and ease of falsification. Valid worries, but for the optimistic the trend promises a massive and revealing new body and way of knowledge.

Neogeography is part of the particularization of power. Individuals participate of their own volition in the production of public knowledge to the extent of their ability to travel, click and access the Internet. If anonymity can be preserved in the individual's use of the Internet, neogeography will deliver new and extensive knowledge about distant places and subjects. Neogeograhy, crowdsourcing, or whatever name survives, is a milestone in the history of technological applications related directly to transparency. The Internet and cell phone, like paper and ink before them, improve the functioning of the liberal social contract, and are, meanwhile, dependent on individual liberty.

See: 110, *Knowledge Gaps*; 111, *Knowledge Cultures*; 80, *Why You Should Like Geography*; 49, *Territorial Scrutiny*; 125, *Human Rights*; 27, *Democracy*; 139, *UAAV*; and 105, *Genocide Geography*.

---

Tai Shan is a great mountain because
it does not scorn the merest handful of dirt.

Chinese proverb

# *Section 109, Hotspotting*

Momma says the secret to good cooking is to serve the food late. Daddy says the secret to winning fights is to pick weaker opponents. This section is about a national-level, or global-level plan to determine what places are likely to suffer events or conditions that anyone else will care enough about to send money, weapons, munitions or especially armed men. It is a public participation method intended to challenge, speed and test the hotspotting efforts of the various national intelligence communities.

Each geography and each conflict is different, so having a better method to predict likely places and contestants makes sense. To win at counterinsurgency, it is a good idea to start early and win fast, if that can be accomplished. If you are an insurgent, you don't need a hotspotting engine; you are already there.

We can use expert opinion to create a simple spreadsheet and a related set of maps to express corporate opinion regarding likely global hotspots, but we can, in the process, retain individual estimates. Results can be compared according to a variety of inputs or participant categories, thus allowing judgments from outside government to be compared to government predictions.

**Definition of Hotspot**: A location where events or conditions are of such concern to a foreign country that the foreign country acts to change them.

Obeying the above definition, selected participants will be asked to identify six degrees of hotspot as follows:

> Degree 5. **Major military deployment** – a foreign country deploys significant military forces expecting they are to use all weapons at their disposal (short of nuclear) to accomplish some objective of the state, and the deployment is expected to last for more than a month. We can call this a Projection Deployment.
>
> Degree 4. **Prolonged military commitment** – a foreign country deploys military assets, expecting to use lethal weapons, but their use is greatly proscribed by their law, and the duration of the military commitment is indefinite. We can call this a Binding Deployment.
>
> Degree 3. **Rapid military application** – a foreign country sends a clearly military asset, which includes lethal force

potential, but the initiative is not expected to last more than a week. We can call this a Prompt Deployment.

Degree 2. **Nonmilitary commitment** -- a foreign country will take actions that include movement to the area of people or things (that could include military units or personnel), but no lethal force is expected to be used except incidentally to the accomplishment of what would be considered generally a non-violent objective. We can call this a Humanitarian Deployment.

Degree 1. **Nonviolent expression** – a foreign country takes an action, perhaps economic, diplomatic, or informational, but the action does not involve a movement of human or physical assets to the area except in the most minor sense (a visit of an ambassador or the sending of a letter).

Degree 0. **Unworthy** -- A zero rating or status means that whatever events or conditions might be likely to occur in a place, no foreign government sees them as worthy of a response.

Not coded **Null** -- A null or non-coded territory means the predictor did not address conditions or events in the place.

In addition to marking places according to the degrees of hotness above, each expert will also be asked to indicate the likelihood of the action happening during a time window two-to-seven years into the future. The experts will be given two levels of likelihood from which to choose:

A. Probably will happen
B. Possibly will happen

The higher levels of likelihood generated by composite maps will be reflected in a 3-D effect on the map image.

With the participant inputs we can create an interactive world map on which degrees of 'hotness' of likely hotspots will be displayed in numeric and color-coded style, along with a 3-D effect to express varying likelihood. It will be possible for the site visitor to create map images reflecting the inputs of any combinations of forecasters, with an option of several pre-designated and automatically updated images of the globe as follows:

– Government opinions created using input from those participants opining from inside-government military/security institutions;
– Non-government opinions created by the set of outside expert forecasters, and;
– A composite of the above.
(It will also be possible for the site visitor to view head-to-head comparisons of the predictive map images.)

The site would invite further voluntary participation on two levels: by petition and qualification on the basis of the submission of curriculum vitae, and as part of an open-to-all public participation.

Nonparticipant visitors to the website would be able to see the map images created by the project, and be able to manipulate the data to create map images using single-contributor data or any combinations of contributions as they wish. Results can be displayed on a continuous basis for each group as well as combined estimates.

Participant forecasters will be able to change their estimates, analyses and predictions whenever they wish, any time of the day, any day of the year. Nevertheless, they will not be able to erase their previous predictions, so that a history of their predictions remains available for comparisons. The idea is not just to hotspot, but to measure and test the hotspotting continuously. The best forecasters will eventually emerge from the evolving data set.

Some area and subject experts can be invited to participate, perhaps even paid, on the basis of their demonstrated regional knowledge. They, like all the participants, would code as many places as they wish in accordance with their own opinion of their own competence to do so. Like everyone else, however, their predictions would remain in the dataset to establish the effect of their expertise on their ability to forecast. Each participant will be given the opportunity to opine as to whether a given deployment or other foreign intervention is a good idea or not.

A 'country,' for the purposes of the hotspotting engine, would be any of the geographic areas listed by the CIA's World Factbook, but the geographic territories about which the participants will be asked to make a forecast would be the county or its foreign equivalent such as the Latin American *municipio* or the Philippine *bayan.* The hotspotting engine, in other words, would code and build comparative images at the level of the county, not the country.

Participants designated as experts would be asked to place their curriculum vitae online, since the credibility of their estimates would rest on the level of their expertise as publicly recognized, rather than on their predictive history, at least until the latter is established by the engine.

Participants would be asked to limit their prognostications to within a time-period running from two years into the future to seven years into the future. That is to say, all predictions would be limited to a five-year period running from two years and ending at seven years after the day of their making a prediction. Every time a participant updated or changed their predictions, the window would move forward accordingly.

Chosen experts would be asked to read and consider a set of factors. They could use the factors or not, or they could use any other factor they think appropriate. They would, however, be invited to explain their predictive ratings and would also be led via the site's input mechanics to a brief taxonomy of potential events and conditions. The experts would be asked to click on elements within the taxonomy, thus giving a rudimentary dataset for comparing reasoning and in order to create data images of hotspot cause/hypotheses (i.e. religious intolerance, corrupt administration, messianic populism, resource taxation, …)

Participants invited due to their recognized knowledge would be invited to read and comment on a list of hypothetical conflict causes, such as the fourteen items (e.g. 'a' through 'n,' listed below.) They will be asked to comment on the list, and will be instructed that they may use the list, reject it, or change it as they wish. The list would not be made permanent and would be reviewed and changed now and then if it appeared appropriate to website owners.

Following are some initial suppositions that might be offered to the participants regarding phenomena likely to lead to foreign intervention. The participants could adopt or reject them as they wished:

a. Being a significant net exporter of energy seems to imply a slight increase in the likelihood of attracting intervention;

b. Lack of commitment of current leadership to electoral democracy might make a place slightly more likely to suffer a foreign intervention;

c. Informality of property ownership in a place can increase the likelihood of internal conflict and perhaps slightly increase the likelihood of foreign intervention;

d. Presence of an illegal armed group with international reach might increase the likelihood of attracting foreign action;

e. Existence of a relatively powerful defending government military may decrease the likelihood of some forms of foreign action;

f. The presence of usual-suspect radicals, like armed Islamic radicals, might slightly increase the likelihood of foreign government action;

g. Some places likelihood of being the target of foreign action are tied to the particulars of specific treaties;

h. An attempt to change control of some key global commerce chokepoint might increases the likelihood of some foreign government action;

i. The presence of a large ethnic or nationalist lobby or voting group in a foreign country could increase the likelihood of a foreign government action;

j. If a country appears likely to gain WMD capability, or significantly increase the power of a WMD arsenal, this might increase the likelihood of foreign government action;

k. Current presence of a foreign military, paramilitary or civic action unit might increase the likelihood that there would be a foreign intervention;

l. Clear vulnerability to and history of natural disasters may indicate a higher likelihood of attracting foreign intervention;

m. Presence or evidence of natural resource reserves can invite intervention;

n. Presence of active, undeterred cells of computer criminals or even genetic experimenters could invite intervention.

Participants would be asked to indicate *what* foreign government might act, as well as what persons, entities or conditions might oppose or assist the intervention.

Some of the parameters of the data collection would be fixed – such as the geographic scale, the timescale, and a scale of definitions for the size and type of interventions pondered (in order to allow data comparison and communicate the logic) – but a great deal of freedom would be offered to participants. Based on their view of things, anything could be reason enough for predicting a foreign intervention into some land. After a while, the predictive capacity of their logic, or the aggregated logic of a given group, would display itself. If it turned out that a group of third-graders were better at forecasting spots where armed conflicts, disasters or some other phenomena were likely to lead to foreign presence, then the engine would be able to show that predictive advantage – and a number of governments could save money by switching analysts. Such an engine would be able to show publics if officials in charge of identifying the right phenomena and doing logical forecasting were earning their keep.

Sufficient clues in locales around the world indicate where peace is possible and where it is unlikely. The engine proposed in this section would be an efficient way to color code the world according to the likelihood that a given locale will experience the presence of a foreign force. To decide if a locale has a social contract that is likely to lead to human flourishing, I suggest the more direct method in *Grading The Social Contract*, but to do that kind of careful description of foreign locales would take a field research program involving people who know how to do field work, can speak local languages, understand and can organize participatory research, grasp the principles of property and land ownership, and are willing to travel.

Few pieces of advice on how to win are more obvious than to choose the right places to go. Current processes and methods for determining the right and wrong places are not good enough. Furthermore, few systems exist for determining who makes the best predictions and analyses over time.

See: 20, *Foreign Support*; 49, *Territorial Scrutiny*; 63, *Cost-Distance*; 68, *Scale*; 25, *Why Humans Don't Fight*; 105, *Genocide Geography*; 48, *Grading the Social Contract*; and 120, *Turducken.*

---

> "You come here with your laptop computers, your malaria medicine and your little bottles of hand sanitizer and think you can change the outcome, huh?"
>
> Danny Archer in the movie
> *Blood Diamond* (2006)[159]

Testing ignorance, begging exploration

# Section 110, Knowledge Gaps

How do you know if you know enough to win, especially about a foreign place? What you don't know can be framed by the following question: Can an ignorant (not dumb, just unknowledgeable) staff person who finds him or herself planning a counterinsurgent, stability, humanitarian or insurgent operation to a foreign land find the requisite knowledge fast enough? If the requisite knowledge is not contained in some easily retrievable dataset familiar to that person -- that is to say, at their keyboard fingertips (public search engines count), in the head of someone in the same building, or someone who can be readily called or emailed, then you can presume that the institution is ignorant, and its effectiveness doubtful. We'll get to what the requisite knowledge is below.

It is hard to say just what the *time-to-knowledge* standard should be: it can't be so much as to harmfully delay or misdirect the planning process. Let's say for argument's sake that a *time-to-knowledge* standard of fifteen minutes initial investment on the part of the staff officer and no more than a 48-hour wait for a key set of facts is acceptable. We're going to use the test subject to see if we (our institution represented in this case by some smart but ignorant researcher) know enough about a foreign place so that we won't make so many mistakes at the beginning of an operation that we can't recover from them.

This section offers a way to test relevant ignorance. It is specifically not about the kind of information sought and processed by secret intelligence agencies in relation to conventional warfare and international confrontations. In other words, this comment is not about knowledge gained by a remote sensor, or that would be the normal purview of spies. That secret knowledge is valuable, but all of the knowledge contemplated by this section is public. Some of that other, secret knowledge might be extremely useful. I'm just not talking about it here.

The process of ignorance testing includes making a map (GIS-based, of course) that shows the world in counties and displays relative ignorance about those counties based on our test subjects' ability to answer a representative set of questions about them. The questions are tracking items -- questions considered *representative* of the kinds of knowledge necessary in order to succeed in operations. The list of questions is not really a list of the most needed things to know about a specific county, or a comprehensive list of what knowledge to seek. *It is not a requirements list.*

Since each place and every mission is unique, there exist thousands of questions that can and should be answered about a given place. Inability of our people to timely answer the tracking questions, however, will warn us of an institutional knowledge gap. You can take the test yourself. Inability to answer the questions is the indicator that tells you your institution doesn't know enough about a particular place. It is not that the questions on the test are the things you have to know, but rather that if you're ignorant of these things, you're probably also ignorant about whatever it is you do need to know.

You will do well to use the county (county, not country) as the level of geographic, territorial resolution for your test, but it could be a higher resolution, like the township. Almost every country in the world has some territorial unit similar in scale to the county.

From a base map of a country of interest (showing counties), pick a county for the test. Choose one that might be of future security interest, then give the name and location to your test subject. Ask him or her to answer all twenty-two of the following questions as soon as he or she can, and note how long it takes to get a good answer. You might want to know the right answers in advance. That might make grading the test a little easier, but it is not necessary.

1. What is the most visited tourist attraction in the county?
2. What families own the most valuable real estate in the county?
3. What is the name and contact information for a person we know and is willing to help us who can speak the language dominant in the county?
4. What three regular open-air public events draw the most attendance in the county?
5. On what day of the year is a thirty-year-old man most likely to visit his mother if she lives in the county (other than her birthday)?
6. Where is the nearest jail that houses more than fifty prisoners?
7. What is the address and location of a morgue in the county?

8. What is the name and contact information for a person willing to help us, who has stood in the county and who personally knows three persons who live in the county?

9. What are the words to the most common three prayers said in the county?

10. What is the second most popular flag design in the county?

11. What is the second most smuggled thing that goes to, through or from the county?

12. What two health issues would a twelve-year-old boy most likely to suffer from in the county?

13. What are the most accessed information media in the county?

14. What is the price of an egg in the county?

15. What is the common distance, for a person of modal income in the county, between that person's kitchen and the nearest source of potable water?

16. What groups or individuals are most likely to be the butt of jokes in the county?

17. What does a man living in the northeastern quadrant of the county use to wipe himself after evacuating his bowels?

18. Where and when is a group of six housewives likely to meet, other than at church?

19. Where would a 22-year-old unmarried male resident go to have sex?

20. What is the most common nickname for a pistol in the county?

21. To whom is a forty year-old man with a family likely to owe a financial debt or tax?

22. Exactly how many motorcycles are ridden in the county?

If you had the time and money to repeat this test over and over, pretty soon you could make a map showing all the counties of which you're effectively ignorant. More than likely you'll find out that you don't need to invest much time or money in the ignorance audit. Your institution probably can answer only a very few of the questions for very few counties anywhere. If you're an insurgent, you or your friends live there, so you not only know the answers to the tracking questions, you know the people who have organized around related grievances.

For any counties you, incredibly, seem to know well, you might zoom the test down further to the level of townships. Next you might physically go or send someone to a township or two just to review that the answers were right. (This means it would be smart for you to pick touristically sweet foreign places for the test. After all, except for a few very places in the world, your institution is equally as ignorant of the nice places as it is of the not-so-nice-places. So if there is any tourist attraction of merit, at least you'll be able to stay in a nice hotel.)

If your test subjects can answer the bulk of the twenty-two questions well and quickly, that's good. The tracking questions, however, are mostly geographic inventory questions. They don't go right at social conflicts -- to the interrelationships, grievances, agents, objects of desire. An idea for that kind of analysis is covered in Section 53, *Hohfeldian Grievance Analysis*. This section assumes that you should not put faith in an analysis of conflict done by a person or office that can't answer the most basic geographic inventory questions.

Don't worry about the test subject or institution getting your list in advance and cheating the test. There are thousands of counties out there. If your test subjects were to build some system that let them quickly derive answers about whatever county you throw at them, you're in great shape. But they won't.

The above text downplays the substantive importance of the individual questions a bit. They were selected to be representative and not specific, but answers to most of them would be operationally useful for many locales. As your ignorance map of foreign counties gets filled in, it can be correlated directly to GIS maps of counties deemed of strategic importance, or of counties that have been spotted as potential foci of human conflict.

See: 66, *GIS;* 49, *Territorial Scrutiny*; 47, *Why the County*; 109, *Hotspotting*; 112, *DIME and PEMISI*; 38, *Cultural Knowledge for What?*; 92, *Land Use Planning*; and 53, *Hohfeldian Grievance Analysis.*

---

> "My mind is a raging torrent, flooded with rivulets of thought cascading into a waterfall of creative alternatives."
>
> Hedley Lamarr in the movie
> *Blazing Saddles*[160]

# *Section 111, Knowledge Cultures*

The kinds of information that people seek, the way they sort through and arrange it, and the way they present findings and opinions are all subject to big cultural and small institutional habits, rivalries and historical divergences. Limitations in knowledge cultures can get in the way of your winning, and breaking out of those cultural constraints might help you win. This topic could drag on forever, so in this section are just a few cherry-picked items you might be able to use to inspect the agility of your personal and your organization's thinking about your irregular war.

A 2010 paper titled *Fixing Intelligence* from the Center for a New American Security starts with the unfortunate sentence, "Eight years into the war in Afghanistan, the US intelligence community is only marginally relevant to our overall strategy."[161] There are reasons why this might be true, as well as a few fixable habits, that are mentioned further below.

**Secret versus not secret**. Because some forms of secret intelligence are so valuable and powerful, everything that can earn a secret label takes on a degree of respect, even while the document marked as secret may be worthless or doesn't need to be so marked. Along with secret-labeled documents come levels of access and exclusive geographies -- rooms, buildings and bandwidth that are for 'cleared' persons only. The abbreviation OSINT stands for Open Source Intelligence, and for a while was a rallying cry for making available more of the vast body of world knowledge onto which nobody had yet stuck a secrecy label. OSINT ultimately became almost synonymous with having secrecy-accredited analysts going onto the open Internet to find information. Today, decades after recognition of the Internet and GIS knowledge revolutions, the formal, unclassified knowledge function supporting the United States military remains in its infancy.

**Government versus academe**. When the big American intelligence organizations were born in the late 1940s, line and block diagrams (organizational charts) with thousands of government positions were created, most requiring some kind of secrecy accreditation. The result was a distancing of American scholars from government knowledge spaces, conversations, decisions, and consequently and worst of all, trust.

**Organigrams versus ideas**. Inside government buildings, knowledge is often constrained by organizational format -- pay and supervision hierarchies, budget flows, and room designs. Maddening or hilarious compartmentalization occurs that leaves holes in the known world. For instance, some years ago it was decided that the Department of Defense would take the lead in fighting illicit drugs. It seemed logical to give the cocaine knowledge portfolio to a team focused on Colombia. The heroin problem went to some Central Asia experts, since that is where most of the world's heroin was grown. Since none of the Central Asia experts spoke Spanish, however, they all but ignored Colombian heroin (at the time satisfying maybe much of the US demand). Complete knowledge about the heroin trade going to the US stumbled for a couple of years because of the line and block diagram. The line and block diagram, with its compartments and hierarchical levels of authority, is very useful for organizing military units. It is not so good for organizing knowledge, but because the organizational culture given to 'intelligence' was a military inheritance, the American government knowledge community got a model that has caused some thought problems.

**Personal loyalty versus intellectual conviction**. This imposition of military organizational design on knowledge processing has secondary effects. For instance, it is traditional military ethos that subordinates support the decisions of military leaders in the hierarchical structure -- the chain of command. It is an ethic that many of us deem noble and necessary. That sense of 'getting behind the decision,' can become a loyalty test expected not just for decisions, but for analyses. This can be an unfortunate ethos for a knowledge organization, especially when the best knowledge may have little correlation to administrative rank.

**Strategic versus operational**. This book mentions a few higher level strategy questions, but it is mostly about movement and placement on the battlefield, identifying and getting close to an enemy so that he can be dispatched, and doing so without creating more enemies.

The gold standard of knowledge for such 'operational art' matters might be something like placing a sniper at a safe shooting distance from a dangerous enemy leader at the moment when that enemy is relieving himself. The gold standard for most intelligence analysts working on what is called 'strategic intelligence' is to have a comment of theirs placed in a briefing folder that a very senior leader might read. This divergence of knowledge glories drags a lot of mental resources away from operational art as understood in this book and toward an expansive frame of subjects and satisfactions that, while often of the highest importance, are often irrelevant or even frivolous. Many points can be gained for a strategic analyst who has made a well-argued prediction regarding an upcoming foreign presidential election. It is not useless effort, but is the kind of thing that absorbs hundreds of work hours even though a wait of a few days will give the definitive answer without any analysis at all. To win at irregular wars, more glory needs to be given to those who derive knowledge tied to operational equations -- to what Maguire offered as aid to understanding the essence of strategy – meaning classic military strategy. To be fair, in the American case, providing the knowledge to kill a top leader of Al Qaeda does not go unappreciated.

**Post-structuralist versus others**. A current fashion in academe favors a freestyle sorting of underdogs and overdogs, the former being good and the latter bad. Assignment of who or what is on the overdog or underdog sides of the knowledge virtue ledger is a constantly changing mix of coded reaffirmations. According to what appears to be mainstream academe, the words *worker*, *resistance*, *anti-globalist*, and *progressive* fall on one side, and *neoliberal*, *colonialist*, *realist*, or *positivist* fall on the other. In a current fashion of social sciences, thinking must be politically competitive if it is to be recognized as scholarly, and research is only ethical if done in service to one side of that competition, the *progressive* side. This competitive reordering of academic life is having a deleterious effect on the production of knowledge in general. Although by no means universal, the tendency in academic circles has been to reject the whole notion of objectivity in favor of competitive intent, a moral infusion that is often no more clearly expressed than as resistance to injustice.

The cultures of academe are subdivided into 'disciplines' but the disciplines and discipline clusters vary country to country. Below is a three column chart with four academic disciplines in each column.

| | | |
|---|---|---|
| Medicine | Mathematics | Philosophy |
| Law | Geography | Sociology |
| Engineering | History | Anthropology |
| Accounting | Biology | Theatre |

It is unfair to use the above selection as a representative sample of the whole universe of disciplines, and it is a shame to leave out what are some of the most useful, like languages, geology, physics, etc. But that doesn't matter, because the chart is only intended here to help make a single criticism, in this case directed at the US Army. The criticism is as follows: Throughout history and across all continents, armies have given special insignia, extra pay, and designated whole corps in accordance with the disciplines listed in the left-hand column. That is because they are so necessary for the efficient and effective conduct of military operations. Those disciplines are in turn obsessed with the disciplines in the middle column, because the middle column disciplines are the food groups for the meals the disciplines in the left-hand column are paid to prepare.

Each academic discipline has its own habits, methods, vocabulary and ethic. Like the various professions that spring from them, they have their own cultures. The disciplines on the left-hand side of the above chart are generally more 'empirical' than those on the right, but those on the left also admire those on the far-right, knowing that all knowledge is grist to their mills. A doctor and his lawyer wife might go out to the theater, enjoy it immensely and learn something useful and enlightening. They would be better off not to suppose that going to the theatre is a substitute for continuing professional education in their disciplines. That, however, is what the United States Army may be doing in its relationship to the various disciplines in American academe. In its approach to insurgent war, army education has been dissipating with the disciplines on the right-hand side of the chart, perhaps failing to keep up with those toward the left. They are all valuable, but some are more valuable than others for winning.

Below is an incomplete list of institutional knowledge sub-cultures, with descriptions of what may distinguish them in terms of how they approach knowledge of armed groups and armed conflict:

**Military**. Military intelligence is based on requirements, collection plans and templates. Intelligence people the world over are enamored of a thing called the Intelligence Cycle, which most of them think is an actual thing spewed full blown from the head of Bismarck, but that actually was invented sometime in the early 20th century as a simplified scientific method that the military might follow. It has many versions, usually depicted in the shape of a wheel turning clockwise and including planning, collecting, processing, and dissemination. It often has other ingredients and flourishes like 'feedback' and 'operational security.' The problem of operational security indeed distinguishes the military knowledge method from academic in that secrecy tends to reduce the feedback. Unlike police work, the military mind usually focuses on a 'unit' rather than an individual, is not interested in proving guilt, and is usually forward-looking in time from the occurrence of events, rather than backward. The military habit does not look to explain why an event happened as much as where the next event will take place.

**Police**. Police seek and follow clues, collect evidence, pursue suspects and help prosecutors build cases. They mostly look backwards in time from the commission of a criminal event. That is not to say they don't try to anticipate a suspect's next moves or try to figure out where he will be, but their investigative time-frame is more about what happened than what is going to happen.

**Business**. Businessmen look for markets, costs, products and prices. They keep accounts, and measure the success of the knowledge process in profit.

**Medicine**. Doctors diagnose from the presence and absence of symptoms. They seek cures. They seek clusters of medical events and try to correlate the clusters to other things, like vectors or habits. They make and keep 'records' and individual histories. Most doctors work at the scale of the individual human body, although there are some that are interested in epidemiological facts. They measure the success of the knowledge process in cures.

**Law**. Lawyers leverage theories about motivations against facts, statutes, cases, and foibles. They like to write briefs and cross-examine witnesses. Their work is constrained by jurisdictions and court dates. How they measure success of the knowledge process depends on the lawyer, but may be in dollars, victories, settlements, convictions, and so on. Legal professional ethic rests on privileged and protected communications with clients, and on a duty to represent aggressively.

**Sports Betting**. Bookies like to find or create environments in which the outcomes they expect are a little more likely than the outcomes other people expect. They depend on the perception of random chance, on someone else's undeserved arrogance regarding the future, and on insider knowledge.

**Espionage**. Spies look for secrets, so they look in hiding places and try to endear themselves to people with special knowledge. They lie. They send code.

**Greek Math**. All dead Greeks knew syllogisms; all Greeks eat souflaki; therefore souflaki killed logic. OK, that's not a valid syllogism, but there are a number of classical rules for sorting truths from non-truths, and a larger number of logical fallacies that are often used purposefully to deceive.

**Academe**. Many scholars still form testable hypotheses and worry over induction, deduction, interpolation, extrapolation, replicability, and terms like epistemology. Many, especially in the social sciences, don't bother with any of that.

Your efforts to know more about your war will be better served if you do not put too many chips on any one of these knowledge culture-baskets, or reject any out-of-hand. A multidiscipline, multi-institutional, multi-profession approach is best. At the heart of your insurgent war analyses, however, put history, geography, engineering and law.

From the preface of George Wells' *World Brain*:

> "Man reflects before he acts, but not very much; he is still by nature intellectually impatient. No sooner does he apprehend, in whole or in part, the need of a new world, than, without further plans or estimates, he gets into a state of passionate aggressiveness and suspicion and sets about trying to change the present order. There and then, he sets about it, with anything that comes handy, violently, disastrously, making the discordances worse instead of better, and quarrelling bitterly with anyone who is not in complete accordance with his particular spasmodic conception of the change needful. He is unable to realize that when the time comes to act, that also is the time to think fast and hard. He will not think enough."

So, according to Wells, you're pretty much ruined, regardless. He's wrong. Fortunately, you are competing against other men. You don't have to be faster than Wells' bear, just faster than the other guy, the bad guy, who lives in the exact same geography you do.

See: 68, *Scale*; 38, *Cultural Study for What?*; 48, *Grading the Social Contract*; 26, *How Violent Groups Form*; 106, *Tourism*; 36, *Engineers*; 1, *What the Pirate Said to Alexander*; and 48, *Grading the Social Contract.*

---

> "I don't care much for facts, am not much interested in them, you can't stand a fact up, you've got to prop it up, and when you move to one side a little and look at it from that angle, it's not thick enough to cast a shadow in that direction."
>
> William Faulkner [162]

It matters how ideas are organized

# *Section 112, DIME and PMESII*

It matters how knowledge is organized. When knowledge is placed in categories, there should be some purpose for doing so. Maybe we choose categories so that other people can easily find information. Maybe we choose them in order to make comparisons of attributes. In other words, we might classify the shoes we sell as pumps, loafers, high-heels, and oxfords; and then subcategorize them according to color and size; and then keep track of the number we sell and the net income by month. We can later go back and find out what the trends and preferences are, so as to better provide what consumers want and thereby make more money. It is important for us to get our categories right, or, as a result of not naming things aptly, we won't make as much money as we might have made. In other situations maybe we want to name categories to help us keep track of common roots and relationships, like a genealogy, or taxonomy of flora. We might pick our categories just because they can help reduce something complicated that we are studying. This can be especially dangerous. We can always make simplifying categories of the complex, even if the complex phenomena being studied really cannot be broken into pieces. That is, we can do things with our language that can't be done in reality. Our categories are a form of imagination. We can easily imagine things as separate that are not, then convince ourselves that they are.

Not only are there a lot of practical reasons to pick good categories for storing knowledge, there are ways to test to see if we have chosen well. For instance, if different shelf stockers independently place the store's shoes in the intended categories, it is a sign that the categories are effective descriptors; that the categories have an efficient relationship to the common language and to the culture of shoe styles, or at least that the employees have been well trained as to the language of the store. Likewise, if sales staff can go find what style shoes they're looking for (just as the shelf stockers had intended) it's a good sign that the shoe categories are reasonable and meeting a purpose. If a sales person can explain the general nature of a shoe model to a customer (or the customer to the sales person) without the model being in front of them, and the sales person can then go retrieve something that meets the description, the whole experience verifies a copacetic categorizing. 'I want a brown, calf-high pump with laces.' Difficult, but if the sales person brings her a pair of Nikes because everything with laces was thrown on the same shelf, then things might not go well.

Here are ten ways to organize knowledge related to irregular armed struggles rather than shoes:

1. The alphabet. Always a favorite, this can be troublesome under translation.

2. Google.

3. Geographically -- It's simple, understandable, comprehensive, hierarchical and categorically unique. This might be called a GIS.

4. Chronologically. This is the way some file systems are done, and is especially powerful in conjunction with number 3., above.

5. The system of knowledge established by the disciplines accepted in US Universities. There are some historical and practical reasons for separating Law from Engineering, for instance.

6. According to Who, What, Where, When, Why, and How.

7. For complicated conflict situations, maybe use something like what is in Section 53, *Hohfeldian Grievance Analysis.*

8. Names of persons associated with an idea, responsible for something, or capable of providing something.

9. According to type of knowledge. For instance, you might try:

   A. Foundational knowledge (objective facts in many categories about places);

   B. Events knowledge (things happening in near time);

   C. Reasoned knowledge (analyses or observations of correlations, anomalies, patterns, trends, systems, complaints, demands); and,

   D. Knowledge about knowledge (metadata?) (How to get knowledge, whether or not to use PMESII, how to impart knowledge, the difference between epistemology and heuristics, and so on).

10. These above ways combined. (Please see Section 109, *Hotspotting.*)

The line and block diagram can be a real thought killer, but it can be very useful for establishing hierarchy, responsibility, accountability or leadership, and for tracing and correlating attributes. It is a known fact, however, that Max Weber, attributed inventor of the thing, is frying in the same little square room in hell as the fellow who invented the cloth office workspace divider.

All militaries love buzzwords and acronyms. When they are used to organize knowledge rather than just make a teaching point, knowledge suffers. A case in point is the almost-acronym PMESII. The letters stand for Political, Military, Economic, Social, Information, and Infrastructure. In some recent doctrinal literature it has had two letters added to make it PMESII-PT, the P and the T standing for Physical Environment and Time. Be careful. Memory devices can be useful, but they are sometimes sold as taxonomies and even methodologies for the study of places and phenomena, when actually they are neither of these things.

It is healthy to be cynical about the laundry list approach to strategery. PMESII, for instance, hardly passes any of the tests for good categories suggested at the top of this section. If a list helps you remember something, great. If it helps you organize a written document, good -- but poor categories pose a danger to good thinking. If PEMISI or any other device speeds and clarifies *your* thinking about a place, don't let this book dissuade your use of it. Consider, however, if an influential phenomenon in the place you are studying can fall into several of the PMEISI categories. That might be a clue to you. If there are a number of themes covered by the sections of this book that are applicable to your irregular war, but that are not well-placed or revealed using PEMISI, that might be another warning. If you are told to use PMESII because 'that's the way the boss wants it,' check to see if the boss is thinking straight, and then decide between obedience and loyalty. If you're the boss, be careful not to hamstring thought with inflexible semantics.

Some instructors at the US Army War College are fond of another mnemonic, 'DIME,' which stands for Diplomatic, Informational, Military and Economic. (Since it is an actual acronym and only has four letters, I tend to remember the order). The school posits DIME as a useful separation of the instruments of national power that might be applied by strategic leaders -- meaning leaders with the wherewithal to influence the application of those elements at a national level. Some War College instructors claim it as a pedagogical device so that senior military officers in charge of the 'M' don't forget that there are other kinds of power that might be more useful and appropriate in a given situation. 'Who holds a hammer sees nails everywhere.' There are some variants to the mnemonic, like MIDLIFE and DIMEFIL, that add other components, but I can't remember what they are. Most military leaders are not so strapped for organizational skill or intellect that they need such a checklist, but the thinking is that it never hurts to remind. Even still, how much help to planning and leading is a buzzword like DIME really going to lend in an irregular conflict, especially a heavily urban one? It might not be a good idea to rest thought on such devices, but if one is helpful, it's helpful.

A city leader or planner, say a mayor, police captain, or traffic engineer, would have to look at DIME and wonder where to put waste engineering, property tax records, land-use and stewardship, or recreation. DIME moves strategy up to 'national' and 'international' importance, but leaves behind a whole realm of matters consequential to military success. DIME, as a parameter for strategic thought, offers little intuitive space for what may be critical instruments of power for winning insurgent struggles. If it is true that DIME does little for the leaders of a city, why would DIME be appropriate for a military leader, or a guerrilla leader, in a world made of cities? Part of the answer (admittedly, the cynical part) can be found in the curriculum of the US Army War College. Or rather it cannot be found. The War College (A wonderful institution, don't get me wrong) barely deals with urban. Things that don't fit well into our laundry lists tend to disappear.

Below is a paragraph taken from the *Globalsecurity.org* website.

> "There is a debate underway to rescind the use of ASCOPE (area, structure, capabilities, organization, people, event) as the methodology to understand the civilian considerations, or "C" in METT-TC. Some argue that PMESII-PT (political, military, economic, social, information, infrastructure, physical environment and time), is sufficient to explain both operational variables as well as mission variables of METT-TC, or at least the civil considerations."

Rather than take a side in that argument, I suggest that the very existence of the above paragraph is evidence enough that something is wrong. There are other approaches, as suggested throughout this book.

See: 53, *Hohfeldian Grievance Analysis*; 111, *Knowledge Cultures*; 110, *Knowledge Gaps*; 109, *Hotspotting*; 34, *Urban or Rural*; 118, *Whole of Government*; 2, *The Line of Retreat*; and 66, *GIS.*

"The state which separates its scholars from its warriors
will have its thinking done by cowards and its fighting done by fools."
Thucydides[163]

Rather than an exclusive 'IC' strategy

# Section 113, National Knowledge Strategy

The National Intelligence Strategy of the United States, at least as expressed publicly, is not a national strategy, but rather only a strategy for the US Intelligence Community (IC). That exclusivity entails a huge opportunity cost. The United States enjoys a knowledge creation and management advantage over most of world -- but it is an advantage that exists outside its federal government's IC. Rather than simply entice quality minds into collaboration with its national intelligence services, the US knowledge strategy (about foreign areas and armed struggles) could become truly national in scope. Comprehensive global geographic experience exists broadly within nongovernment institutions, especially academe, and not within the IC.

The underlying ethos of the American nation is not averse to supplying its public (to include its government) with knowledge of the world, both to avoid the wrong fights and to win the right ones. An inclusive knowledge strategy could coax the product of pent-up exploratory desire on the part of the nation's scholars; would not require additional government line-and-block organizational diagrams, formal requests for information, or masonry and glass architecture; and it might help create a common agenda of discovery. The same condition of untapped capacity -- because of the exclusiveness of centralized governmental intelligence-building processes -- seems to be the case in many Western nations today.

A government could instead state a national knowledge vision, not just an intelligence community vision. That statement could challenge the intellectual comfort that typically grows within a government's intelligence apparatus by pitting the descriptions and predictions of non-government individuals against government employees in fair competitions. It could create stockholders and accountability outside the IC regarding the knowledge on which the government bases decisions about foreign aid, foreign conflicts, threats and interventions into foreign lands. It could engage huge numbers of scholars, students, tourists and business people in collaborative knowledge acquisition efforts.

It would be a knowledge improvement if the United States and other countries established national knowledge strategies, and not just government community intelligence strategies.

See: 109, *Hotspotting*; 108, *Neogeography*; 110, *Knowledge Gaps*; 111, *Knowledge Cultures*; 47, *Why the County*; 115, *Transforming Armed Forces*; 54, *Mercatus*; and 70, *Measuring Effects of Actions on Structure.*

---

**Newsreel announcer**: Accepting responsibility for Klendathu, Sky Marshal Dienes resigns. His successor, Sky Marshal Tehat Maru, outlines her new strategy.

**Sky Marshal Tehat Meru**: To fight the bug, we must understand the bug. We can ill afford another Klendathu.

**Newsreel announcer**: Would you like to know more?

From the movie
*Starship Troopers* (1997)[164]

---

If you don't get the joke, step away from the plans

# *Section 114, R. V. Jones*

Winston Churchill asked young physicist Reginald Victor Jones to defeat German radar and to do so fast. Reggie quickly invented chaff, something we now consider commonplace, rather than something that was actually invented. Reggie understood that knowledge about aircraft locations goes into the radar operator's head by way of a small green tinted screen, and that all it took to ruin the radar was to confuse the operator regarding that little image. Reggie was a genius and one of the winners of World War II. Besides defeating German radar, he convinced the otherwise disbelieving paragons of the British scientific establishment that the Germans had some secret programs ongoing that included accurate long-range rocketry. He was a central author of the deception plans protecting the invasion of Europe. He didn't write much (*The Wizard War: British Scientific Intelligence, 1939-1945*), but in a series of brief, obscure lectures from 1957 to 1975, Professor Jones expressed the nature of his strategic thinking. The titles of two of those lectures bespeak the odd nature of his message: 'The theory of practical joking – its relevance to physics' and 'Irony as a phenomenon in natural science and human affairs.'

As a prankster, Jones thought it therapeutic to trick his physicist colleagues into plunging their telephones into buckets of water (for security reasons). Jones found in jokes all the patterns by which the mind is surprised – delightfully or tragically. His sense of strategy incorporated the idea of creating and anticipating the unexpected. Correspondingly, his advice regarding defense policy underscored respect for strategic irony, especially in the unintended consequences of defensive measures. One of his lecture examples was that of the great pyramids. The Pharos, to preserve their honor as well as their remains, built huge edifices in which to protect their corpses. The effect was to identify the location of their remains and to create a visible promise of great reward to the thief. Ultimately, Egyptian planners had to resort to hiding deceased royalty in the desert.

Professor Jones taught something else. He believed that his sense of humor was linked to his ability to understand, create and anticipate deceptions. His advice was to be wary of those who did not have a sense of humor, that they might not get the big military jokes, might not understand the deceptions inherent in strategy, and so ought not to be on anyone's planning staff. Facing irregular armed conflict, they might not be able to sift through the Magical Realism or the Songs of Chu. They might, as they say, not get it.

Appendix: Thomas Cathcart and Daniel Klein wrote a pair of books with a relevant premise, titled: *Plato and a Platypus Walk Into a Bar* and *Aristotle and an Aardvark Go to Washington.* Maybe military strategy and philosophy run on the same mental circuits as well.

Appendix 2: Hedy Lamarr, born just a few years after Reginald, was an Austrian who became an American citizen and Hollywood star. Some considered her the most beautiful woman in the world. She also dabbled in physics, inventing a frequency jumper that makes radar harder to jam.

See: 8, *The Operational Equation*; 122, *Songs of Chu*; 123, *Thirty-six Stratagems*; 101, *Magical Realism*; 16, *Keeping Secrets*; 117, *Strategic Communication*; 81, *What a Clergy Wants*; and 83, *Conflict Geography.*

"As usual, I'm writing slowly because I know you can't read fast."

Radar O'Reilly from the TV show
*MASH* (in a letter to his mother)[165]

Transformation can still arrive on-time

# *Section 115, Transforming Armed Forces*

**Tailored forces**. The US military has been transforming itself...a little bit. As far as the ground forces go, the Army has some new tank-like vehicles with wheels on them instead of treads, and a few heavily armored trucks that might not be good for much after serving in the current wars in Iraq and Afghanistan. A number of new technologies will emerge from recent combat experiences. Probably of greatest consequence is the normal use of unoccupied, armed aerial vehicles.

Organizationally, the US Army almost changed away from a format based around divisions (as the principal 'unit of employment') with about 16,000 soldiers, to smaller brigades of around 3,500 each. 'Almost' because the divisions were always composed of brigades and the new brigades have ended up reporting to division headquarters that may have several brigades under them. The idea of the brigade-centered army was to enhance speed of deployment and independence of action, but many officers point out that there was always something called the task-force or a regiment or something else, and so the emperor of transformation seemed to lack some clothing. A more transformational phenomenon is exposed in the 2010 Quadrennial Defense Review, however. It shows that the United States admits to having 660 special operations units (Special Forces, Rangers, Seals, Special Recon teams, etc.). This *is* transformational, as these units, much smaller than the division or the brigade, are becoming the new standard unit of employment. The change reflects not only the experiences of the United States in recent years, but similar pressures and responses that have occurred in foreign armies. The challenge of such a transformation is to maintain the elite quality and performance of each 'special' unit, and find enough of the right people to have many such units.

There are other training and 'force generation' aspects to ongoing changes that deserve more attention than they'll get here, but in general, changes in the US military have been less than radical. There are still an air force, a navy, an autonomous marine infantry, a coast guard, and an army. Officers are still created at four academies, or by the ROTC at a number of participating civilian universities, and from the ranks via OCS. Recruiting continues to be accomplished essentially as it has been for decades.

The idea of an expeditionary constabulary force comes up now and then, but is suppressed by those who sense a drain of funding away from the conventional force structure. They may be right. Nevertheless, a force designed and peopled specifically for insurgent, or 'irregular,' war would be better at insurgent war, almost regardless of the specifics of the conflict, than a force designed and prepared for big-war. Conversely it is hard to see how a regular military force would be as good at big war if it is constantly adjusting itself for insurgent-type war.

If the future promises a continuing series of irregular armed conflicts in which an armed force needs or wants to be engaged, then it makes sense to deploy a force optimally peopled, equipped and trained to meet those challenges. It also makes sense to not diminish the big-war making capacity of a military if in fact a viable threat exists for which such a force is needed.

There are four things about the panorama of future irregular wars that especially impinge on the organization of national armed force organization. One is a probable need for great numbers of highly capable special operations units. Another is that high soldier numbers are needed in constabulary, guerrilla, or insurgent type warfare. The third is that the legal environment is very different in irregular war as opposed to regular war, and it is this legal difference that most distinguishes one from the other in terms of training. The fourth is the often recognized but poorly addressed transformation of human habitat from rural to urban.

Of the above four, the legal environment, with its attendant extraterritorial jurisdiction, presents a stronger and stronger strategic argument for creation of some sort of constabulary force appropriately trained in its obligations and authorities, and armed accordingly. In *The Pentagon's New Map*, Thomas Barnett discusses what he calls a 'Sys Admin' force that he distinguishes from a 'Leviathan' force. According to Barnett's vision, the Sys Admin force would submit to the jurisdiction of the International Criminal Court and would not be bound by the Posse Comitatus Act. That idea spreads the concept of international jurisdiction to within the territory of the United States; and relinquishes US sovereign immunity, moving instead toward a jurisprudential status equal to that of many less powerful countries that have decided or have been forced to submit to international jurisdiction.

**What size counts?** Countries will continue to deploy armed forces to foreign lands in order to implement one dimension or another of their foreign policies. Arguably, citizens' military service obligations and opportunities should be tailored to the challenges of insurgent-type war, if that kind of war is foreseen. In other words, transformation in armed forces has its concomitant in the way armed forces are raised. Part of winning insurgent war is to prepare for victory in advance, and for a national State, a piece of that advance preparation is appropriate and sustainable policy regarding military service. To remain competitive, some State militaries may need to induct more people, in all ranks. A major lesson about counterinsurgency, coming from various recent wars, is that it takes a lot of people. A second observation, supporting the same conclusion, has to do with the threat suggested in Section 129, *Nerd Globe*. Direct military action missions will be increasingly assigned to small units of extreme competence and intense preparation to be used against distant point targets. These special operating units, while not ultimately needing large personnel numbers, will depend for their quality on systematic opportunity to carefully select the best candidates from larger pools of competent individuals. In other words, even a force based around elite special operating units will need to count on a large universe of potentially qualified young men and women from which to select.

There may be an inexorable math problem afoot. To get the numbers *and* quality needed to win in a world of insurgent wars and odds-and-ends (but nonetheless serious) threats, armed forces *do* need to transform, that transformation might not include downsizing, and so the administration, culture and politics of service recruitment or obligation might have to be transformed.

Even if 'end strength' were not increased, transformation toward a more competitive force will demand a higher quality *average* service member competence. Besides, another hopefully learned lesson revolves around foreign-cultural competence, a quality of mind that is available in a large immigrant population like that of the United States, but which must be gleaned.

If the speculation is correct that competitive forces will require higher numbers of people with more precious attributes, larger pools of potential inductees will be needed. That, in turn, seems to imply that the pool of inductees represent a broader range of human aptitudes within the available population of young men and women. Furthermore, in the case of both constabulary forces and special operating forces, mental acuity will be a continuously more highly prized ingredient for basic soldiering.

**Academy transformation.** One way to anticipate and accelerate transition toward a force better suited to winning insurgent war is to transform the national service academies. The prescription here, using a US example, is for an increase in the number of students at all of the four national service academies, with the resulting size of the student bodies becoming approximately equal. In addition, the male-female ratio would be made equal in all of the academies.

Attendance in or graduation from one of the expanded academies would not impose a service obligation. That may sound counter-intuitive, but the first reason for eliminating any service obligation is in order to test the schools. Perhaps the most valuable leadership quality to be prized or developed by an academy education is a mixture of resolve and national duty. If the academies are doing their job, a sufficient number of graduates will opt to serve. Theirs will be an emotional obligation and not a legal one. The number of years of schooling should be increased from four to five, with foreign culture education emphasized using the increase. Summer military training opportunities could be made more easily available (and yet also impose no active service obligation). Service upon graduation not only as a commissioned officer but as a noncommissioned or warrant officer should be made an equally honored option.

**An army of one?** What, in this era of nerd power and globalization is an individual's best option to participate and win in today's insurgent wars? This book has in it a number of sections that underline the continuing applicability of the classic principles of military strategy. Disregarding for a moment the realms of philosophy, ideology and political science, and just concentrating on the physical world of movement, position, taxes, and death, it appears as though an individual can be extremely effective as a single-shot weapons system. You, alone, can do a lot of damage – destroy a big target – by taking that last fateful step of committing a well-aimed homicide/suicide. However, getting off a second shot at your enemy is a much harder thing to do without collaborators. To attack again and again, and not have to die, you, alone, would have to select only insignificant targets. When your targets are significant, your risk increases greatly, and Maguire's operational equation becomes imperative. The protection of your route to sanctuary becomes a central operational concern. The likelihood of your being able to attack, win a battle, mount a campaign or prosecute a war is conditioned by the rules of classic strategy. Those rules apply to all kinds of war, and they demand teamwork and leadership. Military strategy does not just happen, so if you want to bring the heat, and also enjoy continuity in your rebelliousness, that is, have any carnal goals of your own, then you will want to be part of a well-led organization. You can join an army or a guerrilla that already exists, or you can start your own.

There is always room to add better weapons and machines, but greater competitive advantage may be available by making step increases in the average quality of the humans in the force. Part of the solution may include a big step toward equal gendering (because of untapped brainpower). Redesign of the experience confronted by individual citizens regarding military service obligation, along with a transformation in the formal military educational institutions, are two options available. In insurgent-type wars, the State holds the advantage of being able to start winning years in advance – if it starts.

See: 54, *Badassoftheweek.com*; 5, *Misleading Counterinsurgency Articles of Faith*; 12, *Protraction and Diligence*; 23, *Mens Rea*; 79, *Suicide*; 45, *Police or Military*; 129, *Nerd Globe*; and 76, *Gendering*.

---

> "I think that, as life is action and passion, it is required of a man that he should share the passion and action of his time at peril of being judged not to have lived."
>
> Oliver Wendell Holmes, Jr.[166]

❧❧❧

A thousand knives for a thousand cuts

# *Section 116, Strategy of Aggregate Tactics*

Success in organized armed struggles can depend on decisions that improve the likelihood of success of many subordinates and supporters during their contacts with the opposition. The decision to use a rifle with a 5.56mm bore rather than one of 7.62mm was clearly a 'strategic' decision, even though the rifle is an essentially tactical apparatus, and no specific campaign or single decisive battle was envisioned when the decision was taken to choose one caliber over another. The decision determined manufacturing processes, the selection of manufacturers, the nature of training and training literature, and even affected gendering (since the M16 was manageable by a greater percentage of women than were the larger caliber rifles). The nature of the 5.56mm weapon may also have shortened average engagement distances in battles. Even if, given the nature of irregular wars, senior leaders were never to make a decision related to a single strategic event, it does not mean they are not making extremely influential decisions.

Allowing 'small battles' to become synonymous with 'unimportant battles' may be part of why many counterinsurgents reject classic military principles as they might apply to irregular conflict. Even an insurgent will categorize some of his small attacks as harassments intended only as economy of force measures, deceptions, expressions of presence and defiance, or to attrite or disperse a government force. While such small battles are mounted in anticipation of bigger ones that the insurgent leader hopes to wage in the future, they are rarely ancillary to or anticipatory of the war effort – they *are* the war effort. One successful form of master strategy is to recognize the aggregate importance of all the little battles, and so seek to make the result of as many as possible decisively favorable.

Certainly national leaders will take some diplomatic and informational decisions that influence large identities, like nations or whole populations. Such decisions are clearly 'strategic.' Senior leaders will take other decisions regarding specific, critical contacts with the enemy or about campaigns involving series of combat actions. Those decisions, too, are strategic in level, scope or import. In an internal war, however, most decisions worthy of the adjective 'strategic' anticipate, comprehend and affect the summed results of many little, even micro battles, which in the aggregate constitute a major outcome.

Colombian FARC leaders recognized decades ago that the land mine was a great leveler of military fortunes. Each time a landmine shortened a soldier's leg, it shortened the culminating points of all government units trying to pursue FARC guerrilla elements in the aftermath of contact. The most effective mine designs, delivery of components, training in their manufacture and placement, and arming became matters for strategic discussion. Although the United States despises them as 'improvised' explosive devices (IED), they are the weapons that have most allowed the survival of insurgent force. They fit the guerrillas' understanding of operational art, and, viewing military strategy as an aggregate of small contacts, the FARC leadership made strategic decisions, hardly improvisational, about explosive devises that would be locally fabricated. As homemade as the individual artifacts may be, nothing could have been less improvisational than FARC use of the landmine as a technology for operational art and strategy.

The Colombian military has made many decisions in recent years that address priorities of effort at the national level. For instance, it decided that one of the first efforts after the end of the truce in 2002 had to be the lifting the FARC's encirclement of Bogotá, which the FARC had achieved in order to mount a progressive siege of that city. Where to concentrate forces nationally, where to take risk with economy of force measures, when to take advantage of rare intelligence that involved international risk (such as the later strike into Ecuadoran territory to kill FARC leader Raul Reyes) and when to commit precious mobility assets – these were not 'strategy in the aggregate' decisions. Nevertheless, many other strategic decisions related to equipment, training, disposition of units, allocations of air transport, or creation of fortified outposts. The Colombian senior leaders made sweeping changes with the understanding that there would be very few large battles, but that if subordinate units of army could win the majority of little battles decisively, the aggregate effect would be more than simple attrition. The senior leaders especially sought that, on every occasion practicable, subordinate army units could pursue FARC units successfully when the latter attempted escapes to sanctuary.

While the success of the Colombian Army against FARC units is ultimately based on its increasing ability to deny FARC elements sanctuary, an inability to do so completely (specifically, to keep FARC units from reaching sanctuary outside the country) is *the* strategic challenge.

See: 11, *Decisive Battle*; 140, *Culminating Point in the Pursuit*; 6, *Classic Strategy and Irregular Warfare*; 108, *Neogeography*; 138, *Roadblocks and Checkpoints*; 89, *The Dot Game*; 129, *Nerd Globe*; and 115, *Transforming Armed Forces*.

---

"From Fort Reno to Fort Apache - from Sheridan to Startle - they were all the same: men in dirty-shirt blue and only a cold page in the history books to mark their passing. But wherever they rode - and whatever they fought for – that place became the United States."

Narrator in the movie
*She Wore A Yellow Ribbon* (1949)[167]

# *Section 117, Strategic Communication*

President Álvaro Uribe of Colombia had a pretty good run as a counterinsurgent president. There is plenty of evidence to explain why. Take, for instance, some of his strategic communication during the summer of 2008. He...

*Gave singer Bosé Colombian citizenship: 'Spaniards are welcome here.'
*Signed a Defense Treaty with Brazil in Leticia: 'How about that, Hugo?'
*Hugged Shakira: 'I'm a guy, she's hot, and she's 100% Colombian.'
*Was often seen working late: 'What good Colombians do.'
*Rode a fine horse and wore a fine hat: 'Your leader is a *Señor*.'
*Looked bookish and concerned: 'A *Señor* is not a clown, like Chávez.'
*Helped organize a mega-march on national day: 'We're in this together.'
*Relieved officers for suspected rights violations: 'We're accountable.'

All in all, President Uribe's argument and argumentation were not about fooling the press, or hiding sins, although he did some of that, too, and there were some things to hide. President Uribe's strategic communication, however, was solid because he knew what his audiences were ready to hear. The messages were not accidental, and, imperatively, they enjoyed a background of concerted action. The year 2008 was one of military victories over the FARC, something that President Uribe had promised, and, if slowly, delivered. In March a cross-border raid (about a mile into Ecuador) killed the senior acting FARC commander and gained a treasure trove of valuable new intelligence. In July, a prized group of hostages was rescued, including three Americans. Soon it was revealed that the iconic leader of the FARC, Manuel Marulanda, had died. The strategic communication was not founded on argument and argumentation, but rather the argument and argumentation were effective because they were backed by successful acts and accomplishments. The fact that the communication was often flashy and entertaining, even while coming from a somewhat dour and applied man, made it fit its culture.

For some, *strategy* implies perfidy, treachery or, at very least, secrecy. Because they might be right, *strategic communications* may be an unfortunate term. To the extent it means the deft use of language, art and imagery by senior leaders in order to further the worthy objectives of a polity, to explain to the polity the reasoning and need for action -- that's nice. To the extent it means how to trick the public media, or how to manage the psychology of a public that the leaders dismiss as incapable of intelligent choice -- that might not be so nice. The word 'spin,' now often used admiringly, used to connote more of this latter, not so nice, aspect of strategic communications. A better term would be 'responsible argument and argumentation.' Many leaders fall so in love with spin that spin grows its own ethical justifications and apologies, tied somehow to belief in a mystical realpolitik blessing. Leaders grow to feel they have a special license for deceptive communicating – to spin. Deceptive communication then becomes confused as strategy itself. Strategy may require deception, to be sure, but strategy is strongest when based on sustainable actions, and then only when the right audience is being deceived. Whatever deceptions Álvaro Uribe might or might not have played on his countrymen, he told them he was going to go punch the FARC in the face, and he did.

See: 101, *Magical Realism*; 114, *R.V. Jones*; 2, *The Line of Retreat*; 125, *Human Rights*;123, *Thirty-six Stratagems*; 122, *Songs of Chu*; 54, *Badassoftheweek.com*; and 113, *National Knowledge Strategy*.

---

> "I prefer an ugly truth to a pretty lie. If someone is telling me the truth that is when I will give my heart."
>
> Shakira Mebarak[168]

Whole of whose government?

# *Section 118, Whole of Government*

'Whole of government' is a term that hopefully refers to: A. Unity of purpose and effort among the various institutions of a State to create or permit a social contract that maximizes human flourishing and builds toward a sustainable balance between material development and the health of the environment; B. Correct weighting of administrative, health and engineering efforts in relation to the coercive or repressive responsibilities of the State; and C. A plan of action intended to create a social contract not conducive to spawning, harboring or empowering smugglers and murderers.

We tend to assume that a comprehensive, unified effort is an obvious prescription for effective counterinsurgency, at least in the long run. The rarely asked question, however, is 'Whole of whose government?' Another lurking question regards who is in charge of this whole government, and a third question is why someone who did not join the military should be expected to do anything the military asks. Sometimes unity of effort translates to 'multi-agency approach,' but again, whose agencies are we talking about and which agency is in charge?

This is where discipline as to definitions comes in. It is an immediately burdened argument that an army fighting in a foreign land is engaged in counterinsurgency. 'Burdened' does not mean wrong, but rather that the burden of proof is against it. In Colombia there is a need for a 'whole of government,' approach to counterinsurgency, but there the challenge of the concept is clearer – a number of institutions within the Colombian State have for decades been populated by more than a few bureaucrats whose sympathies have lain with opponents of the State. Now that's a whole of government problem.

If part of your military is bivouacked in some foreign country, it may be an invited and welcome guest of the local society and government, and have a mission to help that State gain back a monopoly over the granting of impunity, and to create a sustainable society that is not a threat to the United States. It would be reasonable in that situation to argue that your military is a counterinsurgent force, that it is conducting counterinsurgency (and stability operations, nation-building, security assistance, whatever). The government in 'whole of government,' however, is that of the local society, not *your* government. This assertion suggests a pair of paradoxes, one a counterinsurgency operational paradox and the other a counterinsurgent organizational paradox.

The counterinsurgency operational paradox: If a foreign force assumes duties of governance and government services, like providing medical attention, paving streets, establishing courts or fixing pipes, it may very well be seen as accountable – as the cause of dependency, as competitors for work, and as self-serving elements of foreign control. Those perceptions may have some truth to them, a truth sufficient to underpin and foment conclusions that the foreign force is an occupier, not a helper, and therefore a legitimate target of armed resistance. In other words, 'whole of government' may be a logical approach to counterinsurgency, but the wrong 'whole of government' elements and identities can fuel insurgency.

The counterinsurgent organizational paradox: If you have an armed force that is likely to go to foreign lands and stay there for any period of time, how do you design the force? If an armed force is peopled, organized, equipped and trained exclusively to close with and destroy the enemy by firepower, shock action, and maneuver, it will be able to do that mission best. As for the United States military, there exists a constant debate about whether or not a force primarily designed for big combat action can meet other missions, and about how much capacity for nonlethal efforts should be built-in to the force design. How big does the force have to be, will it buy more tanks or more bulldozers, will it train sewage scientists or rocket scientists? So what's the paradox? Senior US military leaders have generally favored maintaining a structure dedicated to winning the kind of wars this book is not about, and to handle ad hoc what they have considered lesser-included challenges along an imagined 'spectrum' of conflicts. Calling for 'whole of government,' however, smells like incapacity. The military argues that others in the US government should participate as counterinsurgent chips because the military obviously does not have the institutional wherewithal. The more the military argues 'whole of government,' the more it says that it is not designed to do counterinsurgency.

In many places and times, military leaders have tended to want to be the ones in charge of 'whole of government' efforts. Leaders of other agencies in 'multiagency' quickly see through this. In the case of United States' presence in foreign lands, most US missions already feature what is called the 'country team,' which is the intended 'whole of representation,' and while there are various perturbations, they are usually, supposedly, led by a civilian.

If you have a military that is going to have regular foreign experiences, design accordingly or support the creation of a separate force that can in any given situation occupy and govern those little chunks of a foreign country that the foreign 'whole of government' is unable to govern. 'Take, Hold, Build' might have to mean, 'Take, Occupy, Fix, Govern, Give Back.' If you really think that doing the latter is going to take a long time, why insist on using a force designed for big-combat?

The 'whole of government' question isn't just about whose government or who is in charge; it is about whether or not the various non-police and non-military elements of a government owe support to the government's police and military in pursuing criminals or destroying enemies. Every effort and every agency of every government everywhere should be counterinsurgent. A true insurgent is fighting against the system within which the government is the most obvious target. When a government is not honest, thrifty, courteous, kind, obedient, helpful, and loyal to its people, it invites insurgents. That assertion made, many elements within even a good government won't see a legal obligation to help in the pursuit of criminals and enemies. Their leaders might vocally ratify their individual members' explicit decisions to not join the police or military because they did not want to participate in the management of violence, and did not want to go away from home. Especially if a conflict is distant and optional, it is easy to see why some people in the rest of the whole of government won't pull on the same rope.

Police and military are special and distinct callings. These identities feature voluntary self-endangerment and a willingness to kill. Part of counterinsurgency can be done by people without this calling, since all good government is counterinsurgent. However, if the counterinsurgency has a military strategy part (perhaps because it has an armed and organized enemy that police cannot handle), that part probably entails a lot of moving and positioning in order to bring death to someone. In my personal opinion, the killing and dying part should not pertain to the rest of the whole of government. Efforts to cajole others outside the military to serve in military endeavors overseas might be seen as sneaky conscriptions.

Good insurgents have determined that their government has become a tyrant. As insurgents gain territorial control, they also are faced with problems of governance under conditions of resource shortages. A foreign force capable of providing interim services might be very welcome – for a while. Bad insurgents want to be the tyrant, and tyrants always preach 'whole of government.'

See: 45, *Police or Military*; 143, *Is It an Insurgency?*; 115, *Transforming Armed Forces*; 27, *Democracy*; 36, *Engineers*; 121, *Commitment of the Reserve*; 109, *Hotspotting*; and 138, *Roadblocks and Checkpoints.*

---

> "Of all tyrannies, a tyranny exercised for the good of its victims may be the most oppressive. It may be better to live under robber barons than under omnipotent moral busybodies. The robber baron's cruelty may sometimes sleep, his cupidity may at some point be satiated; but those who torment us for

our own good will torment us without end, for they do so with the approval of their own conscience."

C. S. Lewis[169]

☙❧☙❧☙❧☙❧☙❧☙❧

The bludgeon game-winner

# *Section 119, Huai Hai Campaign*

Mao was not looking to be the great master of irregular war. He wanted total victory, and thought he would ultimately win by regular battle. Not much has been made of the Huai Hai campaign in English-language strategy literature, and the counterinsurgency literature all but forgets that the Huai Hai battles were the destination of Mao's guerrilla efforts. One professor, Dr. Gary Bjorge at Ft. Leavenworth, noticed the significance of these battles, so with his permission and guidance I paraphrase shamelessly from his *Moving the Enemy: Operational Art in the Chinese PLA's Huai Hai Campaign.*

One of the largest and most consequential wars of the 20th Century was the Chinese civil war of 1946-1949 between the Nationalist government of China led by President Chiang Kai-shek and the Chinese Communist Party (CCP) led by Chairman Mao Zedong. Military forces numbering in the millions fought across the vast space of China in a struggle that ended with the Nationalist government taking refuge on the island province of Taiwan, and the Communists establishing the People's Republic of China (PRC) on October 1, 1949.

The Huai Hai Campaign was the largest and most decisive series of battles of the Chinese civil war. It began on November 6, 1948 and ended on January 10, 1949. It was initially conceived by Communist generals to push Nationalist forces away from the Long-Hai railroad running east of Xuzhou and link together the Communist-controlled areas in Shandong and Jiangsu provinces, but the goal eventually became the final confounding of Nationalist military maneuver options.

The first offensive of the campaign sought to destroy the Nationalist Seventh Army. The second offensive, from November 12 to 16, resulted in cutting the rail line connecting Xuzhou with Bengbu, thereby isolating the Nationalist Second, Thirteenth, and Sixteenth Armies in Xuzhou. These offensives set the conditions for a final victory. Over a period of several weeks, whole armies maneuvered on a grand scale. Maybe this wasn't the largest or most costly campaign in history, but to display the contenders' operational plans requires maps covering thousands of square miles. Five Kuomintang Nationalist armies totaling over a half million men were ultimately surrounded and confronted by the calamity of having failed the basic lesson of classic strategy. The Communists were now the stronger opponent and had compromised the Nationalist's options for escape.

Communist columns pressed inexorably toward the headquarters of the Nationalist military commands at the villages of Chenguanzhuang and Shuangduiji. Due to the rapidly deteriorating situation, the Nationalist commanders finally ordered breakouts, but the decisions had been taken too late, and the attempts were complete failures. A few officers and soldiers did make it through the surrounding net and eventually found their way to Nationalist lines in the South. However, for practical purposes, the entire Nationalist force was either killed or captured, and only a few scattered Nationalist units could still offer resistance. As a result of the loss, the United States stopped assisting the Nationalist Kuomintang government. Soon it would fall to the Communists.

This is too short a summary of such an epic clash, but please notice that the battles revolved around lines of communication and cutting off the enemy's option of retreat. A Huai Hai campaign isn't the destination of all armed struggles. There is only one China, and 1949 isn't coming back. Still, guerrilla struggles often tend toward conventional battles, and insurgent leaders toward conventional military goals. The formula that guerrilla wars develop in three distinct phases may be overdrawn. Still, there is a tendency – from latency, to guerrilla warfare, to position and maneuver. The Huai Hai Campaign was historically decisive, changing the world power balance and setting China on a course of political tyranny and economic mediocrity from which it would not emerge until after Mao's death. It was the last chapter in a book of internal conflict whose earlier chapters were filled with guerrilla campaigns. From chapter to chapter, the essence of military strategy did not change one iota.

See: 138, *Roadblocks and Checkpoints*, 2, *The Line of Retreat*; 6, *Classic Strategy and Irregular Warfare*; 122, *Songs of Chu*; 65, *Smuggling*; 11, *Decisive Battle*; 8, *The Operational Equation*; and 58, *Guerre d'Algérie*.

"There is no shadow of protection to be had by sheltering behind the slender stockades of visionary speculation, or by hiding behind the wagon-wheels of pacific theories."

May-ling (Madame Chiang Kai-Shek)[170]

One kind of conflict stuffed inside another

# Section 120, Turducken

Turducken is a Cajun or faux-Cajun dish prepared by roasting or deep frying a turkey that's stuffed with a duck stuffed with a chicken, which may in turn be stuffed with spices or sausage. The whole thing might even be covered with bacon. The juices and flavors get all mixed together.... mmmm. Not a vegetarian dish. Go on up to Yellowknife or Whitehorse and try the Moosbearbou.

'Turducken' is a good descriptor for some armed conflicts. Military history is replete with examples wherein major contenders engaged in more than one kind of warfare simultaneously. Lawrence of Arabia was doing something irregular in the midst of World War I. General Giap fielded regular armies against French and later United States forces, but also mounted a broad guerrilla campaign. During the American Revolutionary War, General Nathaneal Greene's regular forces coordinated successfully with the militia units and guerrilla methods of the 'Swamp Fox,' Francis Marion. The Napoleonic Wars, classic by default, included the Peninsular Campaigns, which birthed the term guerrilla. These and many others could be termed *turducken* wars. Turducken might be an apt term if a front were established along which two contending regular armies were pitted in maneuver combat, behind which a guerrilla war raged and inside of which international organized crime prospered. (If you don't care for the carnivore analogy, you could use *matryoshka* after the Russian nesting dolls.).

A 1999 Chinese book by Qiao Liang and Wang Xiangsui is titled *Unrestricted Warfare* (or at least that seems to be the best translation. For analysis of the book, see Tim Thomas' *The Dragon's Quantum Leap*). *Unrestricted* is not a reference to, or rejection of international rules of war, as in World War I submarine use, but rather to the idea that all means – political, economic, diplomatic, insurgent, criminal, etc., can and will be used. Beyond 'ends justify the means,' unrestricted implies that the ends justify using any and every means that apply, and in any combination or sequence that produces the best result.

The term hybrid has come into recent fashion as a descriptor of irregular-type wars. (A *hybrid* is generally considered a product of two things that carries some of the characteristics of each of its parents. (A mule is the hybrid offspring of a male donkey and a female horse, for instance.) The use of 'hybrid' as a descriptor of some future warfare could falsely imply contiguity in time and space. Much of what is honored as guerrilla strategy involves the idea of stages or phases. A revolutionary effort, for instance, evolves, according to the literary protocol, from latency through guerrilla operations to a war of movement. This pattern, wherein Mao moves purposefully from organizing secret cells toward the vast campaign of Huai Hai, is poorly contained by the term hybrid. Likewise, if a nation were waging a pitched tank battle on a foreign battlefield, but also contending with an effective and virulent enemy 'fifth column' at home, is that warfare hybrid? Did the activities of the French Resistance make the German's war challenge a hybrid one? If the Iranians build nuclear weaponry, but fund and guide Hezbollah militants in Lebanon, is that hybrid?

*Hybrid* is probably not the best word to use for describing future wars, but if it is or isn't, so what? Part of the upshot is found in how governments organize to meet variable threats to the State. As expressed in other sections, clear distinction can be made between what is police and what is military, at least from a traditional United States perspective. From that point of view, what distinguishes police from military involves differential authorities, obligations, and immunities. Those legalistic attributes express themselves visibly in types of weapons used, organizational design, information cultures and operational practices. In some countries, police-military hybrids exist. Some of these hybrids have long traditions, such as the *carabinieri* of several countries. In the United States, such hybridizing runs into a marsh of issues about the role of federal troops, the National Guard, Posse Comitatus, and the like. A conflict probably isn't a hybrid, but an armed force can be.

*Asymmetry* is another term briefly in fashion for describing insurgent-type wars, and that word spawned its own foreign usage (see Section 98, *Jorge Verstrynge and Pio Moa*). If opponents in a war, battle, lesser armed confrontation, or even a sport, were perfectly symmetrical as to their competitive resources and recourses, the contest would never end, except maybe by dumb luck or divine intervention. We win by unbalancing symmetry. An insurgent is almost always, at least at the beginning of the contest, obliged to be more strategic than his government opponent, that is, to seek surprise and stealth. Patience, observation, and deception are bywords for overcoming what appears on the surface to be an overall government advantage. Advantage is what the competitor seeks, and the word advantage contains within it the notion of asymmetry.

*Anonymity* is the phenomenon demarking the kinds of security challenges you will confront in irregular war, not *asymmetry.* The two terms are related one to the other, since so much of the competitive advantage sought by an insurgent or criminal adversary of the State is achieved through secrecy. The word 'asymmetry' begs the strategy question. Gaining and maintaining advantage in anonymity is a major part of the answer. There is one area, however, where the word asymmetry has greater utility. *Moral asymmetry* is a worrisome phenomenon that lends at least a short-term competitive advantage to the side less constrained by moral standards of behavior. Tactical moral asymmetry is encouraged by revolutionary theory holding that the moral constructs of the enemy can and should be rejected -- that they need not be observed by the morally justified revolutionary. In other words, if you are truly a rebel and not just a crook, you don't just disobey the law, you disdain both the law and the invalid moral structure from which that law sprang. It is partly because of the danger of moral asymmetry that this book delves into 'magical realism' and 'post-structuralism' -- artistic and ideological currents that support moral asymmetry.

In the last decade or so, the vocabulary of English-language irregular warfare doctrine has not been efficient. This section is not a promotion for the fanciful culinary word *turducken* (the Chinese also use *cocktail*); it is a warning that many recent semantic enthusiasms, including *hybrid* and *asymmetric* are no better, and will be short-lived because they invite the question 'So what?' and do not answer.

See: 143, *Is It an Insurgency?*; 115, *Transforming Armed Forces*; 50, *U.S. Persons*; 56, *Militias and Gun Control*; 2, *Anonymity*; 45, *Police or Military*; 82, *Conflict Thresholds*; and 119, *Huai Hai Campaign.*

---

> "The test of a first-rate intelligence is the ability to hold two opposed ideas in mind at the same time and still retain the ability to function."
>
> F. Scott Fitzgerald[171]

A general's big decision

# *Section 121, Commitment of the Reserve*

When and where to commit the reserve is traditionally one of the most consequential decisions the military leader makes. This aspect of classic military strategy is a little harder to apply in insurgent war. When do we send in the reserve in an unconventional conflict? How much of a reserve should we keep? Part of an answer to this question may depend on our having done a few other things first, like having enough resources to begin with, or having found our enemy's lines of communication. None of the principles of military strategy is easy to apply if its sister principles have already been violated.

If you are an insurgent, and you are taking persistent, careful shots at government forces (being sure that you have safe lines of supply and retreat), you will once in a while catch a government unit especially off-guard. These are just the odds. Ten percent of an army's leaders are that army's ten percent most arrogant, lazy, and irresponsible commanders – the bottom ten percent. Sometimes a bottom-10-percent commander, executive officer and senior sergeant all end up in the same unit. Sometimes that army is going to make a simple mistake as to economy of force or care of soldiers, and sometimes Mother Nature or Murphy are just going to align themselves at the right time and place to make things even worse. Once in a while all the disparate chance factors for failure are going to concur to make an otherwise formidable unit unusually vulnerable.

Since you are being persistent and daring in your attacks, it is almost a certainty that uncertainty will eventually favor you, but if you are not ready to exploit the favor by having a ready reserve, you will miss an opportunity that could have vaulted you to an improved level of insurgent power. Luck is where preparation meets opportunity. As an insurgent, you must always prepare for bad luck. That is why you are careful to maintain a secure route of escape. Preparation for bad fortune is your key to survival, but preparation for good fortune is your key to more good fortune. Keeping a reserve force handy in order to take advantage of an unusually successful attack is the classic advice.

Murphy likes bad luck more than good luck, and now and then, in spite of your having trained and planned to keep the lines of retreat of your subordinate units secure to sanctuary, you too have a hapless 10 percent. You also need a reserve to check a pursuing army unit that is closing down the route of escape of one of your guerrilla columns.

A government counterinsurgent reserve force with superior mobility, perhaps provided by helicopters, motorbikes, or mules can lend a great advantage to the counterinsurgent. A reserve force needs something that makes it faster to the points of contact, or it cannot effectively fulfill its role as a reserve, and cannot pursue well. In the past, we kept horse cavalry in the reserve for exactly that reason. Being able to make a quicker decision as to where a reserve should go is also part of the speed formula, so airpower and aerospace power are useful.

In irregular war, timely commitment of a reserve can help turn a battle won into a decisive one. To decisively win a battle in irregular war, the government pretty much has to win the pursuit. Without a reserve, the math of comparative culminating points tells us there often can't be a successful pursuit.

The whole idea of a reserve is subject to that of scale. Step away a bit from 'tactical, operational, strategic,' although that trilogy might apply. After all, scale is a concept that divides more than three ways. Whatever the 'level' of your unit, and whatever the size of the forces engaged, you will want to maintain a reserve fast and powerful enough for you to successfully pursue or to save an endangered retreat. That truth will reign whether you are a single beat cop or commander of a huge tank army. The holding and timely application of a reserve force may be as much the key to winning decisive battles in insurgent warfare as it is in more conventional forms of combat.

See: 11, *Decisive Battle*, 138, *Roadblocks and Checkpoints*; 122, *Songs of Chu*; 140, *Culminating Point in the Pursuit*; 63, *Cost-Distance*; 12, *Protraction and Diligence*; 118, *Whole of Government*; and 8, *The Operational Equation.*

---

> "It is in the use and withholding of their reserves that the great commanders have generally excelled. After all, when once the last reserve has been thrown in, the Commander's part is played...The event must be left to pluck and to the fighting troops."
>
> Winston Churchill[172]

Convincing you to convince yourself

# *Section 122, Songs of Chu*

Legend has it that during the Chu Hang dynasty wars, Liu Bang, leader of the Han, besieged Xiang Yu, leader of the Chu, at Gaixia. Liu Bang had his men loudly sing the local songs of the Chu people. Hearing the songs, Xiang Yu believed his people had joined the Han and that his support had evaporated.

Liu Bang fed Xiang Yu's own existing doubts. It is one of the great classics of psychological operations, an old tale about the power of suggestion. The legend also ties itself to the physical results emphasized throughout this book. In the rest of the story, Xiang Yu tries to make a run for it. His escape to sanctuary fails, Liu Bang's pursuit succeeds, and Xiang Yu, realizing his fate, commits suicide. When faced with a superior force, Xiang Yu did not have a secure route of withdrawal to sanctuary.

Guerrillas or insurgents more than governments are constrained to the basics of the classic military operational equation, and therefore must depend more on technology and be more obedient to the dictates of physical terrain. Without the landmine, the FARC would have been beaten long ago. To survive, Al Qaeda had to seek the most remote area of the Islamic world and live in holes. Being the physically weaker parties, guerrillas will attempt sleight of hand and psychological ploys to misdirect their enemies. It works. Guerrillas have made two generations of government strategists think that the military operational basics somehow didn't apply. The guerrilla's right hand plays songs about religion and legitimacy while his left hand concentrates on the imperative: where on the map to attack and still maintain a secure line of retreat. New songs of Chu help him survive in a world of time, weight, and sudden failure.

By the way, before he flees Gaixia, Xiang Yu tenderly kisses Yu Ji, his favorite hottie concubine, goodbye. This is an obligatory part of the story and part of what makes this such a popular legend, thus revealing that in China as in America, a perfectly good war story has to be schmaltzed up with a romantic subplot or you can't get your girlfriend to go to the movie with you.

See: 8, *The Operational Equation*; 11, *Decisive Battle*; 63, *Cost-Distance*; 31, *Holes in the Ground*; 5, *Misleading Counterinsurgency Articles of Faith*; 41, *Whereabouts*; 67, *Points, Lines, Spaces*; and 29, *Heavy Machines.*

**Young William**: What are they doing?
**Argyle Wallace**: Saying goodbye in their own way, playing outlawed tunes on outlawed pipes.

From the movie
*Braveheart* (1995)[173]

Designed to trick, not bludgeon

# *Section 123, Thirty-six Stratagems*

We won't go over all thirty-six. I'm pretty sure some Chinese general (let's say Sun Zhu since everyone else does) told his doctrine guy he wanted thirty-six stratagems. The guy probably came back and said something like, 'Well, Sir, we can only really come up with twenty-eight distinct stratagems, is that OK?' and the general got himself a new doctrine guy. So there are thirty-six stratagems in Wang Xuanming's *Secret Art of War: Thirty-six Stratagems.* He has another book titled *100 Strategies of War* and so, you see, there might be sixty-four of something you can call strategy that are beyond stratagem.

To unwrap the mystery that is Chinese strategic thinking, I depended on Tim Thomas (*The Dragon's Quantum Leap* and his other dragon books) and Scott Henderson (*Dark Visitor*) whom I have mentioned elsewhere.

Stratagems of the Chinese government should be less of a concern for you (or at least a narrower category of concern) than the strategies of Chinese; and strategies of Chinese less significant than Chinese strategic thinking. Regardless, Chinese stratagems are the heart of Chinese strategic thought, so much so that strategy without stratagem is hard to conceptualize and is rarely applicable to irregular war. Make noise in the East and attack in the West is perhaps the most basic, but a more encompassing angle is perhaps to say that the idea is to get your opponent to want to do what you want him to do.

The Chinese strategic method is to conceive of a specific action in time and space (the objective dimension), but to influence the opponent's mind (the subjectivity dimension) as the latter might affect the objective world. This is what R. V. Jones talks about in the form of practical jokes – of playing to what people want to think or are programmed to think, but with a purpose: to cause action or inaction at a moment in time and place. It is also at the heart of T. Miller Maguire's prompts regarding operational strategy. He is all about the physical security of the physical line of retreat, for instance, but what he alludes to as the essence of strategy revolves around the mindset of the leaders – their perception of the environment, chances of success, and level of resolve – and how to affect those mindsets. Military strategy or operational art do not just happen. The strategy and the decision-making of the strategist are one. So there is no special Eastern magic in Chinese strategic thinking, either traditionally or currently, although it may be that Western strategic thinkers have lost their sense of the essence by denying applicability of the classic operational equation to irregular war.

If you cannot find the enemy or his lines of communication, how can you deceive him as to the proper time and place for his actions or yours? How can you deceive him as to your relative strengths, the security of lines of communication, or levels of resolve? It is not impossible, actually, since you might confuse him into inaction or error regardless of his position, condition, or your own knowledge of them. This is probably an unrealistic hope, since even communicating to him is subject to understanding of the geography.

A few favorites from *The Art of War: Thirty-six Stratagems*:

> Stratagem 28, "Remove the ladder after the ascent. Expose your weak points deliberately to entice the enemy to penetrate into your line, then ensnare him in a death trap by cutting off his rearguard support..."
>
> Stratagem 22, "Bolt the door to catch a thief. When dealing with a small and weak enemy, surround and destroy him. If you let him retreat, you will be at a disadvantage pursuing him."
>
> Stratagem 18, "To catch rebels, nab their leader first. Destroy the enemy crack forces and capture their chief, and the enemy will collapse...."

All 36 are pretty good, and so are the rest of the hundred, and, no, they don't all have to do with the line of retreat.

See: 114, *R.V. Jones*; 8, *The Operational Equation*; 68, *Scale*; 101, *Magical Realism*; 131, *Sea and Aerospace Power*; 117, *Strategic Communication*; 2, *Anonymity*; and 141, *Seven Strategy Strains*.

"The central task and the highest form of revolution is
to seize political power by armed force,
to settle problems by force."

Mao Tse-tung in
*Problems of War and Strategy* (1954)[174]

The United States as insurgent nation

# Section 124, America's Insurgent Stamp

US political and military doctrine on the nature of insurgency and the conduct of government counterinsurgency carries within it a good deal of doctrinaire thinking (or propaganda) characteristically expounded by violent leftist revolutionaries. That thinking generally denies the applicability of the classic rules of military strategy to irregular war. For better or worse, US military doctrine has been insurgent-friendly. Below are a few points of historical evidence. They are selective, anecdotal, and tailored to the argument. They should be repeated with caution; they are not the whole story. Still, after all the disclaimers possible, they tell a core truth about the determinants of tone and bias that often cause modern American counterinsurgency doctrine to be limited in utility and light.

The Declaration of Independence, birthing document of the American Revolution and the United States of America, is unavoidably and undeniably insurgent. It justifies the use of violence to overthrow a constituted government. It asserts indelibly the proposition that an insurgent force, and its use of violence, can be legitimate. This possibility of legitimacy in the use of rebellious force, by corollary logic, planted the idea that the legitimacy of government, derived of its conduct, was a question for constant contemplation. Today, it is all but taken for granted that grooming a perception of government legitimacy is a principle necessity of successful counterinsurgency. The life of that assumption can be traced back through the fact that in North America the dominant, milestone piece of writing on the subject is a call to rebellion.

On June 14th, 2010, the US Army celebrated its 235th birthday, not its 234th, as the nation would on July 4th. From Robert Wright's *The Continental Army* we read that on June 14th, 1775, "Congress adopted 'the American continental army' after reaching a consensus position in The Committee of the Whole. This procedure and the desire for secrecy account for the sparseness of the official journal entries for the day."[175] The military arm of the American insurgency was created by underground movement. America's mechanism for managing insurgent political violence was created before the overt statement of revolutionary intent. It is instructive if not symbolic that in the United States, the 14th of June is celebrated, quietly, every year before Independence Day by many who recognize the day not only as the birthday of a military institution, but perhaps as the de facto birthday of the people's revolutionary enterprise. The fact of secrecy lies at the heart of what makes insurgent warfare unique and difficult, rather than any asymmetry of belligerent capacity or guerrilla style of combat.

In 1785, the new United States of America sent a team of surveyors out west, which from the 'Point of Beginning' near East Liverpool, Ohio began to measure off the land with chains. Tracts were sold at auction in New York, and when the buyer bought, he bought the *fee simple absolute*: all of the rights from the core to the heavens. The government retained only the duty to enforce the social contract on which the ownership rights depended. That revolutionary change in the relationship of the individual to the State answered a royal proclamation that had been sent by King George in 1763 to the effect that no land was to be surveyed west of where the waters ran to the Atlantic. Surveyors like George Washington knew the portent. That order, more than the taxation of tea, differentiated the path toward liberty. The azimuth for insurgency had been set. The survey of 1785 manifested the revolution in law and on maps. The northwest Ordinance, which authorized the survey, made slavery in the new space illegal, this even before it was illegal in New York or England.

The United State's first major military adventure to the south was the war against Mexico in 1848. In that war, clearly of an international character, the invading US commanders found themselves in the midst of indifferent and ambivalent Mexican nationalism, not the fervent, monolithic and decided Mexicanness that is often portrayed. In a context of scattered dissidence and superficial national identity, Winfield Scott found willing subversives to help defeat the 'Napoleon of the West,' General Antonio López de Santa Anna Pérez de Lebrón. America's expansionist adventure into Spanish-speaking lands did not find stubborn opposition to occupation among the populace, but more a mixture of indifference and willing opportunism. That Mexican insurgents might hold the moral high ground, rather than their government, was by the Americans presumed. Rebellion was good.

In the American Civil War, for many American historians and sociologists the crucible of the American nation, we note the publication of General Order 100 on April 24, 1863, also known as the Lieber Code. Fittingly, it was written by a professor from Columbia University, then reviewed and left almost unchanged by a board of army officers before being promulgated by President Lincoln. It is by general consensus the root document of all international laws of war that followed. It may well be the first US paper that can be properly characterized as counterinsurgent doctrine, but it did not deal with resources, maneuver or objectives in stopping insurgency. It dealt with the moral and ethical conduct of the government's own troops. In this respect it was informed by a presumption that a rebel force could be imbued with legal and moral legitimacy. (The form or conduct of warfare, however, mattered more than the political stance of the fighters -- spies, snipers, and guerrillas were all treated harshly)

Jumping to the first 20th century intervention by the United States into the internal conflicts of other countries in the Western Hemisphere, note US support to insurgents of the Panamanian Isthmus, which created space for US construction of the Panama Canal. (You could argue effectively that US intervention into Cuba was the first intervention of the century, and the proposition of American preference for insurgency would be equally enforced using that example.) US support for Panamanian insurgency came after the Colombian congress had declined to sell canal rights at the price offered by the US, a refusal that drew Theodore Roosevelt's now famous invective -- that the Colombian leaders were "homicidal corruptionists."[176] Roosevelt could get away with using such language in part because of popular perception to the same effect, and partly because of considerable evidence that it was true, if unexceptional. Roosevelt also called for a spontaneous revolt, an assertion that was disingenuous at the time and remains a cliché of the American concept of true insurgency.

Selling the American public on the idea of support to an insurgency against a nominally illegitimate government was easy. The move had a patent geostrategic objective, but without the right moral sentiment there might not have been enough reason, even after the 'splendid little war' of 1898 against Spain (splendid in part because, however hapless, the opponent was an established empire), to motivate American public support for the arrogation.

Skipping well ahead to closer conditions and times, we repeat the language of President Clinton's 2000 decision (mentioned in Section 62, *Illicit Commerce*), which stated in relevant part,

> "As a matter of Administration policy, we will not support Colombian counterinsurgency efforts. We will, however, provide support, in accordance with existing authorities and this policy, to the Government of Colombia for force protection and for security directly related to counterdrug efforts, regardless of the source of the threat. This Administration remains convinced that the ultimate solution to Colombia's longstanding civil conflict is through a successful peace process, not a decisive military victory, and believes that counterdrug progress will contribute to progress towards peace."

US perceptions of its national interests in the Western Hemisphere have not necessarily been consistent with perceptions of its interests in other parts of the world, but it is safe to say that President Clinton's policy for Colombia was constrained by the current of American thought that prefers insurgency over counterinsurgency. His decision directive made for poor counterinsurgent military strategy. It is hard to imagine publication of a US military field manual called *Counterinsurgency* in 2000. The United States officially didn't do counterinsurgency.

The selected items provide anecdotal evidence of a permanent current of American attitude. As is typical of the culture, it is but one of many intermixing and cross-flowing currents, but it would be hard to deny that a fundamental preference, a favoring presumption for the insurgent underdog exists in American thinking. This preference allows for a reception, acceptance and internalization of insurgent arguments that might otherwise not happen. Section 5, *Misleading Counterinsurgency Articles of Faith* asserts ten themes that have eased themselves into the basket of guiding assumptions and assertions in US counterinsurgency doctrine. I call the ten 'misdirecting' notions, not because they are wrong, but because they are right enough to throw doctrine off-scent, to mislead. Several of them mislead in good measure because of the American preference for an insurgent starting point. All of them have their utility; most have risen to the status of assumptions and all are over-believed to the point that their matter-of-fact presence causes misapplication of resources, operational impotencies, and the displacement of more important factors. They exist, however, because they reflect who the American nation is.

Before leaving the subject of America's insurgent preference, the following word pairings are proposed for consideration:

Separatism, Counter-separatism
Revolution, Counter-revolution
Insurgency, Counter-insurgency

To be properly confused, please note that a self-styled revolutionary can be the counter-insurgent (this might be the position taken by the Venezuelan or Cuban government facing an internal insurgent movement). How do we, for our own morale and clarity, efficiently deal with these pairings, which are significant in discussions about what kind of fight we might have on our hands? This is one guide:

> In the late 18th century, George Washington won on a revolutionary, separatist, insurgent proposition.
>
> In the mid 19th century, Abraham Lincoln won on a revolutionary, insurgent, anti-separatist proposition.

In both cases, the revolution was about changing the relationship between the individual and the State; success of separatism would in both cases determine the future strength of that revolutionary enterprise; and insurgency in the first case was driven by those opposed to the central State (that of the British King), and in the second case by those supporting it (the anti-slavery Union). At least that's one way of looking at it, and I'm sticking to it.

The American revolutionary movement asserted natural rights of the individual, along with proscription against the tendency of government toward the concentration of power and tyranny. Other movements have come along to cheapen the word revolution, but they are mostly counterrevolutionary (without condemning them entirely by that term). Most of what is called insurgent today is categorized as such because it is opposed to some existing State, but the movement in question can itself be highly statist. People just label as insurgent whoever they think is the underdog, and that means that the idea of insurgent or counterinsurgent is often a matter of scale. In a globalized world, when the United States takes out a tyrannical State, we can argue that the US acts, in historical perspective, as insurgent if not revolutionary. When it supports an oppressive government or defends some other form of tyranny (even at times the product of electoral democracy) perhaps it acts as counterrevolutionary. The notion of global insurgency then comes into play. National governments are often despised by the 'post-structural' insurgent as mere nodes in a much larger capitalist neoliberal structure. Under such a view, the US government plays as a mechanistic, if not lackey force in service to a system that in turn services the arrogant preferences of an elite class of oppressors.

Hopefully, American action will be informed by the same mindset to which Thomas Jefferson attributed the tone and spirit of the Declaration of Independence.[177] Independence was the direct message of the document, but more powerful was the new balance it struck between individual liberty and government prerogative as the source of justifiable action, particularly as to the use of violence. The 18th century geographic and political context required separatism, but that separatism served the revolution, not vice versa. Abraham Lincoln led the same tone and spirit, but, in a changed geographic and political reality, he sensed that the revolution of liberty had to oppose a separatist insurgency in favor of revolutionary insurgency.

Why is this abstract point in this practical book? -- Because this is not a counterinsurgency manual. The United States government will at times be insurgent, counterinsurgent, separatist, or in favor of political unity and sovereign status quo, but hopefully it can remain inspired by the same revolutionary purpose that champions liberty over tyranny. This book is about choosing the right fights, studying the right things, setting the right objectives, managing violence efficiently and responsibly, and closing the deal in time and space. It is not about living in peace, it is about winning it. It is about legitimate violence.

See: 5, *Misleading Counterinsurgency Articles of Faith*; 60, *Slavery*; 6, *Classic Strategy and Irregular Warfare*; 128, *Global Insurgency and Global Trespass*; 2, *Anonymity*; 73, *Property and the Social Contract*; 85, *Gun Control*; and 54, *Badassoftheweek.com*.

---

> "The right of revolution is an inherent one. When people are oppressed by their government, it is a natural right they enjoy to relieve themselves of the oppression, if they are strong enough, either by withdrawal from it, or by overthrowing it and substituting a government more acceptable."
>
> Ulysses S. Grant *Memoirs* (1885)[178]

# *Section 125, Human Rights*

When dealing with the practicalities of human rights issues, you stand to gain competitive advantage by being as geographically and temporally specific as possible regarding both violations and legal processes.

**Basic human rights.** In the midst of an active civil war, you will want to set, announce, and enforce some minimums of behavior for the protection of innocents. Beyond being the right thing to do, it will help you highlight the relative illegitimacy of your enemy. Here is a sample rubric for human rights behavior -- yours, that of your allies, and that of your enemies:

> Children under 15 years of age are a protected category. Involving children in armed conflict is proscribed behavior, a violation of human rights and a crime to be prosecuted. 'Involving' means using children in any capacity, including as shields, hostages, messengers, provisioners, collateral, etc.
>
> The use of landmines, booby traps, and other explosive devices that cannot discriminate as to their target (that is to say, a child might unwittingly detonate and be injured by them) is inherently criminal and a violation of human rights, which will be prosecuted.
>
> The identities of any persons who are detained and deprived of their liberty will be precisely identified along with the reason for their detention. Respect *habeas corpus*.
>
> All human deaths will be investigated. All human remains will be precisely identified, and the fact of a person's death publicized along with the location of the person's known remains. Respect *habeas corpus*.
>
> Obedience to superior orders is not a credible defense for willfully killing another person. Any organization whose member is directly responsible for a human killing must publicly express that organization's grant of immunity to the killer, or investigate the killing as a homicide.
>
> Killers are not released from culpability and liability for crimes solely because their higher authorities express a grant of immunity as to their actions. The expression of immunity

> only establishes by admission the responsibility of the killers' organization as a potentially culpable and liable participant in a killing. That is to say, what the organization granted might not have been immunity, but was impunity.

Why such a simple skeleton? You can always expand the compass of the term 'human rights' and raise the standards of behavior. You might determine that 17 years is a better measure for the protection of children, address the subject of torture, or even set the tormenting of , as an offense.

The above standard leaves open the possibility that a State or an insurgent might protect its agents against prosecution, claiming sovereign prerogative -- with the added flourish that a sovereign need make no justification, legal or moral, since, under a theory of *suma potestas*, there is no higher authority to which the sovereign State must answer. If an insurgent or an established State, claiming such sovereign independence from higher jurisdiction, does not explain its behavior for killing (or other trespass), it nevertheless exposes itself to moral judgment. At some point in an armed conflict, a competing entity will not only say it has a monopoly over the granting of impunity, but also a monopoly on imposing punishment, as well as a monopoly on allowing forensic investigations. Such a power might say, 'If you want to punish people in this territory for some alleged violation of human rights, you will have to force your way past us.'

Some people will argue that a government commits a human rights violation if it fails to stop a human rights violation directly committed by someone else, even its insurgent foe. This has been experienced several times by the government of Colombia. Such an accusation of secondary responsibility asserts that protection of the citizenry is an essential purpose and responsibility of a State. 'Failure to protect' has become a useful, parallel theory of State violation of human rights. Government omissions, inaction or impotence invite human rights charges against the government, making it easier for an insurgent organization to paint the State as a failure. This twist on human rights violation also encourages insurgents to provoke violence.

**Expansive human rights.** People invoke the United Nations Declaration of Human Rights for many purposes. It is a cornucopia of desires, used both innocently and cynically. Rarely is it used a manner that does not judge the ethical performance of armed competitors, and also their objectives, or where on the ground affected persons might enjoy a full range of rights without stepping on rights claimed by others. The Declaration of Human Rights is not a social contract; a social contract is not a list of desirables. A social contract is an agreement about how to peacefully address the distribution of rights and duties. If there is no social contract, then all human rights are subject to forfeiture. Social contracts are strongest when the evidence of rights and duties is accurate, comprehensive and transparent; where there are mechanisms to apply the evidence (such as courts, markets and democratic processes), and the basic rules regarding who can own what (how and to whom rights and duties can be distributed) is in consonance with the expectations of the population as a whole. Although there are some basic human rights that are increasingly recognized on a global scale, there is as yet no global social contract. A social contract requires geographic delimitation -- boundaries.

At some point, human rights, property rights and civil rights amount to the same thing. Perhaps the most basic right to property within English-language tradition is a right to safe use and enjoyment of a place. Human's have a right to exist safely *someplace.* That right is proscribed by the logic of physical separation. We can't all have the same right to peaceful use of the *same* exact place at the same time. Conversely, most of us cannot abide by the idea that there exist humans who have no right to peaceful safety *anywhere.* Mention of this obvious spatial logic leads to another -- that land stays put, but people can move. New theories of 'spatial justice' are at work confounding traditional logic by comparing human material conditions from place to place, and then calling for redistributions of wealth to the *places* of material inferiority. These 'spatial justice' notions depend in part on a curious invention in human rights theory: that not only do people everywhere have basic rights, their claims to a whole basket of rights should be answered without prejudice to their right to stay put (in terms of residence or employment, for instance). In other words, human rights are rights *in situ,* and furthermore, according to many proponents of this line of geographic human rights thinking, when people move, their claim of rights is still not subject to a duty to move.

Such a viewpoint obviously helps the immediate arguments of groups such as organized squatters. An opposing view stresses human movement and separation as options for conflict resolution and material improvement. In other words, this latter view, while it may or may not consider economic rights as basic human rights, does not attempt to suggest that a poor environment (a poor place) necessarily needs to be made better -- the alternative being to empower individuals to have a wider range of location choices that they can make for themselves. Sometimes the best of poor alternatives might be forced relocation.

We cannot effectively outline plans for respecting human rights if we express them in purely legalistic or moralistic terms. They have to be geographical. Thomas Jefferson's vision of a more equitable world required both theory and a place. 'Property,' however, is not a thing or a place; it is an agreement among people about the division of rights and duties within and related to territorially delimited space. Property is where law, economics and geography meet. The practical ethic of a human rights program first has to be about a human right to peaceful existence *in detailed space and time.*

Measuring human rights performance in terms of property, as suggested above, is the theme of Section 48, *Grading the Social Contract.*

See: 53, *Hohfeldian Grievance Analysis*; 144, *Impunity and State Success*; 73, *Property and the Social Contract*; 58, *Guerre d'Algérie*; and 72, *Land Strategy*; 23, *Mens Rea*; 48, *Grading the Social Contract*; and 105, *Genocide Geography.*

---

> "In every civilized society property rights must be carefully safeguarded; ordinarily and in the great majority of cases, human rights and property rights are fundamentally and in the long run, identical; but when it clearly appears that there is a real conflict between them, human rights must have the upper hand; for property belongs to man and not man to property."
>
> Theodore Roosevelt[179]

A cat as good as the king's

# *Section 126, Particularization of Power*

The number of individuals and groups that can exert their will at global distances continues to increase. I call that the particularization of power, as distinguished from the diffusion of property. Both phenomena are tied to globalization. The diffusion of property is the constant division and redistribution of rights and duties that are recognized within human collectives and tend toward increasing formality. The two terms, 'particularization of power' and 'diffusion of property' can be helpful to you in sorting out the nature and possibilities in irregular war.

Today, many individuals can implement their own foreign policy, visiting countries pretty much as they choose, writing congress to restrict aid, sending money to causes, blogging, suing or defending in international courts, or even working for a foreign government. An individual can do all kinds of influential things, often with little regard for the opinions or preferences of government. If he or she can represent a powerful group identity, or has attained great material wealth, he or she can exert influence at global distances. If the individual is nuts and homicidal, he or she can randomly ruin someone's afternoon.

There is a finite amount of attention that can be given by top government leaders to any issue, and when that attention span is occupied, remaining matters of State fall to second then third string bureaucrats. As the rank of the functionary drops, other parts of a government, and influences outside of it, stand to gain a little space. For instance, there is no hope of a unified voice or a *summa potestas* in American foreign dealings; there is more and more of a marketplace for American foreign policy in which the federal government is only a major player. The particularization of foreign policy power, then, is not just related to global redistribution of wealth or new communication technologies, but to ambivalence, involuntary abnegation of power, and the practical limitations of leaders' attention.

Banks, because they process the convertible wealth of other identities (clients, shareholders, creditors, debtors), are some of the most powerful and least understood non-governmental and semi-governmental entities. Through them, agile leaders can translate the cohesiveness of one kind of group into support for the project of another. Banking helps convert money -- hiding the connection between manifestations of debt and credit (cash, commercial paper, electronic inputs) and the manner of their acquisition or accretion. Banking allows what is perhaps the ultimate diffusion of property, and in a way is a paradox of the power of the capitalist system: its life blood, money, can be so easily converted into projects that sicken the system itself. In effect, insurgents can wield un-blessed power, translate it into representational forms of debt and credit, convert those representations into fungible money and then use the newly legitimated wealth to attack. That is really what money laundering is -- changing illegitimate power into legitimate power.

The particularization of power can be anticipated and managed to a degree. When it becomes property, it is a bit easier to see, but in many cases harder to control. In your irregular war, someone is translating power that was not recognized as legitimate or blessed by the system into legitimated property. As soon as illegitimate power is made property, and the laundering is complete, the same anonymity is no longer needed for its use. It is easier for the legitimated system to follow property, but harder for that system to confiscate or deny its use. It is not a black and white world, but in your case you are probably either all about laundering your power into legitimate wealth, or all about trying to keep your enemy from doing the same.

The particularization of power will continue. If you are of a mind to, you can slow it using laws limiting access to places, equipment and privacy. Limiting the conversion of un-recognized or illegitimate power into property, on the other hand, requires more careful study of market mechanisms that depend on the fluid conversion of assets.

See: 130, *Globalization*; 143, *Is It an Insurgency?*; 135, *Bank Robbery*; 73, *Property and the Social Contract*; 132, *Brigands*; 109, *Hotspotting*; 110, *Knowledge Gaps*; and 108, *Neogeography.*

---

> "I give away something up to $500 million a year throughout the world promoting Open Society. My foundations support people in the country who care about an open society. It's their work that I'm supporting. So it's not me doing it."
>
> George Soros[180]

Small war just before air power

# *Section 127, War Nouveau*

The turn of the nineteenth and twentieth centuries witnessed an eclectic, near-simultaneous stew of small wars, all in the context of accelerating globalization. Each contest was unique in terms of cause, motivations of the protagonists, strategic consequence, as well as weapons and methods employed. The principal conflicts occurred at about as great a set of distances from one another as earthly possible, and while their participants were often ignorant of goings-on in other parts of the world, each conflict nevertheless influenced efforts and outcomes in distant theaters. Military strategic thinking drew on centuries of conflict in which the variable of time and distance had changed little. Soon, the radio and airplane, among other technologies, would change all that. For a moment longer, the lessons of Gustavus Adolphus, Marlborough, and Napoleon seemed valid both in form and weight.

Among prominent pieces in the conflict stew in 1900 were the Second Boer War, which pitted the British Empire against a group of transplanted Europeans; Colombia's Thousand Days War, a federal/anti-federal contest; the coalition expedition to put down the Boxer Rebellion in China; the United States' suppression of insurrectionists in the Philippines; the foretelling armed defiance of the 'Mad Mullah' Mohammed Abdullah Hassan in the Horn of Africa; and, throughout 1900, American military governance in Cuba lead by General Leonard Wood.

The year 1900 started what some call the 'American Century.' As a flourish, three events from 1899 and three from 1901 framed it in the following table of fin de siècle events:

| | | | |
|---|---|---|---|
| 1 | 4 February, 1899 | Philippines | Private William Grayson kills a Filipino |
| 2 | 24 August, 1899 | Southern Africa | Boers place an order for six wireless sets |
| 3 | 15-17 December, 1899 | Colombia | Battle of Peralonso |
| 4 | 19-24 January, 1900 | Southern Africa | Battle of Spion Kop, Natal |
| 5 | 2 February, 1900 | United States | Hawaii becomes a US territory |
| 6 | 4 March, 1900 | Horn of Africa | Mohammed Abdullah Hassan attacks Jijiga |
| 7 | 15 April, 1900 | France | Exposition Universelle opens in Paris |
| 8 | 26 May, 1900 | Colombia | Battle of Palonegro |
| 9 | 10 June, 1900 | China | International force dispatched to Beijing |
| 10 | 11-12 June, 1900 | Southern Africa | Battle of Diamond Hill |
| 12 | 16 June, 1900 | Cuba | The Cubans hold local elections |
| 12 | 2 July, 1900 | Germany | First Zeppelin flight |
| 13 | 14 August, 1900 | China | International Relief Force reaches Beijing |
| 14 | 17 September, 1900 | Philippines | Battle of Mabitac |
| 15 | 1 October 1900 | Southern Africa | Dutch De Gelderland recovers Kruger |
| 16 | 27 February, 1901 | Cuba | McKinley signs the Platt Amendment |
| 17 | 23 March, 1901 | Philippines | Aguinaldo captured |
| 18 | 15 September, 1901 | United States | President McKinley killed by Leon Czolgosz |

1. February, 1899. Commodore George Dewey had taken Manila in 1898, but did not allow the Philippine revolutionaries, who sought and expected popular recognition as liberators, to enter the city as victors over the defeated Spanish. This affront notified the Filipinos that the Americans did not intend to grant the locals immediate independence. Tense relations led to an incident in which two American soldiers on guard duty, one of them Private Grayson, killed at least two Philippine nationals, who were looking to provoke an overreaction by the Americans. Legendarily at least, the incident sparked the Philippine Insurrection.

2. August, 1899. Invention of the radio was an incremental process, and recognition of a single most-deserving 'inventor' became a global public controversy, much of the evidence highlighted in patent suits and propaganda. Nikola Tesla, Guglielmo Marconi and Thomas Edison stood out among the contenders. By 1899, in any case, working production models of wireless communication devices were on the market. The Boers immediately recognized the advantages the device would lend to an army in defensive positions, needing to take advantage of internal lines in a large theater. They placed orders for six wireless machines, but unluckily for them, the British intercepted the delivery. The Boers were described by the British popular press of that time as being "solitary, uneducated, solemn people who were resistant to change."[181] Their appreciation of the radio showed they were not resistant to innovation if it involved fighting the British.

Arguably, the most prolific and ingenious were the Americans Tesla and Edison, but this did not prompt the US Navy to apply the device to military purposes quickly. Newly-launched American naval vessels would not incorporate this technology until after 1906.

3. December, 1899. Peralonso was the first significant battle in a federalist/anti-federalist civil war that eventually cost the lives of perhaps as many as 150,000 Colombians. It was a set-piece confrontation of regulars, or as close to regulars as the contenders could afford at the time. The insurgents, the Liberals, sent the government army, the Conservatives, into a ragged retreat. Victory for the Liberals is credited with securing long-term leverage for Colombian liberalism after the war. Nevertheless, an inexperienced Liberal general failed to exploit the opportunity that presented itself. He, like General Meade at Gettysburg, did not, or perhaps could not, pursue the broken Conservative army, preferring instead to recover and marshal strength. The battle (won, but not decisively, even though it seemed to be) lent false hope regarding Liberal military prospects.

4. January, 1900. Earlier, in 1881 during the First Boer War, the British had lost a quick series of battles at Majuba Hill, Bronkhurst Spruit, and Laing's Nek. The Boers won by fighting from fixed positions and using more rapid and effective infantry fire. As a result, in an 1887 military history text (*A Summary of Modern Military History*) T. Miller Maguire stated,

> "Still another point of great importance seems not to have been fully recognized, and this was that rapidity of loading, with increased accuracy and range, would no longer permit infantry in masses approach as heretofore a position defended by troops using breach loading arms....the attempt to move in masses under fire had to be absolutely abandoned."[182]

Maguire' reference, however, wasn't to the lost battles of 1881, but to a Prussian victory over the Austrians in 1866. The Austrians lost because they charged the Prussians, who were waiting in prepared positions and equipped with superior breach-loading 'needle guns.' In other words, Maguire was complaining in 1887 that by 1881 the British hadn't learned a lesson that they could have learned in 1866. At the turn of the century, Maguire was dismayed further. The Battle of Spion Kop in 1900 indicated that the British had still not absorbed the exact same lesson. Maguire lamented a continuing tendency of British tardiness to respond to key technological changes.

5. February, 1900. The transition of Hawaii from island kingdom to member in the American union reached the milestone of official territory, in spite of some American attempts to reject imperialism. US involvement in the Philippines predicated continued possession of the Hawaiian Islands. Dewey had been at a clear disadvantage for coaling and rearming during the events in Manila in 1898. The long Pacific lines of communication made incorporation of Hawaii a logical and comfortable decision for the American strategist, but conditions also had to present themselves to offset American public embarrassment at its own imperialism. A commission appointed by President Grover Cleveland in 1893 had found the United States guilty of dishonorable behavior, but subsequent investigations claimed otherwise, and that competing outside actors, specifically Japan and China, were meddling to influence the outcome. Strategic military necessity occasioned by the Spanish-American War settled the issue. America asserted permanent possession.

6. March, 1900. Mohammed Abdullah Hassan, a Somali, overran an Ethiopian garrison to recover a number of camels the Ethiopians had previously commandeered. Not a seminal historic event, it is instead an emblematic tic mark in a long and successful career of resistance against foreign presence. Hassan was charismatic, astute, and identified strongly with Islamic jihad against Christianity, especially Ethiopian Christianity. Surviving all British and Ethiopian expeditions to discipline or destroy his 'Dervishes,' Hassan operated in un- or under-governed territory that was of secondary importance to the British. The British had larger strategic concerns, beginning with the Boers and proceeding to the Germans, so it was not until after World War I that Hassan felt a level of imperial attention that destroyed his following. Never himself capitulating, Hassan died of the flu in 1921.

7. April, 1900. The official artistic style of the 1900 Paris World's Fair was Art Nouveau. As a style of architecture and applied arts in vogue for perhaps twenty years, it featured floral and nature-conscious themes, flowing lines and softened hues. It reflected optimism and cultural confidence, but at the same time harbored a sense of rebelliousness and defiance against the older design schools. America had its enthusiasts and prime examples, such as Tiffany lamps and Maxfield Parrish illustrations, but other, more technological currents and ideas tempered the American version. A euro-centric style, and a fanaticism for some, Art Nouveau was short-lived, giving way to Art Deco and other Modernism. Art Nouveau is perhaps the first artistic style to be swept along by the phenomenon of globalization, and its spread reflects the Western imperial stamp of the times, even to the extent of America's competent participation, but incomplete enthusiasm. As for France, new imperial adventures in West Africa, Madagascar, Siam and elsewhere generally were going well.[183]

8. May, 1900. In Colombia, only five months after the battle of Peralonso, the Battle of Palonegro dashed Liberal pretensions of fielding military forces able to defeat the Conservative government in open battle. This time the Conservative army won, but, as at Peralonso, the winning army could not or did not pursue its routed foe. After Palonegro, the Liberals felt compelled to pursue a guerrilla strategy that prolonged the war and undermined any moral containment of the horrors about to be visited on the Colombian nation. Military command inexperience and failure at conventional warfare led to a long and destructive guerrilla contest. As a result of national prostration, Colombia would soon be made to concede a huge swath of territory to Brazil in the southeast. The definitive peace agreement was finally signed in late 1902. It would

become known as the Wisconsin Treaty, its eponym the American battleship *Wisconsin*, on which the treaty was signed. The name evokes the American imperial surge as well as the geostrategic consequence of internal war that befell Colombia. It would also lose Panama.

9. June, 1900. Logistical challenges held up the international mission to relieve the foreign legation in Beijing. The principal delay: so many horses and mules had been expended in southern Africa to support the British prosecution of the Boer War.

10. June, 1900. The Battle of Diamond Hill was the last formal, or set-piece, battle of the Second Boer War. Unlike the Colombian battle of Palonegro, it was not especially bloody, with fewer than 250 casualties on both sides. Like Palonegro, its indecisiveness was followed by months of destructive guerrilla war.

11. June, 1900. Cubans successfully implemented General Leonard Wood's Military Order 164, which called for local elections. Suffrage was granted to Cuban males over 20 years old. The elections went well, and maybe they had a beneficial counterinsurgent effect. Wood's war on the mosquito population was definitive, however, all but eradicating malaria and yellow fever as health factors.

12. July, 1900. The first Zeppelin flight lasted for eighteen minutes, and was followed by other, longer flights. Lack of investment or government interest resulted in the ship being scrapped. Not only had the American Century begun, but the Century of Flight.

13. August, 1900. The China Relief Expedition reaches Beijing. The Boxers resisted European commercial exploitation and foreign constraints on Chinese sovereignty. The intentions of the United States government were arguably purer than those of its coalition partners in the sense that the official policy of the United States was one of universal openness and not privileged concessions. The difference may not have been perceptible at the moment; the United States participated in the foreign military coalition. American ability to contribute to the international relief force rested in good measure on the proximity of American units in the Philippines. American diplomatic leverage rested partly on America's commercial engagement with Japan. America's participation in a coalition was rare; perhaps the first time America participated in a multinational force since the American Revolution.

14. September, 1900. One of few Philippine victories in the insurgent war, the Battle of Mabitac involved a futile American infantry charge against a prepared Filipino defensive position. About twenty US soldiers were killed. Pickett's Charge was no more instructive to these Americans than the First Boer War had been to the British.

15. October, 1900. The Netherland's Queen Wilhelmina evacuated President Paul Kruger and his Transvaal government cabinet aboard the *De Gelderland* in open defiance of the British blockade. A European power had identified with the underdog and with common ethnicity, even if not to the extent that it could openly side against the British. Sending the armored cruiser was a gesture, and a bittersweet one at that. Kruger's wife was too ill to travel, and died soon after. Kruger himself died a few years later, still in exile. (And he wasn't even Dutch)

16. February, 1901 The Platt Amendment was made to a US military appropriations act. It partly defined the terms of Cuban-US relations and effectively replaced the Teller Amendment, which had been more of an anti-imperialist gesture. The Platt Amendment mandated that Cuba would contract no foreign debt that could not be serviced from ordinary revenues, and facilitated US intervention in Cuban affairs. It limited Cuba's span of action in foreign diplomacy and prohibited other foreign powers from obtaining basing rights on the islands. It is a milestone in the development of a form of partial American control that would mark some of its relations in the coming century.

17. March, 1901. As a Philippine insurgent leader, Emilio Aguinaldo had a history of being irresolute. He had accepted a payoff from the Spanish and later accepted one from the Americans. His personal capitulation greatly aided a favorable outcome for the United States, and apparently for Aguinaldo himself. He died of heart disease at the age of 94.

18. September, 1901. Philippine insurrectionists/ liberationists hoped for the election of anti-imperialist William Jennings Bryant. When Bryant was not elected, morale among the insurgents slumped. McKinley's assassination by anarchist Leon Czolgosz brought no relief in that regard. McKinley had actually been dubious about America's overseas adventures. He was succeeded by his Vice President, Teddy 'Big Stick' Roosevelt, who was hard to kill.

Art Nouveau expert Paul Greenhalgh opines,

> "Art Nouveau was developed by a brilliant and energetic generation of artists and designers, who sought to fashion an art form appropriate to the modern age. During this extraordinary time, urban life as we now understand it was established. Old customs, habits, and artistic styles sat alongside new, combining a wide range of contradictory images and ideas. Many artists, designers, and architects were excited by new technologies and lifestyles, while others retreated into the past, embracing the spirit world, fantasy, and myth."[184]

See: 131, *Sea and Aerospace Power*; 130, *Globalization*; 93, *Diseases and Disasters*; 99, *Postmodern and Post-structural*; 72, *Land Strategy*; 12, *Protraction and Diligence*; 27, *Democracy*; and 29, *Mens Rea.*

---

> "At Sagamore Hill we loved a great many things – birds and trees and books and all things beautiful, and horses and rifles and children, and hard work and the joy of life."
>
> Theodore Roosevelt[185]

If there's a global system, there's a global rebel

# *Section 128, Global Insurgency and Global Trespass*

**Global Insurgency:** A global insurgency has been afoot for some time – two or three thousand years maybe. Somehow, in the confusion of contemporary arguments and translations, people have begun to identify radical Islamists, deep ecologists, neo-Marxists and other curious bedfellows with global insurgency. That's too bad, because George W. Bush's mention of an empire of liberty was more in line with the heritage of global insurgency. That millennial current of insurgent energy and inspiration has been changing the balance of power between the individual and the collective toward the individual (the power to determine one's fate, compose one's vision of the meaning of life, establish relationships, and improve one's lot). It has clear revolutionary milestones, but has hardly been continual or consistent in its progress or expression. Now and then it has challenged a State, church or some other enterprise, and even destroyed some. It is not inherently against States or other human associations, but rather presumes that they tend toward tyranny and therefore occasionally need to be checked. It is an insurgency because it is about growing and preserving the relative power that individuals have within whatever structure of governance, associational preferences, and entrenched advantages they find themselves. It has old symbols and code words, like *liberty* and *free will*, and its strongest roots have geographic paths that seem to make it more 'Western' or 'Judeo-Christian.' While these latter identifiers may be dependent rather than independent characteristics, Americans are among the most easily engaged in advancing the millennial insurgency today. Partly because America's physical and cultural reach is global, the insurgency is global.

There exists another global current of that does not have as deep a set of roots. It also challenges the power of States (some, anyway) and other associational structures, and for this reason can be ascribed the adjective 'insurgent.' It does not challenge the idea of dominant State power *per se,* however. In fact, it prefers socialism and other designs for centralized decision-making. It is exactly not insurgent in that it seeks to rebalance power toward the State, arguing that human progress will be extended to otherwise abandoned and downtrodden humans if the State has more power relative to the individual. It does not presume that centralized States are inherently likely to abuse power, although it tends to be much more suspicious of churches and businesses.

This second 'insurgent' current manifests itself through a variety of organizational types, most of which depend on and venerate some form of exclusive agency, like a vanguard or a clergy. Although its adherents describe it using the word 'resistance,' it is often anathema to those who would defy and resist the creation of tyrannies, since it explicitly yearns and works toward the concentration of power in small elites. As a global resistance movement, it has taken on a basket of identifiers for what it resists. Accordingly, it describes itself as 'anti-' many things, including neoliberalism, capitalism, and colonialism. The most specific adjective for what the movement resists, and with greatest consistency, is *American*, as in *anti-American*. The movement has a number of intellectual call signs, among them post-structuralism. If a person self-identifies as a convinced post-structuralist, it probably means he or she has bought-in to active anti-Americanism.

The government of the United States does not always proceed in support of the millennial global insurgency described in the first paragraph above, or does it always oppose the resistance movement described in the second and third paragraphs. It is often the opposite. Equally, what Americans do in the world outside the auspices or control of the US Government does not always promotes the millennial insurgency or its counter. However, this bifurcated description provides a way to separate the adversarial notions of global insurgency for the purposes of this book. A global resistance movement exists to which some have applied the distorting descriptor *insurgency*. That un-insurgency does not oppose the notion of concentrated State power, resisting instead only those States that might oppose its imposition of exclusive leadership systems. Chief among the States that it targets is the United States of America. This is logical, since the United States not only can maintain global lines of communication able to support the delivery of physical power at great distance, but every once in a while it goes out to express the American preference for the millennial insurgency.

While there may be 'clashes of cultures' in the world, that concept is not the best foundation for setting the scorecard in the irregular war in which you are likely to participate. It will work better for you to envision the pair of insurgent currents noted above: one a fitful, inconsistent but genuine global insurgency with deep roots, and the other a reactionary amalgam that, when successful, often creates some new tyranny.

When Martin Luther tacked his ninety-five theses onto the door of the Church Castle at Wittenberg in 1517, he set one of the milestones of the millennial insurgency. He told the exclusive agents called the Roman clergy that he wasn't buying it any more. He would deal with God directly and do so in his own language to boot.

**Global Trespass:** There are also two forms of global trespass, *trespass* meaning the violation of others' rights, especially the rights we would suppose people to have in the peaceful enjoyment of their own lands. One of these forms of trespass has a tinge of legality. It is the overreaching and abuse of comparative advantage by those with *de jure* power, either financially or politically. It is what the multinational corporations often do and what dominant governments often do. In other words, having stated admiration for the millennial insurgency whose torch is most engagingly carried by America, it is necessary to insert the disclaimer that everything the second resistance movement (the un-insurgency) does and says is not wrong. It feeds on an existing reality of trespass and injustice.

The second form of global trespass has grown with globalization. It is transnational criminal enterprise. It is hard to claim that it is more or less dangerous to civilization, or to the millennial insurgency, than is the post-structural movement, partly because the two seem to have melded and intertwined to a degree that such an assertion might now be meaningless. Nevertheless, the trespasses can be mapped in space and time, and culpability assigned to actually men.

See: 130, *Globalization*; 100, *What the Foucault?*; 98, *Jorge Verstrynge and Pio Moa*; 124, *America's Insurgent Stamp*; 129, *Nerd Globe*; 46, *Taxes and Debt*; 99, *Postmodern and Post-structural*; and 81, *What a Clergy Wants.*

---

> "Most paranoid delusions are intricate...but this is brilliant."
>
> Dr. Silberman, criminal psychologist in the movie *The Terminator* (1984)[186]

---

Nerds can be bad, too

# *Section 129, Nerd Globe*

In the 2003 Internet article 'Organized Brigandage and the Structure of Life: The Top Ten Threats to America,' the number two threat on the list (David Letterman–style rating) is Math Assault. The assertion was and remains that losing dominance of higher math for almost any amount of time and in any sector of activity can present a grave vulnerability. The one-in-a-million math mind thus becomes the most critical strategic natural resource in the world, at least in terms of national defense or global security. We can divide the kinds of things an aggressive one-in-a-million-mind nerd can do on his evil little keyboard into five parts as follows:

> 1. Overload others' computers so that they don't work. He takes exception to some website, finding it offensive because it insults his nationality, favors someone who does,

seems morally dangerous, is a financial competitor, or who knows why. One of his options is to arrange a denial of service attack in which he overloads the supposedly offending server with so much computer traffic that it chokes on trespassing mips and bips.

2. Sabotage computer systems with viruses, worms, trojans and the like. This is especially annoying when the computers being attacked control things like air-traffic or power stations.

3. Steal valuables...like money, and personal identifications, which are then used to further their criminal enterprise, like stealing more money.

4. Spread propaganda, both commercial and political, to appear all over the place when the rest of us don't want to bother with it.

5. Rig elections. Many electoral territories use electronic voting machines, electronic vote counters, or both.

Obviously these five can overlap, and their effectiveness depends on superior computer skills and ultimately on superior math skills.

The techniques, mental competencies, and formal education needed to commit digital misdemeanors are the same as for digital felonies and digital warfare, and so possessors of these qualities bear watching. As with other crimes, the greater problems arise when bad nerds are organized by leaders with nefarious *mens rea.* What we should not overlook, however, is that the realm of organized math trespass is subject to the same principles of strategy that the mundane, muddy-booted warrior is obligated to observe. Co-relevance of 'virtual' and mundane strategic principles is outlined in the magazine *IOSphere* in an article by Scott Henderson titled 'Mao-e-Guerrilla.'

The classic principles of military strategy and its operational equation are ignored at peril, whether you are Erwin Rommel or Booger Dawson. The trespasser nerd lives in physical space, and his weapons are physical, not virtual. He needs a box, keyboard, server, router, cable, or satellite. He and his equipment are located somewhere. Distance is as important a concept for his actions (and for defense against his actions) as it would be in any other armed competitive activity. The thing to remember from Geography (the academic discipline) is that cost-distance is more important than Euclidean distance. The cost-distances for a trespass nerd, although he may not realize it, are determined by language, legal protection, and emotive or affective welcome. The Chinese hacker does not have to pay much attention to operational security as long as his trespasses are against properties outside those of the Chinese, and especially the Chinese government's domain of national interest, language, and territory. He is not likely to be extradited if he causes a denial of service attack against a website in Australia because he thinks the owners of the website are somehow supporting Uighur separatism.

The competent, funded, malicious nerd will raise his game of competitive strategy from latent stages of guerrilla organizing, to attacking vulnerable targets of opportunity (rarely venturing from his physical sanctuary) to risking extended and external lines of communication in order to establish weapons sites and opportunities for attack outside his sanctuary, into the enemy's geographic depth, attacking enemy lines of communication and even perhaps the enemy sanctuaries. The nerd can do this by overtaking enemy computers with botnet attacks and by planting timed commands in various parts of the enemy physical infrastructure for use at a future date. Perhaps more importantly, the nerd can seek to recruit and incorporate other nerds who can position themselves physically at distant places in order to provide the maintenance and warning necessary without endangering themselves. Know that the supposedly 'virtual' world of computers and math is one of human intention, housed in human bodies, and manifested using physical gear. The distances/weights and timing of the competition is a little different, but it is almost entirely physical, not metaphysical.

Any combination of unfriendly entities -- lone terrorist, brigand, felon, government, or simple pleasure seeker -- can seduce, fund, bully, or otherwise inspire a team of mathematicians to attack files, systems, accounts, and codes. The best mathematicians in the world don't seem to be much brighter than the average Red Wings fan when it comes to identifying the good guys and bad guys in the global insurgency. Loss of math superiority can mean vulnerability to the entire list of the top ten threats and all their permutations and combinations. It can lay a society bare to every terrible manifestation of resentment, disdain, envy, recklessness and other post-structural unworthiness. A large-scale math invasion could irreparably change a country's fortunes.

In other words, some governments will continue building regimes of both criminal and civil law that make hacking and other Internet trespasses more difficult. Depending on their geopolitical analyses, other governments will continue to protect trespass-nerds. Some countries will be obliged to increase diplomatic pressure on governments and NGOs to adhere to, promote and enforce legal restraints on Internet trespass. Shrinking the geographies of cybercrime and easing access to the physical implements of potential cyber trespass through international agreements can make the overall military task more manageable.

Governments, along with nongovernmental partners and allies will have to organize math minds not just for the purposes of passive defense, but offensive mathematical counterattack against trespassers. Finally, governments will prepare resources for the occasional need to visit physical destruction upon some wad of nerds.

The United States and many other countries have the wherewithal to ensure that the best math minds in the world have the opportunity and desire to choose them as home. This suggests governments take active measures to identify the best science and math minds in the world, at an early age, and assure that math education does not lag. The first defense against evil nerdity is to be an inviting attractive place for beautiful math minds to live. Meanwhile and nevertheless, bad nerds on a path detrimental to the safety of a nation must be confronted.

The State has three offensive capacities with which to mount winning strategies against nerds who digitally trespass against it and society. One is mathematical, another is legal/diplomatic, and the third is physical. It will not be enough to build math firewalls and observe safe Internet. There has to be an offensive capability so that the appropriate combinations of offense and defense give the State a reasonable chance against brilliant cyber guerrillas and criminals. Government's service and obligation in the social contract is to provide some modicum of security, and when it does not, the omission engenders self-help and vigilantism. Nerd feuds could get ugly and costly.

Special Operating Forces (SOF) will be called upon more and more often to attack cells of math nerds or even individual math geniuses. Sorry, Booger, but you might just have to go down. Taking Booger (who prefers to be called an 'IT professional') out competently will require observance of the military operational principles, which in turn will require careful study of the physical and human geographies in which counter-nerd operational art will play out.

Although cyber war happens in a physical world, the cost-distances are admittedly distinct. As a result, abstract concepts like spontaneity, collective identity, and democracy can be warped to create practical power advantages. Voting in political elections, for instance, can be achieved in all sorts of new and convincing ways, cheapening and confusing the whole idea of elections. Unscrupulous nerd-handlers can finesse their own rules of legitimacy, create new scams, and change outcomes. For every financial scam we are made to suffer as a globalizing society there may be an electoral scam that is harder to detect. Can the power of higher math be trusted in the hands of the State?

There also exists a related problem that has been developing for several millennia, appears to be accelerating, and could metastasize. It can be called the human presumption to godliness. We keep sneaking up on the biological secrets of life -- cloning, inventing species, promiscuously aborting, inseminating, or redesigning this and that organism. Someone is bound to get scared and angry -- not just at the hacker nerd, but at whomever is perceived to be the mad scientist. The torch-bearing mob at Dr. Frankenstein's door may go global.

See: 67, *Points, Lines, Spaces*; 63, *Cost-Distance*; 59, *Spontaneity*; 8, *The Operational Equation*; 128, *Global Insurgency and Global Trespass;* 2, *Anonymity;* 49, *Territorial Scrutiny*; and 2, *The Line of Retreat.*

---

"You know...
like nunchuku skills, bow hunting skills, computer hacking skills...
Girls only want boyfriends who have great skills."

Napoleon from the movie
*Napoleon Dynamite* (2004)[187]

---

To the chagrin of reactionaries

# *Section 130, Globalization*

The first of two quotations below is from *Karl Marx and Frederick Engels* (1848) and the other from *T. Miller Maguire* (who is featured in Section 8, *The Operational Equation*). A half century apart and a long time ago, the first makes us pause and wonder why being publicly opposed to globalization is such a broach of leftist political fashion. The later comment is more obscure, but together they confirm that globalization is not new to our generations. Maybe not even the pace of globalization is greater now than in some periods during the past. After all, the greatest change in moving weight may have come during the period of rapid railroad network expansions, and then again during the spread of airline service. It may be that, in terms of moving heavy items to some places, we aren't much better globalized today than we were half a century ago. It is possible that in some ways the world is not as 'small' now as it was in the first half of the 20th century, given that today there are fewer active miles of railroad in many areas.

There is no escaping the breathtaking differences in communication brought by the Internet, cell phones and GIS, but armed struggle takes weight, and while informatics have indirectly changed the potential for optimal geographic leverage of weight (that is to say, we should be able to decide more rapidly and precisely where to deliver things that have mass, whether tanks, explosives, food, or arrest warrants), information alone can be unconvincing in armed struggles. We the intransigent need to be shown something with a little heft or we will continue to defy your insults.

From *The Communist Manifesto* (1848):

> The bourgeoisie has, through its exploitation of the world market, given a cosmopolitan character to production and consumption in every country. To the great chagrin of reactionaries, it has drawn from under the feet of industry the national ground on which it stood. All old-established national industries have been destroyed or are daily being destroyed. They are dislodged by new industries, whose introduction becomes a life and death question for all civilized nations, by industries that no longer work up indigenous raw material, but raw material drawn from the remotest zones; industries whose products are consumed, not only at home, but in every quarter of the globe. In place of the old wants, satisfied by the production of the country, we find new wants, requiring for their satisfaction the products of distant lands and climes. In place of the old local and national seclusion and self-sufficiency, we have intercourse in every direction, universal inter-dependence of nations. And as in material, so also in intellectual production. The intellectual creations of individual nations become common property. National one-sidedness and narrow-mindedness become more and more impossible, and from the numerous national and local literatures, there arises a world literature.
>
> The bourgeoisie, by the rapid improvement of all instruments of production, by the immensely facilitated means of communication, draws all, even the most barbarian, nations into civilization. The cheap prices of commodities are the heavy artillery with which it forces the barbarians' intensely obstinate hatred of foreigners to capitulate. It compels all nations, on pain of extinction, to adopt the bourgeois mode of

> production; it compels them to introduce what it calls civilization into their midst, i.e., to become bourgeois themselves. In one word, it creates a world after its own image.

Considering that Marx' and Engle's observations are over a century and a half old, it's pretty insightful stuff. Note the positive aspects the original communists admitted regarding the contribution of the bourgeoisie and the value of globalization. There are some deep ecologists and others today who just don't like globalization, technological progress, or even humankind. They present quite a mental and philosophical challenge. But they are a detail in the panorama of global insurgency. Most of the rest of the participants in the self-styled anti-American version of global insurgency aren't really focused on or enraged about the processes of globalization as such. For some of them, globalization is a tagline for a select number of processes they feel work to the benefit of a small minority of humans and to the detriment of the vast majority. Identifying one's self as anti-globalization doesn't necessarily mark opposition to globalization processes per se, but is rather just a password or entrance badge to communicate solidarity with people who oppose what they think are dominating identities. (Ironically, Marx would have called opponents of globalization reactionaries.)

Marx did not understand property as a social contract or as a conflict resolution mechanism. He did not foresee that the bourgeoisie, if there even is such a collective identity, would actually increase and spread property, or that vastly greater numbers of people would become and consider themselves owners of property. He did not comprehend the modern corporation, or study America. Today's Marxism, however, is only a little bit about Marx. Still, Marx saw injustice, didn't like it, started to think about it, and called for action against it. Some of his original classifications of people were too crude, and his vision overly stuck to his time and place. People then distorted his ideas more, and then, with the auspices of an evil empire, a whole lot of people started adding to and evolving Marxism and Marxism-Leninism. When the empire died, and it looked like we might say goodbye to Marxism, a new group of thinkers dug it up so that now it roams the earth like a zombie, and with some of the same appetites. Today's anti-globalization movement is not all Marxist, but its inspirations and leadership overlaps what Marxism has become, even while it is barely recognizable as early Marxism.

And from *The Gates of Our Empire* (1910):

> "Manifestly the Pacific coast (of North America) is now absorbing the attention of the wisest as well as the ablest of mankind, and what applies to San Francisco in the event of any international dispute would also apply to Vancouver and Prince Rupert, which are a few days journey nearer to Asia than is California. Railways and steamships have almost annihilated distance. Napoleon's men had to walk or ride from France or Spain to Moscow. To-day it takes less time to reach Washington from the most distant nations than it took senators from their respective States seventy years ago, and less time to reach Vancouver than it used to take to get to Galway, and for Dr. Johnson to get to Scotland was a more troublesome task than for a Canadian contingent to get to Africa."[188]

Maguire was a friend of C.E. Callwell whose *Small Wars, Principles and Practice* was a bestseller among British military thinkers. Callwell pointed out that the small wars of which he wrote were those fought by regular against non-regular forces, and that the regular forces were almost always dependent on long lines of supply to base.[189] It was clear to these British that the irregular wars in which they took interest were only interesting because of the strategies made available to a country able to create and exploit the processes of globalization. Maguire was broadly read and was aware of communist ideas, but did not give them significance as a military matter.

Karl Marx and his friends focused on economic effects of globalization, and especially on land arrogations and their revolutionary consequences, but those consequences and the influence of their revolutionary thinking simmered slowly. Fifty years after the publication of the manifesto, Maguire and his buddies were teaching the practical effect of globalization on imperial military strategy, not oblivious to communist theory, but utterly unmoved by it.

Probably the best-known of the globalization measurements today is the 'Globalization Index' produced by A.T. Kearney/Foreign Policy, which can be downloaded at *atkearny.com*. It is a country-by-country ranking using four categories of globalization: political engagement, technological connectivity, personal contact, and economic integration. Although the most globalized technologically, the United States is 71$^{st}$ (out of 72 countries rated) in economic integration. This presents a strange relationship to the anti-Americanism of the neo-marxists, or post-structuralists. Their argument encompasses more than just economics, to be sure, indicting the entire structure of Western culture.

We can suppose all four of the globalization index' categories are fair game for their critical analyses, but economic imperialism is to the anti-capitalists the most consequential sin. Nevertheless, the United States is nowhere near the most involved internationally in terms of economic interdependence and integration. Also, one of the assertions of the Globalization Index is 'there is no turning back the clock on globalization.' This, to the post-structuralist, is an irritating part of a false truth they see foisted on the world by a capitalist, neoliberal, positivist, sexist, neocolonialist monster. In spite of their invective, however, the countries that are apparently benefiting the most, or which have best exploited the processes of globalization, are often small and not 'Western.' It seems, barring Armageddon, that the creators of the Globalization Index and Karl Marx are right – globalization is going to proceed.

Arguments about economics might best be placed to the side when considering globalization. Instead of considering any of the four categories proposed by the Globalization Index, or which countries land in the index's 'winners circle,' go back to what Maguire and Callwell noted about which countries were prepared to move and maintain military mass at distance. This is what really motivates the anti-Americanism of the post-structuralists. In spite of having inherited from Marxist tradition an economics-based conversation, the part of globalization that really galls anti-Americans is the fact that the world is smaller, overall, for the United States military than for any other armed force. The United States and only a few other countries can initiate and sustain military deployments in others' lands. Some would argue, meanwhile, that this US ability to wage war at distance is a fundamental column of the structure that allows the rest of globalization to proceed to the benefit of many lands.

So what? Globalization is, in balance, a positive process. Countries are far more likely to succeed materially if they can globalize. Development plans built on aversion to or denial of globalization (or of market forces) will fail or become tyrannical, and this will be so regardless of interest or indifference shown by the United States. In particular cases of American military involvement, it is an ability to maintain long lines of communication to base that, for better or worse, allows American intervention. Globalization will proceed to the benefit of the world so long as a few countries, and especially the United States, maintain their capacity to fight around the globe.

See: 131, *Sea and Aerospace Power*; 28, *Oviedo*; 63, *Cost-Distance*; 128, *Global Insurgency and Global Trespass*; 95, *Childhood*; 99, *Postmodern and Post-structural*; 100, *What the Foucault?*; and 8, *The Operational Equation.*

---

"My dear Nikolas, perhaps you don't realize that it's tea that has made the British Empire and Dr. Watson what they are today."

Sherlock Holmes in the movie
*Pursuit to Algiers* (1945)[190]

The advantage of optional wars

# *Section 131, Sea and Aerospace Power*

Sir Francis Bacon understood the relationship of Britain's small wars to sea power. The Royal Navy made those land wars optional for the British. It made land war on the British Isles an immensely costly proposition for a would-be invader; it provided a heavy lift line of supply to distant British armies; and it secured a route of withdrawal for those armies in case things went sour. It is never lost on a strategically-minded Brit that William had to load a lot of boats in 1066, or that at Trafalgar in 1805 Admiral Lord Nelson denied Napoleon the opportunity to do the same. On the back of that understanding the British had a pretty good run in terms of strategy and empire, dividends still paying. On one occasion, the distances were so great, the traitors resolute, and the French sufficiently seaworthy that the British lost an insurgency. It happens.

Aside from a possible Spanish-language insurgent movement based on some form of Mexican retro-nationalism, all of US participation in insurgency or counterinsurgency will continue to be allowed by United States sea and aerospace power. United States insurgent warfare is optional, and it is optional because sea and air power give the United States global-length lines of communication -- secure lines of supply and withdrawal. There is no American insurgent or counterinsurgent strategy anywhere outside of North America without the US Navy and the US Air Force.

It may seem that almost all the other sections of this book relate to the labors of men and women in government armies or in land-based insurgencies and gangs, and not so much about sailors, pirates, or pilots. That is the case. The submarine captain will find this book is less about him. Nevertheless, he and his submarine allow continued US presence on foreign soil. A submarine can help win an irregular war. In a given situation it can change the math of whose lines of supply and retreat are protected and whose are vulnerable.

The 'global commons' is a territorial concept that has to be constantly enforced. In part, that's because the operational equation holds true at all scales, and with a common sea, the lines of communications to distant sources of power are easier to keep open. Like the British, the American army officer can presume his global lines of retreat and supply are secure -- a security that exists because of the US Navy, the US Air Force and their allies. Xerxes would be a good witness.

Dynamic and creative use of airspace can provide an almost prohibitive advantage in war, an advantage that in irregular conflicts, although less decisive, goes more often to the counterinsurgent than to the insurgent. The same now applies to the upper atmosphere. In the last few decades we have witnessed two knowledge revolutions. One is the Internet and the other GIS (See Section 66, *GIS*). Both of these revolutions depend for their continued existence on the US Air Force. American ground forces still haven't figured out the real consequences of these revolutions to land power, and, like many things in armed conflict, it is cheaper to break things than to build them. But the US Air Force is probably going to be able to protect the orbiting equipment of the knowledge revolutions long enough.

Governments and insurgents alike understand the lessons of sirs Francis Bacon and Francis Drake perfectly. It is a geostrategic luxury to be able to go abroad to challenge other peoples' holes in ground, roadblocks, and other phenomena gracing sections of this book. Today, the aircraft carrier is a practical fact but for which many violent groups around the world would have little to fear. To many, targeting the USS Cole, though not a carrier, made all the sense in the world.

Air, space and sea power are not more tied to technological change and to machines than is land power, however. They are all woven together. Now, a century from the invention of fighter pilots, their machines are too good for them. The machines can turn quicker and acquire targets faster without a pilot. The cost-points for putting something dangerous in the air have gone down, and the game will soon become cheap enough that poorer peoples can play. Governments with smaller budgets and even insurgent forces are sending up dangerous machines, and sending the issue of local air superiority back into doubt. A few Latin drug lords have shown us something parallel if not quite as ominous in the water, launching flotillas of cheap semisubmersibles capable of independent navigation on the high seas.

Land power, for any country planning to conduct military operations in lands other than its own, is almost entirely dependent on sea and air power. This, historically, has been as true for insurgent or irregular war as for any other.

See: 2, *The Line of Retreat*; 138, *Roadblocks and Checkpoints*; 111, *Knowledge Cultures*; 5, *Misleading Counterinsurgency Articles of Faith*; 7, *Nonlinear Warfare*; 139, *UAAV*; 77, *Sex*; and 8, *The Operational Equation.*

---

> "This much is certain; that he that commands the sea is at great liberty, and may take as much and as little of the war as he will. Whereas these, that be strongest by land, are many times nevertheless in great straits."
>
> Sir Francis Bacon,
> 'On the True Greatness of Kingdoms and Estates' (1597)[191]

> "I do not say the Frenchmen will not come;
> I only say they will not come by sea."
>
> John St. Vincent, First Lord of the Admiralty (1803)[192]

Robbin' nations

# Section 132, Brigands

(This section is adapted from *Property & Peace.*)

Brigandage is evil with social organization and a plan. Brigands (gangsters, organized criminals, thugs, pirates, etc) are often the master employers of terror and terrorists. They combine organizational expertise, aggregated disposable wealth and amorality, and are to be feared in direct relation to the destructive capacity of the weapons that may come into their hands. Bridging what is a police problem and what is a military one, brigandage also straddles the cut-line between civilized-but-unlawful and uncivilized behavior. Sir Michael Howard recommends we use the medieval term *latrunculi* for them, to distinguish the fight against these common enemies of mankind from wars against *legitimus hostis* or legitimate enemies. Physical coercion for profit is wedded by the brigand to the timeless political aspiration of avoiding government regulation and taxation, and of acquiring impunity for criminal acts by any means -- best of all by assuming government power itself.

Governments can become confused or divided by what may be seen as a question of 'public safety' versus what is 'national security,' and so respond inappropriately. Parts of government go 'on-the-take' and further confound successful governance. When states fail initially to confront organized crime, they risk grave errors of omission -- moving from simple irresponsibility or appeasement, to corruption perhaps, then on to criminal negligence -- until the state has neither the power nor the willpower to contain the criminal enterprise. When this happens, a government has forfeited a country's sovereignty, and if that government were supposedly stewarding sovereignty belonging to the people, then it has lost to the brigands the people's status as sovereign owners. Logically, a government losing to brigands (in the fight to maintain a monopoly over the granting of impunity) could more surely relegate a people to slavery than by losing to insurgents or to another country.

Today, some criminal enterprises have global reach, and their day-to-day activities, while perhaps not rising to the dramatic level of the 9/11 attack on the World Trade Center in New York, are often of a similar character and lead to a similar result. Far more people have fallen in Colombia (or Nigeria, Thailand, Sri Lanka, and elsewhere) to the piecemeal terrorism of armed criminal groups than died in the World Trade Center. For decades the Colombian FARC murdered, kidnapped, and bombed on thousands of occasions, finally becoming too powerful to destroy without concerted military effort. Originally motivated by political confrontation, it lost its ideological compass when its funding changed from political donation to drug profiteering. It continued to cloak itself as a revolutionary force engendered and motivated by Colombian social injustice. The FARC 'contextualized' its violence using the argument of political necessity. While that argument is still used by some foreign governments as a justification for accommodations they make to the FARC (accommodations sweetened by FARC money and anti-American sport), the idea of FARC as a champion of justice is all but exhausted within Colombia. The FARC's brigand colors are transparent.

Brigand organizations metastasize, internationalize, and politicize. They call at first for routine compromises of the law, using minor coercion, perhaps justifying themselves as a social rebellion. Their initial presence and activity rarely inspires a reaction at the level of strategy or of military response. When finally it does, it is often too late for a peaceful cure. Many of these organizations plague the world, and as a convenient part of their efforts to establish or feign legitimacy they often disparage, or even target, the United States. Most of the world's countries acquiesce or collaborate with these outlaw organizations to one degree or another, so some foreign banks and governments impede US efforts to curtail outlaw finances -- either because they fear domestic political repercussions or because they gain directly from the illegal enterprise. Others simply disagree with the US view of the nature, progress, or virulence of the problem.

Operationally, most criminal organizations depend on smuggling to one degree or another, and smuggling means routes of movement and speed. Surviving smugglers become experts at logistics. Theirs is the world of lines of communication and the math of escape. Because that geographic math is so often contiguous with the geographic math of military strategy in irregular warfare, the two activities (profit smuggling and politically motivated armed violence) can hardly help but trip over each other.

Government may have to use their militaries to contain and dismantle a corrupted police unit. Military units can become corrupted as well, however, and the police, if ethically healthy, must be readied to capture and jail errant military personnel. This is one reason why the oft-touted virtue 'unity of command' has its limits.

This section, like most of the others, is not oriented exclusively toward the counterinsurgent or toward law enforcement. If you are an insurgent, some brigand may seem like a natural ally because of a shared State enemy. Nevertheless, the Brigand poses a threat to the morale and integrity of your organization, to your best lines of communication, and to both your substantive and perceived legitimacy. Be careful to determine if the alliance of convenience should be you and the brigand against the State, or you and the State against the brigand -- or if the brigand and the State are one-in-the-same. All brigands are smugglers, but not all smugglers are brigands.

Junior Johnson from Wilkes County, North Carolina was a convicted moonshine smuggler, but not a brigand. Junior just liked to drive fast; Ronald Reagan pardoned him in 1986.

See: 1, *What the Pirate Said to Alexander*; 128, *Global Insurgency and Global Trespass*; 45, *Police or Military*; 65, *Smuggling*; 133, *Snipers and Assassins*; 95, *Childhood*; 144, *Impunity and State Success*; and 40, *Rule-of-law*.

---

"And his partners in the posse ain't tellin' off ****...
...Cause damn it feels good to be a gangsta."

Geto Boys from the song
*Damn It Feels Good To Be a Gangsta*[193]

Murderers if no immunity; Convicts if no impunity

# *Section 133, Snipers and Assassins*

Sniping has long been a controversial issue in warfare. Sniping combines a sense of elite status, both technologically and athletically, with stealth. It also gives an impression of one-sidedness, of ambush or surprise. It is so effective and disconcerting that the officers of professional armies have on occasion distanced themselves from sniping as a dishonorable activity, at other times embraced it. Meanwhile, sniping, sharpshooting and regular marksmanship keep closing the gaps among them.

Landmines and snipers are revealing features of irregular war. We refer to the sniper rather than the rifle, while we refer to the landmine rather than the 'emplacer.' Sniping is a more personal act and is more personally risky since, unless done perfectly, it can reveal the whereabouts of the perpetrator and does so within the effective range of an opposing rifle. Snipers have been part of the combat landscape for some time. They are costly because the expert sniper is a physical rarity, must be vetted psychologically, and must be exhaustively trained. The sniper participates intimately in the distance-time-weight linearity of warfare. Most of his activity is movement to the place where he can take a shot, and his art consists of being able to take that shot against a superior unit and be able to escape. The sniper, even as an individual weapon system, must understand and obey the constraints of the operational equation expressed by Maguire. Judging distance is one of the sniper's staple skills.

Explosions are almost exactly not sniping. Their use does not require that the eyes of an emotionally responsive human watch the detonation and effect. The user of explosives can treat the mathematic of operational art differently (being able to begin part of his escape before the detonation), and the moral weight of using explosives is distinct as well. The same professional officer who might eschew the use of snipers due to moral sensibilities might have to reject the landmine outright. In fact, many armies have all but rejected the use of landmines, but still employ snipers.

Because it is such an integral part of a sniper's art that he blend into his surrounding environment, the concepts *sniper* and *spy* begin to converge, at least in urban settings. When snipers are used by an insurgent force, the government might successfully label them simple assassins or murderers.

It is an advantage in irregular war to enjoy superiority in effective, disciplined snipers. That advantage will grow stronger as UAAV's become cheap if not ubiquitous. Leaders in an irregular war should make the status and employment of snipers an issue of direct attention. At some point, influenced by law and diplomacy, a sniper becomes an assassin. My advice is that you not become a sniper yourself unless you can count on being granted impunity by your bosses.

See: 8, *The Operational Equation;* 2, *The Line of Retreat*; 82, *Conflict Thresholds*; 144, *Impunity and State Success*; 115, *Transforming Armed Forces*; 131, *Sea and Aerospace Power*; 136, *Weapons*; and 24, *Ruthlessness and Resolve.*

---

**Vasilli**: In the forest, the wolf lives for three years and the donkey for nine.

**Tania**: That must be a proverb from the Urals, it makes no sense to me.

**Vasilli**: The donkey lives longer because he's more useful.

**Tania**: There aren't any donkeys in the forest, you made it up.

From the movie
*Enemy at the Gates* (2001)[194]

# *Section 134, Luigi Galleani*

Luigi Galleani was born in Italy around 1861, became an anarchist in his teens and moved to the United States in 1901 still practicing and preaching anarchy. He did not come to America to seek a better life or to pursue the American dream. He was a violent communist radical who came to the United States because he could. Other places could repress the vocal anarchist too easily, or had already kicked him out. A lead character in the history of American terrorism, he is an apt biographical focal point for the purposes of this book. Luigi learned the physical operational imperatives of rebellion, and how ideology could both support and offend those imperatives. Always in trouble with the law or a fugitive (he had to escape from an Italian prison in order to emigrate), he was never convicted of a serious crime in the United States. The feds exported him back to Italy in the wake of the 1919 'Red Scare' bombing spree for having promoted the violent overthrow of the United States government.

Luigi was educated, articulate and charismatic. He published a widely circulated booklet on how to make bombs, and a newsletter encouraging 'propaganda by the deed.' One of his mistakes was to let the feds get the mailing addresses of his newsletter recipients during a raid, opening up a number of avenues of investigation and thereby compromising quite a few of his followers. He also made some technical mistakes that blew up a couple of his bomb-makers. Luigi was smart enough not to do the bombing himself.

Two of Luigi's anarchist soldiers, also immigrants, were Nicola Sacco and Bartolomeo Vanzetti. Nicola and Bartolomeo were arrested for murder in 1920, and executed in 1927. Various aspects of their drama are relevant today, bearing as they do on the continuing emotional, philosophical, and political controversy about the relationship of America to the meaning of life. Luigi, too, had been arrested and tried for incitement to riot, but that jury found the prosecution's case inadequate, acquitted him, and the case never became part of popular lore.

For some people, the story of Sacco and Vanzetti is about American hypocrisy... an emblem of the injustices heaped on immigrants as an outgrowth of systemic racism...an epic but woefully common tale of American exceptionalism gone unfulfilled. Galleani's name graces the title to this section, rather than 'Sacco and Vanzetti,' in order to underline operational matters like keeping secrets, impunity, the line of retreat, and the central importance of the guy with the *mens rea.* I also wanted to place the Sacco and Vanzetti saga in a context of identity, sovereignty, and legitimacy. Nicola and Bartolomeo were members of Luigi's violent organization, an organization that funded itself through robbery, used explosives to terrorize and project, and sustained itself within an ethnic geography.

Unlike 'normal' bank robbery or murder defendants, Saco and Vanzetti received high caliber, expensive, and extensive defense counsel. Their status as anarchists and leftist radicals attracted support and solidarity not only in emotional or ideological terms, but in funding and publicity. The support was from a movement within which the lives of Nicola and Bartolomeo were perhaps valued little more than the victims of their bombings. They may not have committed the murders for which they were arrested and tried. The jury may have found them guilty for crimes they did commit, but for which they were not arrested and tried. Their lawyer, a famed socialist defense attorney, built their defense around their being anarchists -- that they were unable to get a fair trial because of public prejudice against their political views. A parallel theme was the generalized injustice inherent in the capitalist system. That strategy helped vault the case onto the world's imagination. Making the case about political blindness and social justice (rather than about a crime) worked, but it might have cost Nicola and Bartolomeo their lives. The probable intellectual author, the *mens rea* guy, died in Italy in 1931 of diabetes or some related complication.

A couple of decades later, Julius and Ethel Rosenberg couriered secrets from Los Alamos Laboratories to the Soviets, accelerating Russian development of their atom bomb. Sacco and Vanzetti had been tried in the shadow of, but not under the authority of the 1917 Espionage Act, but the Rosenbergs were the first to be executed as spies. Their indictment and trial was for decades a controversial cause célèbre whose ledger of ideological positions and proponents read much like those of the Sacco and Vanzetti case. Many commentators the world over would reference the Rosenbergs' fate as an example of a failed social system that had responded to unfounded fear and to ethnic prejudice. For decades, the Rosenbergs' innocence was proclaimed and their execution denounced by left-leaning intellectuals. Ideology aside, it is now beyond reasonable doubt that the Rosenbergs committed the acts for which they were convicted, although public clarification would not come for a half-century after the events -- after the fall of the Berlin Wall. This clarification came with the exposure of the 'Venona files.'

The 'Venona files' is the informal name given to a body of declassified or otherwise uncovered Cold War intelligence files from both the United States and the former Soviet Union. (Several good book titles cover their contents and revelations.) In short, the Venona files not only proved that the Rosenbergs were guilty as charged, the files radically changed the historical record regarding the second 'Red Scare' of the 1950s. The Venona files are nevertheless ineffable in many history and social science departments on campuses today. Few bumps in historiography are so discomforting to the ideological left. The Venona files say, indirectly, that using the word 'McCarthyism' to mean 'political witch hunt' is merely a semantic souvenir of a politicized misread of the actual events.

Senator Joe McCarthy, who became obsessed by what he saw as secret Communist infiltration into American public life, was a delusional paranoiac, and many of his accusations were demagogic and unsubstantiated. Nevertheless, his paranoia fed off a base of facts. The Communist penetration may have been almost as bad as he imagined. There *had* been an extensive secret Soviet Communist penetration into American public life. Having this fact intoned today, much less read aloud, is anathema to the post-structuralist worldview currently fashionable in academe. That worldview would rather have the Rosenbergs, like Sacco and Vanzetti, remain iconic victims of an unjust society, rather than what they were in *deed*: small criminal perpetrators.

Rebels and revolutionaries can be founders of nations, but they have to win. Often pawns of a more cunning and ruthless leader, their personal retreat to sanctuary might not be as well secured as that of their masters. Fortunately or not, honor for the rebel soldier, or at least pity for him as a victim, can be preserved for years, even in the face of the best evidence.

See: 54, *Badassoftheweek.com*; 2, *Line of Retreat*; 16, *Keeping Secrets*; 101, *Magical Realism*; 50, *U.S. Persons*; 143, *Is It an Insurgency*; 72, *Land Strategy*; and 22, *Mens Rea.*

---

Q. Why do anarchists drink herbal tea?
A. Because proper tea is theft.

From The Daily Cocktail, Infoshop.Org
*Anarchist Lightbulb Jokes*[195]

Because that's where the money is

# *Section 135, Bank Robbery*

Bank robbery is a classically romantic activity, something Bonnie & Clyde do, and as difficult as human genius can make it to rob a bank, someone always does. Banks are forts for money. In spite of successful robberies, their existence proves that sometimes defense is or seems more economical than offense, and passive defense sometimes better than active defense. If this were not the case, there would be no banks.

If you have some responsibility for the planning or conduct of some activity related to irregular war, you ought to know where the banks are. These days they might be piggy banks, ATMs, money order stores, computer servers, armored cars, or brick and mortar bank banks. Know where they are; somebody is going to rob them, maybe you – and it won't be well done or well stopped without understanding the escape routes.

Once dollars get into a bank they are not only economically fungible, they become unloved. They become the money of nobody but the system, making bank-robbing more ideologically palatable than robbing from stores and individuals. Centralized account insurance can make it worse, as the depositors then don't care if the bank is robbed. Also, there's more money at the bank for robbers to rob. Here are seven typical bank robbing modi operandi:

> * Enter the local bank building wearing Richard Nixon facemasks and holding some white nylon bags and machine pistols. Tell everyone to get down, leap over the cashiers counter, go to the vault, withdraw cash, stuff it into the bags and then leave, making some violent threats on the way. Jog a block and a half to the getaway car, get in, take off the masks, drive around the block past the bank and away.
>
> * Practice printing money until your bills pass the tests at the local bank counter, then start distributing it and exchanging it for real bills.
>
> * Watch who has bankcards and is buying durable goods with them. Pick up a daughter in one car and the Dad with the bankcard in another. Tell him his daughter is fine, ask him for his personal identification number for the bank card and go to an ATM at a convenience store and withdraw money. Repeat until there is no more money in his account. Let the Dad and daughter go somewhere near each other and not near a phone.

* Learn a lot of math and figure out how to generate your own PIN and break into other peoples accounts without the kidnapping.

* Forget individual accounts and learn a lot more math to break into the banks accounting systems to move money into your account.

* Don't bother with the childish math and get to the uber-math. Learn how to shave points off some kind of reverberated commissions on money market speculation, put it into an algorithm that is timed to make automatic buy and sell decisions at the conjunction of certain dates and market conditions, and… whoosh.

* Mix banking with government and get the government to give your bank money out of its reserves or new issue. This may not seem like bank robbery, but the money is a measure of confidence and the money of the bankers isn't really theirs to begin with. They're supposed to be doing something with it on behalf of their depositors that maintains or increases the financial power of the depositors, so when they do things that reduce the money's relative value, it is almost the same as the counterfeit scheme above, or plain robbery, it just takes a larger scale in numbers and time for the effect to set in.

Now you're thinking that this section has gone too far afield, away from irregular war and toward the murky realm of finance and partisan politics. It is not meant as a sideward comment on the shenanigans and robberies surrounding the United States financial melt-down and bailouts of 2008 and 2009, although they did bother. It is about the geography where your irregular war is unfolding. If you are the insurgent you have to know about the banking system, and it behooves you to rob it. Banks are core places – physical, mathematical and psychological – of the system you think you are trying to overcome. One of the absolute basic services that government performs is the provision of fair measure, and money is the most basic of these. Trust in the money can be imputed as trust in the government. If the government can't maintain the worth of its measures, its legitimacy will wane. It isn't called the 'coin of the realm' for nothing, so, if you're down on the system, you will want to take away its coin. Besides, someone is going to rob the bank, why shouldn't you? You may not have the mental or educational wherewithal to implement the high-end econometric robberies toward the bottom of the above list, but that's OK; you can kidnap the daughters of the people who can.

If you fancy yourself as the counterinsurgent, on the other hand, then you want to know where the banks and bankers are, and, if it is at all in your power, to reshape the geography of money to your best advantage. Depending on the level of commercial development, you may find it advantageous to limit some kinds of transaction to cash, or have certain control technologies placed on banking machinery. If you are the counterinsurgent, the system of exchange is one of the basic things you are supposed to protect, since it is one of the basic things that government is supposed to provide. It may be that the public has lost the sense of linkage between the official money and personal ownership, and so you may want to make that linkage more psychologically meaningful. When a bank is robbed anywhere in your land, that robbery redistributes a little slice of everyone's rights. That slice of power goes to someone who is either an insurgent or a criminal. If a bank is robbed, your enemy gets stronger. So if you do not understand the measurement and geographies of fair exchange, you do not have a grasp on one of the classic means that your enemy has for increasing his power relative to yours.

Bank robbery is more than just another outlaw activity. It moves to the essential purpose of government. If you are an insurgent, you need to figure out how to rob banks.

See: 132, *Brigands*; 17, *Kidnapping*; 129, *Nerd Globe*; 115, *Transforming Armed Forces*; 30, *Control Technology*; 64, *Measuring Power*; 65, *Smuggling*; and 33, *Built Environment.*

---

**FBI Agent**: You're a pretty good judge of size, right?

**Krista**: Size of what?

**FBI Agent**: (shows a $20 bill) What do you think? 6 inches? Under or over?

**Krista**: Under.

**FBI Agent**: Wrong. 6.1 inches. See, I know everything there is to know about money. Thickness: 0.0014 inches; weighs about 1 gram. You know what that means? That means this $20 bill isn't even worth its own weight in Oxycodone.

From the movie *The Town* (2010)[196]

After all, it's about armed conflict

# *Section 136, Weapons*

This book is about armed conflict. We can have violent, organized competition without weapons, but it is called rugby. We can every once in a while stage a big punch up, monkey-style, but over time humans have continually improved their weapons, and this improvement occasionally changes the balance of who is likely to dominate and who is likely to submit.

The cannon is a major historical accomplishment for warring. Its composing innovations accreted over a long period of time, so maybe it was never revolutionary, but it was at least transformational. It is hard to make an arrest with cannon, though, and the people who use cannon don't usually watch their effect in real time. You can extort with cannon, however. Veracruz comes to mind.

The use of artillery can mark a usable threshold between what is 'police' and what is 'military.' In military combat we know that artillery is fearfully effective against infantrymen (soldiers who cannot fly and have no armor worth bragging about). Some soldiers think they are called infantrymen because 'cannon fodder' would have been insensitive. One of the common mistakes in irregular conflicts is for infantrymen to think there won't be artillery, or that enemy planes won't see them.

Howitzers and mortars are variations of cannon designed to send their projectiles on high angles of ascent and descent, thus able to fire over hills and on top of distant targets. You can't make arrests with them, either. Today we are witnessing a hybridization of indirect and direct weapons, which may prove, from more historical perspective, to be a revolutionary step in warfare. The *Predator*, an unoccupied, armed aerial vehicle, is the archetype. (See Section 139, *UAAV*.

In terms of accountability and impunity the most un-artillery weapon is perhaps the pistol. A person has to be pretty close to the target to use a pistol, so the emotional investment and the quantity of resolve needed to use a pistol is much different than for a cannon or an aerial vehicle. However, another weapon that seems dissimilar to artillery, the landmine (or, more broadly, the explosive device or artifact), is closer to artillery on the plane of accountability. No one tries to make an arrest with a landmine. Explosives are often used for pure intimidation, or for making logistics more expensive and causing an overall increase in the costs of an enemy's operations due to force and population protection concerns. However, landmines can also be the backbone weapon for a military operational plan that adheres to the Maguire equation described in section 8 and elsewhere. The landmine can be used to change the relative culminating points of pursuers and pursued, especially in terrain that offers a number of constrictions to movement. If any single weapon or thing has contributed to the longevity of the Colombian FARC, for instance, it would be the cottage industry landmine. If you, as an insurgent, can make it seem morally unjustifiable for the government to use artillery, but still morally justifiable for you to use landmines, you will gain operational advantage.

Lately, inventors have been accelerating efforts to develop nonlethal but incapacitating weapons. Water cannons work, but you have to carry a lot of water. Among the best of the new breed is a sound gun from American Technology Corporation that has seen extensive service in Iraq. Although it is a bit heavy and clumsy, it can make people unbearably uncomfortable, and yet do them little permanent harm (relatively speaking). There are others. Like any weapon, people will find ways to neutralize or minimize it, but the sound gun is the kind of thing that can change the balance of advantages in situations such as a roadblock or building takeover. One of the key advantages that government can have in irregular armed contests is the ability to invent expensive new weapons. Nonlethal choices can change contested geographies (such as building or monument occupations), and change the utility of using certain classes of participants (like small dissent groups populating street barriers). The sound gun or one of its relatives might turn out to be as transformational as the armed aerial vehicle. The nonlethal weapons *can* help make arrests.

Having stated the advantages of new non-lethal weapons, new lethal weapons, like the XM25 airburst shoot-to-behind walls firearm, or armed aerial drones, will likely be seen to have made the greatest impact on winning during and after the conflicts in Iraq and Afghanistan.

See: 19, *Extortion*; 82, *Conflict Thresholds*; 131, *Sea and Aerospace Power*; 125, *Human Rights*; 133, *Snipers and Assassins*; 116, *Strategy of Aggregate Tactics*; 139, *UAAV*; and 24, *Why Humans Don't Fight.*

---

"The only person who could miss with this gun
is the sucker with the bread to buy it."

Peter in the movie
*Dawn of the Dead* (1978)[197]

# *Section 137, Declaration of Counterinsurgency*

The American Declaration of Independence is the seminal document of modern revolution and insurgency. Whatever other significance it has in the history of political discourse, it asserts that sometimes it is legitimate, valid, justifiable, honorable behavior to use violence to overthrow a constituted government. Also in the document, however, are the careful disclaimers about when and under what conditions armed rebellion is justifiable.

What would the counterargument look like? When is it justifiable to use armed violence against a political opponent of the State? This may seem obvious enough, even trivial (it's sometimes called criminal law), and in the best of worlds there is a presumption in favor of the State. Nevertheless, there exists a powerful empathy, greatly America's product, for the insurgent underdog when State opposition can be reasonably painted as a political question or one of relative legitimacy. That empathy has the wonderful effect of changing the burden of proof, and of confusing ethics and equities sufficiently to open space for the insurgent, and to presume him to be noble and the State despicable. This is a good thing -- it keeps government on its ethical toes, but it can also put a mantle of acceptability on what are often just charlatans and evildoers.

A declaration of counterinsurgency might look something like as follows:

> When in the course of human events, it becomes necessary for a people to oppose political bands which have established themselves in violent opposition to the existing social contract and to the government that has been constituted to enliven that contract, a decent respect for world opinion requires that the people should declare the causes which impel them to violently repress such bands.
>
> We still hold these truths to be self-evident, that all humans are created equal, that they are endowed by their Creator with certain unalienable Rights, that among these are Life, Liberty and the pursuit of Happiness. That to secure these rights, Governments are instituted, deriving their just powers from the consent of the governed, that so long as the government is constructive of these ends, it is the right of the people to oppose violent attempts to alter or to abolish it, and to take such actions as to them shall seem most likely to effect their safety and happiness. Prudence, indeed, will

dictate that governments should not answer opposition with violence for light and transient causes; and accordingly all experience has shown that government should suffer even strident opposition, while evils are sufferable, rather than address opposition by abolishing the forms of liberty to which the people are accustomed. But when a long train of abuses and usurpations by an opposing band, pursuing invariably that which evinces a design to reduce the amicable social contract by force, it is the people's right, and the duty of government, to repress and eliminate such a band.

Such has been the patient sufferance of the people; and such is now the necessity which moves them to violently oppose ___________. The history of the ______________ is a history of repeated injuries and crimes, all having the object of destroying the social contract which the people have and continue to embrace, and to supplant that social contract with the establishment of a tyranny of their own selfish design. To justify and encourage opposition to this arrogance, let facts be submitted to a candid world.

Here a list of offenses committed by _________________:

In every stage of these abuses the people have petitioned for redress: Our repeated petitions have been answered only by repeated injury. A band of outlaws whose character is thus marked by every act which may define a tyranny is unfit to be seen as a legitimate counsel or vehicle of political change.

Nor have we been remiss in attentions to reconcile with the _______________. We have issued innumerable warnings and offered various forms of amnesty and plea bargain. We have appealed to what we hoped would be their native justice and magnanimity, and we have appealed to them citing the ties of our common kindred to disavow violence. They have been deaf to the voice of justice and reason. We must, therefore, acquiesce in the necessity, and hold them, as we will hold those who directly support them, enemies.

See: 46, *Taxation and Debt*; 143, *Is It an Insurgency?*; 128, *Global Insurgency and Global Trespass*; 98, *Jorge Verstrynge and Pio Moa*; 14, *Legitimacy*; 5, *Misleading Counterinsurgency Articles of Faith*; 124, *America's Insurgent Stamp*; and 122, *Songs of Chu*.

---

"Once vigorous measures appear to be the only means left of bringing the Americans to a due submission to the mother country, the colonies will submit."

King George III[198]

# *Section 138, Roadblocks and Checkpoints*

Roadblocking is such a typical activity in armed struggles that it should be a central feature of strategic analysis, planning and measurement of success, irrespective of the side of the ledger on which you find yourself. If you want to win an irregular conflict, strategizing roadblocks is probably a necessity. Roadblocks offer a way to effect strategic extortion, steal wealth directly, kidnap selectively, take initiative away from the enemy, and improve chances of enjoying a favorable correlation of force in distant encounters with the enemy. Roadblocks can be quick, only intended to instill fear, or they can be planned to cause some piecemeal and clumsy reaction by the enemy force. They can be mounted through popular movement organizations on the back of some real or trumped-up social question. In this form we can expect them to last for as long as a suitable response fails to mount. A roadblock by a labor union-type of organization, a transport union perhaps, can be placed quickly. These can be extremely costly to overall commerce and industry, and yet can be selectively targeted so that extortion demands can be made to specific individuals. In addition, they can be disassembled before government authorities can assert dominance of the situation.

Blocking the passage of people and things almost always hurts something and someone. Blocking passage *is* violence, and is a popular component of taxation, extortion or just outright robbery. Roadblocks and checkpoints, moreover, adjust the weight of variables within the operational equation. A roadblock planner can apply map algebra to determine the relative cost-distances of effective violent action and an opponent's response to that action. A highway robber can anticipate the correlation of forces likely in the event of a confrontation with the authorities at different points along the road, as well as what security he will need along escape routes from the loci of potential confrontation to safety. His risk analyses will weigh time against the wealth he might happily redistribute by conducting the roadblock. Highway robbery can be profitable if the math is right.

If a government has no strategically practicable plan to address the problem of roadblocks, a smart outlaw can mock law enforcement, and a strategizing insurgent can all but paralyze, and certainly bleed road-bound trade. Roadblocking links the two major strategy options (position and maneuver in anticipation of battle, and extortion). As insurgent, you set up a roadblock as a place of battle chosen by you, and with it you hold the free functioning of the society at risk. The government is all but obliged to respond to a roadblock, and so your action gives you the added possibility of inviting a clumsy response, which you will then further exploit.

It seems everyone everywhere thinks a successful government can assure free flow on roads. The street or the king's highway is psychologically, if not legally, public space. If a group can defiantly collect 'taxes' along a road with impunity, the government will disrespected, and will be seen to fail. If a force can with impunity continue to make movement so costly or dangerous that wealth is held at risk generally, a government will be seen to fail. When a government cannot *effectively* assign culpability to highway robbers or subversives for blocking public ways, the public will quickly assign accountability for the road blockage to the ineffective government.

Government overreaction to roadblocks may at times be the only goal an anarchist or insurgent has, especially if he is clever enough to use surrogates to build and occupy the barriers. For its armed response to the roadblocks, the government will then be painted as the initiator of violence. Blocking people's passage against their will is always a form of violence, but the nimble practitioner of the roadblock can make only the reaction to the roadblock score as violence in the public's eye.

Roadblocks are a central, critical aspect of armed social struggles; perhaps the building block or basic move of an insurgent position and movement operational art. Here is the basic move example: A resistance (insurgent) leader plans a roadblock on a highway 20 miles outside a provincial capital, just on the city side of a road junction. The intersecting road leads to remote areas. He will use a group of radicalized union members, but he doesn't want them jailed, he plans for them to leave the roadblock in the hands of some local supporters when sufficient government force begin to arrive.

The leader knows that in order to dislodge his thirty male and female activists, the government will try to reach the roadblock with at least twenty police or military personnel dressed in riot gear and carrying smoke weapons and clubs. Not wanting to chance failure, however, the government will want to send closer to fifty police. Because of the location of the police stations in the city and the time needed to collect the force, the insurgent can count on at least an hour before a force strong enough to dislodge the roadblock arrives (depending on the time of day). During that hour, the protesters can erect a large barrier on the road about a quarter mile in the direction of the city that will take a backhoe or other piece of heavy equipment ten minutes to remove. In the other direction, at the far side of the junction, they set up a barrier that can be removed quickly, but that stops the traffic going toward the city. So, when the police finally start to arrive with sufficient force, the roadblockers let traffic move across the junction and pile up behind the main barrier, providing them an additional ten minutes. The organizers then pack up and move out along the side roads enjoying at least a fifteen minute head start. They're gone. The protest leaders might even be in sanctuary for an hour before the police get to the junction. More likely they are already stupid drunk while they watch the police chief on TV explain why his troops are shooting teargas at some teenagers.

The cost-distance to the junction for the government was fifty times the pay of one policeman, plus transport for all of them and a backhoe, plus the cost to commerce of having the road blocked for an hour, not to mention having had to keep so many police available in reserve, plus the opportunity costs of not having some of the police where they otherwise might have been. To these costs are added the psychological and political weight of having clever rebels stick it to the Man.

The above simplification gives a basic pattern of roadblock warfare, or the basic move in a roadblock *Go* game. Real operational environments include many routes and potential constrictions, public events and special days, the locations of police stations and public transport, lookout locations, synchronous armed actions, and so forth. The moves can be contemplated and calculated in advance, and often the side willing to do the calculating necessary to get a step or two ahead of their opponent can stay ahead.

In English, we generally refer to police or government roadblocks as checkpoints. The term connotes an event or contraption that is not designed to impede traffic or collect a tax (that's a tollbooth), but simply to conduct inspections. Checkpoints can help crack enemy anonymity, make smuggling more expensive, improve the balance of culminating points in relation to actions and battles, and apprehend fugitives and scouts. They shouldn't just be set up anywhere. If the design is to increase the cost of smuggling, they need to be placed in accordance with an economic analysis of source location, warehousing, transshipment processing, etc.

The viability and efficiency of the inspections, protection of the checkpoint personnel, their rules of engagement, and their vulnerability to corruption should be explicitly addressed in plans, tested and inspected. The checkpoint plan should include an integrated legal concept. In this regard, the government can announce off-limits routes for commercial passage. That is to say, along with major inspection points, the government can make legal checkpoints, inviting licit traffic to flow through main routes. A problem arises when such schemes present targets for terror attack or overburden inspection stations to the point that the economy is damaged.

Bolivia has a lot of space, and a sparse road network. The people of La Paz, one of Bolivia's two capitals, live at an altitude more than twice that of the people of Denver. The *Paceños* (people of La Paz) still live downhill from the half million people who live in El Alto, where the airport and all the communications towers are located, and through which most of La Paz' water comes. If rebels can set up successful roadblocks in El Alto, they can tumble the national government. It happened.

Some places are *trans-modal* locations, that is, places where people or things are moved from one form of transport to another. They are typically used as taxation points, legal and illegal. Whether to government bureaucrats, longshoremen, mafiosos, insurgents or some combination, trans-modal localities present special opportunities for siphoning wealth. When stuff is transferred from a truck to a train or a train to a boat, or even from the trunk of a car to a suitcase, the places where these transfers occur have a regular and often predictable physical signature. They should be identified and considered according to the quality of the opportunity for wealth diversion that they offer. Trans-modal places are special and should be a key feature in place inventories and geographical analyses.

Crime statistics show over and over again that transport-change locations are high crime areas. Even if this were simply a secondary effect of population patterns and the bumping together of territories, there is no getting around the fact that ports and stations and intersections are lucrative places for social stress. They are among the most likely places guiding the logic for locating roadblocks and checkpoints.

See: 8, *The Operational Equation*; 65, *Smuggling*; 131, *Sea and Aerospace Power*; 62, *Illicit Commerce*; 57, *Dogs and Mules*; 139, *UAAV*; *82, Conflict Geography*; and 19, *Extortion.*

---

> "The government of Colombia and even the United States do the same thing... If you don't pay your taxes, you go to jail. Here we don't have jails, so we detain people."
>
> Raul Reyes (dead narco-guerrilla)[199]

Changing the math of distance and moral weight

# *Section 139, UAAV*

The most transformational weapon to come out of the US wars in Iraq and Afghanistan is not the unmanned aerial vehicle, the UAV, but what I would rather call the unoccupied armed aerial vehicle, UAAV (in some documents called the *weaponized UAV*). Finally the killer is watching the kill at a cold distance. The difference is immense, even if, like many changes, it has not yet been fully felt. The UAAV is a big new number in the irregular war map algebra. Think about the basic strategy move in Section 138, *Roadblocks* and how a UAAV could change the game math. Just following the enemy is a good deal, but being able to bring fire on him is a whole different thing. The UAAV brings airpower to smaller, messier conflicts. The thing is, the UAAV is soon going to cause a sea change in what it takes to secure aerial dominance. Lots of countries can make effective little UAAVs, and make them a lot cheaper than the ones the US is in love with these days, like the Predator.

Meanwhile, folk who would never think of throwing on a ruck (so they can sweat walking sixty miles to kill someone) will nevertheless bring death after they set their coffee mugs over to the side of the monitor so they can take some time-in to shoot someone who is two thousand miles away in the face. You can't help but wonder if the guy with the ruck gets the same color medal. No ghillie suits, no crawling into a hide, just a couple of spreadsheet entries.

The real problem isn't the medal, (although the cheapening of valor is no weightless matter), it's the impunity – who grants it and who gets it. The boss is in the room, the machines will tell the forensic investigator who is making the kill decisions, and there is no reason not to keep records, except, of course, to provide impunity. If the enter key pusher is not identified, the hierarchy still will be, so leadership will perhaps be increasingly held accountable when a UAAV kills non-soldier-looking types.

The Smithsonian National Air and Space Museum website stated the following:

> "The US military began experimenting with unmanned aircraft as early as World War I. By World War II, unmanned craft could be controlled by radio signals, usually from another aircraft. Vehicles that could return from a mission and be recovered appeared in the late 1950s."[200]

The US Air Force could have had effective operational UAAVs flying decades ago, but doing so would have meant a radical change in the organizational culture of the Air Force. The alpha male Air Force officer, the guy who goes on to be a general, had, for the most part, to have been a fighter or bomber pilot. Seeing a technology that suggested a new and less athletic path those prime jobs presented a challenge. For decades it was virtual treason to mention the darn things, much less fund programs to develop them. Now the argument is over. Solid circuits don't worry about and aren't limited by the pressure of sharp turns, or by fatigue. What we don't yet know is if the preferred path to generalship will run through the *remote fliers'* toggle-of-death. We can rest assured that cognitive dissonance will cause air forces everywhere to make awkward decisions as they try to maintain their institutional niches.

Section 8, *The Operational Equation,* applies the late nineteenth century observations of a lawyer and historian named Maguire. That era and Maguire's math are relevant partly because his synthesis about military strategy was made just before the advent of the airplane and the changes the airplane wrought in military thinking and practice. The Wright Brothers seemed to make many of the old rules of operational strategy go away, and in fact, the airplane did change the calculus. Lines of communication could be threatened from new angles as well as new speeds. Moreover, in situations where it was hard to achieve victory by applying the classic methods (to overcome his lines of supply and retreat or defeat him in open battle), the airplane made it easier to apply the other strategic approach: extortion. If you didn't have the patience or wherewithal to beat your enemy by position and maneuver, you could perhaps place what was most valuable to him in mortal danger.

The UAAV may force a similar if not as grand an adjustment in military operational math. In irregular war, airpower has perhaps had its greatest effect through changing relative culminating points (especially the helicopter), mostly moving government troops well beyond what would have been the limits of their safe distances. The UAAV does something else, enlarging the geographies of possible points of contact without having to carry additional weight, without the same risk to the attacker, and at a much lower price. The math of culminating points, correlations of force and the geometry of lines of retreat is again being adjusted. Furthermore, the change will not so uniquely benefit government forces as did the helicopter.

You can't make an arrest with a drone aircraft. Perhaps hole diggers, homemade rockets, and international lawyers will be salient features in future irregular armed conflicts. With new arrays of technology in mind, and as to some conflictive places at least, use of the UAAV will carry special juridical and political consequences. Armed engagement with a UAAV inside many countries will quickly test the limits of impunity that might be granted to its operators.

See: 138, *Roadblocks and Checkpoints*; 76, *Gendering*; 133, *Snipers and Assassins*; 2, *The Line of Retreat*; 31, *Holes in the Ground*;
104, *Extraterritorial Jurisdiction*; 82, *Conflict Thresholds*; and 45, *Police or Military*.

---

"...you may fly over land forever;
you may bomb it, atomize it, pulverize it and wipe it clean of life,
but if you desire to defend it, protect it, and keep it for civilization,
you must do this on the ground..."

T.R. Fehrenbach,
*This Kind of War*[201]

ൽൾൽൾൽൾൽൾൽൾൽൾ

A concession to Clausewitz

# *Section 140, Culminating Point in the Pursuit*

The culminating point is a theoretical point in time and space beyond which it would be unwise to proceed with an initiative, such as an offensive, an attack or a pursuit. The term 'culminating point' dates back at least to Carl von Clausewitz, the Napoleonic era, and classic strategy. Of all the concepts of classic strategy that have been dismissed in modern writings about insurgency, this may be the one whose absence is most detrimental.

The operational equation counsels aggressive pursuit (because an inferior force that cannot escape runs the risk of ruin). However, if the pursuing force presses beyond its culminating point, the pursued may turn and counterattack, effect an ambush, or maneuver to cut off the pursuer from the erstwhile pursuer's own line of retreat. Hence, positional, movement warfare revolves in part around the leaders' analyses and intuitions regarding culminating points.

As a matter of military critique, generals are often discredited who fail to press an opportunity to finish off a weaker force. Some will argue that Meade should have pursued Lee after Gettysburg, for instance. These critiques are always speculative observations of a victory that might have been greater. On the other hand, when it is clear that a commander did in fact pass that point of too much risk, it is usually because he was defeated by a counterattack.

The culminating point for a squad in the attack depends in part on the amount of water it carries or if it can be easily resupplied with water. Because the human body so needs $H_2O$, a squad's leader would at some point be taking too much risk if he were to make the squad continue to move forward beyond the squad's water supply. In a severely dehydrated state, the soldiers might be subject to heatstroke, or to an effective counterattack from a well-watered enemy. If this were to happen, if an enemy were to turn and defeat the squad due to its dehydration, we could say that the squad had passed its culminating point.

The distance to the squad's culminating point also depends on many other variables. Ammunition and food are other common limiters of the culminating point. Military expressions like 'water discipline', 'fire discipline' and 'rationing' attest to this. The quality of weaponry, training, morale, and leadership are also contributors to the amount of time and distance before the squad might reach its culminating point. Transportation options also influence the culminating point. A helicopter, for instance, can change the time-distance equation like few other machines. Finally, and this is no small point, initial location on the ground affects the culminating point.

In many situations the landmine can drastically shorten distance to the culminating point. If a squad member steps on a mine during pursuit of an enemy unit up a mountain trail, not only will the squad be immediately weakened, the leader will feel he must take more precautions and move more slowly. The squad's theoretical point in time and space beyond which it is too risky to precede is reduced just by the threat of the landmine.

Why is all this about a theoretical point? -- Because you can design a strategy in such a way that the aggregate of your units' culminating points is advantageous. You can also compare the contributions of various seemingly disparate inputs. For instance, you can determine if the purchase of another helicopter is likely to increase friendly culminating points to an incrementally greater degree than improving the training of your unit leaders or by building a wall somewhere.

Thinking in terms of culminating points can also help determine rough measures of relative unit effectiveness, the reasonableness of an operational strategy, or the relative advantage of positions. It can aid in understanding why certain places are better for building forts and walls.

Getting somewhere is not the same as getting back. Aircraft can take a unit well beyond the culminating point. The French garrison at Dien Bien Phu is an example of a huge violation of classic principles as synthesized into Maguire's operational equation (see Section 8). The French did not assure that, if they were to confront an enemy force with greater strength, their route to sanctuary was secure. In a sense they placed themselves beyond their culminating point *ab-initio.*

See: 116, *Strategy of Aggregate Tactics*, 8, *The Operational Equation*; 2, *The Line of Retreat*; 67, *Points, Lines, Spaces*; 11, *Decisive Battle*; 88, *Sieges and Takeovers*; 7, *Nonlinear Warfare*; and 63, *Cost-distance.*

---

"Next to victory,
the act of pursuit is the most important in war."

Carl von Clausewitz,
*Principles of War* (1812)[202]

Strains on strategy or strains of strategy?

# Section 141, Seven Strategy Strains

There are seven categories, currents, methods, options for dealing with your foe. They are:

1. **Operational Art**. Positioning and movement that seeks the optimal time and place for contact. Cognizant of the practical interrelationship of relative power, distances, technology and resolve, the classic strategist tries to adjust variables of the operational equation to his advantage and to perplex his enemy regarding options, thus driving the enemy to err.

2. **Extortion**. You despair of dominating map algebra and its lines of communication, or you disdain the risks of operational art. You instead hold at risk something of value to your opponent, and convince him that

you are willing to destroy it. You offer to protect or relieve him from that fate if he bends to your will. This course works best if you still pay some respect to the operational art of position and movement, however. Sometimes the word attrition fits in here. Attrition is slow extortion.

3. **Deception**. You deceive your foe into giving up, giving you what you want, or falling into one of the first two options above. Most of the 36 stratagems attributed to Chinese strategic culture involve deception. Some strategists feel that the word strategy refers to this option almost exclusively, or at least that it is indispensable for the optimal functioning of the other options. Some would say if you don't have the power to win battles head-on, that you are relegated to strategy, and they usually mean this kind of strategy.

4. **Negotiation**. You weigh costs and benefits and figure you can offer something to your foe in exchange for something he has or a change in his behavior. It might be that the exchange will benefit both you and your opponent. It is not necessarily a zero-sum world. Trade can be great, create wealth, solve problems. Perhaps he seeks changes in the society or power structure that you are willing to make. More than likely, however, if you are dealing with a foe as characterized in Section 4, *Defining Enemy*, there is not enough time, and you will have to combine this option with one of the first three above.

5. **Argument**. You appeal to reason. You don't have anything to trade, and you either can't or don't intend to deceive. You just have some moral or practical arguments that you feel you can effectively make to dissuade or change the behavior of your foe. This is a great option if he does not fit the definition of enemy around which the rest of this book worries.

6. **Annihilation**. You don't plan to outmaneuver your foe physically, or threaten, deceive, negotiate or argue with him. You don't have to. You have the power and willpower to simply eliminate him from the face of the earth.

7. **Do nothing**. Under this choice we find delay and surrender.
Surrender is always an option. Leave this miserable vale of tears. Delay might work; good things come to those who wait, but, again, our definition of enemy doesn't afford much time.

If you don't wish to surrender, you can't wait, arguments won't work fast enough, you don't have the power or willpower to annihilate your foe, and you don't have anything you want to negotiate away, then you're pretty much stuck with the first three strategy options. Combine them as best you can.

See: 8, *The Operational Equation*; 102, *Negotiations*; 123, *Thirty-six Stratagems*; 122, *Songs of Chu*; 89, *The Dot Game*; 2, *The Line of Retreat*; 6, *Classic Strategy and Irregular Warfare*; and 11, *Decisive Battle.*

---

> "To create a formula or a general rule...that would be appropriate in all situations is absurd. One must be able to think on one's feet to be able to make sense of each separate case."
>
> The Most Humane Human[203]

ശ്ശ

Honor is not private property

# *Section 142, Dignity and Honor*

Do not leave the subject of human dignity at the level of a common sense ingredient in plans and programs, or as a checklist item in the review of the plans, or as a question of tactical cultural courtesies. Instead, make plans that specifically address and incorporate the broader issues of human dignity, and then assure that said plans reconcile with other plans. Study degradations of and threats to the dignity of human identities as they are linked to the places you think you want to stabilize, destabilize, subdue, conquer, liberate, own or protect.

We all have a pretty good idea what the words dignity and honor mean, at least within the context of our own lives, our own institutions and our own society. Like real thirst, however, many of us have not experienced profound lack of dignity, or lack of hope. Our empathy can fail us.

We know that assaults against dignity induce stress, whether the assault is a slow, grinding result of established social relationships, or a more immediate economic or territorial trespass. In any case these can be translated into grievances and, through agency and leadership, into action.

You can highlight grievances, point out assaults on human dignity that have been embedded and hidden in the existing social structure as you find it. (This is sometimes called deconstruction.) You can even increase the sense of insult, or strategize to exacerbate the cause of the grievance in order to bring it to a point of intolerability.

The better plan will be a transparent effort to grow dignity, and to be seen doing so. Anytime you can afford to not offend, don't. In general, older people are not so impatient as to expect indignities to be undone with a stroke, and younger people are not so docile that they are willing to postpone honor for a future generation.

Because they constitute the vast majority of the fighters, the dignity of young men may be of greatest urgency. Their dignity may be tied to that of their parents, siblings, friends and romances. You may, however, not always want or be able to preserve or respect the dignity of young men. For instance, in some societies the dignity of potentially violent young men may be tied to a status quo of submissive indignity for women. It is easy to state the rule, 'Respect everyone,' but dilemmas abound.

This book is greatly about lines of supply, lines of retreat; about physical position and movement, finding and closing with an enemy in order to neutralize and dominate him. It is unapologetically about those things, but they need a bigger reason. Over the long haul they cannot defy basic truths, and one of the basic truths of irregular conflict is the accounting of dignity. On whatever side you find yourself, there one day will be an accounting of how you, your subordinates, your leaders, and your ideas related to human dignity and the structure of life.

It is not that honor and dignity play no role in regular warfare. They do. In irregular conflict, however, the ultimate objective is often an elusive condition of the spirit. Yours may be an existentialist's war. If you cannot express the relationship of what you are doing to the meaning of life, you will want to review your goals to see if that connection is missing. If you cannot say how your goals of closing with and destroying the enemy fit the sustainable balance of dignities (as related to the human identities in the places where you fight) you might want to rethink things. In other words, if you are the leader, and you cannot tell your followers why what they are doing is a fine thing, you might not be the leader. That is not to say, however, that at some scale the honor and dignity of a group of people will not have to be sacrificed, abandoned, postponed, relegated, or even abused and diminished for the safety and dignity of some other identity. Maybe that is the case, and maybe it is a truth you do *not* make transparent.

The 'hearts and minds' approach to insurgency can be too slow at getting to the nub of things. That nub (something probably related to the culminating point) in a given tactical situation might be nothing more than thirst for water and the opportunity to make that dangerous discomfort go away. In urban environments the nub is not usually water, but is very likely camouflage, that is, anonymity. An environment that hides the person can also hide the details of his motivation, and while *whereabouts*, or geographic anonymity, is touted everywhere in this book as a first problem to solve, that solution alone (finding people) is insufficient. What to do with the knowledge about identity and whereabouts remains. If you act quickly, perhaps you can kill your enemy and go home before having to deal much with the question of his dignity. If your answer is not is death or imprisonment, then it is probably tied to dignity. A 'hearts and minds' campaign directed squarely and competently at questions of dignity may be effective, but perhaps only with years of application. Paradoxically, with every ineffectual lingering moment, failure to understand your enemies' dignity will burden your ability to change the balance of anonymity to your favor, that is, finding him.

Even if you only help make it possible for people to evacuate their bowels in a decent way, they will figure out the positive linkage between your behavior and the improvement of their dignity. Humans can be grateful. Still, helping people is not always the way to honor or respect them. Also, being respectful of all people does not mean to suspend judgment, accept all cultures or communions as equal, or pardon trespasses. Respect is a starting place.

See: 79, *Suicide*; 94, *Poop*; 76, *Gendering*; 95, *Childhood,*
51, *Underclass*; 70, *Measuring Effects of Actions on Structure*;
53, *Hohfeldian Grievance Analysis*; and 1, *What the Pirate Said to Alexander.*

---

"Whereas the east coast monuments such as the Lincoln Memorial and the Statue of Liberty speak specifically to ideals, the Protestant Memorial chapel at Fort Leavenworth, Kansas—overlooking the Missouri River at the edge of the Great Plains, with the rails of the Union Pacific visible in the distance—invokes blood and soil."

Robert D. Kaplan[204]

Do you think they may convey immunity?

# *Section 143, Is It an Insurgency?*

Section 124, *America's Insurgent Stamp* notes that Americans like insurgents; America is all about taking it to the Man. When Americans call a situation an insurgency they give some psychological points to the antigovernment side. Here is a kind of litmus test to tell if your war is an insurgency: Do you think the enemy leader has a right under international law to convey immunity to his armed subordinates for killing your armed subordinates (assuming those actions fall within the laws of war)? If you say yes, you put yourself in a traditional State-on-State international war, and it is no longer, if it ever was, an insurgency. If you say 'No, the enemy leader is granting impunity to his people in defiance of my authority,' then yours might still not be an insurgency, but you only then only have to decide if your enemy is merely a criminal, or is instead politically motivated to force change. That distinction is a little trickier.

You'll hear it said (sometimes in pretty huffy tones) that 'insurgency' relates to a goal while 'guerrilla' relates to a method -- or something like that. Sometimes the point is made to argue that more must be done within a battlespace than just combat, 'guerrilla' connoting the combat, and 'insurgency' evoking other efforts including psychological, economic, and social, etc., to gain popular support and not create more enemies. Sometimes almost the opposite argument is made, suggesting that while the type of warfare might be guerrilla, the situation does not call for a full range of counterinsurgency effort. Try not to get caught up in the distinction, as accurate as it may be. 'Guerrilla' is Spanish for small war. Many English etymologies reach it back to the Peninsular Wars of the late 18th century, but the term goes back farther in the Spanish, and yes, there can be guerrilla tactics, guerrilla strategies and guerrilla all kinds of things within a non-insurgent war.

If you get to maneuver a tank brigade against another tank brigade, everything in your battle-space is subject to being blown to smithereens. When you're done, you (hopefully) will go back to the motor park to dust off. You probably don't care if the tiff is called a UN Chapter 6 peace mission, an insurgency, a police action, a punitive expedition, World War III, or what. This book imagines conflicts that don't hold out much chance for that big tank battle to occur. Here we are looking for a separatist, insurgent, brigand, warlord, crime boss -- whatever -- but if any of them *were* to have a tank brigade, the contest would start to be a different creature than what we talk about here. The more useful distinction revolves around the granting of impunity and how much a group has to depend on anonymity to keep defying the State.

For years, Western analysts preferred to view insurgency through the lens of a Marxist-Leninist movement with a unifying ideology, a well-defined cellular structure and a hierarchical central leadership. Many insurgencies of the past half-century had their inspiration and funding from Moscow, Beijing, Cuba, etc. as part of the East-West, Cold War competition (or of the competition between the Soviet Union and the Peoples Republic of China for supremacy in the Communist world). Other insurgencies were discounted and ignored. The wide gamut of motivational and organizational formulae is now more evident, some 'insurgencies' fueled by hate, revenge and psychological stridency, others by gangsterism, and others by the hybrid energies of ideology and profit. The common denominators are their ability to grant impunity to their people within physical space, and to what extent they need to maintain anonymity in order to do so. If they need no anonymity and can still grant impunity, perhaps they are, to that extent, another State. If some foreign government accepts that a resistance group has a right to protect its members from punishment, that group is getting closer to being a State, and if the challenged government also accepts that the insurgent group has the right to protect its operatives from punishment, then the group is looking even more like a separate State.

This book throws most of the irregular armed conflict types and resistance groups into one pot for discussion. Distinguishing them can be comforting, however, so below is a comfort list:

**Armed Insurgency** – Someone is trying to throw out the government by force of arms. They say the government is illegitimate, greedy and corrupt, and justify their use of violence on that basis. They challenge the government's claim on any exclusive power to grant impunity, and attempt to protect their people from being punished by the challenged government.

**Revolution** –Revolutionaries say that the symbols, vocabulary, bureaucracy, institutions, power relationships, legends, – the whole social structure, is built to keep down a particular identity, maybe the proletariat, a race, women, or an amalgam of disaffected groups. If they are right, you might want to make some changes, negotiate, give up or go over to their side. On the other hand, they may be bent on wresting power by force and killing you in the process. If it's an armed revolution, insurgency is a 'lesser included.'

**Occupation and Stability Operations** -- All ground operations are occupation and stability operations. Otherwise, what are they -- 'call in by phone and curse about the chaos' operations? It's just a matter of how long you need to stay and what you want to accomplish.

**Separatism** -- Separatists don't plan on throwing the government out of office, just throwing it out of a place that they claim belongs to them and not to the government or to whomever the government claims to represent. It might or might not be revolutionary, but that doesn't make much difference. There is something about the current ownership they obviously don't like, and that part maybe makes them insurgents. If the separatists are successful, the old government will no longer be able to punish their people, or grant impunity to the government's people, inside the new territory.

**Organized Crime** -- Criminals like the government fine if its people will take the bribe. If the government won't take their bribe, the 'don' is still betting the government can't convict his wise guys, and that it definitely can't convict the don. Criminals often feel the same way toward revolutionaries as they do toward governments. However, crime would be sweeter if they could take over a government for themselves, so the concepts might overlap, and it still doesn't matter.

**Armed resistance movement** -- They don't want a stranger there, the place probably wasn't the stranger's to begin with, and the stranger might not want it either when it comes right down to it.

**Guerrilla war** -- Guerrillas aren't going to confront a stronger force unless they think their line of retreat is secure. They might not have much air power to speak of. They take care to protect their anonymity. They probably dig holes in the ground. They might or might not wear uniforms, or their own uniforms. They might be insurgents, separatists, revolutionaries, or they might not.

You can hold all these concepts together by remembering that if a group does not provide anonymity for its members' personal identification, whereabouts and wealth, you will be able to attack it and its power, and it will not be able to grant its people impunity. They can call themselves anything they want, but pretty soon, if you take away their anonymity, you'll be eulogizing or calling each of them by a tag number. If the group doesn't need anonymity any more, that is, if it can just get in your face, and you can't take away its ability to grant impunity to its people, you're losing. The various definitions of resistance groups are not useless, but don't let the fine distinctions of identity, method and purpose steer you away from analysis of a group's ability to control the balance of anonymities, and grant impunity.

Geography is a simpler discipline than Political Science -- easier to understand. Land rarely lies. If your enemy's line of retreat courses into a foreign territory, where your neighbors allow him sanctuary, then your neighbors are abetting. Your neighbors are helping keep you from asserting a monopoly over the granting of impunity in your place. If your neighbors go further than the mere allowance of sanctuary, and explicitly protect your enemy against punishment for violent acts he commits in your territory, then your neighbors are allies of your enemy. For all logical, operational purposes, your insurgent foe then becomes part of your neighbors' military apparatuses. The basic principles of operational art are grounded in time, space and weight. They tell us that no amount of redefining and grammar is going to change some simple facts. Either an insurgent can maintain his line of retreat to sanctuary or he cannot. However you publicly define terms, go back to the basics of operational art, and the geography will often reveal how much power it will take to win.

See: 45, *Police or Military*; 144, *Impunity and State Success*; 132, *Brigands*; 56, *Militias and Gun Control*; 7, *Nonlinear Warfare*; 53, *Hohfeldian Grievance Analysis*; 65, *Smuggling*; and 128, *Global Insurgency and Global Trespass.*

---

"You learned the dry-mouthed, fear-purged purging ecstasy of battle and you fought that summer and that fall for all the poor in the world against all tyranny, for all the things you believed in and for the new world you had been educated into."

Ernest Hemingway,
*For Whom the Bell Tolls*[205]

**Rooster Cogburn**: I mean to kill you in one minute, Ned. Or see you hanged in Fort Smith at Judge Parker's convenience. Which will you have?
**Lucky Ned Pepper**: I call that bold talk for a one-eyed fat man.
**Rooster Cogburn**: Fill your hand you son-of-a-bitch.

From the Movie, *True Grit*, 2010[206]

A State fails that cannot monopolize the granting of impunity

# *Section 144, Impunity and State Success*

This book is about winning insurgent war or any of the related kinds of armed conflict mentioned in the author's preface. All of them insult, challenge, defy or attempt to destroy governments. In the spirit of having some definition in mind for winning, and therefore some way to measure victory, here is a working definition of State success:

**A successful State
can maintain a monopoly over the
granting of impunity.**

Impunity means exemption or protection from punishment. The word carries a strong connotation of immorality and illegality, and so is distinct from its cousin, *immunity*, which is gained or conveyed for many reasons and purposes, usually within an established system of laws. To grant impunity in advance is to convey a freedom from punishment for anticipated immoral behavior. If you have a monopoly over the granting of impunity, it means that no other person or entity can let anyone 'off the hook' for an illegal act inside your territory. A powerful State maintains a monopoly over granting impunity, but doesn't necessarily grant impunity. Countries in the international system generally claim a thing called *sovereign immunity*. That means no court exists that is competent or has the jurisdiction to punish certain actions done by agents of the government, or perhaps the State. Likewise, one of the United States, or even the US federal courts, cannot punish US federal agents for some acts considered to fall under the protections of sovereign immunity. If, however, an official were the subject of corruption, or were to commit any act that most of us would consider immoral or normally punishable, and yet was protected from punishment, most of us would agree that the operative word is *impunity*, not immunity.

If there are spaces inside a territory where impunity is successfully granted in defiance of a constituted government – perhaps by a mafia don, a warlord or a guerrilla chieftain – the government is failing in those places to that extent. For the purposes of the book, if the State is losing in its efforts to gain or maintain its monopoly over the granting of impunity; the other guys are winning.

A powerful person or organization can let someone off the hook for having trespassed, smuggled, kidnapped, or killed. They can grant impunity in advance, knowing that their agents are going to commit what others will consider illegal or immoral acts. The sovereign immunity granted to a nation's artillerymen is often granted even before those artillerymen are born. If a country can grant such predicted immunity (not considered illegal, but rather a legitimate expression of State power) in reference to acts that might be committed in foreign lands, we'll say it has strategic power. However, if some entity can grant premeditated impunity for acts to be taken inside the territory of an established State, that State, for the purposes of this definition, is not completely healthy or successful.

Other indices of State performance, mostly based on normative standards such as the number of violent crimes, breadth of the political franchise, economic wellbeing and so forth, can be found in the library or around the Internet and are good for something. A definition based on impunity, however, is more appropriate to the discussion of winning violent conflicts. It is more to the point.

An impunity-based definition of State success and failure does not imply judgment about whether or not an organization is good or bad, moral or immoral. A lot of evidence may show that impunity is rampant in a given place. The evidence may include an excess of unsolved violent crimes, failed prosecutions and prison escapes. Lack of transparency in government records also hints to a high level of impunity. The government in such a place may or may not be failing. The impunity we observe may have been granted by the government itself. While it may be an unattractive place, with an irresponsible government, or even be an immoral State, it is successful and not going away soon if no other entity challenges its monopoly over granting impunity.

To win your armed conflict you will secure for yourself the unique ability to grant impunity for violent action within all the geographic space you will call yours. You will secure the capacity to grant your agents immunity from the punishment of others, in advance, knowing that you have the power to absolve those you send out to express your dominating will. To progress, you will concentrate on the management of anonymity, provide it to your people and their informants, and take it from your enemies. Your enemies thus exposed, you will pursue them physically, shutting off their routes of escape, closing their sanctuaries and maybe killing them.

See: 1, *What the Pirate Said to Alexander*; 81, *What a Clergy Wants*; 24, *Ruthlessness and Resolve*; 4, *Defining Enemy*; 72, *Land Strategy;* 2, *Anonymity*; 19, *Extortion*; and 135, *Bank Robbery*.

---

> "Señor Bond, you got big cojones. You come here, to my place, without references, carrying a piece, throwing around a lot of money...but you should know something: nobody saw you come in, so nobody has to see you go out."
>
> Franz Sanchez in the movie
> *License to Kill* (1989)[207]

## RESTATEMENT

There are several conditions and principles likely to reign across all types of irregular armed conflict. A good plan for winning one of those conflicts will address the following seven fundamentals:

•Pick the right place to fight and the right enemy. It is hard to recover from fighting at the wrong place and time against the wrong people. Your enemy has a name and an organization; he is not an amorphous abstraction or a spontaneous reaction. Your enemy is not an idea or a network, he is a man and he is located somewhere. Learn geography.

•Control anonymity. Take it away from your enemy and secure it for yourself. Apply technical and institutional innovations. A regime of accurate, comprehensive and transparent public records tops the list for the counterinsurgent. It is hard to maintain impunity without anonymity.

•Work to cross, close and restrict your enemy's escape to sanctuary. The physical line of retreat to sanctuary should be the central geographic concept of your military operational planning. A successful attack on a sanctuary means it isn't. Battle is decisive when pursuit is successful.

•Create property. Property is the social contract, the contract of contracts that serves to resolve conflicts before they become violent. Property is where economics, law and geography meet. Know who owns what land.

•Respect everyone. This is not abstract concept or luxury. If you do not attend to dignity and honor, your enemy will. The line of your enemy's retreat is covered by people, and so is yours. Set a base of honorable behavior, announce and enforce it. Start with the treatment of children.

•Make something. Bridges, walls, tunnels, and pipelines do not go out of fashion. Humans like them and they help if put in the right places. Either make something that favors your military operational art, or make something useful to the public. Choose or invent the right machines, including weapons and things that change the built environment.

•Listen to advisors who have a sense of humor, not because they are funny, but because deception and humor play on the same mental circuits. Neither believe all your own propaganda nor discard all your enemy's, but when he most insists there is no military solution to your conflict, look harder for it. Wars do not prolong themselves; if you do not want to prolong a conflict, act diligently.

I was sheriff of this county when I was twenty-five years old. Hard to believe. My grandfather was a lawman; father too. Me and him was sheriffs at the same time; him up in Plano and me out here. I think he's pretty proud of that. I know I was. Some of the old time sheriffs never even wore a gun. A lotta folks find that hard to believe. Jim Scarborough'd never carried one; that's the younger Jim. Gaston Boykins wouldn't wear one up in Comanche County. I always liked to hear about the oldtimers. Never missed a chance to do so. You can't help but compare yourself against the oldtimers. Can't help but wonder how they would have operated these times. There was this boy I sent to the 'lectric chair at Huntsville Hill here a while back. My arrest and my testimony. He killt a fourteen-year-old girl. Papers said it was a crime of passion but he told me there wasn't any passion to it. Told me that he'd been planning to kill somebody for about as long as he could remember. Said that if they turned him out he'd do it again. Said he knew he was going to hell. "Be there in about fifteen minutes". I don't know what to make of that. I sure don't. The crime you see now, it's hard to even take its measure. It's not that I'm afraid of it. I always knew you had to be willing to die to even do this job. But, I don't want to push my chips forward and go out and meet something I don't understand. A man would have to put his soul at hazard. He'd have to say, "O.K., I'll be part of this world."

Ed Tom Bell in the movie
*No Country for Old Men*, (2007)[208]

I don't want to be a product of my environment;
I want my environment to be a product of me.

Frank Costello in the movie
*Departed*, (2006)[209]

## SYNTHESIS

A smart general, even if he leads no more than an insurgent squad, protects his lines of communication, and makes sure that as he dares to attack a dangerous foe, he keeps his options for retreat alive. He knows that victory is often achieved only by successful pursuit after battle.

It is never enough to just win battles, either. Sustainable victory means not creating too many more enemies. That is a harder feat to pull off, one which entails administration, engineering, education, indoctrination -- efforts for which regular military units are only partially suited.

In insurgent wars, cultural knowledge cannot be dismissed as a luxury, or relegated to being a secondary concern. Military strategy involves stratagems – deceptions. When civilian things are mixed indistinguishably with military things, plans and deceptions are developed via literature, arts, entertainments, and cultural habits and expectations. Therefore, to not know the culture means not being able to anticipate or develop effective deceptions; which means not being able to implement anything but the most transparent strategies, or recognize and defend against elegant ones.

Some people, although they will admit the importance of cultural acuity, are offended by jokes, especially if they play on the sensitive elements of human thinking like death, ethnicity, or sex. Jokes, however, are created the same as military and political deceptions. If we define Geography as the study of the interrelationship of humans and their environment, then we might logically claim that Strategy *is* Geography -- only adding to Strategy the additional twists of human competition and deception. To shy away from jokes is like shrinking from the subject of deception. If you let your enemy dominate the subtleties of cultural expression, he is likely to get to you before you get to him, and he'll laugh at you. In insurgent types of war, communications are enmeshed in the cultural gearing. If you are ignorant of the culture, chances are you don't get the jokes. How are you, then, for being deceived?

As it is difficult to separate cultural knowledge from military competence in irregular wars, it is likewise difficult to separate ideological and philosophical questions from planning. Activities like building walls and sewers, or doing a thorough inventory of everything and everyone in a place, may not seem to have much connection to vagaries like post-structuralism. Nevertheless, questions about the control and use of spaces -- who will be trusted to decide their use -- who will be able to determine the division of rights and duties on specific pieces of dirt, are responsive to an ongoing intellectual struggle about the correct nature of ownership and leadership. This book looks to the great inventions of Western civilization with admiration. *Property* is the name given to the single greatest set of technologies and relationships for long-term resolution of conflicts, creation of material wellbeing, and the promotion of individual liberty.

The *Songs of Chu* are like strategic chaff. Today the songs seem to share a set of themes: that radically inspired movements cannot be beaten; that military solutions are not available or are inappropriate or immoral; or that insurgencies are necessarily protracted affairs. Post-structuralism is the name of a global piece that includes these stanzas and with them the following refrain: that American power, waning and unfocused, is the bulwark of an evil system which people should resist (as noble insurgents). Post-structuralists enjoy this music, but along with bits of contrived reality to help perplex the engineering mind, they go a step farther to insist that real reality doesn't even exist, and so isn't worth looking for. America will do well not to overvalue the post-structural Songs of Chu, even while it reconsiders its own revolutionary values.

Seemingly indistinguishable from the greater ideological environment is a question often posed as one of *legitimacy*. When dealing with insurgency, there is no way to separate issues of legitimacy from military operational movement and position, or to separate social responsibility from approaches to knowledge. They are all bollixed up. The categories of our thinking, like geography, economics, strategy, law, culture, tactics, postmodernism, or empiricism are all helpful and necessary. As boxes, however, they keep us from freely mixing ideas as we should, and they compete in ways that deny the contribution of other categories. There is no way to keep that from happening, but there are a few things that can speed our thinking in dangerous human competitions. One of the most profitable is to respect time, distance, and weight. Whatever the metaphysicists may find to challenge our assumptions about time and space, for our practical and violent competitive purposes time flows in one direction, and location is fixed.

Great advantage goes to the competitor who takes careful inventories and makes precise and comprehensive maps. In the last few decades two knowledge revolutions have occurred – one is the Internet and the other is GIS. Victory is more likely for those who master both. Successful strategic thinking must reconcile empiricism with solipsism, but you are much more likely to win your war if you build your efforts on a foundation of dogged empiricism, and GIS is the codeword for that devotion. One of the most important objectives of this recommended devotion to GIS-based empiricism is closing with and destroying the enemy. The 'closing with' part is aided immensely by the control of anonymity. The insurgent especially depends for survival on geographic anonymity of his agents, sanctuaries and wealth. (And by the way, if your enemy's sanctuary is in a foreign land from which you can't extract or extradite him, then you might not want to fool yourself into thinking yours is a merely insurgent war.)

If your enemy enjoys a sanctuary, and you don't know where it is or how he gets there, you've got a problem. Many of the other complexities boil down to that one ignorance. In the final calculations of insurgency winners and losers – in the measurements of success or failure – there will be a truth that overcomes all perception management and spin. The side that attains or retains a monopoly on the ability to grant impunity (whether or not it is in fact granted) is the winner. It is ultimately not hard to tell if a government is or is not in control of the granting of impunity within its territory.

The above paragraphs might make it seem as though human conflict is complicated. Maybe it is, but there is no need to let all the trees hide the forest, either. No need to over-think the thing. If you have an enemy, find him and neutralize him. If not, build something, train, or go play golf.

---

"In the immortal words of Jean-Paul Sartre, 'Au revoir, Gopher.'

Bill Murray in the movie
*Zombieland* (2009)[210]

ઊઋ ઊઋ ઊઋ

## ENDNOTES

[1] Richard A. Posner, ed. *The Essential Holmes*. Chicago: University of Chicago Press, 1996, p.82; Oliver Wendell Holmes, Jr. "In Our Youth Our Hearts Were Touched With Fire." *Holmes' 1884 Memorial Day Speech* (An address delivered for Memorial Day, May 30, 1884, at Keene, NH, before John Sedgwick Post No. 4, Grand Army of the Republic). http://people.virginia.edu/~mmd5f/memorial.htm.

[2] Saint Augustine, *The City of God* (edited by Vernon J. Bourke and translated by Gerald G. Walsh, et al.) Garden City, New York: Doubleday and Company, Inc., 1958. p. 88.

[3] IMDb.com. (The Internet Movie Database) *The Pirates of Penzance* (1983) was directed by Wilford Leach, and written by William S. Gilbert and Wilford Leach.

[4] Quotationsbook.com.

[5] IMDB.com. *Nineteen Eighty-Four* (1984) was directed by Michael Radford, and written by George Orwell and Michael Radford.

[6] Richard A. Posner, ed. *The Essential Holmes*. Chicago: University of Chicago Press, 1996, pp. 102-103.

[7] Http://quotes.liberty-tree.ca. 'Protest Quotes /Quotations.' Dwight D. Eisenhower.

[8] Peter G. Tsouras, ed. *The Greenhouse Dictionary of Military Quotations*. London: Greenhouse, 2000, p. 392.

[9] Ernest Hemingway. *For Whom The Bell Tolls*. New York: Charles Scribner & Sons, 1940, p. 284.

[10] T. Miller Maguire. *Outlines of Military Geography*. London: C.J. Clay & Sons, 1899, 21-22.

[11] Ibid., p. 30.

[12] Tsouras, p. 421.

[13] The principal reference for this section is Thomas Miller Maguire. *The Campaign of 1805*. London: William Clowes and Sons, 1912.

[14] Tsouras, p. 422, referencing Nathan Leites, *The Soviet Style of War* (1982).

[15] Russell F. Weigley. *The Age of Battles: The Quest for Decisive Warfare from Breitenfeld to Waterloo.* Bloomington: Indiana University Press, 1991, 'Introduction,' generally.

[16] Carl von Clausewitz. *On War* (Michael Howard and Peter Paret, eds.) Princeton: Princeton University Press, 1976, p. 267.

[17] Central Intelligence Agency (attributed) *Guide to the Analysis of Insurgency.* Unknown:Central Intelligence Agency (attributed), undated, p. 2.

[18] A. Hilliard Atteridge. *Famous Modern Battles*. Cambridge, MA: The University Press, 1913, p. 352.

[19] Great-quotes.com. 'Theodore Roosevelt Quotes.' Quote/939684.

[20] See generally Fishel, John T. and Manwaring, Max G. *Uncomfortable Wars Revisited.* Norman: Oklahoma University Press, 2006.

[21] IMDb.com. *Monty Python and the Holy Grail* was directed by Terry Gilliam and Terry Jones, and written by Graham Chapman, et al.

[22] IMDb.com. *Caddy Shack* (1980) was directed by Harold Ramis and written by Brian Doyle-Murray, Harold Ramis, and Douglas Kenney. Carl Spackler was played by Bill Murray.

[23] IMDb.com. *Fight Club* (1999) was directed by David Fincher and written by Chuck Palahniuk and Jim Uhls. Tyler Durden was played by Brad Pitt.

[24] US Army and US Marine Corps. *Field Manual 3-24, Marine Corps Warfighting Publication No. 3-33.5 Counterinsurgency.* Washington, D. C.: Headquarters, Department of the Army and Headquarters Marine Corps Combat Development Command, 2006, p. 1-11.

[25] William Trousdale. "Dr. Brydon's Report of the Kabul Disaster & Documentation of History: Rendered from Remnants of an Army; by Lady Elizabeth Butler at the Tate Gallery in London" (Dr. Brydon's arrival at Jalalabad on 13th of January 1842). www.kyber.org.

[26] See, for instance, military-quotes.com. Roughly translated: 'I have a catapult. Give me all the money or I will fling an enormous boulder onto your head.'

[27] Dave Barry. *Dave Barry Does Japan.* New York: Ballantine, 1993, p. 7.

[28] Mario Payeras. *El Trueno en la Ciudad* (*Thunder in the City*). Mexico City: Juan Pablos, 1987, p. 89-90.

[29] See http://www.envio.org.ni/articulo/3098; http://www.envio.org.ni/articulo/11; see also Colección de Documentos Históricos, http://www.manfut.org/cronologia/carta1981.html.

[30] Allen J. Christenson *Popol Vuh: Literal Translation*, p. 245; www.mesweb.com.

[31] IMDb.com. *Animal House* (1978) was directed by John Landis, and written by Harold Ramis, Douglas Kenney, and Chris Miller. Otter was played by Tim Matheson.

[32] Robert Lapham and Bernard Norling. *Lapham's Raiders*. Lexington: The University Press of Kentucky, 1996, p. 76.

[33] IMDb.com. *Scarface* (1983) was directed by Brian De Palma, and written by Oliver Stone, et al. Tony Montana is played by Al Pacino.

[34] Richard Saunders (Benjamin Franklin). *Poor Richard's Almanac* (January 1756).

[35] See generally, Michael Howard. *The Invention of Peace: Reflections on War and International Order*. New Haven: Yale University Press, 2000.

[36] John P. Powelson. *The Story of Land: A World History of Land Tenure and Agrarian Reform*. Cambridge, Massachusetts: Lincoln Institute of Land Policy, 1988, p. 308.

[37] Brainyquotes.com. 'American President Quotes, Select Ronald Reagan Quotations.'

[38] Tom Bethel. *The Noblest Triumph*. New York: St. Martin's Press, 1998, p.336.

[39] Brainyquotes.com. 'American President Quotes, All Ronald Reagan Quotations.'

[40] IMDb.com. *The Hitchhiker's Guide to the Galaxy (*2005) was directed by Garth Jennings and written by Douglas Adams and Karey Kirkpatrick.

[41] IMDb.com. *The Matrix* (1999) was directed and written by Andy Wachowski and Lana Wachowski. Agent Smith was played by Hugo Weaving.

[42] IMDb.com. *Tremors* (1990) was directed by Ron Underwood, and written by S. S. Wilson, et al. Burt Gummer was played by Michael Gross.

[43] Doyle, Arthur Conan. *The Adventure of the Copper Beeches*. Electronic Text Center, University of Virginia Library. Http://etext.lib.virginia.edu/, p. 618.

[44] IMDb.com. *West Side Story* (1961) was direct by Jerome Robbins and Robert Wise, and written by Ernest Lehman, Arthur Laurents (additional credits to William Shakespeare and Jerome Robbins).

[45] Brainyquote.com. 'Theodore Parker Quotes.'

[46] Andrew R. Molnar, et al. *Human Factors Considerations of Undergrounds in Insurgencies*. Washington, D. C.: American University Special Operations Research Office, 1966, p. 71.

[47] Political Instability Task Force. 'Internal Wars and Failures of Governance, 1955-Most Recent Year.' *State Failure*. http://globalpolicy.gmu.edu/pitf/.

[48] Jack A. Goldstone, *State Failure Task Force Report: Phase III Findings*. p. v. http://globalpolicy.gmu.edu/pitf/pitfdata.htm.

[49] Daniel C. Esty, et al. *Working Papers State Failure Task Force Report*. P. viii. http://globalpolicy.gmu.edu/pitf/pitfdata.htm.

[50] Jack A. Goldstone, *State Failure Task Force Report: Phase III Findings*. p. vi.

[51] Mauricio Archila, et al. *25 años de luchas sociales en Colombia 1975-2000* (25 years of social struggles in Colombia 1975-2000). Bogotá: CINEP, 2002.

[52] Brainyquote.com. 'American President Quotes, All Ronald Reagan Quotations.'

[53] Brainyquote.com. 'Defiance Quotes.'

[54] IMDb.com. *Snatch* (2000) was directed and written by Guy Ritchie. Mickey was played by Brad Pitt.

[55] A. Hilliard Atteridge. *Famous Modern Battles*. Cambridge, MA: The University Press, 1913, p. 241.

[56] IMDb.com. *The Maltese Falcon* (1941) was directed by John Huston, and written by Dashiell Hammett and John Huston.

[57] Http://www.frfrogspad.com/trsaid.htm. 'The Sayings of Theodore Roosevelt.'

[58] IMDb.com. *Naked Gun: From the Files of Police Squad!* (1988) was directed by David Zucker, and written by Jerry Zucker, et al.

[59] IMDb.com. *The Godfather* (1972) was directed by Francis Ford Coppola, and written by Mario Puzo and Francis Ford Coppola. Don Vito Corleone was played by Marlon Brando.

[60] Elizabeth Margaret Kerr. *William Faulkner's Yoknapatawpha: A Kind of Keystone in the Universe*. New York: Fordham University Press, 1983, p. 12; Google Books.

[61] IMDb.com *Austin Powers in Goldmember* (2002) was written by Jay Roach and written by Mike Myers, et al. Nigel Powers was played by Michael Caine.

[62] Guntram H. Herb and David H. Kaplan. *Nested Identities*. New York; Rowman & Littlefield, 1999.

[63] Hilliard A. Atteridge. *The Wars of the 'Nineties: A History of the Warfare of the Last Ten Years of the Nineteenth Century*. London: Cassel and Company, 1899, p. 437

[64] Geoff Demarest. *Geoproperty: Foreign Affairs, National Security and Property Rights*. New York: Frank Cass, 1998, p. 13.

[65] Quotationsbook.com. 'Quotations by James, William'; Alice Hegan Rice attributes the saying to Charles Atwood Campbell: *My Pillow Book*. New York: D. Appleton, Century, 1937, p. 103.

[66] Quotationsbook.com; Alex Barnett. *The Quotable American*. Guilford, CT: Lyons Press, 2003, p. 277.

[67] Álvaro Garcia. 'The Multitude' in Oscar Olivera and Tom Lewis, *Cochabamba!: Water War in Bolivia multitude*. Cambridge, MA: South End Press, 2004, pp. 65-86.

[68] Ian Hancock. 'What's in a Name.' http://www.utexas.edu/features/archive/2003/romani.html. (accessed October 20, 2010).

[69] J.L. Brierly. *The Law of Nations: An Introduction to the International law of Peace* (Sixth Edition) (Edited by Sir Humphrey Waldock). Oxford: Oxford University Press, 1963, p. 48.

[70] Brainyquote.com. 'William James Quotes.'

[71] Adam Smith. *The Theory of Moral Sentiments*. P. 145.Norderstedt: GRIN Verlag, 2009, p. 145; London: Kincaid & Bell, 1767, p. 273.

[72] Mark Twain. *A Connecticut Yankee in King Arthur's Court*. New York: Harper and Brothers, 1889, p. 337; Google Plain Label Books.

[73] IMDb.com. *Ulzana's Raid* (1972) was directed by Robert Aldrich and written by Alan Sharp.

[74] Associated Press. "Chavez: Civilian Militia Should Be Armed Full-Time." www.foxnews.com. October 04, 2010.

[75] IMDb.com. *The Wizard of Oz* (1939) was directed by Victor Fleming, et al, and written by Noel Langley, et al. The Wicked Witch was played by Margaret Hamilton.

[76] Fall, Bernard B. *Hell in a Very Small Place: The Siege of Dien Bien Phu*. New York: Lippincott, 1967, p. 127.

[77] Galula, David. *Pacification in Algeria, 1956-1958*. Santa Monica: Rand, 2006, p. 262.

[78] Ibid., p. 268

[79] Jorge Verstrynge. *La Guerra Periférica y el Islam Revolucionario: Orígenes, reglas y ética de la guerra asimétrica*. Barcelona: El Viejo Topo, 2005, p. 139 and note 2, p.139.

[80] C.M. Woodhouse. *International Affairs*, Vol. 41 No. 1, 1965, p. 111.

[81] Galula. *Pacification in Algeria.* p. 183.

[82] Ibid., p. 246.

[83] Edgar O`Ballance,. *The Algerian Insurrection 1954-1962.* Hamden, Connecticut: Archon Books, 1967, p. 214-215.

[84] IMDb.com. *Apocalypse Now* (1979) was written by Francis Ford Coppola ,and written by John Milius, et al. Hubert was played by Christian Marquand.

[85] Mark Twain. *Adventures of Huckleberry Finn.* 'Chapter XXII.' www.readbookonline.net.

[86] See generally, Jean François Revel. *The Flight from Truth: The Reign of Deceit in the Age of Information.* New York: Random House, 1992.

[87] Friedrich A. Hayek. *The Constitution of Liberty.* Chicago: The university of Chicago, 1960, p. 14.

[88] IMDb.com. *The Wizard of Oz* (1939) was directed by Victor Fleming, et al, and written by Noel Langley, et al. The Wicked Witch was played by Margaret Hamilton.

[89] IMDb.com. *Office Space* (1999) was directed and written by Mike Judge.

[90] Battle of Arnhem Information Centre. Http://www.market-garden.info/arnhem_battle_information_centre.html.

[91] Comment # 10 on May 22nd, 2010 at 2:40 pm. Http://michellemalkin.com/2010/05/22/mexico-tourism-promoter-running-threatening-ads-in-arizona-newspaper/.

[92] Adapted from a joke at www.physlink.com/fun/jokes.cfm that was credited to Thomas Mayer. Here the physicist is turned into an engineer.

[93] Juan Camilo Bohórquez, et al. 'Common ecology quantifies human insurgency.' *Nature* 462, 17 December 2009. pp. 911-914; *Royal Holloway University of London.* Department of Economics, Conflict Analysis Resources. 'Power Laws and Armed Conflicts.' http://personal.rhul.ac.uk/pkte/126/Pages/Power_Law_research.htm; Kate Julian. 'The pattern behind 'random' terrorist attacks.' *The Washington Post.* http://www.washingtonpost.com/wpdyn/content/article/2010/07/23/AR2010072302434.html.

[94] IMDb.com. *Starship Troopers* (1997) was directed by Paul Verhoeven and written by Eduard Neumeier and Robert A. Heinlein.

[95] See Terrance G. Lichtenwald. "Drug Smuggling Behavior: A Developmental Smuggling Model, Part 1" and "Drug Smuggling Behavior: A Developmental Smuggling Model, Part 2." Thefreelibrary.com.

[96] John Steinbeck. *Travels with Charley: in search of America.* Google Books,p.66.

[97] IMDb.com. *The Core* (2003) was directed by Jon Amiel, and written by Cooper Layne and John Rogers.

[98] See, Karl Marx. *Grundrisse: Foundations of the Critique of Political Economy.* London: Penguin, 1993, p. 524, 538, 539.

[99] IMDb.com. *Zoolander* (2001) was directed by Ben Stiller and written by Ben Stiller and Drake Sather, et al. Derek Zoolander was played by Ben Stiller.

[100] Brainyquotes.com. 'American President Quotes, All Ronald Reagan Quotations.'

[101] Youtube.com. 'Jerusalem by William Blake lyrics'; Hymns.me.uk. 'Jerusalem.'

[102] IMDb.com. *Chariots of Fire* (1981) was directed by Hugh Hudson and written by Colin Welland; To hear the song, go to www.cyberhymnal.org. *Jerusalem.*

[103] Http://ushistorysite.com. 'Dwight Eisenhower Quotes.'

[104] John P. Powelson. *The Story of Land: A World History of Land Tenure and Agrarian Reform.* Cambridge, Massachusetts: Lincoln Institute of Land Policy, 1988, p. x.

[105] Olson, Gary L. *US Foreign Policy and the Third World Peasant: Land Reform in Asia and Latin America.* New York: Praeger Publishers, 1974, p. 42, citing McCune.

[106] Ibid., p. 24. citing *Developing Economies.*

[107] Tsouras, p. 321.

[108] Andro Linklater. *Measuring America: How and Untamed Wilderness Shaped the United States and Fulfilled the Promise of Democracy.* New York: Walker & Company, 2002, p. 258.

[109] Thinkexist.com. 'Frederick Douglass Quotes.'

[110] Samuel B. Griffith. *Mao Tse-Tung on Guerrilla Warfare.* New York: Praeger, 1961, p. 85.

[111] IMDb.com. *Anchorman: the Legend of Ron Burgundy* (2004) was directed by Adam McKay, and written by Will Ferrell and Adam McKay. Champ was played by David Koechner.

[112] See, typically, Katherine Aguirre Tobón and Jorge A. Restrepo. 'Homicidios por género y edad. Colombia, 2005.' (Homicides by Gender and Age) using data from the Colombian National Statistics Department (DANE). Bogotá: Pontificia Universidad Javeriana and The Resource Center for Conflict Analysis (CERAC), 2010; and, International Development Bank. 'Tasas Estandarizadas de Mortalidad para Homicidios por género. Colombia 1980-1995' (Standard Rates of Mortality for Homicides by Gender) in *Dimensionamiento de la violencia en Colombia* (Dimensioning Violence in Colombia). New York: International Development Bank, 1998, p. 7.

[113] Brainyquote.com. 'Hedy Lamarr Quotes.'

[114] Robert Andrews. *The Columbia Book of Quotations.* New York: Columbia University Press, 1993, p. 493.

[115] Tsouras p. 458, citing R. M. Johnston, ed. *The Corsican.*

[116] Tsouras, p. 458.

[117] Http://greatmindsongodreligionandscience.blogspot.com/2009. 'Oliver Wendell Holmes, Sr.' *Great Minds on God, Religion and Science.*

[118] Douglass C. North and Robert Paul Thomas. *The Rise of the Western World, A New Economic History*, Cambridge: Cambridge University Press, 1973, p. 8, and generally.

[119] John Shy. 'Jomini' in Peter Paret, et al. *Makers of Modern Strategy from Machiavelli to the Nuclear Age*. Princeton: Princeton University Press, 1986, p. 171.

[120] Robert Ardrey. *The Territorial Imperative: A Personal Inquiry into the Animal Origins of Property and Nations.* New York: Antheneum, 1966, p. 244.

[121] John R. Umbeck. *A Theory of Property Rights: With Application to the California Gold Rush.* Ames, Iowa: The Iowa State University Press, 1981.

[122] From 'Patriot Games,' an episode of the fourth season of the animated cartoon show *The Family Guy*. 'Patriot Games' was written by Mike Henry and directed by Peter Shin, Pete Michels and Cyndi Tang; See also,

http://familyguy.onsugar.com. 'Stewie Beats Up Brian: Where's My Money?, Parts 1 and 2.'

[123] IMDb.com. *Joe Dirt* (2001) was directed by Dennie Gordon, and written by David Spade and Fred Wolf. Joe Dirt (or Dirté) is played by David Spade.

[124] IMDb.com. *BlazingSaddles* (1974) was directed by Mel Brooks and written by Mel Brooks and Norman Steinberg, et al. Hedley Lamarr was played by Harvey Korman.

[125] IMDb.com. *Zoolander* (2001) was directed by Ben Stiller and written by Ben Stiller and Drake Sather, et al. Derek Zoolander was played by Ben Stiller.

[126] Niccolò Machiavelli. 'The Prince' in Charles W. Eliot, ed. *The Prince, Utopia, Ninety-Five Theses*. New York: P.F. Collier & Son, 1910, p. 38; Google Book Shelf.

[127] IMDb.com. *Khartoum* (1966) was directed by Basil Dearden and Eliot Elisofon, and written by Robert Ardrey. The Mahdi was played by Lawrence Olivier.

[128] IMDb.com. *Guys and Dolls* (1955) was directed by Joseph L. Mankiewicz, and written by Jo Swerling, et al. Harry the Horse was played by Sheldon Leonard.

[129] IMDb.com. *Papillon* (1973) was directed by Franklin J. Schaffner, and written by Dalton Trumbo, et al. Henri 'Papillon' Charriere was played by Steve McQueen.

[130] T. Miller Maguire. *Outlines of Military Geography*. London: C.J. Clay & Sons, 1899, 184.

[131] *Book of Revelations* 21, 12-17. Holy Christian Bible.

[132] Partido Socialista Unido de Venezuela. *Documentos Fundamentales: Libro Rojo*. Venezuela 2010, p. 32.

[133] Robert M. Carmack. *Development and Social Effects of the Guatemalan Earthquake*. 1978.
http://www.crid.or.cr/digitalizacion/pdf/eng/doc3914/doc3914-contenido.pdf. (accessed October 20, 2010).

[134] *Beau Geste* (1939) was directed by William Wellman, and written by Robert Carson and Percival Wren.

[135] Davis, Mike. *Planet of Slums*. New York: Verso, 2006, p. 137.

[136] Ricardo Aricapa. *Comuna 13: crónica de una guerra urbana*. Medellín: Editorial Universidad de Medellín, 2005, p. 10.

[137] Brainyquote.com. 'William James Quotes.'

[138] US Army and US Marine Corps. *Field Manual 3-24, Marine Corps Warfighting Publication No. 3-33.5 Counterinsurgency*. Washington, D. C.: Headquarters, Department of the Army and Headquarters Marine Corps Combat Development Command, 2006, A-6.

[139] IMDb.com. *The Waterboy* (1998) was directed by Frank Coraci, and written by Tim Herlighy and Adam Sandler. Lawrence Taylor is played by Lawrence Taylor.

[140] Richard A. Posner, ed. *The Essential Holmes*. Chicago: University of Chicago Press, 1996, p.86.

[141] Thinkexist.com. 'Joe Namath Quotes.'

[142] Thinkexist.com. 'Merlin Olsen Quotes.'

[143] Thinkexist.com. 'Dick Butkus Quotes.'

[144] Jorge Verstrynge. *La Guerra Periférica y el Islam Revolucionario: Orígenes, reglas y ética de la guerra asimétrica.* Barcelona: El Viejo Topo, 2005, p. 25.

[145] Incompetech.com. John Donne, *Devotions upon Emergent Occasions* (1623).

[146] Arturo Contreras Polgatti. *Conflicto y Guerra en la Post Modernidad.* Santiago: Mago, 2004; Cristián Garay Vera. *La Cameleónica Naturaleza del Conflicto Posmoderno*. Santiago: Ejército de Chile, 2004.

[147] John Donne, *Devotions upon Emergent Occasions* (1623). Virginia Tech Digital Library and Archives.

[148] En.wikiquote.org. 'Henry James.'

[149] About.com. *Outrageously Funny Groucho Marx Quotes*; See also http://simplicius-simplicissimus.blogspot.com/2009/09/21-who-are-ya-gonna-believe-me-or-yer.html. 'Who ya gonna believe, me or your lyin` eyes?'

[150] William Faulkner. *Absalom, Absalom!: the corrected text.* New York: Vintage International, 1990, p. 251.

[151] Bored.com. *Famous Quotes Database*.

[152] Lyricsfreak.com. *Forever Young Lyrics*; See also, *WikiAnswers*. "Who Really Wrote Forever Young by Rod Stewart?" Wiki.answers.com.

[153] United States of America versus Abdulmutallab, United States District Court, Eastern District of Michigan, Southern Division, Case: 2:10-cr-20005; See also *Wikipedia*. 'Umar Farouk Abdulmutallab.' En.wikipedia.org.

[154] See *Wikipedia* 'Fort Hood shooting.'_En.wikipedia.org.

[155] Richard A. Posner, ed. *The Essential Holmes*. Chicago: University of Chicago Press, 1996, p.89.

[156] Robert Ardrey. *The Territorial Imperative: A Personal Inquiry into the Animal Origins of Property and Nations*. New York: Antheneum, 1966, p. 236.

[157] IMDb.com. *Vacation* (1983) was directed by directed by Harold Ramis and written by John Hughes.

[158] Pearl S. Buck. *The Good Earth.* New York: John Day, 1931, p. 260

[159] IMDb.com. *Blood Diamond* (2006) was directed by Eduard Zwick and written by Charles Leavitt and C. Gaby Mitchell. Danny Archer was played by Leonardo DiCaprio.

[160] IMDb.com. *BlazingSaddles* (1974) was directed by Mel Brooks and written by Mel Brooks and Norman Steinberg, et al. Hedley Lamarr was played by Harvey Korman.

[161] Michael Flynn, Matt Pottinger and Paul Batchelor. *Fixing Intelligence*. Washington, D.C.: Center for a New American Security, 2010, p. 7.

[162] Joseph Blotner, ed. *Selected Letters of William Faulkner*. New York: Random House, 1977, p. 222; http://www.mcsr.olemiss.edu/~egjbp/faulkner/quotes.html.

[163] Goodreads.com. 'Thucydides Quotes.'

[164] IMDb.com. *Starship Troopers* (1997) was directed by Paul Verhoeven and written by Eduard Neumeier and Robert A. Heinlein.

[165] Tvloop.com. 'Mash.'

[166] Oliver Wendell Holmes, Jr. "In Our Youth Our Hearts Were Touched With Fire." *Holmes' 1884 Memorial Day Speech* (An address delivered for Memorial Day, May 30, 1884, at Keene, NH, before John Sedgwick Post No. 4, Grand Army of the Republic). http://people.virginia.edu/~mmd5f/memorial.htm.

[167] IMDb.com. *She Wore A Yellow Ribbon* (1949) was directed by John Ford and written by James Warner Bellah, Frank S. Nugent, and Laurence Stallings.

[168] Quotelicious.com. 'Shakira Quotes.'

[169] C. S. Lewis. *God in the Dock: Essays on Theology and Ethics*. New York: Eerdmans, 1970, p. 292.

[170] Thinkexist.com. 'Madame Chiang Kai-Shek Quotes.'

[171] Http://en.wikiquote.org/wiki/Intelligence, citing "Handle With Care", *Esquire Magazine* (March, 1936); but perhaps 'The Crack-Up,' *Esquire Magazine* (February, 1936) www.esquire.com/features/the-crack-up.

[172] Tsouras, page 415.

[173] IMDb.com. *Braveheart* (1995) was directed by Mel Gibson and written by Randall Wallace.

[174] Tsouras, p. 423.

[175]Robert Wright, *The Continental Army.* Washington, D.C.: Center of Military History, 1983, p. 23.

[176] H.W. Brands. *TR: the last romantic*. New York: Basic Books, 1997, p. 483.

[177] See generally, University of Virginia. *Thomas Jefferson on Politics & Government*. http://etext.virginia.edu/jefferson/quotations/jeff0300.htm.

[178] Tsouras, 422.

[179] Theodore Roosevelt. 'The Man In the Arena.' Speech given at the Sorbonne, Paris, France on Apr 23, 1910. Available at *Theodore Roosevelt*, http://www.theodore-roosevelt.com/trsorbonnespeech.html.

[180] Brainyquote.com.

[181] L.L. Fordred. "Wireless in the Second Anglo Boer War 1899-1902." Available from http://ieeexplore.ieee.org.

[182] T. Miller Maguire, *A Summary of Modern Military History, with comments on the leading operations* (London: Simpkin, 1887), p. 27.

[183] See generally, Hilliard A. Atteridge. *The Wars of the `Nineties: A History of the Warfare of the Last Ten Years of the Nineteenth Century.* London: Cassel and Company, 1899.

[184] Paul Greenhalgh. "A New Style for a New Age." *National Gallery of Art.* www.nga.gov; See also, generally, Paul Greenhalgh. *The Essence of Art Nouveau.* New York: Harry N. Abrams, 2000.

[185] Theodore Roosevelt. *Theodore Roosevelt: an autobiography.* New York: The MacMillan Company, 1916, p. 340; Google Book Shelf.

[186] IMDb.com. *The Terminator* (1984) was directed by James Cameron and written by James Cameron, et al. Dr. Silberman was played by Earl Boen.

[187] IMDb.com. *Napoleon Dynamite* (2004) was directed by Jared Hess, and written by Jared Hess and Jerusha Hess. Napoleon was played by Jon Heder.

[188] T. Miller Maguire, *The Gates of Our Empire I: British* Colombia. London: The Anglo-British

Colombian Agency, 1910, p. 54.

[189] See Callwell, C.E. 'Lessons to be Learnt from Small Wars Since 1870' in *Lecture given at the Aldershot Military Society*, Tuesday, March 26, 1895 (London: Gale & Polden, 1895), p. 2.

[190] IMDb.com. *Pursuit to Algiers* (1945) was directed by Roy William Neill and written by Leonard Lee. Sherlock Holmes was played by Basil Rathbone.

[191] Tsouras, 434.

[192] Tsouras, 434.

[193] Lyricsfreak.com. 'Geto Boys: Damn It Feels Good to Be a Gangsta Lyrics.'

[194] IMDb.com. Enemy at the Gates (2004) was directed by Jean-Jaques Annaud, and written by Jean-Jaques Annaud and Alain Goddard.

[195] Infoshop.org. Http://bibliolibertaire.org. 'Anarchist Lightbulb Jokes.' *The Daily Cocktail.*

[196] IMDb.com. *The Town* (2010) was directed by Ben Affleck and written by Peter Craig, et al.

[197] IMDb.com. *Dawn of the Dead* (1978) was written and directed by George A. Romero. Peter was played by Ken Foree.

[198] Thinkexist.com. 'George II Quotes.'

[199] Thinkexist.com. 'Raul Reyes Quotes.'

[200] www.nasm.si.edu. Smithsonian National Air and Space Museum Military Unmanned Aerial Vehicles.

[201] T.R. Fehrenbach. *This Kind of War.* New York: Macmillan, 1963, 454.

[202] Tsouras, 392.

[203] Tsouras, 377; 'The Most Humane Humans,' or, alternatively, 'The Most Human Human' (Ленин - самый человечный человек) is a recurrent nickname in Soviet literature for V.I. Lenin.

204 Robert D. Kaplan. *An Empire Wilderness: Travels into America's Future*. New York: Random House, 1998.

205 Ernest Hemingway. *For Whom The Bell Tolls*. New York: Charles Scribner & Sons, 1940, p. 236.

206 IMDb.com. *The Town* (2010) was directed by Ethan Coen and Joel Coen, screenplay written by Ethan Coen and Joel Coen from the novel by Charles Portis.

207 IMDb.com. *License to Kill* (1989) was directed by John Glen, and written by Michael G. Wilson and Richard Maibaum. Franz Sanchez is played by Robert Davi.

208 IMDb.com. *No Country for Old Men* (2007) was directed, and screenplay written, by Ethan Coen and Joel Coen, from the book written by Cormac McCarthy.

209 IMDb.com. *The Departed* (2006) was directed by Martin Scorsese, and written, by William Monahan, Alan Mak (2002 screenplay *Mou gaan dou*)and Felix Chong (2002 screenplay *Mou gaan dou*), Frank Costello was played by Jack Nicholson.

210 IMDb.com. *Zombieland* (2009) was directed by Ruben Fleischer, and written by Rhett Reese and Paul Wernick. Bill Murray was played by Bill Murray; see also *Tin Cup* (1996) directed by Ron Shelton, and written by John Norville and Ron Shelton; *Happy Gilmore* (1996) directed by Dennis Dugan, and written by Tim Herlihy and Adam Sandler; *The Legend of Bagger Vance* (2000) directed by Robert Redford, and written by Steven Pressfield and Jeremy Leven; *Caddy Shack* (1980) directed by Harold Ramis and written by Brian Doyle-Murray, Harold Ramis, and Douglas Kenney.

## BIBLIOGRAPHY

Alexander, Christopher, et al. *A Pattern Language: Towns, Buildings, Constructions*. New York: Oxford University Press, 1977.

Alexander, Martin and Keiger, J.F.V., eds. *France and the Algerian War 1954-1962: Strategy, Operations and Diplomacy*. Portland: Frank Cass, 2002.

Almario, Virgilio S., et al. *100 Events that Shaped the Philippines*. Quezon City: Adarna Book Services, 1999.

Angarita Cana, Pablo Emilio, et al. *Dinámicas de guerra y construcción de paz: Estudio interdisciplinario del conflicto armado en la Comuna 13 de Medellín*. Medellín: Universidad de Antioquia, 2008.

Anonymous, C. *Guide to the Analysis of Insurgency*. Langley, VA?: Central Intelligence Agency?, circa 1977.

Ardrey, Robert. *The Territorial Imperative: A Personal Inquiry into the Animal Origins of Property and Nations*. New York: Antheneum, 1966.

Archila, Mauricio, et al. *25 años de luchas sociales en Colombia 1975-2000* (25 years of social struggles in Colombia 1975-2000). Bogotá: CINEP, 2002.

Aricapa, Ricardo. *Comuna 13: crónica de una guerra urbana.* Medellín: Editorial Universidad de Medellín, 2005.

Atteridge, Hilliard A. *Famous Modern Battles*. Cambridge, MA: The University Press, 1913.

Atteridge, Hilliard A. *The Wars of the `Nineties: A History of the Warfare of the Last Ten Years of the Nineteenth Century*. London: Cassel and Company, 1899.

Ashworth, G.J. *War and the City*. New York: Routledge, 1991.

Augustine of Hippo. *City of God.* edited by Vernon J. Bourke; translated by Gerald G. Walsh, et al. Garden City: Image Books, 1958.

Aussaresses, Paul. *The Battle of the Casbah: Counter-Terrorism and Torture*. New York, Enigma Books, 2005.

Bacon, Francis. "Essay XXIX -- Of the True Greatness of Kingdoms and Estates," as reprinted in Charles W. Eliot, ed., *The Harvard Classics,* vol. 3. (New York: The Collier Press, 1909) 76-84.

Bailyn, Bernard. *The Ideological Origins of the American Revolution.* Cambridge, Massachusetts: Harvard University Press, 1967.

Barzel, Yoram. *Economic Analysis of Property Rights*. Cambridge: Cambridge University Press, 1989.

Batson, Douglas. *Registering the Human Terrains: A Valuation of Cadastre*. Washington, D.C.: National Defense Intelligence College Press, 2008.

Becket, Ian F. *Modern Insurgencies and Counter-Insurgencies: Guerrillas and their Opponents since 1750*. New York: Routledge, 2001.

Becket, Ian F., ed. *The Roots of Counter-insurgency: Armies and guerrilla warfare 1900-1945*. London: Blandford Press, 1988.

Berke, Philip R., et al. *Urban Land Use Planning (Fifth Edition).* Urbana: University of Illinois Press, 2006.

Bethell, Tom. *The Noblest Triumph: Property and Prosperity Through the Ages*. New York: St. Martin's Press, 1998.

Blainey, Geoffrey. *The Causes of War*. New York: Macmillan, 1973.

Blomley, Nicholas, Delaney, David and Ford, Richard. *The Legal Geographies Reader: Law, Power and Space*. Oxford: Wiley-Blackwell, 2001

Blumenfeld, Samuel L. *Property in a Humane Economy*. LaSalle, Illinois, Open Court Publishing, 1974.

Brierly, J.L. *The Law of Nations: An Introduction to the International law of Peace* (Sixth Edition) (Edited by Sir Humphrey Waldock). Oxford: Oxford University Press, 1963.

Buchanan, James M. *Property as a Guarantor of Liberty*. Cambridge, University Press, 1993.

Burch, Kurt. *"Property" and the Making of the International System*. Boulder: Lynne Rienne, 1998.

Bush, George M. *National Security Strategy of the United States*. Washington, D.C.: The White House, 1993.

Callwell, C. E. *Small Wars: Their Principles and Practice* (reprint of the Third Edition printed in 1906 by His Majesty's Stationery Office). Lincoln: University of Nebraska Press, 1996.

Byman, Daniel, et al. *Trends in Outside Support for Insurgent Movements*. Santa Monica: RAND, 2001.

Campbell, Arthur. *Guerrillas: A History and Analysis*. New York; John Day, 1967.

Cathcart, Thomas and Klein, Daniel. *Plato and a Platypus Walk Into a Bar: Understanding Philosophy Through Jokes*. New York: Penguin, 2008.

Cathcart, Thomas and Klein, Daniel. *Aristotle and an Aardvark Go to Washington*. New York: Abraham's Image, 2008.

Chaliand, Gerard, ed. *Guerrilla Strategies: An Historical Anthology from the Long March to Afghanistan*. Berkeley: University of California Press, 1982.

Cierva, Ricardo. *Historia de España Para Niños* (History of Spain for Children). Madrid: Fenix, 2003.

Clinton, William J. *A National Security Strategy of Engagement and Enlargement*. Washington: The White House, 1994.

Collins, John. *America's Small Wars: Lessons for the Future*. Washington, D.C.: Brassey's, 1991

Contreras Polgatti, Arturo. *Conflicto y Guerra en la Post Modernidad.* Santiago: Mago, 2004.

Crichtin, Judy. *America 1900: The Turning Point.* New York: Henry Holt, 1998.

D. Hittle, ed. *Jomini and his Summary of the Art of War.* Harrisburg, PA: Military Service, 1947.

Dangl, Benjamin. *The Price of Fire: Resource Wars and Social Movements in Bolivia.* Edinburgh: AK Press, 2007.

Davis, Mike and Monk, Daniel. *Evil Paradises: Dreamworlds of Neoliberalism.* New York: New Press, 2007.

Davis, Mike. *Planet of Slums.* New York: Verso, 2007.

Davis, Mike. *Urban Control: The Ecology of Fear.* Westfield, New Jersey: The Open Magazine Pamphlet Series, 1994.

De Blij, Harm. *The Power of Place: Geography, Destiny, and Globalization's Rough Landscape.* New York: Oxford University Press, 2008.

De Soto, Hernando. *The Mystery of Capital: Why Capitalism Triumphs in the West and Fails Everywhere Else.* New York: Basic Books, 2000.

Demarest, Geoffrey. *Geoproperty: Foreign Affairs, National Security and Property Rights.* London: Frank Cass, 1998.

Demarest, Geoffrey. *Property and Peace.* Ft. Leavenworth.: Defense Intelligence Agency Press, 2008.

Denis Judd, 'Part IV The Second Boer War 1899-1902' in *Someone Has Blundered: Calamities of the British Army in the Victorian Age* (Gloucestershire: Windrush Press, 1999)

Dorner, Peter. *Land Reform & Economic Development.* Kingsport, Tennessee: Kingsport Press, 1972.

Duchacek, Ivo D. *The Territorial Dimension of Politics Within, Among, and Across Nations.* Boulder: Westview, 1986.

Dudley, Steven. *Walking Ghosts. Murder and Guerrilla Politics in Colombia.* New York: Routledge, 2006.

Ellickson, Robert C. *Order Without Law: How Neighbors Settle Disputes.* Cambridge, MA: Harvard University Press, 1991.

Evans, Harold. *The American Century.* New York: Alfred Knopf, 1999.

Eyal Weizman. *Hollow Land: Israel's Architecture of Occupation.* New York:Verso, 2007.

Fall, Bernard B. *Hell in a Very Small Place: The Siege of Dien Bien Phu.* New York: Lippincott, 1967.

Fauriol, Georges, ed. *Latin American Insurgencies.* Washington, D.C.: CSIS, 1985.

Fishel, John T. and Manwaring, Max G. *Uncomfortable Wars Revisited.* Norman: Oklahoma University Press, 2006.

Flint, Colin. *The Geography of War and Peace: From Death Camps to Diplomats.* Oxford: Oxford University Press, 2004.

Fowler, Michael Ross and Bunck, Julie Marie. *Law, Power, and the Sovereign State: The Evolution and Application of the Concept of Sovereignty.* University Park: Pennsylvania State University Press, 1995.

Francis Bacon, "Essay XXIX -- Of the True Greatness of Kingdoms and Estates," as reprinted in Charles W. Eliot, ed., *The Harvard Classics,* vol. 3. (New York: The Collier Press, 1909) 76-84

Funes, *El Agua como factor Estratégico en la relación entre Chile y los países vecinos* Santiago, Universidad de Santiago, 2009.

Galula, David. *Counterinsurgency Warfare: Theory and Practice.* Westport: Praeger, 2006.

Galula, David. *Pacification in Algeria, 1956-1958.* Santa Monica: Rand, 2006.

Garay Vera, Cristián. *La Cameleónica Naturaleza del Conflicto Posmoderno.* Santiago: Ejército de Chile, 2004.

George, Rose. *The Big Necessity: The Unmentionable World of Human Waste and Why it Matters.* New York: Metropolitan Books, 2008.

Giangreco, Dennis. *Hell to Pay: Operation DOWNFALL and the Invasion of Japan, 1945-1947.* Annapolis: Naval Institute Press, 2009.

Grau, Les. *Coils of the Anaconda.* Lawrence: University of Kansas Press, 2010.

Greene, Robert. *The 33 Strategies of War.* New York: Viking, 2006.

Griffith, Samuel B. *Mao Tse-Tung On Guerrilla Warfare.* New York: Praeger, 1961.

Gurr, Ted. *Why Men Rebel.* Princeton: Princeton University Press, 1971.

Handel, Michael I. *Masters of War: Classical Strategic Thought.* London: Frank Cass, 2001.

Harries-Clichy Peterson, *Che Guevara on Guerrilla Warfare* (New York: Praeger, 1961

Harris, J. W. *Property and Justice*. Oxford: Clarendon Press, 1996

Harrison, Lawrence E. *Under-Development is a State of Mind.* Lanham, MD: Madison Books, 1985.

Hayek, F. A. *The Road to Sefdom: Text and Documents*. Bruce Caldwell, ed. Chicago: University of Chicago Press, 2007.

Haynes, John Earl and Klehr, Harvey. *Venona: Decoding Soviet Espionage in America*. New Haven: Yale University Press, 2000.

Henderson, Scott J. *The Dark Visitor: Inside the World of Chinese Hackers*. Fort Leavenworth: Foreign Military Studies Office, 2007.

Herb, Guntram H. and Kaplan, David H. *Nested Identities*. New York; Rowman & Littlefield, 1999, 9-30

Hilberg, Raul. *The Destruction of the European Jews*. New York: Holmes & Meier, 1985.

Hobsbawm, E. J. *Primitive Rebels: Studies of Archaic Forms of Social Movement in the 19th and 20th Centuries*. New York: W. W. Norton & Company, Inc., 1959.

Hohfeld, Wesley Newcomb. *Fundamental Legal Conceptions as Applied to Judicial Reasoning*. New Haven: Yale University Press, 1919 (reissued 1964).

Horne, Alistair. *A Savage War of Peace*. New York: Viking, 1977.

Howard, Michael. *The Invention of Peace: Reflections on War and International Order*. New Haven: Yale University Press, 2000.

International and Operational Law Division. *Operational Law Handbook*. Charlottesville, Virginia: The Judge Advocate General's School, 1994.

Jackson, Gabriel. *The Spanish Republic and the Civil War, 1931-1939*. Princeton, NJ: Princeton University Press, 1965.

Joes, Anthony James. *Resisting Rebellion: The History and Politics of Counterinsurgency*. Lexington: The University Press of Kentucky, 2004.

Joes, Anthony James. *Urban Guerrilla Warfare*. Lexington: The University Press of Kentucky, 2007.

Joes, Anthony James. *America and Guerrilla Warfare*. Lexington: The University of Kentucky Press, 2000.

Jones, Reginald Victor. *The Wizard War: British Scientific Intelligence, 1939-1945.* New York: Coward, McCann & Geoghegan, 1978.

Kaplan, Robert D. *An Empire Wilderness: Travels into America's Future.* New York: Random House, 1998.Kent, Edward Allen, ed. *Law and Philosophy: Readings in Legal Philosophy.* New York: Meredith Corporation, 1970.

Kent, Noel Jacob. *America in 1900.* New York: M.E. Sharpe, 2000.

Kilcullen, David. *Counterinsurgency.* Oxford: Oxford University Press, 2010.

Kinzer, Stephen. *Overthrow: America's Century of Regime Change from Hawaii to Iraq.* New York: Henry Holt, 2006.

Klare, Michael T. *Resource Wars: The New Landscape of Global Conflict.* New York: Metropolitan Books, 2001.

Kohl, James and Litt, John. *Urban Guerrilla Warfare in Latin America.* Cambridge: The MIT Press, 1974.

Kopel, David B. *The Samurai, the Mountie, and the Cowboy: Should America Adopt the Gun Controls of Other Democracies?.* Buffalo: Prometheus Books, 1992.

Lai, David. Learning from the Stones: *A Go Approach to Mastering China's Strategic Concept.* Carlisle, PA: Strategic Studies Institute, 2004.

Lapham, Robert and Norling, Bernard. *Lapham's Raiders: Guerrillas in the Philippines, 1942 -1945.* Lexington, KY: The University Press of Kentucky, 1996.

Laqueur, Walter. *The Guerrilla Reader: A Historical Anthology.* Philadelphia: Temple University Press, 1977.

Larson, Gary. *The Far Side, Gallery 3.* Kansas City: Universal Press Syndicate, 1988.

Laveleye, Emile de. *Primitive Property* (translated from the French by G.R.L. Marriott). London: Macmillan and Co., 1878.

Laviana, Juan Carlos, ed. *La Guerra Civil Española Mes a Mes, Volume 1: Así llegó España a la Guerra Civil, La República, 1931-1936.* Madrid: Grupo de la Unidad, 2005.

Lawrence James. *The Savage Wars: British Campaigns in Africa, 1870-1920.* New York: St. Martin's Press, 1985

Lerner, Max. *Ideas For the Ice Age: Studies in a Revolutionary Era.* New Brunswick, NJ: Viking, 1941; Transaction, 1993.

Liang, Qiao and Xiangsui, Wang. *Unrestricted Warfare.* Panama City: Pan American Publishing Company 2002.

Lieberman, Benjamin. *Terrible Fate: Ethnic Cleansing in the Making of Modern Europe.* Lanham: Ivan R. Dee, 2006.

Linklater, Andro. *Measuring America: How and Untamed Wilderness Shaped the United States and Fulfilled the Promise of Democracy.* New York: Walker & Company, 2002.

Linn, Brian McAllister. *The U.S. Counterinsurgency in the Philippine War, 1899-1902.* Chapel Hill: University of North Carolina Press, 1989.

Litteer, Loren K. *"Bleeding Kansas": The Border War in Douglas and Adjacent Counties.* Baldwin City, Kansas: Champion Publishing, 1987.

Locke, John. *Two Treatises of Government and A Letter Concerning Toleration.* New York: Yale University, 2003.

Lucas, Noah. *The Modern History of Israel.* New York: Praeger, 1975.

Macaulay, Rose. *And No Man's Wit.* Boston: Little Brown, 1940.

Mackenzie, Eduardo. *Les Farc ou l'échec d'un communisme de combate.* Paris: Editions Publibook, 2005.

Maguire, T. Miller. *A Summary of Modern Military History, with comments on the leading operations.* London: Simpkin, 1887.

Maguire, T. Miller. *Guerilla or Partisan Warfare.* London: Hugh Rees, 1904.

Maguire, T. Miller. *Notes on the Outlines of Strategy.* London: Simpkin, Marshall, Hamilton, Kent, 1902.

Maguire, T. Miller. *Outlines of Military Geography.* Cambridge: University Press, 1899.

Nosorog, Dean, ed. *Chewing Sand.* New York: Mc Graw Hill, 2005.

Marks, Thomas A. *Maoist Insurgency Since Vietnam.* New York: Routledge,1996.

Marston, Daniel and Malkasian, Carter. *Counterinsurgency in Modern Warfare.* London: Osprey, 2010.

Marx, Karl and Engels, Friedrich. *The Communist Manifesto.* New York: Soho, undated (originally published 1848).

Medina Gallego, Carlos. *ELN: una historia de los orígenes.* Bogotá: Rodríguez Quito, 2001.

Menand, Louis. *The Metaphysical Club.* New York: Farrar Straus and Giroux, 2001.

Melville, Thomas. *Guatemala: The Politics of Land Ownership.* New York: Free Press, 1971.

Metz, Steven and Kievit, James. *The Revolution in Military Affairs and Conflict Short of War.* Carlisle, Pennsylvania: Strategic Studies Institute, 1994.

Moa, Pio. *1934: Comienza La Guerra Civil Española.* Barcelona: Altera, 2006

Morgenthau, Hans J. and Thompson, Kenneth W. *Politics Among Nations: the Struggle for Power and Peace*, Sixth Edition. New York: Alfred Knopf, 1973.

Moroni Bracamonte, Jose Angel and Spencer, David E. *Strategy and Tactics of the Salvadoran FMLN Guerrillas: Last Battle of the Cold War, Blueprint for Future Conflicts.* Westport: Greenwood Press, 1995.

Morrison Taw, Jennifer and Hoffman, Bruce. *The Urbanization of Insurgency.* Santa Monica, California: RAND Arroyo Center, 1994.

Murdoch, Jonathan. *Post-structuralist Geography.* London: Sage, 2006.

Nagl, John A. and Schoomaker, Peter J. *Learning to Eat Soup with a Knife: Counterinsurgency Lessons from Malaya and Vietnam.* Chicago: University Of Chicago Press, 2005.

North, Douglass C. and Thomas, Robert Paul. *The Rise of the Western World, A New Economic History*, Cambridge: Cambridge University Press, 1973.

Noyes, Reinold. *The Institution of Property.* New York: Longmans, Green and Co., 1936.

Ó Tuathail, Gearóid. *The Geopolitics Reader.* New York: Routledge, 1998.

O`Ballance, Edgar. *The Algerian Insurrection 1954-1962.* Hamden, Connecticut: Archon Books, 1967.

O'Neill, Bard E. *Insurgency & Terrorism* (Second Edition). Washington, D.C.: Potomac Books, 2005.

Olivera, Oscar and Lewis, Tom. *Cochabamba!: water war in Bolivia.* Cambridge, MA: South End Press, 2004.

Olson, Gary L. *US Foreign Policy and the Third World Peasant: Land Reform in Asia and Latin America.* New York: Praeger Publishers, 1974.

Pakenham, Thomas. *The Boer War.* New York: Random House, 1979.

Pardo Rueda, Rafael. *La Historia de las Guerras*. Bogotá: Ediciones B, 2004.

Paret, Peter, et al. *Makers of Modern Strategy from Machiavelli to the Nuclear Age*. Princeton: Princeton University Press, 1986.

Payne, Stanley G. *The Spanish Revolution*. New York: Norton, 1970.

Pejovich, Svetozar. *The Economics of Property Rights*. Boston: Kluwer Academic Publishers, 1990.

Penner, J.E. *The Idea of Property in Law*. Oxford: Clarendon Press, 1997.

Plazas Vega, Luis Alfonso. *La Batalla del Palacio de Justicia* (The Battle of the Palace of Justice). Bogotá: Intermedio, 2000.

Posner, Richard A., ed. *The Essential Holmes*. Chicago: University of Chicago Press, 1996.

Stora,Benjamin. *Algeria 1830-2000: A Short History*. Ithaca: Cornell University Press, 2001.

Shrader, Charles R. *The First Helicopter War: Logistics and Mobility in Algeria, 1954-1962*. Westport, CT : Praeger, 1999.

Sheehan, Michael. *Crush the Cell: How to defeat terrorism without terrorizing ourselves*. New York: Random House, 2008

Powelson, John P. *The Story of Land: A World History of Land Tenure and Agrarian Reform*. Cambridge, Massachusetts: Lincoln Institute of Land Policy, 1988.

Preston, Paul, ed. *Revolution and War in Spain 1931-1939*. New York: Methuen, 1984.

Rabasa, Angel and Peter Chalk. *Colombian Labyrinth: The Synergy of Drugs and Insurgency and Its Implications for Regional Stability*. Santa Monica, CA: RAND, 2001.

Record, Jeffrey. *Beating Goliath: Why Insurgencies Win*. Dulles, VA: Potomac Books, 2009.

Rendón, Yoni Alexander. *Comuna 13 de Medellín: El drama del conflicto armado* (Medellín's Comuna 13: Drama of the armed conflict). Medellín: Hombre Nuevo Editores, 2007.

Restrepo, Jorge and Aponte, David, eds. *Guerra y Violencia en Colombia: Herramientas e interpretaciones* (War and Violence in Colombia: Tools and Interpretations). Bogotá: Pontifica Universidad Javeriana, 2009.

Revel, Jean François. *The Flight from Truth: The Reign of Deceit in the Age of Information.* New York: Random House, 1992.

Revel, Jean François. *Anti-Americanism.* New York: Encounter Books, 2003.

Richard Shultz, Roy Godson, and Querine Hanlon. *Armed Groups and Irregular Warfare: Adapting Professional Military Education.* Washington, D.C.: National Strategy Information Center, 2009.

Roger, Philippe. *The American Enemy: The History of French Anti-Americanism* (translated by Bowman, Sharon). Chicago: University of Chicago Press, 2005.

Romerstein, Herbert and Breindel, Eric. *The Venona Secrets.* Washington, D.C.: Regnery, 2000.

Ryan, Alan. *Property.* Minneapolis: University of Minnesota Press, 1987.

Salazar J., Alonso. *No nacimos pa'semilla: La cultura de las bandas juveniles en Medellín* (We were not born for (to sow) seed: the culture of youth gangs in Medellín). Bogotá: Planeta, 2002.

Shrader, Charles R. *The First Helicopter War: Logistics and Mobility in Algeria, 1954-1962.* Westport, Connecticut: Praeger, 1999.

Singh, Prakash, Mendel, William W., and Turbiville, Graham, Jr. *Disaster Response in India.* Leavenworth: The Center for Excellence in Disaster Management and the Foreign Military Studies Office, 2000.

Smith Adam. Edited by Edwin Cannan. *Lectures on Justice, Police, Revenue and Arms.* Oxford: Clarendon Press, 1896.

Smith, Adam. *The Theory of Moral Sentiment: An Inquiry into the Nature and Causes of the Wealth of Nations.* Hamburg: Management Laboratory, 2008.

Stafford, Frank and Palacios, Marco. *Colombia: Fragmented Land, Divided Society.* New York: Oxford University Press, 2002.

Sterling, Brent L. *Do Good Fences Make Good Neighbors? What History Teaches Us about Strategic Barriers and International Security.* Washington, D.C.: Georgetown University Press, 2009.

Stora, Benjamin. *Algeria 1830-2000.* Ithaca: Cornell University Press, 2001.

Tai, Hung-Chao. *Land Reform and Politics: A Comparative Analysis.* Berkeley: University of California Press, 1974.

Talbott, John. *The War Without a Name: France in Algiers, 1954-1962.* New York: Alfred A. Knopf, 1980.

The Invisible Committee. *The Coming Insurrection.* Los Angeles: Semiotext, 2007.

Thomas, Tim. *The Dragon's Quantum Leap: Transforming from a Mechanized to an Informationized Force.* Ft. Leavenworth: Foreign Military Studies Office, 2009.

Tsouras, Peter G., ed. *The Greenhouse Dictionary of Military Quotations.* London: Greenhouse, 2000.

Trinquier, Roger. *Modern Warfare: A French View of Counterinsurgency* (translated from the French by Daniel Lee) New York: Praeger, 1964.

Tuan, Yi-Fu. *Landscapes of Fear.* Oxford: Blackwell, 1979.

Twain, Mark. *The Adventures of Huckleberry Finn.* USA: Book Surge, 2004.

U. S. Army. *Field Manual 100-20, Military Operations in Low Intensity Conflict.* Washington, D.C.: Department of the Army, 1990.

U. S. Army. *Field Manual 30-31, Stability Operations-Intelligence.* Washington, D.C.: Headquarters, Department of the Army, 1970.

U. S. Army. *Field Manual 31-73, Advisor Handbook for Stability Operations.* Washington, D.C.: Headquarters, Department of the Army, 1967.

U. S. Army. *Field Manual 7-98, Operations in a Low Intensity Conflict.* Washington, D.C.: Department of the Army, 1992.

US Army and US Marine Corps. *Field Manual 3-24, Marine Corps Warfighting Publication No. 3-33.5 Counterinsurgency.* Washington, D.C.: Headquarters, Department of the Army and Headquarters Marine Corps Combat Development Command, 2006.

US Army. *Field Manual 100-20, Internal Defense and Development.* Washington, D.C.: Department of the Army, 1974.

US Army. *Field Manual 100-20, Low Intensity Conflict.* Washington, D.C.: Department of the Army, 1981.

US Army. *Field Manual 31-15 Operations Against Irregular Forces.* Washington, D.C.: Department of the Army, 1951.

US Army. *Field Manual 31-15: Operations Against Irregular Forces.* Washington, D.C.: Headquarters, Department of the Army, 1961.

US Army. *Field Manual 7-98, Operations in a Low Intensity Conflict.* Washington, D.C.: Department of the Army, 1992.

US Army. *Field Manual 3-05.130, Special Forces Uncoventional Warfare Operations.* Washington, D.C.: Department of the Army, 2008.

US Marine Corps. *Small Wars Manual.* Washington, D.C.: US Marine Corps, 1940.

Umbeck, John R. *A Theory of Property Rights: With Application to the California Gold Rush.* Ames, Iowa: The Iowa State University Press, 1981.

Valencia Tovar, Álvaro. *Inseguridad y Violencia en Colombia.* Bogotá: Universidad Sergio Arboleda, 1997.

Verstrynge, Jorge. *La Guerra Periférica y el Islam Revolucionario: Orígenes, reglas y ética de la guerra asimétrica.* Barcelona: El Viejo Topo, 2005.

Von Clausewitz, Carl. *On War.* Edited and translated by Michael Howard and Peter Paret. Princeton. N.J.: Princeton University Press, 1989.

Wall, Irwin. *France, The United States and the Algerian War.* Berkeley: University of California Press, 2001.

Weigley, Russell F. *The Age of Battles: The Quest for Decisive Warfare from Breitenfeld to Waterloo* (Bloomington: Indiana University Press, 1991).

Wells, George. *World Brain: The Idea of a Permanent World Encyclopedia.* New York: Doubleday, Doran & Co, 1938.

Wright, Robert. *The Continental Army.* Ann Arbor: University of Michigan Library, 1983.

## GLOSSARY

ALN -- The Army of National Liberation. The ALN was the armed force of the FLN in Algeria.

AUC -- United Self Defense Forces of Colombia -- Colombian guerrilla group (rightist) formed in the late 1990s, now defunct.

Cadastre -- A land or real estate record system, usually concerned with taxes.

CEDA, *Confederación de Derechas Autonomas* (Confederation of the Autonomous Right). .Right-of-center political party or movement in Spain around the time of the Spanish Civil War in the early 1930s.

CCTV – Closed-Circuit Television (monitoring cameras)

FARC -- Revolutionary Armed Forces of Colombia -- Colombian guerrilla group (leftist) formed in the mid-1960s and active today with perhaps 8,000 active members.

ةيرئازج ةروث French -Algerian War Big insurgent win.

EGP -- Guerrilla Army of the Poor. Guatemalan armed insurgent group (leftist), active 1972 to 1997, now defunct.

Ejido -- A form of communal land tenancy, especially in Mexico.

ELN -- National Liberation Army -- Colombian gueril la group (leftist) organized in the mid 1960s and active today with perhaps 1,500 active members.

FLN -- National Liberation Front -- Algerian Insurgent Organization (leftist) active in the 1950s and 1960s, now a legal political party.

FMLN -- Farabundo Ma rtí National Liberation Front- El Salvadoran guerrilla consortium (leftist) active in the 1970s and 1980s, now a legal political party.

GIS -- Geographic Information Systems or Geographic Information Science

GPS -- Global Positioning System

INTERPOL -- International Criminal Police Organization

IPB – Intelligence Preparation of the Battlefield

IPKF -- Indian Peacekeeping Force

LTTE -- Liberation Tigers of Tamil Eelam

M-19 -- 19th of April Movement -- Colombian guerrilla group (leftist) active in the 1970s and 1980s, became a legal political party, now defunct.

Mens Rea-- Criminal intent, herein used as a general reference to the intellectual authorship of violent acts.

ORPA -- Revolutionary Organization of the People in Arms. Guatemalan armed insurgent group (leftist), active 1972 to 1997, now defunct.

Paisa -- A person from a region in Colombia that includes the present day department of Antioquia as well as much of the central coffee-growing region of the country.

PMESII -- Political, Military, Economic , Social, Information, Infrastructure

Post-structuralism – Late 20th century/early 21st century suite of ideas honored by some writers as a distinguishable philosophy. See author's description p. 342.

PSOE -- *Partido Socialista Obrero Español* (Spanish Workers Socialist Party). The PSOE, led by Largo Caballeros and others, the PSOE sparked the Spanish Civil War in 1934.

Quiet-title -- Quiet -title is a formal legal euphemism used for a legal process in civil court that decides definitively the ownership of land. The court 'quiets' the title. Of course, it is not the title that is being quieted.

මහින්ද රාජපක්ෂ -- Mahinda Rajapaksa, President of Sri Lanka since November 19, 2005.

SLA -- Sri Lankan Army

SLMM -- Sri Lanka Monitoring Mission

孟母三迁 -- The Three Moves, a Chinese parable about a mother who loved her son.

URNG -- Guatemalan National Revolutionary Unity. Guatemalan armed insurgent umbrella group (leftist), active from 1981 or early 1982. Coordinated the EGP and the ORPA, now a legal political party.

WWF – World Wide Wrestling Federation (From 1963 to 1979, when it became the World Wrestling Federation, until 2002 when it became World Wrestling Entertainment, WWE.)

ZANLA -- Zimbabwe African Nati onal Liberation Army. Rhodesian/Zimbabwean armed insurgent group (leftist), formed in 1965. Robert Mugabe a leader of ZANLA, is now dictator of Zimbabwe.

# INDEX

## ABOUT THE AUTHOR

Geoffrey Demarest is a researcher in the Foreign Military Studies Office at Ft. Leavenworth, Kansas. He holds a JD and a PhD in International Studies from the University of Denver. He is a graduate of the US Army War College at Carlisle Barracks, Pennsylvania, and of the School of the Americas at Ft. Benning, Georgia.

www.ingramcontent.com/pod-product-compliance
Lightning Source LLC
Chambersburg PA
CBHW080041280326
41935CB00014B/1753
* 9 7 8 1 7 8 0 3 9 9 2 1 8 *